Søren Kierkegaard's Journals and Papers

SØREN KIERKEGAARD'S
JOURNALS AND
PAPERS   Volume 4, S-Z

EDITED AND TRANSLATED BY

Howard V. Hong and Edna H. Hong

ASSISTED BY GREGOR MALANTSCHUK

INDIANA UNIVERSITY PRESS

BLOOMINGTON AND LONDON

This book has been brought to publication with the assistance of a grant from Carlsberg Fondet.

Copyright © 1975 by Howard V. Hong

ALL RIGHTS RESERVED

No part of this book may be reproduced or utilized in any form or by any means, electronic or mechanical, including photocopying and recording, or by any information storage and retrieval system, without permission in writing from the publisher. The Association of American University Presses' Resolution on Permissions constitutes the only exception to this prohibition.
Published in Canada by Fitzhenry & Whiteside Limited, Don Mills, Ontario
Manufactured in the United States of America

Library of Congress Cataloging in Publication Data
(Revised)

Kierkegaard, Søren Aabye, 1813–1855.
Søren Kierkegaard's journals and papers.

Translation of portions of the 20 volume Danish work published 1909–48 under title: Papirer.
Includes bibliographies.
1. Philosophy—Collected works. I. Hong, Howard Vincent, 1912– ed. II. Hong, Edna (Hatlestad) 1913– ed. III. Malantschuk, Gregor.
B4372.E5H66   198'.9   67-13025
ISBN 0-253-18243-3 (v. 4)   1 2 3 4 5 79 78 77 76 75
ISBN 0-253-18299-5 (complete set)

Contents

CHRONOLOGY vii
TRANSLATORS' PREFACE xiii

SUBJECT HEADINGS

Sacrifice 3
Savonarola 8
Schleiermacher 11
Scholarship and Science 16
Schopenhauer 25
Self 36
Seneca 42
Sermons 44
Sex 88
Shakespeare 95
Silence 98
Sin 101
Situation 122
Social-Political Thought 128
Socrates 205
Solitude 225
Sophistry, Sophists 227
Spinoza 233
Spirit 236
Spiritual Trial 257
Stages 273
State Church 321
Stephen 329
Stoicism, Stoics 331
Striving 334
Subjectivity/Objectivity 345
Suffering 366

Suicide 443
Superiority 445
Superstition 447
Teleological Suspension 449
Temptation 450
Tersteegen 452
Tertullian 457
Theologians, Theology 461
Thomas à Kempis 465
Time 466
Toleration 479
Tragedy/Comedy 482
Truth 487
Unchangeableness 505
Unconditioned, the 508
Universalism 530
Upbuilding, the 532
Venture, Risk 534
Vocation 545
Voluntary, the 548
Wit 553
Witness 554
Woman/Man 572
Work 586
World 589
Worship 601
Zachaeus 608

BIBLIOGRAPHY 611
COLLATION OF ENTRIES WITH *PAPIRER* 615
NOTES 623

Chronology

1813

May 5 — Søren Aabye Kierkegaard born at Nytorv 2 (now 27), Copenhagen, son of Michael Pedersen Kierkegaard and Anne Sørensdatter Lund Kierkegaard.

June 3 — Baptized in Vor Frue Kirke congregation (meeting in Helliggeist Kirke) in Copenhagen.

1821

Enrolled in Borgerdydskolen in Copenhagen.

1828

Apr. 20 — Confirmed in Vor Frue Kirke congregation (meeting in Trinitatis Kirke) by Pastor J. P. Mynster (later Bishop of Sjælland).

1830

Oct. 30 — Registered as student at University of Copenhagen.
Nov. 1 — Drafted into Royal Guard, Company 7.
Nov. 4 — Discharged as unfit for service.

1831

Apr. 25 — Finishes first part of second examination (Latin, Greek, Hebrew, and history, *magna cum laude;* mathematics, *summa cum laude*).

Oct. 27 — Completes second part of second examination (philosophy, physics, and mathematics, *summa cum laude*).

1834

Apr. 15 — Entry I A 1 of journals and papers.
July 31 — Mother dies.

1835

Summer in north Sjælland.

1837

Between May 8 and May 12. On a visit to the Rørdams in Frederiksberg meets Regine Olsen for the first time (see II A 67, 68).
Autumn. Begins teaching Latin for a term in Borgerdydskolen.
Sept. 1 Moves from home to Lovstræde 7.

1838

"The Battle between the Old and the New Soap-Cellars" (a philosophical comedy drafted but not completed or published; see *Pap.* II B 1–21).
May 19 About 10: 30 A.M. S.K.'s entry concerning "an indescribable joy" (see II A 228).
Aug. 8/9 Father dies, 2:00 A.M.
Aug. 14 Father buried in family plot in Assistents Cemetery.
Sept. 7 Publication of *From the Papers of One Still Living, published against his will by S. Kierkegaard.* (About H. C. Andersen as a novelist, with special reference to his latest work, *Only a Fiddler.*)

1840

Feb. 1 Census list gives address as Kultorvet 132 (now 11).
Apr. or Oct. Moves to Nørregade 230A (now 38).
June 2 Presents his request for examination to theological faculty.
July 3 Completes examination for degree (*magna cum laude*).
July 19–Aug. 6 Journey to ancestral home in Jutland.
Sept. 8 Proposes to Regine Olsen.
Sept. 10 Becomes engaged to Regine.
Oct. 8 First number of *Corsaren* (*The Corsair*) published by M. Goldschmidt.
Nov. 17 Enters the Pastoral Seminary.

1841

Jan. 12 Preaches sermon in Holmens Kirke (see III C 1).
July 16 Dissertation for the *Magister* degree, *The Concept of Irony, with Constant Reference to Socrates,* accepted.
Aug. 11 Returns Regine Olsen's engagement ring.

Sept. 16   Dissertation printed.
Sept. 28   10 A.M.–2:00 P.M., 4:00 P.M.–7:30 P.M. Defends his dissertation. (Around mid-century *Magister* degrees came to be regarded and named officially as doctoral degrees such as they are now.)
Oct. 11   Engagement with Regine Olsen broken.
Oct. 25   Leaves Copenhagen for Berlin, where he attends Schelling's lectures.

1842

March 6   Returns to Copenhagen.
Nov. 11   S.K.'s brother Peter Christian Kierkegaard ordained.
Johannes Climacus, or De omnibus dubitandum est begun but not completed or published.

1843

Feb. 20   *Either/Or,* edited by Victor Eremita, published.
May 8   Leaves for short visit to Berlin.
May 16   *Two Upbuilding [Edifying] Discourses,* by S. Kierkegaard, published.
July   Learns of Regine's engagement to Johan Frederik Schlegel.
Oct. 16   *Repetition,* by Constantin Constantius; *Fear and Trembling,* by Johannes de Silentio; and *Three Upbuilding [Edifying] Discourses,* by S. Kierkegaard, published.
Dec. 6   *Four Upbuilding [Edifying] Discourses,* by S. Kierkegaard, published.

1844

Feb. 24   Preaches terminal sermon in Trinitatis Kirke.
March 5   *Two Upbuilding [Edifying] Discourses,* by S. Kierkegaard, published.
June 8   *Three Upbuilding [Edifying] Discourses,* by S. Kierkegaard, published.
June 13   *Philosophical Fragments,* by Johannes Climacus, published.
June 17   *The Concept of Anxiety [Dread],* by Vigilius Haufniensis; and *Prefaces,* by Nicolaus Notabene, published.
Aug. 31   *Four Upbuilding [Edifying] Discourses,* by S. Kierkegaard, published.
Oct. 16   Moves from Nørregade 230A (now 38) to house at Nytorv 2, Copenhagen.

1845

Apr. 29   *Three Discourses on Imagined Occasions,* by S. Kierkegaard, published.
Apr. 30   *Stages on Life's Way,* edited by Hilarius Bogbinder, published.
May 13-24 Journey to Berlin.
May 29   *Eighteen Upbuilding [Edifying] Discourses* (from 1842-43), by S. Kierkegaard, published.
Dec. 27   Article "The Activity of a Travelling Esthetician ...," containing references to P. L. Møller and *The Corsair,* by Frater Taciturnus, published in *Fædrelandet* [*The Fatherland*].

1846

Jan. 2   First attack on S.K. in *The Corsair.*
Jan. 10   S.K.'s reply by Frater Taciturnus in *Fædrelandet.*
Feb. 7   Considers qualifying himself for ordination (VII^1 A 4).
Feb. 27   *Concluding Unscientific Postscript,* by Johannes Climacus, published.
Mar. 9   "Report" (*The Corsair*) begun in first NB Journal (VII^1 A 98).
Mar. 30   *Two Ages: the Age of Revolution and the Present Age. A Literary Review* [*The Present Age* is part of this work], by S. Kierkegaard, published.
May 2-16   Visit to Berlin.
June 12   Acquires Magister A.P. Adler's books: *Studier og Exempler, Forsøg til en kort systematisk Fremstilling af Christendommen i dens Logik,* and *Theologiske Studier.*
Oct. 2   Goldschmidt resigns as editor of *The Corsair.*
Oct. 7   Goldschmidt travels to Germany and Italy.

1847

Jan. 24   S.K. writes: "God be praised that I was subjected to the attack of the rabble. I have now had time to arrive at the conviction that it was a melancholy thought to want to live in a vicarage, doing penance in an out-of-the-way place, forgotten. I now have made up my mind quite otherwise" (VII^1 A 229).
           Date of preface to *The Book on Adler* [*On Authority and Revelation*], not published; ms. in *Papirer* (VII^2 B 235-70; VIII^2 B 1-27).
           Drafts of lectures on communication (VIII^2 B 79-89), not published or delivered.

Mar. 13 *Upbuilding Discourses in Various Spirits,* by S. Kierkegaard, published.
Sept. 29 *Works of Love,* by S. Kierkegaard, published.
Nov. 3 Regine Olsen marries Johan Frederik Schlegel.
Dec. 24 Sells house on Nytorv.

1848

Jan. 28 Leases apartment at Rosenborggade and Tornebuskgade 156 A (now 7) for April occupancy.
Apr. 19 S.K. notes: "My whole nature is changed. My concealment and reserve are broken—I am free to speak" (VIII^1 A 640).
Apr. 24 "No, no, my reserve still cannot be broken, at least not now" (VIII^1 A 645).
Apr. 26 *Christian Discourses,* by S. Kierkegaard, published.
July 24–27 *The Crisis [and a Crisis] in the life of an Actress,* by Inter et Inter, published.
Aug. Notes that his health is poor and is convinced that he will die (IX A 216).
  Reflections on direct and indirect communication (IX A 218, 221–24).
Sept. 1 Preaches in Vor Frue Kirke (IX A 266–69, 272).
Nov. *The Point of View for My Work as an Author* "as good as finished" (IX A 293); published posthumously in 1859 by S.K.'s brother, Peter Christian Kierkegaard.
  "Armed Neutrality," by S. Kierkegaard, "written toward the end of 1848 and the beginning of 1849" (X^5 B 105–10) but not published.

1849

May 14 Second edition of *Either/Or;* and *The Lily of the Field and the Bird of the Air,* by S. Kierkegaard, published.
May 19 *Two Minor Ethical-Religious Essays,* by H. H., published.
June 25–26 Councillor Olsen (Regine's father) dies.
July 30 *The Sickness unto Death,* by Anti-Climacus, published.
Nov. 13 *Three Discourses at the Communion on Fridays,* by S. Kierkegaard, published.

1850

Apr. 18 Moves to Nørregade 43 (now 35), Copenhagen.

Sept. 27 *Practice [Training] in Christianity,* by Anti-Climacus, published.
Dec. 20 *An Upbuilding [Edifying] Discourse,* by S. Kierkegaard, published.

1851

Veiviser (directory) listing for 1851: Østerbro 108A (torn down).
Jan. 31 "An Open Letter ... Dr. Rudelbach," by S. Kierkegaard, published.
Aug. 7 *On My Work as an Author*; and *Two Discourses at the Communion on Fridays,* by S. Kierkegaard, published.
Sept. 10 *For Self-Examination,* by S. Kierkegaard, published.

1851–52

Judge for Yourselves!, by S. Kierkegaard, written. Published posthumously, 1876.
Veiviser listing for 1852–55: Klædeboderne 5–6 (now Skindergade 38).

1854

Jan. 30 Bishop Mynster dies.
Apr. 15 H. Martensen named Bishop.
Dec. 18 S.K. begins polemic against Bishop Martensen in *Fædrelandet.*

1855

Jan.–May Polemic continues.
May 24 *This Must Be Said; So Let It Now Be Said,* by S. Kierkegaard, advertised as published.
First number of *The Moment.*
June 16 *Christ's Judgment on Official Christianity,* by S. Kierkegaard, published.
Sept. 3 *The Unchangeableness of God. A Discourse,* by S. Kierkegaard, published.
Sept. 25 Ninth and last number of *The Moment* published; number 10 published posthumously. S.K. writes his last journal entry (XI^2 A 439).
Oct. 2 Enters Frederiks Hospital.
Nov. 11 Dies.
Nov. 18 Is buried in Assistents Cemetery, Copenhagen.

Translators' Preface

Part of the period devoted to the preparation of Volume 4 of *Journals and Papers* was spent in the Søren Kierkegaard Bibliotek of the University of Copenhagen. Therefore we are indebted once more to the University of Copenhagen for the use of the quarters and the materials, to Professor Niels Thulstrup for facilitating these arrangements, and also to the Royal Library for access to its riches of books, manuscripts, and periodicals.

Dr. Gregor Malantschuk of the University of Copenhagen has continued to share in this volume the yield of a lifetime of sensitive, critical reading of all that is available from Kierkegaard's hand. He has written the discussions of central concepts (our translation) found under the topical headings in the notes. For support of this international collaboration we acknowledge the assistance of Rask-Ørsted Fondet and Carlsberg Fondet.

Concentration on the last stage of work on Volume 4 has been made possible by a summer grant from the St. Olaf College Humanities Research Fund and a 1970–71 Senior Fellowship from the National Endowment for the Humanities. Aided and encouraged by these gifts of time, we are now beginning to see dimly the end our seemingly interminable task.

Dr. Oliver Olson has once again provided translations of the German, Greek, and Hebrew passages, and Professor Bert Narveson the Latin. Dorothy Bolton and Chris Wheeler have had a share in the typing. Nathaniel Hong has checked the apparatus, and Todd Nichol assisted in the preparation of the bibliography. Grethe Kjær has continued to give valuable help in various spheres. This volume is graced by the fine original jacket by Karen Elness Foget. To all these colleagues and friends and son we are gratefully beholden.

St. Olaf College   H.V.H.
Northfield, Minnesota   E.H.H.

A history of Kierkegaard's journals and papers and a full account of the principles of this selection from them are given in the translators' preface to Volume 1. Briefly, the entries in the first four volumes of this edition, including the present one, are arranged topically, and chronologically within each topic. Volumes 5 and 6 will contain the autobiographical selections. There will be a complete index. Those who wish to follow the serial order of the entries in the present volume, insofar as that can be done on the basis of the *Papirer*, will find appended a table which collates the entries of this volume with the *Papirer* (see pp. 615 ff.)

Within the entries, a series of five periods indicates omissions or breaks in the Danish text as it stands. A series of three periods is used in the few instances of the translators' omissions.

Brackets are used in the text to enclose certain crucial Danish terms just translated or to enclose references supplied by the translators.

Footnote numbers in the text refer to the editors' notes, which appear in serial order at the end of the volume. Kierkegaard's notes and marginal comments appear at the bottom of the particular page, at the end of the entry, or in a few special cases as a bracketed insertion within an entry.

Diacritical markings, which Kierkegaard rarely used in writing Greek words, have been added.

Kierkegaard's consciously developed punctuation (VIII^1 A 33-38) has been retained to a large extent. This is evident in the use of the colon and the dash and a minimal use of question marks. Pedagogical-stylistic characteristics (change of page, variation of sentence length, and the architecture of sentences and paragraphs) have also been carried over in the main. They are intended as an invitation to reflection and rereading—ideally, aloud.

Søren Kierkegaard's Journals and Papers

SACRIFICE

« 3829 *Yours—Mine*

This is how the Christian—especially one who still is Christian only on the easier terms—might talk to Christ:

I call myself "yours"—not as if I had sacrificed everything to be yours—alas, no—I am an egotist, but you have sacrificed everything in order that I could be yours; I have not dearly bought or dearly expressed that I am yours, but you have dearly bought and dearly expressed that I am yours.

Amazing! Here again as everywhere a complete inversion with respect to the divine. This is just the way the superior one usually talks who perhaps has even cheated another out of his love: I have not done everything in order to be yours, but you have done everything so that I could be yours; in a way, therefore, you are mine, but I am not yours. Alas, and this is the way Christ is cheated somehow by us all. He does everything, sacrifices everything that we may be his—but we do not sacrifice everything in order to be his. And yet grace regards us as his by considering that he has sacrificed everything.

And in this sense the weak Christian calls himself yours.

x^3 A 654   *n.d.,* 1850

« 3830 *The Ancient Church Fathers*

clearly indicate that they still remembered, they still took personally, that there was a time when sacrificing everything was taken literally.

It is so long now since such things were taken literally that to us it has become a fable that such a thing was ever carried out.

We are even afraid of sacrificing something—for fear of tempting God.[*]

Hell, the devil, and everything related are explained as metaphorical expressions—and to sacrifice everything and everything related to that is also explained as metaphorical expression, as hyperbole.

x^4 A 119   *n.d.,* 1851

« 3831

[*]*In margin of 3830* (x⁴ A 119):

We are so far from sacrificing and from simply admitting honestly that it is required, that in order to be perfectly safe we have cooked up a sort of dogma that to sacrifice is "to tempt God."

But the ancient ones, of course, had this mitigation: if someone willed to sacrifice something or himself for Christianity, it was understood—not as it is now, when such a person is ridiculed as ludicrous exaggeration by—Christians!

x⁴ A 120 n.d., 1851

« 3832 *To Sacrifice*

In order to determine whether this or that is a sacrifice, one must always look at the *beginning.*

Many a man, intending to make a profit by some deal or other, has failed and suffered a loss. Then he seeks to reinterpret the result (inverted) in terms of his having made a sacrifice—in order to get some profit anyway, that is, honor and esteem for having made a sacrifice.

Incidentally, the opposite may also be the case—someone begins something with the idea that it will be his defeat (consequently a sacrifice he makes) and Governance thwarts it, or perhaps he did not know the situation well enough.

x⁴ A 129 n.d., 1851

« 3833 *Sacrifice*

Christ is the only sacrifice; no added sacrifice is needed.

The true Christian is the one who becomes a sacrifice in order to call attention to the truth that Christ is the only sacrifice.

Here on the one side we see that to be Christian means to be sacrificed, and on the other side we see the relationship of subordination in relation to Christ.

XI¹ A 159 n.d., 1854

« 3834 *The Idea—To Be Sacrificed*

Not even the most minimal idea ever came into the world without sacrifice.

The artistic imitations or remodelings of what is ideally given are able to bring success and earthly profit.

The less the idea (primitively), the less one becomes a sacrifice, but the closer one comes to winning the temporal.

To serve the idea is to be tortured, to be martyred [*in margin:* Every new suffering is intended to torture forth a new aspect of the idea.] —otherwise the idea cannot be brought out of the synthesis which man is, since in one sense he is animal-man.

But to be martyred in this way, to be sacrificed in this way, is yet again the expression of God's love for this individual. And there must also continually be the element of voluntariness in him; otherwise there is not the proper resilience, and the squeezing out of the idea becomes simply a natural process, not a devotedness as well, a compliance.

XI^1 A 271   *n.d.*, 1854

« 3835 *The Sacrifice*

If a person's life has this formula: enthusiasm but with equally powerful negative reflection—but still enthusiasm, it means that this individual is marked for suffering; he is like a sharpened note, and his life is sharpened for him; he is the sacrifice, which is something quite different from the thousands of spontaneous enthusiasts who have been sacrificed.

How curious that in this category the lowest and the highest resemble each other. In character the lowest is the womanish, the Zerlina-like: I want and I do not want.[1] This resembles the highest, the demonic pathos: I do not want to have anything to do with my contemporaries; I do not want to and yet I do want to—i.e., I do not want to have anything to do with them directly; I want to be sacrificed.

XI^1 A 440   *n.d.*, 1854

« 3836 *The Thought of Being Sacrificed*

does not form associations. I would like to have someone show me an example of men ever uniting for the purpose of being sacrificed, that is, with the idea that being sacrificed has value in and for itself.

The best example, of course, would be the apostles. But I maintain that the apostles were not an association with the purpose of being sacrificed; it was an association of men willing to be sacrificed if it could not be otherwise, but otherwise an association to prevent, if possible, its being necessary.

In one way or another what unites men is the finite; the intention to be sacrificed is fatal to all finiteness.

If I am told that there are examples in the Orient of men who are joined together to be sacrificed, sacrificed by hurling themselves from mountaintops or by throwing themselves under the carriage of the god,[2] then I am obliged to answer that this may well be, but their uniting to be sacrificed in this way is not based on an idea, and they serve no concrete idea by their self-sacrifice.

No, the thought of being sacrificed, the intention to be sacrificed, is the most unsocial of all, quite naturally for the simple reason that uniting together might, after all, lead to some palpable power, which is completely contrary to the idea of being sacrificed.

XI^2 A 10   *n.d.*, 1854

« 3837   *Talking in Spoonerisms*
or
"I am—if it is required of me—willing to sacrifice everything for Christianity"

—Earlier than the end of 1854

If there is any meaning and truth in "giving assurances," the rule is as follows: a man can give assurances of his willingness with respect to whatever is lower than what his life expresses, but not conversely. For example, an officer of the army, the artillery, may say: If it is required of me, I would be willing to serve as a national guard officer. Fine, but the latter is easier than the former. Or—a person who drinks nothing but water may say: Well, if it is required of me, I would be willing to drink wine. It is quite different if someone accustomed to drinking a bottle or a half bottle of wine says: I am willing, if it is required, to drink water. Yes, thanks, my good man—go ahead, for otherwise "assurances" here would be nonsense and something even worse.

The fact is that the things of the world are taken and enjoyed, and then this enjoyment is refined by means of assurances that one is willing, thus producing the appearance that one is such a pious person, such a person of character.

Let us consider this corruption further. "To sacrifice everything for Christianity" and "if it is required." If one does not assume that Christianity directly requires this of everyone, then there is nothing at all to wait for, since it is required, and no doubt everyone readily perceives that a disturbance would contribute to posing the question of being required to sacrifice everything, for in times of disturbance sacrifices are required, in times of disturbance it becomes clear whether the person who gave assurances that he was willing really is.

If someone were to talk this way (giving assurances of his willingness) but did not believe that it is directly required of the Christian at all times—if we then saw him exert his energies and his talents to create a disturbance so there could be the situation in which it would become clear whether or not he was willing, then there would be meaning in his assurances. If, however, we see that a person who gives assurances "that if it is required, he is willing" applies all possible shrewdness and every means possible to prevent disturbance, consequently preventing the situation in which it would have to become clear whether or not he actually was willing—well, then this assurance is nothing but a subtle refinement. A person giving such assurances is disloyal to *the worldliness* which he enjoys as much as any worldling. But the other worldlings are content with being worldlings; they do not enjoy the reputation of being devout and saintly. And he is disloyal to those *earnest characters* who actually sacrificed everything; for if this kind of assurance is sufficient, then their earnestness, after all, gets to be almost a ridiculous overstatement. A faker like this, despite the proverb, "eats his cake and has it too," gets what worldlings do not get, the appearance of sanctity, and he also gets what the devout do not get—all the things of this world.

O, my God, the human heart is exceedingly tricky; therefore let us be extremely cautious about giving assurances that we are willing if it is required! Let our speech be: Yes—yes, No—no! What my life expresses I have the right to speak, but it really is not necessary, for my life expresses it. "Whatever is more than this," to give assurances, "is of evil."

XI^3 B 45 *n.d.*, 1854

SAVONAROLA

« 3838

What Savonarola[3] said about himself—that he was like a hammer in the hands of God: Use it as long as you want to, and when you do not wish to use it any longer, throw it away—is really blasphemy against God. No man can have such a relationship to God. It is too much like an erotic relationship, and furthermore it really attributes change to God. It is as if a girl were to say of her faithless lover: I am satisfied that he loved me for a short time; he cast me away, but I love him just the same and thank him for the brief time he loved me.

It is as if God changed his mind, as if God became tired of a person —but the relationship cannot be of that kind. The error in those words lies in the emotional turn: When you do not wish to use it any longer —for the task in the relationship to God is always the task of faith, to believe that he therefore and nevertheless loves a person just as intensely. Consequently Savonarola must say: Whether you use me or do not use me, help me simply to cling to the faith that you are love; therefore if Savonarola [says] he believes God loves him not *because* he uses him but because God is love, then his relationship to God is not reflected upon, not to mention reflection implying a change, but the nature of God, that he is love.

There is essentially a despair in Savonarola's words, implying that God would not be the same, would not be absolute love in his relationship to a person, if he could no longer use him. Well, so it is with a human being—but how dreadful to think this way about God.

IX A 295 *n.d.*, 1848

« 3839 *Savonarola*

says in a Lenten sermon (Feb. 17, 1495) . . . . .

I will therefore talk with my God . . . . . Forgive me if I speak too familiarly and tactlessly. You, O Lord, who have created all good, have stolen my heart, and deceived me as no man has ever been deceived. For when over a long period of time I beseeched you to show me the mercy of never being under obligation to supervise others, you have done just the opposite and little by little have drawn me into the position where I now stand, without my becoming aware of it. In short, I longed for a quiet life, and you lured me forth with your bait, just as the bird is caught with birdlime. If I had seen it, I would perhaps not be standing where I now stand. My experience has been like that of a fly that stretches toward the light and, flying to a burning light without knowing that it will burn, gets its wings burned. You have shown me your light, and I rejoiced over it. When I was told that it is good to spread this light unto the salvation of souls, I came to the light and singed my wings. I have come out into the deep sea and long to come back to the harbor; I look all around and see no possibility. I will say to you with Jeremiah: O Lord, you have deceived me, and I was deceived, you are stronger than I, and you have prevailed. I have become a laughingstock all the day; everyone mocks me. Jeremiah 20:7.

See Rudelbach, *Savonarola,* p. 154.[4]

But so it is in fact with God's upbringing: he deceives a man into the truth. He grasps the truth in imagination—it looks so inviting, he cannot escape it, he goes along—and now he stands right in the middle of actuality, and the matter is altogether different.

x^4 A 264   *n.d.,* 1851

« **3840** *1. Savonarola*

"The power of faith is secure in dangers, but in danger when a person is secure."

Rudelbach, *Savonarola,* p. 350.[5]

x^4 A 276   *n.d.,* 1851

« **3841** *2. Savonarola*

says somewhere that the person who is truly converted does not care what people say about him, takes courage and says: This is how I want life to be lived in my house.

This reminds me of the words with which my father interrupted all objections to his way of life: This is the custom in my house.

See Rudelbach's *Savonarola,* p. 372, bottom.[6]

x^4 A 277   *n.d.,* 1851

« **3842** *Savonarola—Apologetics*

This is, after all, an apologetic for Christianity. He proves the truth and divinity of Christianity by the transformation which occurs in those who become Christians—the proud become humble, the voluptuous chaste, etc. This is found in *Triumphus Crucis,* II (see Rudelbach, *Savonarola,* pp. 386 and 387[7]).

Such an apologetic in our time would be a satire on us Christians.—x^4 A 279   *n.d.,* 1851

SCHLEIERMACHER

« 3843

[*Observations by Kierkegaard on various excerpts, translated into Danish, from F. Schleiermacher,*[8] Der christliche Glaube . . . , I–II (Berlin: 2 ed., 1830), I, pp. 3–72]:

Page 5, top. If ethics advances this concept of Church *a priori,* I do not see how it will be possible to determine the places in which the individual personages as well as the historical personages are found, for it may very well be that history never corresponded to our conception. If it is advanced *a posteriori,* then in what way is its activity different from philosophy of religion. —The concept "Church" must be advanced in such a way that all kinds of churches fall within it, for otherwise it might happen that we would encounter something which we might call "Church" and which nevertheless could not be subsumed under the concept advanced.

Page 6. *wissenschaftlichen Disciplinen.*[9] These must also be permeated by the Christian spirit, for otherwise will it turn out that we are building with alien material?

I cannot see any other interpretation than that S. clearly places self-consciousness rather than feeling (p. 16) in contrast (to page 8, 2).

The feeling of absolute dependence expressly declares "the source of our receptive and self-active (p. 22) existence [*Tilvær*]. How, then, can one say (p. 26) *das schlechthinnige Abhängigkeitsgefühl in welchem dieser Gegensatz wieder verschwindet*[10] —How can it be said (p. 26) that everything which the subject essentially opposes at the most central point turns out to be identical with him. Nature is also part of this.

[Page 36.] But if the feeling of absolute dependence is the highest, how is this related to prayer? Then prayer is regarded merely as a fiction.

[Page 58.] But how can Schl. simultaneously affirm that Christianity tends toward teleological piety and yet assume predestination.—

[Quotation from p. 70.]

The only qualification I would gladly accept is that it is an effect upon man as a knower, for then revelation is essentially and originally a doctrine.

I C 20 n.d., 1834

« **3844**

[*Excerpts from Schleiermacher continued:*]
1. Human nature such that no redemption can take place.
2. The redeemer such that he cannot complete it.
3. If men are to be redeemed, they must *want* it and actually *be able to receive* it.

[*The following interspersed notes by Kierkegaard:*]
[P. 228:] Does Schleiermacher suppose that man is created sinful. —(Theory of the Fall of the Angels)—*Sichverführenlassen*"[11] (p. 232) presupposes some evil.

Ad page 242—
Since as a rule those who link faith in Christianity to faith in the devil also suppose that the devil led man astray, whereby sin entered the world, it seems to me they could justifiably acknowledge their position.

[Pp. 313 f.] It seems to me that, even if it were unreasonable, one should be able to distinguish between God's direct and indirect activity. The concept of a direct activity implies that one uses means, but the object I use as means must *eo ipso* act as a given over which I consequently exercise a power but which again exercises a power over me, but such a relation cannot be imagined as existing together with God's absolute freedom.

I C 23 (in XI³, p. xxxiv, and in XII) October 1, 1834

« **3845**

Schleiermacher's *Vertraute Briefe über die Lucinde* . . . . .[12]

I C 56 n.d., 1835

« **3846**

Schleiermacher, "*Vertraute Briefe über die Lucinde.*"
Mit einer Vorrede v. Karl Gutzkov. Hamburg, 1835.

These letters are written about a book *Lucinde* published at one time by F. Schlegel. It is not known for sure whether or not this book is by Schlegel, but Gutzkov puts the burden upon everyone to prove that it is not by him. Surely on the basis of internal evidence alone it is incontestable; the characteristically Schlegelian dialectical-polemical language is unmistakable throughout, just as in, for example, *"Versuch über die Schamhaftigkeit."* It is probably a model review and also an example of how such a thing can be most productive, in that he constructs a host of personalities out of the book itself and through them illuminates the work and also illuminates their individuality, so that instead of being faced by the reviewer with various points of view, we get instead many personalities who represent these various points of view. But they are complete beings, so that it is possible to get a glance into the individuality of the single individual and through numerous merely relatively true judgments to draw up our own final judgment. Thus it is a true masterpiece.

I C 69 In October 1835

« **3847**

In margin of 3846 (I C 69):
See *Maanedsskrift for Litteratur,* eighth year,[13] p. 140. An essay by P. Møller.[14]

I C 70 February 1836

« **3848**

Schleiermacher as Stoicism reborn in Christianity.

I A 305 *n.d.,* 1836

« **3849**

That pantheism constitutes a surmounted factor in religion, is the foundation for it, seems now to be acknowledged, and hereby also the error in Schleiermacher's definition of religion as remaining in pantheism, in that he makes the extra-temporal fusion factor of the universal and the finite—into religion.

II A 91 *n.d.,* 1837

« **3850**

Schleiermacher's is basically the first level[15] of genuine orthodox dogmatics (and therefore he will come again to have great importance), however heterodox his position is in many respects, and his position will naturally be significantly modified in that the dogmatic content will be given a completely different, objective qualification and determinateness. Yet in many points his position is right—for example, he has incorporated the concept of wonder in its inwardness within the system rather than, as before, keeping it outside as a prolegomenon;

his whole position is that of wonder, and his entire self-awareness is a completely new Christian self-awareness.

II A 199 December 7, 1837

« 3851

I do not find in the earliest Church the relation of Holy Scripture into which a whole dogmatic development has put it as part of a dogmatic system. This development was supplanted later by Schleiermacher. In Origen's Περὶ ἀρχῶν[16] the question of Holy Scripture is first treated in Book 4, which clearly shows that the whole systematic development was linked essentially to a common consciousness of the faith or something of that order. Since it more or less has been pushed out of the systematic structure, it could just as well be absent from the system without any loss.

II A 242 August 6, 1838

« 3852

[*In margin:* The error in Schleiermacher's dogmatics[17]] is that for him religiousness is always really a condition, *it is;* he represents everything in the sphere of being [*Væren*], Spinozian being. How it becomes [*vorder*] in the sense of coming to exist [*blive til*] and in the sense of being maintained does not really concern him. This is why he is unable to pick up very much from dogmatics. Every Christian qualification is characterized by the ethical oriented to striving. From this comes fear and trembling, and the *you shall;* from this also the possibility of offense etc. This is of minor concern to Schleiermacher. He treats religiousness in the sphere of being.[*]

From this also comes his thesis that feeling is always true. Considered more closely, its truth is actually the truth that it *is*. The whole battle begins with becoming. The question considered in the sphere of "becoming" is: But is that which is—true? In the sphere of being the truth is that it is.

x^2 A 416 n.d., 1850

« 3853

[*] *In margin of 3852* (x^2 A 416):
This also explains Schleiermacher's stipulation of the feeling of absolute dependence as the principle of all religion, for this is again a condition of religiousness in the sphere of being [*Væren*]. As soon as the question becomes ethical, consequently a question of the becoming [*Vordelse*] of this condition, how it comes into existence [*bliver til*],

what I have to do in order that it can come into existence, also how it is to be maintained or how I am to be maintained in it, which also is becoming, then the mark of religiousness is changed. I think it is precisely in this way that Schleiermacher may be said to have falsified Christianity, because he has conceived it esthetically-metaphysically merely as a condition, whereas Christianity is essentially to be conceived ethically, as striving. S. conceives of religiousness as completely analogous to erotic love. But this is a misunderstanding. Erotic love essentially has nothing to do with a striving. But Christianity is in the sphere of becoming. As soon as this is understood, every single Christian qualification is characterized differently than in S. And not only this, but only then do the most decisive qualifications of Christianity appear, and they are lacking in S., or in S. they lack the decisive quality.

X^2 A 417   *n.d.*

SCHOLARSHIP AND SCIENCE

« 3854

Beware of entering too early into the holy wedlock of scholarship and science. Better to live unmarried for a time, even if it is too bad to end up a bachelor.

I A 255   October 8, 1836

« 3855

Thank you, Lichtenberg,[18] thank you for saying that there is nothing more insipid than to talk with a so-called bibliognostic in scholarship, who himself has not thought but knows 1,000 literary-historical details![*] *"Es ist fast als wie die Vorlesung aus einem Kochbuch, wenn man hungert."*[19] O, thanks for this voice in the desert, thanks for this thirst-quencher; like the cry of a wild bird in the stillness of the night, it sets the whole imagination in motion. I suppose it was occasioned by long and tedious prattling with a learned scholarly workhorse who probably deprived him of a happy moment. Worse yet, in the copy that I am reading a marking has been made which disturbs me, for already I have a mental image of some journalist who has carefully gone through this work in order to fill the newspaper with aphorisms with or without Lichtenberg's name, and in this way, I regret, he has robbed me of some of the surprise.

II A 122   *n.d.*, 1837

« 3856

[*] *In margin of 3855* (II A 122):
They keep a list as Leporello did, but what they miss—yes, that is what it is all about; while Don Juan seduces and enjoys—Leporello notes down the time, the place, and the girl's descriptive details.

II A 123   *n.d.*

« 3857

It is strange, yet there are these corresponding phenomena. In a historical period of the world a ludicrous historical thoroughness led the monks to begin their history with the creation of the world, and

16

therefore they never finished. In an age of reflection (ours, namely) reflection gets so entangled in reflection over itself that it finally becomes exhausted in utterly empty, fictitious motions of introduction. They surely should lead into the subject, but they rather lead away, because they are like roadsigns which simply tell the distance but do not specify whether one is moving toward his goal (the capital city) or away from it, or like a clock which is set wrong and may very well measure a period of time accurately but nevertheless gives the wrong time. The inversion is altogether ridiculous—the inverse proportion of brevity of content to length of development in most scholarly works of our time. It is not so much the bad infinity[20] as the miserable infinity.

II A 188 November 3, 1837

« 3858

The sciences at Golgotha under the cross of Jesus or the sanctified sciences. Presented in a dream, in which the sciences come to worship at the cross—translated from the German, Copenhagen, 1764.[21]

The Danish translator's preface. "The book was immediately translated into many languages. In England it appeared on Good Friday in Loyd's Evenings Post." "Golgotha shall be Parnassus."

Si Christum nescis, nihil est si cætera discis.
Si Christum discis, satis est, si cætera nescis.[22]

(N. B. I got the book from Ditlevsen's lending library of devotional books.[23])

P. 7. After her (history) came secular philosophy. Her eyes were somewhat downcast, like one who is bashful and ashamed. However, she finally looked up, deeply moved . . . . . there is truth in the world, but it is like the moonlight.—

> Sometimes one can do nothing but smile when the idea is supposed to be brought out through a ridiculous scientific detail, as on p. 17, where it reads: But in the print of the nails and wounded side the *art of fortification* found completely invincible divine fortresses.

II A 796 November 29, 1838

« 3859

The power of assimilation which an elaborated systematic view gives someone face to face with the phenomenon is certainly to be praised, but the dogmatic *concupiscence* which looks on every woman (the phenomenon)[24] in order to lust after her[25] is extremely depraved, since nothing is impossible to it, is extremely boring, since it has no scope for the youthfully frolicsome individual antics of the phenomenon.

II A 563 September 11, 1839

« 3860 *Scientific Scholarship—Christianity*

I continually say: All honor to scientific scholarship etc.

But the fact of the matter is that scientific scholarship has been the object of a popularization campaign, it has gradually percolated down to the people—and true piety has gone by the board, existential respect has been lost.

Take a child. Instead of ordering him to say "no" to himself in a particular instance, give him a lecture about self-denial, perhaps a historical survey of the different conceptions of self-denial, etc.—the child would go mad.

And the same with the generation in regard to religion—if it is not demented it is dislocated.[26]

There is nothing to do here but split [the crowd] apart, get the single individual aside,[27] and place him existentially under the ideal.

This is my work.

Furthermore, scientific theological scholarship moves in completely false categories, lays everything out in direct categories.

Take the category: Holy Scripture. They say: If it is going to be Holy Scripture, then there must be agreement in every least detail.

Rubbish! This is the human concept of the divine. No, a Holy Scripture requires "faith," and for this very reason there must be disagreement so that the choice of faith can take place or that faith becomes a choice and the possibility of offense gives tension to faith.

Take a purely human situation. If someone had a friend and wanted to test his faith or demand faith, I wonder if he would communicate to him a piece of information on which there was total agreement in every least detail? No, he would say: Does this require "faith"? No, he would put in a few little discrepancies, and then it would become apparent if the friend would "believe."

It is the same with the concept "God-man" as with the concept "Holy Scripture." Scientific scholarship lays this out in direct categories, also; if someone is a God-man, then it must be directly and absolutely certain, says scientific scholarship. No thanks, says God, you have surely forgotten what it is to have faith; there must be no direct recognizability at all, but the possibility of offense.

Scientific scholarship really ought to understand at least that much.

x^3 A 702   *n.d.*, 1851

« 3861 *Clement of Alexandria*[28]

declares that we must substitute the purely human—reflection, scientific scholarship, etc.—for what the apostles had directly through the spirit.

Here is where the confusion lies. It looks as if what the apostles had through the spirit was profundity, speculative intuition—instead of authority. Thus it is forgotten that Christianity is existential.

Simply because Clement of Alexandria must have room for scientific scholarship, he indirectly and without knowing it remodels "the apostle" so that "the apostle" tends to become a qualification of genius,[29] however lofty a place is to be assigned to genius.

x^4 A 110   *n.d.*, 1851

« 3862 *Apology—Apologetics*

Everything gets farther removed from the existential. In former days they wrote apologies; this was in the situation of actuality against the pagans. Nowadays we have a scientific scholarship which is called apologetics, a science of writing apologies.

x^4 A 280   *n.d.*, 1851

« 3863 *Scholarly Study*

Here is an example of how someone can be occupied in a scholarly pursuit without its having the remotest influence on him.

There is a German translation of Epictetus's four books of conversations by a Schultz, 1801, Altona. In the preface to part one he relates that this author has occupied him very much—and in fact he has also worked on the translation of his writings. We would then expect that Epictetus would have had some influence on the man's own being—Epictetus, that man of iron who as a slave said to his master, who was beating him on the leg: If you hit harder, you will break it. And he struck and broke his leg, and Epictetus said: I told you so, didn't I? Epictetus, whose main thesis was: Distinguish between the things which are in our power and those which are not (for example, public opinion these days), and that the latter should not be of any concern to us at all.

In the preface to the second part of this translation, Mr. Schultz writes: *Die gütige Nachsicht . . . . .* whereupon he makes an excuse for having hurried somewhat with the last part because of moving etc. and says (Preface, p. v) . . . . .—*und von Richtern, die noch ein Herz im Busen haben, darf ich nach dieser treuen Darstellung* . . . . . *Schonung erwarten.*[30] Is one to believe that this is a person who had devoted himself to Epictetus for many years—but this is scholarly study.

x⁴ A 409   n.d., 1851

« 3864 *The Confusion of Christianity*

Christianity is *praxis,* a character-task.

By making Christianity into doctrine, an object for passive, brooding meditation, there has arisen this confounded brand of thinkers who use forty pages for their flights of fancy and then on page 41 add: However, this is still somewhat beyond full comprehension. O, miserable waste of time. And even an Augustine is like this!

How clear, how virginally pure, if I may say so, Socrates is *qua* thinker, aided by his strong distinction between what he understands and what he does not.[31] If it has to be stated on page 41 that it is still beyond comprehension, then it is Socratic to save forty pages. But if this were introduced, what would become of all the professors!

x⁵ A 134   n.d., 1853

« 3865 *The Audit*

The audit is imminent, not the audit of Christianity, please note —no, thank you—but the audit of Christendom, of the practically insurmountable rubbish which the preachers and professors have concocted and call Christianity.

The primary requirement for this audit is a person of intellectuality comparable to being an apostle.

This intellectuality, of course, comes long after the apostle, just as being an apostle is also a whole qualitative level higher than this intellectuality, although it actually is the case that the apostle did not have it. I know very well that this will be misunderstood, as if I were speaking disparagingly about the apostle and conceitedly about this intellectuality. But this is a mistake, a mistake grounded in people's not being accustomed to having categories but, on the contrary, being spoiled by prattling with each other about everything.

No, "the apostle" simply does not lie in the sphere of intellectuality in the sense that intellectuality is his power, and it is a general disgrace upon mankind that a scientific scholarship has been erected upon such a book as the New Testament. This is precisely why the audit must also clarify the spheres or clearly separate them, for otherwise it is impossible to throw out all this nonsense which in the name of Christian scholarship has abolished Christianity by confusing what it is to be an apostle with what it is to be a person of intellectuality.

XI^1 A 461   n.d., 1854

« 3866 *Scholarly Research*

Scholarly research is given the appearance of Christian zeal, it is lauded for seeking to penetrate the mass of 1,800 years of history—and thus we do not see that it is a man-made swindle which continually places God at a distance of 1,800 years, that the truth is that we human beings are afraid of finding out to what degree God is the closest of all.

Therefore all this scholarly research—of which it may be said (just as an attorney is said to be a poor lawyer if in bringing one case to a conclusion he does not promptly create ten new ones) that for every problem it solves it creates ten new ones, making it necessary to have more professors etc.

XI^1 A 465   n.d., 1854

« 3867 *To Treat Christianity as a Science*

means to change it into something past or to express that it is no longer something present.

Science, theory, always comes afterwards.

Take another situation. The grammar of a living language can never really be made into a science; this can be done only with a dead language, for the immediate present being of the living language makes the science difficult.

In the periods when Christianity was something present as a religion and a faith—although attempts were made then, too, in the direction of science, they did not really succeed—and simply because Christianity still existed and consequently was not an imperfection.

Only our age has had the privilege of getting a philosophy which *boasts* that Christianity has completely merged with science—that is, Christianity no longer exists.[32]

But inverted as thieves' slang always is, we do not say what is the truth—that Christianity no longer exists. No, we say: What terrific progress! Now Christianity has completely become a science.

XI^1 A 557   n.d., 1854

« 3868 *Eternity—Time*

Although the really great religious figures, whose lives are sheer torment and suffering, can perceive just as well as I and better the infamy of this professional falsification of what it is to be spirit, they do not complain, and they describe their lives as blessed because they are so positive that the suffering is involved in an eternal salvation.

When it is difficult for me not to be annoyed by these professors, let no one misunderstand this, as if it were a perfection on my part, as if I saw something those glorious ones did not see or saw it more clearly. No, no, the reason is that I am not at all so positive that my suffering is involved in an eternal salvation.

XI^1 A 583   *n.d.*, 1854

« 3869 *Ridiculous Scholarship*

Peer Degn[33] says . . . . . "and when it is bound in leather it is called *Aurora* and is *declined like mensa.*" This "and is declined like *mensa*" is scholarship—and completely out of place, merely to betray learned knowledge.

And yet if one took a pencil and went through the books of even so competent a man as Dr. Rudelbach,[34] how persistently one would encounter that kind of scholarship: and is declined just like *mensa.*

Yes, from a Christian point of view, all theological scholarship is a counterpart of this: and is declined just like *mensa.*

XI^2 A 94   *n.d.*, 1854

« 3870 *Theory—Practice*
Doctrine—Existing

Theory, preoccupation with theory, is so far from supporting practice in the ethical sphere (that is, where the task is directed to self-denial, constraining flesh and blood, etc., for medical practice and the like are something else, are not related to character-formation), as if being preoccupied with theory were an aid to practicing it better, that theory here is simply a rascally trick. What Talleyrand[35] said about speech, that it is given to men to conceal their thoughts, can be said far more truthfully of the relation between theory and practice in the domain of ethics. Theory, doctrine, is there to hide the fact that practice is wanting.

Make the ethical as brief as possible—then attention will immediately focus decisively on whether one does it or does not do it, and if one does not, he is exposed in all his nakedness.

But theory, doctrine, produces an illusion, as if one were related to the ethical—by talking about it. Theory and doctrine are a fig leaf, and by means of this fig leaf a professor or clergyman looks so portentous that it is terrifying. And just as it is said of the Pharisees[36] that they not only do not enter into the kingdom of heaven themselves but even prevent others from entering, so also the professor prevents the unlearned man by giving him the idea that it depends on doctrine and that consequently he must try to follow along in a small way. This, of course, is to the professor's interest, for the more important the doctrine becomes, the more important the professor becomes as well, and the more splendid his occupation and the greater his reputation. Generally speaking, the professor's and pastor's spiritual counseling is a hoax, for it is calculated to prevent people from entering the kingdom of heaven.

Just as in the natural sciences and other disciplines with a lot of apparatus it is so difficult to get the dialectical process going, because attention is incessantly being diverted by intrinsically interesting knowledge of details, so by introducing doctrine we try to make it difficult for the ethical to penetrate in a discriminating way in order to see whether one is doing it or not.

The ethical declines whenever it becomes doctrine; introduced by a personality into personal existence, it is taken over by a *Schüler* who transforms it into a doctrine.

When this decline takes place, it is not long before the decline forges ahead and is called "progress"; this is likely to be done by the *Schülerens Schüler*.[37] From that moment on everything is sheer progress. Ultimately even the genuine men of progress, the journalists, take up the doctrine—and now it is unbelievable with what leaps and bounds it progresses.

There is something strange about this talk of making progress. Just as nature is kind enough to hide from cripples and deformed people the fact that they are crippled and deformed, so that they regard themselves as beauties, just so also talk about the progress of a cause usually arises when it is definitely on the decline—and it becomes more and more conceited and loud-mouthed in the degree to which the more and more trivial human trash latch on to it.

XI^2 A 117 *n.d.*, 1854

« 3871

Since the clergyman is paid and has a fixed income, he feels that he has to do something for this money—and he devotes himself to studying and studying and changes religion into a matter of learning —in order to do something and something really good for the money. Alas, if Christianity possessed money, it undoubtedly would gladly give it to the clergyman to cease, for what he is doing is simply the worst thing he can do.

The significance of Socratic ignorance was precisely to keep ethics from becoming scholarly knowledge—instead of practice. There is nothing more dangerous than to transform into scholarly knowledge something which should be practiced. To refrain from doing it is not nearly so dangerous, but scholarly knowledge looks as if it amounted to something and renders performance almost impossible.

XI^2 A 362   *n.d.,* 1854

SCHOPENHAUER

« 3872 *Human—Divine*

A verse by Goethe which I see quoted somewhere in Schopenhauer[38] reads as follows:

> "*Und wenn der Mensch in seiner Quaal verstummt,
> Gab mir ein Gott zu sagen, wie ich leide.*"[39]

This is really incorrect. It is much more likely to be the case that it is human to articulate sufferings and divine to remain silent. Esthetically it is perhaps as Goethe says; ethically, the latter is the case.

XI[1] A 75 *n.d.*, 1854

« 3873

Heraclitus:[40] τῷ οὖν βίῳ ὄνομα μὲν βίος, ἔργον δὲ θάνατος.

Quoted from A. Schopenhauer: *Die Welt als Wille und Vorstellung*, II, p. 584.[41]

XI[1] A 78 *n.d.*, 1854

« 3874 *Docendo discimus*[42]

Schopenhauer[43] says superbly that this is, after all, not unconditionally true—that there are many assistant professors who by lecturing continually *ex cathedra* are themselves prevented from learning anything.

XI[1] A 111 *n.d.*, 1854

« 3875 *Is Not Moral Philosophy like Astrology, Alchemy—a Science that Concerns Itself with Something That Does Not Exist?*

Schopenhauer[44] vigorously attacks treating moral philosophy as Kant did—presenting this ideal *you shall,* ideal virtues and obligations, without regard to anyone's doing it.

No, says Schopenhauer. Moral philosophy, like any other science, must stick to actual life, must present actual life. But—he goes on to say—then one could raise the objection: does not moral philosophy then become a science *a la* astrology and alchemy, a science which concerns itself with something that does not exist.

Schopenhauer himself does not really seem to perceive how extremely funny he is here, for he raises this objection earnestly, rejects it earnestly, and then proceeds to write his moral philosophy.

XI[1] A 112 *n.d.*, 1854

« 3876 *This Honest World*

Schopenhauer[45] says something like this and basically it is excellent: The only honest men in this world are the merchants, for they are still sufficiently honest to admit—that they cheat.

XI[1] A 140 *n.d.*, 1854

« 3877 *On Arthur Schopenhauer*

A.S. *[*In margin:* *Note. Strangely enough, I am called S.A. We, too, no doubt stand in an inverse relation to each other.] is undeniably a significant author; he has interested me very much and, in spite of a total disagreement, I have been surprised to find an author who affects me so much.

I have two objections in particular against his ethics.[46]

His ethical position is as follows: the individual comes to discern the wretchedness of this whole existence through the intellect, consequently intellectually, or through sufferings ($\delta\epsilon\acute{u}\tau\epsilon\rho os\ \pi\lambda o\hat{u}s$), and then decides to slay or mortify the desire for life; here we have asceticism, and through perfect asceticism a state of contemplation, quietism, is attained. And this the individual does out of sympathy (here is A.S.'s moral principle), out of sympathy because he sympathizes with all the wretchedness which existence is, consequently sympathizes with the wretchedness of others, the wretchedness which existing [*at være til*] is.

Here I am obliged to take issue. I could almost rather be tempted to turn the matter around and, please note, also on the very basis of sympathy. Whether someone arrives at asceticism by way of an original intellectuality, because he discerns the wretchedness of everything or, more precisely, the wretchedness that existing is, or he is brought by sufferings to the point where it appears to be a relief to let the whole thing come to a total breakthrough, breaking with everything, with existence [*Tilværelsen*] itself—that is, with the desire for life (asceticism, mortification)—which, with regard to the numerous annoyances, the again-and-again annoyances, can be a relief like breaking into a sweat compared to the distressing heat when one cannot begin to sweat—in both cases I would turn the question: could not this very sympathy hold him back, keep him from going all the way, sympathy with these thousands and thousands who are unable to follow him, these thousands and thousands who live in the happy illusion that life is happiness—and whom he therefore will only disturb, make unhappy, without being able to help them out to where he is? Is it not possible for sympathy to construe the matter this way, too, although I readily admit that right here is a good hiding place for the fraudulence which does not itself dare the uttermost and then creates the appearance of sympathy.

Now the second point, and this is a major objection. A complete reading of A.S.'s *Ethics* makes it clear—he is, of course, that honorable —that he is not any such ascetic himself. Consequently he himself is not the contemplation attained by means of asceticism, but a contemplation which relates contemplatively to that asceticism.

This is extremely dubious; even the most dreadful kind, a corrupting kind, of melancholic voluptuousness may be concealed here, also a profound hatred of man and the like.

It is also dubious in another way, for it is always dubious to propound an ethic which does not exercise such power over the teacher that he expresses it himself.

A.S. turns ethics into a matter of genius—but this is precisely an unethical view of the ethical. He turns the ethical into genius, and although he plumes himself on being a genius in other respects, it has not pleased him (or nature) to let himself become a genius along the lines of asceticism and mortification.

Here I come to a point which S. disdainfully brushes off, namely this "You shall," also eternal punishment and the like. The question is whether or not this kind of asceticism and mortification is actually possible for a man if he does not respect "You shall" and is not qualified by the motif of an eternity, not by his genius but ethically. S., who really gave up Christianity, always praises Indian Brahminism. But he has to admit himself that those ascetics are, after all, determined by a consideration of eternity, are qualified religiously, not by genius, and the eternal confronts them as a religious duty.

* *

To repeat, S. has interested me very much. And so, of course, also his fate in Germany.

S. has properly learned by experience that there is a class of men in philosophy, just as there are clergymen in religion, who under the guise of teaching philosophy live off it, make a bread-and-butter job of it, conspire with the whole secular world, which looks upon them as the true philosophers since, to be sure, they are philosophers by profession—that is, it is their bread and butter. It is quite true that there is such degradation and demoralization everywhere in Christendom that by comparison paganism is divine elevation. S. sees correctly that these esteemed gentlemen are—the professors. In this connection S. is incomparably coarse.

But here it is again. S. is no character, no ethical character, not a Greek philosopher in character, still less a Christian police-agent.

If I could talk with him, I am sure that he would either shudder or laugh when I applied the yardstick to him.

S. has rightly seen that this professional vileness maintains itself by one means in particular—by ignoring what is not of the profession. S. is charming, superbly unparalleled in incisive abusiveness.

But look now! How does S. live. He lives withdrawn and then once in a while sends out a thunderstorm of abuse—which is ignored. Well, there we have it.

No, approach the matter in another way. Go to Berlin, shift the stage for these scoundrels to the street, endure becoming the most notorious man of all, familiar to everyone. Keep up a personal kind of social intercourse with these scoundrels, be seen together with them on the street so that if possible everyone knows that you know one another. This, you see, undermines that vileness of ignoring. This has been my practice[47] here in Copenhagen, in a smaller setting, to be sure; they with their ignoring become ridiculous. And then I have risked still another course of action—simply because I have been religiously commandeered—of my own free will I have exposed myself to being caricatured and laughed at by the whole rabble, the ordinary people and the élite—all in order to explode illusions, and all in order that they may come to perceive that it is not a profane protest that is being made here, one which accepts the help of the rabble, but a divine protest which therefore even dares to spurn the rabble when it wants to applaud a victory.

But A.S. is not at all like this; in this respect he does not resemble S.A. at all. He is, after all, a German thinker, eager for recognition. Yes, it is inconceivable to me that such a brilliant mind as S., such an excellent author, is nevertheless so wanting personally in irony (for stylistically he has a lot), so deficient in the lightness of superiority.

There can be no doubt that the situation in Germany now—it is easy to see, because the literary hacks and porters, the journalists and two-bit authors have gotten busy with S.—is such that S. is now going to be lugged upstage and acclaimed, and I wager 100 to 1 that he will be slaphappy; it does not occur to him at all to cut the tripe to pieces —no, he will be delighted.

Well, it is not so strange after all. Representing a misanthropic view of life as he does so competently, he is then extremely happy, actually happy in a deadly earnest way, that The Scientific Society in Trondheim (ye gods, in Trondheim!) has crowned his prize-essay[48]— it does not occur to him that perhaps The Scientific Society rated it as a bit of rare luck that a German sent them a treatise. *Pro dii immortales!*[49] And when Copenhagen does not crown a second-prize essay by S., he rages, quite earnestly, over it in the preface[50] included in the published version.

To me this is inconceivable. I could understand it if S., in order to have some connection with these societies of scientists, had decided to enter the competition [and had been] amused at being crowned in Trondheim, no less amused at not being crowned in Copenhagen. But not the way S. takes it all!

But this is the way things stand, and it is tragic. S. is concerned outright about recognition; this is what he has desired, this is what he hankers for—he has been treated meanly but has not been broken by it; no, through it he has developed into a very significant author. But to be a person of ethical or religious character—this is not for him at all. The person of ethical and religious character goes about it differently. In the beginning, recognition on the largest possible scale is offered to him—he wants none of it, and here, then, comes the collision.

This is demonstrated above all by the "prototype," the only prototype, the Savior of the world. He begins with their wanting to make him king, but he will not have it; he wants—to be crucified. And yet he has to have that first [possibility] just to be able to demonstrate decisively the religious and to be able to wound his contemporaries decisively in the direction of the religious. If the first [possibility] were not in his grasp, then the question would always remain whether he was not, after all, just a human being who would still rather have been a king, perhaps even someone who in his aspirations was unlucky enough to be crucified instead of getting to be king.

Where ethical and religious character is concerned, the foreground is enormously important. But it goes without saying that when you run through history you very seldom find a person of ethical or religious character.

One thing, however, is indisputable: a secular ambition which one makes a mess of is one thing—it is something quite different to reject the secular triumph which is offered and then to be sacrificed. Only the latter constitutes being sacrificed.

Therefore it can indeed be said that S. is a low-order sacrifice to this whole professorial vileness, but ethically, religiously S. is not a sacrifice—for he would much rather be acclaimed. As mentioned, the foreground is enormously important; it is decisive for the defining of ethical, religious character. The important point here is to make it clear that the suffering is a voluntary choice.

This is genuine, elevated tragedy. But in daily traffic we do the best we can with the tragedy of wanting to be something big in the world—and not succeeding. Here tragedy is like comedy. Pure comedy, elevated comedy or purified comedy, is always of such a nature that we do not laugh at something which in another sense is basically wretchedness. O, but in daily traffic—and the majority of comic poets make a go of it by laughing at wretchedness. And they calculate correctly, since they covet wide circulation, for this corruption, envy, malice, etc. which laugh at wretchedness is far too common.

XI^1 A 144   *n.d.*, 1854

« **3878** *Arthur Schopenhauer*

Just as during epidemics people put something in the mouth in order to prevent, if possible, being infected by inhaling the noxious air, so theological students who are obliged to live here in Denmark in this nonsensical (Christianly) optimism could be advised to take a daily dose of Schopenhauer's *Ethics* to guard against being infected by this drivel.

But in my case it is different—I am protected in another way.

But just as natural eudaemonism must regard Christianity as poison, and wanting to be a Christian as equivalent to taking poison, so also Christianity must regard this eudaemonistic Protestantism, especially Danish epicureanism, as poison. For this reason it would be expedient to take a counter-poison in order to resist, if possible, infection.

XI^1 A 165   *n.d.*, 1854

« 3879 *A Beautiful Metaphor by Schopenhauer*

In the conclusion of vol. I of his *Die Welt als Wille und Vorstellung*,[51] he says that the relation between contemplation and action is exemplified by the actor who, having played his scene, goes down into the theater, sits tranquilly with the spectators and watches the next scenes, even though they are part of the buildup to his death in the last act.

[*In margin:* or as he himself puts it, that alongside his life *in concreto* a person continually leads another life *in abstracto* (vol. I, para. 16).]

XI¹ A 178   *n.d.*, 1854

« 3880 *Suicide and the Stoics*

Schopenhauer writes about it (*Die Welt als Wille und Vorstellung*,[52] I, para. 16),

saying that a recommendation for suicide is blended with their lofty morality "*wie sich unter dem prächtigen Schmuck und Geräth orientalischer Despoten auch ein kostbares Fläschen mit Gift findet.*"[53]

XI¹ A 179   *n.d.*, 1854

« 3881 *Schopenhauer and Christianity*

Schopenhauer belittles Christianity, jeers at it in comparison with the wisdom of India.

That is his own responsibility. I look upon S. as a very important author and one who will also have his importance for Christianity.

There is something false, however, in his gloomy Indian view that to live [*at leve*] is to suffer. On the other hand it can be very good for the contemporary age to be confronted with such a melancholy view in order to become attentive to the essential Christian principle, which Johannes Climacus[54] expresses: to be a Christian is to suffer—something that the New Testament teaches as well.

I have nothing against Schopenhauer's[55] raging violently against this "vile optimism" in which Protestantism especially excels; I am very happy that he demonstrates that this is by no means Christianity. But I object to the thesis that to exist [*at være til*] is to suffer, for Christianity thereby drops out in a way which S. perhaps does not have in mind. To be specific, Christianity proclaims itself to be suffering, to be a Christian is to suffer, but now if to exist at all, to be a human being, is to suffer, then Christianity is robbed of its dialectic, its foreground, an aid in making itself negatively identifiable, then Christianity becomes a pleonasm, a superfluous comment, chit-chat, for if to be a human being is to suffer, then it is certainly ludicrous to advance a doctrine with the formulation: to be a Christian is to suffer.

No, Christianity does not declare that to exist is to suffer. Quite the reverse, and therefore it is erected directly upon Jewish optimism, utilizes as foreground the most intensified lust for life which has ever attached itself to life—in order to introduce Christianity as renunciation and to show that to be a Christian is to suffer, including having to suffer for the doctrine.

There is a second problem in Schopenhauer's view which most likely is a sort of self-contradiction. Let me take another area. Slander, defamation, villainous attacks, etc. know all about prudent caution so that they do not promptly reduce a man to a simple zero and then continue year after year to attack him on the greatest possible scale, for there is a self-contradiction here—if he is a zero, then it is ludicrous to see these enormous measures to annihilate a zero. But this also applies to the whole Schopenhauerian asceticism. Christian asceticism is based on the thought that to exist is not in and by itself to suffer—thus there is meaning in asceticism. But if to exist is to suffer, then asceticism easily becomes eudaemonism, a claim S.[56] himself makes against the Stoics.[*] Take another area. Christianity does not hold that wealth cannot in a certain sense be called a good, and this is precisely why it says: Give everything to the poor. But if someone were to say: Wealth is an evil, show your asceticism by giving away your wealth, there would be a self-contradiction here, for in this case it is not asceticism to give away one's wealth.

In so many areas, wherever there is a dialectic, there is a zealousness which is so zealous in emphasizing the second that in its zeal it takes away the first and thereby basically makes the second impossible.

XI[1] A 181 *n.d.*, 1854

« 3882

[*] *In margin of 3881* (XI[1] A 181):
According to him, asceticism aims at attaining (through mortification of the will to live) a state in which, although one exists [*er til*], it is as if one did not exist—to such a degree asceticism means death to everything. But if to exist is to suffer, then to exist in such a way that it is as if one did not exist, that one scarcely knows whether or not he exists, is clearly eudaemonism—naturally, in a small way—that is, it is the highest form of eudaemonism if one assumes with S. that to exist is to suffer. If to exist is to suffer, eudaemonism of course cannot be

sought in the direction of existing;* it must be sought in the direction of not existing,** and the highest form of eudaemonism becomes the greatest possible approximation of not existing.

> *or in the direction of intensifying "existence" ["*Tilværelse*"].
> **or in the direction of curtailing "existence."

XI¹ A 182 n.d.,

« **3883** *Arthur Schopenhauer*

That he is a significant author, a very significant author, is indisputable, and it must be confessed with joy and gratitude that his life and career are a deep wound inflicted on professor-philosophy.

But yet, in my opinion, he is an alarming sign. For, strictly speaking, he is not what he personally thinks himself to be, which without a doubt would be extremely beneficial if he were: he is neither a thorough pessimist nor is he entirely free from being a Sophist.

He is not a thorough pessimist. Surely what our vapid and effeminate age needed was a genuine pessimist in full character. But look more closely. S. is not a man who possessed the power to be successful, to win recognition—and then threw it away. No, perhaps against his will he was forced to miss out on temporal and earthly recognition. But then to choose pessimism can easily be a kind of optimism—from a temporal point of view the smartest thing to do. —He takes it upon himself to assign asceticism etc. a place in the system. Right here it is apparent that he is an alarming sign of the times. Not without great self-satisfaction he says that he is the first one who has assigned asceticism a place in the system.[57] Alas, this is nothing but professor-talk: I am *the first* to have assigned it a place in the system. To go on, is not the fact that asceticism now has a place in the system an *indirect* sign that its time is past? There was a time when one was an ascetic in character. Then came the time when the whole business of asceticism was consigned to oblivion. Now someone boasts of being the first one to assign it a place in the system. But the very fact that he concerns himself with asceticism in this manner shows that it really does not exist for him, somewhat as Judaism is no longer a religion for the many in our day who esthetically portray the old-orthodox Jewish family life in novels. —S. is so far from actually being a pessimist that he *höchstens*[58] represents the interesting; in a way he makes asceticism interesting —the most dangerous thing possible for a pleasure-seeking age which will be damaged most of all by distilling pleasure even from—asceticism, particularly by regarding asceticism as a characterless spectator and by assigning asceticism a place in the system.

Nor is S. entirely free from being a Sophist. With all requisite abusiveness he hammers away at those job-holders, the professors, and the lucrative professor-philosophy. Fine. But how is S. different from "the professor"? When all is said and done, only in the fact that S. has wealth. But ask Socrates sometime what he understands by a Sophist and just see if he does not answer that undoubtedly making profit on philosophy is enough to brand a man as a Sophist, but it does not follow that not making a profit is sufficient to indicate that one is not a Sophist. No, sophistry lies in the distance between what a person understands and what one is; a person who does not stand in the character of what he understands is a Sophist. But this is the case with Schopenhauer. True, he says it himself and to that extent is to be commended, but that is not enough. And although he says it himself, he seems to forget it when he hacks away at professor-philosophy, but he ought to bear it in mind then, too, if he is really to be in character according to the admission he makes about himself elsewhere.

XI^1 A 537   n.d., 1854

« 3884 *The Law of the Strongest Prevails*
Now Reads:
The Law of the Shrewdest Prevails
(A. Schopenhauer)[59]

Well-spoken by Schopenhauer, and I am convinced that there is more to this than he thinks.

This is what I have always cried out: namely, that Christianity has gotten another aspect of life to fight against than it had earlier, and that the confusion has come about because preaching still takes the old direction.

The wild sensuality, the violence and aggression etc., which Christianity once zealously opposed, has now become shrewd prudence. In order that Christianity may come again, or through its coming again, we will learn to detest shrewd prudence just as mankind was trained to detest violence. (In one of the older manuscripts I have also developed this theme about shrewd prudence as the specific evil [i.e., XI^1 A 145].)

XI^2 A 20   n.d., 1854

« 3885 *"Journalists, Renters of Opinions"*
(*A. Schopenhauer*)⁶⁰

This phrase of Schopenhauer's is really good, and he himself also understood its worth.[*] He points out that although in the outer world the majority would be ashamed to go around in a hat, coat, etc. that someone had discarded, this is not at all the case in matters of the mind. There everybody goes around in discarded clothing. Of course, the great mass of men have no opinion, but—now it comes! The journalists, who live by renting opinions, take care of this deficiency. Naturally, as Schopenhauer rightly adds, what they get is of the same quality generally found in the costumes rented out by the renters of masquerade costumes.

Incidentally, it is a quite simple matter. Gradually, as more and more are forever wrenched out of the innocence of having no duty whatsoever to have an opinion and into the "duty" (it is every man's duty, says the journalist) of having to have an opinion: what are the poor people to do! An opinion becomes an article of necessity for the whole great public—and so it is that the journalist offers his assistance —by renting out opinions. He operates on a double track: first he drills it into them with all his might that it is necessary for every man to have an opinion—and then, then he recommends his own assortment.

The journalist makes men doubly ludicrous. First by making them believe that it is necessary to have an opinion—and this is perhaps the most ludicrous aspect of the matter: one of those unhappy, inoffensive citizens who could have such an easy life, and then the journalist makes him believe that it is necessary to have an opinion. And then to rent them an opinion which despite its flimsy quality is nevertheless put on and carried around as—an article of necessity.

XI² A 58   *n.d.*, 1854

« 3886

[*] *In margin of 3885* (XI² A 58):
Note. In one respect I almost resent having begun to read Schopenhauer. I have such an indescribably scrupulous anxiety about using someone else's expressions without acknowledgment. But his expressions are sometimes so closely akin to mine that in my exaggerated diffidence I perhaps end by ascribing to him what is my very own.

XI² A 59   *n.d.*

SELF

« 3887

According to Christian doctrine man is not to merge in God through a pantheistic fading away[61] or in the divine ocean through the blotting out of all individual characteristics, but in an intensified consciousness "a person must render account for every careless word he has uttered,"[62] and even though grace blots out sin, the union with God still takes place in the personality clarified through this whole process.[63]

II A 248   August 20, 1838

« 3888

There are men whose corruption is not brought about by external damage but which develops, like rottenness in certain fruits, in the heart, in the core.

II A 297   November 13, 1838

« 3889

The states of a man's soul *ought to be* as the letters *are* in dictionaries—some are very strongly and copiously developed, others have but a few words listed under them—but the soul ought to have a full and complete alphabet.

II A 337   January 23, 1839

« 3890

That Christianity is the opposite of pantheism can be seen also from the caricature that accompanies it. The caricature of pantheism is obviously the evaporation of the person brought about by luxuriousness, the poetic world that the individual projects, in which authentic conscious existence is surrendered and everything is poetry, in which the individual is at most like a flower woven in damask cloth. The antithesis to Christianity is hypocrisy, but this is obviously based on the reality [*Realitæten*] of the moral concepts: personality, responsibility.

II A 464   July 1, 1839

« 3891

What it means to damage one's soul.[64]

If you could manage to spin an ingenious net around yourself and everything you held dear so that nothing would be able to penetrate it, no dangers etc.—and if you lived securely within your fortification —but damaged your soul. . . . .there is an external corruption obvious to everyone—there is an internal corruption that secretly devours the soul's strength.

Faith—Hope—Love

When common sense takes the place of these, one damages his soul —somewhere else the expression "lose oneself" is used.[65]

III A 139   n.d., 1841

« 3892

Aristotle also represents love of self as the highest, that is in the good sense (see 9:8, 10:7):[66] "Every man's true self resides in this part, namely, the thinking part."[67] Therefore he recommends the contemplative life as the highest happiness,[68] but happiness, again, is the goal of everything[69] and [he] defines happiness as an intrinsically desirable *activity* (see 10:6).[70] See 10:8 about the felicity of the gods.[71] It is readily seen here that Aristotle has not understood this self deeply enough, for only in the esthetic sense does contemplative thought have an entelechy, and the felicity of the gods does not reside in contemplation but in eternal communication. —Aristotle has not perceived the qualification of spirit. Therefore he recommends even external goods, although only as an accompaniment, a drapery, but at this point he lacks the category for making a consummating movement.

IV C 26   n.d., 1842-43

« 3893

What is the self that remains when a man has lost the whole world and still has not lost himself.[72]

The preachers must surely know this; after all, they preach about it every Sunday.

IV C 77   n.d., 1842-43

« 3894

The most dreadful thing that can happen to a man is that he himself becomes ludicrous in the essentials, that he discovers, for example, that the substance of his feelings is drivel.[73] In his relation to another person a man can easily run this danger—for example, by believing shouts and cries etc.[74] Here everything depends on being well constructed.

IV A 166   *n.d.*, 1843–44

« 3895

Suppose a man who customarily greets you is walking with a very prominent man and does not greet you. Is this pride? Far from it—it is because he himself is dubious of being able to sustain the comparison; Goethe would not have done it.

VI A 132   *n.d.*, 1845

« 3896

Empedocles supposed that there were two kinds of insanity—the one had its basis in physical illness, the other in the purification of the soul.

See Ritter I, p. 571.[75]

In a note he quotes Coel. Aurel., *De morbis chron.*, 1,5: *Empedoclem sequentes alium (sc. furorem) dicunt ex animi purgamento fieri, alium alienatione mentis ex corporis causa sive iniquitate.*[76]

VII^1 A 47   *n.d.*, 1846

« 3897

The strayed sheep—a picture of the wretchedness of going astray; the lost penny[77]—a picture of the wretchedness of getting lost in the world. In the one there is more guilt, in the other more suffering. A poor, insignificant man so easily loses the conception of himself, as if he were nothing, he who is disregarded by all. But Christ seeks the lost penny; the lost penny is more important to him than the 99.

VIII^1 A 625   *n.d.*, 1848

« 3898

Antoninus,[78] who as a Stoic naturally sanctions and recommends suicide, nevertheless disapproves of the martyrdom of the Christians (XI, 3). He insists that the willingness of the soul (to die, to do away with itself) ought to be the consequence of one's own conviction, not mere opposition, as with the Christians; no, this willingness ought to express itself with deliberate dignity, and, in order to convince others, without all this tragic pomp. Thus what he really disapproves of is the whole Christian view of contending with the world. What he is asking for is a sustained selfishness which does not choose death in order to serve a cause etc. but because at present it appeals most to the self. The

Stoical self is the most isolated self; it would therefore presumably be a mistake for his death to serve a cause. No, his death must merely satisfy himself.

IX A 373 *n.d.*, 1848

« 3899

In relation to the good as well as to the evil, to the demonic as well as to the religious, it is a matter of being a substantial ego—that is, a substantial egoity, subjectivity. The majority of men do not have sufficient subjectivity for Governance really to get a hold on them, and therefore they become in the most profound sense neither good nor evil, but a mixture. The same egoity who is a despot, a tyrant, a great figure of that sort, can be a truly religious person—but in that case this egotism is crushed and placed under God in unconditional obedience. —The lives of most men are like the grass—only the trees catch the storm, and they experience a great deal, but the grass experiences practically nothing.

The person who in the crucial moment of his life, when it is a matter of completely involving himself with God and taking the *coup de grace,* turns to another human being—his religiousness will become human sympathy. For a man cannot essentially grasp or believe in anything higher than that in which he himself has his life.

It may be said that to take refuge in another human being at such a moment is natural, human, modest, is one's duty. But the question still is whether it is not also a lack of confidence in God—for God is nevertheless the closest of all to a person. But it is a venture. One who does it in this manner—at that moment his religiousness will promptly take on a resemblance to cruelty. This is definitely Christianity. If the way of human sympathy were the truth, then, to be sure, Christ's life and the life of every apostle are a misunderstanding. To be sure, an apostle also speaks mildly. Certainly, and at other times he speaks severely; he alters his mode of speaking. But while he alters his mode of speaking in this way, his life remains unaltered, every everlasting day expressing the rate quoted, that he is not dabbling in sympathy but lets it come to a head, to the point of being put to death, to the point where others become guilty of a murder.[79]

X^1 A 65 *n.d.*, 1849

« 3900

Luke 9:21. Peter answered: You are the Christ of God. "But he charged and commanded them to tell this to no one." Here we see how

Christ held to his incognito, still very clearly a teleological reticence implicit in his coming in the form of a servant.

Luke 9:25. What does it profit a man if he. . . . .*but loses or forfeits himself*; to lose oneself does not mean flatly to get rid of oneself, it means to retain oneself in damaged condition.

x^1 A 255   *n.d.*, 1849

« 3901

The only legitimate tears are those cried over oneself. Praised be the one who can say: Myself—that is the only object I have found worthy enough—or wretched enough—to cry over.

x^2 A 87   *n.d.*, 1849

« 3902 ***What Is Required in Order to Look at Yourself with True Blessing in the Mirror of the Word***[80]

[*In margin:* What is required in order to look at yourself with true blessing in the mirror of the Word.   New.]

(1) You must know yourself beforehand. For he who does not know himself cannot recognize himself, either; you are continually able to recognize yourself only to the extent that you know yourself.

A certain kind of preparation, therefore, is required. It is also physically true that a person who accidentally sees himself in the mirror, or if someone without his knowing places a mirror where the image he sees is a reflected image of himself—does not recognize himself.

Paganism required: Know yourself. Christianity declares: No, that is provisional—know yourself—and look at yourself in the mirror of the Word in order to know yourself properly. No true self-knowledge without God-knowledge or [without standing] before God. To stand before the mirror means to stand before God.

(2) But do not be afraid to see yourself. It is well known that men are afraid to see themselves physically, that superstition thought that to see oneself was an omen of death.

And so it is spiritually: to see yourself is to die, to die to all illusions and all hypocrisy—it takes great courage to dare look at yourself—something which can take place only in the mirror of the Word, for otherwise it very likely will become a fraud and one's self-knowledge like the whacks Sancho gave himself.

You must want only the truth, neither vainly wish to be flattered nor self-tormentingly want to be made a pure devil.

(3) You must conceive an implacable hatred for the self which the mirror shows as being that to which you should die, the old man.

x⁴ A 412   *n.d.*, 1851

« 3903 *My God, My God, Why Have You Forsaken Me!*

These words signify that the prototype [*Forbilledet*] is not characterized by Stoicism or Stoical self-satisfaction but that he must and will hold out beyond the leaping-off point (suicide) of the Stoic, who wants to exclude all impressions other than the impression of himself and, when he can no longer manage that, prefers to destroy and annihilate, if possible, his self.

These words are consoling to those who imitate [Christ]. Where was there ever a martyr who in the most agonizing moment or in a moment of weakness was not on the verge of losing his conception of himself, as if he had been abandoned by God. But at the time his life truly seems to be infinite despair. He is lost for this life; he himself has made it agony—and a better world, yes, that might seem to him to be even greater agony, to have to live a whole eternity and have the impression, be hounded by the memory, of having lost his conception of himself.

This, you see, is why the prototype consoles by showing that this, too, belongs.

In a certain sense it may be said that to feel abandoned by God belongs to the proper emptying out of the human being standing face to face before God, so that the martyr is not motivated by human self-satisfaction.

But if this belongs, there is nothing depressing in having to be reminded that one has undergone this human suffering of feeling abandoned by God, of losing the conception of oneself, precisely because having suffered the uttermost gives one the conception of himself again, on the highest level.

XI¹ A 285   *n.d.*, 1854

SENECA

« 3904

As far as I can remember, it is Seneca[81] who says the remarkable words: *Quæ latebra est, in quam non intret metus mortis.* —

II A 153   *n.d.,* 1837

« 3905

The beginning of Seneca's treatise *De ira*[82] is rhetorically beautiful. To show how inhuman and unworthy of man anger is, he forms a proposition with the antitheses: man is born for mutual support, anger for corruption etc. (this is in chapter V); thus man—and anger —are placed in opposition to each other.

X^1 A 493   *n.d.,* 1849

« 3906

At present I am reading Seneca's letters and find them excellent, the little quotations from Epicurus which are incorporated are also splendid.

In the 22nd letter[83] a passage from Epicurus is quoted, which among other things states: "From the most difficult of situations there is hopefully a happy way out, if one does not hurry before it is time or procrastinate when it is time."

X^3 A 29   *n.d.,* 1850

« 3907

Seneca's 22nd letter[84] quotes a Stoic: He is not a man of courage if his courage does not increase under difficulties.

X^3 A 31   *n.d.,* 1850

« 3908

Seneca's 26th letter.[85] Quoted from Epicurus: "Prepare yourself for death; it is better that it approaches you now, or you, it." Thus Seneca is saying that it is a glorious thing to learn to die. You perhaps consider it superfluous to learn something you can use only once? This is the very reason we must prepare ourselves. That which cannot be experienced in advance must be continuously learned if we want to understand it.

For the most part Seneca's letters are pithy.

x³ A 35   n.d., 1850

« 3909

Seneca's 53rd letter:[86] "Why does nobody admit his mistakes? Because he is still ensnared in them. The person who is awake or waking up tells his dreams—to confess one's mistakes is a sign of healing. Let us wake up, then, in order to be able to convince ourselves of our mistakes."

x³ A 36   n.d., 1850

« 3910

Plus dolet, quam necesse est, qui ante dolet, quam necesse est.

Seneca, Ep. 98.[87]

x³ A 452   n.d., 1850

« 3911

Seneca: *quare vitia sua nemo confitetur? Quia etiam nunc in illis est. Somnium narrare vigilantis est.*

(Epistle 55.)[88]

x³ A 481   n.d., 1850

« 3912

Seneca[89] says:

It is not really courageous if the courage does not increase with the danger.

x³ A 601   n.d., 1850

SERMONS

« 3913 *Miscellany*

Outline for a sermon on I Timothy 3:16.[90] *Introduction.* All the rest of the points enumerated (ἐφανερώθη ἐν σαρκί etc.) are purely historical and are reported just like other events; (1) but these words, "He was believed on in the world," is this also merely a historical report, a news item, which you have just as others do by way of second-hand reports—or is it something far deeper for you, can you and your life also be a testimony for yourself and for others to the accuracy of these words: He was believed on in the world. Is this faith so living and so firm within you that even if the world did not understand you, you could still say: He was believed on in the world. If it is not, if the firmness of your conviction about these words is more or less conditioned by what others say, then remember (2) that after these words, "He was believed on in the world," comes: "He was taken up in glory." This existence was given as a time for transformation—"You shall judge the angels"—many nations in the world to whom Christ did not come—you do not want to blur the statement with that—was he not offered to you—do you know the ways of providence—were you not among the many who were called—or will you console yourself because that was the case with many others, also—will you blur your grief over the death of a father by the thought that every day 100,000 die on this earth—you must not tempt God—would that this hour might help you to be able to say: He was believed on in the world.

II A 1   *n.d.*, 1837

« 3914

That was the prayer.[91]

The text should be, "John, who preaches in the desert."

Devout Listeners:

What have you come to the desert to see? This is the earnest preliminary question with which John as the forerunner of the Lord prepares the way for him in the minds of the people and calls the Jews to reflection ..... At times when we come up to this holy place to proclaim the Word we may likewise be tempted to ask: What have you come out to see? Was it [to see] a man dressed in fine clothes, did you want to hear a sermon embellished in human fashion with worldly pomp and glory ..... look for that in your own social gatherings ..... and if I were low enough for that, I would still wish that I eventually might muster the strength of Samson to wreck the magnificence of the temple and like him I would not care even if it meant my own ruin. ..... *Was it a reed tossed to and fro by the wind?* Was it a sermon calculated to promote the daydreams of the lethargic and to lull to sleep those still awake ..... look for that in the marketplace and streets ..... But the truth is that just as such a sermon is, according to the desire of many, compliant to the wind, so also shall it be cast away like chaff before the winnowing shovel; the Lord has everything in his hand. No, my speaking shall be like wild honey—its clothing like the wool shirt John the Baptizer wore, rough and sharp, perhaps to many a severe talk. —Yet, after all, you are not seated in a temple built with human hands; even less should you take up residence in euphemistic phrases.

II A 286 *n.d.*, 1838

« 3915 *Sermon Delivered in the Pastoral-Seminary*[92]

Father in heaven! Draw our hearts to you so that our longing may be where our treasure is supposed to be,[93] turn our minds and our thoughts to where our citizenship is—in your kingdom,[94] so that when you finally call us away from here our leave-taking may not be a painful separation from the world but a blessed union with you. But we do not know the time and the place,[95] perhaps a long road still lies before us, and when strength is taken away from us, when exhaustion fogs our eyes so that we peer out as into a dark night, and restless desires stir within us, wild, impatient longings, and the heart groans in fearful anticipation of what is coming, O Lord God, teach us then, fix in our hearts the conviction that also while we are living, we belong to you.[96] Amen.

Philippians 1: 19–25

It is from his prison in Rome that the apostle Paul writes to the congregation in Philippi the letter from which our text is taken. Truly, if the beginning of the letter did not inform us of the fact that he was living as a prisoner in chains[97] in the emperor's palace, we would certainly have no idea of this from the words just read. For it is not the thought that the prison gate might open just once again for him to be led to death that calls forth his sorrowful longing to depart and to be with Christ.[98] His words sound to us as if he were living free and unfettered in the world, as if in the midst of his never-resting activity he had surrendered for a moment to solitary contemplation of the meaning of life and death. He longs for the congregation[99] he had established, for the scores of people he had led from the way of destruction to the knowledge and blessedness of truth, he longs for the congregation he loved, he longs for the Lord and Master who had called him back from the way of destruction, for the Lord and Master who loved him. Thus he stands before our thoughts, sunk in contemplation, a beautiful picture, elevating and strengthening, an object our eyes can rest upon— not as a faithless, disappointing illusion which disappears from our sight in the hour of peril, when a storm rages in our breast, but on the contrary [an object that] shines even more clearly. He stands high above the world like Moses[100] of old, lest he gaze longingly at a promised land he could never set foot upon; he considers the blessing he had propagated round about the world, and from afar he hears the prayers and supplications of the devout,[101] the congregations' hymns of praise for him, their founder and father in Christ. But he does not take this honor in vain. The earth does not imprison him; the world is too narrow for him. Powerful longings, a holy homesickness, turn his gaze toward heaven, and he, the apostle Paul, who could rejoice in a labor the significance of which few could match, imperishably memorable as that of no others, he nevertheless knows a beyond which is even greater, even more blessed. He does not have intimations (and how could a mere intimation bring him to want to abandon such a life?)—no, he knows that to depart this life and to be with Christ is ever so much better.[102] Consequently he is not wishing to go away because life has become a painful burden, the world vanity, his apostolic call foolishness. Truly he had not lived in vain, he had not done battle with the air.[103] His longing is sound and strong, the object of his longing consciously, firmly, unshakably fixed. His longing does not waste away his powers, does not make him unfit for his task. Strengthened, his thoughts turn to his call; rejuvenated, he feels new life in himself. And this, he says, I know and am positive of, that I shall remain and continue to be with you all, for the sake of your progress and joy in the faith.[104] As if he had as yet accomplished nothing in the spreading of Christ's name, he hurries ahead to new activity. Forgetting what is behind and reaching for that which is before, he hastens toward the goal.[105] He grieves over the many who lost the faith and went about as enemies of the cross of Christ[106]—if only his voice might reach their ears! He recalls with grief the infirmities of the congregations that needed to be strengthened in order to advance firmly along the way. He who describes himself as being a debtor to both the Greeks and the barbarians,[107] the wise and the unwise, yearns to make Christ known among the Gentiles again and to praise his name among the nations, to shout to them: rejoice, you Gentiles, with his people, and again: praise the Lord, all you Gentiles, and praise him, all nations.[108] He makes himself again a servant to all. He wants to preach the gospel again not because he is looking for a eulogy but because necessity impels him, and he has become everything to everybody in order, by being everything, to be able to save some.[109] And this same apostle, who witnesses that if our hope in Christ is only for this life then we are the most wretched of all men,[110] proves also by his life that he hoped for this life too; for if to live in the flesh, he says, procures for me the fruit of my labor, then I do not know what I should choose;[111] his conduct teaches us that he knew what it is to make the most of the time.[112]

Such observations and reflections as these, which the apostle expresses in the text just read, have at no time completely disappeared from the earth. For even if there always have been many whose busy pursuits have not given them the opportunity to reflect upon what lies beyond, whose distracted minds could never collect themselves for earnest meditation, many who, enslaved in the service of the moment, diverted for a brief hour, infatuated by the lust of the eye and the world's vanity, and now, vanished like fleeting shadows, snatched away in the confusion of life, many who grew old among us but learned nothing, experienced nothing, found out nothing, whose lives disappeared without a trace in the world, in whose inner being life itself had left no impression, many who flitted erratically about, who thought themselves free and yet were the most wretched slaves of time—still there are always many left who do not completely reject such thoughts. Some of these soon found out that basically it was wasted labor to think about that which is beyond, that the time given to such reflection was really lost, since the insight gained was regarded as nothing. They did not keep this cleverness to themselves; they gladly involved others in it, would gladly be guides for the deluded ones. Activity in the world became their watchword. But then when everything went wrong for them, when insurmountable obstacles mocked their most zealous efforts, when unforeseen difficulties brought their greatest expectations to nothing, they despaired without hope in life, without hope in death. And when at times a longing for a hereafter stirred within them, it was an effeminate sigh, a plaintive, weak cry which was unable to strengthen and nourish because it had nothing to hold on to. Or they expanded the idea of activity in the world to include the conception of the enthusiastic cooperation of the race in a common goal. They bade everyone welcome who would join the immortal host which with the courage of youth would perfect its task. But the single individual who could not become quite intimate with such thoughts, who concealed an inexplicable private secret for whose glorious revelation[113] he sighed—they had no time to wait for him, they had no comfort for him, except to advise him to surrender and forget such thoughts, to quell these longings by intoxicating himself in the contemplation of the immortal achievements of the race. They let him wither and die. And when the individuals had used up their energies in this type of joint action, when they felt that they were no longer able to follow the young crowd that was supposed to solve his riddle, again the crowd had no comfort for them. Their time was over, they were indeed superfluous; yet like someone buried alive they had the consolation that death would be more compassionate and when it came would free them from their last pain and only joy, the memory of a life that was over and never more to be experienced. The age demanded new powers, and as nature squanders what it produces, as it coldly and indifferently blows to the winds the fertile pollen which hides within itself the life-germ of a whole world, just so the human spirit is prodigal with rational creations.

Others did not let go of such observations so easily; they were not so readily convinced, not so quickly enlightened. They struggled, as it were, to halt time's hurried flights, to make the transient moment stand still, in order to devote themselves deeply and intensely to such deliberations. No moment was to go by unused, but every day their reflections began all over again, their lives were consumed in constant deliberating and scrutinizing, they never came to choose because they were never finished with their uneasy calculating. Without balance, without significance, their lives were tossed about between equally empty thoughts. They yearned to get away from a life whose meaning they did not understand; they yearned for a life whose meaning they misunderstood. Like clouds emptied of water,[114] their thoughts were driven by every wind, and their yearnings became unfruitful labor pains. Intoxicated by dreams, they passed through time like shadows. And if they chanced to wake up and with grief perceived that this life, even if it had any meaning, was forfeited by them, they consoled themselves with an insipid and sterile vision of a life beyond which would compensate for what they had lost. Without the strength to live, too timorous to bear the burdens of life, they tried to fake a courage which dares to hope. They yearned to get away from this world, they yearned for a blessedness this earth cannot give but heaven alone possesses. And when they had embellished these expectations with their sickly fancies, when they had shaped for themselves a heaven as they wished it to be, their longings became more and more intense; then they felt convinced and were ready to convince others of the same thing—that to die is gain.[115] No doubt they avoided getting their own ideas mixed up with the thoughts of the Lord's apostles, that to be with Christ is far better.[116] And this did not disturb them, for their heaven was far more glorious, far more merciful, far more hospitable, much less limited than the apostle in his day and from his vantage point was able to imagine. All of them—to a certain extent like the apostle—now pondered the meaning of life and death, but they were not clenched between strong and powerful thoughts[117] but were confused and irresolute, shattered by contradictory thoughts, as unlike the apostle as possible. It is therefore with an earnestness which judges the secular mind, the frivolous effort, the vain longing, but which also consoles the troubled dejection, lifts up and braces the depressed longing and the shattered hope, that the apostle offers the words of our text:[118] "I am hard-pressed between the two. My desire is to depart and be with Christ, for that is better. But to remain in the flesh is more necessary on your account."

And we, Christian friends, we will not cleverly hide behind the apostle's words in order with his power to apprehend the worldly wise in their foolishness; we will humble ourselves under his apostolic authority and we will let his words judge the conflicting thoughts, let his discourse punish and discipline our misled minds; but we will also let his words comfort and calm the fearful heart that does not wish to be without God in the world,[119] that longs to be beyond with Christ, but which is troubled by the thought of how weak it still is and how unstable. Therefore, with the help of God and guided by the apostle, we will consider together the meaning of the words:
for to me to live is Christ and to die is gain.[120]

We will reflect in what sense one may say *for me to live is Christ* in order to be able to add: *to die is gain.*

In Scripture we find expressions and ideas that are used with a special emphasis, metaphorical descriptions that sharply define the contrast between the Christian and the secular and uncompromisingly confirm the separation. They describe the situation in the world before Christ as one of ignorance, darkness, death; they describe the individual before Christ as lost, ignorant, dead. But in the fullness of time for the second time there sounded over the earth: let there be light. He was the Lord Jesus Christ, the Prince of Life,[121] who himself is life; he brought the believers from death to life, from darkness to light. Even if these contrasts do not recur so strongly in the consciousness of those of us who in our earliest life were illuminated by the truth of Christ, who were preserved in the body of the Christian community, who did not need to wait longingly for the break of day but merely needed to look about us, to open our eyes to become present to the truth, yet this contrast is experienced by every believer to a greater or lesser degree. Or was there not a time also in your consciousness, my listener, when cheerfully and without a care you were glad with the glad, when you wept with those who wept,[122] when the thought of God blended irrelevantly with your other conceptions, blended with your happiness but did not sanctify it,[123] blended with your grief but did not comfort it? And later was there not a time when this in some sense guiltless life, which never called itself to account, vanished? Did there not come a time when your mind was unfruitful and sterile, your will incapable of all good, your emotions cold and weak, when hope was dead in your breast, and memory painfully clutched at a few solitary recollections of happiness and soon these also became loathsome, when everything was of no consequence to you, and the secular bases of comfort found their way to your soul only to wound even more your troubled mind, which impatiently and bitterly turned away from them? Was there not a time when you found no one to whom you could turn, when the darkness of quiet despair brooded over your soul, and you did not have the courage to let it go but would rather hang on to it and you even brooded once more over your despair? When heaven was shut for you, and the prayer died on your lips, or it became a shriek of anxiety which demanded an accounting from heaven, and yet you sometimes found within you a longing, an intimation to which you might ascribe meaning, but this was soon crushed by the thought that you were a nothing and your soul lost in infinite space? Was there not a time when you felt the world did not understand your grief, could not heal it, could not give you any peace, that this had to be in heaven, if heaven was anywhere to be found; alas, it seemed to you that the distance between heaven and earth was infinite, and just as you yourself lost yourself in contemplating the immeasurable world, just so God had forgotten you and did not care about you? And in spite of all this was there not a defiance in you which forbade you to humble yourself under God's mighty hand? Was this not so? And what would you call this condition if you did not call it death, and how would you describe it except as darkness? But then when hope, heaven's messenger, penetrated this darkness, when your soul felt renewed, when you felt the vigor of new life stir within you, and when the abundance of God's grace overwhelmed you, then you felt so happy, so rich, so content, so assured of your fellowship with God, so strong in faith, so burning in spirit, so powerful in withstanding all the crafty onslaughts of the tempter,[124] so blessed that it seemed to you as if all anxiety and restlessness, all strife and trouble, all fear and doubt, lay behind you, were fought out and conquered, far behind you, as on a still and hallowed evening, yes, as if even the last enemy[125] were vanquished, as if you did not even need to bow your head in order to wander through the valley of death, but as if heaven were open and your hand already stretched out for the jewel, for the victor's crown which is set aside for all who keep the faith[126]—did you not then burst out in jubilation: *I who was dead, I live?*[127] And if then you would not forfeit this blessedness, would not shrewdly surmise that the whole thing was a celestial joy that visits the joyless abodes of men in a happy moment in order to refresh one with its sweetness but quickly vanishes and no one knows from whence it comes or whence it is going,[128] and you would not let your soul again become cold and indifferent at the thought that there was no one you could thank for it, if you would not have it this way but on the contrary with profoundly humble thanksgiving assured yourself that God was present, that you not only were and lived and moved in him[129] but that he was present now as from the very beginning, when he loved the world in Christ,[130] if you perceived that the yawning abyss which separated you from your God was filled up, that a way had been made which connected you and him, by which comfort and strength could descend to you, and that this way was your Lord and Savior, Jesus Christ, who is the truth and the way and the life[131]—did you not then say *for me to live is Christ.* But the apostle adds these words: *to die is gain.* We have no desire to tear away the anxious soul's last comfort, we do not doubt that the penitent thief was with Christ in paradise[132] that very same day; but you do not believe, either, my listener, that such transfigured moments would disappear so that they are recognized no more;[133] you know very well that they contain a promise for the time to come, that in them you have the Spirit's pledge for the time which is coming. And if in such a moment you were to say: *to die is gain,* this would be a distrust of God, rooted in a fear that heaven's abundance would not always be so plentiful, its mercy not always so readily available, its grace not always so willing to witness to itself. But you became aware of another voice, also, deep within, a gratitude which desired to feel how much you owed your God, a fervor which desired that your life might thank him for it, a love of neighbor[134] which desired by God's help to be an instrument for saving even if only one single human being and for hiding the multitude of sins,[135] and then you cried out: *for me to live is Christ.* And you even confessed that your peace and your salvation were a gift of grace which no life, no deed, which the whole world could not earn or deserve, and you brought your thank-offering in shame and with averted face because you felt how cheap it was, because you felt that God's grace and love became even greater by the fact that he would notice it, and so, after all, it was not untruth, vanity, and pride in you if you desired to live. And was it not the same with Paul? From the moment our Lord and Master had stopped him on the way of perdition and had hurled the blinded and proud Saul to the ground in order to raise up the humble Paul[136] and draw him to himself, from that moment he found no more rest on earth. He proclaimed the Word by day, he worked by night. He witnessed in the heavily populated regions, in the noise of cities, he witnessed in the still recesses of prisons. He witnessed to the wretched and despised among the people, he witnessed to princes and kings, in Jewish synagogues, in pagan assemblies, he witnessed on land, he witnessed on the sea, he witnessed in life and he witnessed in death.[137] My soul is strangely moved; it is alarmed by the powerful pictures which glide by in imagination; it again sighs despondently: *to die is gain.* But you, my listener, you surely know that these great men, God's chosen instruments, were not in the world in order that we should be appalled by our own wretchedness but in order that we should praise and thank God. You know that no man can add one inch to his height.[138] You know—and this is sufficient for you—that you too are called with a divine call,[139] that the spirit is the same even if the gifts of grace are different;[140] you know that you too are God's coworker.[141]

There is a *godly grief;*[142] weary of the world, it does not draw its nourishment from it, esteems it no more, is not diverted by its multiplicity, is not disturbed by its noise, but quietly and deeply seeks God in its grief. This also is a testimony. There is a *joy,* a victory over the world; even if the world is not aware of it, even if in the hour of death it does not radiate in glory before the eyes of all, it witnesses aloud in the stillness of the night. There is a *hope;*[143] light as a bird it glides over the precipices, a hope of God's glory. There is a *soul-strength;* it is not tested in strife with external enemies but is tried in combat with the clever wisdom of the passions, with the blind impulses of the instincts. There is a *gentleness,* a mildness, an indestructible essence of the quiet spirit;[144] it witnesses more powerfully than many a loud confession, it does not incite opposition, it moderates and appeases it. There is a *love* which loves first of all;[145] there is a love which loves enemies,[146] a love which loves in life and loves in death. There is a *compassion* which visits the fatherless and the widows,[147] which gives away everything for the sake of Christ.[148] There is a *sympathy* which walks poor and empty-handed through life, which does not own gold or silver;[149] it owns only one earthly treasure, a precious linen cloth[150] with which it wipes away tears, it owns only one great riches—tears. There is a *reconciliation;* it wins the most beautiful victory in the world, it wins the vanquished ones.[151] There is *a peace;* lack of appreciation and scorn do not disturb it, it survives all strife; to the world it is an inexplicable riddle, a peace of God which passes all understanding.[152]

All these testimonies have first and foremost, now and for all eternity, one witness—the Spirit, who witnesses in heaven;[153] but besides they are all a promise for this life, here and now. Alas, but we all carry the Spirit in fragile vessels,[154] and when at times our work seems so insignificant, when, sunk in quiet melancholy, we sigh in humble grief over our having been given so little, we may at times impatiently complain about it; if now and then our own weakness occasions sometimes willful and sometimes unintentional misunderstanding, then it seems to us that the holy name is disgraced rather than glorified by us; when it seems that our witness denies rather than confesses our Lord and Master, dare we then justly say: *to die is gain.* Let the apostle Paul answer: "For I think that God has exhibited us apostles as least of all, like men sentenced to death; because we have become a spectacle to the world, to angels and to men . . . . . to the present hour we hunger and thirst, we are ill-clad and buffeted and homeless . . . . . we have become, and are now, as the refuse of the world, the offscourings of all things. I do not write this to make you ashamed, but to admonish you as my beloved children." Let him talk to us: "I urge you, then, be imitators of me."[155] Your mind will again find strength, your courage again be raised up to bear witness, even if it is ignored, misinterpreted, disdained. And even if you feel that your external, your visible appearance corresponds very imperfectly to your inner life, that your secular life is shot through with infirmity, that much which is thought to be good can be turned to evil,[156] O, it is precisely then that this inner life is all the more important. About this, too, you say: *for me to live is Christ.*

And even if the thought that we are all members of one body,[157] that we are all debtors to one another, calls upon you again to perfect the external revelation as far as you can, you still know that you stand alone, that there is an inner life within you, and you know that it is your blessedness that this life be unfolded and delivered up in all its richness. For of what use is it to you, even if you could witness not merely in words but also in your external life so that others accepted your witness, but you did not have the witness within yourself. Of what use is it to you if you could convince them about that which you yourself did not accept, if you could fortify them in that in which you yourself vacillated (therefore we say with the apostle, we seek to win men, but before God we are revealed).[158] There is a life within you; it is not seen, it is not heard, it avoids all scrutiny, it flies away from the world; in the midst of the world's confusion you are alone with your God. Yet even if this thing I mention is a secretive and obscure thing, it is not strange and unknown to you. Scripture talks about it with significant presentiment. This life is a concealed life; it is hidden within us, for our life is hid in Christ;[159] it is revealed in us, for this life is Christ in us. It is not our life, it is the Spirit's life in us,[160] it is a divine growth. There is a *benediction of prayer;* when your lips are dumb but your heart has overflowed, there is a benediction of prayer which possesses the assurance of prayers answered, there is an assurance of prayers answered which holds fast to God, because the Spirit given to each person individually[161] is the one who prays within you, because the Spirit comes to the aid of your frailty when it comes forward with unutterable sighs, and he who searches hearts discerns the Spirit. There is a *blessedness of contemplation;* it unites what God has united, it links together what God has linked together[162]—man with God and God with man; it shows you the image of your Lord and Master, the image of man in God and the image of God in man; it humbles you with the representation of your unlikeness, and you sink to your knees in adoration; it raises you up with the hope of likeness, and you rise up humble and full of confidence. There is a *presence of God* in us. Your mind is not restlessly agitated, does not drift in longing, is not shaken by a fleeting anxiety; your thoughts do not strain after heaven; your God takes up residence within you, is within you beyond all measure, is present within you, even if you notice it first of all with his disappearance.

In addition, this life has a growth, an unfolding, a coherence, a constancy within itself, a constancy which is not seen;[163] you perceive only its individual expressions but anticipate expectantly their inner connection. For just as this life flees the world, so it also avoids your own scrutiny, will not be possessed by it. For self-scrutiny breeds unrest and unrest breeds spiritual trial and spiritual trial breeds despondency and despondency halts the growth and grieves the Holy Spirit.[164] Only God knows this life, and it is not yet revealed what we shall become.[165] And when this life spreads more and more abundantly within us, when it attains mature manhood and the full-grown development of the fullness of Christ,[166] when even if the external nature is wasting away the internal nature is renewed every day:[167] then indeed we dare to say: *to die is gain*—not because death frees us from all the hardships of the world, but because in death we win a complete and undisturbed possession of that which here in life we had only in part and uncertainly.[168] And what was hidden and concealed in life, God, who sees in secret, will give us openly.[169] Then you will not wander away from here, for you were already away; then you will not wander to strange places, for you will come home; then you will leave nothing behind, for you take everything with you; then you lose nothing, but you win everything. Amen!

III C 1   *n.d.*, 1840–41

« 3916

Text: I Corinthians 2:6–9: Yet among the mature we do impart wisdom, although it is not a wisdom of this age or of the rulers of this age, who are doomed to pass away. But we impart a secret and hidden wisdom of God, which God decreed before the ages for our glorification. None of the rulers of this age understood this; for if they had, they would not have crucified the Lord of glory. But, as it is written,

> What no eye has seen, nor ear heard,
> nor the heart of man conceived,
> what God has prepared for those who love him,
> God has revealed to us through the Spirit.[170]

Prayer

Father in heaven! Well do we know that you dwell in light and that your essence is brightness, but for that very reason you are also dark (even in your revelation) and like a secret we are unable to utter. But then it is for our consolation that you see in secret and understand from afar. So test even our hearts, and according to the secret which each one's heart conceals and according to the way you understand it, make it clear also to him in proportion to his keeping the secret and his love for you.

The apostle Paul knew many, widely different ways of varying his speaking about the same truth—in order that he might commend it to men and if possible to win some. He did not do it for the sake of gain at all, for he had learned to dispense with and to do without the earthly without missing it. He did not do it for the sake of honor and esteem, so that some might name themselves after him and be adherents of Paul.[171] On the contrary, he consoles himself with the thought that he had baptized only one single person and consequently had avoided every occasion for regrettable misunderstanding. He did not do it with deceit in his heart, for he was open before God. He humbly confesses before God and men that he was the least of the apostles,[172] untimely born, not worthy of being called an apostle. But when it becomes necessary, when the word of one who knows how to debase himself is not listened to or heeded, then he shows that he is also powerful in word and authoritative in speech, that even though he humbles himself under God's mighty hand and gladly endures the doormat role of an apostle in the world,[173] he himself nevertheless has not forgotten that he is an apostle who dares to step forward; he affirms his worthiness and the doctrine he proclaims against every worldly, usurping obstacle (II Corinthians 10:5). When the Jewish Christians thought that they had an advantage, a firstborn's right which made them more pleasing to God and justified them in putting Christian freedom in the chains of ceremonies, Paul condemns this bent for quarreling and vainglory, he who dared put his trust in the flesh more than anyone else, born of the tribe of Benjamin, Hebrew of the Hebrews, a Pharisee according to the Law, who had done what even they had not, had persecuted the Christian community—but who still regarded all this as vanity and bitterly repented the last. If certain individuals in the congregation would be precipitous, as if they had already laid hold on perfection, then the old fighter, conscious of who he is, joins them out on the racetrack in order to let them measure the distance between themselves and the one who still did not think he had obtained perfection but only pursued it.[174] —If the congregation is inflated with a sense of security as if it would easily win what the apostles, like abandoned men, had to work for day and night without seeing any other reward than to be like garbage in the world[175] and to harvest the congregation's ingratitude, then he rages for a moment in order to remind them that he who has been swept up into the third heaven,[176] with fear and trembling works out his own salvation.[177] He acted this way only out of love, only that he might win men not for himself but for the truth. He incited no one, and in all that happened to him in his long life he found no occasion to arouse unhealthy passions in the believers. Even when he stands in chains before a miserable prince, his words do not seek to arouse bitterness, he does not incite, does not point to his chains in order to condemn; he has forgotten the chains and the world's injustice against him, forgotten all this out of concern for the truth, whose witness he is. He wishes that even that miserable prince were like him, wishes it so forgivingly that he adds—but without these chains.[178]

It was the same in relation to the pagan Christians. Paul was strong enough to keep the doctrine from being tossed about by every wind, but in the presentation, in the adaptation, he knew how to use every breeze in order that truth's unchanged word might find harbor in some heart. He has not rushed forward to throw over the pagans' altars, he has not scorned their wisdom, he has not thought this to be the way to become imperishably remembered for his zeal. From their poets he used lines[179] which were on the lips of the people so that his teaching might reach the heart through this channel. He has paused at their altar in order to interpret the truth of his teaching in and through the enigmatical inscription which was the pagans' highest wisdom.[180] But if when they sought to misinterpret this loving self-denial, this concerned long-suffering, which loved men and desired their good, when a worldly wisdom wanted to help him meet them at a halfway point in his explanation, when the luxurious, empty-minded life in the locality sought to take Christianity in vain, regard it like everything else, with its customary lack of discrimination, then he was again true to himself, to his teaching, to his responsibility for future ages. He did not bargain, he did not make a compromise with vague words, he did not surrender the doctrine to be corrupted and to degenerate in protracted intercourse with pagan sagacity, he broke off from reflection's long family register which wanted to help him advance the truth in the world in a way different from the way it entered the world, the way he himself had accepted it. He did not vacillate; he confessed that the teaching he proclaimed was an offense to the Jews and a foolishness to the pagans.[181] Even if half the world had derided him and the other little half had taken offense, he would not have changed a thing, not a whit, even if he must then have taken the teaching with him to the grave without winning a single one.

He incites no one, seeks no proof for the truth of the doctrine in that it is an offense to the Jews and foolishness to the Greeks, but he knows that the teaching is the truth. This to him is the main point. He knows that the other will happen with the foolishness of this preaching, since the Jews ask for signs and the Greeks seek wisdom (I Corinthians 1:22). He does not self-tormentingly crave this gloating certainty of the truth of the teaching—that it always scandalizes someone or arouses someone's scorn, as if this were his task in the world and as if he had only then accomplished it. O, lies and foolishness can also arouse offense and scorn. He knows the teaching is the truth, and if all the world accepts it, this will not convince him the more, even though it is the desire of his heart and his prayers; if the opposite happens, this will not enervate his conviction, exhaust his enthusiasm, extinguish his spirit.

Paul had to struggle this way expecially in the congregation founded in Corinth. Into this flourishing commercial city, which as a result of its shipping trade and its location maintained a living connection between the East and the West, flocked a great multitude of people from all corners of the world; different in language and in culture, they mixed with the inhabitants and by contact and controversy produced ever new diversities. In the congregation, as well, this diversity sought to assert itself in factions and parties, and in particular a pagan wisdom sought to press ahead as teacher of the truth. In his first letter to this congregation, from which the text that was read aloud is taken, Paul fights vigorously against this and seeks no amicable accord with the wisdom with which he neither had nor wanted to have any fellowship. We have heard his words read. Zealous for what had been committed to him, he does not want the doctrine of truth to worship strange gods or to beg the assistance of magnificent words; he confesses that even though he spoke wisdom among the mature, he nevertheless did not speak the wisdom of this world, the wisdom of the rulers of this world, which shall be put to shame, but proclaimed the secret wisdom which was hidden from the beginning of the world, hidden from the eyes of the rulers of the world, since they crucified the Lord of glory.

What if Paul had lived in our day! His concern for men would certainly have led him to find many a means hidden from us, but I wonder if, when this became necessary, he would have changed the definite, incorruptible word that offers peace, I wonder if one who had been contemporary with him and knew the earlier times would have missed not only the teaching but also Paul? Certainly not. But what results from this for one who is to speak in the congregation? Is he supposed to lead you, my listener, out of the holy house, perhaps, out into the streets and byways, or remain in the courtyard, in order to haggle and trade with worldly wisdom, not for your sake, for what would this benefit you if it still is not true, not for the sake of truth, for it aspires only to be proclaimed pure and unadulterated, but for vanity's sake, that the speaker may appear glorious in the eyes of the world? On the other hand, here in the sanctified place where you indeed know that this wisdom is a secret which was a secret, which was proclaimed as a secret and consequently continues to be manifest in secrecy, should he here try to parrot* the apostle's strong words and in this way foolishly make a big noise, disgracing the apostle and himself? Praised be the man who knew how to strive for the truth, the man who did not wash his hands and let the truth be crucified,[182] praised be the man who for forty years, night and day, bore up in actual danger, in hunger and nakedness, without a fixed place on this earth, renouncing everything, abused, persecuted, scorned, cursed.[183] But a man would indeed be a fool if he strove in the same manner although his danger was altogether different, not the danger of not fulfilling his apostolic calling but of not saving himself. Let the apostle keep the strong battle words which penetrate through to confirm the separation. But if we want to repeat his words after him, would it not be as when a child puts on the armor of the mighty one in order to play warrior—would not the opponent soon discover that it was a child

---

*In margin: to copy the apostle's strong words.

hiding in there; would not the opponent likewise soon discover that it was a weak soul, an impotent thought** housed in the powerful words! Would this not be detrimental, just as it was essentially beneficial that Paul began what he would complete gloriously, began a struggle in which no terror would convince him that he still had not sufficiently consulted with flesh and blood, had not properly finished with himself, since he already would be finished with everything in order to begin to battle with the whole world.

Let us therefore rather apply the words to ourselves and talk each one with himself in particular about what he hears, not what relation the teaching has to the world but what his relation is to that secret wisdom. For this, indeed, would be the most tragic of all, if what was to the Jews an offense and to the Greeks foolishness, to Paul God's power unto salvation, if this were to become an empty sound upon his lips, loud talk in his mouth about its being an offense to the Jews and foolishness to the Greeks! Would not this be just as tragic as it would be if he knew about that mystery of godliness which Paul mentions elsewhere:[184] that God was manifested in the flesh, vindicated in the spirit, seen by angels, preached among the nations, believed on in the world[185] but he did not know if he himself believed it.

Therefore the discourse will stick to your sphere, my listener, and will consider

Your Relation to the Secret Wisdom

This secret wisdom proclaims *what no eye has seen.*[186] Did you see it, my listener, or was yours the relation not of one who saw it, even though offended,[187] not of one who saw it, even though he mocked, but of one who did not see it at all, or saw it as everything else in the world, something which tempts neither to offense nor to mockery? In that case, although seeing, would you not be like one who does not see. Should it be this way—that the wondrous would become so natural that there is no moment when offense prowls around in your soul, when mockery secretly plots against you in order to disturb your perception? Even an apostle was not far from being scandalized, but he became all the more zealous an apostle, because since he loved God the offense he felt had to serve to his good. Let us not make the wondrous all too natural; then what we are speaking about is perhaps no longer the wondrous, and what we say is not what we mean to say. Two wrong

---

**A tiny voice

ways have been mentioned: offense and mockery, for when the wondrous does not become the saving factor, it tempts a man either in defiant cowardice to lose himself and be offended or in cowardly defiance to revenge himself by mockery. For if he demands a sign—but the wondrous is the sign not in human boldness but in divine condescension—then he is offended, as Peter was; and if he seeks wisdom, then he mocks—just as Sarah laughed[188] when the promise was announced to her.

Did you see it, my listener, or do you merely say: Blessed are the eyes that saw it,[189] and even this, how do you say it? The glory of which we speak was not pleasant to the earthly eye, since it was an offense to the Jews and foolishness to the Greeks. Consequently the eye that saw it was not the earthly eye but the eye of faith, which looked trustingly through the terror in order to see what the earthly eye did not discover, what the seer was unaware of, what there was to see, just as the disciples did not see it when they walked to Emmaus,[190] and Mary Magdalen[191] did not see it when she stood by the grave—in order to see what would trouble earthly eyes if the seer knew what he should see. Now it is certainly true that the eye of faith is always blessed when it sees the object of faith, but when you count it blessed, you are not speaking of seeing what may indeed be glorious to have seen, what fortune, what circumstances give one man opportunity to see and deny to another. When you count as fortunate the man who saw what the earthly eye is pleased to see and do it without envy but in all good will rejoice with the fortunate, then we extol you for not becoming impatient and coveting, for not becoming envious out of want, and thus your joy over the fortunate one contains your own eulogy. If, on the other hand, you count the eyes of faith blessed because it saw the object of faith, then you may either cunningly misunderstand yourself and what you say, as if something external were at stake, or you may instantly feel a secret reproach, so that you speak as if you had been denied the opportune hour to see what the believer in that far-off time saw, a secret reproach so that you misuse a word which applies more particularly to times past, prior to the fullness of time, which desired to see what the believer saw,[192] but what the believer will not cease seeing if he himself wants to see. You must—if you are honest—feel a dissatisfaction with yourself for using that word as a hiding place for unbelief, as if you would have seen at some other time[193] in the world what only faith sees, as if you, whose lukewarmness is strong only in misconstrued praise, would have avoided offense and mockery if that glory about which we speak had forced itself on you so that you might see.

Did you see it, then, my listener? With what? Was it by means of that beautiful power in the soul which consoles and gladdens, the childlikeness in us, that beautiful power which calls forth longing's desired form, the beloved picture of memory, more than a deceptive presence of the past—but also alarms with the frightful images of fear and presentiment? This power undoubtedly has great capacities, but what it produces is still your own work, even though what is produced acts in a secondary way by the power you gave it. And what this power brings forth the earthly eye may indeed have seen in one way or another, but the object of faith cannot be seen by the earthly eye, and consequently it does not manifest itself in the pictures of the imagination either. Would it be desirable that the object of faith be the kind of form which—something you yourself certainly have experienced—fails to appear when you need it most; for when security and stillness and quiet, in which the picture comes into existence, vanish, when struggles and strife begin, then nothing appears except what anxiety [*Angst*] and terror conjure up. And even if such a form appeared, it still would not be able to calm the strife, for what the imagination forms is a unity without structure. Thus if you wanted to imagine a king[194] but he was not dressed in purple—for then imagination would be able to help you, even if you had never seen a king—but dressed as a poor man, if you wanted to imagine him as not in a palace—for then imagination would help you, even if you had never seen its gloriousness—but with the poor and scorned folk, and if there was no hut so poor but that he could, as it were, walk upright in it, and there lived in the hut no one so wretched but that he manifested to him also that he was the king—would you be able to picture this? Or at this point would not the imagination despair? Even if you had read carefully what has been disclosed and preserved in writing, would you not still try in vain to picture to yourself the glory which was an offense to the Jews—for even if the king had wanted to visit the poor, which would be no problem, he would have transformed the poor man's hut into a palace—the glory which was foolishness to the Greeks—for if that noble king became unrecognizable only by wearing wretched clothing, and if the human shape as such were not already a disguise even though he was attired in purple, or if the wretched clothing had been a distinguishing mark which in a different way distinguished him more than all earthly magnificence—yes, then a Greek would certainly not mock.

But if you now saw this glory of which we speak, then I understand how you saw it—that you saw it believing. Faith itself is, like the object of faith, an offense to the Jews, because they demand that it be proved by a sign; whereas the wondrous itself wants to be the object of faith, to the Greeks foolishness, because they seek wisdom, but faith itself is a secret and only an apparent foolishness.

This secret wisdom proclaims *what no ear has heard.* Have you heard it, my listener—and how? Was the proclamation perhaps not secret because the word of which we speak, at one time whispered in remote places, is now proclaimed from the rooftops?[195] Does the secrecy consist in this? If a man confides a secret to another and through his carelessness or malice the secret gets out, then it is revealed, and it would be foolish if the two men thought that they still had a secret. But the secret wisdom is indeed only for the one who has ears to hear,[196] for only he hears.

Did you hear it then, my listener; or were you—not like the one who was offended but still heard it, not like one who mocked but still heard it—but rather one who hearing did not hear,[197] heard a breeze that drifted away, tempting no more to offense than to mockery. Therefore the one who was offended heard better; and the one who mocked did not forget so quickly. For the former was in a relation to what he heard, an unwilling surrender from which he could not tear himself away, and the latter continually had to defend himself with mockery against that which he managed to hold at a distance only in this way. So if you perceived nothing unto offense, although not until the moment when, saved in unconditional surrender, you discovered how close it had been, if you perceived nothing to mock, although not until the moment when in blessed devotion you consented in secret—then it is indeed doubtful not only whether you were in the proper relation to this word but whether you were in any relation to it at all.

Did you hear it, my listener, or do you merely imagine that you heard it; do you listen to it and say: Blessed are the ears that heard it? Yes, fortunate the ears that heard what the earthly ear wishes to hear, but we are not speaking about all this. What you crave to hear you have indeed heard; it is heard again and again; it is heard at all times in many places, and you need not say—who mounts up to heaven to fetch it down for us.[198] But then it was not the hearing itself that you extolled, but perhaps the one you counted blessed was the one who had ears to hear and they heard, for hearing always requires an ear, but the one who has ears to hear with has an inner ear. Yes, fortunate is he whose ear was opened to catch the innermost harmony, and if you count him happy to whom this is given, then we will again extol you for not pettily wishing that everybody should lack what you lacked. But of this we will not speak. The word was not a magnificent word such as tickles the earthly ear—then how could it be an offense to the Jews and foolishness to the Greeks? It was not inflamed speech, glowing with fire, for more than anyone else the Greeks comprehended the beautiful, and the fervor of enthusiasm inflamed the Jew. So it was not the earthly ear which heard but the ear of faith which, amid the temptations to offense and mockery, listened to hear the word of faith. Yes, blessed the ear that heard it. But how can you count it blessed because it heard what neither time nor space keeps anyone from hearing who has been informed of the proclamation.

Did you hear it, then, my listener, and how did you keep it? For one who merely hears the sound hears only physically, and even if it were human speech he wanted to hear, he would not really hear it if he did not hear something more, and even if he heard in a different way but heard nothing as soon as the something more began to speak, he still would really hear nothing. Did you keep the word with that upright power in the soul which adds nothing and takes nothing away but meticulously and unfailingly gives back to you what you have committed to it. Could you wish to commit the word to this power? Yes, it is upright, but when the struggle begins and your soul becomes restless, then you would certainly perceive that you resorted to memory [in vain[199]], because it too shares in the confusion. Furthermore, memory does not quite belong to you; it is in foreign service, dependent on something not in your power, for time blunts it and little by little tricks out of it what was confided until the final hour comes in which you most need the word of which we speak. Did memory succeed in keeping what you wished kept? To be sure, this particular word is something past, spoken many centuries ago, and this faculty is able to take hold of the past,[200] as it were, bring it to the foreground again, plain and present as a memory, without omitting anything, but also without forgetting that it is something past. If this is forgotten, then that which was confided is indeed changed, as if one distinctly remembered an event but forgot that it happened many years ago. But that word of which we speak is indeed just as much something present as something past, for otherwise it would not be wrong to count the ear blessed that heard it many years ago in preference to the believing ear that heard it yesterday.

But if you did not hear the word in a way by which it cannot be heard, then we know indeed how you heard it, that you heard it with the ear of faith. For like the word, faith is an offense to the Jews, since they demand a sign which would foreshadow the future, but the future is precisely the present, and to the Greeks foolishness, since they seek wisdom, but the present is precisely the past, which nevertheless is present without being a repetition.

This secret wisdom proclaims *what did not arise in any man's heart.*[201] Was it in your heart, then, my listener, as that which did not arise therein, or was it present in such a way that it did not tempt to offense and to mockery and had never done so?

But who has comprehended the human heart! Even the one who perceived it most clearly in his own breast, even he who knew how to listen most alertly and discern its every movement and every impulse within it, even he would end as he began: nothing is as incomprehensible as the human heart.[202] And if someone were to ask him what it is that cannot arise in a man's heart, he would be astonished at the question and would be able to answer only by asking for time to reflect, and upon the expiration of that time he still would not have answered. But if no man is able to propound everything that can arise in a man's heart, yes, if it never occurred to anyone to want to do it, who knows then if that wisdom might not have arisen in some man's heart, if there might not be or have been a solitary man in a nook of the world, if there might not be or have been a man in the noise of the city, in whose heart it arose? My listener, we do not speak this way in order to persuade the whole world, we speak only of your relationship to the secret wisdom, and if someone else were to think that decision on this question ought to be postponed until every thought which has arisen in any man's heart has been explored and examined, this certainly is not your relationship.

Was that secret wisdom in your heart, or do you merely say: Blessed is the heart that kept it? Surely you do not do this, since you well know that the means by which it is kept[203] is the same as that by which it is received, and the means is the same for every man and ready for use by every man who wills it.

If that secret wisdom was in your heart, was it in your heart without having arisen there but yet in such a way that you perceived none of the human heart's passive[204] [suffering] opposition in offense or active opposition in mockery, then it is doubtful whether it really was the wisdom of which we speak. Was it perhaps magnanimity on your part that you, as if to honor it, said: Truly nothing like this has ever arisen in my heart—but this was only a bold, enthusiastic expression about something for which you were indebted to another; yet there was nothing to preclude its arising in your heart, even though this clearly was not the case, even though it was laudable that you would not ungratefully attribute something to yourself falsely. Even if such wisdom did not arise in your heart, yet it got in there in such a way that it could not possibly encounter or could have encountered the misunderstanding of offense or mockery. But this impossibility is sure proof that such wisdom is not the wisdom of which we speak. For the possibility of offense and mockery certainly does not prove the wisdom but proves the impossibility of its having arisen in a deeper sense in your heart, even though it got there accidentally through someone else. Then it would perhaps be magnanimous if a person were to say that about another wisdom, but with respect to that about which we speak, where would the abundant magnanimity be or the authorization to talk big. For if you, saved, rest in that wisdom, then indeed the possibility of offense and mockery would have exhausted human magnanimity in such a way that it would have nothing, nothing at all, to appeal to, but could only humbly accept what would be the power of God unto salvation.

Was that secret wisdom in your heart, my listener, as that which did not arise in your heart but perhaps gradually became so natural to you that it was as if it had arisen in your heart? O, if a person did hide in his soul a word which once saved him in life's need! Perhaps the word was simple and elemental, perhaps it became clear to him through pondering on it, perhaps he could clearly, lucidly, with all the force of language, explain it to everybody, but one thing he could not do—he could not explain how it arose in him precisely in the hour of need; he could expatiate upon all its later influence on his life, but he could not explain how, precisely when the need was greatest, the help had been most available to him in this word. I wonder if he, even though he grew old and superannuated, would ever come or would want to come to the point where the word had lost that secret power for him? Or if a person had a secret friend, and it was very beautiful to hear him bear witness to how this friend had helped him many times and in many ways throughout a long life, but he could not explain how that friend had found him, since he himself searched the wide world in vain—I wonder if he would ever come or want to come to the point where his secret relationship had lost its wonderfulness! Or if there was a compassionate person to whom you once had owed everything and no one could without deep emotion hear you tell how his concession had not only been your salvation but the origin and source of your welfare, but you could not explain how, and every time you thought about it, about your debt, you still always said as you did the first time —it is impossible even though true—I wonder if you would ever come or wish to come to the point where that wonderful settlement would become less wonderful; would you, I wonder, understand or wish to be able to understand someone who would assist you to the explanation that you never had been so very indebted, after all, that your debt was only apparent, since the concept of it had been dissolved by the fact that all men are indebted in the same way and that your expression of thanks was an illusion? It is the same with that secret wisdom; even if it explained everything to a man, opened his eyes to see, opened his mouth to speak, expanded his heart to comprehend the abyss, I wonder if it would still ever become manifest to a man in any other way than in the secret. On the contrary he would certainly mutilate and spoil everything for himself by wanting to forget, by mendaciously wanting to defraud the wonderfulness of the origin. And every time he wanted to work himself back to that origin in his soul, he would again see the offense and the mockery standing beside the narrow entrance which is faith's.

But if that secret wisdom was in your heart as that which did not arise in it, then we do grasp how it was there, that it was in your heart by faith. For faith is, as it is to the Jews, an offense, because it will not cause a split in your being but will reconcile you with yourself, and, as it is to the Greeks, foolishness, because it will reconcile you with yourself, but not by yourself.

* *

My listener, this discourse has not roamed about in the world looking for a fight, it has not wanted to conquer anybody, and it has not even wanted to support anyone, as if there were a battle outside. It has remained with you, has not intended to explain something to you, but secretly has wanted to talk with you about your relation to that secret wisdom. O, that nothing might disturb this for you, neither life nor death nor things present nor things to come nor any other creature[205]—nor this discourse, which, if it has done nothing else, still has sought that which is indeed of first and last importance—to help you have faith, as Scripture says, between yourself and God (Romans 14: 22).

IV C 1   *n.d.*, 1844

« 3917 *Theme for a Friday Sermon*

Luke 24:51. *"While he blessed them,* he parted from them."
        It is really about the Ascension, but this is always the way Christ parts from men.²⁰⁶

VIII¹ A 260   *n.d.*, 1847

« 3918

For a Friday sermon the following words could be used from Gerhard, *Meditationes sacræ,* no. XIX, *De coenæ dominicæ mysterio:*
    *Mirari non rimari sapientia vera est.*²⁰⁷

VIII¹ A 261   *n.d.*, 1847

« 3919 *Text for a Friday Sermon*

        Our citizenship is in heaven.²⁰⁸
. . . . . We are especially aware of this today—for every time these words are repeated: Our Lord Jesus Christ "on the night when he was betrayed,"²⁰⁹ the congregation steadily draws still closer around him, as if the traitor were coming nearer again.

VIII¹ A 265   *n.d.*, 1847

« 3920 *Text for a Friday Sermon*

    I John 3:20: "Even though our hearts condemn us, God is greater than our hearts."²¹⁰
Is it not this which is expressed today: in the confession of sin we all step forward today—and consequently we condemn ourselves—but God is greater.

VIII¹ A 266   *n.d.*, 1847

« 3921 *For a Friday Sermon*

Every holy day is a break in the ordinary (and this is good), but the holy day itself is an ordinary break and in turn can so easily grow into a habit. But Friday is originality's break.

VIII¹ A 285   *n.d.*, 1847

« 3922 *Friday Sermon*

Text: I have earnestly desired to eat this passover with you.²¹¹
Theme: the truly inward longing to go to communion.²¹²

VIII¹ A 287   *n.d.*, 1847

« 3923 *Text for Friday Sermon*

He lives that he may always make intercession for us.

VIII[1] A 324   *n.d.*, 1847

« 3924

From Friday Discourse no. 1.[213]

In the night when he was betrayed. It is midnight; the city sleeps, the populous city is as if dead, everything is quiet and peaceful in the night. Only treachery, which walks about at night, is sneaking around in the dark; only evil, which turns night into day, awakens now as if it were day; only "the high priests are glad" (Luke 22:6) that the darkness has conquered and may conquer "without making any uproar."[214] In "the great room" he is sitting at the table with his apostles for the last time. (Luke 22:6).

Was not used—a mistake here, also, since it is evening, not midnight. Yet it says in John 13:30 that it was night.

VIII[1] A 386   *n.d.*, 1847

« 3925 *Text for a Friday Sermon*

In remembrance of me.[215]

1. Do this in remembrance of Him—this is to His honor and glory; therefore it is required, just as God requires that you shall remember the Sabbath day and keep it holy.

2. Do this in remembrance of Him—because to remember Him, His remembrance, is your redemption. He, the Redeemer, never requires anything of you except what is for your salvation; it is to His honor and the same is your salvation; it is for His sake and it is for your own sake: O wondrous uniting, to do two things at one time this way.

VIII[1] A 498   *n.d.*, 1847-48

« 3926 *From a Possible Friday Sermon*

..... But you who are now assembled here to share in the Supper in remembrance of our Lord Jesus Christ, which was instituted that night, you have yourselves prayed that he will present his sufferings and death before your eyes in a living way. O, there are perhaps those who pray that they might be allowed to see what kings and nobles desired in vain to see, one of his days of glory—do not repent of your choice—but he nevertheless would choose the truly better part who chooses first and foremost that the horrifying might appear to him in a living way.

VIII[1] A 506   *n.d.*, 1848

« 3927 *The Pharisee and the Tax-Collector*[216]

> The one lifted up his eyes
> the other cast his eyes down
> how one who truly prays looks up
> and how he also looks down.
>
> VIII[1] A 635   *n.d.*, 1848

« 3928 *Friday Sermon*

On Wednesday evening when I had my discourse[217] ready for today,[218] I almost threw it away and chose this theme, which has gripped me so powerfully.

It should be based on this passage in Hebrews:[219] We have a high priest who is tempted in all things without sinning.

How Christ put himself in our place.

(1) A person who is suffering always complains that the one who wants to console him does not put himself in his place. One person can never quite do this in relation to another—there is a boundary. But Christ did it.[*] He was God and became man; consequently he put himself in our place. And in every way he put himself in the sufferer's place. If it is poverty and need—he too was poor. If it is ignominy etc. —he too was scorned. If it is fear of death—he too suffered death. If it is sorrow over someone who has died—he too wept for Lazarus. If it is sadness for the confusion and corruption in the world—he too wept over Jerusalem.[**]

(2) Tempted in all things—yet without sin. He was tempted just as you are. Here it is exactly the same, that one who feels the temptation says that the other person does not understand him, does not put himself in his place. But Christ set himself in your place. To be developed.

(3) And yet without sin. In this respect he did not put himself in your place. Yet in another sense he did: Christ's *atoning* death, he died for you, suffered the punishment of sin in your place.[†]

IX A 266   September 1, 1848

« 3929

[*] *In margin of 3928* (IX A 266):

He *is able* to have sympathy for our frailties—for he was tried in like manner (this is the condition for sympathy), and he must have sympathy for our frailties, for it was precisely in order to have sympathy for our frailties that through his own voluntary decision he was tried in all things.

IX A 267 n.d.

« 3930

[**] *Addition to 3928* (IX A 266):

Yes, in one sense he more than put himself in our place, for the hardest of all is to have been rich and then to become poor, when one has been happy and then to become unhappy; no man was ever tried in such a reversal as he: to be God and then to become a poor servant, to come from heaven down to earth.

IX A 268 n.d.

« 3931

[†]*In margin of 3928* (IX A 266):

(3) He put himself completely in your place, was tempted in all things in the same way—yet without sin.

..... And when punitive justice here in the world or in the judgment hereafter seeks the place where I, a sinner, stand with all my guilt, with my many sins, it will not find me; I no longer stand at my place, I have left it and another stands at my place in my place; I stand saved beside the other, Him, my Redeemer, who put himself in my place—therefore accept my gratitude, Lord Jesus Christ.

Here presumably the discourse is essentially finished—and then just a few words to those who are going to communion.

IX A 269 n.d.

« 3932 *The Difference between the Pharisee and the Tax-collector*[220]

(1) The tax-collector stood far off by himself. The Pharisee presumably had chosen the top place, where he stood by himself.
(2) The Pharisee talks with himself.
   The tax-collector talks with God.
   To be sure, the Pharisee fancies that he is talking with God, but it is easy to see that it is a delusion.
   This is a big difference.
(3) The tax-collector looks down.
   The Pharisee presumably looks proudly upward.
(4) The Pharisee *thanks* God—and yet actually blasphemes him.
   The tax-collector accuses himself, prays—Honors God.
(5) The tax-collector went home justified.

Assuming even that the Pharisee went up justified—the manner he went up into God's house became a fault which he in any case took home. Probably it escaped him completely that among other things his fault was going up into the house of the Lord in this way; if he had stayed home he would have had one fault fewer.

IX A 272   n.d., 1848

« 3933 *Text for a Friday Sermon*

Just the verse from the gospel about the tax-collector and the Pharisee:[221]

but the tax-collector stood far off by himself and did not even dare lift up his eyes, but said: God, be merciful to me a sinner.

You, however, are now closer—you are now about to go up to the altar, even though you are still far off. But in a sense the altar is the place where one is nearest to God.

In margin: In the inwardness of the consciousness of his sin (and this inwardness determines the distance) the Christian stands still farther away—and yet at the foot of the altar he is the nearest to God it is possible to be. This being far off and near while the Pharisee in his arrogant rudeness was near—and far off.

"He went down to his house justified." This is to be used in the conclusion.

X^1 A 428   n.d., 1849

« 3934

In his sermon for the First Sunday in Advent, Zacharias Werner[222] says: Christ signifies one who is anointed; but there are only two classes of men who are anointed, priests and kings—and Christ is both priest and king, thus he is the anointed one in a double sense.

X^2 A 26   n.d., 1849

« 3935

Zacharias Werner[223] (in his sermon for the Third Sunday in Advent) put it superbly: John is the voice crying in the wilderness—and there still are wildernesses, our heart is a wilderness.

X^2 A 28   n.d., 1849

« 3936 *Texts for Friday Discourses*

No. 1. I Corinthians 11: 31–32.
No. 2. Matthew 13: 45–46.

The kingdom of heaven is like a man.

[*In margin:* How remarkable that the kingdom of heaven is compared to a man—one would rather think that the kingdom of heaven is something on the outside, into which a man is received. But the kingdom of heaven is also "within you"²²⁴—therefore it can be compared to a man. The unity of the subjective and objective, that the most objective thing, the kingdom of heaven, is compared to a man.]

He found a very costly pearl—and he went and sold all that he had and bought it.

But if he found it, he did not need to sell anything in order to buy it, for it was already his.

Here we see the true Christian proportions. It is grace, which you cannot buy, cannot earn—it must be given (just as he might find the pearl)—and only then can it be bought, only then can you sell all that you have in order to buy it.

It is the same at the altar.

No. 3. Revelation 3:20.

It is told that after his resurrection Christ once came through locked doors into a room where his disciples were assembled.²²⁵ This picture has often been misused to show the zeal with which Christ seeks souls, that he even goes through locked doors (the indifferent or the hardened). But this is untrue.

He stands at the door and knocks.

If anyone hears my voice and opens the door, I shall come in to him and sup with him and he with me. To be sure, the Communion supper is a visible event, these actual men kneel at the altar and each one receives the bread and the wine—but it still does not necessarily follow that Christ sups with every such person. *No, only with him who hears Christ's voice* (to be developed, yet in a quite different way than in the earlier "My sheep hear my voice"),²²⁶ *only with him who opens the door* (the door of the heart, for the door of the Church stands open to all and can be opened by one person for another, but the door of the heart can be opened only by the single individual himself). *I shall go in to him* (it certainly is true that in the Communion, following the invitation "Come," you come to Christ, but it is truly the Lord's Supper only when Christ comes to you) and sup with him and he with me (for it is not you who sup with Christ, but Christ first sups with you, and only then do you sup with him. Grace is everything).

X^2 A 50   *n.d.*, 1849

« 3937 *Texts for the Friday Discourses*

No. 1. Matthew 28:5. "Do not be afraid, for I know that you seek Jesus who was crucified."

That the sinner's first relation to Christ is one of flight from him, fear of him.

See journal NB 11, p. 186 [i.e., x^1 A 473].

No. 2. Luke 18:13. "But the tax collector . . . . . would not even lift up his eyes to heaven."

First of all, the meaning of this is to be delineated. Then Christ's words to the man blind from birth (Luke 18:42) are to be used as a counter theme: Look up (the text, unlike the Danish version, Receive your sight, reads ἀνάβλεψον), your faith has saved you.

The significance of this looking up, of confidently looking up; this, after all, is the way we speak to the sick, the downhearted, the troubled, when we want to encourage them to hope: Look up!

Being unwilling to lift up his eyes to heaven is a sign of having lost confidence, but Christ gives confidence: Look up.

[*In margin:* Luke 21:28. Now when these things begin to take place, look up.]

No. 3. Matthew 8:8. "But the centurion answered him . . . . . Only say the word, and my servant will be healed." Or, as it says in an old hymn,[227]

> One word from you heals
> for all eternity.

To need a word, sometimes even in relation to one person, for example, the word "Yes" for the beloved, the word of forgiveness from one you have wronged, etc.

But so it is with Christ's words at the Lord's Supper.[228] Many of his words to his contemporaries are preserved; but the words at the Lord's Supper are spoken directly to us. This is my body which is given for you.

x^2 A 51   *n.d.*, 1849

« 3938 *The Fourth Sunday in Advent*[229]

Supposedly no connection can be found between the Gospel[230] and the Epistle.[231] But it is there if one considers what John the Baptizer says of himself: He who has the bride is the bridegroom; the friend of the bridegroom rejoices greatly at the bridegroom's voice;

therefore this joy of mine is now full. So a possible theme here is: the perfect joy—and this would correspond to the Epistle.

And then for the Epistle the theme could be:

The Perfect Joy, Joy in the Lord.

(1) The joy of reconciliation through meekness (verse 5). The most beautiful joy.

(2) The joy of freedom from cares (verse 6). The most blessed joy.

(3) The joy which is the peace of God. This is the most perfect joy [*in margin:* the most *trustworthy* joy]:

(a) it passes all understanding, so indescribable is it; (b) it keeps hearts and thoughts in Christ Jesus, so different from all other joy, which we must care for lest we lose it, but instead this joy watches over us, keeps us—what trustworthiness!

X^2 A 274 *n.d.*, 1849

« 3939 *"The Prodigal Son"*——*"The Father"* ——*"The Brother"*[232]

Three Discourses

Or perhaps a completely new form could be chosen: Godly diversion (light reading) for upbuilding.

[*In margin:* It is no novel; the story is very short, and there is not a word about romantic love; there are no female characters—no, a situation like this would never occur to a novelist: a father and two sons, no more and no less; it is an utterly simple story.]

1

The Prodigal Son

Let us begin at the beginning; the beginning is: he wants to go out in the world; he is tired of staying home, seeing the same old things and hearing the same old things. It is an old story. This is how it looks to the young; there comes a moment when "father's house becomes too cramped." So it is even for a girl when she peeks out of the window of her father's house (for the girl has to be satisfied with getting permission to look out the window once in a while; she does not get permission to go out the way the boy does); she thinks she will find what she is looking for in the distance, and this is really the reason why the young girl "sighs" in the midst of all her happiness; but with this she does not object to staying quietly at home in her father's house, her longing is simply a quiet inwardness, a wealth for her whole life.

But the son has to get out, take his leave.

Now for the story.

[*In margin:* After having received "his" share of his father's goods (yes, it would be possible to argue about his right, but we can talk of that another time, and since the father, who was the closest to the situation, raised no objection, we will not either), he travels to foreign lands. If he fails out in the world, he will in any case not be able to say that it was because his father was miserly and strict, stood in the way of his advancement and denied him money for travel abroad.

So he goes traveling. We see at once that this is no novel—the story rushes off all too rapidly to the catastrophe. I use this foreign word properly, I believe, for there really is upheaval in the story. He goes traveling—and not only do he and the story arrive in that foreign country, but at that very moment we are at the end of the story, at least the first part. It could easily be shown that the striking brevity of this part may have a deeper meaning, for the more quickly a wastrel goes through his money, the more of a wastrel he is, and thus it is a self-contradiction to prolong the story of the greatest wastrel's squandering through many volumes. Nevertheless in making such observations we, too, will try to be brief.]

If he had stayed near his father, he certainly would not have squandered so much. Thus his misfortune was that he traveled so far away—but yet perhaps it was his salvation, for the father was not close enough at hand to prevent the school he had to go through from getting to be a serious matter.

Ordinarily fathers do not understand this and do not have the high-mindedness to send their son away or to understand that he must go away: and so it all amounts to nothing in particular.

From first to last the prodigal son's social life was bad—he spent his money on prostitutes—and he ended taking care of swine—his social life was approximately of one piece.

It is a mistake to regard him as the prodigal son only when he has run through his money; he was that just as much when he was squandering it on prostitutes.

"He came to himself"—see, now the journey abroad is over; it actually ends not with his returning home but with his coming to himself. And from now on we begin to talk in another vein about the prodigal son.

2
The Father

Usually all the attention is concentrated on the prodigal son and the father is almost forgotten.

But this is unfair, for this father is truly a very remarkable man.

If you want to know exactly what is remarkable here I shall tell you, and please pay attention to it. The remarkable thing is that when he got himself a prodigal son—precisely then he really became a father in earnest. Other fathers want to be fathers all right—when the son is a well-behaved child—but when one's own son is the prodigal son, then the father says: I do not want to be his father any longer; let him paddle his own canoe. No one wants to be the father of the prodigal son—but this father, this remarkable man, he really wanted to be the father of the prodigal son; it is almost as if he did not care so much about the prodigal son's brother, the well-behaved son. Was this not remarkable? And if a teller of fairy stories ever had the right to end his story with this phrase: "Was this not remarkable?" then I have the right to conclude this point of departure the same way. The prodigal son appears often enough in actuality, but God knows how many times there appears in actuality a father like this; I wonder if he does not really belong in the fairy story—and in the gospel? And why in the gospel? Because the father who is being talked about is actually God in heaven.

But let us begin over again in order to scrutinize this affectionate father and learn to know him.

The son wants to go out in the world, finds his father's house too cramped. In a certain sense it was perhaps ingratitude toward the father, but there is not a word about this. On the contrary, the father has so affectionately identified himself with his son that he has not thought of himself at all.

So the son demands that the father divide the estate with him. How unjust—the son has no right to demand the least thing. How ungrateful—it is almost like saying to the father: I really wish you were dead. And if it would have made the son happy and truly benefited him, the loving father would gladly have wished himself dead, too.

So he divides the estate with him. Rarely does it happen that a father is willing to do this, but if he is, then it is "Goodbye and don't come back." But this father has no limits to what he will put up with, and he still continues to be a father; fatherhood does not hang loosely on him as a title. The son wants to go away—he is the father; the son wants him to divide the estate with him—he is the father; the son leaves —he is the father; everything is lost, the son is lost—he is the father. But now, if you insist on variety in order to be intrigued, then we will promptly call a halt, for then this father is the most tiresome man on earth, and I can merely say for your comfort that such a father very seldom appears in actuality.

All this will have to be gone through bit by bit.

3
The Brother

We are automatically accustomed to picture this one as the hardhearted son, to shrink away from his hardheartedness, and to feel ourselves superior to him. If we want to have any benefit from the gospel story, we ought to be careful about doing this and be especially careful not to do it automatically.

Humanly speaking, he is justified. On that point there is no discussion: his dissatisfaction is not at all overdone, is kept within proper bounds; justified he is, humanly speaking. Let us not therefore use this gospel on Sundays simply to make believe that we are not at all like this brother. There is one reason for his dissatisfaction which is not readily seen, for he is indeed a good son, does indeed love his father, and thinks he deserves to be loved more by his father. Therefore it is not even because he is angry with the brother, but because the brother, and a brother like that, is preferred at his expense, inasmuch as the father's joy reaches such a height that it almost seems as if he had only one son, the prodigal son, as if the other son were displaced, as if the father said (the reverse of other fathers, who do not want to be the father of the prodigal son): I do not want to be the father of the righteous son. Here I want to call to mind one thing often seen exemplified in both trivial and important ways: that the bad child is often favored, is promptly thanked if he is ever a little bit good, and thus the most advantageous thing to do both in the family and in the greater life in the state is almost to be the bad child. What must be noted in the case of the prodigal son is that there was a genuine conversion.

My objection to the brother is actually this: when he sees that his father is so indescribably happy, out of love for his father he ought to enter into his father's joy.

In general we have here an example of the difference between fatherly love and brotherly love. To be developed.

Then develop thoroughly everything available about this brother.

Also to be used, perhaps, the parable of the two brothers, one of whom said: Yes, and did not do it; the other said: No, and did his father's will.[233]

x^2 A 325 *n.d.*, 1849–50

« **3940** *Theme for a Sermon:*[234]

The Proclamation of the Word

to be developed on the verse in the old hymn[235] (O great God, we praise you):

> The prophets announced him,
> The apostles proclaimed him,
> And the martyr-host celebrated you
> In the hour of death, solemnly.

This is authentic preaching; this is what it is to witness; the Sunday nonsense has no great meaning.

There is something in the verse which, although probably incidental, could be used: announced *him* and proclaimed *him*; only in relation to the martyr-host is Christ himself present, and therefore it reads: it celebrated *you*. There is also a present tense about the martyr-host, a not-yet-finished character, so that new martyrs may come. On the other hand, in our day it is no doubt just as ridiculous to sing such things as it is for the night watchman on a winter evening to shout at 8 o'clock: *Now* darkness blinds the earth and *day departs.*[236]

x^2 A 333 *n.d.*, 1850

« **3941**

Hugo d. St. Victore's commentary on the words: Many are called but few are chosen, is excellent (see Helfferich, *Mystik,*[237] pt. II, p. 319).

The story of Ahasuerus, who repudiated Queen Vashti because of her pride.

Then he ordered that beautiful young virgins be brought together from the whole kingdom. They were to be brought to the one in charge of the harem and adorned in beautiful garments. Then for six months they were anointed with balm and myrrh and for six more months with other spices and ointments. Then they were presented to the king so that he could choose one. "Thus many were chosen so that one could be chosen..... The king's servant chose many to beautify; the king chooses only one for his apartment. The first choice fell upon many according to the king's order; the second, only one, according to the king's will."

The story is found in the Book of Esther, chapter II.

x^2 A 350   n.d., 1850

« 3942 *Theme for a Friday Discourse*

At the altar there is: (1) **forgetfulness** (for *your sins*, the past), (2) **remembrance** (of *Christ's love*, the eternal as the life to come).

x^2 A 597   n.d., 1850

« 3943 *The Gospel: The Great Banquet*[238]

[*In margin:* I have been thinking of preaching on this Gospel and have therefore been looking into it somewhat.]

[*In margin:* See p. 177 (i.e., x^3 A 155).]

Theme:
The Earnestness of Life

That this is not finite aims, especially when finite aims obstruct the eternal, but also that mediation is a delusion, for if seeking the eternal "first" is going to be an earnest matter, then the finite aims for the most part go by the board.

As we read the Gospel *here* today, each one understands what is readily understood—and he admits that these are excuses, poor excuses which ought not hold a man back. But right now we are here in God's house, in a quiet hour, as it is called. Out there, where there is no stillness whatsoever, there the very excuses just quoted are practically the earnestness of life—and the only excuse for this is probably the fact that out there the supreme invitation goes unheard, as if it has pulled back from the actuality of life and is pronounced only in special quiet hours.

But is it not the Gospel's invitation which is really in the wrong, coming as it does at inconvenient moments, the very moment someone stands and is about to be married, when a person is busiest of all with his secular enterprises etc.; of course the invitation could come at a time when there is nothing else to take care of, in an idle moment, perhaps in a quiet hour; the Gospel demands too much! —Yes, the Gospel introduces an either/or, and does it deliberately, with the intention of creating the appropriate tension for a choice. However gentle the Gospel is, however lovingly it extends the invitation, it nevertheless has not lost the idea of itself.[*]

The remarkable thing is that it was a wedding to which they were invited, and yet they excuse themselves by saying that they have to go to a wedding[239]—consequently, two weddings. And God is so gracious that he describes his relationship to men by a relationship of erotic love.[**]

x^3 A 107   n.d., 1850

« 3944

In margin of 3943 (x^3 A 107):
Prayer
Father in heaven, you who received our earliest promise, to whom in baptism we promised that we would not forget our promise, forget that we are betrothed, forget to come to your wedding—whatever we might find as our excuse is a matter of indifference, for the crucial thing would be that we do not come to the wedding [*in penciled brackets:* we who do not, like those in today's Gospel, excuse ourselves from accepting the invitation but have indeed accepted it, solemnly promised to come, so that if we do not come, our guilt is even greater].

x^3 A 108   n.d.

« 3945

[*] *In margin of 3943* (x^3 A 107):
It could be said that this is a curious sort of invitation. An invitation leaves one free to come or not. And then when those invited courteously excuse themselves, the inviter has them slain.[240] —But this is God's royal prerogative. The latter is not the amazing part but rather the first, that he condescends to invite us.

x^3 A 109   n.d.

« 3946

[**] *In margin of 3943* (x^3 A 107):
Nevertheless it may be observed that in the Gospel about the great banquet[241] it is not stated that the invitation was to a wedding, and in the Gospel about the king who prepared for his son's wedding[242] mention is not made of the excuse that he had taken himself a wife but only that one went to his field and another to his business. But it really makes no difference.

x^3 A 110   n.d.

« 3947 *The Gospel, the Great Banquet*²⁴³

Theme

Who bears the greatest guilt: those in the Gospel who excuse themselves from accepting the invitation—or we who have solemnly answered: Yes (in baptism) and promised to come and then do not come because of the same hindrances as in today's Gospel.

x^3 A 111   *n.d.*, 1850

« 3948 *The Great Banquet*²⁴⁴

[*In margin:* see pp. 86, 87 (i.e., x^3 A 107–111).]

One could ask what right the inviter had to have the ones invited put to death because they did not come²⁴⁵—after all, that is a peculiar kind of invitation.

As far as we ourselves are concerned, we must honestly say that we have it coming, for we, after all, promised in baptism to come.

If one does not want to emphasize this, then the answer is to be found in the fact that the inviter is God, who after all does have proprietary rights over us men.

x^3 A 155   *n.d.*, 1850

« 3949 *"The Missing Penny"—"The Strayed Sheep" —"The Prodigal Son"*²⁴⁶

3 Christian Discourses

(1) The missing penny. Here there can be no talk about straying. A penny can only be missing—it cannot stray. Furthermore, a penny is not at all to blame if it is lost; if it is lost, it is the holder's fault or the fault of the person who was supposed to take care of it. Finally, a penny cannot do a thing about helping itself get found again. No wonder, therefore, that the owner is so happy to find it, for he himself is to blame for losing it; thus in no sense does he rejoice on behalf of the penny—it is altogether on his own behalf, also because the guilt and the confusion involved in losing it are now made good again.

(2) The strayed sheep. There is no mention of how it happened; its loss has no history of that sort. The story begins by saying that it is a strayed sheep. Yet it is obvious that in a sense a sheep can be to blame for its own loss by leaving the shepherd, even though the shepherd also may be reproached for not watching. Consequently the sheep itself is able to do something to bring about its loss. It can do

nothing about its rescue. The shepherd must go out and look for it. Finally he finds it and in such bad condition that he has to carry it home. The shepherd's joy is great, but very likely it is not wholly on the sheep's behalf, inasmuch as the shepherd possibly has something to reproach himself for because of not having taken better care of the sheep.

(3) The prodigal son. Here the story begins by telling how it happened that he became lost, and he is entirely to blame for it. Next, he himself has to do something toward his own rescue: return home [*vende Hjem*] to his father to repent [*omvende sig*]. Finally, the father's joy is wholly on behalf of the son. The father has nothing to reproach himself about; he has done everything for the son; and the son is of such an age that the father could not with a good conscience treat him like a child but must let him undertake life by himself.

There is, therefore, a progression *from* the joy of the woman who lights the lamp, sweeps the house, finds the penny, and calls her neighbors and friends together—*to* the joy of the shepherd who goes out and looks for the straying sheep and finds it—*to* the joy of the father in regaining the lost son.

This is the kind of joy there is in heaven over one sinner who repents. *In just this way,* for God possesses all us men in the same way someone possesses many, many coins, knows exactly how many he has, and immediately misses the lost one. God is a shepherd to all us millions of men, just as the shepherd who watches his sheep, knows each one, and discovers at once when one has gone away. As a father loves his child, so God loves each man, knows exactly how many children he has, and misses at once the lost child. Ah, if someone possesses millions and millions of pennies (as God possesses men), he is perhaps tempted to assume that the relationship must be different from that of the woman who possessed only ten pennies and therefore must have been readily aware when she lost one. Or if someone possesses millions and millions of sheep (as God possesses men), he is perhaps tempted to assume that the relationship must be different from that of the shepherd, who does not have so many sheep and therefore must easily miss the one. But when it is a child! Is it conceivable that a father could have so many children that he would not know how many he had and would not at once miss the one who is lost! It certainly is possible that a man could possess so much money that finally he would not know what he had and would become indifferent to it, although he nevertheless must be said to have money. But if a father had so many children that he became indifferent to the fact and did not even know how many he had—then he would not be a father.

x³ A 213   n.d., 1850

« 3950 *A New Turn*

by Pastor Paulli.²⁴⁷ Today (Second Christmas Day) he preached about Stephen. He was well aware that this was not something to be "admired." More properly, it should be presented for imitation or for humbling. But Paulli did not make this turn. No, we should not admire it but "give God the glory." This may indeed be said, but the Pharisees said the very same so they would not receive the impression that Christ had healed the man born blind.

x³ A 695   n.d., 1850

« 3951 *Theme for a Sermon or Four Sermons*

Four lines which I read somewhere in Scriver;²⁴⁸ he calls them a verse, although they do not rhyme, and he relates that he read them over a door or someplace like that. At most we limit ourselves to writing a little something over the entrance to a tomb, which, after all, can be of no use to the dead, since it is behind them.

(1) *As you believe, so do you live.* *

Thus it is not as is usually thought—that a person's faith is immaterial to his life, that a person can believe one thing and his life express something else. No, even if your mouth says something else, what your life expresses is your faith.

(2) *As you live, so do you die.*

Death, after all, is a possibility at any moment—and late conversion a dubious thing.

Dying is not something in itself but is the product of one's life. Not something which happens to one but something which belongs to one's life.

(3) *As you die, so do you depart this life.*

To die is not to disappear, get mislaid in the ground, etc.

(4) *As you depart this life, so do you remain.*

Frightful earnestness: Consequently it is decided, and as it is now so will it remain. Who has sufficient strength to bear the weight of this thought. Only a criminal is convicted for life (thus only for these few years, not for eternity)—the moment the sentence is announced he almost swoons. And yet he does not interpret it absolutely literally; he immediately slips in the idea that a reprieve is possible in due time. But in eternity there is no time. If two friends or two lovers are separated and say to each other: we will never see each other again—they are overwhelmed. Yet they do not interpret it literally even in that initial moment. They slip in the idea that the future has many possibilities and a lot can happen in that time. But in eternity nothing happens—everything remains as it is, and there is no future—and yet an eternal future. Frightful earnestness!

x^3 A 706 *n.d.*, 1851

« 3952

In margin of 3951 (x^3 A 706):
* It is the old Socratic way: when someone says that he understands that this or that is right and does not do it, then he does not understand it either. Affirming and reaffirming a conviction is ridiculous when action is the only permissible affirmation. This is readily apparent in a finite situation. If a capitalist were to affirm and perhaps explain in a very persuasive talk that right now the only sound thing to do is to buy 3% bonds—and he himself buys 4% bonds: I wonder if it is his conviction that this is the sound thing to do.

x^3 A 707 *n.d.*

« 3953

In margin of 3951 (x^3 A 706):
Perhaps this is done best as confessional discourses with strong use of the situation in the confessional: as an individual before God.

x^3 A 708 *n.d.*

« 3954

Addition to 3953 (x^3 A 708):
(1) In the world around us it is enough for you to say that you believe this or that; we are not able to check a person in that respect. But here you are before God and the judgment of eternity will be: as

86   SERMONS

you lived, so have you believed; it will do no good to say: Lord—faith is recognized by its fruits.[249]

x³ A 709   n.d.

« 3955

Addition to 3953 (x³ A 708):

(3) Consequently[250] you are immortal. Do not take the trouble to doubt it or to have it proved.[251] You are immortal. You will depart this life—and eternity is not a land of shadows—but of clarity, of transparency,[252] where everything is made manifest, is held up to the light—and going to confession is the same—consider carefully; you are alone before God, and he is sheer clarity, he lives in a light which no one can penetrate, but he is a light which penetrates everything. O, use the moment, voluntarily will to become completely open; afterward it is too late when in eternity you are obliged to become completely open.

x³ A 711   n.d.

« 3956 *Theme for a Sermon*

"Not that I have grasped it—

but that I am grasped."[253]

x³ A 777   n.d., 1851

« 3957 *Theme for Sermon on the Second Day of Easter*

The words in the Gospel of Luke 24:24: "Some of those who were with us went to the tomb, and found it just as the women had said; *but him they did not see.*"

This: *but him they did not see.*

It was just the same with the disciples who walked to Emmaus while Christ walked along with them—but him they did not see.

So also with us. Here a little skirmish about historical knowledge, which also comes and looks and finds it exactly as related—but him it does not see.

x⁴ A 523   n.d., 1852

« 3958

Come to me, all who labor and are heavy-laden etc.[254]

To put an end to the mendacious way in which preacher-squawking uses these words, all that is needed is to introduce as commentary the words of Christ[255] in which he repudiates the one who insisted on burying his father first, as well as Christ's other utterances in that passage.

XI¹ A 83   *n.d.*, 1854

SEX

« 3959

Here should be considered the whole question of hermaphroditism, which greatly occupied the older dogmaticians, and of the deep importance of sexual differentiation for the classical-antique worldview, the purely sensual element in their love.
See Scotus Erigena, *de divisione naturæ libri quinque. Oxonii* 1681. II, p. 53: . . . *saltem post ruinam suam de spiritualibus ad corporalia, de æternis ad temporalia, de incorruptibilibus ad caduca, de summis ad ima, de spirituali homine in animalem, a simplici natura ad sexuum divisionem, ex angelica dignitate et multiplicatione ad pecorinam contumeliosam corruptibilemque secundum corpus generationem suum miserabilem interitum, tali poena admonitus etc.*[256]

II A 797 Dec. 17, 1838

« 3960

It is obscene to present a woman scantily dressed instead of depicting her naked as the Greeks did, for the lustfulness consists in the draperied concealment which evokes the imagination. It is indecent to have dressing and undressing onstage go so far as to show the actress in a slip, for it makes no difference how many clothes she has on underneath and that the slip is actually nothing more than an outer garment—it is all a matter of the necessary connections in the association of ideas.

II A 427 May 29, 1839

« 3961

This could be a very interesting problem: to what extent do the feminine and the masculine characters reach their ultimate in the negation of discretionary differences, in indifference to sex-differences and the difference of individuality (here seen, of course, as representative, as difference in ideas) based on them, just as the highest titles and terms of address are of themselves androgynously elevated above the contrast of differences ("Your Majesty" applies to both the king and queen, "Your Royal Highness" to both the prince and princess, "Your Grace" to both the count and countess), a transcending of differences not conceived ridiculously as in the late Vadskiær's immortal wedding poem:²⁵⁷ Yes, if there were neither skirt nor trousers, the difference would disappear completely; she is called Fredrik, he is called Louise —or in an even more profound concretion of this contrast.

II A 478   July 15, 1839

« 3962

Only the animal can remain naïve in the sexual relationship; man is unable to because he is spirit, and sexuality, as the extreme point of the synthesis, promptly rebels against spirit.²⁵⁸

V B 53:27   n.d., 1844

« 3963

..... for a moral marriage is by no means naïve, and yet it is by no means immoral. This is why I always say that it is sin which makes sensuality sinfulness.²⁵⁹

V B 53:28   n.d., 1844

« 3964

..... for they win neither Greek serenity nor the bold confidence of the spirit.

The sexual is not sin; when I first posit sin, I also posit the sexual as sinfulness. It does not follow as a matter of course that I sin by marrying, since on the contrary I strive to eliminate the contradiction.[*] The individual for whose arrival I am responsible does not become sinful through me but becomes that by positing sin himself and then himself positing the sexual as sinfulness.

[*] *In margin:* to transform a drive into the moral; for the sexual is the sinful only to the extent that the drive at some moment manifests itself simply as drive in all its nakedness, for this can occur only through an arbitrary abstraction from spirit.²⁶⁰

V B 53:38   n.d., 1844

« 3965

A psychological observation on the love of boys in antiquity.

The reason pederasty was so common in antiquity and actually not condemned was probably due to the corruption of paganism, but psychologically there is something else to remember.

In the relation between man and woman, the sexual, there was no place at all for the intellectual; the woman was too inferior for that, too inferior in man's opinion, at any rate, as is the case throughout the

Orient. The relation is only sexual. So the intellectual was introduced in connection with the love of men, as Socrates[261] says, that is, still in an innocent sense, and then it degenerated into that depravity. But the intellectual had no place in loving the opposite sex.

In Christendom intellectuality has been more or less included in the love of woman. The big question is and will be whether this whole admixture of intellectuality and such a drive is not morally dubious, and whether it does not develop a refinement which is not much help in loving one and keeping to this one alone when *per abusum* intellectuality is added to it in this way.

x^2 A 536   *n.d.*, 1850

« 3966 *Another Dishonest Use of Christianity*

Men seem to have a good many and very different preoccupations. But if one were to be named that could be called the one and only thing which preoccupies men, it would have to be: sex, sexual desire, propagation, and the like: for, after all, men are primarily animal.

This is why all that human hypocrisy is able to invent comes together at this point as at no other. If you really want to learn to know human hypocrisy, then pay attention to men in this area. For precisely because we stand here on the lowest level, something they are ashamed to acknowledge for what it is—precisely for this reason hypocrisy is active right at this point.[*] This accounts for the lofty talk about the profound seriousness of propagating the race, also about the great benefaction of giving another person a life, etc., all calculated to refine the sensuality of lust.

The great benefaction of giving another person life. Well, watch out now. A worn-out lecher, an old man, with scarcely any sensual power left—the truth is they are unable to control the fire of lust, but this is hypocritically expressed by saying that they intended to perform the great benefaction of giving another person life. Thanks! And what a life, a miserable, wretched, anguished existence, which is usually the fate of such progeny. Is it not splendid! Suppose that murdering, pillaging, and stealing were transformed in like manner into the greatest inestimable benefaction! And what is putting a man to death compared with bringing such a miserable creature into this life! For no matter how universally it is regarded as sad (which as far as I recall one of my pseudonyms says somewhere,[262] or is found somewhere in my journal, or in any case is a remark I made a long time ago) that there is greater guilt in giving a life than in taking it—even though this is universally regarded as sad with respect to a life destined to be sickly —it is still not often expressed. Nevertheless this hypocrisy about a great benefaction is persistently maintained; the child supposedly will never be able to thank sufficiently for it—instead of the father's never being able to rectify his guilt sufficiently, even if he went on his knees in tears before the child.

But now to the hypocritical use of Christianity. This is giving the appearance that Christian parents—and in Christian countries we are all Christians—beget Christian children—but in that case it gets to be identical with receiving an eternal salvation. Aha! Consequently the meaning of Christianity has come to be the refining of the lust of the procreative act.[**] Otherwise one would perhaps stop, see if he possibly could control his lust, hesitate to give another person life merely to satisfy his sexual desire—ah, but when one begets eternal, eternally blessed creatures, then, after all, the best thing one could do, the most Christian thing one could do, would be to occupy another all day long, if that were possible.

XI^1 A 219   *n.d.*, 1854

« 3967

[*] *In margin of 3966* (XI^1 A 219):
In the sexual relation man is not on a level lower than the animal, but *au niveau;* and there is nothing further to be said on that, we are indeed animal creations. But what makes man frequently sink lower than the animal on this point is the nauseatingly hypocritical solemnity with which he refines this relation; the male who quite simply lives with a female because of his sexual drive at least has the superiority that he does not refine it by means of hypocritical solemnity.

XI^1 A 220   *n.d.*

« 3968

[**] *In margin of 3966* (XI^1 A 219):
The person who has learned to shudder at the thought of how difficult it is to enter into the kingdom of heaven and that only few are saved no doubt loses the desire to beget children and take upon himself the new responsibility of whether or not they will be among the few who are saved. If he should be moved to beget children, then Christianity is obliged—however strange this thought is—to make begetting children a condition [of new responsibility] for his eternal salvation.

XI^1 A 221   *n.d.*

« 3969 *The Sexual Relation*

The lower a man's level of consciousness, the more natural the relation.

But the more intellectually mature a person is, the more the life of consciousness prevails, the closer one gets to the point where Christianity and any similar religious and philosophical view are situated, the point where abstention becomes the expression for spirit.

Between these two extreme points lies the halfway state in which the sexual relation had lost its immediacy and one does not will to move toward spirit.

Here one feels the need (in part this can be regarded as a kind of modesty, in part as perhaps a bit of hypocrisy or sometimes a refined hypocrisy) to resolve to get married—for reasons.[263] The fact that a man has reasons is supposed to spiritualize the marriage somehow, make it something higher than the satisfaction of a drive.

Nonsense! Either quite simply and wholly the satisfaction of drive or spirit.

The Vicar of Wakefield begins like this: I was ever of the opinion that the honest man who married and brought up a large family did the state more service than he who continued single and only talked of population increase.[264]

Here we have one of the reasons for getting married: to raise children to serve the state—*risum teneatis amici!*[265] No, the point is this: with the growth of culture, man somehow grows away from the drive as the life of consciousness increases, in any case grows away from the immediacy of the drive. A certain intellectual embarrassment *in specie* (not to be confused with spontaneous modesty, *pudor*) arises in man. This is why he must have reasons to hide behind, however poor a hiding place they provide, as, for example, this very transparent screen of raising children to serve the state. To serve the state! Yet perhaps there is something to it, perhaps the state is rightly conceived as a stud farm—and kings ought not be compared to shepherds but to studmasters.

I disagree with the rest of the statement in *The Vicar of Wakefield*. By remaining unmarried and only talking about population increase or, more correctly, by remaining unmarried and precisely by talking against population increase, I believe I am doing the state (which is sinking under overpopulation and which demoralizes with the numerical) a greater service than if I, were it possible, begot 170,000 children.

With regard to the Vicar's saying that he *brought up*, I willingly concede that it no doubt is a kind of service to the state to bring up the contingent he places in the field, that his conduct is a service to the state if it is compared with what is done by those who limit themselves merely to doing the state the big service of encumbering it with a flock of children.

XI¹ A 259 *n.d.*, 1854

« 3970 *The Propagation of the Race*

To give life is supposedly—as it is in fact said to be—the greatest benefaction to a child; thus it supposedly also enriches existence [*Tilværelsen*], is an enrichment.

Let us see if Christianity has the opposite view instead, that to propagate the race is a corroding.

Even if Christianity otherwise had nothing to say against propagating the race, one of the old Fathers of the Church would probably speak as follows: Refrain from propagating the race, control your drives and lust, for remember that every time this drive is satisfied, Governance must give an immortal soul to the animal-creature which is the fruit, thus you are dragging one more immortal soul down into this misery, down into this enormous danger, from which, it is true, he possibly may be saved through Christianity, but where he can also be lost eternally.

This interpretation, you see, is quite different from the hasty, optimistic, and diverting one about childbearing as an enrichment of existence. It drains, it vitiates, it pulls more and more souls down into this existence. On the basis of what lies ahead, propagation seems to be an enrichment, for after all there is a steady increase; but on the basis of what lies behind it, it is a minus, more and more are constantly being pulled down into corruption.

The lie is focused on this point about the propagation of the race; if sin comes thereby, the lie really becomes fully operative at the same time. The mere fact that we have embellished the satisfaction of the most powerful lust—which is practically life for the majority of men—the mere fact that we have also embellished the gratification of this lust as the greatest benefaction, a benefaction for the child, for society, an enrichment of existence, in short, the most exceptionally sublime, moral, and extremely beneficial act possible—just this shows what a scoundrel or what a henchman a man is. Now that is just great, this is what is called double valor—it is sweet soup not only with jam in it but with jam on it. It is fast becoming an outright, an unpardonable offense for a man not to give himself completely—if this were possible—to doing nothing else night and day but begetting children, which, after all, is the greatest benefaction to the child, to society, to mankind, to existence, and perhaps even to God, who says: The more the better!

Yes, here is the headquarters of the lie. This is why the child has to be filled with all this talk about a wonderful world, that life is intended for rejoicing, for enjoying, etc., which, in fact, is what the child by nature is inclined to accept (Schopenhauer[266] is right in saying that every man is born with the fallacious idea that the destiny of this life is to be happy), but which also has some connection with the parents' inevitable predicament if they had to explain that it is an evil world, that the condition of this life is suffering, also that the child came into existence through the gratification of a lust etc.—if it occurred to the child to ask: Why then did I come into existence?

Sexuality is not merely ambiguous in that it can be looked at in two ways, but it can be looked at in a hundred different ways, and there is always a bit of a lie; it is something hidden, which precisely for that very reason is extremely dangerous, built entirely on a lie, and woman's element is also a lie.

XI^2 A 202   *n.d.*, 1854

SHAKESPEARE

« 3971

In Shakespeare's *A Midsummer Night's Dream*, II, 1, a flower is given the name (in Tieck's translation,[267] p. 213):
>Lieb im Müssiggang
>*Ihr Saft getraüfelt auf entschlafne Wimpern*
>*Macht Mann und Weib, in jede Kreatur,*
>*Die sie zunächst erblicken, toll vergafft.*[268]

IV A 194   n.d., 1842

« 3972

It is strange that in *Macbeth*[269] Shakespeare uses a sleepwalking scene[270] to give us intimations of Lady Macbeth's remorseful conscience. I believe the effect would have been even greater if Shakespeare had presented Lady Macbeth as one who herself knew that she sleepwalked and then never dared relax in sleep for fear of betraying herself. In such a nighttime hour, when she had sent everyone away, when she would wish the whole world a safe and undisturbed sleep but dared allow herself only a nap, in this nocturnal anxiety when she merely dozed and woke up every moment, her torment would show up in all its dreadfulness.

IV A 50   n.d., 1843

« 3973

It might be interesting to interpret Lady Macbeth this way: she does not sleepwalk, she does not dare sleep, she fears that she will betray something in her sleep.

Scene at midnight: she sits alone in her room, anxiously walks around checking to see that all doors are locked (she becomes melancholy and distraught, checks the doors many times, for it seems to her that she had forgotten it the preceding time); thus she is almost like a sleepwalker as she sits there:

Sleep, sleep, dreadful invention, horrible necessity, you, the only power that I fear, you who have managed to do something no human being has done—tear my secret from me, you cunning wizard, who gets a person in his power and makes him inform on himself; so while I sleep you have the power, you manage to do what no one else succeeds in doing—no, I am still awake, I will not sleep—and yet I must sleep, O dreadful necessity, why can I not do without sleep as I have learned to do without the heart's emotions, which to others are a necessity. But I sleep behind locked doors; the paneling is designed to stifle every sound—and yet where can one hide, even the walls have ears!

N.B. This could perhaps be done better with an individual like Cromwell, or the passion could perhaps have a more feminine quality.

Sleep, you may come and lie with me and deprive me of what no man can deprive me; when I am dissolved in your embrace, you look deep into my innermost soul, into this abyss where only I myself dare look when I know that I can keep everyone from looking down there. —Alas, my head is so weak, I need rest, and yet in the split-second when consciousness leaves me and sleep comes I can betray everything; alas, that a split-second has this power over me, a split-second which the necessity of sleep cruelly requires. Why do I dread sleep as a curse when for others it is the greatest blessing—am I cursed? If only I could go without sleep all my life! It is inhuman! I almost shudder at becoming a spirit in this way. O, if I cannot do away with it, the horror of taking it into my confidence! Excruciating wakefulness! Still I need it. No, I need to die, I need that last sleep, the sleep of death, my only sleep; if I know it is the sleep of death, then I will dare lay down my head on the pillow. Why? Because then death will take care that everything becomes quiet. —I hate Lady Seymour.[271] I suspect that she takes exception to my precautions (I must eventually lie and give false reasons for the arrangement of my bedroom)—but I dare not ask, I shudder to think of betraying something that way, and yet I would give anything to know what she thinks!

VI A 67 n.d., 1845

« **3974**

In margin of 3973 (VI A 67):
She always has domestics who cannot understand English, usually Frenchmen, out of dread that they might learn something, but gradually her torture finds expression also in French. Therefore the scene could begin with a few French words.

VI A 68 n.d.

« 3975

From the standpoint of the humorous it is right that Hamlet swears by the fire-tongs;²⁷² this holds equally for the opposite. For example, if one were to say: I wager my head that there is fully a 4 shillingsworth of gold on the binding of Heiberg's *Urania*.

> The contradiction lies in the pathos: to stake one's head, and then 4 shillings, and it is intensified by the predicate "fully."

VI A 124   *n.d.,* 1845

« 3976

Othello's lines²⁷³ in which he says to Desdemona just before killing her:
Has Desdemona pray'd tonight?
are an indescribably moving and harrowing form of insanity. He does not say "you" but speaks as one speaks to a child: Has William done this and that?
They are masterly lines.

IX A 40   *n.d.,* 1848

SILENCE

« 3977

I would like to establish a silent order like the Order *de la Trappe*, not for religious but for esthetic reasons, in order that all the chatter which is heard at present might possibly be silenced.

III A 100   n.d., 1841

« 3978

When Amor left Psyche he said to her: You will give birth to a divine child if you keep silent, a mere human if you betray the secret.[274] —Every human being who knows how to keep silent becomes a divine child, for in silence there is concentration upon his divine origin; he who speaks remains a human being. —How many know how to keep silent—how many understand what it means simply to be silent.

IV A 28   n.d., 1842-43

« 3979

Silence in the individual life is like a woman's virginity, and the one who violates it is like a woman who will begin a second love, and a woman who will begin a second love is like a broken flower.

V A 51   n.d., 1844

« 3980

The threshold of consciousness or, as it were, the key, is continually being raised but within each key the same thing is repeated. It is well known that a cannonade makes one unable to hear, but it is also well known that one can become so accustomed to the roar of cannon that he is able to hear every word.[275] Thus in our age, for example, much more than in the time of the Greeks, the stillness in which we hear is a noise. This noise would have been enough and more for the Greeks, but we speak just as one in the midst of a cannonade would say whatever he wishes, since the cannonade for him would be stillness.

V A 96   n.d., 1844

« 3981

In the last writings he has adopted the principle of silence. "Silence is genius,"* he says. But he does not develop this thesis in greater detail; on the whole he seems to have abandoned himself to touching tangentially for a moment all sorts of disparate things and then publishing it all in one book—no, in four books at once. With silence, however, it is a rather simple matter. Silence is the way of interiorization for us ordinary human beings.[276]

*In margin: this must be in the preface to Studier.[277]

VII² B 261:18 n.d., 1846–47

« 3982

That one can confess Christ also by being silent and that this was the view in the early Church can be seen, for example, in Ignatius, *Epistola ad Ephesios*, ch. XV.[278]

VIII¹ A 3 n.d., 1847

« 3983

"To be silent" means while reflecting to be able to speak, that is, about everything else imaginable, for otherwise it is conspicuous and suspicious for someone to be silent, and then it is not exactly silence, not complete silence.

X¹ A 124 n.d., 1849

« 3984

How gripping—God says to Moses:[279] Why are you shouting so loudly—and Moses was being silent. Silence can be that heaven-scaling.

I read this in Luther's sermon[280] on the Gospel for one of the Sundays after Easter: Hitherto you have not prayed in my name.

X¹ A 394 n.d., 1849

« 3985

In situations where my silence will make me seem worse than I am, I should be silent—for instance, giving alms in secret. Where my silence will make me seem better than I am, then I should speak—confession of sin. The good a man does he should, if possible, keep to himself; the evil he has done he should speak about.

Incidentally, with respect to the latter some very unusual conflicts arise for the voluntary. If a man carries the heavy consciousness of a sin, but it has not become known and perhaps is the kind that does not come under the jurisdiction of civil authorities, should he go on his own and publicly confess it.²⁸¹ Here a certain kind of Christianity will declare that this is tempting God: he can, after all, bear his punishment with quietness and in other respects let his life honestly serve the good.

—X² A 43 n.d., 1849

« 3986 *Language, or Language Betrays Them*

Although all of them, when they are supposed to act, discuss it with "the others" and all that—they all nevertheless say depreciatively of someone: He went and discussed it beforehand with "the others."

Consequently they betray themselves, betray their awareness of the fact that authentic intensive actions spring from an individual and from silence.

—X⁴ A 16 n.d., 1851

« 3987 *The God-Relationship (Silence)*

It is true even in human relationships that if an otherwise nobody of a girl, as we unkindly put it, has the capacity to be absolutely silent about her relationship to her beloved, does not talk about it to a single other person, this gives her a certain worth, gives her a winsomeness in the eyes of her beloved.

God loves silence in the very same way.[*] He does not want this driveling to other men about one's relationship to God. It may well be conceit to do this—and this is displeasing to God. Or it may be motivated by cowardice and lack of faith, because one is distrustful or is perhaps afraid, if I may say so, of getting into trouble sometime—all of which displeases God. If someone says that if a person is more advanced than another, it is very cordial to let that other person share in his God-relationship, God is opposed also to this, for it is conceit. What conceit! God says, have I not had it proclaimed that every man, unconditionally every man, can turn to me—and therefore that other persons can certainly do it as well.

—XI² A 142 n.d., 1854

« 3988

[*] *In margin of 3987* [XI² A 142]:

Silence in the relationship to God is invigorating; absolute silence would be like a jack or the point outside the world of which Archimedes²⁸² speaks. Talking about one's God-relationship is an emptying that weakens.

—XI² A 143 n.d.

SIN

« 3989

Sin cannot arise out of man alone any more than one sex alone can produce a new individual; for that reason the Christian teaching about the devil's temptation is correct. There is a second factor, and this is also why human sin is specifically different from the devil's (original sin—the possibility of conversion). The other thesis would contradict the analogy.

I A 3   n.d., 1834

« 3990

Von Baader[283] does contend that evil is older than man, but nevertheless he thinks that evil has entered the world through man, so that the corruption of nature is contingent upon man's fall and that man's return to God will carry the world along, but here (p. 84) he seems to assert that evil has entered the world through other, nonhuman, beings.

Should God's productions be called immanental or emanental? Human creation may well be called an emanental production, and if it presupposes a ground as the locus (p. 87), where is this? Here, it seems to me, the question of the creation of matter becomes urgent.

I C 31   n.d., 1834-35(?)

« 3991

It is not merely because there is a human race that the world required a stage for sin and another for the consciousness of sin (if I may put it that way); the life of the individual manifests the same. First sin, and often, when it has ceased *de facto,* the consciousness of sin comes.

I A 92   October 11, 1835

« 3992

Frequently the reading of medical case histories can produce an effect related to presentiment—yet two factors are already present

102   SIN

here: in a way the makings of sickness are present in the fear—for it is difficult to say which produces the other—there is a certain receptivity so strong that it is almost productive—

Also the effect which executions, for example, produce.—

The many phenomena which are evoked by the doctrine of the sin against the Holy Spirit.—

All sin begins with fear (just as fear of a sickness is a disposition toward it—see Schubert, *Symbolik*[284]); however, the first human beings did not begin with it—there was no original sin.

II A 19   n.d., 1837

« 3993

Does not original sin—rendered possible by Adam's fall and actualized through the thereby conditioned family relationship (continuity of the race), referred to in Romans 5:13, 14 in the expression "that all men sinned in Adam," and maintained in its ecclesiastical orthodox consistency, eliminating every Pelagian restriction (*cum hoc non ideo propter hoc*—on the contrary, a *cum hoc et propter hoc*[285] at one and the same time)—does it not of necessity lead to the doctrine of the Church, of its superabundance of good works, of the blessing it possesses (according to the Catholic conception it leads to this and leads to this as the only adequate conclusion)? Or to what extent is there correspondence between the two parts of that parallel drawn in Romans 5 between the first and second Adam? Or is there something corresponding to the doctrine that all sinned in Adam and that some are saved in Christ, if in the one case sin is placed in relation to the whole race, is seen from the standpoint of race, and in the other Christ is placed in relation to every single individual? (For it certainly does not illuminate anything to say that just as individual human beings are declared to be sinners only insofar as they submit to universal humanness and make universal human nature their own, just so the children of the second Adam are exonerated only insofar as they share in him —since in this it is forgotten that the one is a necessity and the other a possibility repeating itself for every single individual). Or is the state in this world already such that we are supposed to be like angels, a state which usually is said to come to pass only in the next world? Or is this not the same problem which meets us on the phenomenological level, where the restless, worried individual wants, as it were, a middleman, something we must declare to be unprotestant. Or does not original sin consistently condition the doctrine of the Church—for otherwise what is hereditary would have no influence upon the given in society

—or are individuals emancipated and the concept of the Church abolished?²⁸⁶ In this respect I believe Günther²⁸⁷ has something under the doctrine of works. Herein is the philosophical meaning of the doctrine of a superabundance of good works in the Church's lap, of a christening present on the Christian's cradle, as conditioned by the generation's development antithetical to Adam's relation to the race. —One can connect this with intercession, the inexpressible need to plead for mercy as the unhappy dead seek appeasement with the living (the ecclesiastical dogma of requiem mass for the dead); see Kerner, *Eine Erscheinung aus dem Nachtgebiete der Natur*, 1836, p. 214.²⁸⁸

II A 117 July 11, 1837

« 3994

My conception of the relation between *satisfactio vicaria*²⁸⁹ and man's own expiation for his sins is as follows. It is certainly true, on the one hand, that sins are forgiven through the death of Christ, but on the other hand a person is not snatched as if by magic out of his old condition, the "body of sin" which Paul talks about (Romans 8:25). He has to go back the same way he came, while the consciousness that his sins are forgiven buoys him up, gives him courage, and prevents despair—like someone who in the full consciousness of his sin denounces himself and then with confident courage goes to meet even a criminal's death* because he feels that it must be, but the consciousness that the case will now go before another and more lenient judge sustains him. He walks the dangerous way (which indeed can be thorny enough even with the consciousness of the forgiveness of sin, for one so often forgets it) and will not tempt God or claim a miracle from him.

II A 63 n.d., 1837

« 3995

Addition to 3994 (II A 63):
* As Luther²⁹⁰ also says of a sinner somewhere in his *Tischreden:* "*Er starb mit fröhlichen Herzen in seiner Leibesstraffe.*"

II A 64 August 26, 1837

« 3996

In margin of 3994 (II A 63):
One must go back the same way he came, just as the magic spell is broken by the musical passage (the elf king piece²⁹¹)—something one can learn from the elves—only when it is correctly played through backwards.

II A 65 October 11, 1837

« 3997

I will turn away from those who only lie in wait to discover that one has done wrong in some way or other—to him who rejoices more over one sinner who repents than over the ninety-nine wise ones who never have need of repentance.[292]

II A 66 n.d., 1837

« 3998

What is the real meaning of the words in Genesis 3:22[*]: "Behold, the man [Adam] has become like one of us etc.," the words Erdmann[293] (Bauer's *Zeitschrift,* II, part 1, p. 205) uses to justify further his speculative view that the fall of man, looked at from one side, is a forward step?

[*] *In margin:* See I John 3:2, where likeness is the result.

II A 90 n.d., 1837

« 3999

For something to become really depressing, there must be first of all, in the midst of all possible favors, a presentiment[294] that it might just be all wrong; one does not become conscious of anything very wrong in himself, but it may lie in the familial context; then original sin displays its consuming power, which can grow into despair and have a far more frightful effect than the particular whereby the truth of the presentiment is verified. This is why Hamlet[295] is so tragic. This is why Robert *le diable,*[296] driven by a disquieting presentiment,* asks how it could ever be that he does so much evil. —The blessing is changed into a curse. —It is an extremely poetic governance which makes the girl dumb, she who alone can comprehend what is behind Robert *le diable's* assumed madness (his penance).

> * When Høgne,[297] whom his mother had conceived by a troll, sees his image in the water,
> he asks her why his body is shaped that way.
> See *Nordiske Kæmpehistorier* by Rafn,
> II, p. 242.[298]

II A 584 n.d., 1837

« 4000

Sin is committed in secret, but scarcely does one know it before the clamor, even though weak, begins, the torch is lit, by which one's arena, like the wild animal's, is steadily decreased.

II A 604 n.d., 1837

« **4001**

Have you really felt the consolation in the reflection: God tempts no one.[299] Have you felt the suprahuman strength, the preternatural greatness, which you get in the face of sin at the thought that it is your own flesh and blood or its temptations which have been vanquished once and for all (to be sure, God exposes a person to tests [*Prøvelser*] in order to strengthen and mature him—temptations [*Fristelser*] aim to break, because the tempter believes the one tempted will succumb). But have you also felt humbled by the thought: He is not tempted, not by anyone[300]—why do you lift up your voice to heaven, almost defiantly challenging heaven—why do your thoughts assault heaven—do you believe your troubles are so great, your grievance so just, your sighs so deep and so gripping that God must be tempted by them?

II A 310 Christmas Eve, 11 o'clock, 1838

« **4002**

In margin of 4001 (II A 310):

Why is even your prayer so belligerent; is it not because you believe that your grievance is so just that your voice must resound through heaven and call God from his hidden depths in order to accommodate you. Then heaven closes up against such presumptuous talk with the words "God is not tempted, not by anyone."[301] Such talk is as impotent as your arm. But when you humble yourself before God and say: My God, my God, great is my sin—your cry reaches heaven . . . . . then heaven is opened once again, then God, as the prophet says, speaks down to you through his window saying: Just a little while, just a little while, and I will etc.; then Christ's words come to you as they came of old when Christ said of Lazarus: This sickness is not unto death;[302] no, on the contrary, it is unto life.

II A 311 n.d.

« **4003**

The whole doctrine of original sin is presented in the Catholic Church[303] as so essentially irrelevant to the single individual that it could be compared best to the outer title-page, which is cut off when the book is bound, and for that reason *justitia originalis*[304] is also so far removed from the person that this is best compared to a splendid binding that bears no relation to the book.

II A 446 May 27, 1839

« 4004

Christianity was the first to advance the concept of synergism, and finitude receives its validity first in Christianity. Speculation acquires its true fulcrum first of all in Christianity, and freedom its reality [*Realitæt*]. Christianity's first qualification of synergism is *sin*. Sin, therefore, is not simply finitude, but in sin there is an element of freedom and of free finitude.

III A 118 *n.d.*, 1841

« 4005

What is sin: the pact of an evil conscience with the devil—and what has a memory like that of an evil conscience?

III A 226 *n.d.*, 1840–42(?)

« 4006

Just as the conception of God develops from the human spirit through its relation to itself and to the world, so the conception of Christ develops through the consciousness of sin.[305] This, more than the historical revelation, was what paganism lacked.

IV A 189 *n.d.*, 1844

« 4007

Strangely enough, the purer a young girl is, the more readily she acknowledges her sinfulness. This has gratified me very much, because in thinking about sin and putting everything under sin I really had the greatest difficulties with this phenomenon; with the rest of us it is easy enough.

V A 59 *n.d.*, 1844

« 4008

Sin in a man is like the Greek fire[306] which is not extinguished with water—but in this case only with tears.

VI A 30 *n.d.*, 1845

« 4009

If a child were told that to break a leg is a sin, in what anxiety he would then live, and he would probably break it more often and even regard coming close to it as a sin. Suppose it were impossible to overcome this impression from childhood. Out of love for his parents, he would carry on as long as possible, lest their mistake become appalling because of his ruin. It is like hitching a horse to a load too great —straining, it pulls with all its strength— and topples over.

Such "misguidance" about the nature of sin is often found, and the source may very well be someone with the best intentions.[307] For example, a man who has been very debauched and, wanting to deter his son from the same, interpreted the sexual drive itself as sin—and forgot that there was a difference between himself and the child—that the child was innocent and therefore must necessarily misunderstand. Unfortunate one, who in this way would be hitched, even as a child, to pulling and hauling through life.

VI A 105   n.d., 1845

« 4010

At first perhaps a person sins out of weakness, yields to weakness (alas, for your weakness is the strength of lust, inclination, passion, and sin); but then he becomes so despondent over his sin that he perhaps sins again and sins out of despair.[308]

VIII^1 A 64   n.d., 1847

« 4011 *For a Friday Sermon*

To be desired: that which seeks to draw us away from God might in fact lead us closer to him. Sin does indeed seek to draw us away— but in the Atonement it is precisely the consciousness of sin that leads us closer to God.[309] There is hope of conquering evil when its every assault only leads us closer to God.

VIII^1 A 284   n.d., 1847

« 4012

Christianity presupposes that, before there can be any question of really hearing what it teaches, the hearer has advanced so far in high-mindedness and in the power of the spirit over worldly things that all this about poverty, although he himself is poor, about sickness, although he himself is sick, about abasement and insult and persecution and grievance etc. does not preoccupy him very much, and then Christianity proclaims "the forgiveness of sins." Christianity presupposes that a man has progressed so far that he has only one sorrow—sorrow over his sins—and then it proclaims reconciliation. Light the lantern and go around all Christendom and see if you find ten men who actually have only one sorrow—sorrow over sin! And on Sunday Bishop Mynster says: How very rare is the person who properly understands that sin is the corruption of man—and on Monday he makes out as if everything were just as it should be, that the whole country is Christian.

VIII¹ A 473 *n.d.*, 1847

« **4013** *Two Forms of Sin*

(1) a man sins out of weakness
(2) then out of despair.
In the strict sense this is the sin.³¹⁰

Here, also, is the Atonement. A man doubts that the sin he committed out of weakness can be forgiven. All is lost, he thinks, and thus he sins. Therefore it takes the Atonement to bring him to a halt.

VIII¹ A 497 *n.d.*, 1847–48

« **4014**

In the older theology there was much discussion about sin being so great because it is against God and therefore hell-punishment has to be eternal. A later age found this to be foolish; for sin is just as great whether or not it is against God. Fundamentally, this is a most unspiritual and materialistic view. If sin, then, is an external fact, is it not also a conception, and does not the one who has a developed conception sin more than the one who has a dim conception, and does not the one sin most deeply who, although he has a developed conception of God, still persists in sin.³¹¹

VIII¹ A 662 *n.d.*, 1848

« **4015**

"Over what does a man groan; every man groans over his sin."³¹² How rarely this occurs, how rarely this is ever understood, for one who sorrows over his sins—that is, over what he calls his sins—perhaps nevertheless forgets if he does not have other particular sins; yes, he perhaps overlooks that the way in which he sorrows over his sins is a new sin, the sin of impatience, for example.

IX A 313 *n.d.*, 1848

« **4016**

There are, as I have pointed out elsewhere [i.e., VIII¹ A 497], two forms of sin—the sin of weakness and the sin of despair; a person sins out of despair over having been weak or over being weak enough to sin. The latter form is sin proper. Therefore this is the sin Christianity has aimed at. The doctrine of the Atonement is essentially related to this despair, the Atonement wants to halt this despair; only such a person actually comprehends the Atonement—that is, feels a need for it.

IX A 341 *n.d.*, 1848

« 4017

Blosius, *Consolatio Pusillanimium*, p. 381.
"*Satis rogat, qui morbum* (sin) *agnoscit; vehementer rogat, qui plorat et confidit.*"[313]

IX A 429 *n.d.*, 1848

« 4018

It is true that Christianity must be presented in such a way (here lies the possibility of offense) that if the consciousness of sin does not drive a person, he must be mad to get involved with Christianity. An end must be put to all the coddling nonsense that Christianity satisfies the deepest longings, etc. No, only "the struggle and distress of the anguished conscience"[314] can help one venture to will to have anything to do with Christianity; otherwise Christianity is and must be unto offense.

X¹ A 133 *n.d.*, 1849

« 4019

There is only one thing a person should become really earnest about—his sin. With respect to all other lamentable matters, the more lightly they are taken the better. But to take one's sin lightly is a new sin, which simply shows that here *is* earnestness.

X¹ A 195 *n.d.*, 1849

« 4020

There is the Christian definition of sin which Christ[315] himself expresses: The Holy Spirit will convince the world of *sin, that it has not believed.* Sin is not to believe. It is presented this way in *The Sickness unto Death*[316] also.

X¹ A 348 *n.d.*, 1849

« 4021

The sinner's relation to Christ is like the woman's love-relation to the man. The first stage is a pain, a suffering—for the womanness has still not surrendered itself; it has selfishness within itself and shudders at the thought of the man's superiority. In the same way the sinner at first shudders at the thought of coming so near to the Holy One, to be before him every moment. There is still selfishness in the sinner, and right here is the essential root of offense. As soon as he completely surrenders, this becomes his most blessed consolation—that at every moment he has Christ with him—his Savior and his Redeemer.

x^1 A 433 *n.d., 1849*

« **4022**

It would seem calamitous enough not to know the time of one's visitation—and yet this is also presented as something to be punished, or that for which one is punished. For instance, in the Gospel for the Tenth Sunday after Trinity.[317]

In this sense sin is ignorance, but a punishable ignorance.

x^1 A 627 *n.d., 1849*

« **4023**

The most terrible punishment for sin is the new sin. This does not mean that the hardened, confident sinner will understand it this way. But if a man shudders at the thought of his sin, if he would gladly endure anything in order to avoid falling into the old sin in the future, then the new sin is the most terrible punishment for sin.

There are collisions here (especially in the sphere of sinful thoughts) in which anxiety over the sin can almost call forth the sin.

When this is the case, a desperate wrong turn may be made. Vigilius Haufniensis[318] has described it thus: Penitence loses its mind. As long as penitence keeps its head, what should stand eternally fast does stand fast—namely, that the sin must be overcome. But in his despair it may not enter the unhappy man's head that since the new sin is in fact the most terrible punishment of sin he perhaps ought to put up with it.

No doubt this is how to understand what quietism has taught, that a man may be saved and yet continue in sin. In deadly anxiety he trembles before the new sin—but since it is in fact the punishment, despair takes him prisoner, as if there were nothing to do.

Here we see the difference in the ways temptation [*Fristelse*] and spiritual trial [*Anfægtelse*] should be fought: in the case of temptation the right thing may be to contend by avoiding. In the case of spiritual trial one must go through it. Temptation should be avoided; try not to see or hear what tempts you. If it is spiritual trial, go straight toward it, trusting in God and Christ.

Since in our time people have no idea at all of spiritual trial, anyone who suffers from it in our time would also be regarded as a very extraordinary sinner.

x^1 A 637   *n.d.*, 1849

« **4024**

The sinner, who after all was a woman and a sinner,[319] dared go to see Christ at the Pharisee's house, where the Pharisees were all together at a feast—Nicodemus,[320] who regarded himself as a righteous man, dared go to him only at night.

x^2 A 29   *n.d.*, 1849

« **4025**

This really seems to have been spoken by a father confessor. Zacharias Werner[321] declares in his sermon on the Fourth Sunday after Easter:

"Many good but despondent Christians denounce themselves in the confessional for all kinds of sins which are not sins at all or are of no significance whatsoever. No, rather denounce yourself for your true sins; rather say: the sin of despondency, for despondency is a sin, and it can end with mistrust in God's grace and mercy, which is a fearful sin."

x^2 A 74   *n.d.*, 1849

« **4026**

How infinitely profound it is—and is not this really the reason for my calamity and the calamity of all, that we have no real conception of what sin is in God's eyes.

Speaking of Christ's suffering and death, Arndt[322] (as well as the old devotional books) says that we ought to contemplate them in order to get a conception of what sin means to God. I trifle with it and have no real pathos-filled idea of how revolting sin is in the eyes of God—this I must see in Christ's sufferings for sin.

Here again is the dialectical: his sufferings are not supposed to reassure first but to terrify first, to terrify me. In this way Christ teaches first of all brokenness—that he may then reassure. But with his sufferings he makes me aware that I must really profoundly feel the horror of sin.

The truth of the religious can be illuminated by a not inappropriate illustration, by considering the concept of the aristocratic, a courtier, and then forgetting what ought to be forgotten. Think of having insulted the king: who will despair more over having done it—a peasant or a courtier? Will it not be the courtier, beyond comparison? It is the same with the religious. The saint understands what sin means—I, a sinner, trifle with it; this very trifling is part of my sin.

x^2 A 400   n.d., 1850

« 4027 *Another Example of Dialectic*

Christianity makes sin the most dreadful thing—and then wants to have it removed. A more lenient view (Leibniz,[323] for example) wants to make sin more benign, defends it—and then, quite properly, we remain hung up in it; it becomes an everlasting imperfection inseparable from being human. The result is to take sin off our hands.

x^2 A 403   n.d., 1850

« 4028

Julius Müller's answer to the explanation that sin is weakness is excellent: Is it not in fact observed that evil gives intensified energy. For support he points out that Plato characterizes ἡ ἀδικία as τὸν ἔχοντα: (τὴν ἀδικίαν) μάλα ζωτικὸν παρέχουσα, καὶ πρός γ' ἔτι ζωτικῷ ἄγρυπνον. [*In margin: Republic,* X[324]] (see Julius Müller, pt. I, *Die Lehre von der Sünde,* p. 119, note).[325]

In earlier journals [i.e., IX A 419;] I have myself pointed this out, that the good no doubt gives energy, but also the sensitiveness of eternity, which is why the good and the innocent suffer so deeply. Evil (precisely through despair) gives a desperate zest for life and strength (while the good longs to be out of this life). I have pointed out why baptized Jews are particularly good examples of this kind of energy, because very often they have no religion at all and in despair interpret this life as being the only life allotted to them. This gives impetus.

x^2 A 404   n.d., 1850

« 4029

With regard to much mental anguish, it may be said that perhaps the particular fault the sufferer accuses himself of is really committed first at the present time, but in quite another way. There was a person (he was a Catholic who had become a Lutheran; Kofoed-Hansen[326] told me about it) who confessed that he had sinned against the Holy Spirit by having betrayed his convictions in a weak moment, and that for him there was no mercy. Perhaps the sin against the Holy Spirit was rather the pride with which he would not forgive himself. There is also a severity in condemning oneself and not wanting to hear about grace which is nothing but sin. As I pointed out to Kofoed-Hansen, Anti-Climacus[327] has already called attention to this.

x^2 A 429 *n.d.*, 1850

« **4030**

[*In margin:* Julius Müller. *Die Lehre von der Sünde*, p. I, pp. 457 ff.[328]]

There is an excellent little section on evil, on sin as the incomprehensible, the impenetrable, the world's secret—precisely because it is the groundless, an arbitrary discontinuity. I am also happy to see that he quotes Daub, who also explains it in *Judas Iscariot* this way and is not disinclined to place evil under a special definition of the miraculous, although he later abandoned this view and conceived of evil as the negative, for example in his book *Hypotheser om den menneskelige Frihed.*[329]

J. M. is absolutely right in saying that the "incomprehensibility" of sin is not based on limited knowledge so that the task should be that we are to continue speculating and then finally get enough knowledge. No, its incomprehensibility is its very nature.

It can also be quite simply illustrated as follows. If we take a man who at one time was abandoned to a sin and now is delivered—and ask him whether he is now able to comprehend how he could sin like that, he will answer: No, and now less than ever. The more pure a man becomes, the more incomprehensible evil becomes to him.[*]

I can demonstrate this incomprehensibility of sin in another manner. Anti-Climacus[330] has correctly pointed out that with regard to evil possibility and actuality have the reverse of their usual relation; ordinarily actuality is higher than possibility, but in relation to evil actuality is lower than possiblity; the good as possibility is the imperfect, as actuality the perfect, but the evil as possibility is better than evil as actuality.

But to comprehend evil is to dissolve actuality into possibility (see Johannes Climacus[331]); but if actuality *in casu*[332] is lower than possibility, then it is impossible to comprehend, for sin genuinely *is* only as actuality, but to comprehend means to dissolve in possibility; consequently it is impossible to comprehend it, for dissolved in possibility it is not evil. The good can be comprehended, because there is a direct relation between possibility and actuality, although of course it must be remembered that the good in possibility is a lower form; to comprehend the good is qualitatively distant from realizing it.

x^2 A 436 *n.d.,* 1850

« **4031**

[*] *In margin of 4030* (x^2 A 436):
Therefore we find that when a person ponders his sin or his having sinned, he described his condition rather as one of intoxication. He sank or his consciousness sank as if into darkness. Here we have the qualification: the groundless. Yet two things must not be forgotten —that the evil can have frightful energy in a man, energizing him to want to plunge into this darkness, and also that it is essentially a matter of the will and is in the realm of responsibility. But just as the drunkard is guilty of being drunk because of drinking strong liquor to an excess —although the drunkenness itself is in fact a sinking below consciousness—so it is also with sin.

x^2 A 437 *n.d.*

« **4032**

The difference between a pagan and a Christian is not that the latter is without sin; the difference is how he regards his sin and how he is kept in the striving. When a pagan sins—and precisely the more profound and noble he is—there is a dreadful halt in striving; he sinks into depression, broods introspectively over his guilt, and the sin then perhaps gets more and more power over him, so that he despairingly sinks deeper and deeper. The Christian has a Savior; he takes refuge in "grace"; as with a child, his sin is transformed for him into a fatherly punishment intended to help him go forward—and he perhaps makes the self-assured step forward right now. Bold confidence is truly not irresponsibility but is trust in grace. The fact that a man quickly dismisses thought of a sin of weakness can be irresponsibility, but it can also be bold confidence because he has such a deep and trusting conception of "grace."

x^2 A 456 *n.d.,* 1850

« **4033 *Romans 7***

The most severe condemnation of sin, and right here begins the Redemption, by saying the same thing but in another way.
Romans 7. Obviously the most dreadful form of sin is reached when sin has taken away a man's power completely and has him in its power against his will. All voluntary sin is thus far less appalling simply

because it is apparent that he had the power to act otherwise. It is the same with the individual's own condition: there is an inherent hope of salvation through his own powers, that he could have done otherwise, but when he can only say, sin has such power over me that it is against my will, then despair is right at the door.

And yet here, here begins the Atonement and the Redemption. He then says: Take courage, it is not you who wills the evil, it is the power of sin in you; take comfort in Christ.

Astonishing—that the most frightful accusation from the one side is the exculpation of compassion from the other.

It is easy to see that this doctrine can be taken in vain. Yet the danger is not so great if we remember one thing: what is supposed to happen is that a person comes out of his sin. The frightful abuse of the doctrine occurs when one continues in sin and justifies it by saying it is against his will.

X^2 A 467 *n.d.*, 1850

« 4034

Julius Müller[333] properly formulates the problem of original sin (*peccatum originale*) and guilt. He shows that guilt and sin are correlatives—ergo, where there is sin there is also guilt; if one has admitted A, he must also admit B.

And it is also correct to give this the formulation that original sin is sin, or that original sin *is*. Therefore the condition from which actual sins necessarily come is also sin. It is very simply stated in the categories: cause and effect.

He also points out correctly how the syllogism about guilt and sin can be turned around in *Pelagian* fashion to just the opposite. Guilt and sin are correlatives; now it is impossible to think of my sin in relation to something I have not myself committed—ergo, there is no original sin; thus by denying the concept guilt I deny original sin on the basis of the same thesis: that guilt and sin are correlatives.

X^2 A 472 *n.d.*, 1850

« 4035 *Original Sin*

On the whole, as I see it, "original sin" is an expression of the fact that Christianity uses God's standard. God sees everything *in uno*.[334]

It is this which lies most deeply as the basis of the possibility of offense in relation to and inseparable from every single qualification of the essentially Christian: that Christianity is of God's devising,[335] that at every single point it does not forget that God is along and as participant is what he condescended to be; from this it admittedly follows that we—humanly speaking, if you please, we poor men—must put up with the fact that God's standard is employed. The first consequence of this is that we are under a standard which no man by himself dreams of or thinks about (here the Augsburg Confession[336] is masterly in declaring that on his own a man has no true idea of how deep a corruption sin is, that he must be informed of this by a revelation—and quite rightly so, because it is a part of sin to have only a shallow notion of sin and also because only God, the Holy One, has the truly divine idea). But in the second it comes again,[337] for then it is also promised to man that he may become God's child.

x^2 A 473 *n.d.*, 1850

« 4036

That a person wants to sit and brood and stare at his sin and is unwilling to have faith that it is forgiven: is this also guilt in that it is a minimizing of what Christ has done.

x^2 A 477 *n.d.*, 1850

« 4037

Here is an error in Julius Müller.[338] He is right in maintaining that sin and every manifestation of freedom (the younger Fichte[339] has already repeatedly stressed this) do not occur of necessity (no, neither before nor afterward; see *Philosophical Fragments*)[340] but must be experienced.

Fine, now he should have swung directly into the ethical-religious, into the existential, to the *you* and *I*. Earnestness is that I myself become conscious of being a sinner and apply everything in this respect to myself. But instead of that he goes into the ordinary problems about the universality of sin, etc. But if it is to be experienced, then I must either know all, and in that case, since the world goes on, the whole thing becomes a hypothesis, which perhaps held water until now but does not for that reason hold water (as I see Prof. Levy writes in an article about the maternity hospital)—or I must also understand what Johannes Climacus has developed in *Concluding Postscript*,[341] that with regard to actuality every individual is essentially assigned only to himself; he can understand every other individual only in possibility.

x^2 A 482 *n.d.*, 1850

« **4038**

On closer inspection it becomes apparent that original sin, which is an article of faith, is actually not an intensification, rightly understood, but a mitigation, marked by the fact that there is an Atoner who has made satisfaction for the whole race.

But it must be maintained that the universality of sin cannot be a matter of knowledge; it can only be believed; it is a communication of revelation. Beyond that I have to concentrate all my earnestness solely on this—that I am a sinner.

x^2 A 483   n.d., 1850

« **4039** *Sin-consciousness Binds to Christ*

They all deserted Christ, even the apostle[342] denied him—only the thief[343] on the cross remained faithful to the end and in the final moment, but then of course he was bound by the consciousness of sin and the situation of death.

x^3 A 180   n.d., 1850

« **4040**

In margin of 4039 (x^3 A 180):

But nevertheless what faith! To believe that the one who was under the same sentence, insulted, mocked, spit upon, cursed, nailed to a cross—to believe that his words had significance, that he could be God who gives one a place in Paradise,[344] to keep this faith when it comes to the point where the crucified one himself cries out: My God, my God, why have you forsaken me.[345] (Tersteegen[346] has called attention to this.)

O, there is so much talk that Christianity is direct communication. For a man suffering the insults and curses of all, condemned as a criminal, nailed to a cross, to say: Believe on me, I am God—God in heaven, is this in fact *direct* communication!

x^3 A 181   n.d.

« **4041** *Something Dubious about the More Proficient Proclamation of Christianity*

Almost every one of the prominent personalities in the Church had previously been a sinner in the stricter sense of the word. It is precisely this which contributed to giving them the impression of Christianity—they literally needed Christianity.

But now there is silence about this and instead an emphasis upon a universal human sinfulness.

118 SIN

The conditions Christianity banished when Christ proclaimed it must still be the ordinary conditions. But at that time it was in fact the publicans and sinners (consequently those called sinners in the stricter sense of the word) who took their stand with Christ.

X³ A 199 *n.d.*, 1850

« 4042 *What It Is That Binds Us to Christ*

It is a power which is called sin. If you want to be saved from it, then turn to Christ. He is salvation, even though the salvation is otherwise bitter, humanly speaking, but if the sin within you is in truth more bitter, then there is surely nothing to think twice about.

A final hour is coming, the hour of death. Christ promises you an infinite good, the blessedness of heaven. Would you dispense with that for something else? Well, then choose him. But then he reserves the right to have the disposal of your life here in the world, he makes life more difficult for you—but he also helps you to bear it.

X³ A 341 *n.d.*, 1850

« 4043

The whole point—something about which one can never adequately pray to God—is that a person must always have clearly in mind an infinite conception of the loathsomeness of sin and an infinite conception of what an infinite good eternal salvation is. If one does not have these, he is overwhelmed by sufferings, is enervated, thinks these conditions too dear a price to pay for eternal salvation. So he squints at the fringes, keeps his ears open—and in this way is able to hear from the millions that a person can be saved on far cheaper terms. O, the most dangerous place for a true Christian to live is—Christendom.

X³ A 376 *n.d.*, 1850

« 4044 *The Sinner*

The [woman who was a] sinner[347] is present almost as if only in effigy, and yet she is the one around whom the action centers—the one who is present.

X³ A 566 *n.d.*, 1850

« 4045 *What Sin Cries to Heaven?*

The very one that hides most secretly and most quietly within.

No, what the adulterers, murderers, and thieves do cries out already here on earth and does not really cry to heaven.

X³ A 688 *n.d.*, 1850

« **4046** *Iranæus*

declares that it is true that death is the punishment of sin (consequently a part of God's righteousness), but it is also an expression of God's grace and mercy. Precisely thereby God upset, as it were, the devil's apple cart—he thrust death in between and thereby put an end to sin. If man continued eternally or were eternal, the devil would have conquered. But now sin's punishment, death, establishes a boundary to sin in another sense (grace and mercy).

See Böhringer, *Die Kirche und ihre Zeugen*, I, pt. 1, Irenæus, pp. 237-38.[348]

x^4 A 133   *n.d.*, 1851

« **4047** *Augustine*

What is so often advanced as an excuse for man's sin—namely, weakness, ignorance, being overpowered by the sensate, etc.—Augustine turns quite masterfully when he says that far from being a defense or an explanation of sin it is much more the punishment of sin; sin is not to be explained as a result of this weakness, this eclipse of the understanding—no, this is to be explained as a result of sin, the punishment of sin. "We do not call sin only that which is generally called sin in the most essential and rigorous sense—namely, a voluntary and conscious fault, but we call everything sin which is a *necessary result* of such a fault and thus is its punishment." See Böhringer, I, pt. 3, p. 408.[349] Böhringer is correct in saying that Augustine interprets the relation in such a way that the particular will is not external to but enclosed within the condition in which the person finds himself.

See ibid., p. 490, top.

x^4 A 173   *n.d.*, 1851

« **4048** *Theme*

When a man is sick or indisposed, the first thing he does is to send for the physician, and medication is what he wants; spiritually it is just the opposite—when a man has sinned, the last thing he wants is the physician and medicine.

x^4 A 534   *n.d.*, 1852

« **4049** *Spiritual Sins*

How far the world is from being spirit is seen also in the fact that the very sins regarded as the most frightful by Christianity are not regarded as sins by the world but are almost admired: for example, cunning, wickedness with ingenuity, subtlety, etc.

What the world regards as sin and makes an uproar about is either stealing and anything related to the security of property and possessions, or it is sins of the flesh, indeed, precisely that which Christianity regards as most pardonable. A man who tricks and swindles day in and day out but otherwise is an extremely cultivated gentleman belonging to the society of the cultivated—if he has the bad luck to get drunk once—heaven help him, it is an irreparable loss, and he himself condemns it so severely that he perhaps, as they say, never forgives himself, while it probably never occurs to him that he should need to be forgiven for all the tricks and frauds and dishonesty, for all the spiritually revolting passions which make their home within him and are his life.

XI² A 6 n.d., 1854

« 4050 *Isolation*

That Christianity is unconditionally related to isolation (the single individual) is evident also in the fact that Christianity's presupposition is always the consciousness of sin, that it begins by proclaiming the forgiveness of sin.

But the consciousness of sin is the unconditionally isolating. Even the most primitive originality is not so isolating, at most is still an anticipation oriented to the others, does not touch the essence of the personality on the deepest level. Even the most exceptional human misfortune and suffering are not as isolating; others participate in it by their being men, and it ends in fact with death, does not touch the essence of the personality on the deepest level.

Sin alone is the unconditionally isolating. My sin does not concern one single human being except me and touches my personality on the deepest level.

In this way we see how nonsensical it is to say that states and nations and countries and abstractions are Christian, also that little children are Christians. Christianity has been made into something in which Christianity's presupposition can never be present, its *sine qua non*:³⁵⁰ isolation, the single individual.

XI² A 14 n.d., 1854

« 4051 *Original Sin—Christianity*

Just when a man has reached the age when he perhaps might have the maturity capable of becoming aware of the essentially Christian view of original sin, that the propagation of the race is sin, that for the spirit to exist [*være til*] as animal-creature is an ambiguous good, etc. —precisely at that time or a few years before, he himself, in the role of father, is busy hammering into his children's heads what a benefaction it is that he has given them life, or he is in full swing enjoying his children's joy of life, which, after all, Christianity has never denied, for the child is only an animal-creature, and Christianity understands that for spirit it is suffering to exist as animal-creature, which explains why Christendom has very shrewdly abolished the qualification "spirit" with respect to being man and thereby has made life easy, marriage to be life's earnestness and significance (which procreation is for the animal-creature)—and then still continues to call itself Christian.

Just as in the fairy tales the woods creatures withdraw themselves and give instead some nonsense to one who tries to investigate them, so too existence withdraws and deceives men by tricking them into race propagation whereby their lives are placed in parentheses, and these parentheses expand into millions and it continues from generation to generation, while existence remains no more transfigured than before and Christianity is shoved completely outside.

All this talk about Christ's having made satisfaction for original sin does not, after all, prove that Christianity wants race propagation. For all expiation and atonement is still always focused backward and not forward. Just as with actual sin, if one's sin was stealing, then he makes atonement for the past, but this still does not mean that in the future he can steal as much as he wants to. So also with making satisfaction for original sin—it certainly does not mean that now in the future man can be just as gay as he wants to be with respect to race propagation. No, Christianity blocks the way with the single state. Your father's guilt which brought you into existence, it says, has been atoned—but now stop, the Atonement does not mean that you are to go and do the same as he: the making of satisfaction does not give you a free pass in this matter.

XI^2 A 242 *n.d.*, 1854

SITUATION

« **4052**

The situation is decisive. If in a situation of actuality I say what the pastor says on Sunday and what everyone at that time approves, all are insulted, embittered, indignant with me, or they find it embarrassing. It is considered to be uncultured, an indulgence in personalities, to say to him personally the very same thing which he himself thinks is all right if said in a general way. The pastor says: Do not worry about tomorrow, and we all approve. If I were to say the same thing to a merchant who had gone bankrupt that very day, he would take it as a personal insult. The sermon is on sacrificing everything for the truth, and we all approve. If tomorrow I were to say to the same pastor—with reference to the utter disgrace he would incur by acting as he ought to: Here is your opportunity, as you said yesterday, to sacrifice everything for the truth, the pastor would say: I must say it is highly inappropriate, somewhat embarrassing and boorish, to indulge in personalities this way; and the whole town would think that the pastor was right, the same town that wept with the pastor when he wept and preached about suffering for the truth.

X^1 A 17   *n.d.*, 1849

« **4053** *A Situation*

Only in the situation of actuality is it possible to get the true impression of the essentially Christian. At the time when Christianity was persecuted, to accept Christianity meant immediately being listed among the banished; then the situation was cut out to make a man reflect on whether he wanted to be a Christian or not. In the dead calm of a commonplace illusion, when everything is given over to internal decision alone, a person can become anxious and fearful—is he really a Christian, may he not be deluding himself.

I will now imagine myself to be a man who says to himself: It is easy to see that what is declaimed in churches by paid professionals is not Christianity. On the other hand, I know what Christianity is. Here and now I am going to place this right in the middle of Christendom (for my own sake as well, as that I may produce the situation of tension necessary for an infinite decision). Christendom, of course, will become enraged, and I will come close to being persecuted. But this is what I need in order to confront to my benefit the question of whether or not I want to be a Christian, and this is actually what Christendom needs.

Has a man a right to do this? It is a concern for the truth which guides him, and in my best judgment he does have a right to do it.

But I still do not dare avail myself of such an answer.

I believe that if a man is going to be used according to that standard, Governance helps him by constraining him.

Governance, educating him, leads him on little by little; he does not arrive at such a momentous decision by virtue of an *arbitrium*.

Generally speaking, the proper consolation for those who are actually being used as instruments is that in one sense their suffering is against their will. Just as Plato[351] says in the *Republic* that only those should rule who have no desire to rule, so also a man is used by Governance for the very thing he in a certain sense is most disinclined to do. For instance, Governance uses the most sensitive men for almost the cruelest jobs, the weakest and most anxious for the toughest jobs, just as he used Moses,[352] who quite rightly appealed to his being anything but a speaker, used him for the mission to Pharoah.

X^2 A 13   *n.d.*, 1849

« **4054** *A True Christian*

may involve himself in secular affairs essentially only in order to deceive—that is, to create a situation for introducing Christianity. If, for example, a true Christian has a striking talent by means of which he can make a big hit, he may do it for a few years, win all the honor, esteem, and fame possible—in order to throw it all away suddenly, now after having made sure of getting a hearing which can constitute a situation in which Christianity can make an impression.

X^4 A 397   *n.d.*, 1851

« **4055** *The Situation Decides the Issue*

When Christ says to the leper or to the two blind men (Matthew 9:28): Do you believe that I can help you, and they are then healed in the power of their faith—and when we now say: I believe that Christ is able to help me, the two are not at all comparable. Now Christ is not in the form of an insignificant servant anymore, in his incognito,[353] the obstacle which was needed so that faith could become faith.

And yet in Christendom we pretend as if it is as easy as falling off a log; we talk about faith as if believing that God can help us is the same thing as believing that this particular man with whom I stand and talk, this man in the form of an insignificant servant, the sign of offense,[354] that he can help.

XI[1] A 562   n.d., 1854

« 4056 *The Medium for Being Christian*

The Situation

Ventriloquism is a way of speaking so that it cannot be determined who the speaker is; the words are heard, but as if they were unattached, as if there were no speaker.

But in a far deeper sense all speaking with the mouth is a kind of ventriloquism, an indeterminate something. The deception is that there is, after all, a definite visible figure who uses his mouth. But take care. Language is an abstraction.

In order for speaking actually to become human speech in a deeper sense, or in a spiritual sense, something else is required with respect to being the one who speaks, two points must be determined: the one is the speech, the words spoken, the other is the situation.

The situation determines decisively whether or not the speaker is in character with what he says, or the situation determines whether or not the words are spoken at random, a talking which is unattached, which in a deeper sense is true of all talking that is situationless.

And yet it is this very situationlessness which negatively characterizes all Christendom and makes all its Christian professing a delusion, ventriloquism, so that one actually could just as well use a machine.

But it is precisely this shirking which is so common among men —they say what is supposed to be said—but shun the situation. I knew a man who was in public life, was a member of popular assemblies, but almost never spoke. He managed by telling his neighbor what should be said at the meeting. This is deficiency of character through absence of situation.

So also with Christendom. From a Christian point of view, to confess Christ is to do it in the situation Christianity assigns: the actual world. To confess Christ is not to say it on Sunday in a quiet hour, or in private conversation in the peaceful living room, etc. The matter is not improved by the shameless claim that one is, after all, declaring Christianity objectively.

To declare it objectively is just another attempt along the line of ventriloquism, for it is speaking in such a way that it is impossible to identify who is speaking, it is a shrouding of one's *I* in the disguise of a third person or an abstract *I*.

An illustration. There is a particular word—to say it to the tyrant is mortally dangerous. What does one do, then? —One plays the game of saying the word—yes, absolutely right—but not to the tyrant. This is how children play—and this is the way those profound men of earnestness like Bishop Mynster et al. are Christians.

XI^2 A 106   *n.d.*, 1854

« **4057** *Martyrdom—Asceticism*

That Luther altered Christianity by changing the concept of martyrdom as not having intrinsic worth, I have pointed out elsewhere [i.e., XI^1 A 193].

Then somewhere else [i.e., X^5 A 99] I have called the asceticism of the Middle Ages situationless.

Commenting on this, I would say that it is quite true that the asceticism of the Middle Ages is situationless and that the Christian must go out into the world in order to be sacrificed.

But from another point of view, the idea of being sacrificed can easily be made sophistical, as if it were up to a man's understanding to discern where a sacrifice is needed.

No, the Christian view is that sacrifices, in fact, are always needed, and asceticism is really the view of life that regards God as the unconditioned and believes that before God this world is immersed in evil, is not a happy playground but a penitentiary, and asceticism voluntarily endeavors to express this idea of the world that God has.

What made the asceticism of the Middle Ages situationless was really the fact that direct recognizability had been introduced, that one wanted to be honored and was honored for his asceticism. Well, *das ist was anders!*[355] This, you see, allowed the union of two alien elements: an ascetic—who is afraid of losing his life, afraid of martyrdom. His asceticism was in fact not pessimistic but was a cunning contrivance to achieve public distinction, to *live* admired, almost idolized. Far from incurring the hostility of men (in love to God), he had much the same relation to them that a juggler has to his public, and although he was an ascetic he perhaps clung harder to this life than any juggler, loved the admiration of men more passionately than any actor.

XI² A 161 *n.d.*, 1854

« 4058

To a discourse, to a word, also belongs the situation during which or in which it is spoken. If the situation is different, one does not say the same thing but something else, perhaps even the opposite, even though the word, the discourse, is the same.

As far as the essentially Christian is concerned, in Christendom the situation in relation to the New Testament is completely changed. When we go on as usual and use the pathos-filled expressions of the New Testament for the existential, especially the polemical existential, it becomes either nonsense or hypocrisy, and thus the Sunday church service treats God as a fool, since in his Word it is obviously understood differently, while we either muddleheadedly or sanctimoniously say the same words.

Example. "So every one who acknowledges me before men" etc.[356] In the New Testament the situation is one in which the world has polemical relationship to being a Christian; therefore to confess Christ is the expression for the highest venture. In Christendom we are all Christians, benefits and advantages are bound up with being Christian, careers and offices and livelihoods are bound up with being a clergyman—and then we go on talking with pathos about confessing Christ to the world, and the pastor declares that he is doing it: this is either drivel or hypocrisy.

In a little article by Brammer (in Hjort's *Kirketidene*)[357] "He who does not confess" etc. etc. is pointed out as one of Bishop Mynster's Bible texts.

O, it is abominable to go on as usual in this way and actually use God's Word in treating God as a fool.

XI² A 319 *n.d.*, 1854

« 4059

In every word Christ speaks (likewise the apostle) the situation must be taken into account—namely, that Christ is the one persecuted, misunderstood, hated, humiliated, etc.

For example, Christ says: Believe in me; only believe in me and you will be saved—*aber, aber*[358] the one spoken to must, after all, carry this out in the situation of contemporaneity, but then suffering is unavoidable.

Here is the fundamental confusion in the use now made of the New Testament: we take the words without the situation, or even in an opposite situation; in this way the words acquire a different meaning and have no relation to the person.

XI^2 A 343   *n.d.*, 1854

SOCIAL-POLITICAL THOUGHT

« **4060**

Should a great man be judged according to principles different from those used for every other man? This question has often been answered with "Yes," but my opinion is "No." A great man is great simply because he is a chosen instrument in the hands of God. But the moment he fancies that it is he himself who acts, that *he* can look out over the future and on that basis allow the end to justify the means— then he is small. Right and duty hold for everybody, and trespassing against them is no more to be excused in the great man than in governments, where people nevertheless imagine that politics has permission to go wrong. To be sure, such a wrong may often have a beneficial result, but for this we are not to thank that man or the state but providence.

I A 42   December 23, 1834

« **4061**

There is a remarkable connection between Protestantism and the modern political point of view. It is a battle about the same thing, about the sovereignty of the people—which is why it is also interesting to see that the genuine royalists—insofar as they do not have one view on one matter and an essentially different view on another (in an individual both must be based on the same principles)—tend toward Catholicism.—

October 13, 1835

For Luther's view on this, see Clausen and Hohlenberg's *Tidsskrift*, III, pp. 548 at the bottom and 557.[359]

I A 93   *n.d.*

« **4062**

A peculiar kind of monkey is the so-called Entellus (*Semn. Entellus*), which is light gray but has a black face and hands . . . . . The French naturalist Duvaucel had great difficulty in getting to shoot these Entellus monkeys in Sumatra because the natives regarded them as transmogrified princes and princesses with divine powers.

Dansk. Ugeskrift, IV, p. 338 (in a paper by Escricht on "Apes").³⁶⁰

I A 133 n.d., 1836

« 4063

The contrast between the romantic period and our age of reason is clearly apparent in the following. Whereas the former dwelt mainly on the thought of a great tree³⁶¹ which towered to the heavens (in order to connect heaven with earth—the ash tree Ygdrasill—the giants?), our age seeks to get everything to spread out in plain sight, side by side. Whereas the former sought to get the whole generation merged, so to speak, in one individual, our age tries to get all nations to stand alongside one another—the so-called cosmopolitan system. No one raises the objection that romanticism, too, was a kind of cosmopolitan view, for the difference is that the romantic period emphasized more the idea of the great sublimity etc. of this single individual, whereas our age emphasizes more the thought of the multiplicity, the diversity, which is joined together in a unity. Thus while that period adhered to nationality, with every nation epitomized, so to speak, in its representative, our age places greater emphasis on the idea of the multitudinous individuals who are united in one state, the plurality of interests which intersect here—consequently, on *multiplicity.*

I A 139 March, 1836

« 4064

The orthodox appeal to God and conscience—something mysterious—cut away the connecting link. —The Romans made Augustus god —humbling themselves before god—noblemen—grand toward others.

I A 180 n.d., 1836

« 4065

The wish commonly expressed during the French Revolution to see the last king hanged with the gut of the last priest is reminiscent of Caligula's wish³⁶² to see the heads of all the Romans sitting on one neck so that they could be cut off with one stroke.

I A 246 September 20, 1836

« 4066

Since every development, in my opinion, is finished only with its own parody,³⁶³ it will soon become apparent that politics is the parody in the development of the world—first of all, genuine mythology (God's side), next, human mythology (man's side), and then a realization of the world's aim in the world (as the highest), a sort of Chiliasm,[364] which meanwhile brings the individual politicians, carried away by abstract ideas, into contradiction with themselves.

I A 285   November 20, 1836

« **4067**

Parody (as the final stage in the development) is apparent also in the way childhood is repeated in old age: "to be in one's second childhood."

I A 288   *n.d.*, 1836

« **4068**

Just as education or upbringing is for the purpose of having the individual experience the growth of the past, so also every nation has a stage in which it passes through what the world has experienced in its development, a stage before it *comes of age world-historically*, and—just as during the period of upbringing—the more this hidden life is kept out of the *world debate*, the better it is, the more distinctive it is.

I A 289   *n.d.*, 1836

« **4069**

Although we personally do not exert much effort to shape society, do not work jointly toward a common goal, but on the contrary are quite egotistically isolated and separated, we are nevertheless always interested in lives bound together in this way (monks—thieves—robbers—bourgeois life—the religious life's monstrosities or parasites???—political life in revolution—chivalry); at least the associative element manifests itself in our day in external ways, for example in fund-raising (English Bible societies—associations to support the Greeks—foundations for morally depraved persons—).

I A 304   *n.d.*, 1836

« **4070**

When the dialectical period (the romantic) has been passed through in world history (a period I could very appropriately call the age of individuality—something which can also be demonstrated historically quite easily), social life must again play its role to the utmost degree, and ideas such as the state (for example, as the Greeks knew it, the Church in the older Catholic meaning of the word) must of necessity return richer and fuller—that is, with all the content that the residual diversity of individuality can give the idea, so that the individual as such means nothing, but all are links in the chain. This is why the concept of Church increasingly makes a claim, the concept of a fixed objective faith etc., just as the propensity to found societies is a forerunner, although up to now a bad one, of this development.

I A 307   December 11, 1836

« 4071

Politicians——Spartans——a contrast in the sacrificing life.
The gospel's teaching about the law is similar.

I A 308   n.d., 1836

« 4072

The romanticism in Solon, who wanted his laws to be in force no longer than 100 years.

I A 309   n.d., 1836

« 4073

When the state acquires its proper significance, to be exiled will become—as it was with the Greeks—the most severe punishment.

I A 310   n.d., 1836

« 4074

Once again there is new life on Amager Square, and the multi-colored floral carpet of the street crowds is spread out there. At twelve o'clock last night a man in shabby clothes was picked up there because, as the night watchman said, he had been abusive to a number of people; the watchman making the report had not seen it, and they probably had no right to strike the arrested man, and no one protested it—no one knows it. Today everything is the same in the marketplace; it is still Amager Square—what is that compared to Denmark, Europe, the earth, the world.

II A 618   n.d., 1837

« 4075

There are two directions of circulation in the state—the one process leads from the heart to the extremities (the government officials), the other from the extremities to the heart (the municipality, representation in the provincial chambers) but nothing abstract.

II A 668   n.d., 1837

« 4076

There are certain arrangements in the state (certain authorities) which originally were in continual fluctuation in the life of the state but which because of the ossification in the life of the state are said to govern the *casus* just as prepositions do, although strictly speaking they do not—they are prepositions that have become adverbs.

                                          II A 669   September 29, 1837

« 4077

Hatred of monarchist principles has gone so far in our day that people want to have four-part solo parts.

                                          II A 680   December 31, 1837

« 4078

Even if everybody were very fond of the government, even if everybody were willing to do everything, one may nevertheless be sure that somewhere there is some mistletoe[365] which in a blind (anonymous) man's hand is aimed against this unity.

                                          II A 703   February 12, 1838

« 4079

At present the state is obviously suffering from an abdominal attack (*tiers etate,* bellyache)—previously it was a headache.

                                          II A 705   February 19, 1838

« 4080

The role the common prostitute (the Goddess of Reason) played in Paris is not so strange, for where is it more natural for public opinion to incorporate itself than in a common prostitute; nor is it the first time this has happened, for as a matter of fact even Simon Magnus[366] palmed off a woman who was a common prostitute as his first published thought (the first to be made *publici juris*[367]).

                                          II A 219   *n.d.*, 1838

« 4081

When the Jews were persecuted by Philip the Fair of France, they emigrated and later drew out their money by means of bills of exchange; nowadays, when Jews are tolerated everywhere, they are emigrating from Germany (the new Germany) and draining off the resources of the old Germany by printing pirated editions.

                                          II A 257   September 8, 1838

« 4082

It is remarkable—something that has recurred in the political development, something that is so prototypical in the development of the first crusade—that a Walter v. Habennichts³⁶⁸ leads them, except that in the political development there is not a single such individual but the entire militia is made up of those who more or less are *Habennichts*es.

II A 272 October 10, 1838

« 4083

It is a witty coincidence of history that at the same time that papal power is at its peak (Innocent III) there lives a king immortalized by the appellation "without a country"; popes and kings have always found it difficult to eat together out of the same dish, but that time the pope had eaten calamitously of the king's portion—that is, his country.

II A 274 October 11, 1838

« 4084

Our constitution more and more resembles that of the Chinese— the only thing still lacking is that we prohibit emigration.

II A 290 November 2, 1838

« 4085

Our politicians are like the Greek reciprocals ($\dot{\alpha}\lambda\lambda\eta\lambda\hat{\omega}\nu$), which lack the nominative, the singular, and all subjective cases—they can be thought of only in the plural and in declined cases.

II A 710 n.d., 1838

« 4086

We cannot deny [that] the politicians [exercise] a certain vigilance and watchfulness over everything—the fact is that they, like bad pennies, are everywhere.

II A 735 n.d., 1838

« 4087

The politicians charge me with always contradicting; yet in this they are my superiors, for they always have one more they contradict —namely, themselves.

II A 754 n.d., 1838

« 4088

But the liberals have, as it says in the fairy tale,³⁶⁹ a tongue and an empty head, like the tongue in a church bell.

II A 774 n.d., 1838

« 4089

The story about clever Else could be printed in its entirety—otherwise the caption could be used: What a clever Else[370] we have!

II A 775   n.d., 1838

« 4090

Precisely because politicians overlook continuity, they admit only two of the three marks of the validity of the public spirit,[371] *consensus* and *universalitas* (and even these in a rather trivial and arbitrary sense), but completely overlook the third—*antiquitas*.

II A 783   n.d., 1838

« 4091

The Christian can toss around a lot in the world and have dealings with it, but his religion he must keep to himself, just as in buying and selling the Jews used Roman money with the head of Caesar, but in the temple they used their own coinage.

II A 323   January 8, 1839

« 4092

.....then he rode over to him and whispered: "Major, you are making an about-face"; whereupon the major shouted with a commanding voice: "Battalion, about-face!" and so he kept on going wrong, to say nothing of the whole battalion's ending up in the wrong position. This, you see, is the trouble with politicians—it is always the "whole battalion," while it is only they themselves who should make an about-face.[372]

II A 378   March 3, 1839

« 4093

In many ways the Church Fathers' descriptions of demons fit the politicians of our day. They lived in the air (they are far too windy to be able to keep their feet on the ground); they lived on the smoke of *offerings* and *incense*; they were very mobile and could *pass over the whole world in a hurry*.

II A 436   May 21, 1839

« 4094

The liberals are like the tailor in heaven (see the fairy tale "The Tailor in Heaven"[373])—in order to punish a single abuse which they notice from our Lord's usurped throne, they grab God's footstool and hurl it down to earth—yes, to punish it they would willingly destroy the whole world.

II A 460 n.d., 1839

« **4095**

The same contempt for every element of knowledge, insofar as it is purely human, which finds expression in Tertullian[374] in the words: *credo quia absurdum,* is repeated in a similar negation of the reality [*Realitæt*] of the civil world when Tertullian says that a denunciation and the resulting death sentence are for the informer an act of murder. See de Wette, p. 215.[375]

II A 467 July 3, 1839

« **4096**

If the orthodox and the politicians were to combine against the state, I suppose that things would turn out for them as they once did for two lads who wanted to swing a third and against his will wanted to swing him really high. They aimed too low, missed contact, and when the energy directed from both sides did not find the expected pressure of his back, they ran head-on into each other, but the boy in the swing sailed unscathed over both of them.

II A 481 July 20, 1839

« **4097**

..... Therefore the king is no *incarnation,* not a being we should worship; he is a weak, fragile human being like the rest of us, but he is king *by the grace of God,* and it is this religious boundary which limits and terminates the state, and thereby all the abstract nonsense about the wisest individual of all is demolished, because all differences in human wisdom are still relative and vanishing over against the divine wisdom of Divine Governance which calls and designates the individual.

II A 531 August 8, 1839

« **4098**

In margin of 4097 (II A 531):
and in the historical situation (conditioned by Divine Governance), in which the king must be regarded as the people, the "we" he uses is not merely a *pluralis majestatis,* i.e., a *singularis,* but in truth a *pluralis:* i.e., the *intensified state-consciousness.*

II A 532 n.d.

« **4099**

Although the development of the state which has the divine in itself not as potency but as *primus motor* has monarchy as the last (and lowest) factor (patriarchs, judges, kings, and including a repetition of the judges in the prophets), because monarchy is most incorporated into the world, ordinary human evolution has monarchy as the intrinsically highest, as that to which every other form of the state strives; whereas in the other sequence of development it must be regarded as a decline. —It is the same development which in the sphere of knowledge permits the system to be regarded as a decline and proverbial wisdom as the first and highest, whereas in the other sequence the system is the highest.

II A 573   September 19, 1839

« **4100**

Regarded as a state, North America is structured just the opposite to European states. It develops in length and breadth (the discontented conquer or buy new tracts and establish themselves there), the European in height and depth, genuine organization.

III A 106   n.d., 1841

« **4101**

..... and losing oneself atomistically in life's social throng, and as you once very wittily observed, when the idea of society really ascends, communication will become so intense that even to the experienced eye the human race will become an ocean where it will be impossible to distinguish between the hordes of infusoria who previously formed isolated existences.[376]

III B 41:2   n.d., 1841

« **4102**

Imagine a king who ruled over a happy nation, a kingdom where peace and prosperity really seemed to have taken up residence, imagine him saying to himself in one of his solitary moments: I have the allegiance of my people, they praise and bless my regime, and yet what have I done and what am I doing. If, then—in order to do something —he did not resort to something that destroyed his people but calmly told himself: I have the responsibility, my crown does not weigh heavily upon me, but yet the responsibility does rest upon me—if he said and felt this, then he would also be justified in enjoying all the approval a grateful people could shower upon him.³⁷⁷

III B 41:18   n.d., 1841

« 4103

Orthodoxy has never gone so far overboard in idolatry as was done during the empire period with the emperor's image: one who struck his slave while he carried on his person a silver drachma imprinted with the emperor's image was condemned for high treason. (See Philostratus, *Leben des Apollonius v. Tyana*, p. 185.³⁷⁸ Cited by Suetonius, *Vita Tiberii*, 58.³⁷⁹)

IV A 7   n.d., 1842-43

« 4104

In Aristotle's *Ethics*, bk. V, ch. 10,³⁸⁰ there are many examples of the way kings have brought revolutions upon themselves. Frequently there are many interesting collisions, a plentiful profusion for a poet.

IV A 9   n.d., 1842-43

« 4105

It is a psychological oddity. Vindex instigated a revolt against Nero. What embittered Nero most of all was that he had said that Nero was anything but a zither player and was more of a zither player than he was a king. Nero was offended that Vindex regarded him as a bad zither player.

> Philostratus, *Apollonius af Tyanas Levnet*, 5, 10, p. 430 in translation.³⁸¹
> In the note Dio Cassius,³⁸² LXIII, 22-24, is cited.
> Sueton., *Vit. Ner.*, 41.³⁸³

IV A 13   n.d., 1842-43

« 4106

Just as Tordenskjold tricked the Swedes concerning the number of his troops by having the same soldiers march around on another street and march by again, just as on New Year's the indefatigable activity of firemen³⁸⁴ darting through the streets congratulating everybody must make one think the fire department is enormous, although it has not increased, so also one would believe that our age is profoundly stirred, that our age really has something to say, but it is merely the same old empty phrases marching around the corner and coming back again, these empty phrases: This is what the times require, a long-felt want, danger stands at the door. So today it is a new hymnbook[385] that the times require; Heiberg[386] thinks it is astronomy —perhaps astronomical psalms ought to be selected for the supplement. —I believe the age has only one requirement, namely, to be taken by the nose. This need will certainly be satisfied.

V A 77 n.d., 1844

« 4107

It is clear that the place politics occupied in Greece has been taken in Christianity by religion (genuine folk Christianity), which is a subject for discussion and is influenced by discussion. Therefore in a purely formal way Aristotle's *Rhetoric* will throw much light on religious problems. The whole question of being and nonbeing, which is not found at all in Aristotelian philosophy (his οὐσία πρώτη and δεύτερα, see *Categories*,[387] are something else entirely), he transfers to rhetoric, as that which is supposed to produce conviction. πίστις,[388] in *pluralis* he uses πίστεις.

VI A 1 n.d., 1844–45

« 4108

.....Instead of conscience and God's Spirit to get a community by means of the brutish miasma of men, a something which sweats out of them in the pressure of crowds, a something which is called public opinion, and by philosophers: the objective spirit.....

VI A 26 n.d., 1845

« 4109

The new development in our time cannot be political, because politics through the *representing* individual is dialectical in the relation between the generation and the individual, but in our time each individual is already on the way to being too reflective to be able to be content with merely being *represented*.[389]

VII¹ A 17 n.d., 1846

« 4110 *The Dialectic of Community or Society Is as Follows*

(1) the individuals who relate to each other in the relation are individually inferior to the relation.

> Just as the separate members of the body are inferior to the body; the particular heavenly bodies in the solar system.

(2) the individuals who relate to each other in the relation are individually equal in relation to the relation.

Just as in earthly love each one is a separate entity, but the need for the relationship is the same for both.

(3) the individuals who relate themselves to each other in the relation are individually superior to the relation.

As in the highest form of religion. The individual is primarily related to God and then to the community, but this primary relation is the highest, yet he does not neglect the second.[390]

See also *Concluding Postscript*, p. 327[391]—that the task is not to move from the individual to the race but from the individual through the race to achieve the individual.

See an article by Dr. Bayer, *"Der Begriff der sittlichen Gemeinschaft"* (in Fichte's journal, 1844, XIII, p. 80[392]). His tripartition is: *Beziehung, Bezug, Einheit.* (See pp. 80 and 81.)

VII¹ A 20   n.d., 1846

« 4111

All questions ultimately will become communistic. In an article sent from Jutland the *Kiøbhposten*[393] reprinted some adverse German opinions of Madvig's Latin grammar. So they write for tavern keepers etc. about Madvig's Latin grammar (an extremely little known quantity) and about the opinion of some German professors (a very dubious quantity). Finally a tavern keeper thinks something like this: Why shouldn't I be able to have an opinion about Latin and Greek? Such things are merely relics from the Middle Ages and the caste system. Don't I pay high tuition for my son in the grammar school? Shouldn't I be a judge of Latin and Greek, then, or at least have an opinion about them.

VII¹ A 54   n.d., 1846

« 4112

Schelling[394] is right when he says in the preface to Steffen's *Nachgelassene Schriften:* "When it has come to the point where the majority decides what constitutes truth, it will not be long before they take to deciding it with their fists."

VII¹ A 63   n.d., 1846

« 4113

In our day almost the only form of aristocracy left is the sneaky kind. The aristocrat sneaks through the streets, has no desire to exist for anyone else but his clique, and then on a few great occasions for the admiring crowd. But this really means taking his distinction in vain. One ought to exist for all men and not caste-consciously and egotistically to seek his own advantage; even if a person is mocked by the crowd, he is still a memento to them. The sneaky aristocracy really have a tacit understanding that most men are garbage, are lost. The sneaky aristocracy do not egg on the crowd as the old aristocrats did, proudly showing themselves to the mob—no, they secretly engage in treachery. God knows how they will justify it in eternity.

VII^1 A 163 *n.d.*, 1846

« 4114

It is all very well that by living only in certain select circles one is able to live securely, aloof from the crowd etc.—but does one have the right to live this way? Did Christ live this way? Has any really noble man ever lived this way? Or is wanting to evade the fact that one is a human being just like all the others anything else than abominable self-love.

VII^1 A 212 *n.d.*, 1846

« 4115

Our liberals are the greatest cowards and know only how to talk. They write about the proceedings of the government;[395] then if it is pointed out that they do not act, they answer that they are not, after all, the government. If they are then asked why they never once turn their weapons against the demoralization in which as journalists they are so deeply implicated, they answer: Well, we cannot have anything to do with the demoralizing of the public. *Summa summarum*, total meaninglessness, not one single solitary person of character.

VIII^1 A 79 *n.d.*, 1847

« 4116

The world situation will change also in this respect that every future effort at reformation, if the person involved is a true reformer, will be directed against "the crowd," not against the government. Government (royal power) is really representation and to that extent Christian (monarchy). The dialectic of monarchy is in the world-historical sense both practiced and established. Now we are in the process of beginning somewhere else, that is, with the intensive internal growth of the state. Then comes the category "the single individual";

this category is so linked to my name that I would like "that single individual" to be placed on my grave.

With this in mind, I must attach great significance to the bread-riots[396] around Europe this year; they indicate that the European constitution (as a physician speaks of a man's constitution) has completely altered; in the future we will have internal disturbances, *secessio in montem sacrum* etc.[397]

It all fits my theory perfectly, and I dare say it will come to be seen how *exactly* I have understood the age—alas, that is the worst crime a man can commit, for rubbish and half-truths are what the age demands —and then that the truth be derided.

VIII[1] A 108 *n.d.*, 1847

« 4117

In margin of 4116 (VIII[1] A 108):

It is one thing when the people, the crowd, the opposition are involved in controversy with the king, the government (this is what we call politics); it is something else when there are disturbances within the state similar to those in a house where the residents on the various floors begin to fight—not with the caretaker but among themselves. *Controversies on the various floors, from the basement all the way up to the attic, but among themselves.*

VIII[1] A 109 *n.d.*

« 4118

What makes my position in public life most difficult of all is that men are not at all able to grasp what it is I am fighting. Most people believe that taking a stand against the crowd is utter nonsense, for the crowd, the majority, the public are, after all, the saving powers, those freedom-loving societies from which salvation shall issue—against kings and popes and public officials who want to tyrannize over us. *Ach, Du lieber Augustin.* This, you see, is the result of centuries of fighting against popes and kings and the powers that be and, on the other hand, regarding the people and the crowd as holy. They do not dream that historical categories change and that now the crowd is and will be the only tyrant and the root corruption. —But to the crowd, of course, this is the most incomprehensible of all. —The crowd is sick for power and considers itself fortified against all reprisals, for how is it possible to get hold of the crowd. —What we call the opposition here at home still lives on in the old stuff and nonsense about fighting the tyranny of the government. When a policeman makes the most trifling mistake, for which he is punished by his superiors to boot, there is a big uproar; but if the public, the crowd, the rabble, public opinion, etc., year after year is responsible for the most nauseating atrocities and misuse of power—yes, the opposition dares not talk about this. Either it cannot comprehend that they are atrocities, since the idol of the opposition does them, or it sees them but does not dare to complain because it is cowardly. —Nowadays if someone is censured for a minor infraction but, please note, censured by the king, by a high official etc., everybody sympathizes with him—he is a martyr. But if a man is insulted day in and day out, persecuted, mistreated (mental cruelty) by the stupidity, curiosity, and insolence of the crowd, the rabble, and the public, then this is quite all right, it is nothing at all.

There is no doubt, you see, that a sacrifice is needed at this point. Yes, we are so backward that a lot of sacrificial victims will have to fall before men are made aware that the trend is altogether different from the reformation movement that had to do with a pope, a king, a general. On the whole it is enormously narrow-minded and by no means to the honor of the honorable reformer's *judicium* to believe that a reformation could revolve around getting one single man overthrown —for in that case the world would be a wonderful world.

No, then the ancients understood the issue better, understood that the crowd is the dangerous power. And history is turning back again to the ancient forms. Europe will not have war—but constant internal disturbance (the plebes—the patricians).

If men had not become immersed, with the momentum of some centuries and the passion of habit, in the fixed idea that a tyrant is a single man, it would easily be perceived that to be persecuted by the crowd is the most burdensome of all, because, after all, the crowd is indeed the sum of the individuals, and therefore every individual adds his little part, but the individual does not consider how much it amounts to when all the individuals do it.

Has not philosophy taught us long enough that the world has taken up reflection. This is true, and for this very reason no individual (king, pope, etc.) can ever again become a tyrant. Tyranny must become a relationship of reflection. You see, here we are confronted again by the category: the crowd, public opinion, etc.

To repeat, it will be a long time before the person who is going to contend with the masses gets a little pathos over to his side—that is, a few who are able to understand the reality of this battle.

Socrates, to my way of thinking, is and will continue to be the only reformer I acknowledge. The others I have read about may have been inspired and well-meaning, but they were also notably narrow-minded.

VIII^1 A 123 *n.d.*, 1847

« **4119**

Whatever the subject or sphere, it is the minority, the very few, some few individuals who know; the many are ignorant. This is certainly clear as daylight, for otherwise one would have to conclude that every man knows everything. Simply because this is not so, every man has or ought to have his subject, be it great or small, complicated and difficult or less difficult, which he knows about so that he is the teacher and the others—the many, the majority—the learners, and in this way every one of us has his own subject. —But what does the daily press do? The way it communicates everything it has to communicate (it makes no difference what the subject is—politics, criticism, etc.) presumes that it is the many, the majority, who are informed. This, you see, is why journalism is the most corrupting sophism that has ever appeared. People complain that now and then there is an occasional inaccurate article in a newspaper—but that is a trifle. No, this whole basic form of communication is false. —In ancient times the masses were sensually buttered up outright with money and bread and circuses—the press has intellectually-spiritually buttered up the middle class—we need Pythagorean silence. Much more necessary than temperance societies that abstain from drinking alcohol are temperance societies that abstain from reading newspapers. —The ridiculousness of *Fædrelandet* wanting to be aristocratic—and then be a daily paper. No, if the publisher wants to be an aristocrat, he will have to let the paper fold up. To be an aristocrat among journalists is like being an aristocrat among tramps.

VIII^1 A 134 *n.d.*, 1847

« **4120**

Historically considered, it may be said that the fate of funeral orations is to find the inappropriate occasion. A tavern-keeper is buried, and there is an oration—the same with a major-general. But the truly great, the nobility of the human race, seldom get a funeral oration: they are usually executed—and no funeral oration is arranged. The tavern-keeper is buried like a hero—the hero is crucified and buried secretly.

VIII^1 A 222 *n.d.*, 1847

« 4121

The whole effort to assert each individual living language by itself—this dispersal method does nothing but take us backward, is a retrogression. It is a familiar fact that America has the most languages because every nationality speaks its own language. But this is not a perfection. One learned language is the best.

The Grundtvigian nonsense about nationality[398] is also a retrogression to paganism. It is unbelievable what foolishness delirious Grundtvigian candidates are able to serve up. Th. Fenger[399] says, for example, that no one can be a true Christian except through nationality. And Christianity specifically wanted to do away with paganism's deification of nationalities! But what does Fenger know about paganism; and as for Christianity, what else does he know but blustering around with the Grundtvigians!

VIII[1] A 245 *n.d.*, 1847

« 4122

The category "to continue to stand"[400] can be used in connection with Asia. The Jews continued to stand; China has continued to stand; India has continued to stand—on the other hand, the category for Europe is: to fall. Rome fell. Greece fell.

VIII[1] A 279 *n.d.*, 1847

« 4123

One ought to travel in China for ten years and then come home and write an interpretation of Europe from the standpoint of China—comparative description of nationalities—China is a caricature of Europe. The caricatured consequence of absolute monarchy, which is the deification of existence, is to prohibit emigration. —The nature of the examination in China, that the central figure in the novel is a person up for his examination—that "the button" (distinction) is not the symbol of worthiness but is worthiness, so that if a person is unlucky enough to lose his button, he also loses his honor. —The law is a personification which, when a crime has been committed, requires that someone be executed, regardless of whether he is the one actually guilty. —The world is square; China is the innermost square.

Vertically in margin:
N.B. I cannot help thinking that this has been noted before someplace else [i.e., I A 313]. The idea of China has intrigued me.

VIII[1] A 280 *n.d.*, 1847

« 4124

Reflection no. VII in part two[401] about mercifulness is also rightly turned against communism. It is no art to speak of such things in ordinary expressions which mean nothing, but here the matter is given a completely different turn which is certainly Christian.

VIII[1] A 299   n.d., 1847

« 4125

If someone is going to be a *persona publica* these days, then taking exception to being overwhelmed occasionally with abusive language is like taking exception to or misunderstanding what it means for an officer in the fire-brigade to be splashed. The main point is that he direct well; the spray on his coat has no positive significance. He takes his coat off at night—and in death he lays aside the overcoat on which the insults still rest—they get no closer than that.

VIII[1] A 321   n.d., 1847

« 4126

All these pastoral conventions, general assemblies, societies, in short, all the sociality in our age, are directly analagous to the drinking-song period, manifestations of the need for meaninglessness and immaturity to feel like somebody or feel happy and secure in existence by clinking glasses together and toasting each other. F. Fenger,[402] who now scurries over to Skaane (see the latest *Kirketidende*) to find an occasion to bring together in the theological sense also, the politically "scattered men," would naturally in the age of the drinking song have sung "my full glass"[403] etc., clinked glasses with doughty comrades (*fi faldera*) just as energetically as he now operates in conventions etc. Only the age of the drinking song was far more innocent than our age.

VIII[1] A 382   n.d., 1847

« 4127

All this apprehension of Germany[404] is an hallucination, a game, a new attempt to flatter national vanity. One million people who honestly admitted to being a little nation, and now before God individually resolved to will to be what they are, is an enormous power; here there is no danger at all. No, the calamity is something else altogether; the calamity is that this little nation is demoralized, divided in itself, nauseatingly envious man to man, unruly toward everyone who is supposed to rule, malicious toward everyone who is anything, impertinent and undisciplined, riled up to a sort of rabble tyranny. This produces a bad conscience, and therefore people are afraid of the Germans. But nobody dares speak about the root of the calamity—and so people flatter all these unhealthy passions and become self-important by contending against the Germans.

A nauseating period is ahead for Denmark. A market-town mentality and mutual petty cantankerousness toward one another; ultimately one will be suspected of being German if he does not wear a certain kind of hat, etc. On the other side is the communist revolt; everyone who owns a little will be singled out and persecuted with the collaboration of the press.

This, you see, is Denmark's calamity—or this is Denmark's punishment, a people not truly God-fearing, a people who only have town-gossip for a national consciousness, a people who deify being nothing, a people among whom school boys are the judges, a people among whom those who should govern are afraid and those who should obey are impertinent, a people who each day provide new evidence that there is no public morality in the land—a people who must either be saved by a tyrant or by a few martyrs.

VIII^1 A 531   n.d., 1848

« **4128**

Up to this time *the people* or *the folk* has been the dialectical factor in the development of the human race. "The people" is like the material in the process of manufacturing, the stock-on-hand, to which there is a continuous addition (number) and from which, then, comes what is to be—that is, individuals or a few individuals, but so enormously much is wasted [*spildes*], but this is not the fault of Governance, who has ordained everyone to become an individual, and therefore we say that it is forfeited [*forspildes*].

The people has been the impetus. The people is the force which has demolished kings and emperors; kings and emperors again have sometimes used the people to demolish the nobility or the clergy. The people has demolished the clergy, and the clergy has used the people to demolish the nobility, and the nobility has used the people to demolish the clergy. But always "the people."

Now comes the last and final development; the concept "the people" itself becomes dialectical. It is now "the people" which must be demolished. How is it to happen? Well, here is the category: the single individual.

The process of bringing up a human race is a process of individualization. This is why the race first of all has to be cut up into three estates—but then finally the chopping of this enormous abstraction, the people, into pieces begins with the help of the "single individual."

Anyone who is able to think can understand this. But the majority are unable to think; if they are to hold on to a thought they immediately have to have a few others along who strengthen each other in believing that it is right, otherwise they do not dare think it. When this is the case, it is certainly impossible to think this thought of the single individual—for this thought certainly cannot be thought *en masse*, since its very intention is to break up the mass.

VIII^1 A 551 *n.d.*, 1848

« 4129

Addition to 4128 (VIII^1 A 551):

Yet it will be a long time before world history arrives at the single individual. First of all, the nation-states have to be broken up into smaller pieces. The more development, the less state. If everybody is to share in the governing, the state must be very small.

VIII^1 A 552 *n.d.*, 1848

« 4130

The government ignored the opposition and thereby amounted to something. The opposition has not grown any smarter: it ignores the rabble insurrection in the press—which thereby amounts to something and becomes the downfall of the opposition.

VIII^1 A 556 *n.d.*, 1848

« 4131

The idea of genuine equality, essential equality, has been given up; equality has now become a political question discussed throughout Europe.

Consequently every one of the older forms of tyranny will now be powerless (emperor, king, nobility, clergy, even money tyranny).

But another form of tyranny is a corollary of equality—fear of men. I have already called attention to this in the last discourse of "The Gospel of Suffering."[405] I called attention to it again in the third part of *Christian Discourses*, no. 5.[406]

Of all the tyrannies, it is the most dangerous, in part because it is not directly obvious and attention must be called to it.

The communists here at home and in other places fight for human rights. Good, so do I. Precisely for that reason I fight with all my might against the tyranny of the fear of man.

Communism ultimately leads to the tyranny of the fear of men (just see how France at this moment is suffering from it); right here is where Christianity begins.

What communism makes such a big fuss about Christianity accepts as something which follows of itself, that all men are equal before God, therefore essentially equal. But then Christianity shudders at this abomination that wants to abolish God and create fear of the crowd of men, of the majority, of the people, of the public.

VIII[1] A 598 *n.d.*, 1848

« 4132

Every movement which is actually to be a forward step must originate with one person—so that it may be clear that God is along in the game, that the whole thing actually originates with him. Every movement and change that takes place with the help of 100,000 or 10,000[407] or 1,000 noisy and rumbling and buzzing and yodeling men (all of it resembling stomach rumbling and stomach gas) is *eo ipso* untruth, a forgery, a retrogression. Here God is along but very confusedly, perhaps not at all, perhaps rather the devil. But the sensate man always makes a mistake and pays attention to externals, sees that this and that change has taken place in the external. God help us. The only thing to pay attention to is the God-relationship, and perhaps we have distanced ourselves from it even more. A mediocre ruler provides a much better condition than this abstraction, 100,000 buzzing un-humans.

VIII[1] A 599 *n.d.*, 1848

« 4133

And when an abstraction such as this[408] has made its creatures the government, then they obey, as it is called. Yes, and why? Because it flatters their arbitrariness that the government they obey is of their own making. It is like a pagan worshiping the god he himself has made —it is about the same as worshiping oneself.

VIII[1] A 600 *n.d.*, 1848

« 4134

Ultimately all world history will become nonsense. Action is completely abolished; if anything happens it is all incidental. The stronger power does not act, does not know for sure what it wants, does not say it definitely—even less is there any individual man at the head, a hero. No, as an abstraction the stronger constrains the weaker one *in abstracto* to do something passively—and this becomes the event. The castle in Paris is stormed by an indefinite mob that does not know what it wants, with no definite ideas. Then the king flees—and then there is a republic. Nonsense. Here at home 15,000 people advance on the castle,[409] singing. They have not requested a minister: Hvidt; no, they have used utterly vague terms about surrounding the throne with democratically-minded men;[*] even less have they requested responsible cabinet ministers. Then Frederik VII is upset, appoints Hvidt et al. as cabinet ministers, makes them responsible—and the people jubilate; it is a victory of the people. To me it seems something rather to weep over, over all the brutish cowardice, where not a trace of personal courage is to be found.

VIII¹ A 606 *n.d.*, 1848

« 4135

[*] *In margin of 4134* (VIII¹ A 606):
Hvidt et al.[410] should never have been and should never have demanded to be anything other than folk-tribunes with admission to the council-of-state on the one issue (nationality[411]).

VIII¹ A 607 *n.d.*

« 4136

The French republic is a gift of fate. It is built on an untruth and must then begin with the untruth that people make each other believe that this was what they wanted, what they intended—although it is well known that they wanted nothing, had no intention.

In a conversation with me the night before, Tscherning[412] was able to understand this—the next day he was himself a cabinet prime minister by the very same method, exactly as I said of the French Revolution, that it was like an engagement made at a ball in a giddy moment when one did not know what he was doing.

VIII¹ A 608 *n.d.*, 1848

« 4137

The tragedy at this moment is that the new ministry needs war to survive,[413] needs all the agitation of national feeling possible. Even though we could easily enough have peace—if the ministry is not completely stupid, it must see that *it* needs war.

VIII¹ A 609 *n.d.*, 1848

« 4138

And when it is all over with Holsten,[414] when nothing comes of it—when we get around to digesting the fact which the agitations of one evening[415] saddled on the state—when blood everywhere is astir for patriotism, and the masses fermenting: what then?

VIII[1] A 613   n.d., 1848

« 4139

At this moment there must, of course, be no opposition, no resistance to the government—and why? Because the opposition has come into office![416] Long live human stupidity! And this is called freedom.

VIII[1] A 614   n.d., 1848

« 4140

There is something melancholy for me in the fact that I actually believe that the old public officials, simply because they are men who have been brought up morally, men who have a notion of what it is to obey, are better able to submit to obeying even such a fantastic ministry,[417] which is surely unparalleled in Europe, than young people are able to submit to obeying the old.

It is like a family in which the parents have not been able to get the children to obey—so the parents say: Well, now, you take command and let us obey—it goes better. And with the parents' respect for what it means to obey, it actually does go better for a moment. O, but the untruth of it! And eventually it must itself give birth to calamities.

It touches me very deeply, but I do really believe that that proud old ruler who truly was born to govern and learned it by obeying and disciplining himself—I believe that Bishop Mynster[418] can better perform the feat of obeying Monrad[419]—than the young Monrad has ever been able to do his duty in obeying the old Bishop.

VIII[1] A 615   n.d., 1848

« 4141

And during all this agitation not a word about religiousness has been heard—not a single one. Who in all the world would think that Denmark is a Christian country. I wonder if any of those who are now going into war[420] actually think of settling their account with God. O, it is so remote that hardly any pastor even dares call it to mind.

VIII[1] A 618   n.d., 1848

« 4142

There is an excellent proverb in *A Thousand and One Nights*:[421] He who refuses to be ruled by his own will be tyrannized by a stranger.

This is found at the end of volume III, in one of the parables of the animals that conclude the volume.

VIII[1] A 624   *n.d.*, 1848

« 4143

Little by little as reflection increases in the development of the world and individuals also become more and more subjectively reflected, every subjectivity for itself, it will appear all the more disproportionate for one person to be king. "The king" is actually a common noun, belongs essentially to natural states in which the individual is not reflected in himself, in which it does not occur to the king, as in Russia, that his personality should influence the governing of the country, that a new personality will again alter the whole organism.

VIII[1] A 636   *n.d.*, 1848

« 4144

Of all tyrannies, a people's government is the most excruciating, the most mindless, unconditionally the downfall of all greatness and elevation.

A tyrant is still a man[422] or an individual man. Ordinarily he does have an idea, even though it is most unreasonable. A person can at least think over whether or not the idea is worth the trouble of letting oneself be put to death for it if it collides with his own thoughts. And then he adjusts and lives. —But in a people's government, who is the ruler? An X or the everlasting blather: whatever at any moment is or has the majority—the most insane of all determinants. When one knows how a majority is attained and how it can fluctuate—and then to have such nonsense be the government!

A tyrant is still but one individual; consequently, if a person feels like it, he can arrange to avoid him, live far away from him, etc. But in a people's government, how shall I escape the tyrant. In a certain sense every man is the tyrant, if he can only create a multitude, a majority.

As an individual man a tyrant is so elevated, so distant, that with him a person has the right to live as privately as he wants to. It would never in all eternity occur to an emperor[423] to bother about me, about how I live, what time I get up, what I read, etc.—ordinarily he does not even know that I exist. But in a people's government "the equal" is the ruler. He occupies himself with such things as whether my beard is like his, whether I go out to Deer Park the same time as he does, whether I am just like him and all the others, and if not—well, then it is a crime —a political crime, a crime against the state!

A people's government will at most only be able to create a few martyrs, from whom it profits as Joseph's brothers profited from Joseph.[424]

To live under such a government is the best conditioner for eternity, but the worst torment as long as the government lasts. There can be only one longing—that Socratic wish[425] to die and to be dead. For Socrates had to put up with this mindlessness that numbers rule, that we are not all equal before God (for what does anybody in a people's government care about God!) but are all alike before number! And number is the very evil that is also used so significantly in the Book of Revelation.[426]

A people's government is the true picture of hell. For even if one could last out its torment, it would still be a relief if one got permission to be alone; but the torment is that "the others" tyrannize over one.

VIII[1] A 667 *n.d.*, 1848

« 4145

When some 1,800 years ago the people shouted: Crucify him, crucify him[427]—this voice of the people was the voice of God (*vox populi, vox dei*), for the voice heard at the same time: "Father, into thy hands I commit my spirit"[428]—this was not the voice of God.

IX A 29 *n.d.*, 1848

« 4146

How appalling, after all, is the relativity of concepts: that two men, individually, can sincerely (humanly speaking) thank God for opposite things. On the Great Day of Prayer the Prussians hold a church service and preach that their piety has been pleasing to God and this explains their victory on Easter day.[429] Visby preaches that God must above all punish the impiety of making an attack on Easter day.[430]

This is the way the concepts of right and wrong fluctuate, and the calamity is that humanly speaking both sides mean what they say.

IX A 31 *n.d.*, 1848

« 4147

The dangerous aspect of insidious vilification is that it takes considerable imagination and dialectical power to grasp it at a given moment and see what it is. Most people distinguish none of the parts—and therefore the vilification steals forward undetected little by little every day. At first the vilification makes an impression and men become aware of it, but it comes dressed up as "nothing at all," "an innocent joke," and the like, so that people do not notice anything, until they are gradually brought to a point of injustice against an individual in a way they have never dreamed of.

And no one dares say how things are; if there is someone who suffers under this mistreatment, it is supposed to be fantasy and exaggeration—naturally, because a loathsomeness like this, from which one despairs of rescuing the community, must be nothing—otherwise a person would have to confess his own powerlessness and the majority their complicity.

IX A 61 *n.d.*, 1848

« 4148

The reason why the world does not advance but goes backward is that men consult only with each other instead of each one individually consulting with God. Basically the generation lives on and eats away the traditions of a vanished past. But these traditions become thinner and thinner, there is no new infusion from on high, that divine flowing is constantly diluted more and more by this merely human agreement between man and man—ergo, the world goes backward.

IX A 117 *n.d.*, 1848

« 4149

What is destroying Denmark is neither the new nor the old government but the fact that the country, small as it is, even smaller through demoralization, has become a market-town where every government is an impossibility, because envy keeps a watch on anything that is something, so that only contemptibility can have a kind of power or only an approximation of a martyr can rule, not to mention a martyr.

What brought in a new government[431] was not wisdom, patriotism, and the like, but an expression of this demoralization. And what will overthrow the new government will again be envy,[432] caprice, pettiness, and the like; it is not the noble, the good, which triumphs —no, it is the same demoralization which has taken on a new shape.

In this respect Goldschmidt[433] is not undistinguished. He is like a cholera fly to cholera; it cannot be said that it is he who produces the demoralization (and everybody else is good) but that he makes manifest that there must be demoralization. He is and remains the characterless instrument of envy and demoralization. He has nothing to lose, cannot be attacked, or envied, either; he is safeguarded by means of contemptibility—and then he gnaws and gnaws. And a good many representatives of the old regime think this is fine—because the new government is the victim. How tragic that there is no character at all, no reflection, no consistent point of view anywhere in Denmark, but everything is momentary passion.

IX A 303 *n.d.*, 1848

« 4150

Chateaubriand's *Memoirs* has a superb motto taken from Job: *sicut nubes ... quasi naves—velut umbra.*[434]

IX A 309 *n.d.*, 1848

« 4151

What I have so often said jokingly—that it does not make any difference what government I live under just so I get to know who it is, who is *Imprimatur*[435]—it now occurs to me that this is really Christianity. For in the story about the tax coin Christ[436] asks: Whose likeness is this, who is *Imprimatur?* Christ clearly means this: If you want to be a Christian, then snap your fingers first and foremost and above all at politics; whether the picture you see on the coin is named Peter or Paul, is a native or an alien—forget it—give him the tax and do not waste a single moment on such squabbling, you who as a Christian have enough to do giving God what is his due, for the emperor's image is on the tax coin, but the Christian bears God's image and therefore does with his whole person what he is commanded to do with the coin —gives himself wholly to the one whose image he bears.

IX A 353 *n.d.*, 1848

« 4152

That a man acts with the thought of being victorious here in the world and then is victorious—yes, this the world understands and shouts bravo. That he acts with the thought of being victorious but fails, this the world also understands; it understands his first intention and now judges him in a different way, whether his action was rash or not, but it understands him. But that a man acts, makes the step with the thought and consciousness: I must lose, fall—this the world regards as lunacy. For the world has no conception of duty or of the obligation of the God-relationship; its explanation is limited to prudence. That a man sees that evil has won at one point or another and he now says to himself before God: you cannot possibly be victorious, but you must act, and by acting you will come to suffer; consequently you must act and with the thought that you will suffer—yes, in the eyes of the world this is lunacy; the world will say that this is hating oneself, and Christianity answers: the Christian must hate himself[437]—for the sake of Christ.

Incidentally, here we see an analogy (yet remembering that qualitatively there is no analogy) to the saying about Christ, that he suffers for our transgressions[438] and bears our sins. To be specific, when in a certain situation evil has gotten the power and the others keep still, participate in it, and then the good is to be expressed, the relationship is turned right around in such a way that the good comes to suffer the punishment the others should have suffered. The evil world in all probability punishes the good on account of that for which the world itself should be punished.

When a whole city with the cooperation of a newspaper with thousands of subscribers makes gossip and nonsense public opinion —and then someone stops it,[439] they say it is doltish to want to talk about something no one cares about. Consequently—what a surprising reversal!—he becomes the only one, he who is obliged to act simply because the evil would have attacked practically everyone. But it is always better that one suffers than the whole people,[440] and better that one gets the blame and the others go free.

IX A 364 *n.d.*, 1848

« **4153**

Basically, I am too ideally brought up also in this respect that I go about simplemindedly with the thought that everything should be done to make men aware, with the thought that every individual human being is a prodigious object,[441] that not a single one, to say nothing of 1,000, is to be wasted. Well, good night! Basically the objectivity with which most men know about things is appalling; yes, their daily lives express that there are thousands and thousands and thousands who simply go to waste, a prey for all the crafty and cowardly seducers of the people—and no one raises a protesting voice. Yes, on the whole people would roar with laughter if someone were to say in earnest that it is a man's duty (therefore *also his*) to improve the world. O, good Lord, they would say— so you want to be a reformer; no, my friend, you are too insignificant for that etc. etc. Yet (and this is a new confusion) they would have nothing against it if a clergyman —that is, someone who talks generally—or a textbook says that it is a man's, every man's, duty to work for the improvement of the world. They will listen to it readily enough, especially, preferably, from someone anonymous. But if someone wants to do it—consequently a single individual (when action occurs, the single individual appears)—people find it ridiculous. That is, they do not find it ridiculous to place an X together with the ideal, but to place a single individual together with it—that is, at most they want the highest to be talked about, but if it is to be done, it must be done by the single individual—and this they find ridiculous. Here we see the more profound significance of anonymity and sociality: they are for the purpose of warding off the ridiculousness of an individual's willing it (that is, in order to make the true impossible). They think it is wonderful when an anonymous someone talks grandiosely about the highest; they imagine that an anonymous someone is more than an individual; in any case they do not get the impression that an individual will do it.

It is really dreadful—the despair with which men like that view the world as abandoned once and for all, and, as in a fire, everyone merely tries to snatch what he can and avoids dangers. One has only to look at their actions to see that this is so; in their words and speeches they are philosophers, optimists, who praise this as the best of all possible worlds.

It is exactly the opposite with the Christian; he teaches that the world is immersed in evil, but nevertheless he does not abandon it but risks everything to contribute something so that it might become better and the good might come.

IX A 445   n.d., 1848

« **4154**

That supreme power is impotence is seen in the impotence of Christ, the only one who never got justice, for even his death became a benefaction, even to his murderers.

IX A 449   n.d., 1848

« **4155**

In the sphere of finitude the power of superiority is in fact impotence. Socrates had the power of superiority, and that was why he was executed; if he had been an ordinary man and had wept and blubbered in court, flattered the people, he would not have been condemned.[442] So it is that the strong one, who can bear lightly, with a smile, all the mistreatment of base meanness, is for this very reason the one without power; if he were the weak one, he would have sympathy on his side, and he would not come to suffer at all.

IX A 453   *n.d.*, 1848

« **4156**

It is quite curious, come to think of it. If I compare my life with a judge's (omitting, of course, the qualitative difference between us), the difference is that in former times the judge came in order to judge the government. My frontline has been the very opposite. This has not been understood (is regarded as strange for a man living a private life); I myself have scarcely understood it deeply enough, but now in 1848 and afterward it is very clear that if providence is going to send prophets and judges in the future it must simply be to help the government, to assist so that there may be governing at all.

And what has Mynster actually done in this respect? Yes, he has sat and enjoyed ruling, giving away official appointments, etc.

X^1 A 96   *n.d.*, 1849

« **4157**

One solitary man cannot help or save an age; he can only express that it is foundering.

X^1 A 171   *n.d.*, 1849

« **4158**

Just as Christ[443] tells the rich young ruler to sell all his goods and give to the poor, so one could also speak of the requirement to give all his rank and dignity (that is, the earthly, temporal) to the poor in order to express equality.

X^1 A 269   *n.d.*, 1849

« **4159**

It is really so. If you wish to reduce the speed of *infinity*, if you are afraid that it is taking you too far, then accept just one follower; with each single follower you accept, you reduce it more and more. In the finite world it goes just the opposite; men believe that their cause gains more and more speed the more followers they acquire—this may be true, but this kind of speed is merely extension within the moment, a lingering speed, not the accelerating kind, so far from being real speed that it is delay. In the same way man's hustle and bustle is delay.

X^1 A 350   *n.d.*, 1849

« **4160**

The fact that almost everything is communicated by the press has confused everything. Everything has become impersonal. This is why states have collected an inorganic sediment, an enormous mass of sediment: the crowd, which no one gets involved with because the teachers are not persons but are authors, who, hidden from everyone's eyes, send out a few thoughts into the world.

The only conflict has been with the government, because the government could judge the press; but the real conflict of truth, conflict with the crowd, the public, the abstractions (the evil, the stronghold of the lie) seems to be completely forgotten.

x^1 A 356 *n.d.*, 1849

« **4161**

The meaning of the words that the woman was given to the man for community[444] is not, I dare say, that the relationship to the woman as such was in itself community; it probably refers to the family relationship, offspring, and in this elemental sense it is said that the woman is community and that she brings community along with her.

What is the idea "community"? It is not the association of several people of the same age; it is rather a unity which shows various ages in the most intimate interrelation. Thus: the grandparents, man and wife, children of various ages—this is really community.

This is "community" and a beautiful unity, too. Each age has its own eccentric possibility—therefore the different ages provide a corrective for each other. For example, how beneficial the child-adult corrective is, restraining a person from becoming pure spirit or from becoming too serious etc.

It could be a fine and engaging task for a psychologist to reckon and tabulate the possible combinations of ways in which one age group essentially provides a supplement and corrective for the other.

x^1 A 369 *n.d.*, 1849

« **4162**

Public life in the state is divided into two parties. The one party grabs the offices, power, and influence for itself, but under the solemn appearance of being useful, that this is the earnestness of life. Then there emerges a new party (the opposition); it finds a new role—to be the martyr, to bring sacrifices etc.—which it does do with the most scrupulous exactitude, depending on how large the subscription list is.

x^1 A 522 *n.d.*, 1849

« **4163**

To "achieve actuality" also means willing to exist for every man, as far as one reaches.

On Sunday the pastor preaches about loving "the neighbor"—but in so-called actuality every man as such has a certain relativity in which he lives; the others do not essentially exist for him.

From a Christian point of view I do not have the right to ignore existentially one single man. I have the right to ignore an anonymous writer, to ignore the public and all such fantasies, but not actual man.

The tragedy is that if one is not willing to ignore the whole crowd —he becomes the sacrifice, for this class of society neither has the presuppositions to understand a person, nor do they have or give themselves time for it, nor can one manage to talk with every single one; and a journalist can confuse them at any moment anyway. To exist for the crowd, when one has something true to communicate and does not wish to deceive (for *mundus vult decipi*[445]) means *eo ipso* having to become the sacrifice.

Here is a collision: Christianly one has no right to ignore one single solitary man; but if one is not willing to ignore the crowd, one incites it against himself.

x^1 A 632 *n.d.,* 1849

« **4164**

[*In margin:* Rudelbach on the Church constitution, para. cxxxi, pp. 243 etc.[446]]

This book has the merit of having shown that the state church gave rise to or contributed to giving rise to the proletariat.

How much there is to this Rudelbach seems not to have perceived.

In Christendom life is completely unchristian also in terms of what it means to live together with the common man and what this involves.

In this respect my life is like a discovery—alas, in a certain sense I can say that it is a dearly purchased discovery. It is unchristian and wicked to base the state on a substructure of men who are totally ignored and excluded from personal association—even though on Sunday there are touching sermons about loving "one's neighbor."

x^1 A 669 *n.d.,* 1849

« **4165**

A strange nemesis hangs over the Pharisee (in the Gospel about the Pharisee and the tax-collector[447]). Ignoring others is indeed pride, and yet it is the proud Pharisee who notices "this tax-collector;" whereas the tax-collector humbly ignores the Pharisee.

X^1 A 682 *n.d.*, 1849

« **4166**

The advance of civilization, the rise of the large cities, centralization, and what corresponded to all this and essentially produced it—the press as a means of communication—have given all life a completely wrong direction. Personal existing vanished. To take life's dailiness quite literally as one's scene of action, to walk about and teach in the streets, was set aside more and more, finally became utterly ridiculous exaggeration.

All reforming, insofar as there was any, now took a onesided direction against government.

To reform "the crowd"—well, no one thought of that; finally everyone fully and completely agreed that such an idea could originate only in a lunatic asylum—and yet this is the genuine idea of what it means to reform.

The "crowd" was allowed to stand, and it was actually this category, or it was the press with the help of this category, that reformed the government with the help of the crowd.

The result has been an increase of the inorganismic in the states. This becomes the public, and here is also the proletariat.

But to want to reform the crowd—yes, now when men's eyes are finally beginning to open a little, everyone shrinks back, is paralyzed with fright.

And yet this is what it really means to reform. And here is the real scene of martyrdom. What is persecution by the government compared to being persecuted daily, every hour of the day, by these thousands and thousands.

Fear of man dominates to the extent that merely to draw men's attention to oneself is one's downfall, regardless of whether it is for a good cause or for nothing at all or for a crime.

But these days it is impossible to work for the good, the true, and the like according to a proper standard without drawing attention to oneself, and thus one's downfall is certain.

"Attention," especially since it is dementedly potentiated with the aid of the daily press, is the demolishing principle which will slay "the single individual." On the other hand, only "the single individual" can work in truth for the truth.

If Christ lived today, "attention" would make the most desperate effort, even if it might not be able to succeed in suffocating him. Every day every paper would have an article on him. Every insignificant detail about him would be spread all over the country in 10,000 copies. Everything possible would be dug up to make the situation demented.

And yet it is along this path that the world will go forward. If not, Christianity is a chimera.

The pattern of life in our day expresses that Christ is a chimera, for it expresses that it is a collective which is used for evolutions, not the single individual, but Christ was truly no collective, and he does not preform collectives[448] either.

O, in vain, in vain do I testify and strain my life to the uttermost. The few who in some measure understand me do not *dare* to understand me. If they understand a little of me, they promptly get busy making it clear to a collective, and then everything is confused again.[449]

Meanwhile there are 1,000 clergymen who have turned Christ into money, make a living out of "the truth suffers in the world." And these clergymen are or aspire to be knights of the Order of Denmark etc. And the whole country is Christian, that is for sure, and now we are going to have a synod called together to reform the Church.[450] Good heavens!

x^2 A 7   *n.d.*, 1849

« 4167

It is really worth noting that if one reads the description of the future found at the conclusion of "a literary review of *Two Ages*,"[451] he will realize how quickly and exactly it was fulfilled two years later in 1848, and how no one took any notice of it at the time it was written, but everyone believed that everything was secure, that both "the system" and the states were just about at the height of perfection.

x^2 A 52   *n.d.*, 1849

« 4168

The whole concept of a "Christian" state is actually a self-contradiction, humbug. This being so, it is in turn a misunderstanding that it appoints and pays "teachers" of Christianity. Certainly I have the right to be paid for being a teacher of Christianity (a laborer is worthy of his wage), but then there must be some actual Christians, so that by accepting the wages I also give assurance that they are Christians, that I *qua* Christian and teacher dare accept these wages. But I must not receive my wages through a third party which in an emergency uses secular power to get me what is owed to me, a third party which in a deeper sense says goodbye to being a Christian and merely maintains the fiction that we are all Christians, so that the pastor, appointed by the state church, comes to a congregation with a stipulated salary, and it makes no difference if there is perhaps not one single Christian in the whole congregation, if no one goes to church etc.: the pastor preaches according to schedule and the state sees to it that he gets his wages.

The state is related to the category "the race"; Christianity is related to the category "the single individual"; in this alone it is possible to see that they are heterogeneous.

In respect to everything secular, including art, scholarship, and science,[452] etc.—there I rightly have something to do with the state.

We now see how mistaken the efforts of the clergy are, even wanting to be paid directly by the state. If a person cannot instill in men a sufficiently great idea of the importance of Christianity that they voluntarily pay, then one should not take their money either. Christianity is too high-born to be patronized by the state. If the individuals in a state were to sink so deep that they had no sense for art and scholarship, and the state then said: Well, it cannot be helped, you must pay for it just the same—this is quite in order and commendable. But Christianity is infinitely elevated above the state; if people reject Christianity, then the punishment must be that they do not get to hear Christianity.

If we ever tried to get serious about this, I believe it would work. If it really ever happened that the proclaiming of Christianity was silenced, its time would surely come again, instead of an appearance which is now maintained by the pitiable thing palmed off as Christianity.

X^2 A 240 *n.d., 1849*

« **4169**

Here is another way men often deceive themselves: in private conversation and association they say of this one and that one, he is a bad man, or, his life is detrimental to the good, to the cause of Christianity—but publicly they say nothing, and then they count it as a kind of leniency on their part, a considerateness. Well, thanks for that. To do it in public would be burdensome, an inconvenience, perhaps a risk. What double duplicity.

I have established a principle for myself: not to waste my time going about privately saying that someone is a scoundrel and the like. If I regard him as that and the matter to be important, I make it public. But to go around like that and prattle privately is too paltry for me and too nauseating.

x^2 A 292 *n.d.*, 1849

« 4170

True religiousness cannot form a party or a clique, for it is an association of persons who do not covet anything either separately or together, but each one is willing to be sacrificed and now associates only to that end; thus the one encourages the other to sacrifice more and more. As soon as someone wants to have something, he is *eo ipso* out of the association.

x^2 A 351 *n.d.*, 1850

« 4171

It is obvious that one of the factors in Christ's death was that he repudiated nationalism, wanted to have nothing to do with it. Nowadays the orthodox are—the true nationalists; they produce theories about Christian states and Christian peoples. If any people *qua* people could claim to have the title of being related as such to Christianity, then it certainly would be God's chosen people—and yet they collapsed and became an everlasting memento that Christianity is not related to nationality. But how convenient—precisely when nationality is the order of the day—it fits in neatly to posit the religious: and then orthodoxy becomes recognizable precisely by being genuinely supernationalistic.

Grundtvig,[453] who has always hated discipline and rigorousness, has also produced a theory that the true Christian takes part in everything—he has presumably forgotten the metaphor about those who run in the race[454] and are abstemious in everything. It is unbelievable what nonsense they have made out of the story of the wedding in Cana. The Grundtvigians, to be consistent, must be upset by the fact that Christ was not married, let alone many times. This "taking part in everything" is, after all, a delusion; one will not admit what another admits, that it is beyond the powers of a man to be equal to everything.

x^2 A 356   *n.d.*, 1850

« **4172**

Everything is understood politically (but "they" do not necessarily have a great understanding of politics), with the result that the religious person comes to be hated as being proud, aristocratic, and the like. The religious person expresses that there is a God; the life of the religious expresses first of all: Please make room; it is the expression of respect. Of course it is not an expression of respect for "the public" and concepts like that, just the opposite. But it is nevertheless the expression of respect—namely, for God. Yet no one takes time to perceive the second thing, that the religious man is as far removed as possible from being proud, aristocratic, etc., that he bows in true humility and adoration, seventy times deeper than any politician. But as I said, the second is not perceived, is not understood, and so one shouts about the religious man: a proud aristocrat!

x^2 A 391   *n.d.*, 1850

« **4173**

With Christianity everything has been placed in the realm of the spirit. The stage is now continually the realm of the spirit.

But now Christianity has actually been changed into a universalized tradition, an atmosphere.

The present situation is analogous to ancient times. The negative principle was fate, a principle of nature. Fate was envious of the individual, especially of the prominent individual. The insignificent individual was not pursued by fate. In tragedy fate crushes the hero, but the chorus is oblivious to the blows of fate.

In the realm of the spirit the analogy now appears. The general concept "public" and the like, an abstraction,[455] is fate, negatively oriented against the individual, but only against the outstanding individual. The chorus in a sense no longer exists, since the chorus is really the public. The insignificant individual lives happily in the public, while this abstraction levels the outstanding individual.

This is the battle of the future, except that the individual will not be of the tyrant type but the religious individual, whose intention is precisely to free the individual, but the public does not understand this.

Yet there is also an ambiguity in "the public," for although it is itself the leveling power,[456] it is also the spectator, the chorus. This relation is rooted in irresponsibility.

x^2 A 394   n.d., 1850

« 4174

It is dangerous to live in times when the world tide is turning. It is likely to take a generation or two before there is an awareness of where the evil lies and that the attack must be altered. Thus they who represent a somewhat more noble, suffering form will profit, for then they will in fact triumph and in addition enjoy honor as martyrs. In the states this is the case with the opposition which, suffering, once fought at the head of the "mass," at that time weaker, against the more powerful "government." Now for a long time the "mass" has actually been dominant in the state. Those who stand at the head of it are by far the stronger, and yet they reap martyr-glory and honor. It is the same with the natural scientists, who still want so very much to play the game of enjoying martyr-glory and esteem, too, while in fact natural science is dominant and theology was dethroned long ago.

x^2 A 395   n.d., 1850

« 4175 *The Christian "Congregation"*

In order to describe where it is to be found, I know of nothing more illuminating than an analogy which in certain respects is *sans comparaison*. The world of crime forms a little society of its own, lying on the other side of human society, a little society which ordinarily also has an intimate solidarity not altogether common in the world, perhaps also because each one individually feels expelled from human society.[*]

It is the same with the society of Christians. Each one individually —by accepting Christianity, consequently by becoming a believer, that is, by accepting, yes, by staking his life on the absurd—has said farewell to the world, has broken with the world. The society of those who have voluntarily placed themselves outside society in the usual sense of the word is all the more intimate precisely because each one individually feels isolated in "the world." But just as the company of criminals must carefully watch out that no one comes into the society who is not branded as they are, so also in the society of Christians: they must watch out that no one comes into this society except the one whose mark is that he is polemical to the utmost toward society in the usual sense. This means that the Christian congregation is a society consisting of qualitative individuals and that the intimacy of the society is also conditioned by this polemical stance against the great human society.

But when in the course of time and in the steady advance of nonsense it turned out that to be a Christian is synonymous with being a human being, then the Christian congregation became the human race—good night, Ole! Now the Christian congregation is the general public, and in the eyes of every cultured clergyman, to say nothing of the lay people, it is offensive to talk about "the individual."

x^2 A 478   *n.d.*, 1850

« 4176

[*] *In margin of 4175* (x^2 A 478):
Or let me take another illustration. The individuals who are so conspicuous and prominent among a people that they must bear the burden that even the most insignificant trivialities in their lives are interesting and become material for town and newspaper gossip—in short, the individuals on whose renown the bestial contemporary age bestially lives as far as conversation is concerned—perhaps such individuals also constitute a small society; perhaps the pressure of enduring this and also the nausea at common human bestiality make the association more intimate. But this little society lies on the other side of "society"; the basis of the association is, among other things, a common consciousness of the way each of the individuals is in a certain sense deprived of ordinary human rights, for example, permission to be left alone, etc.

x^2 A 479   *n.d.*

« 4177 *Every National Existence Needs Means of Diversion*

In monarchies people were satisfied with the theater, Tivoli, and the like.

But then the world became so dreadfully serious—that is, altogether secular. Now there had to be entirely different means of diversion. On the one hand the blissful illusion for each one individually: I am a part of the state government, perhaps my voice decides the fate of the state (yet when it gets down to brass tacks, it is maintained, as at present in Parliament[457] on the question of the president's taking part in voting: it is unjustifiable to require a man to vote on the condition that his vote determines the issue—something my brother[458] has used like a clumsy fool, so his whole attack amounted to nothing and merely gained him praise and commendation), and on the other hand the tension of actuality: that actual human beings are playing here, not as in the theater, that their fate is to be decided by voting etc.

x^2 A 486 *n.d.*, 1850

« 4178

In contrast to what was said about possession in the Middle Ages and times like that, that there were individuals who sold themselves to the devil, I have an urge to write a book:

Possession and Obsession in Modern Times

and show how people *en masse* abandon themselves to it, how it is now carried on *en masse*. This is why people run together in flocks—so that natural and animal rage will grip a person, so that he feels stimulated, inflamed, and *ausser sich*.[459] The scenes on Bloksberg[460] are utterly pedantic compared to this demonic lust, a lust to lose oneself in order to evaporate in a potentiation, so that a person is outside of himself, does not really know what he is doing or what he is saying or who it is or what it is speaking through him, while the blood rushes faster, the eyes glitter and stare fixedly, the passions boil, lusts seethe.

What depth of confusion and corruption, when at the same time it is praised as the earnestness of life, as cordiality, love, yes—as Christianity.

x^2 A 490 *n.d.*, 1850

« 4179

The railroad craze is altogether an attempt à la Babel. It also fits together with the end of a cultural period; it is the last lap. Unfortunately almost simultaneously the new era began, 1848. The railroads are related to the idea of centralization as a potentiation. And the new era is related to dispersion in *disjecta membra*.[461]

Centralization will probably also be Europe's financial downfall.

x^2 A 497 *n.d.*, 1850

« 4180 *The Fate of Denmark*

In the government of the state and in almost all contexts older men and in part much older men stood at the head. They governed with the thought: It will surely hold out as long as we live. O, demoralization gets dreadful encouragement when nobody takes the reins with vigor and with a keenness for decision.

In other areas of public life there were again older men who, by doing nothing, fought to maintain the appearance that they were what they once were: for example, Heiberg,[462] and many others. Again encouragement for the onset of demoralization.

Fædrelandet[463] has also been in this situation for a long time. It feels that at any moment it may close up—and therefore it will not act decisively. It was already this way at the conclusion of Christian VIII's rule, and now again after the unnatural boom of 1848.

Encouragement everywhere for the onset of shabbiness and meaninglessness.

Denmark's downfall is easy to recognize, that is—prognosticate. A physician cannot have more certain symptoms of the presence of physical putrefaction than a psychologist has here of mental disintegration. For a moment a war and a flaring nationalism[464] cast or did cast a cloak over the true condition. It is not the Germans who would eat us, O no. It is we ourselves who are internally disintegrating. Public life is carried on in a lurching between *envy* and *pity*, but no pathos, no enthusiasm for greatness, no gratitude etc. *Flyveposten*[465] is therefore an altogether normal phenomenon. It maintains itself by responding to this alternation. Where envy[466] is concerned, it tolerates everything—so says the "good-natured" Dane, so we must certainly do something for him again—we subscribe.[467]

x^2 A 498   *n.d.*, 1850

« 4181

It can be a dreadful thing to see a single individual so feverishly tossed about, but then imagine the whole of public life! Para. 14 is being discussed—*en passant* a question is raised about the whole constitution as a detail, and then it is discussed as a detail under para. 14.

The discussion goes on and para. 15 is just completed—and then comes the news that the government in power since last year has been overthrown by a people's rebellion. Then comes a new government. It gets almost to para. 9.

This is the rational state, the pride of the human race, the fruit of enlightenment, the product of the daily press (that priceless good).

x^2 A 506   *n.d.*, 1850

« 4182 *"Actuality" as It Actually Is*

It is the mass that actually rules the state, and with the cooperation of the daily press chatter[468] is the absolute power.

God preserve us, an appearance of earnestness is indeed maintained, but this is the lie, and the case is that chatter is the only thing ever listened to. Take anybody—an artist, a poet, a scholar, a clergyman, a state officeholder, a journalist, and the like, attack one or another of his enterprises, show that it is—and let us assume that it is —a shabby thing: such an attack amounts to nothing, is largely confined to the sphere of society that is engaged in the same enterprise, and is soon forgotten, and in any case the larger part of society is quite uninterested in such things.

No, let "chatter" begin. Write whatever nonsense you want to about him, write the kind of rubbish schoolchildren call "poking fun," that he spilled on himself at the table yesterday, sketch him with a towel around him, do it regularly every other day for 14 days: now that fearful monstrosity, the rabble, gets interested—this is something for them. These thousands and thousands roar with laughter or howl with joy like beasts of prey over the booty. This attack, you see, is dangerous —and in neurotic anxiety the people shout: It is nothing.[469]

Moses[470] was a tormented man, and why? Was he persecuted by tyrants? No, no, compared to his sufferings that is almost only childish tricks. The most tormented man, and why? Because it was his mission to set a *slave-minded* people *free.* He had to endure daily the bestiality etc. of this slave-minded people—in order to set it free. —This really struck me today, but also the kind of a man Scripture made him out to be—that *Holy Scripture* calls him the most tormented man.

Yet back to "actuality," the rational, the Christian state, which still has many high-flown epithets, all of which are the most offensive sarcasm.

So "chatter" is the power; just as in mythology night is everybody's mother, so is chatter the womb, particularly for the modern states with complete freedom, freedom for all chatter to come forth, and freedom for all to chatter away.

That this is the way is as certain as the earth. But the fact of the matter is that one cannot ever get it said.

How should one say it so it can be heard? In the daily press? Pyt —it sees to it that no such communication goes through it.

And so life goes on. "Earnestness," "the truth," "candid opinion," etc. lead a hidden private existence—for almost everybody knows a good deal better. Talk with them, each one individually, with the legislator, the journalist, the deputy, et al.—talk with each one privately, then you get to hear his indignation over intrigue in the legislature—but in the legislature, that is, officially, there he is careful not to talk about such things, there he talks movingly about the advantages of this free constitution for promoting truth etc. You get to hear another man's indignation over the daily press—but in the daily press (for he himself uses the daily press) that is, officially, he does not mention such things—such trivialities would not be worth talking about officially. Splendid! Officially evil is strengthened by the great means of communication; privately, confidentially, the good and the true are permitted to have a little of their due.

And thus society is trapped as if in an obsession. The majority actually do not detect or in a more profound sense notice anything, for since they never act officially or talk officially on the basis of their true understanding but on the basis of falsity, things go very well for them in the world. Meanwhile they flatter themselves in private over being in the know about the lying and the deceit. In truth this is terrible flattery, terrible, for this will be their very judgment in eternity—that they privately knew better; if they did not have this consciousness, they would be less guilty.

X^2 A 571 *n.d.*, 1850

« 4183

This is the measure of what a man is: for how large a portion of his contemporaries does he dare to exist, allowing his life to be judged by them.

In this respect a person could go through a whole scale of relativities from those who exist for only a very few (for example, a woman, then those who exist for constantly greater and greater, more and more numerous constituencies) to the highest qualification, the God-man, who posits the quality "man" and therefore must and will be judged by unconditionally every man, everlastingly divinely assured that he, precisely he, expresses the quality: what it means to be *man*, whereas all other men do not express the quality but this together with an admixture of relative contingencies.

Courage is to dare to will to exist for the whole range of one's contemporaries. Of course the natural, comfortable thing is to exist only for a particular circle that holds the same views as one's own; to exist for them signifies "the togetherness" that provides life with earthly security. How many are there in a generation who know what is what; to them the important thing is in every sense to have solidarity with others, a few others, many others. But the heterogeneous person who dares to exist for others must be absolutely sure of himself (and assured most of all by the help of the consciousness with God) that he is man; for otherwise the judgment will soon be declared that this heterogeneity is lunacy and the like.

But the courage to venture to exist for the whole range of one's contemporaries is also punished, or, more correctly, is also distinguished by this, that the courageous one may get into trouble. This is difficult to avoid, simply because a particular judgment about such a man may take shape and then this gets circulated about him, but if the majority are to be along in the judging, then there must come a sort of criss-crossing among the judgments, and this alone is enough to confuse the whole thing. It is different with regard to one who exists only for a smaller circle. This group is in complete harmony with him about what it is to be a man. This is in agreement with the judgment of him going the rounds. For the others he *essentially* does not exist; they are therefore satisfied with conveying further the group's judgment. Let me take an example. A scholar who is extremely careful not to exist for anyone other than scholars lives a very concealed life etc.: a judgment about him grows among the scholars. Gradually many other people besides the scholars get to know something about him, but since he has not given these others, these many others, occasion to judge, they limit themselves to putting that judgment in circulation: *relata referre*.[471]

To arrange one's life in this manner is the only prudent thing to do. (This is the case with Bishop Mynster.) I doubt that a man has, in the religious sense, permission to do this; in any case he should make an admission. From the Christian point of view, however, it is precisely the task for every generation to get the question of what it is to be a man more clearly and more adequately defined, for the question of the relation between God and man will emerge all the more profoundly. Anyone who has his life merely within a particular circle contributes nothing to clarifying the question of what it is to be a man and bringing it closer home; he merely helps himself through life in the best way, investigating nothing more profound, but grabs hold of a few habits related to being a man of that sort and puts everything into that. He lacks primitivity altogether.

Since the God-man alone expresses qualitatively what it is to be man, it is of utmost importance to him to exist for every man, unconditionally every man. In a way it might seem that the God-man must become an extremely abstract man. And this is the case: he is literally nothing.

We could now go through all kinds of human relativities in detail in order to establish to what extent such a relativity could be commensurate with the God-man, so that he could have been the God-man in that relativity.[472] Since qualitatively he is essentially just as far from and just as near to every moral relativity of what it is to be man, it might seem inconsequential which he chose. And one could indeed say: He chose a differential, since he chose to be a poor and insignificant man rather than to be prominent. But this is not true, for he was not a poor and insignificant man in contrast to prominence and wealth; if that were the case he would have belonged to the solidarity of the poor and insignificant. He was purely and simply man, who felt no pressure to own anything (consequently he was not poor) and found blessedness in being nothing (consequently he was not insignificant, either). He could just as well have been rich and prominent if there would not have been class solidarity right away and if wealth and prominence were not dubious qualities with respect to being man.

x^2 A 643   *n.d.,* 1850

« 4184 *Clique—and Community in the Idea*

The law of the clique is: the closer two people come together, the more intimately, all the more well-disposed is their judgment of each other, and all the more leniently they interpret everything as perfection. In relation to the idea the law is: the closer you come, the more rigorous becomes the judgment. If you want a more lenient judgment, which makes the relative amount to something or overlooks imperfections—then get a little farther away; rigorous judgment means making distinctions and it increases with proximity. A clique is an impossibility this way.

x^3 A 26   *n.d.,* 1850

« 4185 *The Shift in the Interpretation of Christianity also Occasioned by the Year 1848*

The conflict about Christianity will no longer be doctrinal conflict (this is the conflict between orthodoxy and heterodoxy). The conflict (occasioned also by the social and communistic movements) will be about Christianity as an existence. The problem will become that of loving the "neighbor"; attention will be directed to Christ's life, and Christianity will also become essentially accentuated in the direction of conformity to his life.

The world has gradually consumed those masses of illusions and insulating walls with which we have protected ourselves so that the question remained simply one of Christianity as doctrine. The rebellion in the world shouts: We want to see action!

X^3 A 346 *n.d.*, 1850

« 4186 *The Single Individual—Togetherness*

Being an individual is a higher form of existence than "Let a few of us get together in a group." This is the view particularly of Christianity, and from the Christian point of view it holds true particularly of greatness that if there is no individual in a given generation capable of it, then it will not occur in that generation, for through togetherness it is an impossibility.

But this "Let a few of us get together in a group" makes life easier and more comfortable etc.

I have nothing against anyone's choosing to do so for this reason, but I do oppose the mendacity which has turned the whole thing around and made being an individual into fanaticism, untruth, and the like—but has made togetherness (the easier life) into truth, into the highest. It is nauseating to hear or to read the conceitedness with which every registered student, graduate, shopkeeper's apprentice, et al. disrespectfully talks of being an individual as something inferior and defective. And it is no less nauseating to see how those who ought to know better cowardly and effeminately support this mendacious inversion.

But I want the truth. I will not strain one single person's life more than he has been accustomed to until now—but he has to be honest, he must declare that the easy life is the highest life.

X^3 A 529 *n.d.*, 1850

« 4187 *The Refined Immorality of the Age*

There is no one who will venture, no one who will sacrifice anything, no one assumes a strenuous undertaking—well, let the matter rest there. But then they have gone further yet. They have even ascribed to themselves that most exalted role of reformer, the very title. Let a few of us get together and do some reforming, but very carefully so that there will be no danger, no sacrifices to make, but each one will become a titular reformer.

Everything is taken in vain. The government's decorations and medals are so common that only not having a decoration is conspicuous. It is the same with all other distinctions. To be a reformer, zealous for reforming, is a distinction everyone wears in his buttonhole, something like a popinjay ribbon at the popinjay shooting—and it is no more inconveniencing than that, either, to be that kind of reformer.

Communism shouts that ownership is thievery—yes, to own the title of reformer in that way is in truth thievery.

— x^3 A 575 *n.d.*, 1850

« 4188 *A Strange Contradiction*

The entire age is radical, wants to begin from the beginning in everything, therefore wants to do away with tradition: and look, in daily life, in practice, it is apparent that the same people understand very well that in everything the thing to do is to get the assistance of a little tradition. A shopkeeper, for example, advertises every day in the newspaper, hoping by this continual reiteration to gain the power of tradition, which otherwise would not be achieved for some years.

It is the same practically everywhere. Yes, one can say that it is the practice in the world of commerce these days to establish tradition by artificial means.

What they want to do, then, is do away with the traditions which inconvenience them, the venerable old traditions, and then as soon as possible themselves provide substitute traditions, traditions established by artificial means.

The radicals abhor everything called custom—and yet that is precisely what all the journalists and the like are working on: the art of foisting customs on the public in the shortest possible time—but, please note, customs which suit these benefactors of the human race.

— x^3 A 587 *n.d.*, 1850

« 4189 *Give to God the Things That Are God's*[473]

But everything is God's, so that to give to God the things that are God's is to give him everything, even that which belongs to Caesar, inasmuch as I obey Caesar out of fear and love of God.

— x^3 A 603 *n.d.*, 1850

« 4190 *Nonsense*

Stilling[474] told me that someone—it probably was a clergyman—had stated to him that *Practice in Christianity*[475] was an arrogant usurpation, "an arrogant usurpation for an individual to talk that way."

Fine! Ultimately they are going to want an association, a committee to present ideals.

O, what abysmal nonsense! Either there has to be an individual who presents ideals—or they cannot be presented at all. When there are many—there is relativity.

The tragedy of the age is precisely that society has completely strangled ideals. Finally it is an individual who in the most modest manner makes the attempt—but an individual, as stated, it must be—and then it is called: an arrogant usurpation by an individual.

Basically there is an instinctive craftiness in this remark. For the very last thing they want is ideals; people want to remain in the sphere of social haggling. But ideals can be set forth only by an individual—ergo, they try to intimidate the individual not to dare and thus they slip out of the ideals. Perhaps they may still find there is something to the question—and appoint a committee, or drive around in a spacious four-seater Holstein carriage—looking for ideals.

x^3 A 607   n.d., 1850

« 4191 *Christianity—the State*

Guizot[476] says: The only policy for the state is to be indifferent to all religion.

This goes along with the old Christianity, which declared: Christianity is indifferent toward each and every form of government; it can live equally well under all of them.

Alas, but the inversion today is that the state wants to play the aristocrat as if it did not need religion—whereas it is religion which does not need the state. This is the thanks Christianity gets for being used by statecraft to organize the states.

x^3 A 679   n.d., 1850

« 4192 *Publicity*

Total publicity makes it absolutely impossible to "govern." For all "government" is grounded on the idea that there are a few individuals who are more insightful than others and for that very reason are able to see so much farther that they are able to pilot; but total publicity is grounded on the idea that everybody should "govern."

That this is the case no one has understood better than the daily press, for no power has guarded the professional secrets of its internal organization, who its collaborators are, what its actual aims are, to the same degree as the daily press, which at the same time has continually cried that "the government" should be public. Quite right; the press really wanted to dispose of "government"—and then it would itself govern, which is why it also assured for itself the concealment which is necessary in order to—govern.

x^3 A 690   n.d., 1850

« 4193 *The Clergy*

When a society goes to pieces the way it did in '48, it is not the fault of kings and nobility—but is essentially the fault of the clergy.

Christianity has nothing to do with the state but continues in the original apostolic tradition—or, if it wants to get involved with the state and in that way also profit from it, then it becomes a state church, and then the clergy have to guarantee the state a sufficient foundation of politically indifferent, that is, actually religiously engrossed, good citizens.

They were the ones who in former days were the mainstay of the state. Christianity is political indifference; engrossed in higher things, it teaches submission to all public authorities.[477]

In former times this religiousness provided the states with good, quiet citizens who were not occupied with wanting to rule or wanting to control the government.

But religiousness disappeared. The newspapers and public life in general did everything to sweep everyone into political interests—and the clergy never thought of forming or were able to form an opposition, not in the manner of Tryde,[478] by flirting with politics and taking part in discussions, no, but by developing the interest of the religious, which is political indifference.

Nowadays everything is politics, and the clergymen are the first to run for parliament.

If someone speaks up and tries to explain that it is "the crowd" which must be opposed, the clergy may perhaps think there is something to that, but the clergy themselves are just as vote-hungry as the others.

This is why I have never wanted to let the matter rest here. In order to approach the matter radically, I have launched an attack on the clergy, but without attacking anyone personally. Certainly the clergy do have an enormous responsibility.

But I am not really understood. The faith I have in the rightness and the ultimate victory of my cause is shared by no one, but in our day faith is extremely rare anyway. The few who are more or less in agreement with me would say: Let us unite together against the crowd. But I see very well that the evil lies deeper than that. Although I definitely oppose "the crowd" and believe that it is the clergy who actually should be used, I by no means begin by promptly joining up with the clergy as such but begin by attacking them. But human hustle and bustle and prudence are also the very opposite of faith.

— x³ A 746   n.d., 1851

« 4194 *The Clergy*

ought to be an executive power in society by being in character. The greatest possible error arises when the clergy become teachers.

— x³ A 754   n.d., 1851

« 4195 *The Clergy*

are an executive power. Imagine, in order to get a proper notion of the confusion, imagine that the police, instead of acting, began to *teach* about thievery etc.

— x³ A 773   n.d., 1851

« 4196 *The Highest Is the Abnormal*

Nowadays the most inferior can easily counterfeit it.

But the abnormal, which is the highest, has the enormous pressure of the intervening ethical.

The lowest now wants to take this away—and be the highest—without all the dangers.

To that end they have hit upon this: Let us form a group.

— x⁴ A 31   n.d., 1851

« 4197 *The Supremacy of the Mass*

It is easy to see that the form of the world has changed qualitatively. No longer can it be said that one person rules over the others. If there is to be governing, it must be indirect or inverse—that is, through suffering.

An example of the indirect rule is the poet, who by introducing ideals forces men back within their boundaries.

— x⁴ A 40   n.d., 1851

« 4198

In margin of 4197 (x⁴ A 40):

That the mass is to be confronted by the ideal through the aid of a "poet,"[479] that this is also an advance, means that everyone is to be a single individual and that as a single individual he relates himself to the ideal, means equality before the ideal, means human equality and humanity.

A single individual ought not be a ruler with direct recognizability[480] as such. This is a lower form of human existence, and the power hunger of the mass can no longer endure it.

No, when he says: I am a poet, only a poet—he is saying: Look at me and see that I am not great, I am not the ideal—but look at the ideal.

Yet a person somewhat more developed must be used as the "poet" in order to produce the indirect impression by way of the ideal; if it is positive that he, too, is a contemptible fellow according to human standards, he makes no impression and he does not in any way help the ideal make an impression.

Consequently the more developed person, instead of wanting to enjoy having his advanced development be recognized (by being a ruler directly, being admired and obeyed), must have resignation enough to hide it in unrecognizability (incognito) with the help of the ideal, which quite rightly also reduces his bit of precociousness to nothing.

This again is what I have intimated in the conclusion of the review of *Two Ages*. O my God, how clear it all is to me! I can never be thankful enough for what has been done for me, so infinitely much more than I had ever expected, could have expected, or dared to expect!

x^4 A 41   *n.d*

« 4199 *Voting*

All finite matters are suitable for voting. Nothing infinite can be decided by voting. A decision by voting means only that the matter has a terminal point, not, in the infinite sense, that it is now decided. In the sense of the infinite, a decision through voting results in nothing. The matter is simply terminated.

x^4 A 43   *n.d.*, 1851

« 4200

Does one dare vote in purely formal agreement together with those with whom he otherwise disagrees without calling attention to the fact that this agreement is a misunderstanding; is this not a concealment?

Strictly speaking, one dare not do this. But since I always argue with people only *e concessis*,[481] I will say: Well, if someone is concerned only with being an out and out politician, then I have no objection. For politics is sheer externality, and the fundamental difference between one externality and another is not so qualitative that it is necessary to raise a cry of alarm. Moreover, in many respects politics is devoid of conscience.

But if one is supposed to be a Christian in the most rigorous sense of the word, then he dare not conceal the fact that this agreement is a misunderstanding, that is, according to Christianity's concepts of purity from intrigues, a concealment; therefore he must either call attention to this—or surrender the claim of wanting to be regarded as a Christian in the more rigorous sense of the word.

x^4 A 47   *n.d.*, 1851

« 4201 *Reply*

..... Well, if the matter is of such a nature that it is suitable for settlement by voting, then I am willing to vote—although I otherwise neither dance[482] nor vote.

Once I spoke in a general assembly and then asked that a vote be taken. It was in the student assembly, and the question was about prohibiting the playing of badminton, which [prohibition] I opposed.

x^4 A 51   *n.d.*, 1851

« 4202 *Religious Upbringing*

With regard to all externality (which I myself as an individual am unable to eliminate or which does not make me feel conscience-bound to become a martyr in order to eliminate it), the law is this: the task is simply by means of an inward turning to become indifferent to this kind of change, to draw the mind away from preoccupation with it.

This business of forming a little group etc. is a forgery, is also, looked at purely from the point of view of discipline, like the pupil's inattentiveness during the lesson or, more accurately, like his sitting passively in class.

Everywhere there is and must be existentially an either/or. And the demoralization of our age is precisely the continuous substitution of quantification.

x^4 A 63   *n.d.*, 1851

« 4203 *Handbook for Voters*

A satire on the whole odious practice could be written under this title.

On the whole it is tragic how little thinking is done in the world. The form of government is changed; everything, everything is changed

—and the only thing they have no doubts about, the only firm and fixed thing, is faith in the kind of decision arrived at by voting.

There are some extremely interesting and important problems here with respect to showing the limitations of voting, where the use of voting is nonsense, just as it would be nonsense to use a steelyard for weighing gold. And the fact that mankind acknowledges only voting as a means of decision shows how deeply the human race has sunk, how purely secularized it has become.

x^4 A 65   *n.d.,* 1851

« 4204 *The World's Wisdom or Worldly Wisdom Abolishes Character*

In his autobiography Franklin[483] says regarding a project of public utility which he proposed anonymously early in his life: Here I learned, as I later experienced, how right it is, when one wants a cause to be promoted, not to place oneself at the head of it but to have "a man who has an active interest in our situation etc."[484]—that is, the abstract, an X. —Well, I suppose that is the most prudent way; it is related to the fact that human craving for power, leveling, cannot bear to have anyone stand at the head. And this has abolished the ethical, which insists upon the *person* and would condemn this prudence as disgraceful cowardice.

In a similar vein he says that one of his friends made him aware that he must become occupied with humility. Franklin says: That is just what I did, without actually becoming more humble because of it. But my manner of speaking changed; I spoke less frequently in definite opposition to anything; I generally used such expressions as: I believe that one might suppose etc. Franklin adds, "After that, I was much more successful in carrying through what I wished to carry through."[485] Naturally, for this humility is a compliment to the human craving for power which will not tolerate character.

x^4 A 68   *n.d.,* 1851

« 4205 *Theories of the State*

Instead of all these hypotheses about the origin of the state etc., we should be more occupied with the question: given an established order, how can new points of departure be created religiously?

x^4 A 72   *n.d.,* 1851

« 4206 *Fichte,* Ethics[486]

Part I, p. 780. In connection with the French motto: Liberty, Equality, *Fraternity.*

This fraternal love becomes that before which property, marriage, family, and even the diversity of talents and capabilities are supposed to disappear. *"Die Bruderliebe wird plötzlich als gleichmachende, revolutionaire Gewalt proclamirt: ein seltsamer Selbstwiederspruch!"*

And now he shows that in a certain sense justice equalizes, love does not.

He could have developed this more powerfully, showing that it is love that preserves difference, because love does not seek its own but what is the neighbor's; not only does it not covet what is the neighbor's but, on the contrary, rejoices that he has it or has what I do not have or am not.

But the most dreadful hoax of modern times is that egotism passes itself off as love, so that love becomes the demander instead of the giver. It is love if someone says: If everyone else has this or that advantage and I am the only one who does not have it, then I rejoice that the others have it. It is egotism to say: If I do not have this advantage, then no one else ought to have it either.

Here again we see what I have always maintained—that the whole modern trend is a disastrous caricature of religiousness—it is politics.

Human equality—yes, Christianity does indeed want this! In two ways: either that you—if you are the one who has drawn the shortest straw—patiently reconcile yourself to the fact—for in this way the distraction is essentially removed, or that those who are favored with the good themselves resolve to give up something or everything. But Christianity always wants the influence to come from the good—how could the differences in earthly life ever become so important to Christianity that it would want quarreling and contention because of them.

But politics is egotism dressed up as love, is the most frightful egotism, is Satan himself in the form of an angel of light. To tell the truth, a person well-favored might say: Let them take everything away from me—but let them at least be honorable enough not to do it in the name of love. Too often have we shuddered over the contrived and cunning cruelty with which the clergy in its time handed over a heretic to secular authorities—in order not to have any dealings themselves with capital punishment (as if they did not already have something to do with it anyway!)—and even added: they prayed that the shedding of blood might be avoided—which meant that the convicted one should be burned! O, but it is just as cunning when the most dreadful egotism, this released demon, passes itself off as love and, while it is leveling everything, demands to be worshiped and idolized as love.

x^4 A 83   *n.d.*, 1851

« **4207 *No Reformation***

The method of proceeding is very simple and in the true Christian spirit.

It is quite in order to ask everyone—the tax-collector or the gravedigger, it makes no difference, if possible every last person in the country, the most wretched and poverty-stricken as well as a professor and the most distinguished people—are you the reformer?

If the answer is categorically "No," then the matter is decided, and then in a genuinely Christian spirit one simply turns against this alternative: getting together a group that wants to reform.

x^4 A 97   *n.d.*, 1851

« **4208**

..... cannot be formed according to the paradigm of balloting (voting, voting with discussion, voting without discussion—voting, from, in, with, upon, by voting) or be done according to the popular song: Let's get together, hurrah, hurrah, hurrah! Street-lighting and clothes and, with all due respect, the sanitation department can be reformed in this manner, but let us be men:[487] Christianity does not lend itself to reformation in this way.

x^4 A 102   *n.d.*, 1851

« **4209 *Amazing!***

Once the objection against Christianity (and this was right at the time when it was most evident what Christianity is) was that it was unpatriotic, a danger to the state, revolutionary—and now Christianity has become patriotism and a state church.

Once the objection against Christianity (and this was right at the time when it was most evident what Christianity is and the objection was made by the genuinely keen-eyed pagans) was that it was antihuman—and now Christianity has become humanity.

Once Christianity was an offense to the Jews and foolishness to the Greeks, and now it is—culture. For Bishop Mynster[488] the mark of true Christianity is culture.

And now if Dr. Rudelbach[489] will give up his office and step forth as a solitary man, get rid of misconceived collaboration in the form of political favor, and declare that he is no Christian and that Christianity does not exist at all—that would be something. But this whole muddle of voting by every Tom, Dick, and Harry, which allows for a host of illusions—no, this is nonsense.

X^4 A 126 *n.d.*, 1851

« **4210** *Ambrose*

The demand was made that he surrender a church to the Arians. The emperor's envoys come to Ambrose in the cathedral and demand it, reminding him that it is the emperor's prerogative. Ambrose answers: "If the emperor demands my property, my fortune, I shall not oppose it—although it all belongs to the poor. But the emperor has no right to what belongs to God. If you want my possessions, take them! My life—I am ready to follow you! If you want to put me in chains and lead me to death—with pleasure! I shall not encompass myself with people as with a wall. *I shall not embrace the altars in order to live, but I shall rather sacrifice myself in order to save the altars.*"

Böhringer, I, pt. 3, p. 29.[490]

X^4 A 155 *n.d.*, 1851

« **4211** *Vinet*

I have now obtained *Der Sozialismus in seinem Principe betrachtet* by Vinet,[491] *übersetzt von* Hofmeister.

Reading his preface to the little book has been enough.

He is not the man. He is a brilliant author who writes something about the single individual but is not in character, does not operate in character, is not existentially higher than all discussion—no, no, he writes something which he then submits to public opinion; he palavers with the public in the usual author fashion.

But nevertheless there is spirit.

X^4 A 185 March 9, 1851

« **4212**

In margin of 4211 (X^4 A 185):

It was Vinet for whom Rudelbach[492] shouted in his book on civil marriage, saying that Vinet and I are in agreement. Curiously enough, I then requested a book by him from the University Library. It was on loan. Some time later it was sent to me. A few days later the librarian told me that the one who had had the book would like to have it again.

I returned it at once. It turned out that Martensen[493] was the one who had had it. It was a large book by Vinet in French and for that reason I did not read any of it. But today I myself have obtained the little book that I had ordered.

x^4 A 186   March 9, 1851

« 4213 *Collision of Conscience—the Established*

It is said (and rightly so, from the Christian viewpoint) that it is paganism and the destruction of all truth unceremoniously to allow the individual to become absorbed in the state and that the individual with conscience is above the state.

(*In margin:* Vinet[494] also presents it this way.)

It is emphasized that the heroes of the human race are individuals who have collided with an established order in a matter of conscience.

Right, right! Ergo, you say, all laws which are able to constrain conscience ought to be abolished.

No, no, no! A dreadful error and dreadful demagogic flirtation and sentimentality! No! Why did those men become heroes? Precisely because there was the established order that could bring pressure powerfully to bear and by this pressure upon the single individual brought out the truth in him, made it a matter of conscience with the result that he did not make a mistake and go off half-cocked.

See precisely for the sake of conscience I need constraint. I love greatness—O, with indescribable envious admiration —but I hate rubbish—and again in this realm the attempt is made to interpret everything in terms of rubbish.

x^4 A 187   *n.d.,* 1851

« 4214 *The Passion Story*

At most they feared that Christ might become dangerous to the emperor; yet Pilate feared no longer when Christ was flogged—and then he became dangerous not merely to the emperor but also to the emperor's gods.

From a religious point of view, the greatest impotence is the greatest power.

Therefore Christ has no scepter in his hand, only a reed, the symbol of impotence—and yet at that very moment he is the greatest power. As far as power is concerned, to rule the whole world with a scepter is nothing compared to ruling it with a reed—that is, by impotence—that is, divinely. A sovereign in purple robes is not nearly so great as a sovereign in rags, which is why we in fact sometimes see that the sovereign who really feels himself to be a power prefers to rule in an old cloak etc., even if he actually is able to dress in purple. This is a very weak analogy to the divine order: the greatest impotence is the greatest power, for the analogy is still only a game of abolishing the insignia; divinely it must be in earnest, in all earnestness, and physically understood it must be the greatest impotence.

X^4 A 209 *n.d.*, 1851

« 4215 *Politics*

Statesmanship in modern states is not: how one *manages to be* a cabinet minister, but: how one *manages to become* a cabinet minister. More one does not know—so one actually consumes his wisdom in a kind of introductory science to becoming a cabinet minister. This will lead to the disintegration of states, for there is really no governing or ruling.

In former days, when life was quieter, there were only a few who could hope to become cabinet ministers, and they had the time to prepare themselves to be that. Nowadays the possibility is open to everyone, and the urge to become a cabinet minister is so great that it takes a whole new skill to force one's way through, if possible, to become one. They train for this, consume their time and effort in this study—and then someone becomes a cabinet minister but does not know any more. He could say, naïvely: I have not prepared myself to be but to become a cabinet minister, and in this respect I certainly have shown that I was clever.

X^4 A 249 *n.d.*, 1851

« 4216 *My Position*

One of two situations usually prevails. Yes, this is the case in almost every place I have read about: a polemicist either makes "the people" the fixed point, the truth—and attacks the government, or, belonging to the government he rants against "the people." Both forms, it is easy to see, belong to secular struggle; there is no double danger.

What is my position? Do I attack "the government"? No, no. But I say: You do not govern; it is indefensible of you to let the workers deprive you, and you clergymen, you especially, you are swindling

Christianity by flirtingly, politically making it agreeable to the crowd instead of teaching with authority.

My polemical aim is really at "the crowd." But I do not have the safeguard of being a public official.

How then am I going to get anyone really to listen to what I have to say? The rulers are not willing to listen to it. And "the people"! After all, I cannot complain to the people that the rulers are not ruling adequately; if one is going to talk to the people about the "government," it must be in terms of maintaining that the government is tyrannical or abuses its power in another way—whereas my complaint is that the government does not use its power as it should.

How can I hope to get anyone to want to fight under conditions such that there is no possible reward or profit, but the displeasure of both sides is practically unavoidable. All who want to help me promptly mess up my cause by making it partisan in one direction or the other, and therefore I cannot use them.

What I give expression to is a religious battle, and how strenuous and exhausting it is can be seen simply in the fact that I scarcely am able to get anyone to have sufficient self-denial to understand how thankless the battle is.

x^4 A 268 *n.d.*, 1851

« 4217 *The Incident in France*

The crucial reply (this the Emperor of Russia will understand) is really that the soldiers said: We are soldiers. Their being addressed: Citizens—and that they therefore dare not shoot—is thereby set aside until later.

Napoleon is no hero. This needs no proof. But there is proof in that the night before the coup d'etat, between two and four, he ran about agitatedly asking the adjuncts and sentries whether or not they had heard anything, namely, the signal he was expecting. The old Napoleon could sleep before the battle. A hero carries his task intensely, very quietly, without others' noticing how heavily it weighs. The new Napoleon lacks this intensive calm within himself—he is like a gambler, tense as a gambler, not self-contained like a hero.

x^4 A 447 *n.d.*, 1851

« 4218 *The Income Tax—the Temporary —Count Sponneck*[495]

The finance minister has presented the income tax plan to Parliament.[496] He believes this money is needed; this is the financial side of the matter. He believes that an income tax will be an appropriate way to raise it, and he is also of the opinion that it will be willingly accepted since it will be only temporary.

It is the error of this idea that I would like to point out.

It is a very common notion and tactic (it appears in big affairs and small) that in proposing some change or other one will much more easily get those concerned to accept the proposed change if he adds: The change will be only temporary. This also makes good sense. But, as in everything human, this too has a limit, and when it is overstepped, there is no longer any sense in talk about its being only temporary.

It is not difficult to determine this limit. Wherever a *restitutio in integrum*[497] is possible or is possible without much difficulty through the termination of the temporary, it makes sense to say that the proposed change will be more readily acceptable because it is only temporary. But where this *restitutio in integrum* is difficult, very difficult, impossible, this kind of talk is meaningless—for example, if one wanted to hang himself temporarily, meaning that hanging—which generally can be a very serious matter, a step one does not take without mature reflection—would not be so dangerous if one did it temporarily. Or take a lesser example. A man proposes marriage to a girl; perhaps she does not think it a suitable match, but she does decide to consider it. Then a second fellow crops up—a fast worker, a smart, gallant young man, a devil of a fellow. He proposes marriage and adds that he suspects that she will be all the more inclined to accept since it is his intention that it be only a temporary marriage. A temporary marriage! I think the girl will answer: No, thank you, even if I were otherwise not disinclined to enter into this marriage, I must decline if the condition is that it be only temporary.

Thus the point that it was supposed to be only temporary proved to have the very opposite effect—instead of making the girl more inclined toward this change, it set her more definitely against it. And why? Because marriage is such a decisive step, involving such consequences that when it takes place no *restitutio in integrum* is possible. And if no *restitutio in integrum* is possible, then it is frivolous, fraudulent, and thoughtless to say that the matter is not so dangerous, after all, since it is supposed to be only temporary, for in that case it is not temporary, no matter if one says it ten times in order to get the person concerned to acquiesce or become entrapped.

No doubt a moralist could do much good by pointing out the frivolous misuse of "the temporary" so characteristic of our age. Instead of concentrating mind and thought on the earnest decision—and then letting it be in earnest, something new has been concocted: the gravest and most radical changes may be accepted as if they were nothing "since it is supposed to be only temporary." O you Sophists! If they are the kind of decisions in which no *restitutio in integrum* is possible, then what?

So it is with the income tax, and especially in Denmark, with its small-scale operations, where pettiness is always so close at hand. It is in fact an extremely important decision, a radical change in our whole social life—if it takes place, it cannot be undone again within one generation. And then the finance minister is of the opinion that it is so much easier to accept since it is only temporary.

Everyone with any sound thinking at his disposal will certainly take the opposite view—if it is to be only temporary, then vote: No! There will always be many objections to the income tax, but, good heavens, if it is necessary, then let the matter be put forth in earnest and as earnestness; but if it is supposed to be merely temporary, then it is really meaningless.

The finance minister may be right in calling the tax temporary, for it may be possible to drop it in a few years. But the fact of its having been an income tax cannot be dropped. The change in our social conditions will have taken place—even if the income tax were to last only fourteen days, it nevertheless will have taken place. Here again it is evident that the temporary (if one thinks soundly) in such situations where a *restitutio in integrum* is impossible has just the opposite effect: the very fact that it is supposed to be only temporary is reason enough to make one more definitely opposed to it. In something that in any case is to be only temporary, there is actually nothing similar to prompt such considerations.

My point is very simple: precisely that with which the finance minister has intended to advance the cause or, more correctly, to get it going and slip it over on the people, perhaps also get the people to walk into the trap—precisely this is what the protest ought to be against. And I believe this will happen if there is a predominance of sound thinking in Parliament. At some time let the extent to which we ought to have an income tax be decided in earnest, but let us not make ourselves as ridiculous as that suitor who thought the girl would more readily decide to marry him since he intended the marriage to be only temporary, or like that man who believed that hanging himself was not so decisive a step, since it was his intention to do it—only temporarily!

X^6 B 257   *n.d.*, 1851

« 4219 *Caesar*

See the brief essay on Caesar and Alexander by Fr. Schlegel (*S. Werke*, IV, p. 307).[498]

Caesar publicly admitted his similarity to Cataline; when he was reproached for having promoted some men of very low birth to the highest places of honor, he answered that if assassins and robbers had been useful in upholding his power and prestige, he would have rewarded them in the same manner.

See p. 310. Caesar made no bones about his power-seeking disposition and was always quick to quote Eteocles' words in Euripides:[499] "For the sake of dominion one may indeed do wrong; otherwise do right."

X^4 A 575   *n.d.,* 1852

« 4220 *The Highest Christian Pathos*

The words of the Epistle to the Hebrews[500] express it: They refused to be comforted and to be helped.

Only this pathos can carry Christianity through, can hold it to the divine apex so that it does not run downhill like a coach; only in this pathos is the essentially Christian bottled airtight, inaccessible to all commerce with the heterogeneous. As soon as the thought of human assistance arises, of not refusing the help of men,[501] all is essentially lost, faith in martyrdom as having value in and by itself, and Christianity runs downhill until, just as the Rhine ends in mud, it ends in the mud of politics. Take an air pillow—a pinprick is enough. If you clip a large hole with a pair of scissors, the situation is not altered essentially—it is no longer airtight.

This change really came in with Luther. He was the Christian hero who blinked, certainly not because of lack of courage; no, but ensnared in the idea that it is godliness to be made happy in this life, faith in the unconditioned value of martyrdom vanished. He did not refuse the assistance of men—in his hour of death he repented of it.

Here the change entered in, and from then on Christianity became more and more politics. The formula is very simple: a cause which is served by the refusal of human assistance—yes, it may be arrogance, but it may also be God's cause; but a cause which is served in such a way that one accepts the assistance of men is politics. To set God's name to it does not turn the scales any more than to say: Now in God's name I am going out to steal, or—in the name of our Lord Jesus Christ I shall go and hang myself.

X^5 A 115   *n.d.,* 1853

« 4221 *To Struggle with "the Many" and To Struggle with a Tyrant*[502]

Perhaps the second is easier.

In struggling with a tyrant, the resistance fighter will be understood by men, and this is an enormous help; whereas the whole conflict with "the many" is an obscure sort of battle.

What makes struggling with "the many" particularly exhausting is that in struggling with a tyrant—well, a decisive point is reached, he is taken prisoner etc., from now on it is not in his power to escape. But struggling with "the many" begins all over from the beginning every single day. A person can pull out, hide, move somewhere else, etc. Consequently every single day the task must be shouldered anew, and every single day there is, so to speak, the tempting question: Spare yourself, aren't you tired of the whole business, isn't this self-inflicted torture? Truly, in order to struggle with the many and to stick it out the determining factor must be the God-relationship—for this very reason no one understands this kind of battle. This understanding, however, will be inescapably necessary in the future if Christianity and God are not to be completely abolished and the fear of men placed upon the throne.

X^5 A 136 *n.d.*, 1853

« 4222

According to the New Testament there is discord between God and man. Christianity, of course, opposes every effort directed at fusing men into a compact mass directly over against God—therefore everything called state church, folk church, Christian nations, etc. etc.

But generally speaking all effort is in this direction; consequently it is not a weak effort in the direction of the essentially Christian but an enterprise directed against Christianity.

But, of course, if there is no state church, folk church, Christian nation, etc., then there are no big jobs, no high official ranks, nor the whole load of prevarications and excuses and illusions in which we live as utter pagans—and, please note, call it Christianity.

XI^2 A 391 *n.d.*, 1853–54

« 4223 *The New*

Christianly, newness comes from God; *politically,* it comes—from the street.

XI^1 A 17 *n.d.*, 1854

« 4224 *Establishing a Party, Forming a School, etc.*

Why do I do nothing along this line? It is certainly clear that Socrates did it and Christ even more so.

The answer to this must be: establishing parties, forming schools, togetherness etc. is precisely the error of our times; consequently, in the interest of the truth, this must be pointed out as forcefully as possible.

Yet this answer is not conclusive. But the point is this—establishing a party and forming a school may be something inferior to what I am doing (as with the whole political *Treiben*[503] of our time), and it can be something superior, as with Socrates and Christ.

It depends on the situation in which or the stage at which a person does it. It is certainly easy to see that to establish a party and found a school is to acquire more or less palpable power—in this case a person may wish to found a school and party for purely egotistical reasons. Understood in that way, my position is superior.

But if suffering is intrinsic to the truth, if a person is initiated into the true forms of the truth only through suffering, then it holds that both for the sake of truth and, properly understood, for his own sake, one should not unseasonably acquire palpable power in such a way that he thereby avoids suffering.

As far as Christ was concerned, he certainly was aware that he would become the sacrifice, he was divinely sure of himself—as a result he could found a school with the greatest equanimity. As for Socrates, I dare say that when he began founding a school he was so far advanced and his life so abandoned that he actually was sacrificed.

In forming a school, the person not matured this way, not so far advanced, whose life is not thus marked, can easily deceive himself as to whether or not it is egotism that determines him—rather than concern for the truth.

XI^1 A 18 *n.d.*, 1854

« 4225 *Opposition*

To be in the service of the established order is to have palpable power; to establish a party and in this sense be the opposition is to have palpable power—but this is not serving the truth.

I do not belong to the established order as a civil servant, thus have neither salary nor power nor position. On the other hand, I have not only not established a party but have lined myself up against acquiring a party and furthermore have taken up combat against the opposition.

XI¹ A 30   n.d., 1854

« 4226 *Society's Remoteness from Christianity —and Yet We Are All Christians*

The state is morally disintegrated—this is the situation.

If the 1,000 clergymen at least made an attempt to make an ethical impact, that would still be something.

But, no, this does not happen—they dare not, which again expresses how deeply society has sunk.

If it happened, if it were done competently, it would be something at least, and from a purely pagan point of view, the state would still be helped. But it would nevertheless be a long way from Christianity.

Yet this never happens—and then we are all Christian.

At one time I thought of turning my efforts to this ethical task—but I could never get permission for this—because of the clergy (Bishop Mynster).[504]

So I was forced to concern myself more and more deeply with what Christianity is—and now I see what a dreadful distance there is between society and Christianity.

It is always society itself which helps make me become aware—by doing me injustice.

XI¹ A 54   n.d., 1854

« 4227 *Representation—Association*

Once upon a time to be a man meant something like this: the generation made every effort to raise up and support a few eminent individuals. In these the rest of the people envisioned themselves. By way of these eminent individuals (to whom they were all related) the concept of the infinite elevation of what it meant to be man was maintained—that it really meant to be in kinship with God.

Gradually the inferior element in the race triumphed; envy ascended and came to the top. Now everything was changed. Through the power that lies in numbers they wanted first and foremost to get rid of all eminence, and through numbers (by being a group, a crowd, a party, etc.) they wanted to upgrade themselves.

It was successful. But as always when something accursed succeeds, on closer inspection one sees that it succeeded by way of degrading the whole race. All the power used to advance through numbers leads univocally to the degradation of the whole race. And so it is. Given what it means now to be a man, it is nonsensical, ludicrous (almost as ludicrous as it would be if such a thing were to occur to a cow or a horse) to talk about immortality, eternity, being in kinship with God.

XI^1 A 93   n.d., 1854

« 4228 Substitute, Curious Substitutes

In these days everything is a substitute; we help ourselves along with substitutes—and with extremely curious substitutes:

..... to insist on truth, this would be too much; one must not pull the bow too tight—so one helps himself along with the official lie, which is, after all, a kind of truth. To insist on virtue, this would be too much; let us not be unreasonable, it gets one nowhere—so one helps himself along with refined villainy, which is also a kind of virtue. It would be futile to insist on unselfishness—so one helps himself along by hidden, hypocritical selfishness—which is also a kind of unselfishness and resembles it perfectly.

Curious substitutes—even the most flagrant lie, the most outrageous crime, the most obvious selfishness—are less reprehensible than these.

XI^1 A 98   n.d., 1854

« 4229

Society does not presume (as I understand the Chinese do) only five cardinal virtues (civility is the fifth)—no, society presumes, sets up but one: civility.

XI^1 A 99   n.d., 1854

« 4230 Double Leveling, or a Leveling[505] Which Cancels Itself

By means of the daguerreotype it will be easy for everyone to have his portrait made—formerly only the distinguished were able to do this; and at the same time every effort is made to make us all look alike—therefore, only one single portrait is needed.

XI^1 A 118   n.d., 1854

« 4231 The Human—The Divine

Man is "a social animal,"[506] and what he believes in is the power of association.

Therefore the human idea is this: Let us all unite—if it were possible, all the kingdoms and countries of the earth—and this pyramid-union, rising ever higher and higher, carries at its peak a super-king —he must be regarded as being closest to God, so close in fact that he approaches so near to God that God is worried about him and pays attention to him.

Christianly, the situation is just the reverse. Such a super-king as this would stand farthest from God, just as God is exceedingly opposed to the whole business of the pyramid.

Christianly, God chooses and is closest to the despised, the castoffs of the race, one single sorry abandoned wretch, a dreg of humanity.

He hates this business of the pyramid. For just as God is infinite love and his paternal eye readily sees how cruel this human pyramid-idea can easily become toward the unfortunate, the ignored, and the like in the human race (which is the very reason why the God of love looks after them), he is in the same way too infinitely wise a majesty not to see that if this idea of the pyramid got the slightest acceptance, as if there were some truth, even the smallest crumb of truth, to the idea that as the pyramid rises higher one comes still closer to God, then man would not be able to relinquish the idea of some day raising a pyramid so high that he will believe himself able to shove God off the throne.

So God pushes over the pyramid and everything collapses—a generation later man begins the pyramid business again.

XI^1 A 330 *n.d.*, 1854

« 4232 *Christianity—The State*

Imagine this. Suppose that a coachman sees an absolutely remarkable and utterly faultless five-year-old horse,[507] an ideal horse, snorting and as full of mettle as any he has seen, and he says: "Well, I cannot bid on this horse, nor can I afford it, and even if I could it is quite unsuitable for my use." But after a dozen years, when that remarkable horse is spavined and spoiled etc., the coachman says: Now I can bid on it, now I can pay for it, and now I can make enough profit from it, from what is left in it, so that I can properly see my way to spending a little for its board.

It is the same with the state and Christianity. Of the lofty Christianity which entered into the world, every state is obliged to say: "I cannot buy this religion; not only that, but I will say: God and Father, save me from buying this religion; it would surely be the ruin of me." But when after a few centuries Christianity had become spavined and decrepit and on its last legs, spoiled and muddle-headed, then the state said: See, now I can bid on it; and smart as I am I can see very well that I can use it and profit from it enough so that I can properly see my way to spending a little to polish it up.

If only Christianity, in return for the refurbishing, would play on the state the practical joke of becoming itself again: "Ugh! God and Father, save and preserve us—any state can see that this religion is my ruin." The coachman is sure that he has made a shrewd buy; he runs no risk of the twenty-year-old nag's getting back its five-year-old mettle again, which according to the unanimous opinion of all coachmen would not serve a coachman any more than the state is served by—the eternally young Christianity.

XI^1 A 366   n.d., 1854

« 4233 *A Philosopher on the Throne*

is what Plato[508] wanted. Our age teaches us that a dramatic poet on the throne is a dubious matter.

I mean Louis Napolean.[509] As a poet he realizes that during the review in Boulogne it would create an extraordinary effect to have a courtier arrive on the run with news of the capture of Sebastopol. All right, so it is arranged.

The result, of course, is that the next day all France has *Katzenjammer*,[510] just as after a drunk.

But Napoleon is excellent for prostituting the generation. This generation of windbags deserves a windbag *en gros*[511] for an emperor. How excellent, too, that all mankind's great inventions (railroads, telegraph, etc.) tend to develop and encourage windbaggery. Yet in the process men may turn away from this sort of thing.

XI^1 A 507   n.d., 1854

« 4234 *Numbers–the Idea*

The idea always relates to one, one person is enough, and Christianly everyone can be that one.

Eternity does not count; it is quality, and therefore it is not a matter of numbers, although there are numbers.

When two joined together are related to the idea, number begins, because two indicates number.[512]

Finally the numbers become so overwhelming (when they have reached the millions) that the idea is removed and can be advertised for in the lost and found column in the newspapers.

This is how things stand. In any case, this swindling use of language must be halted and changed: joining together in order to serve the idea better, the truth better, to be able to be spirit better. No, in the realm of ideas and of spirit numbers subtract.

But people join together because they cannot endure being the single one. *Ja, das ist was anders!*⁵¹³ But then let us say it this way and get some truth into the relationship instead of twisting the idea the wrong way and jamming it, making it impossible to be related to spirit at all.

Sociality belongs to the animal definition of being a human being, and it is the cunning device (in every case, instinctively cunning) by which joining together has been connected with spirit. This has made Christendom spiritless or spirit-abandoned and to such a degree that it is jammed, for by confessing that the joining together is out of weakness one is still relating to spirit.

XI¹ A 536   *n.d.*, 1854

« 4235 *Drivel—Maltreatment by Ridicule*
—Persecution by the Public

If I had time, I think I would write a book about this as a guide for future officials of Christianity, because this is what we are headed for, here is the evil, and it is good for an official to have in advance the most concrete possible conception of the suffering and danger.

What makes this kind of abuse so scurvy and thereby exhausting is that it is altogether devoid of factuality, has nothing to go on, but always has the cover-up of being nothing.[*] This again has the result that many who otherwise would restrain themselves out of a sense of shame think that they can participate in this or at least gloat when such things happen to a man, and the person concerned cannot in all decency speak about his mistreatment, for it is designed precisely to destroy his conception of himself.

And yet this abuse is so odious that it is comparable to fights between wild beasts in pagan times, except that this is within culture and refinement or polish, and it is covered up by the hypocritical appearance of being nothing at all, which is even more infamous; it is like being cast to the wild animals and having to fight them, except that here men undertake to be the beasts and at the same time hide their infamy under its being nothing at all.

What has weakened and weakens governments and renders them impotent is that they are able to use only massive means. But massive means *first* of all to place responsibility on those who use them and, *second,* to give pathos and recognizability to those against whom they are used.

But as the world grows older and consequently more demoralized, infamy also becomes greater. Then the public becomes the tyrant, one who hypocritically hides under being nothing—and then assassination makes its appearance. The insidious attack whereby responsibility is evaded (for, after all, the public is nobody) and the insidious attack whereby the one persecuted is deprived of pathos, the pathos of recognizability. Miniscule means, but many to use them, slight but continuous, something not worth talking about but which everybody talks about, saying it is not worth talking about, a trifling matter but over a long time—this is what is used. In the most loathsome way the public is power, power like bedbugs or a foul smell, which always has the advantage of denying pathos to the one being abused. What a nauseating kind of blood-lust—the thirst for a man's blood, not like a lion's or a tiger's, no, but like that of a louse or a legion of lice! The most loathsome of all kinds of tyranny—the tyranny of lice, and the most loathsome of all the bootlickers of tyrants, you timeservers of tyrants, of the lice: "the journalists." Praise be mankind! It advances in culture and refinement.

Of course, the public naturally wants to have only secret knowledge of this state of affairs—for if this were made known, it would constitute an attempt to divest the public of its power. Therefore the public fosters the impression that there is nothing. But generally the public knows the true situation very well. The public is well aware, for example, that four shillings is very little but that a subscription of four shillings over the whole country is a great deal. The public also knows that one of these ordinary men is *so viel wie nichts,*[514] but that 10,000 such ditto ditto are a kind of power. And so it is in many situations. But in connection with slander, the ridicule of envy, gossipy prattle, etc., the public does not want to be informed—partly so that there can be no question of responsibility, partly, as stated, in order not to lose its power.

As far as I am concerned, I do not complain. For one thing, in the course of time the whole thing comes to mean something different to me, becomes a welcome occasion for a love-understanding with God. After all, gifts from God ought to be the most precious of all to a man, and if he now happens, *si placet,*[515] to have the singularity, *si placet,* that his gifts are in the form of tortures, may it not still be the same, that they are from his hand.

But even if this were not the case, I still do not complain; as a psychologist I am satisfied. A physician who would complain that the disease he is treating is malignant would be a queer fellow. No, I have wanted to get to know men, and I could not have been more strategically placed to gain a knowledge of men, which has had infinite value for me, although at the same time it teaches me, I must say, that there is very little value in men.

XI^2 A 23 n.d., 1854

« 4236

[*] *In margin of 4235* (XI^2 A 23):
Note. And it may be noted that one can endure the persecution of the public if one makes himself secure by having a high office and is thereby a power or if one is a rich English gentleman. But in neither case is there a true official of Christianity. No, to be nothing and then to receive what a cabinet minister may receive—this is the proper Christian context, making sure that the official is not a politician who transforms Christianity into politics.

XI^2 A 24 n.d.

« 4237 *The Condition of Things in the Established Order*

How fundamentally corrupt everything is is shown by the fact that everyone more or less clearly knows, but no one will say, that all, guilty in varying degrees, stick together loyally like conspirators to prevent its being said—how false the established order is.

This again explains why one single person is enough; only one person is needed to say it right out. This is the nemesis hanging over such dishonesty, that one person is sufficient—just let it be said, heard, and everything is changed, then fire is set in the haunts of the philistines.[516]

But of course for this reason it can be rather dangerous to have to be the one to say it, yes, perhaps for this very reason the danger is greatest.

When the conflict is between a clearer insight and one less clear but honest, the struggle seldom gets to be very intense. No, but where it is personally known that things have gone bad and everything is done to conceal the fact and to prevent its being said—it perhaps becomes the most dreadful crime to say it.

Take an illustration: go to a businessman who believes that he is sitting pretty—but you know that he is bankrupt; tell him so . . . . . well, he certainly is not happy to hear it, but he no doubt gives in. But go to a merchant who has known for a long time that he is bankrupt, has underhandedly and cunningly been doing everything possible for a long time to hide the fact that he was bankrupt—show him that he is bankrupt: it will no doubt become a life and death struggle.

The point is that where the deficiency is in knowledge, the truth does not, after all, become a charge against one's character; but where knowledge is present, then the truth becomes criminal.

The dangerous collisions in the world never have occurred where only knowledge was lacking, but always where those actually involved knew very well themselves that they were championing something false, and these collisions get to be the most dangerous of all when those actually involved carry along crowds of men who to a certain extent lack knowledge and to that extent are not entirely dishonest.

My own life has already contributed an illustration of this. When I at one time took on *The Corsair,* there was not a single person in the whole kingdom who had not more than once repeatedly said in private conversation: The paper is an outrage; something ought to be done about it. But—it must not be said publicly. Here is a study of rascality in human demoralization. In private conversation we hypocritically say, "It is an outrage," when, please note, it is guaranteed that envy publicly continues to have its triumphant organ—and this is why there is indignation if someone goes and says it publicly. On the other hand, in every generation there are men who by their position, by their place in society, are committed to witnessing against demoralization. But they, you see, have deserted—and thus it became a crime, an act of madness, that I said it publicly.

But wherever it is not knowledge that is lacking but there is a conspiracy (in which the most different people are interested for different reasons), one person is sufficient, one person who says it. But it is also the most dangerous kind of business.

XI^2 A 85 *n.d.,* 1854

« **4238 *The State***

That the state in a Christian sense is supposed to be what Hegel[517] taught—namely, that it has moral significance, that true virtue can appear only in the state (something I also childishly babbled after him in my dissertation[518]), that the goal of the state is to improve men—is obviously nonsense.

The state is of the evil rather than of the good, a necessary evil, in a certain sense a useful, expedient evil, rather than a good.

The state is human egotism on a large scale and in great dimensions—so far off was Plato when he said that in order to become aware of the virtues we should study them in the state.[519]

The state is human egotism in great dimensions, very expediently and cunningly composed so that the egotisms of individuals intersect each other correctively. To this extent the state is no doubt a safeguard against egotism by manifesting a higher egotism which copes with all the individual egotisms so that these must egotistically understand that egotistically it is the most prudent thing to live in the state. Just as we speak of a calculus of infinitesimals, so also the state is a calculus of egotisms, but always in such a way that it egotistically appears to be the most prudent thing to enter into and to be in this higher egotism. But this, after all, is anything but the moral abandoning of egotism.

The state cannot go beyond this; so to be improved by living in the state is just as doubtful as being improved in a prison. Perhaps one becomes much shrewder about his egotism, his enlightened egotism, that is, his egotism in relation to other egotisms, but less egotistic he does not become, and what is worse, one is spoiled by regarding this official, civic, authorized egotism as virtue—this, in fact, is how demoralizing civic life is, because it reassures one in being a shrewd egotist.

Higher than this the state cannot go, and considered as moral upbringing and growth this must be regarded as very dubious.

Thus the state is continually subject to the same sophistry that engrossed the Greek Sophists—namely, that injustice on a vast scale is justice, that in a very peculiar manner the concepts turn around or flop over,[520] that what counts is to practice it on a vast scale. Furthermore, the state is continually subject to the skepticism that quantity or the numerical defines the concept, that the greatest number is equivalent to the truth.

And then the state is supposed to be counted on to develop men morally, to be the proper medium for virtue, the place where one really can become virtuous! In fact, for such a purpose this place is just as strange as would be the claim that the best place for a watchmaker or an engraver to work is aboard a ship in a heavy sea.

Christianity therefore does not believe that the Christian is to remain in the body politic for the purpose of being morally improved —no, in fact it tells him in advance that it will mean suffering.

But in thieves' slang, of course, the state is said to be morally ennobling—thus we are perfectly secure against anyone's suspecting that the authorized egotism is not virtue.

Generally speaking, it can never be emphasized strongly enough that the immediate, the unrefined, the imprudent, etc., are never as corrupt as the shrewdly prudent. A brazen lecher, blazingly licentious, is perhaps not as corrupt as the lecher who observes decorum. A swindler who, as the saying goes, skins another man, is perhaps not as corrupt as the person who knows precisely how far he dares to go with his swindling and still preserve the reputation and esteem of being a highly respectable man.

XI^2 A 108   *n.d., 1854*

« 4239

If the "pastor" is bound by oath to the New Testament, he cannot defend being paid as he is now, because it is thoroughly unchristian for a third power to intervene between pastor and congregation, to compel the congregation to pay a certain amount, to use the police to collect it, etc.—this the pastor cannot defend if he is bound by oath to the New Testament.

But if he will not bind himself by oath to the New Testament, then the state will presumably not pay him.

XI^2 A 292   *n.d., 1854*

« 4240 *A Teacher of Christianity*

Only in one instance can a teacher of Christianity who is bound by oath to the New Testament justify letting himself be supported by the "state"—namely as a prisoner under arrest, and, please note, a prisoner under arrest for the sake of Christianity.

XI^2 A 352   *n.d., 1854*

« 4241

I do not say that the state cannot in a certain sense be served by the kind of Christianity which is the official Christianity today—if it were only served a bit more competently—on the other hand the state certainly would not be served by the true proclamation of Christianity. But what I do say is that Christianity cannot be served by calling such a thing Christianity; therefore Christianity must demand first and foremost that the pastor preach that what he has hitherto proclaimed as Christianity actually is not Christianity. But this again will be advantageous to the state, for only Christianity in the eminent sense can be dangerous to the state. Thoughtless and idea-less toning down, such as in the official proclamation of Christianity, cannot serve the state—it demoralizes; but modification, yet with just enough truth in it that it is made clear that it is a toning down—this again will have so much rigorousness about it that, looked at from the state's interest, it will be beneficial to the state.

XI^2 A 356   n.d., 1854

« 4242 *"Christian" : "State"*
or
The Union for Mutual Destruction

This is the way it must be if the union is to be of benefit: Christianity, that heterogeneity to finitude, *"resignation"* (for we will not here consider Christianity in its highest truth as the impatience of martyrdom), should provide the counterweight to finitude, the state.

The finite, finite objectives, living for finite objectives, easily cause too great and too fast a pendulum swing either in craving (for the fortunate) or in despair (for the unfortunate). Therefore eternity should be continually introduced counteractingly.

But inasmuch as Christianity came to be served in homogeneity with all finite objectives (something achieved especially in Protestantism, especially in Denmark), Christianity essentially dropped out, eternity dropped out; that which was supposed to represent the eternal became exactly like all other finite things, a living for finite objectives.

The result was that the pendulum swing of finite objectives became extreme, that human existence, so to speak, ignited spontaneously, which is the significance of the 1848 catastrophe and explains why eternity dropped out and why serving it became finitized.

The Christian state does indeed fancy that it takes Christianity along, but this is a misunderstanding. Let me speak metaphorically. Imagine a machine so constituted that there are two wheels originally designed so that the one wheel turns opposite to the direction of the other and by this turning interlocks in counteraction with the turning of the other wheel—if then someone were to claim to have such a machine, demonstrate that it did indeed have both wheels, but, please note, they did not turn in opposite directions but turned together: this would not be true; it is not the same machine.

It is this very heterogeneity of Christianity as "resignation" which is the saving factor for the state. But then Christianity must actually be served in heterogeneity. The ruination of the state is the absorption of Christianity as homogeneity, served by public officeholders, personages of rank, professionals, in short, just as all other finite things are served. "The state" is "politics"; what it needs is something else which is not politics. But Christianity served in homogeneity with all other finite things is also politics.

Therefore the union became the ruination of the state, and of course the ruination of Christianity as well, for only in its heterogeneity is it what it is; the protection of the state (*si placet!*[521]) [is] its ruin.

How is it possible then that this union can come to pass, a union which both simple Christian honesty and true human wisdom must condemn: it is mutual destruction?

This, you see, is what human shrewdness leads to—and here also is its punishment!

The state thought it prudent to accommodate this teaching of eternity and instructions about another world in order to tranquilize people and thus be better able to control them. The state (presumably because of overweening ambition) would not want to accommodate Christianity in its truth (as resignation in character); it would rather have it up to a point, have it in its power, determine how it is to be accommodated—everything is shrewdness. But this shrewdness is not merely short-sighted, it is blasphemy against Christianity.

On their part the clergy thought that it was very prudent to accept the protection of the state. The clergy understood, all right, that it is considerably more pleasant to be a hired servant of the state than to serve Christianity according to the understanding of the New Testament. But this prudence was short-sighted, and it was blasphemy against Christianity.

Therefore the punishment came: the pendulum swings of finitude became more powerful. [*Changed from:* finitude's impatience set fire to the whole thing, a kind of spontaneous combustion.]

What the craving, fortunate ones needed in their impatience was to get to see that there is an eternity, a goal of eternity to live for: this is tempering. But they failed to see that; they merely came to see that describing eternity and living for the goal of eternity were made into a finite endeavor just like any other, rewarded by all the things of this earth.

What the despairing ones needed to come to see was that there is an eternity, a goal of eternity to live for, and that the things of this earth are gladly renounced for the sake of this goal. But they failed to see this; however, what they did come to see was that describing eternity and living for the goal of eternity were made into a finite endeavor just like any other, rewarded by all the things of this earth.

After all, the state, certainly from earlier experiences, ought to have learned this much from God's administration, that what the people really need is not to be made fools of, that it is a sin to exploit what unfortunately is true—that men want to be deceived—and that it also is shortsighted, for when the goal is reached it always ends with frightful revolutions, the punishment for the shortsightedness of shrewdness and for the outrage of wanting in this way to make capital of Christianity for finite ends and for wanting to "use" the divine as an element in statecraft.

XI^3 B 126 *n.d.*, 1855

SOCRATES

« 4243

In Clausen and Hohlenberg's *Tidsskrift for udenlandsk theologisk Litteratur*, 1837, no. 3, pp. 485–534,[522] there is a fragment of an article by Baur[523] on the Christian elements in Platonism which drives right into my own study of irony and humor; this must be the case particularly with the portion omitted from the journal,[524] since one of its particular tasks is to develop the concept "irony." (To what extent Baur has become conscious of the Christian contrast in humor[525] I still do not know, of course, as I have not read the article.) In his parallel between Christ and Socrates on page 529 [p. 528] there are some very good things. Just as in paganism the divine usually belongs only to the subjective representation, and thus always has the human [p. 529] as its presupposition and foundation, so that precisely this, the human subjectivity of the divine, is paganism's greatest characteristic, just so even such a remarkable personality as Socrates is regarded only from the standpoint of the human.

II A 186   November 1, 1837

« 4244

In the case of Socrates it was an irony of fate or of life that Xantippe frequently made him celebrated, that he was more or less henpecked.

Also his similarity to his most ill-tempered enemies, the Sophists, with whom he could easily be confused.

Socrates was the ugliest of men.[526]

III B 8   n.d., 1840–41

« 4245

How abstract Socrates' dialectic was can also be seen in the basic law for the dialectical movement, which is that only two things can be the opposite of each other (*principium exclusi medii inter duo contradictoria*[527]). See *Phaedrus*, p. 218;[528] *Protagoras*, p. 155;[529] *Republic*, Schleiermacher, pp. 245, 246 etc.[530] (the dichotomous throughout the *Sophist*).[531]

III B 27   n.d., 1841

« **4246** *Caricature*

Socrates was the ugliest man in Athens and had the most shrewish wife around—one more reason for him to spend so much time on the streets. He was first a sculptor but gave up this profession when he began playing the genius. He had a little property (perhaps he had invested it on good terms with one or another of the businessmen or shopkeepers with whom he associated); no doubt he ate into his capital later, and therefore it was no wonder that he always was at hand when a banquet took place (for this reason both Xenophon and Plato have a symposium, however different their interpretations otherwise are); he did not wish to have any fixed occupation and therefore, in order to have his future secured nevertheless, he wanted to be maintained as a pensioner in the Prytaneum, and in this way he would pass through the two categories vagabonds are accustomed to pass through—that of being a capitalist and of being a pensioner.

He was a lecturer who never left the city (see *Crito,* Heyse, p. 150 middle and bottom;[532] see *Phaedrus,* Ast, I, p. 133, Phaedrus's speech[533]).

He was very absentminded; for this reason some have wanted to explain the ambiguous passage in Aristophanes' *Clouds* as an absentminded error. See Rötscher, p. 284 etc.[534]

The whole collection of quotations in Süvern, p. 3 etc.,[535] Rötscher, p. 277 etc.[536]

He was discontented with the established order; therefore he loafed around everywhere; this also had a basis in his unfortunate marriage, for although he had the benefit of his wife as riding masters have of wild horses by learning to constrain them (See Forchammer, p. 49, bottom[537]), it was nevertheless natural that he often sought out strangers, all the more because he seldom saw strangers at home (the story about Xantippe's getting angry; see Plutarch 11, 41 A, B[538]).

He was not constituted like other men, was never sick, not even during the horrible plague during the time of the Peloponnesian war. See Heinsius, p. 5.[539]

He learned to dance when he was sixty years old because the motion was so superb. (See Diogenes Laertius.[540])

III B 30 *n.d.,* 1841

« **4247**

Actually it was Cato who first declared that Socrates was a *Schwatzer*[541] who wanted to turn things topsy-turvy for his people. See

Plutarch in *Life of Cato*, ch. 23. (found in the Danish translation, III, p. 450.⁵⁴²)

IV A 199   *n.d.*, 1842–43

« 4248

In his *De genio Socratis,* Plutarch⁵⁴³ tells that Socrates' father had received the oracle about his son stating that he must compel him in no way but allow him to follow his inclinations completely.
See Tennemann, *Geschichte der Philosophie,* II, p. 30 note.⁵⁴⁴

IV A 200   *n.d.*, 1842–43

« 4249

Two quotations concerning his relation to Xantippe, which I have never seen referred to otherwise but found in Antoninus, *Philosophus ad se ipsum,* XI, para. 23 and 28.⁵⁴⁵

> Moreover, I have indicated the best of *Diogenes Laertius*⁵⁴⁶ in my copy of the Danish translation. The article in Bayle⁵⁴⁷ also contains a few things.

IV A 202   *n.d.*, 1842–43

« 4250

Something of the former in the dialogue *Alcibiades primus* (about how Socrates went looking for Alcibiades), although Schleiermacher⁵⁴⁸ rightly assumes this dialogue to be spurious and the interpretation of Socrates incorrect but useful.

IV A 203   *n.d.*, 1842–43

« 4251

That Socrates is supposed to have gotten up in the theater during the performance of *The Clouds* is told by Aelian, *Var. hist.,* II, ch. 13 (found in Flögel, *Geschichte der comischen Literatur,* IV, p. 64⁵⁴⁹).

IV A 204   *n.d.*, 1842–43

« 4252

Socrates is mentioned as using the parable
> Aristotle, *Rhetoric,* II, ch. 20.⁵⁵⁰ The same passage is usually cited as an example of an incorrect analogical conclusion. See Trendlenburg,⁵⁵¹ *Erlaüterungen zu den Elementen der aristotelischen Logik,* Berlin, 1842, p. 79.⁵⁵²

IV A 205   *n.d.*, 1842–43

« 4253

Socrates' discourse on death in Plato's *Apology* is mentioned in Plutarch's *Consolations to Appolonius*, para. 12 etc.[553]

IV A 206   *n.d.*, 1842–43

« 4254

Socrates' answer to Archelaus

    Aristotle's *Rhetoric*, II, ch. 23 (in the little translation, p. 199[554]); see also Antoninus, *Philosophus*,[555] the portion cited in this volume.

IV A 207   *n.d.*, 1842–43

« 4255

There are very important passages in Flögel, *Geschichte der Hofnarren*, pp. 96, 97.[556]

IV A 208   *n.d.*, 1842–43

« 4256

See the conclusion of Aristophanes' *The Frogs*.[557]

    For it is excellent not to sit with Socrates, gossiping and denigrating the art of poetry etc.

IV A 209   *n.d.*, 1842–43

« 4257

In *The Wasps*, ll. 1075–79, Aristophanes[558] himself names the evil of which he wanted to cleanse the state with *The Clouds:* idleness and legal trickery.

IV A 210   *n.d.*, 1842–43

« 4258

Socrates has also been depicted by two other comic poets: Ameipsias in the comedy *Konnos* and Eupolis.[559] See Krag's translation, p. 272.[560]

See the same book, p. 268, note: it is impossible to repudiate completely the Roman's harsh words[561] declaring that he talked about virtue, corrupted the morals, and as a citizen was dangerous to public freedom.

IV A 211   *n.d.*, 1842–43

« 4259

Plutarch[562] relates (*vitæ paralelæ: Aristides*, ch. 1) that Demetrius of Phaleron reports that Socrates not only owned his own house but also had accumulated funds amounting to 70 minas, which he had deposited at interest with Cato.

IV A 212 n.d., 1842–43

« 4260

What Socrates says in the *Cratyllus* is beautiful—namely, that to be deceived by oneself is the worst of all, for when the deceiver does not go away even for a moment but is constantly present, how could it fail to be dreadful?

Cratyllus, para. 428. Schleiermacher translation, II, 2, p. 104.[563]

IV A 124 n.d., 1843

« 4261

Do you not know that suicide is called *an outbreak* because the living are imprisoned, and it is called desertion because "the living are soldiers on duty."[564] (Socrates).[565]

V A 113 n.d., 1844

« 4262

I wonder if Socrates was that cold; I wonder if it did not hurt him that Alcibiades could not understand him.[566]

V B 4:3 n.d., 1844

« 4263

Socrates knew this, and frequently it certainly does take Socratic boldness to see it again, as it took boldness to see it then, as it took boldness to understand then that Alcibiades did not owe Socrates more than Socrates owed him, something which in its presently adopted formulation is easier to grasp—that one person, insofar as he is a believer, does not owe another person anything, but both face to face with the god owe him everything.[567]

V B 23:1 n.d., 1844

« 4264

Socrates is thought to have been so popular and one hears a lot of excited babbling about this:[568] Nonsense! All that about walking and talking with shoemakers and tanners etc. was ironically directed against the "academic philosophers," and it amused him that it appeared as if they spoke the same language (he and the shoemaker) because they used the same expressions—but Socrates understood something entirely different by it.

VII^1 A 65 n.d., 1846

« 4265 *Why Did Socrates Compare Himself with a Gadfly?*[569]

Because he wanted to have only ethical significance. He did not want to be admired as a genius who stood apart from others and who therefore essentially made the lives of others easy, since they might say: It's easy enough for him—he's a genius. No, he did only what every man can do; he understood only what every man understands.[570] Therein lies the epigrammatic quality. He bit hard into the individual, constantly compelling and teasing him with this universal. In this way he was a gadfly who prodded by means of the individual's own passion, who did not permit him to admire and admire, comfortably and effeminately, but demanded himself from him.[571] When a person has ethical powers, people will gladly make him out to be a genius merely to get him out of the way, for his life contains a demand.

VII^1 A 69 *n.d.*, 1846

« 4266

The fact that many of Plato's dialogues end without a result has a far deeper basis than I had thought earlier.[572] They are a reproduction of Socrates' maieutic skill which makes the reader or hearer himself active, and therefore they do not end in a result but in a sting. This is an excellent parody of the modern rote-method which says everything the sooner the better and all at one time, which awakens no self-action but only leads the reader to rattle it off like a parrot.

VII^1 A 74 *n.d.*, 1846

« 4267

Socrates feared most of all to be in error.[573] If physiology and the natural sciences had any enlightenment to give on the concept of spirit —how would I dare omit studying them. But simple Socrates would also quite correctly regard this science as a delusion (sham-science) and out of fear of being in error would leave it alone—yes, renounce it, so that he would not come to waste his whole life in a conceited and bustling approximation.

VII^1 A 193 *n.d.*, 1846

« 4268

Men really cannot be blamed for resisting every time "a gadfly" (Socrates[574]) through his own strenuous existence makes a demand upon them. Yet this battle really is not for altar and hearth but rather for sofa and bedstead.

VIII¹ A 154 *n.d.*, 1847

« 4269

If Socrates' defense is not as I believe it to be—irony, in order to make game of everybody—then the argument against its authenticity arises: it is unlikely that Socrates would want to defend himself.

VIII¹ A 281 *n.d.*, 1847

« 4270

The difficulty with Socrates is not to understand his teaching but to understand Socrates himself: how much more so with regard to Christ. By this a period is put to all speculation, for its secret is to turn the whole thing around.

VIII¹ A 490 *n.d.*, 1847

« 4271

Socrates, although called a popular philosopher, *quoad doctrinam*, is and was and will be *essentially* unpopular. How many have understood, how many are there in each generation (and in this sphere the progress of a generation accomplishes nothing at all; for every individual the task begins from the beginning) who understand that thought could have such power over a man that he went to his death for thought, acting upon it. This is the heroic, and the heroic is essentially just as unpopular in every generation. But the heroic is related to every single individual; every single individual could become a hero. Heroism is not connected with the differences between man and man (to be a genius, artist, poet, of noble birth etc.)—no, heroism is virtuosity in the universally human. Heroism is being great in that which everyone could be.

To call Socrates a genius is a profound stupidity. If he had been a genius, he would not have been related to the universally human (that is, to every man) but would have been on the outside and thus would not have been a gadfly.[575]

VIII¹ A 491 *n.d.*, 1847

« 4272

Socrates' smile.[576] This smile was thought to be malicious, but it was not. It was because his one and only joy and pleasure was to have it out with another and to question him empty—this was why he smiled. Think of an artist (who of course has nothing to do with cross-examining others). The moment an idea for a great work of art really becomes clear to him, he smiles. It is the same with a thinker when he has really comprehended something. If fishing were not so prosaic an art, the fisherman would also smile when the fish bites. This is the smile of intellectuality.

VIII^1 A 520 n.d., 1848

« 4273

Socrates[577] loved young men, and why? Because there is a breath of the infinite in them, and it was this he wished to preserve.

Take Mynster,[578] he really does not love young men; he loves demoralized men, men who are demoralized by having to make finite goals into the earnestness of life—they can also be dominated.

X^1 A 591 n.d., 1849

« 4274

In the sermon on the Gospel for the Fourth Sunday after Easter, Zacharias Werner[579] says that he pointed out in the sermon on the two who walked to Emmaus that Christ was being asked questions constantly. And in today's Gospel he says in turn: None of you asks me, "Where are you going?"

Here, perhaps, is a feature of the contrast between Christianity and paganism: Socrates is the questioner and Christ is the one who is questioned.

X^2 A 67 n.d., 1849

« 4275

What Socrates[580] really meant by wanting to have "the poets" expelled from the state was that by writing in the medium of the imagination instead of precipitating men into ethical realization in actuality, the poets spoiled them and weaned them or kept them from it.

One could be tempted by and large to make the same charge against "pastors" today.

Yes, compared to Socrates Plato himself is a misunderstanding. Only Socrates managed to hold his uncompromising position of continually expressing the existential, constantly remaining in the present —thus he had no doctrine, no system and the like, but had one in action. Plato took his time—with the help of this enormous illusion there came to be doctrine. By degrees the existential disappeared from view and the doctrine grew dogmatically broader and broader.

x^2 A 229 *n.d.*, 1849

« 4276

Talleyrand[581] (when Mirabeau described what attributes a deputy ought to have and meant himself) said, "You forget one—he ought to be pockmarked." He would have been still more ironical if he had said: You forget *one, but of course it is self-evident*—he ought to be pockmarked. That would have been more Socratic.

x^2 A 248 *n.d.*, 1849

« 4277

Socrates is actually a martyr to the numerical, the sacrifice that voting has demanded.[582]

x^2 A 449 *n.d.*, 1850

« 4278 *Socrates*

It is nevertheless clear that it was Socrates' very defense which embittered the judges and made them condemn him to death.[583]

Socrates had been regarded as an eccentric who as such was allowed for the most part to shift for himself.

Then he was accused. The accusation itself did not mean much. But then the accusation-situation became the situation which made it clear what there really was to Socrates. The elevated self-esteem with which he related ironically to the *summa summarum*[584] of the whole popular assembly, unwilling to defend himself but only jesting with them: this actually became the deciding factor. His behavior as the accused had embittered the people to the point where he was actually condemned for this behavior and the accusation was transformed into the occasion.

This was also correctly perceived by Wieland in his *Aristipp und seine Zeit,* II, pp. 12 and 18;[585] there are also some good observations on pp. 38, 39, 40, but from the other side; here the question also arises, but very briefly, whether Socrates out of solicitude for the Athenians, ought to have run away (one is reminded here of H.H.'s two essays[586]); see also pp. 55 etc.

x^2 A 598 *n.d.*, 1850

« 4279 *Socrates—the Ideal*

Socrates did not have the true ideal, neither the conception of sin[587] nor that the salvation of man requires a crucified god. The watchword of his life therefore could never be: The world has been crucified to me, and I to the world.[588] Therefore he maintained irony, which expresses only his elevation over the world's shabbiness. But for a Christian irony is insufficient; it can never come up to the dreadful fact that salvation means God crucified, although for a time irony can be used in Christendom for awakening.

x^3 A 253 *n.d.*, 1850

« 4280 *A Socrates in Christendom*

Socrates could not prove the immortality of the soul. He simply said: This matter occupies me so much that I will order my life as if there were an immortality—should there not be any, all right, I still will not regret my choice, for this subject is the only thing that occupies me.

How much Christendom would already have been helped if there were someone who said and did the following: I do not know if Christianity is true, but I want to order my whole life as if Christianity were the truth, risk my life on it—if it is not truth, all right, I still will not regret my choice, for it is the only thing that occupies me.

x^3 A 315 *n.d.*, 1850

« 4281 *A Passage in My Dissertion*

Influenced as I was by Hegel and whatever was modern, without the maturity really to comprehend greatness, I could not resist pointing out somewhere in my dissertation[589] that it was a defect on the part of Socrates to disregard the whole and only consider numerically[590] the individuals.

What a Hegelian fool I was! It is precisely this that powerfully demonstrates what a great ethicist Socrates was.

x^3 A 477 *n.d.*, 1850

« 4282 *Plato's* Republic, *Book VI*[591]

Here someone raises an objection to Socrates, who praises philosophers, that the common opinion is that some of philosophy's adherents are incompetent and others, the majority, are quite contemptible—to this Socrates answers that this is because so many incompetents have usurped the name of philosopher.

But here Socrates does not reduplicate his polemic view of life: that the common opinion (of the crowd) regards the true good as foolish; here Socrates simply accepts the common opinion as correct, whereas the mistake is rooted in the fact that so many incompetents have pushed themselves forward as being philosophers and want to be regarded as that. Naturally Socrates must therefore assume that the true philosopher would also be recognized as such by public opinion, but this is directly contrary to Socrates' polemical view of life and contrary to what his own life witnesses.

x⁴ A 250   *n.d.*, 1851

« **4283 *Socrates*⁵⁹²**

would not use the speech which was offered him. He found it inappropriate, beneath his dignity, to use this artfully contrived, elegant presentation—he wanted to speak *ex tempore*. And the person in whom a point of view is a life, an existentiality, a presence, will also have enough well-considered remarks to give at any time if he merely, so to speak, turns on the faucet; he will also be suspicious of the elaborately prepared speech which both distracts him personally and leads the listener's thoughts to something other than what is important.

From a religious point of view, speaking ought to be *ex tempore* also for this reason. This way a person is unable to have at his disposal all those cunning and cautious turns and shadings of speech with which one protects himself, but it is far better for him just to come out with it.

Furthermore, it is beneficially humbling for a man to talk *ex tempore*. It can very easily be pure pleasure to sit and compose, and it is again a pleasure to be conscious that one is not saying a single word that is not painstakingly, artistically chosen.

Finally, if a person actually is able to work out a speech in detail, it becomes a wasted labor, for not one in a thousand in the audience is advanced enough to be able to listen at that level. The listener will forget one point after the other and miss most of it. And the speaker also wastes far too much: first the time used in composing the speech and then all the time spent memorizing it.

x⁴ A 314   *n.d.*, 1851

« **4284 *Socrates***

How normal! First he occupies himself with nature (natural science, astronomy, etc.) and then goes over to dealing with men as an ethicist and stays with that.

In our modern times it goes just the other way. We begin by being involved with men and, tired of that, turn to nature. For example, Rousseau.

x⁴ A 319 *n.d.*, 1851

« 4285 *Socrates' Way of Life*

It is told that he never went out of Athens (that is, from the time he began to philosophize ethically), and he himself declares somewhere in the introduction to one of Plato's dialogues[593]: One learns nothing from the trees, but one can learn something from men in the city. I will not ask: But did he learn anything from men? I am thinking of something else.

Consequently he continually moved about in the human swarm. This can express his power, express that he could hold on to his thoughts in the midst of the swarm.

But it can also be an expression for his weakness, his limitation—that in one sense he needed men.

The point is this. Socrates is a skeptic, but a skeptic who is ethically in character. But a skeptic nevertheless. His life is a hypothetical experiment, and the heroic character of it is this enduring to the end, his becoming a martyr for it, but again in character, without pathos, etc. —thus one gets the impression: it could be a unique experience to be condemned to death.

He is a skeptic. His reflection has quite appropriately reached the point where it stops.

If Socrates had lived as an ascetic in rural solitude, it is a question whether he would have endured it.

Simply because he is brought to a standstill at the infinite negative—he has to be in the swarm, he needs men in order to carry on his experiment with them, ever new men, even as a fisherman needs fish.

This fills his life, it is true, but one could also ask whether he himself did not need it in order to fill his life.

x⁴ A 333 *n.d.*, 1851

« 4286 *Ignorance—Faith*

Socrates believed that he was divinely commissioned to show that all are ignorant—quite right, at that time divinity had not let itself be heard from.

But after the revelation has been shared with men, the question is (*ad modum* the Socratic: Do you know something or do you not know something): Do you believe or do you not?

x⁴ A 334 *n.d.*, 1851

« 4287 *Dying to the World*

was indeed also Socratic.
Theaetetus: διὸ καὶ πειρᾶσθαι χρὴ ἐνθένδε ἐκεῖσε φυγεῖν ὅτι τάχιστα. φυγὴ δὲ ὁμοίωσις θεῷ κατὰ τὸ δυνατόν.[594]
Quoted from Meiners, *Ethik,* I, p. 211 (Göttingen, 1800).[595]

x⁴ A 463 n.d., 1852

« 4288 *Socrates*

He is still the only one of his kind, a true intellectual hero. In pathos he is so self-contained that he never shares pathos in common with others but always prevents this communication by means of irony —so little does he need others.

He is sentenced to death. We read Xenophon's *Apology*[596] and sense Socrates throughout. He is preoccupied with the thought that he is an old man now, seventy years old, thus death can never come at a more opportune time. Furthermore, drinking poison is a pleasant mode of dying.

Just as someone might say: My stomach has been out of order for several days; I believe I will take some pills for my digestion—so Socrates drinks the poison. O, you grand master of irony!

Cicero (in *Tusculan Disputations*[597] says it splendidly: He (Socrates) drinks the poison as if he were drinking to quench his thirst. I would add (this appears in *Phædo*[598]): He drinks it festively as if it were a delight.

x⁴ A 467 n.d., 1852

« 4289 *Inversion*

was characteristic of Socrates even in his time, but of course a whole quality lower than in Christianity, a developed philosophy of inversion.

Aelianus[599] (in *Variæ historiæ*) tells of an artist who was commissioned to paint a rolling horse. The artist painted a horse in full jump. When the owner complained and said that was not what he had ordered, the artist replied: Turn the picture upside down and you will have what you asked for. —This, says Aelianus, is the way Socrates talks; he must be understood inversely.

This is excellent! When I wrote my dissertation on irony I had not read Aelianus, but how remarkable that nobody brought him to my attention!

x⁴ A 490 n.d., 1852

« 4290 *Socrates—the Others*

Socrates always talked only about food and drink—but basically he was always talking about and always thinking about the infinite.

The others always talk about the infinite, and in the loftiest tones, but basically they are always talking and always thinking about food and drink, money, profit.

X^4 A 497   *n.d.*, 1852

« 4291 *Socrates*

How sublime! He is accused among other things of not fearing the nation's gods. He is condemned to death. His friends want to help him get out of prison. No, answers Socrates,[600] if I were to flee, it would, after all, substantiate the accusation that I do not fear the nation's gods!

X^4 A 530   *n.d.*, 1852

« 4292 *Socrates*

In books, articles, sermons etc. we often find this phrase: Time does not permit us to develop this further etc.

How infinitely witty Socrates[601] was. When he was condemned, after the sentence was passed, he tells the judges that he is well aware that he will not be able to convince them of his innocence, "because the time is too short for that" or he has "conversed with them for too brief a time." However, he assumes that if there were not such a rush and he could converse properly with them, he would certainly be successful.

X^4 A 598   *n.d.*, 1852

« 4293 *The Authentically Socratic*

In his defense Socrates[602] does not say a word in the beginning about the sacrifices he has really made—no, he says that because he has been so busy going around working with the single individual, "he has not had time to occupy himself with politics or earning money, but has lived in extreme poverty."

With pathos one may say: I have lived in poverty in order to serve my cause; irony puts it this way: I have not had time to earn money.

X^4 A 599   *n.d.*, 1852

« 4294 *Socrates*

The new literature about him is engrossed in the question of the extent to which he does or does not agree with the Sophists. If it is assumed that he does, then it is hard to explain that he was the Sophists' most dangerous opponent. But if he was the Sophists' most dangerous opponent, then the old order would surely have been delighted in him, and then his being condemned becomes inexplicable.

The matter is quite simple. The Sophists were the most dangerous enemies of the old. And Socrates was the very man to make cabbage soup of them. In order to be able to do a thorough job of it, he had to move so far out that the old order became anxious and afraid of him. The Sophists can be radically slain only by the Socratic; but this radicality is again too much for the old order, for something old and a radical cure are not compatible.

My own life has taught me this, even if on a smaller scale. The party or the parties of change are dangerous to the established order. It is clear, and Mynster[603] himself acknowledges it, that I am the person who can best cope with them. But, but in order to do it I must take the matter so far out that Mynster becomes almost afraid of me. Mynster thinks it is enough to do a bungling repair job, a little piecing and patching—but a radical job—no, that is too much.

x^5 A 69 *n.d.*, 1853

« **4295** *Contrasts*

Bernard of Clairvaux preaches crusades; under the open heavens (see the passage in Böhringer[604]) thousands and thousands are assembled; he cannot even finish before the crowd roars: The Cross, the Cross[605]— —this is working in the direction of the animal-category, to work men together into—a crowd.

O Socrates, you noble wise man. In the midst of the crowd, surrounded by these thousands and thousands, you work—to split up the "crowd" and to seek "the single individual"—this is the spirit-category of what it is to be man.

Bernard is a Christian, and this takes place in Christendom—and Socrates is a pagan—and yet there is more Christianity in the Socratic approach than in Saint Bernard's.

x^5 A 133 *n.d.*, 1853

« **4296** *Socratic Ignorance*

also means: primitivity, inwardness; it means: away with all this rubbish of historical knowledge about how these thousands and thousands, the others, have conducted themselves, lived, etc.—I will be alone with the idea.

And what "Christendom" needs on the largest possible scale is simply one man (not an aping of what it means to be a man, an aping of "the others," the historical etc.), one man—and then the New Testament—one man alone with God's word, this secured by Socratic ignorance.

XI^1 A 15 *n.d.*, 1854

« 4297 *Socrates—Christianity*[606]

Socrates is right: if a man does not do the right, it is because he does not understand it; if he understood it, he would do it—ergo, sin is ignorance.

Christianity is right: sin is guilt. It is quite correct that if a man does not do the right it is because he does not understand it; if he understood it etc. etc. But he does not understand the right because he is unable to understand the right, and he is unable to understand the right because he does not *want* to understand it—see, here it comes.

Only by treating everything as criminal has Christianity coped with the world and managed to maintain justice.

XI^1 A 318 *n.d.*, 1854

« 4298

Father, forgive them, for they know not what they do.[607]

The Socratic view that sin is ignorance[608] is not implied here.

XI^1 A 334 *n.d.*, 1854

« 4299 *O Socrates,*

you were and are, after all, the only philosopher in the realm of the purely human.

The so-called Christian philosophers—what muddleheads! Take the much acclaimed Augustine! Somewhere[609] he argues with the Donatists something like this: What do a dozen men like you think you are against the whole Christian Church, as if a dozen men like you possessed the truth. O Socrates, can this be called a philosopher! He argues concerning truth on the basis of numbers. And a Christian thinker! Whereas Christianity is related to the category of the single individual.

XI^1 A 371 *n.d.*, 1854

« 4300 *Socrates——Alcibiades*

Why did Alcibiades[610] weep when Socrates spoke ("When he speaks, my heart pounds, pounds more violently than the Corybantes', tears stream from my eyes")?

Without a doubt Alcibiades was a man who knew how to express himself, knew how to choose the appropriate expression. Now if Alcibiades looked upon Socrates as an ironist with an unparalleled ability in playing tricks, it would be odd to speak this way of him; Alcibiades might rather have said: One could almost die laughing listening to Socrates.

Why did Alcibiades weep, then? It is easy to see that Socrates, simply because he was a true ironist, used irony to conceal the ideals. But at times he had also brought them out in the open. It was at such times that he so deeply moved Alcibiades.

Alcibiades wept, tears streamed from his eyes, his heart pounded violently—for the simple reason that Socrates brought him to the agony into which a frivolous intellectual lacking in character can be brought by a man of character. Alcibiades had enough ideality and intelligence to be seized and enthralled by the ethical ideal which Socrates presented—but he could not master his lower nature. Therefore it became a matter of tears and a pounding heart—if, as Socrates would probably have said, it had become a matter of ethical action, the tears and the pounding of the heart presumably would have stopped.

XI^1 A 428   *n.d.,* 1854

« 4301 *What Is Deceptive about Socrates*

What is deceptive about Socrates is that his irony is so witty and his intellect so superior that a person is tempted to forget completely that what he is dealing with is simultaneously a matter of life and death.

We read Plato's *Apology* and are enthralled: how extremely witty he is, how pointed every word, how perfect—alas, we who are spoiled by that cursed notion that to be an author is the greatest of all are tempted to read him as if he were an author, a witty author who probably would even get an A-plus from the journals—but for Socrates the stakes are life and death.

On a smaller scale something like this is apparent in my life. For my personal existence has much greater value and is strenuous in a way quite different from my writings. But this is completely misunderstood by this theatrical generation, who, like the elf-maidens, are hollow in the back and no doubt also date their origin from theatrical marriages.

But Socrates is the only one of his kind! Such a cultivated intellect, so very subtly educated and sharpened that presumably such a man would need all the coddling and all the remoteness from actuality that a poet, an artist, needs—and then to be the toughest character in Greece, one who does not produce in a study but in the most crucial actuality, with everything at stake and face to face with death, infuses this subtle intellect so subtly into every line, so magnificently into even the most unimportant turn.

What my pseudonyms frequently say could be said of Socrates: His life is not a drama for men but for the gods; spectators such as he required are found almost as rarely as a Socrates.

Socrates would himself understand this in the same way; for here we see how true and how Socratic was this Socratic principle: to understand, truly to understand, is to be. For us more ordinary men this divides and becomes twofold: it is one thing to understand and another to be. Socrates is so elevated that he does away with this distinction —and therefore we are unable to understand him, understand him in the most profound, the Socratic, sense. I can depict Socrates at a distance, but I doubt that as a contemporary I could have endured him.

Outside of Christianity Socrates is the only man of whom it may be said: he explodes existence, which is seen quite simply in his elimination of the separation between poetry and actuality. Our lives are such that a poet portrays ideality—but actuality is a devil of a lot different. Socrates is an ideality higher than any poet is able to poetize it, and he actually is this, it is his actuality. This is why it is all wrong for Oehlenschläger[611] to want to poetize Socrates. In relation to Socrates "the poet" is a completely superfluous person who can only become an object of ridicule, a laughing-stock, when he does not keep the proper distance but even wants to poetize him. What does it mean to poetize? It means to contribute ideality. The poet takes an actuality which lacks something of ideality and adds to it, and this is the poem. But, good God, Your Lordship, there is no need at all to add anything here; Socrates' ideality is higher, and it is that precisely by being actuality. This is why the poet, when he wants to poetize, finds himself in the same situation as the orator Johannes Climacus[612] tells about, who at the climax of his address confuses the direction and ascends from the higher to the lower; the poet pulls Socrates down—yet I have enough of the Socratic in me to understand that I did not get Oehlenschläger to understand this.

What a wonderful Socratic difficulty! In order to poetize a man it is surely necessary first to understand him. But Socrates himself says: "To understand is to be." O dear poet, if you were able to understand this it would never enter your head to poetize it. Consequently it can be poetized only if it is not understood, or to poetize Socrates is *eo ipso* a misunderstanding, and to praise a poet for having poetized Socrates in a masterpiece makes a fool of him.

A great character but lacking an equivalent intellect can be poetized by poetically adding that equivalent intellect or, conversely, by poetically adding something of character to a superior intellect. But where intellect and character are equally superior, there is nothing for the poet.

How ridiculous for a poet to want to seize hold of Socrates—Socrates' whole intention was to put an end to the poetic and to apply the ethical, the whole point of which is that it is actuality.

XI^1 A 430   *n.d.*, 1854

« **4302** *Enthusiasts*

Lessing[613] makes an accurate observation someplace that the word *Sværmer* [enthusiast] is derived from the word *Schwarm* [swarm] and therefore indicates sociality, this urge to run together in flocks—and thus he cannot be called an enthusiast.

A solitary enthusiast is something so marvelous, a phenomenon as rare as a meteorite, that there is only one such—Socrates.

A solitary enthusiast is just as odd as mixing fire and water, or speaking of a chaste voluptuary or a solitary good mixer, or keeping a liquid in a bottomless vessel! Marvelous Socrates! To keep the highest enthusiasm, to keep it in the most brilliant reflection and wisdom —just as marvelous as keeping liquid in a bottomless vessel. It does not work for the rest of us; if the vessel has no bottom the liquid runs through—and in proportion to the development of our reflection and sagacity something is subtracted from our enthusiasm.

Marvelous Socrates! That was quite a feat you performed, something entirely different from Columbus's egg and all those in a certain sense plebeian tricks. And therefore your feat—O, how I admire you for that righteousness which eternally protects you against the fraternity of the rabble and the mob of professors—your feat differs from the plebeian tricks, for it is no trick at all to do them afterward. No, no, you glorious one, it remains just as difficult—and one thing is certain, no one has done it after you, although every one of that pack of professors and assistant professors no doubt believes he has gone much farther than you, that pack I assume you were quite secretly speaking of when you, as Alcibiades[614] says, continually spoke about pack-asses.

XI[1] A 448 *n.d.*, 1854

« **4303** *Socrates*

It is said that Sardanapalus[615] had the following put on his grave: "I took all the pleasures of life along with me," about which even a pagan[616] has brilliantly observed: How was it possible; even while you lived you could not hold fast to a single one.

It is not possible to take everything along to the grave in this manner; this way the only achievement is to have everything pass through one and have nothing at all to take along to the grave.

No, Socrates is the only person who solved the problem: he took everything, everything, with him to the grave. Marvelous Socrates, you performed a feat which remains eternally just as difficult, if anyone should want to repeat it; you left nothing, nothing, nothing, not even the thinnest thread of a result which a professor could grab onto; no, you took everything along to the grave. This way you kept the highest enthusiasm closed up airtight in the most eminent reflection and sagacity, kept it for eternity—you took everything along. Therefore the professors are disparagingly saying of you now—O, Socrates!—that, after all, you were only a personality, that you did not even have a system.

XI[1] A 449 *n.d.*, 1854

« **4304** *Socrates*

It is related that the father was enjoined by the oracle not to constrain the child.[617] How ingenious! For Socrates, after all, is precisely the subjectivity who is supposed to overthrow Greek objectivity, an ideal heterogeneity.

XI[1] A 527 *n.d.*, 1854

SOLITUDE

« **4305**

It is disastrous enough to be taken by surprise when one is seeking solitude. Yet it depends on whether one is surprised by a wanderer who has lost his way or by a group that probably only seldom comes there, but to have found one's solitary nook and then suddenly to be surprised by a solitary person who is looking for the same thing is just as disastrous as to become the object of an insane man's fixed idea or the fixed idea of a hysterical* female.

In margin: *Politivennen* writes this word *hylsterisk*.[618]

VA 61 *n.d.*, 1844

« **4306**

It is a frightful satire and an epigram on the temporality of the modern age that the only use it knows for solitude is to make it a punishment,[619] a jail sentence. How different from the time when—however secular-minded temporality has always been—men believed in the solitude of the monastery, when they honored solitude as the highest, as a qualification of the eternal—and nowadays it is detested as a curse and is used only as a punishment for criminals. Alas, what a change!

VIII[1] A 40 *n.d.*, 1847

« **4307** *An Excellent Remark by Stilpo,*

which reminds me of what I have said continually, that men have to be taken aside, if possible into the confessional, before there is any use in talking to them about Christianity.

Someone asked Stilpo[620] if the gods found satisfaction in our worshiping and offerings. Stilpo answered: "You are very flippant about this; let us go aside if you want to talk about such things."

I remember having given the matter a similar turn myself. It was up at Gjødvad's.[621] There were a number of us present, including Martin Hammerich,[622] who talked in this cavalier manner about a Christian subject. I answered him: What you are saying sounds fine out here where we are several people in a group; were there still more, it would sound still better. However, if you will go into the adjoining room where we will be alone, you will find that it sounds very mediocre.

In other respects Stilpo's interpretation was something quite different; his main point was that when talking so cavalierly about the gods, one ought to find an out-of-the-way place where he would be sure that the gods did not hear—but such a place is not to be found.

I am reminded of that incomparable story which I have put away some place.[623] A disguised clergyman (who went about disguised simply because of a greater effectiveness in converting people) arranges a tryst with a loose woman. One thing you must promise me, he says —it must be a place where no one, no one can see us, because—imagine the risk I take if we are discovered. She promises. He comes at the appointed time. She takes him to several rooms which she regards as safe, but he thinks otherwise. Finally she takes him out of the city to a remote grotto and says: Here no man can see us; it is possible only for God to see us. The clergyman answers: How do you suppose that God can see us; he is the last one I would want to see me—and thereupon he began to preach so powerfully about God's omnipresence that the woman gave up her former profession. (I got this story from Abraham à St. Clara.[624])

x^3 A 425 *n.d.*, 1850

SOPHISTRY, SOPHISTS

« 4308

Protagoras's[625] proposition that man is the measure of everything is, in the Greek understanding, really a parallel to the witticism of a noncommissioned officer out on the commons. Since the hawker did not have the half-pint measure handy and there was no time to waste because roll call was being sounded, he said: "Just give me the bottle; I have the measure in my mouth."

VII¹ A 235   n.d., 1845–47

« 4309 *The Official Proclamation of Christianity in Christendom Is Sophistical*

To illustrate this, a few words about the ancient Sophists.

To understand them it must be remembered that they were not as Plato represented them. In Plato they are turned inside out. Their essence and innards are disclosed; whereas their actuality was simply cunning, shamming, hypocrisy. After all, it would be a foolish, stupid —and stupid the Sophists were not—self-contradiction on the part of one whose secret was: the task is to appear righteous and good but not be that, for there is certain misery in being that*—it would be a curious self-contradiction, then, to lecture directly about this oneself, for then it would be impossible to put on an appearance, and what was done would be neutralized. No, in actuality they are fighting simply to save appearances: they praise the good etc. (thereby approximating the appearance of being that—but they were not that and thereby they gained all earthly advantages). In his *Geschichte der Wissenschaften* (Lemgo: 1782), part II, p. 208, Meiners[626] describes their lives, according to Philostratus. That beautiful moralistic tale about Hercules at the crossroads is attributed to Prodicus, a Sophist. Gorgias promoted harmony among the Greeks at the Pythian and Olympian games. Hippias described the battles and deeds of the heroes, the famous men, the wise counsel Nestor gave to Neoptolemus after the capture of Troy. Furthermore, the Sophists changed according to the situation: in

Thebes and Sparta they declaimed about virtue, extolled virtue and virtuous men—for this appealed to the people there. In Athens they expatiated on the advantages of poverty and exile, because such rhetoric was appealing there. (See Meiners, I, p. 209. In the note he refers to the passage about Athens: Isocrates in Helen. Encom.) —In short, they were *rhetoricians* and *orators.*

Just as with preachers nowadays, the point is to appear devout but not to be that—for to be devout—well, that entails misery, persecution, etc. In the quiet hours they declaim so movingly—they are moving, they have the appearance of being devout—but in actuality, in character, they shun it—and acquire the goods of this world. But be cautious, take care that no one finds out—the point is to give the appearance. And they do this for money, which both Socrates and Aristotle allege to be a mark of sophistry. And by thus achieving the appearance of being devout, good, righteous, they contribute inversely to the truly righteous man, who suffers as if he were impious and unrighteous. Socrates, too, presents it this way, that the last spiritual trial for the person who in truth wills to be the good is to be treated and regarded as the very opposite, as if he were evil, and he must suffer as such. "He is persecuted or crucified or burned—until he learns too late that the point is not to be the good, no, but to seem to be that."

The appearance of being the good is comedy acting. And comedy acting is all the world is able to take. This, you see, is why these rhetoricians and orators make such a hit.

O Socrates, Socrates, Socrates!

* Note. It was not without deep feeling that I read again the quotation from Plato's *Republic*[627] where the Sophist presents this formulation. Socrates did see the truly ethical so clearly—alas, and then think of Christendom, which is far ahead of Socrates!

x^4 A 466   *n.d.*, 1852

« **4310** *The Sophists*

In the second part of Meiners' *Geschichte der Wissenschaften,*[628] in the section on the Sophists, right at the end, I see that the Sophists later (after Socrates' death) sank in esteem to the point that they were not even allowed to be witnesses in court.

Splendid, splendid! Just as it is nowadays with the police in France! And so shall it also be, God willing, with journalists!

x^4 A 469   *n.d.*, 1852

« 4311 *The Sophist in Oneself*

·If a man were to have his own way, he would never become earnest about anything; the Sophist in him always substitutes illusion, evasion, etc. for earnestness.

A person reads or hears or somehow comes by himself to consider what unconditional obedience and devotion God must demand: that he not only is supposed to endure patiently the adversities he sends but that he is to accept them as good gifts, as gifts and presents even more glorious than all earthly good fortune, etc. This is moving, a certain tone is created—and presto! the sophistical idea pops into his head that this frame of mind should be so very pleasing to God that he no doubt will send good gifts, good fortune, happiness, etc. in another sense.

O, sophistry! sophistry! Is this not like the man who went past a tavern without drinking a glass of "schnapps" and rewarded himself by going into the next tavern and drinking one—so he not only got his schnapps just the same but also got it as his reward—which is so ingenious that he ought have still another glass of schnapps as a reward (for his shrewdness).

X^4 A 476 *n.d.*, 1852

« 4312 *Sophistry*

In the sphere of the ethical and the ethical-religious, anyone who does not himself existentially express what he teaches, or at least call attention to this, inform against himself, and explain his own position in the matter—every such person is a Sophist, and all such communication is sophistry.

He who himself expresses existentially what he teaches is a "teacher"; the next class could be called assistant teachers, their value is in testifying to the truth, pointing out what it is to be a teacher, but admitting that they themselves are not that.

Alas, the situation today is that there is not one single "teacher," and I am the only one who could be called an assistant teacher. And this is called Christianity.

X^4 A 484 *n.d.*, 1852

« 4313 *A Resource against Sophists*

If you want to protect yourself against falling into the hands of Sophists, then act in the following way, which is according to Christ's words[629] "You will know them by their fruits"—ask yourself: Who is speaking? What kind of a life is he living? Practice this continually. As soon as you hear a pronouncement, an exhortation, a sermon, you must say to yourself: Who is the speaker? What is the nature of his life? You must practice this in order to save yourself from the illusion that Christianity is an objective communication instead of a life of imitation and discipleship, and therefore it will sanction no so-called objective proclamation but rather a proclamation in words—with the life of the proclaimer as the commentary.

Suppose an apostle has declared: The life of a Christian is sheer joy and happiness. And then the allegation is made: A Christian's life is sheer joy and happiness. But remember that you are now to ask: Who is speaking? What kind of a life is he living? You find out that the speaker is a man who in a state of wretched poverty has been persecuted for a good many years, in short, has had suffering such that you could endure scarcely a fortnight. So you conclude: When such a man says this, then joy and happiness must be taken to mean something extremely lofty, far different from what we call joy and happiness. —Now take some examples of objective proclamation. The manager of a dance hall puts a sign over his door: A Christian's life is sheer joy and happiness; here there is sheer joy and happiness, and this is what the apostle declares a Christian's life to be. —Or a man who has amassed money and material abundance by proclaiming Christianity, enjoys every possible worldly pleasure, refined by the sheen of sanctity because he is an ecclesiastic—imagine him saying: A Christian's life is sheer joy and happiness. Simply ask yourself: Who is saying this? What kind of a life is he leading? —and you will readily see the Sophist. In order to understand the apostle's words properly you must always have his life before your eyes. It is hypocritical objectivity to take his word.

Another example. Paul[630] says: The laborer deserves his wages. Remember, now, you are to ask: Who is the speaker? What kind of a life is he living? The speaker is a man who did not take one farthing for proclaiming the doctrine, although he worked harder than 1,000 pastors do these days, a man who preferred to earn the bare necessities of life by means of a simple trade so that he could proclaim the Word gratis.

Now take a clergyman with a salary of 10,000 dollars who says: The laborer deserves his wages. Well, it is entirely true, objectively true, but immensely untrue that it is Paul who says it, for Paul's life is indeed an essential part of the declaration. Paul and Christ and the other apostles, who lived in voluntary poverty, must have meant by the assertion that the laborer deserves his wages something different from the purely secular interpretation that a laborer tries to earn as much as possible by his labor.

So it is. Yet the congregation ought not be stingy with the teacher. No, the congregation should be willing to give in abundance; but "the teacher" ought to say: I dare not accept it. Holy Scripture tells us what we should understand by the word "wages" in the lives of the saints, which provide a commentary on their words. When Christ bids the teacher to live in poverty (imitation) and the apostle nevertheless declares: The laborer deserves his wages, it is easy to see what is meant by wages: just as much as poverty needs to sustain life. The apostle comments on this by being unwilling to accept even that wage. However, as stated, the congregation should be glad to give in abundance, but the teacher should declare: I dare not accept any more.

x^4 A 555 *n.d.*, 1852

« 4314 *Sophistry*

Indulging in esthetic, imaginary passion, someone protests in the strongest terms that he is willing to sacrifice everything, if it is required —and at the same time he employs the toughest common sense to forestall at all costs any catastrophe, any situation which could make evident whether or not he will live up to his word—this is sophistry. He gains all the earthly advantage—and the appearance of sanctity as well. This is the very same as the Greek idea of doing what is unjust under the appearance of justice.[631]

It is situation, especially catastrophe, which discloses to what degree a person's protestations are the truth within him, are his personal character.

Once in a while providence comes upon the Sophists from behind and helps them—by providing the situation, and then they are done for.

Generally it is a very strange way of talking—to be willing to sacrifice everything, if it is required. It is in the New Testament; consequently it is required, namely, if you are voluntarily willing to do it; otherwise God has neither required it nor will he require it. What does this mean: if it is required of me? Presumably the Sophist means, if I am compelled to do it—then, then I will sacrifice everything. Yet the Sophist is and continues to be true to himself to the very end—always reward; for if something is taken from me, when I am compelled to give it up, then there is still always the reward of giving the appearance of sacrificing it.

x^4 A 608 *n.d.*, 1852

« **4315** *Sophistry*

No man can be the truth; only the God-man is the truth.

Then comes the next: the ones whose lives express what they proclaim. These are witnesses to the truth.

Then come those who disclose what truth is and what it demands but admit that their lives do not express it, do not try to hide this, but to that extent still are striving.⁶³²

Here it ends. Now comes the sophistry.

First of all come those who go on as usual and objectively teach the truth but go on as usual in that their lives do not express it.

Then come those who even alter the truth, the requirement, cut it down, make omissions—in order that their lives can correspond to the requirement. These are the real deceivers.

X^5 A 35   *n.d.*, 1852

SPINOZA

« 4316

With respect to being, see also the passages I have indicated in my copy of Spinoza[633] and my notes to it found on small sheets in the copy.

IV C 69   *n.d.,* 1842–43

« 4317

Spinoza in *Præfatio tractatus theologico-politicus,* p. 88.[634] ..... reliquis autem hunc tractatum commendare non studeo, nam nihil est quod sperem, eundem iis placere aliqua ratione posse; novi enim quam pertinaciter ea præjudicia in mente inhærent, quæ pietatis specie amplexus est animus; novi deinde æque impossibile esse vulgo superstitionem adimere ac metum; novi denique constantiam vulgi contumaciam esse, nec ratione regi, sed impetu rapi ad laudandum vel vituperandum. Vulgus ergo et omnes, qui iisdem cum vulgo affectibus conflictantur, ad hæc legenda non invito, quin potius vellem, ut hunc librum prorsus negligant, quam eundem perverse, ut omnia solent, interpretando molesti sint, et dum sibi nihil prosunt, aliis obsint .....

The final sentence contains
an advance apology.

VII¹ A 39   *n.d.,* 1846

« 4318

..... jam dudum enim res eo pervenit, ut neminem fere, quisnam sit, num scilicet Christianus, Turca, Judæus vel Ethnicus noscere possis, nisi ex corporis externo habitu, et cultu, vel quod hanc aut illam ecclesiam frequentat, vel denique quod huic aut illi opinioni addictus est, et in verba alicujus magistri jurare solet.

Spinoza, *Præfatio tractatus
theologico-politicus,* p. 85.[635]

VII¹ A 250   *n.d.,* 1846

« 4319

In March 1846.
See journal JJ, pp. 274, 276, 278, 280
[i.e., VII¹ A 23, 29, 31, 34, 35].

Spinoza's *Ethics.*[636]

Spinoza may well be right in his whole introflected method—that the *finis*, the τέλος is itself *appetitus:* that *beatitudo* is not *virtutis præmium men ipsa virtus*—the question is only whether his whole ethics is not to be charged with a duplicity, that he simultaneously (in order to do away with theology) contemplates everything at rest and then also (by virtue of the definition's *suum esse conservare*[637] gets finitude in process: that is, the concept of motion is lacking here.

It is certainly true that *truth* must be understood *in and by itself*, and that therefore all means fabricated for assistance in comprehending it better and more easily are an illusion, as, for example, miracles, because for the believer miracles are indeed truth, but they are not truth for the one who has not grasped the faith. (I myself have pointed this out several times in *Concluding Postscript.*[638]) In the same way *virtue* must be desired *for its own sake.* But if the individual is not originally disposed to this—something Spinoza, after all, denies—the question is whether or not he himself can do anything. Spinoza himself does in fact speak of a way to this *perfectio;* he himself defines *lætitia* by *transitio, in perfectionem,* and specifically stresses *transitio,* consequently transition, movement.[639] But right here is the duplicity. The first, seen *sub specie æterni* gives immanence. But if Spinoza wants to speak of actual individuals as he indeed does, then he must *eo ipso* admit that the maximum is still to know this* and to strive to approximate it, but, please note, in existence, which in fact *yields* theology by separating the *acquiescenstia* of immanence *in se ipso* and through its becoming producing the opposite, a nisus, a drive, and thereby an interest.

In margin: *in abstracto.*

VII¹ C 1   *n.d.,* 1846

« 4320

In margin of 4319 (VII¹ C 1):

In *Cogitata Metaphysica, pars* I, p. 60,[640] Spinoza himself says (in the paragraph *quare aliqui bonum metaphysicum statuerunt*) that a distinction has been made between *rem ipsam et conatum qui in unaquaque re est ad suum esse conservandum*[641] and that this is a misunderstanding. But here it is again—then the entire ethics is revoked, all his guidance for the wise etc.

See also *Cogitata Metaphysica, pars* I, p. 57,⁶⁴² *conciliationem libertatis nostri arbitrii et prædestinationis Dei humanum captum superare.*
       where he himself passionately affirms
       something incomprehensible.

                                                         VII¹ C 2   n.d.

« 4321

Addition to 4319 (VII¹ C 1):
Spinoza wants to develop or draw the existence [*Tilværelse*] of God from the idea of God and believes that he thereby obviates the pathos-filled intermediate clause (that God cannot deceive) which Descartes needed in order to give reality [*Realitet*] to thinking.
                                   Opera omnia, pp. 5 and 6.⁶⁴³
One cannot have any certainty about anything without first having an idea about God; but one cannot have an idea about God as long as one does not know whether the primary source of our nature has formed us to be deceived. Spinoza⁶⁴⁴ answers: The first is admitted, the second denied. I can have an idea about a triangle without knowing whether the primary source of human nature has formed us to be deceived. In exactly the same sense I can have the idea of God and from it derive existence [*Existentsen*].

                                              VII¹ C 3   n.d., 1846

« 4322

Addition to 4321 (VII¹ C 3):
P. 11, Axiom X.⁶⁴⁵
It is different with human thinking, which must have a basis for its having come into existence and for its continuing, because after its coming into existence [*Tilblivelse*] its nature does not involve a necessary existence [*Existents*] any more than before it came into existence, and therefore it needs the same external creating power in order to continue as it did previously in order to begin.

                                              VII¹ C 4   n.d., 1846

SPIRIT

« **4323**

Of what real use is it to have much spirit if one is physically weak. In fact, what do people care about spirit. Most men unconditionally are and continue to be animal-creatures. The only one they really respect is a big-boned fellow who can fight and swear and brawl. The kind of modesty and shyness which is always connected with spirit they regard as tomfoolery. Basically they have a dim notion that those richly endowed spiritually are more delicately constructed—and therefore they almost rejoice in the awareness of their raw strength over against this weakness.

VII[1] A 168   n.d., 1846

« **4324**

It can be a bit gruesome for me to have to live regularly and associatively with men who actually regard everything called spirit and everything called moral modesty in the interior life as make-believe, because anything like that does not exist for them at all. A person like that may very well be deceptive, but he does not affect them at all; they respect only physical force. There actually are people with whom it is gruesome to associate. Every concern that is not physical is ludicrous to them.

VIII[1] A 334   n.d., 1847

« **4325**

Of all anguish, the greatest is this—to have the task of being spirit and then to have to live among men.

IX A 38   n.d., 1848

« **4326**

What does really explain the change in the apostles, who a few days previously were despondent and fainthearted and now suddenly gained the faith and courage and resoluteness to risk life and everything for Christ's sake? The answer is usually: the communication of the Holy Spirit on Pentecost,⁶⁴⁶ and this change is offered as evidence that a miracle must be involved.

Meanwhile another side of the matter must be pointed out. As long as Christ was with them, they could not really abandon their earthly expectations (as Christ⁶⁴⁷ says, he had to go away in order that the *Spirit* could come). Then when He⁶⁴⁸ died the death of the cross and was buried, it became earnest for them; every earthly hope was now lost—and right here is their rebirth and regeneration. Christ's most solemn assurances of his suffering and death do not help; the fact that it is he who says it, the fact that he is personally there with them, precisely that makes them unable really to believe it. It must become earnest. Here we see the difference between direct and indirect communication; when he was actually dead, then there was indirect communication.

From this we see how preposterous the charge is (which is found also in the *Wolfenbüttelschen Fragment, Vom zwecke Jesu und seiner Jünger*, I, para. 32 and 33⁶⁴⁹) that the apostles had changed their view and did not make him a redeemer of the world until after his death, instead of an earthly Messiah which they took him to be at first. This is quite true, but the fault is not Christ's; he had said it plainly enough to them, but they could not understand it.

This means that *Spirit* can be communicated only indirectly. As long as he was personally with them, however plainly he said it, they still misunderstood—not until he was dead, not until then did they themselves become spirit and understand him. The situation must be present.

And so it goes with every man. There is here the distinction between understanding in possibility (an understanding which is always a misunderstanding) and understanding in actuality. If a person has conceived an ever so self-sacrificing plan, as long as there is not the earnestness of actuality, he cannot protect himself against the substitution of an earthly hope, that he might just possibly be victorious in this world. He has not yet become spirit. It is impossible to become spirit in "possibility." Only when it becomes actuality and every earthly hope is actually lost is he born again to understand truly what he had somewhat understood from the beginning, yet in such a way that misunderstanding slumbered within.

Then the spirit becomes integrated as spirit and now has purely spiritual powers. It perhaps looked easier in possibility, but it has in fact become easier in actuality, because the spirit now is in essential, complete unity with itself.

x^1 A 417 *n.d.*, 1849

« **4327**

The trouble with me is that I have lived too ideally or too soberly ideally. If a person thinks he is going to die tomorrow, he either says: Let us eat and drink,[650] or he tries to fill out the present day with more ideal impressions. If a man goes on living this way year after year, he misses out on all earthly advantages. Here we see a miniature commentary on: Seek the kingdom of God first.[651] The physical-mental idea that a long life lies ahead of one etc. prompts a man to become, as it is called, practical and to accommodate himself to life etc. But the spiritual idea is to live today. The category of "a long time ahead" is a much lower category than that of "today"; the long time ahead, these thirty to forty years, is a physical-mental qualification and no proof that man has an immortal spirit; it simply corresponds to the animal instinct of foresight, but "foresight" belongs to the physical-mental level.

x^1 A 652 *n.d.*, 1849

« **4328**

I Corinthians 2:15. The spiritual man judges all things but is himself to be judged by no one. This means that the spiritual man has the power and the key to interpret all lower modes of life. This being the case, he cannot be judged by anyone, only by that which is superior to him.

x^2 A 65 *n.d.*, 1849

« **4329** *The Gospel about the Ten Lepers*[652]

How the nine were healed of their leprosy—and then caught an even worse leprosy: their ingratitude and unthankfulness.

    The difference between sickness of the body and sickness of the spirit.

Sickness of the body reveals its own identity. The leper did not need to be told that he was sick—so he cried out to Christ for healing.

But that ingratitude was a sickness never occurred to them (a new intensification of ingratitude); they thought they had no need of Christ in this case.

The danger with sickness of the spirit is just that a certain degree of health is required in order to become aware and to know and acknowledge that one is sick.

x^2 A 103   *n.d.,* 1849

« 4330

It is indeed a true and suggestive expression that I have heard R. Nielsen[653] use a number of times: there is an infinite difference if one goes to an auction with the intention of being willing to bid 100 dollars —or if one when he enters the auction hall immediately bids 100 dollars —there is an infinite difference especially in the sphere of the spirit, where the price is always what it ought to be or one gets just what he pays for.

x^2 A 327   *n.d.,* 1849–50

« 4331

To me this, too, is an inexplicable form of absence of spirit—how a person can have a definite religious impression at a particular date and hour: at Christmas to be full of Christmas joy and not give a thought to Good Friday, on Good Friday to be deeply sad and then not have any other impression. It is the best proof that one's religion is something completely external.

x^2 A 379   *n.d.,* 1850

« 4332

Basically most men live in the same duplicity with regard to spirit as to natural phenomena. Science explains that the sun stands still and the world revolves around it—in everyday talk we continue to say: The sun rises and sets. Thus science basically presents a view *toto coele*[654] different from that which we imploy in everyday use, from that which the pastor preaches etc., and particularly in connection with the latter instance the most curious kind of affectation appears, since almost everybody says that it is all right to use such notions in popular presentations, although almost everybody is informed about the "scientific." For whom, then, is the popular lecture given?

x^2 A 424   *n.d.,* 1850

« 4333

The question in relation to Christianity is always to what extent a person must be transformed in the direction of becoming spirit so that he dares appropriate grace.

The situation at present is insane; actually it is nothing but refined paganism. A person remains within all the qualifications of sensuousness and the secular mentality, exists in them, willingly acknowledges that he is far behind (this is called repentance) but stays on the same spot, and then introduces "grace" as—as the new patch on the old garment.

On the other hand, if a person must be decisively developed to be "spirit" so as to dare appropriate "grace," then God knows how many there will be in each generation who actually feel any need for or have any use for Christianity. If I must actually die to my dearest desires, renounce everything that makes earthly man happy, then I do indeed, humanly speaking, become as unhappy as possible—and then the question is whether I am "spirit" enough that I actually have use for Christianity.

There is a shameful abuse fostered by the division: the law terrifies —the gospel reassures. No, the gospel itself is and must be terrifying at first. If this had not been the case, why in the world did it go with Christ as it did when he said: Come to me[655]—and they all went away, they fled from him.

It becomes more and more clear to me that only an apostle can in the stricter sense proclaim Christianity, for only he has the authority to be rigorous in this way. A man does not have this authority and therefore must compromise. Only a person who in the more rigorous sense is himself transformed to "spirit," only he can no longer understand, does not want to understand the confounded nonsense, the infirmity in which the rest of us are trapped, with the result that we coddle ourselves much too much and *rest* in grace too soon, and rest in it apart from striving instead of resting in it to be renewed for renewed striving.

X^2 A 445   *n.d.*, 1850

« 4334

In the external world the farmer does not make the mistake of believing the tares to be wheat, making a great fuss about the tares, harvesting them, taking them in, and letting the wheat lie and rot in the field. With regard to things of the spirit the mistake is usually made in this world of regarding tares for wheat. Now this, of course, is not so strange, for, from a spiritual point of view, even in the wheat field there are always many more out-and-out tare blossoms to be found than wheat stalks in the tare fields of the world. And then the result *a parte potiori* or *majori fit denominatio*,[656] since by far the great majority are tares, is that tares are wheat and wheat is tares; if not absolutely all then at least the great majority prefer this—and the majority are, after all, the truth. Since concepts in the spiritual world do not have an external actuality but are conceptions, the opportunity is unceremoniously seized and the concepts are relabeled according to what is most convenient to the majority.

x^3 A 241   *n.d.,* 1850

« 4335 *An Incomprehensible Arithmetic Problem*

Take a combination of five people, each of whom puts ⅝ of his capability into working jointly for the same cause—and take one person who does not have more ability than each of these five but puts all his abilities to work: who will achieve the most.

All sensible men will unanimously bet on the combination; I bet on the one person.

Putting all one has into something is vastly different from a high total of fractional efforts; it is dedication, it is spirit—the other is human muddling.

But how many are there in our day who sense what is of the spirit?

x^3 A 493   *n.d.,* 1850

« 4336 *Rigorousness—Mildness*

In his sermon on the Gospel "the good shepherd," Luther[657] does not develop the text properly.

He speaks—and in the strongest terms—of Christ's taking to himself the crushed and broken spirits—all quite true.

But now see if the same sermon declares that the minute a person becomes a Christian there will be persecution for the sake of the Word, that this is inherent in the Gospel, and therefore the Word must be dearer to a person than his life. Furthermore, that Christ at times even leaves his own in the lurch, a new suffering apart from the persecution by the world and of inner anxiety. Furthermore, that the suffering is so great and fearful that it truly is a matter of not being offended by Christ.

But, my God, is this doctrine then so mild.

O, no, this is half information that people run around with—well, not Luther, for he knows how to exercise a restraining influence—but that is the way it goes in ordinary preaching.

242   SPIRIT

The matter is quite simple. If I were spirit, I would consequently be so strong that I would have but one single concern—for my sin and for my soul's salvation. If this is true, then Christianity is as mild as mild can be, for what is milder than this—that in this respect I have nothing at all to be concerned about, that satisfaction has been made.

But unfortunately I am not a pure spirit, or I am not spirit; I am flesh and blood, a weak human being—and so Christianity is exceedingly rigorous. For Christianity will not introduce its mildness as a matter of course (this would be taking it in vain) but first of all desires to transform me into spirit.

If a man who has not a trace of the qualification of spirit in him could understand this, he would be obliged to flee Christianity as the greatest plague. Yet, no matter how indifferently and faintheartedly he involves himself with Christianity and wants to begin the course of becoming a Christian, there is always some spirituality present.

But what has Christianity come to these days? And then there are 1,000 clergymen, and scarcely one of them ever has time to read through in earnest a book that might enlighten them about something in the mildest way.

I stand, of course, as one impotent—I have no livelihood to give away, nothing to distribute, no profit to offer; my only interest is that there may possibly be a little love of truth in someone.

X^3 A 579   n.d., 1850

« 4337 *The Ascending Difficulty in the Life of the Spirit*

The farther one advances, the more difficult it becomes. It is not only that the world's opposition increases—this is easy to understand—but one is hit by so many little misfortunes, life's little irritations which he has been spared up to now and from which he feels he ought to be free especially now. One can interpret this to mean that he is on the wrong road and should take another. O, but have faith, and you will see, you will gain the courage to understand it differently—that these things happen simply as an assistance in the task, so that it may be served with more purely religious powers. The more significant the task is, the more God must control the one he is dealing with, lest there be a mixed-up genius who gets hold of the most dangerous of tasks.

Consequently these distresses are the *conditio sine qua non*[658] for becoming entrusted with such tasks.[*]

When a rider wants to ride his horse properly, a sharp bit is used, and perhaps he reduces the horse's food ration. The horse probably had secret thoughts that just the opposite would happen. But if the rider and the horse could talk together, the rider would say: Only with the help of a sharp bit can you learn to step like a parade horse. Even if you would promise me ten times over and determine ever so honestly to carry yourself like a horse on parade—it will not work; no, if you are to step like a parade horse, you must be assisted—and this is the reason for the sharp bit. And the same goes for the reduced rations.[659]

x^3 A 596 *n.d.*, 1850

« 4338

[*] *In margin of 4337* (x^3 A 596):

It does not follow that a person is to endure this incessantly, but the idea is that the divine is the exact opposite of the human: when someone is to have a difficult task, he is indulged in all other respects —no, then still more torments must be added, otherwise he will not be able to carry out the task.

x^3 A 597 *n.d.*

« 4339 *A Singular Difficulty*

It is said that if you have worldly goods etc., then be happy about it—but, declares the pastor, you must also consider that they can be taken away from you at any time, and, declares the pastor, this consideration will assist you in achieving true enjoyment.

Here, again, things are upside-down. If a person is actually able to maintain that all this over which he is humanly happy can be taken away at any moment, if he actually can maintain this at every moment, then he is essentially "spirit" and at that very moment these worldly goods will actually have no meaning for him.

Here, as usual, the pastor takes the loftier definition, makes it seem as if becoming "spirit" were a direct good instead of being a good only from a spiritual point of view, and therefore a good from which we men who still have not become spirit actually shrink.

The idea that to be spirit (being able to understand at all times that all this over which I humanly rejoice can be taken away from me) and at the same time still be able really to rejoice in it is a modern invention, the basis of which is that one is never existentially in earnest about maintaining the thought that it can all be taken away at any moment—thus the thought never really disturbs one's enjoyment of worldly things. The moment a person is in earnest about becoming spirit, certain consequences immediately appear—the whole worldly infatuation vanishes.

If we, in our present way of life, are to be truthful before God, we would have to talk like this: I understand very well that to become spirit is really the requirement, but could you not grant me a little indulgence, permit me the grace of not having such thoughts come too close to me, for I would so much like to enjoy the things of this earth, and, Lord God, I do not pretend to be stronger than I am—I am only a child.

x^3 A 705 *n.d.*, 1851

« 4340 *Spirit*

is the power a person's understanding exercises over his life.[660]

The person who has perhaps a false conception of God but yet observes the self-renunciation this false idea requires of him has more spirit than the one who perhaps even has the most correct scholarly and speculative knowledge of God but whose knowledge exercises no power at all over his life.

x^3 A 736 *n.d.* 1851

« 4341 *The Church—Sociality*

Richard Rothe in his *Die Anfänge der Christlichen Kirke*[661] deduces the idea of the Church directly from human nature. It is supposed to be grounded in the social instinct that is part of human nature.

Without wanting to deny the reality [*Realitet*] of the Church or that Christianity affirms it, I would take objection, however, to this kind of deduction.

To be specific, Christianity is related to spirit—and sociality is related essentially to the mind-body synthesis. Aristotle[662] says correctly that "the crowd" is an animal qualification. Christianity teaches also that eternal life is simply not social.

Society cannot be deduced from "spirit," and the Church exists precisely because we are not truly spirit or pure spirit. "The congregation" is an accommodation, a concession in view of how little we are able to endure being spirit.

But this is something quite different from that hasty deduction.

x^4 A 226 *n.d.*, 1851

« 4342

From him who has not, even what he has will be taken away.

SPIRIT 245

In the first place, having must be understood to mean having acquired; whoever has acquired nothing (this is related to the parable of the entrusted talents[663]), from him even what he has will be taken, that which he has as a given; thus the one talent was the given, and since he had acquired nothing, the given was also taken away from him.

And this, in fact, is the law of the spirit for all possession: only in acquisition is there possession; if nothing is acquired, the given also is taken away.

x^4 A 486 n.d., 1852

« **4343** *Christianity*

..... When someone has become wretched and unhappy in this life to the point where there can be any question of his becoming a Christian in earnest, one of two things will happen.

Either he will not succeed in pressing through and attaining the triumphant joy of the spirit but will nevertheless continue to relate to Christianity, and the world will ridicule him for making himself unhappy

Or he will press through and attain the triumphant joy of the spirit. And then what Christ[664] prophesied to his disciples will be fulfilled for him also: "You will be hated by all for my sake, indeed, the hour is coming when whoever kills you will think he is offering service to God." He will be put to death—in Christ's name, in order to serve Christ! —He will be cursed and hated, the epithet "egotist"[665] will be shouted at him from first to last. In a sense I can understand that the world must talk this way. What egoity there is in the divine's wanting to be loved as God, according to Christianity, wants to be loved—to the point of one's hating father and mother! And what egoity there is in the true Christian—to love himself so much that in order to save himself and to look to God he is—egotistical!—enough to hate the world, himself, the generation, his friends!

No, the world hates nothing so much as it hates the one who expresses what spirit is. One hundred thousand thieves and robbers are not so dangerous to the sensuousness in which the sensate has his life as one single true Christian who, by expressing what spirit is, explodes the whole secular mentality.

x^4 A 508 n.d., 1852

« **4344** *Infant Baptism*

To a certain degree infant baptism is part and parcel of a charming parental conceit.

It is, however, a misunderstanding to think that a child owes his parents his existence [*Tilværelse*] qua spirit. No, but let us be nice about it; qua animal-creature he does owe them his existence.

But the parents want to flatter themselves by imagining that they have begotten a Christian and therefore the child has to be baptized immediately.

No, it is also part of the earnestness of Christianity that it forces itself disruptively, with the decisiveness of eternity, between parents and child: the decision to become a Christian comes far later in life.

But in "Christendom" this wholesale confusion begets parents who perhaps do not have the remotest impression of Christianity, and they beget Christians—and so it goes.

x^4 A 617   *n.d.*, 1852

« **4345 *The Sensate—the Spiritual***

Plato says (*Phaedrus*, 250) that sight is the sharpest of all the senses, but wisdom is not seen by it because a love would thereby arise so powerful that it would become a kind of sensate concupiscence.

Similarly, if the sign of the relationship to God were success and prosperity, this really would be a sensate intoxication. But this is why the very opposite is the case.

Generally speaking, there is nothing more dangerous than this confusion, when the sensate is substituted for that which is considered to be spiritual, for example, when sensate love is mistaken for Christian love.

x^4 A 632   *n.d.*, 1852

« **4346 *Spirit—Is To Believe That Others Have Had the Spirit***

The true relation is: to be able to testify from personal experience that it is a Spirit who makes a person know that it is more blessed to do without than to get, that to suffer is more blessed than to be victorious, that to renounce is more blessed than to enjoy.

The next relation is this: unable to testify from one's own personal experience (because one has not ventured so far out that "the Spirit" is reached), one nevertheless modestly and humbly believes that what these glorious ones testify is the way it is.

Absence of spirit is to say goodby to everything about any such Spirit; shamelessness is to want to be a Christian anyway; blasphemy is to go so far as to mock such a Spirit and still want to be a Christian anyway.

x^5 A 37   *n.d.*, 1852

« 4347 *Irony*

How ironical this is! —Imagine a man who under the domination of flesh and blood goes on living in the self-complacement self-satisfaction that "if it really mattered, I could easily do it."

O, I wonder if just one person could be found among us who has any idea at all of what is involved in a battle when it becomes earnest! The apostle[666] says, "We are not contending against flesh and blood, but against principalities and powers"—yes, because battling with flesh and blood comes to be a battle with principalities and powers.

But we have managed things advantageously in such a way that we have completely abolished becoming spirit in the Christian sense. Thus we feel fine, we even boast that we do not know anything of these enormous battles and temptations and even draw the conclusion that, Christianly, our way is the right way!

What profound nonsense, confusion, and hypocrisy!

XI^1 A 34 *n.d.*, 1854

« 4348 *Mediocrity*

From the purely human point of view the most prudent thing is always to make life as trivial as possible (as devoid of ideas, as spiritless or as devoid of spirit as possible)—for the more mediocre, the easier life becomes.

Perhaps someone could go further and think that this would be most prudent to do also because one might thereby manage to avoid being noticed by God, to stay clear of his criterion, for if one is just a specimen, a unit in an enormous number, how is God's eye going to fall upon him?

Yet one deceives himself if he thinks this way. For this very reason Christianity approaches from the opposite side and makes man responsible—to the accounting of eternity—for whether or not he has applied the Christian criterion to his life.

XI^1 A 211 *n.d.*, 1854

« 4349 *Man*

according to Christianity is a fallen spirit who by way of punishment was degraded to being animal.

Nevertheless spirit is required in order to comprehend the humiliation properly; the trivial and the bestial are thoroughly happy to be animals, that is, they really do not notice it.

If Christianity had not come into the world, men would never have become properly aware of this tragic secret, for Christianity is needed in order to explain the true situation to man, that he originally had been something quite different, that is, how deeply he had sunk by having become animal. Man does not hit upon such a thing by himself, and only the most eminent individuals outside of Christianity have had intimations of such a conception.

Now it is clear in what sense Christianity is good news and how bestial Christendom is. Christianity is the good news that opens a man's eyes to a misery of which the natural man has no intimation. Christianity is the good news which makes this earthly existence the greatest misery for a man and also makes it the most agonized strenuous effort—in fear and trembling—and then, yes, then Christianity is the good news about the eternal.

Does this resemble the Christianity of Christendom?

XI[1] A 363 n.d., 1854

« 4350 *I——Third Person*

To be *spirit* is to be *I*. God desires to have *I*'s, for God desires to be loved.

Mankind's interest consists in alleging objectivities everywhere; this is the interest of the category of race.

"Christendom" is a society of millions—all in the third person, no *I*.

XI[1] A 487 n.d., 1854

« 4351 *The Measure of Spirit*

This is how we talk. A man proudly declares: I am not a single man but a man with a family—perhaps a big family. From a spiritual point of view, a single man is more.

This is how we talk to God. Someone steps forward and says: We are not a few individual men, we are a nation. From a spiritual point of view, an individual is more before God; this is precisely what Christianity is and that any person can be this individual.

How ironical that every man is intended to be an Atlas who carries a world—and then to see what we men are; alas, and how tragic that we ourselves are responsible for being what we are!

XI[1] A 498 n.d., 1854

« 4352 *The Life of the Spirit*

To live so strenuously that even though one's life is not merely irreproachable but by human standards is extremely rigorous and pure and yet nevertheless to speak of his body as "the body of sin" (as does

Paul)⁶⁶⁷—this is spirit. Just as what is not of faith is said to be sin,⁶⁶⁸ so also as soon as the body is not at the service of spirit, does not will what spirit wills at every point, even the least, at every moment, even the briefest—it is the body of sin.

But there is not even an intimation of such a thing in our day, when all life is mediocrity and living in harmony with the flesh is called Christianity.

Of course, the very fact that spirit is involved makes the body more insubordinate. In its own way the body is, if you please, a decent sort of fellow. It does not make much trouble if it is permitted to jog along in its own routine—that is, in flat mediocrity. And the favorable results of this kind of treatment are regarded as proof that the method is right or, as it is said, is truly Christian.

Yes, in a certain sense what the atheists maintain (and the orthodox indirectly)—that Christianity is a myth—is true; yes, it is a myth, a fable, that there have been men who existed [*existeret*] by such a standard; it is a myth, because, after all, the "nation of boys"⁶⁶⁹ who call themselves Christians these days are the true humanity, even the highest humanity, since it is positively the most recent instance of the mounting perfectibility of the human race. If we did not have bones of the mammoth, we would, of course, insist that the historical account of such animals was a myth, a fable—at least all the animals belonging to the animal species would do this.

XI¹ A 524   *n.d.*, 1854

« **4353** *Do You Want To Be a Power?*

I daresay everyone wants that, but just listen now to how the truly powerful person might speak.

"If anyone asks me what absolute power I possess, I answer: the only true power. For to be in command, even to be at the head of 500,000 men and 1,000 cannon, is only relative power: suppose someone comes along with 600,000 men and 1,500 cannon. No, my absolute power is the only true power—and when I ponder it, it seems so easy to attain that it is inexplicable that not everyone is what he infinitely wants to be. For this is my power. Do they want to laugh at me—I am ready! Do they want me to be imprisoned—I am prepared, and so much so that I will gladly relieve the state of the trial costs, for human justice is a tedious waste of time, and as some author⁶⁷⁰ has said, the attorneys for the prosecution and for the defense are comparable to Harlequin and Pierrot; therefore just a word, a hint from the authorities, and I will take a carriage, pick up the executioner myself, and the two of us will go out—the chaplain as well as guards and policemen are unnecessary. But if there is a request for carrying it out someplace where a large number can be assembled, I will not object but only ask the authorities to consider that if the purpose of the public execution is to deter, then it would no doubt be best that mine take place as secretly as possible so that it may not have the very opposite effect."

This, then, is what it means to have power. Do you want it? Or why do you not want it? Alas, we live such wretched lives these days that we are all spoiled by reading and hearing this kind of talk and very likely admire it as poet-talk—but it never even remotely occurs to us to act accordingly. This is why it is even dangerous for a person of character to have this poetic talent, for it is so easy to take his poetry and ignore everything having to do with character. Poetic talent together with character is dangerous in the same way that it is dubious in logic to illustrate the laws of thought with interesting examples—because often the important point is easily forgotten.

XI[1] A 538 *n.d.*, 1854

« **4354 *To Be Spirit***

Flesh and blood or the sensate—and spirit are opposites. Thus it is easy to see what it is to be spirit, that it is to will voluntarily that which flesh and blood shrink from most—for spirit and flesh and blood are just as opposite as, to use an adage, the ends of a sack.

From what do flesh and blood shrink most of all? From dying. Consequently spirit is to will to die, to die to the world.

Incidentally, it is easy to see that to die to the world is a whole exponential power higher than to die, for to die is only to suffer, but dying to the world is voluntarily to force oneself into the same suffering; furthermore, dying is a suffering of rather short duration, while dying to the world is for a whole lifetime.

This also explains how it happens that so many become Christians, as the saying goes, on their deathbeds. This is a dubious matter. Christianity is a pessimism, but on the deathbed, when everything for this life is lost anyway—to choose Christianity then makes it almost a kind of optimism; it is something like the kind of generosity with which someone threateningly required at pistol point to hand over his money chooses to give the affair a turn and say that he generously offers it as a gift. What Christianity wants to do away with is flesh and blood's attachment to life, it wants man to be spirit, and this is expressed by dying to the world; but when a man lies on his deathbed and then grabs at Christianity, it is almost like flesh and blood's last gimmick. Here there is no assurance at all that a transformation has actually taken place, the transformation of becoming spirit. For what gives assurance that a transformation has taken place is just this—that the situation expresses that he is alive and well. But the situation of a dying person is something quite different—or, more correctly, there is no situation in the sense that the very situation is part of the expression of spirit. This is why it happens that someone who snatches at Christianity on his deathbed reverts to his old self if he does not die, thus demonstrating that no change had taken place.

XI^1 A 558 *n.d.*, 1854

« 4355

"I came to cast fire upon the earth"[671]

How fearfully true are Christianity's metaphors. To cast fire upon the earth. Yes, for what is a Christian? A Christian is a person who has caught on fire.

On Pentecost this comes again—spirit is fire; tongues of fire settled upon them.

Spirit is fire. This is in accord with language usage. An example from a completely different world, which for that very reason illuminates ordinary language usage. In Kruse's adaptation of *Don Juan*,[672] Don Juan says of Elvira: "In her eyes there flames a *fire* that seems to be from another world," and this is why "his heart pounds at the sight of her."

Spirit is fire. Therefore the expression: to burn out to spirit (in Baggesen:[673] "burned out to spirit"). Alas, but in the fire Christianity wishes to light not all are burned out to spirit, a few are burned out to ashes—that is, they do not become spirit in the fire.

Spirit is fire, Christianity is fire-setting. And by nature man shrinks more from this fire than from any other. For even if someone were a victim of fire ten times, if only his zest for life does not die out, he perhaps can still get to be a prosperous man and enjoy life. But the fire Christianity wants to light is not intended to burn up a few houses but to burn up the zest for life—burn it out to spirit.

Spirit is fire. From this comes the frequent expression: As gold is purified in fire, in the same way the Christian is purified. But fire must not be regarded merely as the fire of "tribulations"—that is, something coming from the outside. No, a fire is kindled in the Christian, and by means of this or in this burning comes the purification. Thus there was a demonic ingenuity in the most horribly shocking atrocity perpetrated on some of the first Christians—burning them as torches along the road. One can almost hear these inhuman emperors scornfully say: After all, Christ wanted to cast fire upon the earth, so let the Christians serve as torches.

XI^2 A 41   n.d., 1854

« 4356 *Spirit Power—Sensate Power*

To become and to be spirit power is very arduous and fraught with danger besides; so men prefer the easier and more profitable way: to become sensate power by simple addition. This art is practiced more and more commonly these days and has the harmful result that it will be more and more difficult in the future for spirit power to penetrate. If men lived as they did formerly, each one shifting for himself in a simple routine, then it would be easier for spirit power to get hold of them. But nowadays there are factions and parties, numbers, sensate power everywhere. Just as the invention of gunpowder altered the conduct of war, so also this change—that we deal everywhere with sensate power—will, if possible, alter the battle of the spirit. This, however, cannot be done, for if the spirit changes and becomes like its opponents, it is no longer spirit. Consequently the only result possible is that it will be more difficult for spirit to break through; as was stated, gunpowder altered warfare and did away with personal bravery, and similarly in the realm of spirit the human race is inclined to abolish personality—that is, abolish spirit and make personality impossible—that is, make spirit impossible.

In the sensate realm the change was irresistible. When one nation conducts war with cannons, there is nothing for the other nation to do but get cannons or surrender. It is assumed that the same thing will happen in the world of the spirit. If so, this will mean that spirit no longer exists.

XI^2 A 62   n.d., 1854

« 4357 *The Present Human Race*

is so devoid of spirit that men no longer have any self-esteem oriented to being "spirit"; the only self-esteem they have is more or less along the lines of animal-creatures.

Remember those departed officials of Christianity who thought to crush men by calling them hypocrites, ungodly men, etc.—this would not affect men in our day in the least.

The metaphorical expression "fornicators" used in the Bible is not effective either, for fornicators do have self-esteem *qua* animal-creatures.

No, we must change our way of speaking. Somewhere else [i.e., XI^2 A 186] I have suggested a provocative figure of speech, namely, that they are spiritual cuckolds—the analogy is simply to being a cuckold who lives on with his wife in matrimonial cohabitation although he knows he is being cuckolded continually—and this corresponds precisely to having a religion which one himself regards as a fable but, spineless wretch that he is, does not have the courage for the one or the other. This sort of charge provokes and also has the good quality of prostituting them in the eyes of women, which they dread so much, since, as stated, self-esteem *qua* animal-creature is the only self-esteem they have and the relation to the opposite sex has been made into the meaning and earnestness of life—into true Christianity.

XI^2 A 198   *n.d.*, 1854

« **4358 Talent—Spirit**

If a man with talent is actually to become spirit, he must first of all acquire a distaste for all the satisfactions the talent has to offer—just as a lad apprenticed to the pastry trade has permission from the start to eat as many cakes and cookies as he wants—in order to acquire a distaste for cakes and cookies.

XI^2 A 228   *n.d.*, 1854

« **4359 Irony in Relation to Spirit and What Is of the Spirit**

There is no qualification of spirit without the presence also of some irony. The sensate view of life maintains that what makes a person want to think about life is the idea that the more he thinks about it, the easier life becomes for him. The presence of spirit means that the more a man contemplates life, the harder and more strenuous it becomes for him. "He who increases knowledge increases sorrow"[674] —yes, and the strenuousness of existing.

"But then all this about spirit is madness"—yes, absolutely right. But precisely this is the negative sign of spirit, and the way to make life easy is not to have spirit—so selective is spirit.

Money, earthly power, etc., this the sensate man knows all about; he aspires to it because in his opinion—and he is partly right—to possess it makes life easier. If accumulating money categorically meant that for every thousand there would be more suffering and hardship —well, then the sensate man would probably refrain from it—as he in fact does with respect to spirit—happy that over the centuries this way of life is traveled more and more as the one and only soundly celebrated way, that is, remaining practically pure animal-creation is the way to make life most comfortable.

Spirit placed together with a life as animal-creature yields suffering; the more spirit the more suffering. This is why Christendom has taken it upon itself (with the help of its perfectibility!) to improve Christianity. The qualification "spirit" is allowed to drop out entirely (to introduce it Christ came into the world), and thus we are Christians, Christianity flourishes all around the country; there are 1,000 generous appointments for teachers (but according to Christianity being a teacher must not be a livelihood), marriages are solemnized before the altar (but Christianity is the single state), children are begotten into Christianity and brought up in Christianity and baptized as Christians etc. etc.—Christianity everywhere—that is, everywhere there is the very thing to which Christianity is diametrically opposed.

But admittedly life certainly does become easier; the scene in Christendom, particularly Protestantism, is idyllic—begetting of children, fat livings, busyness in this world, politics.

XI^2 A 246 *n.d., 1854*

« **4360** *How Did It Happen That Christ Was Put to Death?*

I can answer this in such a way that with the same answer I show what Christianity is.

What is "spirit"? (And Christ is indeed spirit, his religion is of the spirit.) Spirit is: to live as if dead (to die to the world).[675]

So far removed is this mode of existence from the natural man that it is quite literally worse for him than simply dying.

The natural man can tolerate it for an hour when it is introduced very guardedly at the distance of imagination—yes, then it even pleases him. But if it is moved any closer to him, so close that it is presented in dead earnestness as a demand upon him, then the self-preservation instinct of the natural life is aroused to such an extent that it becomes a regular fury, as happens through drinking, or as they say, a *furor uterinus.*[676] In this state of derangement he demands the death of the man of spirit or rushes in upon him to slay him.

XI² A 279 *n.d.,* 1854

« 4361

Spirit is restlessness;[677] Christianity is the most profound restlessness of existence—so it is in the New Testament.

In Christendom Christianity is tranquilization "so that we can really enjoy life."

XI² A 317 *n.d.,* 1854

« *Tranquillity*

Man desires tranquillity so that he may enjoy (*nil beatum nisi quietum*[678]—*Epicurus*).

God (according to Christianity) does not want men to have tranquillity—spirit is restlessness.[679]

Here alone there is an irregularity in Protestantism inasmuch as it tends exclusively toward tranquilizing.

XI² A 353 *n.d.,* 1854

« 4363 *To Become a Christian,*

according to the New Testament, is to become "spirit."

To become spirit, according to the New Testament, is to die, to die to the world,[680] for according to the New Testament no man is born as spirit, and after the natural birth to be man is to be body and mind. Therefore dying to the world is the crisis in which one becomes spirit.

For the natural man the most dreadful thing of all is to die; to die to the world is even more dreadful and agonizing, more agonizing than all other human misery and wretchedness.

Yet God wills it so out of love: you, O man, neither do you have God's conception of the dreadfulness of sin nor of the gloriousness of salvation—if you did, you would at least not complain about God's having mercy on you in this manner.

It is out of love—blessed is he who is not offended.[681]

*   *

This is what it means to become a Christian according to the New Testament.

Now ask yourself, among these thousands or among these thousand pastors, have you seen one single one who fits this description in even the remotest manner, or whose life is not essentially patterned in the very opposite way, not on dying to the world but on enjoying life? Then ask yourself if it seems too much to propose that we at least should admit this.

XI^2 A 378 *n.d.*, 1854–55

SPIRITUAL TRIAL

« **4364**

If I remember correctly it is in *Minna von Barnhelm*[682] that Lessing has one of the characters say that a sigh without words is the best way to pray to God. That sounds fine but actually means that one does not really dare or does not want to get involved with the religious but merely wants now and then to gaze out upon it as upon the boundaries of existence—the blue mountains. If one puts on the religious for everyday use, then spiritual trials [*Anfægtelser*] are bound to come.

VI A 2   n.d., 1844-45

« **4365**

As long as there are many springs from which to draw water, troubled concern about possible water failure does not arise. But when there is only one source! And so it is only when Christianity has become a person's one and only spring that spiritual trials [*Anfægtelser*] also begin. Spiritual trial is the expression of a concentration upon Christianity as the only object. This is why most men have no spiritual trials.

VIII^1 A 47   n.d., 1847

« **4366**

Addition to 4365 (VIII^1 A 47):

In the metaphor of spiritual trial there is a besieged city which has only one spring. The first[683] must be included. This is what men want to omit. They want to have an easy life and then believe in Christianity, believe in Christ's reconciliation. But believing in the Atonement is illustrated symbolically by the Jews when they were attacked by serpents[684] in the wilderness and Moses raised up the sign of the cross. Believing in the Atonement means: bitten by serpents, while the bites pain and tempt men to think only of this and of the possibility of getting the serpents killed—then to believe. Not everyone bitten by serpents can make up his mind or find the grace to believe the Atonement.

VIII^1 A 48   n.d., 1847

« **4367**

May 5, 1847

The difference between sin and spiritual trial [*Anfægtelse*] (for the conditions in both can be deceptively similar) is that the temptation [*Fristelse*] to sin is in accord with inclination, [the temptation] of spiritual trial [is] contrary to inclination. Therefore the opposite tactic must be employed. The person tempted by inclination to sin does well to shun the danger, but in relation to spiritual trial this is the very danger, for every time he thinks he is saving himself by shunning the danger, the danger becomes greater the next time. The sensate person is wise to flee from the sight or the enticement, but the one for whom inclination is not the temptation at all but rather an anxiety about coming in contact with it (he is under spiritual trial) is not wise to shun the sight or the enticement; for spiritual trial wants nothing else than to strike terror into his life and hold him in anxiety.

VIII[1] A 93 *n.d.*, 1847

« **4368**

There is a "Savior" not merely so that we can resort to him when we have sinned and, relying on him, receive forgiveness, but precisely for the purpose of saving the rest of us from sinning.

It is a very special spiritual trial [*Anfægtelse*] when a person in the strictest sense sins against his will, plagued by the anxiety of sin, when he has, for example, sinful thoughts which he would rather flee, does everything to avoid, but they still come—it is a special kind of spiritual trial to believe that this is something he must submit to, that Christ is given to him to console him as he bears this cross, plagued as he is by a thorn in the flesh.[685]

No, this is still a kind of despair. By faith in Christ he shall and must become the master of these evil thoughts.

The verse about the thorn in the flesh can occasion this kind of misinterpretation. There are instances when a man can truthfully say: I know that I do not call forth these evil thoughts, I know I am doing all I can to counteract them—consequently, it is continually against his will. But nevertheless Christ exists not merely to console him but to save him from the power of these evil thoughts.

IX A 331 *n.d.*, 1848

« **4369**

In margin of 4368 (IX A 331):

But if a half-educated clergyman comes running up with instructions that the sufferer must become the master over these thoughts, then he does not know at all what he is talking about and would, if he were permitted to do the counseling, merely drive the sufferer crazy; there is a whole dialectical process left to go through before he can arrive at what the clergyman is preaching about.

IX A 332   n.d.

« 4370

The above-mentioned spiritual trial [*Anfægtelse*] is very painful and excruciating and, in addition, dialectically complicated almost to the point of madness; if it may be thought of in this way, it is, to define it teleologically, an educational torture which, whatever else, is intended to break all self-centered willfulness.

It is in fact a kind of obsession. Humanly speaking, the sufferer is completely without guilt. He himself does not, as in sin, deliberately provoke these thoughts; it is just the opposite, these thoughts plague him. In his anxiety he flees from them in every way; he perhaps strains to the point of despair all his powers of ingenuity and concentration in order to avoid not only them but even the remotest contact with anything that could be related to them. It does not help; the anxiety becomes even greater. Neither does the usual advice help—to forget, to escape, for that is just what he is doing, but it merely nourishes the anxiety.*

In order to endure this agony, a specific kind of religiousness is needed, is required, which humbly and without breathing a word submits it to God somewhat like this: Before you, O God, I am nothing; do with me as you will, let me suffer all this which almost drives me to madness; you are still the one to whom wisdom and understanding belong, the loving Father. Such a religiousness is required in order to hold out. If this agony collides with a passionate self-centered willfulness which cannot become nothing before God, it must end with the sufferer losing his mind.

Consequently the sufferer endures with the help of religiousness. But now comes the consciousness of freedom with responsibility. In itself the suffering is perhaps the most tortuous of all sufferings for a free being, thus to be as if unfree in the power of something else. But the responsibility of freedom asks: Is a person not responsible for his thoughts, then? This concern breeds new anxiety, since the suffering now also seems to become guilt. What shall he do now? Here the understanding is again exposed to a collision, and if there is self-centered willfulness and obstinancy in him, he loses his mind. The very thing which otherwise should help a man—namely, that he becomes anxious and afraid and flees from the evil—is precisely *in casu*⁶⁸⁶ that which throws him into the power of those evil thoughts. The more anxious he becomes, the more power they get over him.

Here it once again takes the specifically religious to hold out. In addition to his other sufferings he must suffer having every man as a third party regard him as guilty and summarily say to him: You must try to escape such thoughts—which he has been trying to escape with an almost insane ingenuity. He suffers further from being unable to get a foothold, whether this is suffering or sin, for he is alone with God, and who dares then be so certain. He is again brought as if to madness. He does everything to flee, he trembles at the mere thought of the remotest association of ideas which could bring forth those thoughts again—and then on top of all this he is supposed to be guilty. In a moment of impatience it must seem to him as if children torturing a butterfly could not inflict worse torture than he is suffering. If all the self-centered willfulness does not die within him, he loses his mind. In a moment of impatience he perhaps could almost wish this in order to put an end to the self-contradiction in the agony.

What is he to do now? Nothing; be silent and wait in prayer and faith. One thing he must do: not despair of the possibility of salvation, not—abandon God. People talk of abandoning oneself, but this is rubbish; it is a matter of abandoning God.

If there is any guilt in his suffering, it must be in his terminating too quickly and resigning to the suffering, but yet with the stubborn thought that he must now give up waiting for it to be taken away. No, this is precisely what he must abandon.

No man knows when help will come, no man knows whether it will come in a short time or in forty years. But the help will consist in this that "the Savior" comes to mean something different to him. With all his power the sufferer has probably avoided having these evil thoughts come upon him in prayer or when he thought of God, assuming that this must be a monstrous sin. And yet his salvation lies right here, in his acquiring the frankness to think these evil thoughts together with God before God—in order to dispose of them. His salvation lies in his getting a Savior or in his Savior's coming to exist for him so that he dares say to him: These evil thoughts haunt and hound me, not letting himself be frightened by the notion that naming these is the same as having them again.

When this will come to fruition for him or this will be granted to him, no man can say. One thing is sure, and every man of experience knows this, that grace too has its time and its times, that there comes a moment [*Øieblikke*] when that which a man has sought after year in and year out suddenly is granted and comes to fruition.

The impatience in which his self-centered willfulness must lie is that in one way or another he wants to see an end to this matter—that is, he wants to have it explained, even if this explanation is that there is no explanation and none can be expected in this life. He wants to resign himself humbly to this and still believe God, love God. He is not, then, like those who defiantly abandon God—on the contrary he needs God continually in order to endure this suffering and the meaninglessness of it. But he wants to have it settled that his suffering is and will remain meaningless, so that he can now concentrate all his energies upon bearing it patiently, humbly. But God will not have it this way; it is easy for God to see a little self-centered willfulness in this, for God wants him also to hope continually in the possibility of salvation and that in whatever moment it is offered to him he will receive it with the same joy as in the first moment. In a certain sense this no doubt increases the suffering, creates the tension in which he is kept suspended (and in which the self-centered willfulness is supposed to die) even more exhaustingly. For the more profound person it is undoubtedly a kind of relief to get it settled and certain that help is not to be expected, that the task is to bear it in silence. But the task is also to hope against hope.[687] This is precisely why day in and day out he repeats his suffering; every day he must hope—against the understanding—that God will nevertheless help him, and this he must endure year after year. This is what it is to be educated, to learn obedience: never once to resign oneself willingly to the very worst as conclusive, to get permission to do this and yet in readiness for this to be obliged every day also to hope to God that it might nevertheless please him. The merely human hope has been exhausted for a long time; a hope like this is therefore a religious work, a new obedience which is demanded of him, which really lets him feel in what sense God is master. When a person finds it easier to bear the hardest conclusion as conclusive (for the fact that there is a conclusion is precisely the relief), then to be obliged to hope this way year after year, which only strengthens the awareness that up to now no help has come—to hope in this way means precisely that any resting in a conclusion is continually disturbed: this, you see, is what it is to learn obedience.

IX A 333 *n.d.,* 1848

« 4371

[*] *In margin of 4370* (IX A 333):
For what is often maunderingly maintained with respect to criminals—that an overpowering urge drives them to steal etc.—is relevant in quite another way to thoughts, and the big question is always to what extent a man is absolute master over every thought—that is, over the thoughts or thought processes which arise in or pass through his head; the thoughts which *preoccupy* him are another matter.

IX A 334 n.d.

« 4372

Because religion is not taken seriously nowadays in Christendom, there is never a hint about spiritual trials [*Anfægtelser*]. Life is just not lived religiously; this can be proved indirectly by the disappearance of spiritual trial.

In the words of the preachers, *every* man ought to relate himself to God in *all things,* ought to refer *everything* to God. Yes, *every* man—that is, John Doe, and everything—that is, X. In this way, to be sure, one does not discover spiritual trial; and nothing more is done now—at most it is preached about.

Spiritual trial is the divine repulsion in the *quid nimis*[688] and can never fail to appear if one is to exist religiously, consequently as an actual, definite, particular man—for example, I, Søren Aabye Kierkegaard, thirty-five years old, of slight build, master of arts, brother-in-law of businessman Lund,[689] living on such and such a street—in short, this whole concretion of trivialities, that I dare relate myself to God, refer all the affairs of my life to him. No man has ever lived who has truly done this without discovering with horror the horror of spiritual trial, that he might be venturing too boldly, that the whole thing might really be lunacy.

But to preach that in all things *every* man *always* ought to refer *all things* to God—yes, as stated, this does not result in spiritual trial.

Every man who will shut his door, become conscious of himself in his total concretion—and then think of God, the infinite one—and then refer—not his life, this is too grandiose—no, refer this or that of his life to God: if he does not discover spiritual trial, then call me Matt.

Luther[690] says that as soon as Christ has come on board the storm immediately begins; this storm is spiritual trial, which Luther attributes to the devil. This, however, is more childish than true. No, it is spiritual trial because it seems to the person himself as if the relationship were stretched too tightly, as if he were venturing too boldly in literally involving himself personally with God and Christ. And, indeed, this is in fact so elevated and so daring that ordinarily one would be regarded as insane, insane with pride, if he were to blurt this out on Monday—but on Sunday and especially if one is a pastor, one may very well talk about this in generalities.

The hiddenness which the religious man seeks (lest he be surprised at prayer and flush and feel sheepish, quite like a young girl) is therefore probably of an erotic nature, modesty with regard to one's feelings, but it can also be cowardice, which does not dare to be too earnest, which looks fine on Sunday in the preacher's sermon and which on the basis of geography[691] is the case with all of us, since, of course, we are all Christians.

X^1 A 22   *n.d.*, 1849

« 4373

There is something dialectical here. It can be a spiritual trial [*Anfægtelse*], but it can also be true that a man demands too much of God, wants to be far too much spirit and thus in a certain sense wants to love God more or differently than God can allow and will tolerate, if in connection with all his suffering and temptation [*Fristelse*] he always wants to be helped only spiritually. There are innocent human aids (diversion, physical recreation, etc.) which a man dare not disregard without demanding too much of God.

But there is something dialectical here. For sometimes there is an unwillingness or there is in a person a human indolence which is unwilling to be spirit and which promptly grasps at the easier expedients and then says that it is sometimes because it does not dare demand too much of God. But sometimes it can also be a spiritual pride, or it can be an overstrained dejection which actually demands too much of God and of itself. To the former one must say: No, do not spare yourself, just persevere. To the latter: Do not presume too much, or do not become a self-tormentor.

Certainly a great, great deal of suffering and spiritual trial which can be blown away by human expedients can become almost a world event if it is going to be endured or conquered by spirit alone. What is strenuous is the infinite transparency[692] before God. The human expedients are all calculated to draw attention outward. In many respects what is a wife, for example, but an excellent diversionary means, likewise mechanical activities, association with others. But as diversionary means these are all dangerous, for they virtually attack ideality.

Ideality's truth is this: each human being is the one and only human being—but what an alleviation it is to know that one is a unit among ten, thousands, millions. How easy life finally becomes—almost nothing.

Yet, to repeat, the diversionary means could be necessary. But, of course, the proud and the dejected get immersed in them too easily if they are spiritually permitted to do so.

Let us take such a person. He says: But if I am going to submit unconditionally to everything, ultimately the spirit must surely help, or is spirit not absolute? Yes, of course, but take care, you are not completely spirit. On the other hand, he can be tortured constantly by the thought: But if I just hold out a moment more, perhaps spiritual help will come—and that is just what I want. But this must be answered as follows: Certainly you are somewhat right; it is not commendable for a man to say right away: If only I could get some help, become satisfied, it makes no difference whether it is with the help of the spirit or by means which divert away from spirit; but it is still true that absolutely no man has the right to say: I insist absolutely on being helped only by spirit, for if he had the right to will something absolutely, then it must be this: to be helped, and then to be grateful for diversionary means.

No doubt the rule for spiritual advisers generally should be to advise a person not to spare himself but to endure being and becoming spirit. Genuinely spiritual persons are so rare that they can be handled appropriately as exceptions.

The norm, therefore, is: in a few exceptional cases recommend diversionary aids, but as a rule prescribe aids of the spirit, for men use diversionary aids all too promiscuously of their own accord. The exceptions are the sick, for whom diversionary aids are prescribed; most people are much too robust, so the operation is precisely to make them a little sick, a little weak—by prescribing that they use the aids of the spirit.

X^1 A 452 *n.d.*, 1849

« 4374

There is also an anxiety about sin which avoids Christ, at least to a certain extent, and yet is related to him. It is quite in order that a person who wishes to continue his sin avoids Christ. But it is another thing for a person who in his anxiety about sin avoids if possible every temptation [*Fristelse*] or every occasion for temptation—one would think he would be unconditionally constrained to seek Christ and there find rest. But this is not always easy and not always readily understood. In his anxiety he may sometimes think that there is a safe place where he can avoid temptation; if his understanding thinks it has discovered this place, he becomes more calm and the temptation actually retreats. All of this is fine and, humanly speaking, he is even to be commended. But there is still a little deceit involved. He thinks (and right here is the anxiety of spiritual trial [*Anfægtelse*]) that it is impossible for him to continue to survive the temptation; if his understanding guarantees that it has found a place where temptation (which is assumed to come from without, and precisely this is part of "the anxiety" and shows that there is still some honesty in him, for if the temptation originates within himself, then it would be impossible to find any such place) cannot reach him—then he is secure. But what does this mean? Even if he prays and ever so fervently calls on Christ's name, Christ is still not a Savior for him. He struggles on his own as well as he can, employs, honestly, we may say, all his understanding to avoid the temptation, and thereby secure evades the actual danger and then, perhaps, gratefully submits it to Christ. But the faith that Christ would help him conquer this temptation he does not have.

This is one of the most tormenting forms of spiritual trial.

X^1 A 477 *n.d.*, 1849

« 4375

Humanly speaking, Job's wife was in a certain sense right. For humanly it is in truth an enormous additional burden to suffer this way and then also be strained by the thought that God nevertheless is love. This is almost enough to make a person lose his mind—and, humanly, it is far easier to despair—period.

In sufferings and spiritual trials [*Anfægtelser*] there are actually combinations such that the thought of God and the thought that he nevertheless is love make the suffering far more strenuous. Here it is a case of faith being tested, of love being put to the test, whether one really loves God and really cannot do without him. Humanly speaking, a person who is experiencing such suffering is justified in saying: The whole thing would be far less agonizing to me if I did not have the idea of God along with it. The pain lies either in being left helpless by God, the omnipotent, who could so easily help, or in the crucifixion of one's understanding, that in spite of all this God is love and that what happens is for one's own good. Humanly speaking, it is dreadful to be like a sparrow or even less with regard to having an interpretation and fragmentary understanding about something he presumably can pass judgment on—his own suffering. The alleviating aspect of despair is its unmitigated agreement that the suffering is unbearable. The strenuousness of the idea of God is to have to understand that not only is the suffering to be endured but that it is a good, a gift from a God of love. Think of it! When a person inflicts suffering upon another man and then himself wants to be the cruel one who says: This is cruel—there is relief in this. But if the person who inflicts the suffering says: This is a benefit—that, humanly speaking, is enough to drive one out of his mind.

Yet this is only a spiritual trial, which can be dreadful enough as long as it lasts. But blessedly to endure with God. The first lesson is simply a matter of immediately grasping the God-idea, and then one gains alleviation. In the second lesson (and here lies the real spiritual trial) it is as if the God-idea itself intensified one's agony. Here it is a matter of enduring in faith. If you do not let go of God, it will still end in your blessedly agreeing with God that this suffering was a benefit. For God will be in the right, unconditionally; O, but the height of blessedness is to agree unconditionally that God is right precisely when, humanly speaking, there seems to be a case against him. God wants to be believed, unconditionally; but He, the Infinite One, cannot do anything other than jack up the price of faith[693] infinitely high. How blessed to believe—the higher the price the more blessed it is to believe—the more dearly you buy faith, the more blessed it is. How sad and shameful to have bought the highest of all for the lowest bargain price, if this were possible: how blessed to have bought it at the highest price. Even a lover speaks in this way; he is not happy to have gotten the beloved as a bargain; the more he paid the happier he is—the very price is his joy. Yet in erotic love there is always a possible irregularity, that in the long run the price might interest him almost more than the beloved, but this is impossible with faith.

Lessing[694] must have had something similar in mind when he said that he would choose the left hand, continuous striving. But he was wrong insofar as this is a little too erotic and smacks a little too much, also in relation to truth, of wanting to regard the price as being more valuable than the truth. But this is really a kind of selfishness and can easily become a dangerous, yes, a presumptuous error.

X^1 A 478 *n.d.,* 1849

« 4376 *Concerning Spiritual Trial* [Anfægtelse]

[*In margin:* concerning spiritual trial]

Simply because the essentially Christian in the more rigorous sense is in many ways related inversely to the universally human—Christian love from a human point of view is like cruelty (and yet again love), sympathy is a higher kind of rigorousness, and yet again it is sympathy, except that here there is a sort of dialectical middle term, whereas ordinarily the essentially Christian and the directly human run together—for this very reason the horror of spiritual trial consists in this that when a person feels weak he turns around and goes back to the purely human, and he is not far removed from seeming to have to repent of what in a crucial sense is more essentially Christian, as if it were out-and-out cruelty, out-and-out rigorousness, out-and-out price, etc.

This is how God keeps the Christian in his power. The school of spiritual trial is a frightful school. Spiritual trial can also express itself in such a way that it seems as if one should indeed repent for having ventured so far out, just as for a sin, for having come in contact with spiritual trial at all. For the person who does not get involved with God decisively is *eo ipso* exempt from spiritual trial. In a weak moment venturing so far out seems to be pride, and pride ought indeed be repented. And yet Christianity is precisely this—to become decisively involved with God.

Spiritual trial is a terrible thing. Yet I owe it to truth to testify that an intimation of a higher and more blessed understanding constantly smolders therein. It is almost like the suffering of having something in mind and not being able to express it. We have a presentiment of bliss —but for the time being it expresses itself only in the most horrible agony.

X^2 A 189 *n.d.*, 1849

« 4377 *Spiritual Trial*

Just as a woman, because she is far too intensely preoccupied with thinking about her one and only beloved, suddenly has almost a feeling of revulsion for her beloved, whom she really does love, so also there is a religious spiritual trial, also found described by older writers, in which a disgust for the religious sets in, although it is still the highest reality [*Realitet*] for the sufferer, but he has been occupied too much with it. There is nothing to do here but to have patience and to be quiet; then the joy comes again and all the more strongly.

x^2 A 590 *n.d., 1850*

« 4378 *The Tactic against Spiritual Trial* [Anfægtelse]

James 4:7: Resist the devil, and he will flee from you.

This, then, is the tactic. Not the reverse: Flee the devil—this can be the tactic only in relation to temptation [*Fristelse*].

Here we see that spiritual trial lies a whole quality higher than temptation. Humanly speaking, it is always an alleviation to have a possibility for, and deliverance in, flight from the danger. This is not the case with spiritual trial. But from this, again, a new spiritual trial is born, because for a long time it will seem to the spiritual combatant as if he perhaps had taken on too much, as if he perhaps ought to have tried flight. This again is a spiritual trial. Spiritual trial can be fought only with the rashness of faith, which charges head-on. But in his weak moments the believer grows uneasy and fearful over this rashness of faith, as if it were even a way of tempting God, which again is a spiritual trial.

x^4 A 95 *n.d., 1851*

« 4379 *Spiritual Trial* [Anfægtelse]

The majority of men no doubt live essentially without religiousness, or at most have religiousness in the same sense as they go to the theater now and then, which is nul-religiousness. As far as they are concerned, spiritual trial is completely out of the question.

Then there are a few individuals who do have some religiousness, who live their daily life within religious conceptions. They live somewhat like this: God is the one they depend upon to make everything go well for them, provided they themselves are circumspect, prudent, stay out of all dangers, etc. Here spiritual trial is completely out of the question.

Then comes authentic Christian religiousness—whether or not a religious person like this is to be found, I do not know; I have never seen one. This religiousness believes with the N. T. that truly to keep close to God definitely means suffering in this world, that religiousness means to will to witness for the truth, to suffer, to sacrifice—all, of course, without the conceit of meritoriousness. But inasmuch as they venture out in this way, for them the mark or the sign of the God-relationship is the opposition of the world, persecution, suffering. This is spirit, and the witness of the spirit bears them up. But in dull and lackluster moments they sink down from this high intensification—and now the change takes place—it seems to them that the world's opposition perhaps proves that they are wrong, it is perhaps arrogant of them to have ventured out this way, so that they almost repent and regret as guilt what was their most honest enthusiasm. This, you see, is spiritual trial. The natural man tends to believe that having everything go well is the sign of his relationship to God. "Spirit" recognizes God's relationship in the opposition, in suffering, and has the courage and faith for an interminable polemic; Luther[695] illustrates this when he quite correctly proves that he is the true Church from the fact that they are a despised little flock, that the true Church always is marked by suffering, and those who persecute the true Church instead of suffering thus become the triumphant false Church. (The passage is from *Geist aus Luthers Schriften: Kirche*, 5780.) But in every dull and lusterless moment the spiritual man sinks down to being the natural man, and then comes spiritual trial.

He who egotistically wants only to live in clover and have God help him to profit can never experience spiritual trial. For if he is a big success, he will be so bewitched that he will be blind to his true condition. If he fails, if this perhaps helps him to become aware of his true condition, and he now repents his former life, this is not spiritual temptation, because to repent of something bad implies a very good straightforward intention. Spiritual temptation consists in this: it seems as if one must repent of his best. And it is enough to make one lose his mind. For God in his Word sits, so to speak, and lures a man out, or commands him to venture out—and then when he momentarily lets the man go, everything turns around for him.

x^4 A 411   n.d., 1851

« 4380 *A Psychological Observation*

We are brought up in Christianity so leniently that one may actually be faced with a spiritual trial [*Anfægtelse*]: whether or not trying one's hardest to have the kind of integrity Christianity demands (not wanting to use the usual shabby means, not wanting to make a profit, not wanting to sing with the birds one is among, etc.), whether or not this may even be against God, whether or not this is arrogance, pride, wanting to be better than others, so that instead of being pleased, God disapproves of my striving.

You see, for us what God wants and what we must do unconditionally is no longer unconditionally firm, but "grace" has been introduced wrongly, all too soon.

X⁴ A 431   n.d., 1851

« 4381 *Amor and Psyche*

I am reading the story in Apuleius⁶⁹⁶ again this very day. The fourth test which Venus assigns Psyche is to get the box from Proserpine—and the dangers along the way consist mainly of meeting such sights and objects as will move her to sympathy and therefore delay her and hold her back.

I have observed in other legends, too, that in relation to the extraordinary, what in Greek style might be called the divine venture, is shaped by delaying factors or something which tempts [*frister*] one to remain behind, tempts one to sympathy.

And rightly so. For dangers and the like scare the ordinary human being back. But then there are the brave ones. Dangers and the like do not scare them, and therefore spiritual trial [*Anfægtelse*] is given the shape of sympathy. And usually it is precisely the brave ones who are disposed to show sympathy for others. Ordinary persons probably could not be detained so easily by sympathy even if they themselves had the courage to meet the dangers, but it is the brave ones who are most indulgent in the direction of showing sympathy.

Take an example. To identify oneself with an idea. Well, the ordinary man is kept by fear of danger from risking such a thing; he cringes back and would rather be content with being a copy of others. But the brave one. Quite right, he does not cringe before the dangers. But note—such a thing cannot be done without making some people unhappy—and here in the area of sympathy lies the spiritual trial.

X⁴ A 462   n.d., 1852

« 4382 *Thoughts That Try the Spirit*
    [anfægtende Tanker]

Quite simply, the tactic is this: be completely indifferent to them; the most absolute indifference to them is itself the victory. Such thoughts want to make you anxious, want to worry you to the point where your spirit is so weak and cowardly that you imagine that you are responsible for them; they want to worry themselves into you, foist themselves on you so that you will listen to them, brood on them, etc., and all this amid the torment that you have the responsibility. Once they have made you think this, the devil is loose. Therefore be absolutely indifferent; be more indifferent to them than you are to a little rumbling in your stomach. Or get angry, as angry as you can get when someone rings your doorbell at an inopportune time and you rush out and say: What kind of an uproar is this! —That is, get angry just short of being afraid, for this is precisely what should be avoided.

Temptation [*Fristelse*] is best fought by running away, avoiding it. But this does not work with thoughts that try the spirit, for they pursue you. Here the tactic must be: do not get frightened, remain utterly calm, absolutely indifferent.

Thoughts that try the spirit (which are entirely in order when a person is to be placed under tension commensurate with the tension of being a Christian and also under the tension of the imagination) do not appear at all these days among Christians, particularly among Protestants, particularly in Denmark. Of course this is even regarded as progress, yes, progress backward, the kind of progress the physician talks about in *Barselstuen:*[697] The patient is dead, but the fever has completely left him—in the very same way thoughts which try the spirit have vanished, but so, of course, has Christianity.

XI^2 A 30 *n.d.*, 1854

« **4383** *Thoughts That Try the Spirit*

are related, as mentioned before [i.e., XI^2 A 30], to the imagination— pure rationalists do not know about such things.

They are best compared with *flatus* (wind). As such they are nothing but can certainly make one uncomfortable as long as they last.

And, to continue the analogy, just as those who suffer from abdominal distress must take care to have a thorough evacuation every day, so a good evacuation in the form of action-in-character is the best remedy against thoughts that try the spirit. It is in the time prior to action, when one has not made up his mind or is not clear about what he is supposed to do, that such tormenting spirits turn up, just as the morning and evening twilight is the time for ghosts. They are: possibility, a product of possibility—the best remedy against them is: actuality.

XI^2 A 33 *n.d.*, 1854

« **4384** *Thoughts That Try the Spirit*

When I say that the interpretation that suffering connected with becoming a Christian comes from the devil is not a truly Christian interpretation but that suffering comes from the God-relationship itself, this must of course be understood with the addition that in one sense suffering also comes from the individual himself, from the fact that his subjectivity cannot immediately and completely surrender to God.

In older and better devotional literature we read much about thoughts which try the spirit [*anfægtende Tanker*] and cause the individual to suffer, thoughts described as burning arrows and ascribed to the devil. But this is not a truly Christian interpretation; such thoughts come from the individual himself, although innocently.

The fact is that when God loves a man and a man is loved by God, this man *qua* selfish will has to be completely demolished. This is what it means to die to the world;[698] it is the most intense agony. But even if the religious person in accord with his better will is willing enough to do this, he can neither promptly nor completely get his will, his subjectivity, into the power of the better will[699] in him, and therefore, after first making a most desperate resistance, it still continues to watch for a chance to disorganize the whole revolution that dethroned it.

No religious person, even the purest, has sheer, purified subjectivity or pure transparency[700] in willing solely what God wills, so that there is no residue of his original subjectivity, a residue still not wholly penetrated, a remote portion of residue still uncaptured, perhaps as yet not even really discovered in the depths of his soul—out of this come the reactions.

But as the old devotional literature rightly teaches, the individual is completely innocent in this. Far from being something to be charged against him, these thoughts which try the spirit prove that he has really become thoroughly involved and engaged. The police are totally innocent when by really involving themselves in a case they uncover more and more crime, but the police are guilty when their inactivity makes it appear as if there were no crime. Thus physical security and mediocrity are completely ignorant of thoughts that try the spirit—this in fact is its guilt and fault, its new crime, proof that it has no intimation at all of what the essentially Christian task is, for dying to the world, slaying his will, are truly not the kind of operation which can go on unnoticed, as if it were nothing.

XI^2 A 132   *n.d.*, 1854

STAGES

« **4385**

Just as there are people who, like fashionable French shops, display everything they have, so also there are those with intimations of something profound but whose profundity is still only like that of a drop of water or a mirror—everything in it is a reflection.

I A 52   April 3, 1835

« **4386**

It is very interesting to see the results of the practical life-examinations passed by very great individuals. For instance, a Goethe[701]: *"Vanitas vanitatum vanitas." Ich hab' mein Sach auf Nichts gestellt Juche* etc.; a Kingo:[702] "Farewell, then, world, farewell"; a Herder,[703] for example, in a little poem in the English style where he relates that only two flowers remain for him—love and friendship; Schleiermacher:[704] My soul's spiritual pulse will beat with the same brisk stroke until I breathe my last, etc.

I A 121   February, 1836

« **4387**

I have pointed out the juxtaposition of Sancho Panza and D. Quixote, D. Juan and Leporello, Faust and Wagner; similarly Figaro is a contrast to a stock character; so also in the fairy tale a nurse usually accompanies the princess as an adviser.

I A 122   February, 1836

« **4388**

Lest a person become haughty over being able to change, he must assume that it is with divine assistance that this can be done. Tieck[705] tells a story (in his novel, *Der junge Tischlermeister*, Berlin, 1836, I, in the beginning) about a man who quit drinking but who then soon believed that he was a prophet.

I A 167   June 6, 1836

« **4389**

Foreknowledge—hints in life—of various kinds dependent upon one's attitude toward it—anticipation of st. [studies?], for example, how many books have I bought because of an odd inclination and left lying until—also events inverted *fata morgana*. Reminded of a scene in Scribe. Also in *Faust*. Also in sickness—

I A 183   *n.d.*, 1836

« 4390

In life very much depends upon being alert to catch one's cue.

I A 279   *n.d.*, 1836

« 4391

May it not seem right to do as that ancient sect[706] (see Church History) did—go through all the vices simply to have experience of life. —

I A 282   *n.d.*, 1836

« 4392

The square is a parody of the circle; all life, all thought is a circle, but the petrifaction of life results in crystalline forms which never become circles. This is why it is so characteristic of the Chinese, for whom everything is fossilized, to regard the earth as square and their kingdom as the innermost square—this is something for square heads. —

I A 313   December 24, 1836

« 4393

Addition to 4392 (I A 313):

I wonder if there is any crystallization at all in the form of a circle; if this is the case, then the matter is clear, since the squared tends to remain fixed—to die.

I A 314   January 8, 1837

« 4394

There must be a stage in the development of mythology which corresponds to that whole period in childhood when the individual is so minimally separated from the whole that he says: Me[707] hit the horse —the stage in which the individual is so minimally separated from the whole that he comes to view only in fleeting moments, something like *"die Wellenmädchen"*[708] in the sketch found in the Wollmer prints (*Vollständiges Wörterbuch der Mythologie*, plate CXV),[709] where the individual is correctly portrayed and rendered graphic as a procreative power in the process of becoming.

I A 319   January 7, 1837

« 4395

I hope that gradually the momentary consolation and gratification —which is nothing but the bush that shot up and shaded Jonah[710] (at the time of his formidable call to proclaim doom to the people of Nineveh; and as long as we have the same call, so to speak, with respect to ourselves, we may enjoy the same solace to the utmost) only to wither right away—will be followed by a far deeper calm, with the result that the surface may be painfully disturbed but the deep inwardness is unaffected.

I A 321   January 17, 1837

« 4396

There are many people who arrive at conclusions in life much the way schoolboys do; they cheat their teachers by copying the answer out of the arithmetic book without having worked the problem themselves.

I A 322   January 17, 1837

« 4397 *Something about the Page in "Figaro," Papageno in "The Magic Flute," and Don Juan*[711]

Tonight for the first time I shall see *The Magic Flute*. It has occurred to me that it might have significance with respect to Don Juan and might fill out a stage between him and the Page in *Figaro*. I am of the opinion that in these three stages Mozart has consummately and perfectly presented a development of love on the level of immediacy.

(1) The Page in *Figaro* is the first level in the development. This is the level of undefined, awakening desire in an unconscious conflict with the environment: it is a play of colors from which gradually there develops a pure color: it is the level not of a given *I* but of the becoming *I* with its searching feelers. Just as all coming into existence [*Tilblivelse*] is a polemic, so also is life itself: on the first level [it is] not conscious but is a continual approximation of consciousness. It identifies itself in a way with the world (the child's "me"),[712] but precisely because it is a life, a development, precisely for that reason there is an endless approach toward definite conscious desire, yet without its thereby appearing as a final factor, since it rather comes all at once as a new point of departure and cannot be explained by everything that has happened previously. All the abundance of life and the full range in which it moves on the different levels of its development are presented: the whole horizon of life with all its variety is presented (but simply

because the *I* is not given, the question could perhaps arise as a conclusion at the highest stage of approximation: Why did one not see the earth, which after all is also a celestial body in the heavens)—therefore, like the plant imprisoned at one spot, it exhales its longing, sheds forth the fragrance of its desire, but the longing and desire are not so definite that they wrench him from the earth in order to find what is sought after. On the contrary, it seems as if the objects of his desiring glide past him in great numbers, and if he wants to grasp at a particular one and at the same time leave it alone, it is not because it disappears before him—in such a case his desire would either be so intense that it would suddenly wrench him loose from the earth in which he sprouted or else he would follow the vanishing object of desire with the yearning gaze of Ingeborg—but because something just as glorious and beautiful appears that very moment, something which, as it too vanishes, is succeeded by something equally glorious and beautiful, etc.—and this again is not because everything in all the fully developed abundance is equally beautiful, but because the individual at this point has not detached himself and therefore cannot establish any criterion, not even that of the plant which closes up in bad weather or at a profane touch (because the plant does not have desire in this sense). —And how could I better express this than to recall the Page's rapture over every girl he sees along the way, indeed, even reacts the same way to old Dr. Bartholo's housekeeper. From the foregoing the basis of what is distinctive in the melancholy of this level should be evident, that it arises because the whole fullness of life presses down and, so to speak, overwhelms one; whereas the melancholy of another level (the romantic) can express itself, inasmuch as the individual, pursuing his vanishing object, is as if brought to a standstill by what it would call the poor, prosaic world.

That which is not taken up into the idea is the accidental and the unessential, which results from the reception of a foreign additive when it [the idea] is represented in a particular personality. This is the case with the Page, in that, so it seems, he is deeply *forliebt*[713] with the Countess, but this is accounted for in part by what I have just emphasized, and in part by the fact that the Page in *Figaro* has gone a little beyond the very middle point of that stage, and in this way a glimpse of one side of the third stage is given. —So it is in Papageno's duet in the fourth act, which shows that Mozart has filled out Papageno's position with inner consciousness. (Perhaps all his wanderings were for that purpose? Silence is imposed upon him, a sojourn with Isis and

Osiris, where the fugitive must settle down). Instead of the first and second stages being rounded out in the third stage as in Don Juan, Mozart has an individual at this point arrive at gratification. The Page's infatuation is to be interpreted in the same way, although it is not so obvious.

Note: In the awakening of the Page's love is there not something unbeautiful with respect to the as yet undeveloped sensuousness? May this perhaps be explained as being more natural in Italian life?

But the longing becomes more definite or, more correctly, by means of a contradiction (a continuous desire and an all too great gratification which is still not gratification), the first stage must move into the second stage. The longing detaches itself from the home soil and takes to wandering. The heart beats faster, the objects appear and disappear more rapidly, but still before every disappearance there is an instant [*et Nu*] of pleasure, brief but happy, gleaming like a firefly, inconstant and fleeting as a butterfly, countless kisses, but so hurriedly enjoyed, as if he tore them away from one girl in order to give them to the next one, and yet with occasional darts of desire for a deeper satisfaction which, however, never gets time to take form as such.*

(2) *Papageno in "The Magic Flute"*** This is the second stage, just as the perpendicular direction of plant life is superseded by the horizontality of locomotion. Melancholy does not take form at all as on the previous level, because the desire following upon the pleasure is satisfied at once by a new pleasure—even if not completely (see above) yet in such a way that the remaining desire is again gratified by a new pleasure—even though not completely—and so on and on endlessly. It is not the melancholy stare, fixed upon itself, as it were, which seemingly cannot forget the past object upon the presentation of the new —and so on endlessly; it is like the concentration of the soul in the eyes all at once for an instant—a single object—and then concentrating on the next, and so on endlessly, but yet in such a way that the full concentration does not take place because almost at the same instant a new pleasure presents itself.

(3) Now we approach the third stage, Don Juan, who is the unity of both stages and is the final stage of the development of immediacy (by calling it immediacy I wish to indicate that as striving it has not yet reached consciousness of its relation to the world, but magnetically

---

* It is the level found in plants with the male and female on the same stem.
** Skjærvæk in *Apothekeren og Doctoren*[714] is somewhat analogous to Papageno.

seeks its gratification). This stage is a unity of the two previous ones, in that the deep, infinitely melancholy draining of the whole fullness of love (like the horn from which Thor[715] drank at Loki's, the horn with its tip in the ocean) is united on one side with the exuberant variety, and therefore all the striving is infinite in intensity as well as in extensity and thus in constant contradiction with itself.[*] Moreover, I do not believe that the first aspect (intensity) is sufficiently emphasized in the adaptations we have of Don Juan, although significant clues in this respect are found, of course, in Mozart.

Just one more observation: naturally, all three stages, being immediate, are purely musical,† and any attempt in another presentation is likely to endow them with far too much consciousness.

(Note: Does not the more mediated love-life begin in Faust, insofar as he reproduces Don Juan?)

I C 125   Thursday afternoon, January 26, 1837

[*] *In margin:* Through this contradiction appears the significance of married life—debauchery (for this does not enter into the first stage).

In margin: †I mean, specifically, that the immediate (lyrical) level is completed through a steady ascent in music (prose—immediate musical verse —reflective musical verse—music). All the reflections about this are so sparse, because it is by far an *einfachere*[716] medium for one's expression. The significance of music in the treatment of the insane. Music completes the immediate level, just as actions another, concepts another.

« **4398** *Something about Life's Four Stages, also Concerning Mythology*

The first is the stage in which the child has not separated himself from his surroundings ("me").[717] The *I* is not given, but [there is] the possibility of it, and to that extent it is a conflict. It is gestalted in vague and fleeting outlines, just like the sea-maidens the waves produce only to form new ones again (see a copper etching).[718] I would like to think that all these profuse and fleeting forms will be formed into a unity by a stroke of magic, these multitudinous elements standing alongside each other in childhood, crowding each other out in order to enter into the eternal present of the *I;* in childhood there is an atomistic multiplicity, in the *I* there is the one in the many. As far as I know mythology, this stage corresponds to the Oriental mythologies. It is the divine fullness which streams down like the golden rain on Danaë's lap; to use an expression from dogmatics, it is the original righteousness which, as the Catholic dogmaticians believe, was given to man—in superabundance, if I may say so. But as life by means of an endless approximation comes closer to self-consciousness, the more apparent the conflict becomes. And thus in addition I get the multiplicity which has been regarded as adequate justification for calling these mythologies romantic, yet only somewhat analogous to what I call romanticism, since the genuinely romantic stage is the reproduced first stage. But at this point life still has not gained self-consciousness, still has not gained a center of gravity within itself, and thus the multiplicity exerts a pressure. Just as in a room with a low ceiling (it is relatively the same, however high or low it is) an extremely complicated and overcrowded painting on the ceiling seems to press down and gives one the feeling that it is sinking down, just so is the heaven of the Orientals, whereas the Greeks' light drawings and beautiful forms produce harmony and serenity.

But after this turmoil comes a peace, an idyllic well-being. It is the youth's satisfaction in family and school (church and state); this is the second stage: Greek mythology. Here is genuine equilibrium, here the divine is merged in the world (see a lot of paper scraps on this) in such a way as it never has merged or ever will, either before or after in the world's development, although this is indeed the case in the single individual's development, for in what I specifically call the romantic a question arises about a satisfaction lying beyond the world and which therefore cannot be found in the world, and even in the fourth stage [it is to be found] only in the form that there is still so much given in the world which is adequate if one is modest and unassuming (resignation), yet there is little to hope for; at least this is the way Christianity, which certainly has the greatest historical significance regarding the solution of this issue, has answered it. Yes, fundamentally Christianity has everything to hope for, so the expression "little" really refers to the philosopher's struggle.

Note: Observations on the last two stages are to be found among my papers.

Note: The system has only three stages: immediate, reflective, and unity. Life has four.

Note: To what extent does Hegel include my first two stages, since his first stage (the immediate) as pure abstraction is actually nothing, and all philosophy before its retrogressive systematic movement must begin with the conflict; in his system he perhaps has the conflict between the *I* and the world as the first stage but not the corresponding

« 4399

One must not be in too much of a hurry with his rebirth, lest it go as it did with the sorcerer Virgilius[719] when he was going to rejuvenate himself and to that end had let himself be put to death (hacked to pieces), and then, through the carelessness of the one who was supposed to watch the kettle, it was opened too soon, and Virgilius, who at this point had just become an infant, disappeared with a doleful wail.

II A 152   August 31, 1837

« 4400

It would be interesting to follow the development of human nature (in the individual man—that is, at various ages) by showing what one laughs at on the different age levels, in part by making these experiments with one and the same author, for example, our literary fountainhead, Holberg, and in part by way of the different kinds of comedy. It would—together with research and experiments concerning the age level at which tragedy is most appreciated and with other psychological observations about the relation between comedy and tragedy, why, for example, one reads tragedy alone by himself and comedy together with others—contribute to the work I believe ought to be written—namely, the history of the human soul (as it is in an ordinary human being) in the continuity of the state of the soul (not of the concept) consolidating itself in particular mountain-clusters (that is, noteworthy world-historical representatives of life-views).

II A 163   September 20, 1837

« 4401

In Grimm's Irish fairy stories[720] (which he says, referring to the English original, were gathered from the people with their idiocies and mainly in *verba ipsissima*)[721] it is remarkable that on the subject of the "quiet people," "the goblins," after they are first deprived of the innocence of imagination and the question is raised as to their being good or evil spirits in their relations with human beings, both answers are given: [p. 20] Die Mahlzeit des Geistlichen: Leute, die sich auf solche Dinge verstehen, sagen, das stille Volk sey ein Theil jener aus dem Himmel verstossenen Engel, die nun auf Erden festen Fuss ge-

first analogous stage, and his peace is not Grecian, which can correspond only to a prior stage, which is my first one but Hegel's last.

I C 126   January 27, 1837

fasst haben, während ein anderer Theil grösserer Sünden wegen, an einen viel schlimmern Ort noch tiefer gesunken sey ..... p. 42. Die Flasche: In den guten Tagen, wo das stille Folk sich noch haüfiger sehen liess, als jetzt in dieser ungläubigen Zeit.⁷²² Yet this question is by no means answered with bourgeois meticulousness, but the latent irony (see book two, no. 2) actually makes it impossible to know whether to smile at those frightened by these creatures or at those who want to master them with their great presumed superiority. At any rate we usually find these creatures taking not a malicious but rather a sarcastic vengeance.—

II A 169   September 29, 1837

« **4402**

In margin of 4401 (II A 169):
just as it is remarkable, after all, that during the time when these creatures lived in legend in the naïveté of the most prolix imagination —at the same time the question is raised about their being good or evil spirits. But for one thing we should be pleased that this question was raised but also promptly dropped: *das mag dahin gestellt bleiben* (Grimm, p. 20),⁷²³ and for another [we should note] that while in those days the fear of God was greater and for that reason abhorrence of evil greater, there also was a certain childlikeness in the conception of good and evil with respect to God's standpoint as well, and I daresay that there is a deep melancholy in the Middle Ages' concept of sin, but also some roguishness (just as we see in children the hope which is always so lively here—and also the marvelous receptivity for genius that is present in this), which in no way should be confused with the trivial, sophistical sensibleness of our prosaic age, in which we are constantly losing in the idea the more we win in actuality—that is, we get historically actual hypocrites etc. and all those dreadful vices, because we will not be satisfied with getting them in legends, in the manna of tradition.—

II A 170   n.d.

« **4403**

On the whole there are two movements which young life has to go through, movements perpetuated in the Middle Ages and accessible for consideration in an unconscious contemporaneity—the age of chivalry and scholasticism.

II A 218   April 4, 1838

« **4404**

Genuine depression, like being splenetic, is to be found only in the highest circles—this expression understood in the first case in the spiritual sense.

II A 721   April 14, 1838

« **4405**

It takes some time before we really settle down and feel at home (know where everything has its place) in the divine economy. We grope around amid a multiplicity of moods, do not even know how we should pray; Christ does not take on any definite configuration in us[724]—we do not know what the cooperation of the Spirit means, etc.

II A 756   July 7, 1838

« **4406**

It is not only in the history of art that the Dutch distinguish themselves by their *Stilleben*[725] but also just as much in a spiritual sense, in tone* and color equally characteristic (Beguines, etc.).

*The Lollards got their name from their low funeral song; who would not be prompted by it to think of the four insane brothers in Claudius,[726] and what more deadly kind of *Stilleben* is there?

II A 279   October 26, 1838

« **4407**

The life of every individual also has its Genesis and then its Exodus* (its exit into the world), its Leviticus, when the mind turns toward heaven, its Numbers, when one begins to count the years, its Deuteronomy.

In margin: *See Luke 9:31.

II A 321   January 6, 1839

« **4408**

In patience let us gain our souls (see Luke 21:19).[727]

II A 339   January 28, 1839

« **4409**

Longing is the umbilical cord of the higher life.

II A 343   February 1, 1839

« **4410**

In a spiritual sense, too, there comes a moment when we feel that we ourselves achieve nothing at all, when we go as if naked* out of our self-scrutiny,** as we did formerly from the womb—

II A 357   February 8, 1839

« **4411**

In margin of 4410 (II A 357):
*And then like Adam we must say with deep sorrow: I heard your voice in the garden and saw that I was naked, and therefore I hid myself. Genesis 3:10.

II A 358   n.d.

« **4412**

In margin of 4410 (II A 357):
**But it is also necessary in order that good can create something out of us, for God always creates out of nothing and needs neither material nor our self-conceit—neither suitable nor unsuitable material.

II A 359   n.d.

« **4413** *Bibliography*

1. *The Book of Nature.* This book is very voluminous and as yet no one has succeeded in getting it bound; therefore an attempt has been made with duodecimo—sextodecimo editions which were believed to contain the most important things, leaving out all of nature's tiresome repetitions. The last attempt[728] to get the whole work completely collected and bound in fifty trustworthy leather-bound volumes, *systeme de la nature,* failed completely, and nature was all too natural to wear a French corset.

2. *The Book of Oblivion.* Although in *The Book of Nature* nothing is forgotten, just as in nature nothing is forgotten, in *The Book of Oblivion* nothing is forgotten which ought to be forgotten. This book is kept by an auxiliary corps of all sorts of secretaries of all sorts of ages, all sorts of nations, all sorts of points of view; it is kept with painstaking scrupulousness, set in tasteful German type and elegant lapidary style; with appropriate type and emphases it is one calligraphic masterpiece. At the same time it is an ideal which in spite of Herculean efforts is by no means finished; not until the world is so aged, so advanced in years, that it really can make up its mind on everything, not until the art of writing has become so speedy that it can instantaneously commit it to paper, a *litteris tradere,* and have it preserved, only then is it finished.

3. *The Book of Life.*

II A 459   n.d., 1839

« 4414

Young man,⁷²⁹ you who presumptuously depend upon your strength, perhaps at some time it will be said of you as of the rich man: you have enjoyed your wealth—some time when adulthood and age approach and assert their claims.

II A 500   n.d., 1839

« 4415

..... When one turns around in order to interpret life behind him, even though what he inspects is exactly what he has experienced, and however circumspectly he has lived through it, however often, for the sake of the *way back,* he has impressed upon himself that the road which now goes to the right must then go left, and all the bends and turns conform to this rule—one still has trouble at times making head or tail out of it, because so much of it appears entirely different than it did earlier, just as one continually experiences on walking tours that when he has reached his destination and takes the same way *back,* the whole region appears entirely different. How much more true this must be in the world of the spirit, where no external tangibility at all is assumed outside oneself, but where everything depends upon one's thought, thinking clarifying itself.

II A 515   July 26, 1839

« 4416

Precisely because Don Juan is presented musically, his natural genius is emphasized; if a more reflective Don Juan is wanted, one could employ arbitrariness so that he seduces a girl not because she happens to stir him but because she awakens a pleasant memory and for diversion he wants to see if it can be realized—or she awakens a pleasant memory—to remain beyond his grasp forevermore.

III A 189   n.d., 1841

« 4417

What speculative validity does the old saying *opposita juxta se posita magis illucescunt*⁷³⁰ have in relation to the total structure of human life, to what extent is it merely a practical esthetic rule. If it has speculative validity, then the duality of life is posited.

IV A 4   n.d., 1842-43

« 4418

We ought to be as enthusiastic as Dion was when with a few companions he went to war against Dionysius. To take part in it, he said, was sufficient for him; if he were to die the moment he landed, without achieving a thing, he would still consider that death to be happy and heroic.

See Aristotle's *Politics* 5:10
(in Garve, p. 468).[731]

IV A 10   *n.d.*, 1842-43

« 4419

Augustus seems to have died very happy; in the hour of death he recited a Greek verse which means: *plaudite;*[732] Suetonius[733] quotes it: Δότε κρότον, καὶ πάντες ὑμεῖς μετὰ χαρᾶς κτυπήσατε.[734]
See Leibniz, *Theodicy*, para. 261.[735]

IV A 18   *n.d.*, 1842-43

« 4420

How is this [the relation between the speculating subject and historical existence] related to the world-historical development used so much now? In all ages man has had everything; the transaction takes place in cognition, feeling, and will; they rank equally high. There are two goals: every man is τέλος, and the world-historical development is τέλος, but this τέλος we cannot penetrate.

IV C 93   *n.d.*, 1842-43

« 4421

A pathos-filled transition—a dialectical transition.

IV C 94   *n.d.*, 1842-43

« 4422

The development of life is a strange retrogression; the child cudgels his brains to understand the most difficult things; the adult simply cannot understand the most simple.

IV A 52   *n.d.*, 1843

« 4423

Everyone has his hobby-horse and when his well-saddled horse is led out to him, up he goes, and then it is giddap and gallop.

IV B 57   *n.d.*, 1843

« **4424**

The ability to busy oneself continually with the same thing is a good sign, for it is only gypsies[736] who never come back to a place they once have been. (See *Preciosa*,[737] where the old gypsy woman says this.)

V A 76   *n.d.*, 1844

« **4425**

To be concerned about oneself.

VI B 175   *n.d.*, 1844-45

« **4426**

The spontaneous or immediate religious person does many things which the infinitely reflected religious person, when he does the same things because they are fine, must interpret half humorously and half penitently. For example, the immediate religious person goes to church three times every Sunday. He presumably does not build his salvation on that (then he would be irreligious or would not know what he is doing), but he is nevertheless happy to be able, as it were, to make a little repayment to God in return for all that God can do for him (the relevance of Socrates' words[738] when he would not accept an invitation to come to King Archelaus because he could not return the favor—in the same way many people do not become involved with God because they feel they will become a mere nothing). In the Old Testament, in Mohammedanism, in the Middle Ages, meritoriousness in the innocent sense, good works, appears. —The infinitely reflected religious person does the same things—for example, goes to church three times every Sunday, but interprets this in a purely humorous way and with a willingness to repent at once—in a humorous way, because he cannot omit it, because he cannot grow weary of hearing His Word and being in His house—half penitently if it should nevertheless be that he repeatedly needs new stimulation in his God-relationship.

VI A 52   *n.d.*, 1845

« **4427**

It is sometimes said that if one does not remain the same,* then there is no immortality. God knows how it is going to go with the kind of people who already in life are changed an incredible number of times.[739] (Plutarch's little article on the word $\epsilon\iota$ in Delphi, para. 18,[740] is very good.)

In margin: *after death.

VI A 71   *n.d.*, 1845

« 4428

> *Movement; Repetition; Decision*
> a trilogy
>
> VI A 112 n.d., 1845

« 4429

It is commonly known that the genuine pearl is formed by dew absorbed into the mussel.⁷⁴¹ But according to Ammianus Marcellinus⁷⁴² it makes a difference whether it is morning dew or evening dew that is absorbed. —It is the same with men: the noble individualities of hope or of memory.

VI A 114 n.d., 1845

« 4430 *The Dialectic of Admiration*

The esthetic-sensuous man admires the strange, that which has no relation to himself; the ethical man admires what has an essential likeness to himself—the great, that which can be the prototype of what he himself ought to be; the religious man admires God, who is of course the absolutely different but still is that with whom he ought to have likeness through the absolute unlikeness.⁷⁴³ (Adoration.)

VI A 123 n.d., 1845

« 4431

In the conscience—there God has the power. Let a man have all the power in the world—God is still the master there. One with power who knows he has the power speaks to the powerless like this: Do exactly what you wish, even let it appear that you are the one with power—the real situation remains a secret between you and me.

VII¹ A 45 n.d., 1846

« 4432

Amazing! There outside the city lies the garden of the dead—a little smallholder's plot, scarcely as large as a smallholder's plot, and yet it accommodates the whole content of life. It is a condensed reproduction of actuality, a concise epitome, a pocket-edition!⁷⁴⁴

VII¹ A 57 n.d., 1846

« 4433

The quality of an individual can be measured by the distance between his *understanding* and his *willing*. What a person is able to understand he must also be able to constrain himself to will. Between understanding and willing lie excuses and evasions.

VII¹ A 68   n.d., 1846

« **4434**

When the sea lies still, deeply transparent, we extol its purity and delight in this sublime picture. So also with a man's soul—when the lower, finite, and complex elements in it are in motion, it is like muddied water, is murky, opaque, has no depth, but when it is quietly deep in willing only one thing, it is pure as the transparency of the sea. Therefore we compare the soul with water, and the image is appropriate: stillness is purity, when all that is impure sinks, purity is transparency, transparency is depth.[745]

VII¹ B 192:12   n.d., 1846

« **4435**

When the sea rages in storm and the sky is hidden, when sea and sky blend as one in the turmoil, we do not say that the sea is pure, however terrifying this drama is. Not until they are distinguished in peace, when the sky arches high over the sea, which deeply reflects it, not until then do we say that it is pure. Purity is not in the blending-into-one of the raging storm but in distinction. Therefore we compare the soul with the sea. When in the unity of confusion it arrogantly breaches the distinction between good and evil, it is riled and impure, but when the good like the fortress of heaven arches high over the soul, which deeply reproduces this oneness, we say it is pure. Distinction between good and evil is unity, confused unity is doubleness—ask a child about it if wisdom no longer is able to understand what a child understands simply! It is an image we use—is it perhaps inappropriate because the distinction between good and evil is not physical like the distinction between sea and sky,* or is it inappropriate because the sky is, after all, not the good and the sea the evil; if however the distinction is there and it is in a man's power to commingle it in the unity of confusion or humbly fortify the distinction in the purity of his heart—then the metaphor is indeed appropriate![746]

In margin: * but spiritually, therefore invisibly, hidden in the soul's invisibility.

VII¹ B 192:13   n.d., 1846

« **4436**

To will the good for the sake of reward is double-mindedness. But purity of heart is to will one thing. When a fog hangs over the sea, of what good is it that the heavens are high and bright; we still do not say that the sea is pure. Similarly there is a fog that hangs over willing the good; this fog is willing the good for the sake of reward. Reward is so far from helping a man to will the good in truth, that aspiring to reward, just like the fog, creates a separation: the good in its heavenly splendor remains far away from him, and his impure soul remains in the fog of reward. But the fog does not always come right away in the morning hours; sometimes it comes only later in the day, sometimes not until evening.[747]

VII[1] B 192:15 *n.d.*, 1846

« 4437

... This dizziness is quite simply a metaphysical sublimating of the esthetic, outside of the ethical. The ethical is and lives and moves in the distinction between good and evil; the esthetic is rooted in the quantitative: the great, the amazing, the daring, the dizzying; and the metaphysical is devoid of interest.[748]

VII[2] B 256:19 *n.d.*, 1846–47

« 4438

Instead of coming out of the tension through resolution and action, reflection holds him more and more firmly in it.[749]

VII[2] B 266:26 *n.d.*, 1846–47

« 4439

There is something very profound in the stories about the Mount of Venus,[750] that the person who went there was not able to find the way back. It is always difficult to find the way back from lust.

—Something similar is found in legends, that one under the spell of enchantment had to play the same piece backward, and every time he made the least mistake he had to begin this work all over again backward.

VIII[1] A 17 *n.d.*, 1847

« 4440

Sirach 2:12

"Woe to the timid hearts and the negligent hands, and a sinner who walks two roads."

VIII[1] A 22 *n.d.*, 1847

« 4441

The fact that the rifle clicks means not only that it does not go off (the negative) but also that with every click the spring loses more and more of its tension (the positive in the negative).

VIII¹ A 67   n.d., 1847

« 4442

There is so much exhortation to intimacy, but this kind of talk is again one of those deceitful fabrications. In a secular sense much intimacy does in fact make life easier—that is, more banal and frivolous. But do I have a right to make my life slovenly this way. By having only God as one's confidant, life becomes terribly strenuous—but is not this precisely what I should do. But there is confusion everywhere. Stealing can perhaps make a poor man's life far more comfortable—does he therefore have the right to do it? Similarly, it is extremely doubtful to what extent intimacy between man and man concerning the highest and the deepest things[751] is permissible; one thing is sure, it loses through this familiarity. What God can require of me no friend dares to require of me; and what I am constrained to do by having God alone for my confidant, the friend can promptly help me to chisel down.

VIII¹ A 78   n.d., 1847

« 4443

What a difference there is between the powerful puff of an animated breeze at the beginning—and a steady wind which uniformly fills the sails so that you advance steadily under full sail.

VIII¹ A 95   n.d., 1847

« 4444

An artist, a poet, a scientist, etc. may very well live admired through a whole lifetime, and it is accidental if such a one is persecuted or derided. Every such person relates himself differentially to the universally human, and, since his production is in the medium of the imagination it does not essentially touch existence.[752] But essentially an ethicist must come to be persecuted; otherwise he is a mediocre ethicist. An ethicist relates himself to the universally human (consequently to every man, and equally, not differentially), and he relates himself to human existence as a requirement. If the ethicist sees that men tend to admire him (which is quite all right for a poet, an artist, etc., since the relation is to that which differentiates), he must himself perceive that this is a deception, a lie. Men ought not admire an ethicist; they ought to be precipitated by him into the ethical life. The minute men are allowed to admire an ethicist, they make a genius of him—that is, the differentiated—and ethically this is nothing but the most dreadful deception, for the ethical life is and should be the universally human. An ethicist must constantly insist and emphasize that every man is just as capable as he is. Now, you see, the relation is changed. Instead of exacting men's admiration (something men are quite willing to give, especially when it suits their indolence, as by saying: It is easy for him—he is a genius, etc.), he demands of them existence. Then they become furious. They would rather admire him in order to get rid of him—that is, the sting in his existence; but the humanity in him, his declaring that every man is just as capable as he is—this is what is hated and makes men want to get him out of the way.

This, again, is why they honor him when he is dead, for now the sting rooted in contemporaneity is taken away. That which they object to when he is alive they eulogize when he is dead. If the ethicist gives in during his lifetime, the world momentarily thinks well of it, but it is not long before the world itself declares that it was, after all, weakness on his part—this much understanding of the ethical life the world does have. But if he refuses to give in, the world is embittered, but when he is dead the same world says: He was, after all, right.

VIII¹ A 160 *n.d.*, 1847

« **4445**

The child plays with the doll, but then a child becomes the doll when the child becomes the mother.[753]

VIII¹ A 208 *n.d.*, 1847

« **4446**

When a ship is to be piloted out of the harbor, first of all a rope is thrown out and a couple of sailors in a boat row with it to fasten it to a piling, and in this way the ship is pulled: and if a human life is to be commenced properly, a rope must be thrown out first of all—that is, there must be a dead and departed one[754] who assists in setting this life in motion. Any existence which does not have the assistance of a dead and departed one becomes a trivial existence or a great one in a purely worldly sense . . . . .

VIII¹ A 306 *n.d.*, 1847

« **4447**

6. The basis for erotic love is a drive, the basis of friendship is inclination, but drive and inclination are natural qualifications, and natural

qualifications are always selfish; only the eternal qualification of spirit expels the selfish; therefore there is still a hidden self-love in erotic love and friendship. When the girl is able to love only one person, one single man in the whole world (something the poet rejoices to hear and to celebrate), this is indeed erotic love, but this erotic love certainly is the most glowing expression of preference. Although neither the girl nor the erotic love are conscious of it, self-love lies hidden in preferential love, especially when it is ardent. To relate to one single human being in unconditioned impetuous preference is to relate to oneself in self-love; implicit in such a preference is a conscious or unconscious obstinacy which arbitrarily wants to have its own will. To be permitted to love this one person is the gratification of the love passion and of preference, but at bottom also of self-love; to despair if it is denied is the very proof that the erotic love was self-love. But precisely because this escapes erotic love, it is able to come up with the giddy expression: to love another person more than one's self; alas, for the lover still has not learned to love himself in the truth and earnestness of eternity.[755]

7. Here, too, there is no occasion for despair, as in the case of the lover not getting the beloved, for the neighbor is every man, and this is so far from being a natural qualification, an impulse of drive or of inclination to love the neighbor, that on the contrary one shall love him.[756]

9. And this neighbor is every man; if he is not every man, then preference is part of the definition. The neighbor is not one who is more distinguished than you, since to love him because he is more distinguished can very easily be preference and to that extent self-love; neither is the neighbor one who is inferior to you, since to love him because he is inferior can very easily be the condescension of preference and to that extent self-love. No, to love the neighbor means equality. In relation to the distinguished person it is heartening that you dare, yes, that you must love him as your neighbor; in relation to the inferior person, it is humbling that you are not to love him as the inferior person but as your neighbor; and both of them you are to love as yourself.[757]

10. In the ardent perception of preference the beloved is "the other person" or the friend; in the earnestness and truth of equality the neighbor is "the other person," and it makes no difference if there are thousands or only one if that one is "the other person."[758]

12. And it is this Christian love that discovers and knows that *the neighbor* exists and, what amounts to the same, that everyone is this, for

if it were not a *duty* to love, then the concept "the neighbor" would not exist, either.[759]

VIII[2] B 71:6, 7, 9, 10, 12 *n.d.*, 1847

« **4448**

When a man possesses all worldly goods, does his life then express that if there were no eternity he would be the most wretched of all?

For we pay no attention to the fact that he says it.[760]

We must ask how he has gotten these goods. Has he earned them himself, consequently gone after them; if so, this, too, is dubious. Earthly goods are in great demand, and a person can hardly acquire them without having to make many a shabby concession. One does not become honored without having to kowtow sordidly many times etc.

But such a life has made itself as secure as possible here in our world: what does it mean, then, that he would be the most wretched of men—if there were no eternity?

IX A 37 *n.d.*, 1848

« **4449**

When a few children are together all day long, they play with each other or do what they usually do, and this relationship with each other, this relativity, becomes actuality to them, an actuality in which they are, so to speak, each one respectively, of significant magnitude. But what happens—suddenly there comes a message that little Peter, Christian, Søren, Hans, or whatever the person is called, must go home. In this way the absolute disruptively intervenes. It is the same with adults—that is, with the religious man in his life together with adults. Now he goes and talks with the other earnest men about what he wants to be in the world, that he wants to be this and that, and it seems to the other earnest men that he is an earnest man, almost as earnest as the others. But what happens—suddenly there comes a message that he must go home—that is, the God-relationship asserts itself. This, you see, is why the truly religious man can never engage in the strange sort of earnestness which is common in the world, that which leaves out the God-relationship. The child cannot be allowed to get stuck in the illusion that the relationship with the other children is the whole thing—for then comes the message that he must go home.

IX A 194 *n.d.*, 1848

« 4450

A person can also win honor and esteem by being very God-fearing. Therefore in this connection self-denial insists upon disconcerting a little. But on the other hand one has a duty not to go too far, lest the whole thing mislead instead of leading and guiding. Furthermore, if a person is careful that it is true Christianity he proclaims, it will be more difficult to fall into the danger of winning honor and esteem. And above all a person must take care humbly to express that in fear and trembling he himself is committed to the religious life so that the impression is not given that he is superior to it. I could give some examples of this sad situation.

IX A 204 *n.d.*, 1848

« 4451

If a person took into account what it means in relation to God (and a man is in fact related to God in everything) to lose patience, or that to lose patience is to lose it in relation to God, no one would dare have the cheek to do it. The one who is superior (the chief in relation to a subordinate, the father in relation to the child, the benevolent person in relation to the one who accepts his benevolence) may speak of losing patience—but, merciful God, how can a man want to lose patience in relation to God! Consequently, even if God will have patience with him, he would no longer have patience with God. What nonsense! I wonder if anyone could endure this thought! But the point is that men do not think through their thoughts, they become impatient, say that they have lost patience—and completely forget with whom they are speaking.

IX A 342 *n.d.*, 1848

« 4452

There is so much talk these days about the individual's phases of development, that the individual goes through many phases, that it has become sufficiently muddled to be popular on the basement level of society. Goldschmidt[761] is now the rage, is the admired individual who is going through many phases. His first phase is "The Corsair." He personally and his public still less do not seem to know that there are certain phases followed by a period, a full stop. To speak of his first phase is about like saying: My first phase was seven years in a house of correction—or, I became a public prostitute, that was the first moment. Such phases others take to be subtractions.

IX A 494 *n.d.*, 1848

« 4453

In a spiritual sense or spiritually understood, to grow does not mean to become greater but to become less. The child is a purely spontaneously qualified egotist and is certain of himself in a quite different way than adults, who have only moderately involved themselves with the infinite. Spiritually understood, all developmental growth does not consist in being added unto but in being subtracted from, all the probabilities and the like which I have and which are my strength in immediacy. We see here how stupid is all this yelling about the positive. This is why it is also the highest religious act to become nothing before God. The tragedy of the majority of men is by no means that they are weak but that they are too strong—genuinely to be aware of God. A tree, an animal is even stronger—and therefore it is not at all aware of God; a stone is the strongest of all and therefore is completely unaware of God.

X^1 A 50 *n.d.*, 1849

« 4454 † †
†

With respect to a merely human prototype—and here there can, after all, be no question of worship—there is no time for admiration—get busy right away at the task of imitating him. The ethical truth of the matter is just this—that admiration is suspiciously like an evasion. With respect to Christ, however, this cannot be the case. Here it is again apparent (as I have so often pointed out in *Concluding Postscript*)[762] that the Christian-religious is a unique sphere where the esthetic relations reappear, but paradoxically, as higher than the ethical relations, but otherwise this is all reversed. Esthetically (taking here only the relation to a human prototype) admiration is the highest; wanting to imitate has no place in the esthetic. Then along comes the ethical and says: As a matter of fact, wanting to imitate is decisive; admiration has no place or is an evasion. Then comes the paradox-prototype (the God-man). Here we have the esthetic paradox again. If I want to proceed directly to be ethical about this, I take this prototype in vain. Here it is a matter of worship and adoration first and foremost

—and only through worship and adoration can there be any question of wanting to imitate. Here must [sic]
[*in margin:* unless the prototype himself helps the one who is supposed to imitate him. And in one respect no one can imitate him, yes, cannot even think of wanting to imitate him (it would be blasphemy), inasmuch as the prototype is the Atoner and the Atonement.]
[*A page torn from the journal.*]
x¹ A 134 *n.d.*, 1849

« **4455**

As soon as the religious leaves the existential present, where it is sheer actuosity,[763] it immediately becomes milder. The process of religion's becoming milder and thereby less true is directly recognizable by its becoming a *doctrine*. As soon as it becomes doctrine, the religious does not have absolute urgency.* In Christ the religious is completely present tense; in Paul[764] it is already on the way to becoming doctrine.

One can imagine the rest! And with the tendency to become essentially a matter of doctrine, the complete departure from the religious begins, and this trend has been kept up for God knows how many centuries.

In margin: * Note. There comes to be more and more delay before I get around to doing it, and finally (when the religious has become doctrine completely) it all becomes total delay.
x¹ A 383 *n.d.*, 1849

« **4456** *The Basic Error*

in Christendom is actually that people have wanted to make all religious education Christian education on the ridiculous presupposition that all men are Christians because they are baptized as children.

Just as Christianity historically entered the world after having a whole pre-historic religious development in the background, so a man, if he is going to get a decisive impression of Christianity, must first of all go through a whole religious school. Christianity is truly too spiritual for a person to begin with it right off. What discipline is presupposed in order to understand truly so that it is a personal truth that sin is the only tragedy, together with the related truth that Christ alone is Savior.

In Christendom it would be most proper to build a number of

chapels for the teaching of Jewish piety without ever naming the name of Christ; for many this in itself would amount to quite a lot.

This is my unswerving position: the little bit of piety in Christendom is Jewish piety (a clinging to this life, a hope and faith that God will bless them in this life, etc., so the proof that a person is God's friend is that things go well with him in this world), and yet they always put Christ's name to this.

x^2 A 80   *n.d.*, 1849

« **4457** *On the Occasion of H. H.*[765]

[*In margin:* On the occasion of H. H.]

No matter how one conceives of simplicity after (on the other side of) reflection, it is never exactly like the simplicity of immediacy or spontaneity; it will be recognizable precisely by the continuous accompaniment of reflection, but it will be ethically subordinated.

This is the difference between the martyr of immediacy and the martyr of reflection; therefore the immediate martyr cannot have genuine sympathetic collisions.

It is easy enough to make out as if one had thought reflection through; then the simple conclusion comes forth just like a simple conclusion of immediacy, never striven for by any reflection. This looks splendid, but it is the same sort of rubbish as all the Hegelian talk about doubting[766] and then arriving at certainty etc.—only those who have never attempted anything indulge in such talk, only those who are most remote from attempting it in earnest.

x^2 A 279   *n.d.*, 1849

« **4458**

It is characteristic that religiousness (as it is always presented in the more rigorous devotional books) regards it as piety to long for death. And in our time there is a tendency to criticize this, to try to make it seem almost ludicrous, to boast about hanging on to this life.

Here again as everywhere almost the exact opposite of religiousness is achieved while the game of playing at religiousness still goes on. The matter is quite simple: basically belief in eternal life is lacking and death is feared—therefore the all-out attempt to maintain high zest for life and mutually to strengthen each other in it.

x^2 A 313   *n.d.*, 1849

« **4459** *Ascending Forms of Religiousness*

(A) The individual relates to God so that it may go well with him on earth—consequently to profit from the God-relationship in an earthly sense.

(B) The individual relates to God in order to be saved from sin, in order to triumph over his inclinations, in order to find in him a merciful judge—consequently in such a way that the relationship becomes altogether undialectical and the individual alone has benefit from this relationship.

(C) It is required that the individual must confess in word and in deed (self-denial, renunciation of finite aims) the faith in which his salvation lies, but the confession will have the result that the individual suffers, humanly speaking makes himself unhappy. This is where the dialectical aspect of gaining benefit from the God-relationship comes in; in his weak moments the God-relationship must appear to him to be a misfortune and a detriment since, humanly speaking, he would be rid of a lot of suffering by omitting the confession, the words of the confession as well as the deeds of the confession. But if at some point the individual gets so mixed up that he almost feels as if it were he who is doing God a service (as if it were not proper for God to require infinitely and as if God were not acting infinitely beyond compare on behalf of the individual, which [to him] is as nothing compared with his suffering), then the individual in every such moment as this is ungrateful and stands in danger of being blasphemous. I would advise a person in such confusion to avoid the danger momentarily and to confess his ingratitude rather than have this frightful thing happen— to blaspheme by venturing, venturing in the illusion of being able to do God a service.

Note. It is not said that the dangers in confessing the faith were present only in Christianity's early period; alas, the same thing will still befall every honest confession, but the fact is that we are cunning and by all sorts of illusions evade decisive confession in word and deed.

X^2 A 318   *n.d.*, 1849

« **4460**

An eternal symbol of the relation of the God-fearing to God (that this is education) is embodied in a characteristic of the language of God's chosen people: It must be read backward.

To exist [*existere*] backward is actually the most rigorous religiousness, the strongest expression for the way God constrains. He who is turned forward, boasting in exalted tones about what he will do in the future etc.—he is by no means rigorously religious.

No, backward—at each moment he perhaps has scarcely more than a day to live, scarcely an hour—and to live this way is religiousness. But this can only be read backward.

Moses[767] saw the back of God, not his face—that is, there is no agreement in advance, the religious man is only the unconditionally obedient instrument—and then afterward he sees how God has used him. To know that God is using one—this would be a dangerous thought for a man to have; this is why he does not get to know it until afterward.

x^2 A 642   *n.d.*, 1850

« 4461 *Christianity—Modern Cures*

It is fortunate, after all, that we have the old devotional books to hold to. How in the world would we acquire these mental states in our age. That which made its appearance by treating man as spirit, all these conditions of soul, inwardness—is cured nowadays by vacation trips to a spa, by leeches, bloodletting, and all that—but we are all Christians.

x^3 A 79   *n.d.*, 1850

« 4462 *What Does It Mean To Be a Christian?*

It means to walk under the eye of the Heavenly Father, therefore under the eye of the truly loving Father, led by Christ's hand, and strengthened by the witness of the Holy Spirit.

O, blessed companionship! If it is not like this, then we ourselves bear the guilt for it—because this is how God wants it to be.

We ourselves bear the guilt for it—what a comforting thought,[768] for it means, after all, that change is possible.

x^3 A 394   *n.d.*, 1850

« 4463

In the sermon on the Epistle for the Tenth Sunday after Trinity Luther[769] says somewhere: One must either curse Christ or acknowledge him as Lord.

This is absolutely right. The inverted passion of adoration is to curse. —And the basis for this again is that Christianity, understood in a purely human way, is an affliction. (*Odium totius generis humani.*)[770]

x^3 A 396   *n.d.*, 1850

« 4464 *The Difference between the Poetic
—and the Religious*

It is no wonder that wine (external conditions and the like) inspires—but that water (self-denial, renunciation, and the like) inspires:

yes, this is religiousness. And this is the difference between existing religiously and existing poetically.

x^3 A 512   *n.d.*, 1850

« **4465 *Whipping***

The fact that a driver whips his horses[771] can have distinctly opposite meanings; it can mean that the horses are supposed to run, but it can also mean that they are supposed to stand still. Let us not forget the latter meaning.

x^3 A 662   *n.d.*, 1850

« **4466 *Chrysostom***

In a letter to Theodorus of Mopsuetia he makes this splendid observation:

"If the Christian does not do himself harm, nothing will harm him, he is impregnable."

See Neander's *Chrysostom,* pt. I, p. 15.[772]

x^3 A 745   *n.d.*, 1851

« **4467 *Human Self-Contradiction***

Someone becomes a poet, a virtuoso, through a crime (as is told of Paganini, for example)—he is aware of the ethical, that this is precluded. A person can become that through innocent suffering without any objection on the part of the ethical, but not through a crime. And yet perhaps he is the very one who is aware of the ethical; perhaps it is just this punishing or judging unrest of the ethical which makes him into a poet, a virtuoso.

But in any case it is ethically precluded. The ethical has to deliver him, a penitent, to the religious for reforwarding. Ethically it is precluded. It is as if the esthetic said to a man: You are a poor devil; there is a man at such and such a place—get up the courage to kill him and you will be as rich as anybody, and no man will ever know. The ethical would be obliged to say: No, stop! The minute you have killed him, you must give yourself up to the police, pay everything back, and then be condemned as a murderer.

x^3 A 791   *n.d.*, 1851

« **4468 *A Procession***

In a beautiful way Scriver[773] takes the words "their deeds follow them" quite literally—as if they walked behind in a procession—perhaps for want of any other funeral procession.

This can be continued, for when the rest of the procession goes home again from the grave, this procession goes on following.

This can be continued further, for if this procession and its continuation are eternally valid, the continuation follows.

But this procession is not to be called a voluntary procession; here one can say with the philosophers: It follows by necessity. It is both a procession [*et Følge*] and a consequence [*en Følge*].

x^4 A 59   *n.d.,* 1851

« 4469 *The Extraordinary—the Universal*

The extraordinary must sacrifice and must find his satisfaction therein, just as he also must be absolutely certain that this is his task.

Within the universally human one ought to admit humanly his earthly desires, be out-and-out human, strive for their fulfillment, and then let God decide if he will subtract anything. But the place for the extraordinary must be kept open.

x^4 A 125   *n.d.,* 1851

« 4470 *Augustine*

speaks in a later book about his earlier passion for the theater. He points out the self-contradiction of esthetic grief in that one involuntarily breaks off where action should begin. He says that tragedy is supposed to awaken compassion, "but what kind of compassion is it when the onlooker is not called upon to rush assistance but is only invited to enjoy the pain ..... Miserable me, I loved this enjoyment of pain! But what kind of love is love of pain! For I did not wish to suffer what I might see performed but only let myself be moved a little by it superficially, and thereafter there came an inflammation just as when one scratches himself with his fingernails. This was my life, O God!"

See Böhringer, I, pt. 3, p. 110.[774]

x^4 A 160   *n.d.,* 1851

« 4471 *The Purely Human*

It is unbelievable the way the purely human is boldly appealed to nowadays in contrast to Christianity.

But what is it that we call "the human"? It is volatilized Christianity, a culture-consciousness which Christianity has deposited. Consequently it is due to Christianity—and then it is asserted in contrast to Christianity.

The humanists ought to be challenged: produce, then, the purely human—for the human that we now have is Christianity's, even though we do not want that, but you cannot justly take it as yours in contrast to Christianity.

x^4 A 235   n.d., 1851

« **4472** ***Christianity Is Needed First and Foremost***

in order that I may become aware, in order that I may learn how I need it.

Christianity is usually presented as follows—they say, for example, that Christianity teaches an Atonement, and it is expected that men will surely accept it.

No, no, I must first of all learn from Christianity how I stand in need of Christianity.

Christianity is God's conception of sin and justice etc. If I go along and relax languidly in my purely human conception of what sin is and of God's justice, how in all the world could it ever occur to me that sin is something so dreadful that Christ's suffering and death were needed to atone for it.

This is the infinitely deep agony of misunderstanding in Christ's suffering. We human beings go on living in our own thoughts, think we are very well off, that sin is not so bad, etc.

Then comes Christ and wants to save us: he does everything out of love, yes, but continually applies God's conception of what sin is.

In this way, from a human point of view, he first of all makes men unhappy—but when we have been willing to let ourselves be taught what a dreadful thing sin is, and about God's justice—yes, then he is our Savior.

In your agonies, my Lord and Savior, will I first learn and see how dreadful sin is. When I have learned that, then follows the next: how I stand in need of Christianity.

But first of all I must learn from Christianity how I need Christianity.

Yet even in lesser relations between man and man there is a somewhat similar situation. A lover needs the beloved not merely in order to love him or her but first of all to become aware of what it is to be in love, and this will be especially true where one of the parties is somewhat languid.

x^4 A 251   n.d., 1851

« **4473** ***Mood***

What a heavy weight the essentially Christian conception lays upon a man.

Man has a natural and spontaneous hope and faith[775] that if he only makes an effort he will surely be victorious. And then Christianity comes along and says: You fool, or you cheeky fellow, do you not see what "the prototypes" express, do you imagine yourself to be better than they? And what do "the prototypes" express? That downfall is being victorious. Know this—if you manage to reach merely a modest degree of perfection, your downfall is certain, and the more you succeed, the more certain your downfall. O, it is enough to despair over! To turn over thoughts like these for only one hour is more exhausting than enormous efforts in the spontaneous hope of being victorious. To think that by working one works against himself, that one can easily be victorious by leaving the work alone, by relaxing, by being self-seeking like all the others, by using scurvy means as the others do—but that if I managed to use unconditionally pure means and only such means, then my downfall would be unconditionally certain!

It is just as if Christianity would kill all courage, all delight, every hope in a man. Yes, all spontaneous courage and delight and hope—this is called dying to the world.[776]

But I wonder if Christianity therefore wants you to stop striving? No, you *must*.

Or is Christianity without courage? O, no, but it is so infinitely high that it is almost as if it were not intended for men but for heroes. Where merely human hope[777] and courage expire in hopelessness and lack of courage, the essentially Christian courage begins. Only one thing is certain—downfall, and this is what he is working toward with enormous effort and total sacrifice. Wonderful courage!

O, you thousands and thousands who hustle around busily—and are also Christians, have you also understood this or merely had an intimation of it.

The fact that I have been initiated into what would be called melancholy thoughts practically from childhood has had an enormous influence on me. From a merely human point of view it is absolutely certain that to succumb and to go under should not be the guiding principle in life, is precisely what should be avoided. For me, however, the Christian idea that to be victorious is to go under has been perfectly clear, although I did not understand it in the beginning as clearly as later.

If I did not have Christianity, I would steer my life differently. I would turn aside, be lenient with myself, saying: Now you can venture no farther, for then you will go under. But then Christianity comes along and explains that to go under is precisely what is required, to win is worldliness.

And this is the doctrine which has become the religion of a whole country and people, and there are thousands of teachers with a livelihood—and yet nothing is more sure than this—the one who merely in some small measure manages to "seek the kingdom of God *first*" will not succeed in securing a livelihood. If our Lord—if I dare speak this way—is high and mighty about this and says: You must seek my kingdom first—then concern for securing a living is also high and mighty and says: You must seek me first and foremost, otherwise you will get nothing—something all the prototypes in fact express, for it is true they did not die of hunger, but what they had was so meager that it could hardly be called a living.[778]

This alone is shocking enough. Yet there is still another difficulty. Suppose—let me imagine this possibility—that I succeed in attaining something of this loftiness: it seems to me that I must then become alienated to all men, they would hate me (alas, this is what Christianity in fact predicts), it would seem to them that I wanted to destroy everything they held dear.

And this doctrine, which fills me with fear and trembling, is now accepted by all these millions and millions, among whom there are millions who perhaps have scarcely a half hour a year to spare in which to think over their inner life—but Christians they all are.

X^4 A 291   *n.d.*, 1851

« **4474** *Lessing's Conception of Christ* **(Wolfenbüttel Fragments)**[779]

The root of this conception is obviously a psychological observation.

Lessing cannot get it into his head that a man would begin by being religious, or rather, by being originally religious, first of all—but that this is a later stage. Then the pattern is like this: a person has earthly goals, wants to be king—fails, and then reinterprets his whole life, pretends it was his original idea to want to suffer, so he still has that gain.

If we disregard Christ, then there is, of course, a certain truth in Lessing's view.

In the first place there is the truth that in one sense the religious cannot be the first [stage] in a man, for the religious is a dying[780]—consequently there has to be something to die away from.

In the second place, it is often the case that a frustrated secular striving will be composed in a new form afterward and be an original religious striving.

Yet there are some purely human lives in which the religious actually is the first [stage]. They are the suffering ones who from the very beginning have been set outside the universal by a special suffering, who are denied the enjoyment of life, and who therefore must either become purely demonic (in an evil sense) or become essentially religious persons.

x^4 A 335   n.d., 1851

« 4475 *An Earlier Age—Our Age*

A psychological observation

Why is it, I have wondered, that whereas authors, poets, et al. in earlier eras produced their most important work in their later years, it is characteristic of our age to begin with the climax, also a distrust of life; thus almost everyone considers quitting early, a professor for a few years, a poet for a few years, an actor a few years etc.—in short, as if the tasks were not enough for a whole life.

I think it can be explained this way, that instead of being character tasks, all tasks have become virtuosity tasks. This is why they are not enough. The ability to express the highest, to understand the highest, to present it, etc., can be achieved before thirty. But to do it—that changes everything and gives one a task large enough for the longest life.

But this is not what they want. They want to scintillate with virtuosity—and sneak away from character. This is why they turn aside.

From this comes the teaching approach, that villainy—there where someone lays down his life, suffers everything, along comes a wretch who takes the teaching, the objective teaching (the subjective is to suffer; it is the unimportant, the inferior), and makes a success.

x^4 A 430   n.d., 1851

« 4476 *Can I Understand?—Do I Want to Understand?*

The entire sphere of intellectuality and everything pertaining to it is recognizable by the formula that I must ask with respect to it: Can I understand it? The task here is to understand; the differences between man and man are rooted in this, that one man can understand more than the other, understand more easily, more quickly, etc.—

genius and talent—and if I do not possess this difference, then there is nothing further to say about it.

The ethical and the ethical-religious sphere is recognizable by the formula: Do I want to understand it? Here, therefore, there are no differences.

The ethical and religious sphere must above all assimilate nothing to which this genuinely applies: Can I understand it? The moment it does, the ethical is altered, has lost authority, procrastination has set in.

The ethical, therefore, cannot be served the same way the intellectual is, by saying: Just work at it and you will come to understand; give yourself a little time and it will come, etc. No, no, of everything about which it genuinely holds true that there is a question as to whether I understand it or not, it also holds true that it is not the ethical; such things do not belong to the ethical, the ethical therefore can be served only by something of the police variety: You scoundrel—not wanting to understand, you hypocrite, etc.—or by irony, which cunningly operates with the help of: You can understand very well, but you do not want to.

What profound cunning, therefore, to make science and scholarship out of the ethical and ethical-religious! What profound subtlety when it is said that the preacher must have comprehended the newest philosophy in order to satisfy the demands of the time. To be sure, for the demand of the time is simply to get free from the ethical demand —so it is best to apply science and scholarship, which politely operate along intellectual lines: to be able to understand.

x^4 A 461   *n.d.*, 1852

« **4477** *Intensification*

In these journals I have often pointed out that "man" never really rests at ease before he gets the wrong made into dogma—not until then does he believe he is absolutely fortified against the right. To be separated from the right only by the partition: I cannot, I recognize what is right, but I dare not—one fears, and perhaps with justification, that this will not hold up in the long run. So he removes the right still another interval from himself: the right is presumptuousness, etc.—and now he is satisfied. One does what he pleases in the wrong; and the wrong also enjoys honor and esteem as the right.

A similar intensification is to hate the good, hate God—and thus Scripture declares that love of the world is hatred of God.[781] The same thing happens here as in the other intensification. If anything, one wishes to be rid of the good, be rid of God. One fears, however, that this will not be adequate protection against them, so there is nothing else to do but to hate them—in order to protect oneself against them.

x^5 A 24 *n.d.*, 1852

« 4478 *Progress in Becoming Or in Being a Christian*

Take a person who is born in Christendom and consequently is brought up, nourished, or coddled in the mitigated kind of Christianity which is handed to the child and which the child to some extent makes for himself even if given stronger food.

God is the good, the giver of all good gifts (in the direct sense), love, unspeakable love. And in this beautiful, childish joy and confidence the child rests, and it satisfies the young person completely.

The more he has identified himself with this, the more frightful becomes the pain when the God-concept is to be lifted a quality higher; "when the child must be weaned,"[782] the more he has identified with this, the more frightful becomes the suffering which is the "dying to the world"[783] related to God's being "Spirit" and as such God has a completely different idea about good gifts than a child or youth has. This suffering may become more intense in "Christendom" than it was for the pagan who became a Christian, because the pagan had not been induced to think that he was a Christian—he abandoned one god or idol in order to embrace the true God. But in Christendom we have the dreadful situation that it is the same God, that after one has been spoiled first of all by Christianity concocted as cake, this must now become something taken in earnest, that consequently one is not to turn to a new God and a new doctrine, but it is the same God and the same doctrine, and yet so infinitely different—O, it is so alluring then to want to go back to the child and the youth instead of going forward.

Meanwhile—and this now is the second stage—he cannot, does not dare, do otherwise, he still chooses to cling to God, although it appears to him to be sheer suffering and pain. He does indeed hear that God promises a Spirit who will make a person's suffering into a blessing, but as yet he has not experienced this—and to be sure it does not come posthaste like that, either, for then it could easily become a matter of practical prudence to choose suffering.

So he chooses to cling to God, although the prospect is sheer suffering, even though he perhaps has an intimation that faith will surely come and then the blessedness, also, and in any case he does have eternity.

Personally he has made up his mind. But then comes a new pain—the pain of sympathy. If, then, he cannot, does not dare, do otherwise than choose God, even on the condition that it is sheer suffering, he finds it difficult and sad if he must declare this to others and consequently make them just as unhappy, humanly speaking, for this life. He would be happy to hide his inner suffering and proclaim a milder gospel to the others, those he loves; to them he would gladly grant all the joys of this life. —It is quite natural for him to feel this way, since as yet he himself has experienced only the pain of clinging to God—yes, for him it can almost be treachery or at least an unkindness toward others to continue to cling to God on these terms, as if he were not indebted to them, and it would be preferable to abandon God rather than make both himself and them unhappy. —Alas, this collision of sympathy can become extremely painful.

Finally there comes a breakthrough in this man, and he experiences the blessedness of suffering: blessed it is to suffer.

From now on everything is in order; how could it ever occur to him to shrink from having to proclaim Christianity to the others, to the loved ones—indeed, it is blessed, blessed to suffer. His concern now is of another kind: that he can get the others, the loved ones, far enough out—instead of his earlier fear of wrenching them out. Now he wants the others far out, out where he is, and why? Because it is blessed to suffer, because he fears on their behalf that they might sometime, if not now then in eternity, repent that they did not come to experience the blessedness of suffering, fears that they might reproach him for being lenient with them out of mistaken love, even if they perhaps once asked for it and thanked him for treating them leniently.

X^5 A 82   *n.d.*, 1853

« 4479 *An Immediate Relation to God —The Universally Human*

The Jews believed that to see God was death;[784] the pagans that to see God was punished by madness—it was punished, and yet it was the supreme grace and blessedness. This is what it means to have an immediate relationship to God—it is *eo ipso* to be sacrificed; as I have often said [i.e., X^5 A 17], it means to be hit by the sunstroke of the unconditioned—the greatest possible human suffering and a superhuman blessedness.

Ordinarily we human beings do not have an immediate relationship to God. His will is proclaimed to us *in abstracto* in his Word and the like, but I, this concrete I, am not told: In these concrete circumstances you are to do this and this. No, every single individual must, so to speak, translate God's commands *in concreto*. One way this takes place is with the aid of the *understanding*.

Thus every ordinary person (for whoever is granted an immediate relationship to God is freed of all concern in this respect) is responsible to God both for using his understanding and for the way he uses it.

Must a person therefore also use his understanding in relation to doing the will of God? Most assuredly, to want to venture in such a way that one's understanding is obliged to say: This is certain ruin, is thrusting oneself on God, is deliberately wanting to have an immediate relationship to God (but they who actually have an immediate relationship to God do not have it by having forced themselves upon God but by God's having chosen them)—this is tempting God.

But if a man is to use his understanding in this way, do we not then have a thoroughgoing secular mentality, which egotistically employs its understanding, and cowardliness?

No, so far as the latter is concerned, it is sufficiently clear that a person is by no means exempted from venturing because he is forbidden to venture out into certain destruction. No, if a person ventures, there is the *possibility* of destruction; this is called venturing.

As far as the former is concerned, Christianity teaches that a man must hate himself, and in such a case there is no danger of his using his understanding egotistically.

At the same time the ordinary person cannot, dares not, yes, must not venture in the same way as the one who has an immediate God-relationship, for the one who has an immediate God-relationship is freed from all responsibility, simply has to obey the order. If the order results in plunging him to his ruin, he has no responsibility. On the other hand, since every ordinary person has a responsibility not to plunge himself into certain ruin, and since it can, again, be difficult for him to decide when it is a matter of certain ruin and when not, and since he must nevertheless venture and yet also hate himself, the difficulty is enormous and can really teach a man to feel at all times that he needs grace. At times it may even be necessary to be lenient with himself and thus to use his understanding—but then he must immediately inform God of this.

Let me give an example. Christ[785] says to the rich young man: Sell all that you have. If this rich young man has seen God in Christ, he is then in the situation of having an immediate relationship to God, he, as a concrete person, has an order, a concrete order, from God. If that young man has not seen God in Christ, he is essentially in the same situation as every subsequent rich young man who reads this story, to whom Christ, to be sure, does not plainly say: "You" are to go and give everything to the poor.

It is quite easy for the person who has an immediate relationship to God to know what he must do and in this respect to be free from responsibility—alas, but then the order results in suffering, in being sacrificed. The rest of us are perhaps spared sufferings, at least sufferings on that scale, but then we have the suffering in connection with comprehending what the orders are, and thus we have the responsibility.

X^5 A 95 *n.d., 1853*

« **4480** *The Most Beautiful Sight*

If there were a man who had achieved perfection in the art of always being able to discern the task, discern the task in everything and at all times, never without composure, never without courage (Socrates was the man who attained the highest)

—if there were such a man, then to see him related to God, who knows how to assign the task at all times, at every moment, in all things:

—this would be the most beautiful sight of all!

It is even a beautiful sight to see a man with a willingness to learn this art from God.

What stops and delays and plagues and torments men is that they always stop without being able to transform what confronts them into a task. They wish that this and that may succeed—it fails: well, then the task is to make the best of it. A person expected so much from a happy marriage—and got an ill-tempered woman: well, then this is the task. O, Socrates! There were thousands who, nagged and scolded and despairing, out of indignation at the ill-tempered woman became ill-tempered men, thousands who sank under it, thousands who, quietly sighing, put up with it, a few who bore it patiently—but there was only one so ingenious that he promptly saw that this was the task: I am happily married; this was precisely the madame I needed for my training.

Always to see the task! Today you were prepared for a melancholy day—and see, it turned out to be a smiling day: fine, then this is the task, perhaps just as difficult as the opposite. The very moment you have firmly established it as the task, the same moment the scene is changed and you encounter something so fatal that you do not want it at any price, and it is doubly tormenting because this day so *unexpectedly* had become a pleasant day: well, then this is the task.

To worship God is a royal service.

How is a royal courtier different from an ordinary citizen? In this that each day the ordinary citizen is simply himself: if he is a cheerful, jolly brother, then that is what he is; if he is a sulky fellow, then that is his life. It is different with the royal courtier. He begins unconditionally from the beginning, so to speak, every morning, begins with nothing, but (his perfection is related to this) if possible with the possibility of everything. First of all he must see the majesty, and then the art is to be able to be related correctly to what the majesty is at every minute, at every moment, without having the least thing fixed and nailed down, without any stiffness or rigidity in his joints.

It is a feat, meaningless and empty, of course, inasmuch as this majesty is neither more nor less than another human being.

But in the relation to God this feat is life's deepest meaning.

XI^1 A 456 *n.d.*, 1854

« 4481 *Do You Want To Be a Significant Person?*

Well, who doesn't? If so, then become involved with God, but do it first of all, without having millions between yourself and him—and you will find yourself to be such a significant person that the slightest fault will be punished as if it were the most outrageous crime.

"How," you ask, "can this constitute being a significant person?" My friend, can you not grasp that it cannot possibly mean anything else than that, that you are a most significant person, since everything is done so scrupulously.

XI^1 A 457 *n.d.*, 1854

« 4482 *Play—Earnestness*

This is the game we humans play. It is generally conceded that life for a countless host of men is wasted trouble.

But there are some who are supposed to express earnestness, that which is earnest. This is how they behave: having secured and continually securing their animal existence, they occupy themselves, as it is put, with the eternal. Profound earnestness! From a Christian point of view, it is nothing but a game, and it is just as foolish to call this earnestness as to call eating cake asceticism.

No, earnestness means that you cannot truly have anything to do with the external without its ruining the temporal, your animal existence, for you more and more.

"But under these conditions you will not get anyone at all who wants to have anything to do with the eternal." My friend, do not talk to me like that. I did not invent Christianity. If you have any objection to make, perhaps you would address yourself to His Majesty, God in heaven.

XI^1 A 472   *n.d.*, 1854

« 4483 *A Good——Which Hurts*

This is how I could dialectically and accurately describe what Christianity is according to the New Testament. The phrase also shows how difficult in a certain sense it is for a man to enter into it, for anyone can understand a good which helps and will jump at it, but that anything which hurts should be called a good is crazy and is impossible to accept; it would be easier to accept if it were bad, for then it would make sense that it hurts, but that it hurts and is also supposed to be a good is too much.

Man is a synthesis, a composite of the lower and the higher, and from birth on he is almost completely in the power of the lower. The pleasant—and the unpleasant—are what determine him, and it remains just about that way throughout life for most men. Or how many would there be in any generation, to take but one example, who would be capable of approaching the desire to know in such a way that they would declare: It will not bother me whether this knowledge ends with making me happy or unhappy; I simply want to know? Or how many would be capable of being able to persevere in wanting to penetrate deeper and deeper into a knowledge which they later perceive must necessarily make them unhappy? No, the lower nature in a man plays the master: is it pleasant or unpleasant, that is the question, and as soon as it becomes unpleasant, this is the signal to break off.

With divine knowledge of human nature, Christianity is designed for the higher part of human nature, but in such a way that the lower nature will experience unhappiness because of it.

Here we immediately see something worth noting, that the distinction which has been introduced in Christendom with respect to accepting Christianity: great capacities, much understanding, etc. or meager capacities—this distinction has no place here. The distinction between man and man with respect to accepting Christianity lies somewhere else: to what extent is your life dominated by the pleasant and the unpleasant, how far can you force yourself into something unpleasant—but after all the simple man, a servant girl, a foot-soldier can do this just as well as the highly gifted.

Christianity, then, has aimed at the higher nature in man and proclaims itself to be a great good, the highest, the unconditioned good. Let us dramatize this. The same moment "man" hears this proclamation, the animal, the lower nature in him, which is immediately ready and willing when it is a matter of grabbing hold of a good thing, simultaneously says: Wonderful, wonderful! To which Christianity must answer this lower nature: No, my friend, you actually have nothing for which to thank; on this occasion you will reap unhappiness.

So we have here a good—which hurts. What then? Retreat is blown; man thinks something like this: This is really nothing for me, it is a kind of madness and to call it a good really makes a fool of a rational creature and earnest man.

Originally there was no help to be had from rubbish and nonsense; with divine authority a few were ordered through—consequently this good which hurts even went so far that when a person would not enter into it by way of the good, evil was used—and yet it was a good, the highest good.

Then it ended; Christianity had been introduced. Now divine authority was no longer to be used; men were supposed to proceed on their own to help themselves and each other into this highest good which hurts. Divine authority was no longer used; God wanted to see what honesty there was in "man."

In the course of centuries a change took place in Christianity, it was abolished, or, to show that man also can be paradoxical, it was abolished in such a way that, as the saying goes, it lived on and blossomed. Christendom is almost as much a paradox as the phrase: a good which hurts, for Christendom is the paradox that Christianity is abolished and yet lives on.

So Christianity was abolished. In order to get men to accept Christianity *en masse* and joyfully, the diabolical mark of identification "which hurts" was removed and Christianity was proclaimed as a good, an outright good, without—as the late Bishop Mynster said—beating around the bush, which is certainly unseemly in relation to such an earnest matter as the highest good, and any earnest person readily sees that it is nothing other than a lack of earnestness to connect "which hurts" to "the highest good."

This is how Christianity conquered! As fishers of men the apostles were nothing but bunglers compared to the fishermen who now began to fish. Thus Christianity won a complete victory—that is, it became complete nonsense. A horde of muddleheads, dressed in "long clothes"—I mean preachers and professors—proclaimed Christianity as the highest good, the unconditioned good for man's upbuilding, contentment, and diversion.

This is the situation at present. All are Christians; Christianity is the highest good—

—now there must be a little beating around the bush (with Bishop Mynster's permission)—this "which hurts" should be introduced.

Now I am really not utterly lacking in knowledge of human nature, and knowing both myself and men, and the situation being what it is, I have thought it perhaps easiest to get people to accept Christianity by proclaiming it as an evil which hurts—just to get the clause "which hurts" included.

"God forbid," I hear the preachers roar. "God forbid—to preach Christianity as an evil and then expect to get people to accept it, Christianity an evil, this invaluable good—." O, would to God you would stop your mouths and the whole proclamation of Christianity! [*In margin:* As Anti-Climacus[786] says, "It is not worth a pickled herring" —it is so disgustingly sweet.]

The matter is quite simple. When the point is to include the dialectical "which hurts" and when the situation is what it is in fact— that men are hopelessly mixed up in and by this preacher-nonsense about Christianity simply as the highest good—then it is a mitigation to proclaim it as an evil. "An evil which hurts"—this compounding does not paradoxically strain the understanding.

If this were put into practice and we actually included the dialectical "which hurts," the sign of spirit, and thereby managed to cut off this nonsense, then it might be possible to achieve the truly Christian, that is indeed a good, but, but a good which hurts. This compounding once again strains a poor human being—so high up does Christianity lie.

"Grace" is taken in vain; by proclaiming Christianity solely as grace, Christianity has been rendered meaningless. If, then, men are as spoiled as this and the dialectical "which hurts" is to be introduced, then it is easiest for men to begin by proclaiming Christianity as an evil which hurts—that is, as law. Not until this is put into practice can we talk about this infinitely high truth: a good which hurts, a grace which hurts.

XI^1 A 475 *n.d.*, 1854

« **4484** *God's Compassion on Man in Christianity*

This is how the matter stands in the New Testament. God is touched to see man in all his wretchedness and need, constantly plagued by the fear of death (for this is the situation in paganism and Judaism, and not as we have falsified it in Christendom by appropriating the consolation of Christianity without taking its responsibilities); so God has compassion on man. "I shall" (he could very well think aloud in this way) "I shall have compassion on you and make your thinking about death the most precious of thoughts—the outcome, of course, will be that this life becomes more painful than ever."

Always, if you please, this misrelation between God and man, something which cannot be avoided; what God calls consolation becomes in another sense a strenuousness.

XI^1 A 478 *n.d.*, 1854

« **4485**

"God made man upright, but they have sought out many devices." This is an excellent quotation from Ecclesiastes.[787]

XI^1 A 481 *n.d.*, 1854

« **4486** *The Steps in Being a Christian*

The beginning is the consciousness of sin. It is this which teaches a man to flee to God. And now Christianity proclaims Atonement, and Christianity is then sheer gentleness and alleviation.

When this is practiced and rooted, it goes further and we must suffer for the doctrine; to be a Christian means to become unhappy in this life in a very special sense. This is of infinite concern to God, for now it is a question of being loved. He, of course, does it out of love, but nevertheless it can be just as painful for a man.

If this pinches and a person opposes God too much, the prior stage, the consciousness of sin, is used to constrain. As I said somewhere else [i.e., XI^1 A 311], it is easier to suffer for one's sin than to suffer because one relates himself to God. If I am unable momentarily to endure this suffering, suffering because God in love makes me unhappy, God lets go of me for just a moment and I come to suffer for the sake of my sin, which then is a kind of relief and also a chastisement, until there can be a beginning again.

XI¹ A 564 n.d., 1854

« 4487 *Sorrow over One's Sin*

The true sorrow over one's sin is—to reform. The sin can be forgotten, or an attempt made to forget it in new sins, the one displacing the other, or in diversions—but in vain. The true sorrow and the true forgetting is—to reform.

XI¹ A 574 n.d., 1854

« 4488 *Relapse—Progress*

The true consolation for a relapse is—that by the help of God it became a step forward, that you may say: Without this relapse, I would not have advanced as far as I have.

XI¹ A 575 n.d., 1854

« 4489 *Restlessness*[788]

As the fisherman after setting out his net makes a noise in the water in order to drive the fish in that direction and catch all the more, as the hunter with his band of beaters encircles the whole terrain and then scares up the game in great numbers and drives them to the place where they are to be shot—so God, who wants to be loved, hunts men by means of *restlessness*.

Christianity is the greatest, the most intense, the most powerful restlessness imaginable; it disturbs human existence at its deepest level (such, in fact, was the effect of Christ's life), it explodes everything, bursts everything.

So it is that God uses restlessness—he utilizes unrest to hunt men who will love him. But the difference from the fisherman and the hunter is that God does not use restlessness to capture all the more, does not use it for the sake of numbers, but for the sake of intensity—that is, when the greatest possible restlessness is brought about, in the tension there can arise within a person the intensity which really can love God.

But man loves rest, security. However, it is certain that in security, at rest, no one can become a Christian, and it is no less certain that no Christian can remain in security and at rest. If one is to become a Christian, there must be restlessness, and if one has become a Christian, restlessness continues.

XI² A 29 n.d., 1854

« **4490** *Christianity—Christendom*

Think of a medicine generally known to have a very specific effect —for example, a laxative.

A physician who is fully informed about this goes to another country where—and imagine his amazement—all the physicians use this medicine as a remedy for diarrhea; every druggist knows about it, and every physician uses it this way.

Our physician says: But how is this possible? If the patient gets this medicine, it must certainly be evident at once that it has the opposite effect. The answer: The patient gets a good big dose of it, and it has a slow-down effect—and this is the way we have practiced from time immemorial.

Then the physician says: May I see the medicine. It is brought to him, and he examines it—well, *das ist was anders;*[789] this is not at all what I am talking about but, quite right, is an equally well-known medicine which has a slow-down effect. But how in the world did kaopectate come to be called epsom salt?

So it is with Christianity in Christendom. In the New Testament Christianity is the most intense unrest[790] possible—God in heaven has not been able to find one more intense. And in Christendom Christianity is used—as a tranquilizer.

"But how is this possible?" the physician must say. "How is it possible, if someone takes just a little dose of New Testament Christianity he promptly perceives that it does not have a tranquilizing effect." "Well, the only answer to that is that around here we all use Christianity this way, and we all feel the same effect—it is tranquilizing." "May I learn a little more exactly what you understand by Christianity?" When he finds out, he answers, "Aha! The riddle is solved! I do not deny that such a thing has a tranquilizing effect, but I doubt that it is Christianity."

XI^2 A 42 *n.d.,* 1851

« **4491** *Seeing the Task*

How different understanding is from acting is perhaps seen best of all in the fact that in the very moment a person resolves that he henceforth will see his task in everything and will not let himself be disturbed by anything—that he then is most fearful that something might happen in that very same moment which would give him an occasion to carry out his resolution.

The resolution, the thought of willing from now on into the future is like a large-denomination bond—one is very reluctant to offer it on the exchange because he is secretly bothered by a suspicion that the whole thing will go to pieces for him and the rich wealth of the resolution will dissolve into less than nothing.

XI^2 A 73   n.d., 1854

« 4492 *Half Is More than the Whole*

These words by Hesiod[791] come closest to what Asaph[792] says: Do not give me riches. To want the whole is dangerous; it is safest to have the half.

In spiritual matters the opposite holds: to have the half is to lose the whole.

But in the sensate world the half is to be preferred, and all finite prudence is based on halfness.

XI^2 A 225   n.d., 1854

« 4493 *The Quality of Man*

was that Christianity wanted to change

Man always uses the substitute: change the model—the quality remains the same.

Mankind has embraced Christianity in this way, but this makes a fool of Christianity and of himself.

In fact, the longer Christianity lasted in Christendom, greater and greater became the choice of different models available, a scholarly knowledge of all these many models and their mutual relationships—all serving to divert attention from what Christianity is—a change in quality.

Christendom does everything to draw attention to the model—Christianity concentrates everything on the quality.

Thus through the centuries Christendom has furnished millions and millions of Christians in every possible model and continually has thousands of men and women in action begetting little Christians in the various models. Christendom can best be looked at as an enormous factory. Eternity, which asks only about quality, is embarrassed (if it were possible for eternity to be embarrassed) amid all this abundance.

Christianity aimed at a change in quality. The result of Christendom appears to be that in Christendom the quality of what it is to be man has become even lower than it was before Christianity entered the world, something that is concealed, however, by the cunning importance given to the question of the model. It is easy to see that nothing protects one so well against the examination which is concerned with quality as diverting attention to the variety of models, and true Christianity was zealous to become informed here, to get into polemical action here—not simply against flesh and blood (which Christianity proposes, since it aims at a change of quality) but against opinions and scientificities[793]—which explains why the religious controversies in Christendom best reveal that as far as the quality of man is concerned, it is all ancient, pagan, Jewish, or even worse.

XI^2 A 232 *n.d.*, 1854

« **4494 *To Have Religion***

Regrettably most men live only in the finite and for the finite.

It is precisely *religion* that should lift them up and out of this kind of life, which is unworthy of a being who is in kinship with the divine, draw their minds up and away from this downward-turned living which, also according to the pagan view, is proper only to animals.

But it is readily apparent that this does not happen, that instead of letting themselves be lifted up by religion, men drag religion down into finitude and the finite, talk and think about it and possess it the way one talks and thinks about and possesses the finite.

With respect to everything finite it is quite right that if one cannot have the best, one can make do with the inferior. For example, if one cannot afford to drink the finest Bordeaux wine, he can make do with a lesser wine, and so it goes with everything finite, although there is a limit even here: the wine which is served may be so bad that one may say: No, it is better to drink water.

But religion has an inverse relationship to the finite, simply because religion is supposed to elevate men.

Either/or holds true of religion: either prime quality, or really no quality at all; either with all your heart, all your mind, and with all your strength, or really not at all.

But men do not relate to religion this way; they treat it as if it were something finite, are well satisfied with having religion in a driveling and mediocre way.

But to have religion in this way is not merely not to have religion, no, it is the most dangerous and culpable kind—it is irreligion. If you look at it more closely you will see that it really is contempt for religion. Religion insists on being an either/or for a person; to treat it as if it were like beer and food etc. is fundamentally to scorn it, which is quite different from decisively willing not to have religion.

The point is to get this made clear to men. But this is a difficult thing in itself, and doubly difficult when 1,000 state-authorized tradesmen and their families make a living deluding men into thinking that this impious mediocrity is true Christianity.

This *impious* mediocrity. I have here added to mediocrity an adjective which may be considered inappropriate, however disparagingly one may otherwise truthfully talk about mediocrity. Therefore the point is to drill it in that "religion" must brand mediocrity as the most culpable kind of impiety, the worst possible insult to religion, a far more serious offense than decisively rejecting religion.

Try to make out what Christ thinks about mediocrity! When the apostle Peter, that intrepid man, when he well-meaningly wanted to keep Christ from being willing to be sacrificed (and compared to the mediocrity I am talking about this cannot be called mediocrity), Christ[794] answers: Get behind me, Satan! You are an offense to me. He declares that he is an offense to him, and he calls him Satan, says that his idea is inspired by Satan!

In the world of mediocrity in which we live it is assumed—and this is one of the ways used to safeguard mediocrity—that only crackpot boldness etc. should be deplored as offensive, as inspired by Satan, and that the middle way, however, is secure against any such charge. Christ and Christianity are of another mind: mediocrity itself is the offense, the most dangerous kind of demon possession, farthest removed from the possibility of being cured. To have religion, especially the Christian religion, on the level of mediocrity is the most unqualified form of perdition and has protected itself best—how frightfully ironic—against the possibility of being saved.

XI^3 B 148 July 5, 1855

STATE CHURCH

« **4495** *State–Church*

Here lies the whole secret!

At one time there must have lived a few rogues, as Holberg[795] says, who duped the state into thinking that the suffering and death of Jesus Christ and eternal salvation were something which could be used to raise money.

Great! So the state undertook—Christianly!—to make a complete deal with Christianity.

In Denmark, for example, there are 1 1/2 million inhabitants. They bring in about 600,000 or 700,000 rix-dollars a year. This is used to pay pastors etc.

But the point is this—from a Christian point of view, no man and no society, either, has the remotest right to intrude between the suffering and death of Christ and another man and intervene financially between them.

The state is equally wrong in both forms; from a Christian point of view both are high treason.

If there is a person who feels the desire and need to hear about the suffering and death of Jesus Christ, the state has no right to butt in and say: Fine, pay ten rix-dollars and we will arrange it.

No more so in the other form. If there is a person who has no desire to hear about the suffering and death of Jesus Christ, the state has no right to say: "Well, it makes no difference whether or not you want to hear it—that is up to you, you will not be forced to hear it—but you will damned well pay the full ten rix-dollars, for we have taken it upon ourselves to make a deal with Christianity." This ought not and cannot be. The situation should not be as it is at present—if a man does not want to pay, the police are required to collect the ten rix-dollars. On the contrary, the situation should be such that if anyone comes and demands the ten rix-dollars from such a person, he should be able to send for the police and insist on being protected against this, just as against any other swindle.

Christianity is the highest earnestness. Therefore (as always with the highest) it is recognizable by a negative criterion, by something seemingly lower. From a Christian point of view men ought to have the right in this life to conduct themselves entirely as they themselves wish —the state, something far lower, cannot concede its constituents this kind of freedom in civil matters—but, but, but (here comes the earnestness!): you individual, every single individual, you are on the way to the accounting of eternity.

But the fact is that judgment, the accounting, and the earnestness of eternity have completely vanished, and therefore, to get a little bit of earnestness, police are called in to help. What an abysmal depth of nonsense! Nonetheless we are on our way to an accounting in eternity.

Here it is: the highest earnestness and rigor (the judgment of eternity) are recognizable by the highest freedom: in this life, as far as this matter is concerned, you are permitted to do entirely as you wish.

This is Christianity. The other is a human invention. Essentially, eternity is removed, and then the attempt is made to introduce a little police-earnestness.

To me this is as simple and clear as possible. Once again I make the most lenient proposal—that we at least are so honest toward Christianity that we openly admit how the matter stands.

XI^1 A 63   *n.d.*, 1854

« **4496** *State-Church*

Calling oneself a Christian* has become such an important condition for advancing in the world that most likely one could not get permission to earn his living by maintaining a house of prostitution without proving that he is baptized and is (that is, calls himself) a Christian. Accordingly, to earn a living in this manner may certainly be conceded, says the state, but only on the premise and assumption and condition that you are a Christian. God in heaven!

Incidentally, how characteristically incongruous: the state, which permits that trade if one is a Christian—and Christianity, which from the fact that one earns his living in this way proves that he is not a Christian even though he has been baptized a hundred times. Thus the state requires the condition that he be a Christian and then permits him that by which Christianity proves that he is not a Christian.

* This expression is actually regarded these days as synonymous with being a Christian.

XI^1 A 74   *n.d.*, 1854

« 4497 *The Secret*

Christianity is renunciation of this world—let the state hire and pay even as many as 100,000 men to attack Christianity—this is not dangerous.

But let it hire and pay ten to proclaim Christianity—this is dangerous. Here is the secret—in this way under the name of Christianity one gets precisely what is not Christianity. The danger lies in getting it under the name of Christianity.

Any proclaimer of this kind has a secret, a confounded secret; after all, he cannot come right out and say what Christianity is, for then he implicates himself as well as his accomplice, the state. So it must be concealed—and then this becomes Christianity.

There is one thing which Christ must unconditionally exclude: financial assistance. But Satan knows that there is only one way to annihilate Christianity—by means of financial assistance. And it becomes all the more dangerous the more solemn and refined it becomes—that of course it is not the money one cares about—which means that a person hypocritically wants to have even more than money—that is, in addition to money the honor and esteem of not caring about money—something which probably does not usually appear in any activity outside of the Christian domain.

XI^1 A 102   *n.d.*, 1854

« 4498 *Pastor in the State Church*

But, you perhaps say: I preach true Christianity and therefore it is no concern of mine how corrupt the rest of the state church is.

No, wait a minute! After all, the state church has been made possible only by the fraudulent manner in which the appearance that we are all Christians has been conjured up. You have no right to avail yourself of this in order to get the secular assurance and security that a public official in the state church has.

XI^1 A 105   *n.d.*, 1854

« 4499 *The Wrong Turn That Was Made in Christendom*

———

The time (to take a definite point in time) when Christianity was elevated (that is, degraded) to a state religion—if at that time there had been someone who with human honesty had said: I see that the world has really gained the upper hand, that this is no longer New Testament

Christianity, but I am not the God-man or an apostle, and it takes more than human power to put a stop to this—well, then, I will go along with it, but it must be made known that this is not New Testament Christianity—O, how far different everything would have been.

But instead of that there was a prudence which sought to conceal. What nonsense that is! God is spirit, Christ is the truth, Christianity is the truth—and yet we serve it by trying to conceal the true condition.

No, to New Testament Christianity and to truth one can be truly related in only one of two ways: *either* we do indeed have this teaching *or* we truly confess that we do not have it.

But prudence thought that the latter would never do; it would be too dangerous. Splendid! Christianity was originally truth, and now it has become Christendom: the danger is that the truth of the matter comes to be known.

XI^1 A 348   *n.d.*, 1854

« 4500 *Has Not the Whole Business of Christendom Been Caused by a Confusion?*

Christianity came into the world when Caesar Augustus[796] levied taxes on the whole world—one could be tempted to believe that Christendom has made a mistake, that it confused these two simultaneous events and thought that it was Christianity which came into the world for the purpose of levying taxes on everyone.

XI^1 A 534   *n.d.*, 1854

« 4501 *The State, the State Church*

Since the state, as mentioned earlier [i.e., XI^2 A 108], is the higher egotism or the calculus and reflection in egotism of individual egotisms, it is easy to see that Christianity fell into good hands when it was taken over by the state. And how comical that this whose whole point is quantity should take it upon itself to look after the interests of that whose whole point is single individuals.[797]

Since the higher egotism has now taken over Christianity, it has probably sized up the whole matter something like this.[*] If there are individuals in the society who obstinately claim to be the true Christians in contrast to others, this must be regarded as culpable egotism, something my state has the task of persecuting, for I hate all egotism and strive to eliminate it (with the help of a higher egotism). To want to be a Christian in this way shows a lack of public spirit and civic virtue; the good citizen wants nothing for himself but wants everything in common. Obviously such men are to be regarded as criminals. But since their guilt does not involve the supreme good in society: money and the security of property, the highest level of severity is not required. However, they ought to be punished. Generally speaking, for single individuals to be engaged in particular personal matters is and always will be bad practice in the state, untidy and disorderly—this alone is a crime. The state takes over Christianity and then requires (for the subjects' best interests, which the state is always looking after), also for the sake of order, that everybody be a Christian just like everybody else—a requirement it emphatically intends to be kept.

So far the state. But the egotisms which were satisfied and completely acquiescent to the state's taking over Christianity probably reasoned something like this.

Wanting to be a Christian under difficult and strained conditions—that is, the condition of having to suffer for the doctrine—is a mistaken egotism. No doubt this egotism has the satisfaction of thinking that the others, after all, will be damned, but nevertheless it is a mistaken egotism. Gold, too, can be bought at too high a price. No, a reasonable calculation of the relations among various egotisms indicates that the most prudent egotism for all of us is: We are all Christians. Therefore, in order to prevent all this continual inordinate bickering, the only right thing to do is for the state to take over Christianity. This, in fact, is why we have the state. When the state takes over, an end is put to bickering, and then, too, everything is taken care of better. In fact, this is true of any situation. Take street lighting, for example—each resident or group of residents could have a light and take care of it, but that would be a mess; no, let the state take it over, and we will pay a fixed fee. Similarly it is also the right thing for the state to take over Christianity, take over everything dealing with eternal salvation, and we will pay a fixed fee. This provides a certain sense of security as well and therefore has a tranquilizing effect. Eternity, after all, is like another part of the world—and to have to come sailing in as an individual person—no, coming to grips with a world is nothing for an individual person to do. We see this in other things, too. Suppose a man here in Denmark is so unfortunate as to have a court case in Italy—it is just about the same as losing it, for it is an individual against a whole country. It is a quite different matter if he is lucky enough to get Denmark interested in the case through its diplomatic channels, for then it is sure to be all right. Why? Because it is country against country. And it is the same with eternal salvation; the matter is too earnest to be taken care of by an individual (in fact, the position of Christianity is that the earnestness lies precisely in this, that it shall be taken care of by the individual, that the matter is too earnest to be taken care of by an abstraction)—no, let the state take the thing over, let it vouch for us and guarantee that we are Christians, that salvation is assuredly ours: this is reassuring. The other is so horrible—just think of an individual human being, a man here in the city as an individual —and then this enormity: another world—to penetrate that is inconceivable. But the state, there you have something, there you have a power, and when it gives the guarantee, well, then something comes of it.

XI^2 A 111 *n.d.*, 1854

« **4502**

[*] *In margin of 4501* (XI^2 A 111):

Note. So the state established a kind of eternal principle that every child is born more or less a Christian. Just as the state undertook to take care of eternal salvation for the Christians (*si placet*), it also undertook to do the whole job, also to produce Christians. Just as production by machine is on a much larger scale and more accurate than by hand, so also generation after generation the state delivered an assortment of Christians, all with the factory stamp of the state, each Christian an accurate copy of the others, so accurate that the heart of every manager of a factory must leap to see what matchless heights of accuracy the art has attained. The main point in Christianity is that man is spirit and spirit is diversity *per se;* Christianity's infinitely sublime thought is that each Christian becomes a Christian by different ways and means— always diversity, which is precisely what God wants, he (a detester of all mimicry, which indicates the absence of spirit) who is inexhaustible in creating diversity. So the state took over Christianity, and the main point in being Christian came to be the greatest possible factory-made uniformity. Curiously enough, in a way God and the state have one thought in common, nevertheless: both want to do the supervising— it is, in fact, the task of the ruler. But God as the infinite concretion oversees with absolute ease, is not afraid of losing track if he allows diversity. No, just by wanting to have diversity everywhere he expresses his majestic confidence in being able to maintain supervision. The state, which is not completely secure, desires as much uniformity as possible—for the sake of supervision.

XI^2 A 112 *n.d.*

« 4503 *The State Church—The Folk Church*

Every effort to produce a Christian state, a Christian folk, is *eo ipso* unchristian, anti-Christian, for any such effort is possible only by reducing the criteria for being a Christian; therefore it is diametrically opposed to Christianity and is oriented toward providing the mask that we are all Christians, thus making it so easy to be a Christian.

XI^2 A 373   *n.d.*, 1854–55

« 4504 *The Church State and the State Church
The Two Forms of Swindling*

May 23, 1855

Through Christianity, God, the Almighty, Ruler of heaven and earth, the present reigning Majesty of majesties, wanted to bring up and educate men. Obviously he knows all about ruling. His idea was to want to rule with the help of eternity as background: an eternal salvation or an eternal damnation.

Appalling, so appalling that the human race shook and trembled under the pressure of the majesty of this ruler.

Time passed, but soon lust for power, human ambition—the passion which is perhaps strongest in man when he has learned to vanquish the purely animal nature—turned its attention to Christianity to see if it could cunningly take possession of it and then with respect to other men play our Lord, who rules with the help of eternity as background.

The really great attempt in this direction is the pope. His idea is to rule men by means of eternity, for it is he, Peter of the keys or Peter of the lies, who controls eternity. Splendid!

The other effort in this direction is that of the state. This falls more into the sphere of the negligible, and no doubt the state actually got into this strange situation *bona fide*. However, the state certainly cannot be acquitted of gradually having gotten the idea in its bonnet that it might, after all, be a good thing, in order to rule over men better, to have eternity up its sleeve, thus being a citizen and being a Christian become identical, being what the state would call a good citizen is synonymous with being a good Christian, consequently absolutely sure of eternal salvation, and being what the state would call an unruly subject is synonymous with being a poor Christian who would go to hell were it not for the increasing prevalence of the slothful view that we are all saved.

Both of these efforts, according to the Christian point of view, are in the category called swindle: the attempts are not a kind of nose-thumbing at God himself but a way of deceiving other men by pretending to be God.

XI² A 410 May 23, 1855

« **4505** *The Drones*

One of the metaphors Socrates[798] continually uses in the *Republic* to designate harmful members of society is drawn from the beehive.

This metaphor perfectly fits Christendom and its official clergy; they are merely consumers, they live off Christianity and yet give the appearance of building up and serving Christianity, while their zeal and enthusiasm never reach any farther than what pays. This is the most dangerous kind of counterfeit renunciation.

XI² A 416 *n.d.*, 1855

STEPHEN

« **4506** *Stephen*
*When he had said this, he fell asleep*⁷⁹⁹

(1) He fell asleep. How quiet. A person can sleep restlessly, but then he cannot be said to have fallen asleep. But to sleep quietly symbolizes quietness. How quiet. How quiet—doubly so because of a raging mob that fumes violence and murder—and he, he sleeps. His Lord and Master⁸⁰⁰ slept in the boat while the storm raged—the disciple imitated him: sleeping at that moment.

(2) He fell asleep. How powerful—yes, or seen from another side, how powerless, how powerless you are, sinful world, how powerless in all your noise and rage; what do you accomplish by it—look, this is what you accomplish: he sleeps! Be sleepless yourself in your bitterness, succeed in disturbing everything—but not him, not the sleeping one! How powerful to be able to sleep at that moment, and not only to sleep at that moment but to lay himself down to sleep at that moment. How little it usually takes to disturb a man's slumber—and then to be able to sleep this way. You are almost to be laughed at, world, for your impotence: he sleeps, he sleeps through the whole affair, he does not resist, no, far from it, he sleeps. He does not answer—no, far from it, he sleeps, he does not get involved with you at all—no, far from it, he sleeps; he is as if far away, far removed, absent—he sleeps.

(3) When he had said this, he fell asleep. What was it he said? He said: Father, do not hold this sin against them. This, then, is the formula—then one falls asleep; as we tell a child to say his prayer aloud and go to sleep—so he went to sleep, he went to sleep saying this. He prayed for them. He had prayed for himself again and again; his whole life to the very end, his sufferings, were praying for himself. Now there is only a moment left, a minute: he prays for his enemies. Yet it must be confessed that the shorter the time allotted, the easier it is, perhaps, to resolve to pray for one's enemies; if he had lived longer among them, it perhaps would not have been so easy to pray for them.

But we learn from him—to pray for ourselves, to pray for our enemies—and then to fall asleep.

So sleep then, sleep sweetly (to be continued).

[*In margin:* They saw that his face was like the face of an angel—so it is in death.]

For 1,800 years he has been famous and eulogized; but he cares nothing about that—he sleeps.

x⁴ A 434   *n.d.,* 1851

« 4507 *Stephen*

Theme: What is required to be able to pray for one's enemies?⁸⁰¹

Praying for one's enemies is the greatest of all—therefore it is so intensely embittering in the situation of contemporaneity.

x⁴ A 435   *n.d.,* 1851

« 4508 *Stephen*

In margin of 4507 (x⁴ A 435):

Theme: When the world shuts its doors to a man—heaven opens up to him.⁸⁰²

Introduction: The animal does not see heaven at all. The pagan (the erect) did see heaven,* but only the Christian sees the open heaven, especially the martyr—and for him the world shuts its doors on the greatest possible scale.

* But of paganism it must be said in another sense that paganism is: the closed heaven—but the world stands open to it all the more. The two are counterparts, either/or: to whom the world opens, heaven closes; to whom the world closes, heaven opens—now you can choose.

x⁴ A 436   *n.d.*

« 4509 *St. Stephen's Day*

The Christmas festival begins and ends with angels: yesterday the angels announced that a Savior was born—today Stephen witnesses to it, and they saw that his face was like an angel's.

[*In margin:* But if someone says: "Angels, no one has seen angels, that is just something for children"—answer: Rubbish, nonsense, hold your tongue—just see to it that you become like Stephen, that your face is like an angel's face—then the rest of us will get to see an angel.]

x⁴ A 438   *n.d.,* 1851

STOICISM, STOICS

« **4510**

The Stoic philosopher Empedocles[803] has said somewhere: "Be abstemious in vices."[804]—

II A 331   January 17, 1839

« **4511**

The contradiction in connection with Zeno's development of ethical concepts is of great interest. He declares that the highest good is indifferent to time, and he also says that the good man, the virtuous man, is the one who does the good throughout his whole life. Only the virtuous man can possess the highest good, and thus there is still a time qualification. (See Tennemann, *Geschichte der Philosophie*, IV, p. 89, p. 93 note, p. 134)—a modification of it on p. 145.[805] It is particularly noteworthy that this same teaching permitted suicide.

IV C 54   n.d., 1842–43

« **4512**

What I wish in a man is what a Stoic uses in an evil sense: εὐκαταφορία εἰs πάθos[806] (see Tennemann, *Geschichte der Philosophie*, IV, p. 129, note).[807]

IV A 44   n.d., 1843

« **4513** *Stoicism*

There is, however, a curious self-contradiction in Stoicism. We are taught that the Stoic takes earthly sufferings, adversities, etc. so lightly that they simply do not exist for him—and then suicide is still recommended as the ultimate avenue of escape. But one of two things: either suicide is ridiculous, for it is surely ridiculous to do a something on the occasion of nothing, or suicide is a sensible step—that is, a step in which there is a kind of meaning, but then it is thereby proved that sufferings do exist for the Stoic and are not as nothing to him.

Here, however, we see the union of pride and cowardice. By continually having cowardice as an open means of escape, a person keeps himself at the peak of pride as long as possible. Thus pride is like a bankrupt man's wasteful extravagance during the whole period he knows that he will go bankrupt. It is not a matter of pride changing to cowardice when suicide takes place—no, all the time pride was sustained by the thought of suicide, the pride was cowardice.

However, having suicide in reserve naturally has a certain power to make life intensive. The thought of death condenses and concentrates life. If we did not know how intensively Napoleon[808] lived, we could deduce it from the fact that he always went around with poison.

Here again we see Stoicism as a false edition of the essentially Christian. For it is quite true that Christianity also makes life intensive with the thought of death, imminent death, perhaps tomorrow, perhaps today. If this does not lead to "let us eat and drink," it leads to using the day today with enormous intensity. But then the essentially Christian gets still another weight to bear—that death may possibly remain far removed. This is what is so dreadfully strenuous, this alternating.

x^3 A 14   n.d., 1850

« 4514 *Epictetus*

What I particularly object to in him is that he shows that he is a slave. The dreadful knowledge that he is a slave and then the fact that it is settled forever weighs him down with such despair that through it he manifests the pride of Stoicism.

To be sure, only horror to the point of despair develops a person to his maximum—although of course many perish under the treatment, but it is also beneficial for a man to be dealt with so harshly.

Already in Epictetus's first words[809] I hear the slave: Some things are in our power, others are not; understood thus, there is a frightful passion in these cold words; we hear the slave groaning in chains, or we hear the groaning from the time when he, as a slave, had to learn this, learned how to practice this distinction.

The distinction is correct, but the passion with which it is practiced is something very different.

To be sure, nowadays we are old women compared with antiquity, and a good share of the trouble no doubt consists in our not learning anything from our unhappiness—because the external pressures are so mild and we do not have the character ourselves to make ourselves unhappy—but nevertheless character can also be purchased too dearly, in a certain sense can be purchased at the cost of character.

x^3 A 643   n.d., 1850

« 4515 *Stoic Suicide:*

ἠνοικτὰ [sic] ἡ θύρα, τὸ ἀνακλητικὸν σημαίνει.⁸¹⁰ Arrian III, 10 and 13. Quoted from Meiners, *Ethik,* I, p. 164.⁸¹¹

x⁴ A 464   *n.d.,* 1852

« 4516 *Marcus Aurelius—Epictetus*

How insignificant Marcus Aurelius' writings are compared to those of Epictetus!⁸¹² Marcus Aurelius' writing really has no genuine character; it is almost as affected as a professor's. No, it takes a slave to write with the loftiness of Stoicism; this is really the only alternative. Marcus Aurelius took care of himself in so many ways—by being emperor.

x⁴ A 576   *n.d.,* 1852

« 4517 *Christ Is "the Mediator"*

The untruth of Stoicism is also evident in the Stoics' wanting to be related directly to God (without a mediator).

x⁴ A 577   *n.d.,* 1852

« 4518 *Stoicism—To Die to the World*

It is not always great sufferings which enable us really to die to the world. No, they can also give zest for life, spiritual zest for life.

No, the most deadening of all are the miseries of finitude, trivialities and the like.

Stoicism was, after all, profound. As a matter of fact it permits suicide only in this situation (see Zeller, *Die Philosophie der Griechen*).⁸¹³ It does not permit suicide in order to escape great dangers; why should it! No, but the really deadening, this stultifying deadening—here suicide is permitted, for here it is as if there were nothing for "spirit" to do.

This is precisely what Christianity is alert to. When Stoicism would say: Now you have the right to kill yourself—precisely there is the real dying to the world—if one is to endure going on living.

Stoicism has an enormous resiliency in being able to endure sufferingly many things from which a man would ordinarily shrink. But its resiliency can nevertheless fail—here, then, comes suicide—the resiliency of patience breaks—and here comes the essentially Christian act, to die to the world.

x⁵ A 63   *n.d.,* 1853

STRIVING

« **4519**

To what extent can a person, with regard to the highest level of self-renunciation (where it consequently is not a question of natural qualifications, genius, being able to, etc.), have the right to say: I can go no farther, or, I cannot go that far out?

The matter is quite simple. Since every man's life must be conceived as a striving and he cannot do everything *ein, zwei, drei,*[814] it can be altogether true and be God-fearingly true (since the very opposite is presumptuous) for a man to say: At this moment I cannot go farther out. But he ought to admit this to himself, not try to forget it, not dissipate himself away from it; it ought to become a burr which helps him farther by keeping him awake and in the striving.

x^1 A 429   *n.d.,* 1849

« **4520** *"I do not box as one beating the air"*[815]

No, truly, when one pummels his own body, "subdues his own flesh," he never beats the air. Everyone who pummels others is boxing, yes, but perhaps in the air.

x^3 A 684   *n.d.,* 1850

« **4521** *"They all run the race"*[816]

Alas, times and situations differ. There was no doubt a time when this text might have been an occasion to preach about mistaking the goal, that it is no use to run if one is running the wrong way, and this, no doubt, is what Paul had in mind.

But nowadays the theme would have to be: No one is running; everybody is sitting in cozy ease.

x^3 A 685   *n.d.,* 1850

« **4522**

In margin of 4521 (x^3 A 685):

Well, in a certain sense, no doubt, all are running. They are running after money, honor, status, women. They run with gossip, rumors, loose talk, with lies, fiction, and trifles; they run now to the east and now to the west, panting on their activistic errands etc.—but they are not running on the racetrack.

x^3 A 686   *n.d.*

« **4523 "Grace"**

From a human point of view, there is something crippling about "grace," for striving, denying self, etc., if accorded merit, satisfy the merely human in a quite different way. But to have to strive, deny oneself, sacrifice everything—and then in spite of that it is still "grace" —this is, humanly speaking, ever so paralyzing.

x^4 A 191   *n.d.*, 1851

« **4524 "Works"**

Take a weak analogy. Imagine a girl in love: for a time she will find it sufficient to express her love in protestations, but there will come a moment when this will no longer satisfy her, when she will long to embrace her beloved. This means that she requires a stronger expression of pathos. So also with the believer in relation to God—expressing his gratitude in words, perhaps even in more elegant and artistically chosen words (and this is an utterly wrong direction), he will finally reach a point where he must say: I cannot stand it, this no longer satisfies my need; you must, O God, permit me a far stronger expression for my gratitude—works.

Even if this were not required, it must be just what the better man himself must desire—although the fact that it is required frees him from any anxiety about whether or not it is pleasing to God.

Which is which? Is it God's intention with Christianity merely to humble man by the prototype [*Forbilledet*] (consequently the presentation of the ideal) and to console him with "grace," but in such a way that Christianity is a means of expressing explicitly that there is no kinship between God and man, that man is supposed to express his gratitude the way a dog expresses it to a human being, so that worship becomes more and more true, more and more pleasing to God, the less it occurs to man to want to resemble the prototype, the more he can refrain from any attempt in this direction and simply and solely rejoice as an animal creature, for this was precisely what God wanted with Christianity—he wanted to express that in his infinite elevation he could no longer involve himself with man in the way man once childishly imagined, that he neither was nor could be in kinship with man but nevertheless was compassionate toward him, was really pleased up there in heaven to see him rejoice as an animal creature, and could not tolerate one thing only—man's frightful presumptuousness in wanting to be like the prototype? Is this the meaning of Christianity?

Or is Christianity's intention just the opposite? Does God wish to express precisely that he wills to be in kinship with man and just for this reason desires gratitude and worship which is in spirit and in truth—namely, imitation [*Efterfølgelsen*]?

The latter is certainly the intention of Christianity. But the former is a crafty invention by us men (even if it may have its more beautiful side) in order to slip out of the true relation to God, because this in its first stage actually is suffering.

How can this be? Because what God in his infinite love wants with man is so infinitely high that at first it becomes suffering—and we have no desire to get into that, and therefore we contrived the invention that true worship is not to presume to want to resemble the prototype. Let me speak symbolically. Imagine a powerful emperor; he bestows all his love on a peasant lad, and, O, an emperor's love is so great that it is not satisfied until the peasant lad is adopted as the emperor's son and becomes his successor [*Efterfølger*]. Let us now talk quite candidly. I wonder if the peasant lad would not think to himself: "This can get to be real torture; if the emperor really loves me, let him express it by doing what I want, let him give me a good farm so that I can marry Catharine, and I shall thank him all my life. But for me, a simple farm boy, to be swept into high society where I feel completely alien—this is close to being the greatest torture." No doubt this is just about the way he would talk to himself. But to the emperor he would probably say (for hypocrisy and being human are almost inseparable): What you want to do for me is far too much; I am both too humble and too modest to dare aspire to such things (but it is not he, after all, who aspires to it; it is the emperor who stands and invites him, yes, desires it); I would be speechless with joy if you would give me a well-equipped farm. —Now if the emperor did not palpably embody visible power to this peasant lad so that in a way it was left up to him to determine the relationship, the outcome would be that he arranges things in such a way that he gets the farm, praises the emperor's love, and explains that out of humility he does not aspire to be the emperor's son.

So it is also in the relationship to God. God simply wants—O infinite love!—a person to be in kinship with him in Christ. But for this to happen, one has to die to the world.[817] Aha! But man likes so much to enjoy this life. What does man do then? He contrives the invention that it is God's love which helps us enjoy this life, and that it is humility on man's side not to aspire to be in kinship with God.

You see, it's the old story! But is this right? Is it right to take advantage of God's declaring himself to be love, as if one could do what he wanted with him—"After all, he is love"? Or is it not God's intention to stir us to do his will precisely by revealing himself as love?

Here comes the hypocrisy again! God is love, says Christianity. Man avails himself of this and says: God is love—this is Christianity—but by this understands something quite different from what Christianity understands.[818]

Concerning the relation of my work as an author to Christianity, this must be said.

Overwhelmed by the impression of these millions of Christians, who I still believe will all be saved, I, because of my reckless and also melancholy[819] nature, and for many other reasons, have thought of first making a move in such a way that we at least admit that we are not Christians but only approximations.[820]

The official preaching such as it is nowadays is nothing but an illusion; the original rigorousness, heroism—well, how could I ever think of getting it introduced again, I am no hero;[821] so I thought: Well, then let it become official that we are not Christians at all, that Christianity is too high for us, that at most we can only tolerate "imitation" [*Efterfølgelsen*] as something we get permission to halt as soon as it hurts a little; let it become official so that God can get hold of us again, so that we can find out if this can stand. But the thing I opposed most of all was and is the nauseating deceitfulness of pretending that what is current now is Christianity.

I believed that this step had to be taken first. This done, we would perhaps come to see that we ought not relax but go on through.

Here, where I first began, is where Mynster should have come in; it would have been most beneficial for him. This he failed to do, and he, through the tragic insight into his prudential Christianity which I later had the opportunity to gain, was the very one who has forced me farther out.

x^4 A 639   *n.d.*, 1852

« 4525 *Through God We Are Capable of All Things*[822]

Even if these words can be misinterpreted, it can never be a misinterpretation to apply them the way God himself demands in his Word; here it is absolutely clear that even if we think we are incapable, we can do it through God. But the whole thing has been so wrongly and atrociously misinterpreted that we are not far from explaining it as presumptuousness—if someone, trusting in God, ventures to will what God commands in his Word. Yes, it has really gone so far that we have not merely abolished Christianity, but abolished it as presumptuous—of course, for otherwise one would not be quite sure that it is abolished.

X⁵ A 5   n.d., 1852

« **4526** *Nitpicking*

There is nothing more dangerously destructive to everything than this hearty nonsense which "tries and tries a little bit"—no, it is a swindle.

The most dangerous thing in a school is that shirking and whining get a foothold; there is nothing more difficult to eradicate.

This is why it is part of good discipline to designate shirking and whining qualitatively by the severity of the punishment in order to get a whack at it.

With respect to defiance, insubordination, indolence etc. the discipline needs to do no more than decree the punishment; with respect to shirking and whining, the discipline must first of all really turn it into guilt.

XI¹ A 167   n.d., 1854

« **4527** *Infinite Striving Propped Up by Finite Striving*

To prop up infinite striving with finite striving is like swimming in a life-jacket. It also has the advantage that one does not venture too far out, for one thing, because temporal goods are always found in the crowd and thus one cannot strive for them by coming out of the crowd, but to stay in the crowd also makes one feel secure, and for another, because the life-jacket is always there to haul one back to land.

But, of course, eternally this is a most stupid thing to do—how strange all these shrewd ones will feel when their shrewdness is shipwrecked on eternity.

XI¹ A 212   n.d., 1854

« **4528** *Effort*

The idea demands, and Christianity even more definitely, that you must express the unconditioned, strive in the direction of the unconditioned.

And then one is . . . . . no, I will not talk impatiently this way, I will not say: And then one is placed in the world where everything is mediocrity. No, no, it is precisely for this reason that one is put into the world where everything is mediocre (in order to be able to express the unconditioned; how infinitely consistent!), for in such a world you will come to suffer for your striving in the direction of the unconditioned—and therefore this very suffering belongs with a truly unconditioned striving.

But it is true that everything is mediocrity. There is the harmless mediocrity—these thousands and thousands—and in fact they are the best. Then there are the scoundrels, the aristocratic envy which takes advantage of the mediocrity of these thousands or the fact that they are unable to grasp anything else but mediocrity. Yes, I have experienced how the inability of men to understand anything other than mediocrity has been exploited as applicable to my true adherents, so that my cause is drawn back into mediocrity.

This is exhausting! O, just as one who is accustomed to play for high stakes and one who is accustomed to fight with sharp weapons must find it agonizing to have to live in a city, in a country, where they play passionately for peppernuts and maneuver passionately with blank cartridges, so is this life full of agony. And just as they could long to be away from such wretchedness, so may one long to be gone, long for the company of those glorious ones who also played for high stakes while they lived, those for whom the meaning of life was simply to put down the highest possible stake.

XI^1 A 266 *n.d.*, 1854

« 4529 *Christianity Is Restlessness*

We all laugh when the comedy[823] shows the family in a four-seated Holstein carriage pursuing the young girl running swiftly over the ridge out into the wide world.

And yet this is only a meager metaphor of how ridiculous Christendom is.

The ideals, the prototypes—yes—no fleetfooted young girl is so quick; with the restlessness of eternity, with the passion and impatience of the martyr, they hasten out of this trashy world— — —and Christendom! A four-seated Holstein carriage drawn by two horses is probably saying too much for Christendom, because, after all, the carriage is moving. No, if one were going to illustrate Christendom's pursuit of the ideal one could (like the Jew who asked if they had a

340   STRIVING

carriage with five benches) imagine a Holstein carriage with 140 benches and one horse up front* going up a hill—that is, sliding back down a hill, yet claiming that this expedition is pursuing the ideal, a claim also that it is moving forward, which is recited by the clergy, one of whom is sitting on each bench.

XI¹ A 397   n.d., 1854

« 4530

In margin of 4529 (XI¹ A 397):
*Note. The horse, of course, by arrangement with the ecclesiastical ballet-master, is provided for the sake of appearance so that it may truthfully be said: Everything is fine. We are making an effort, we are driving—after all, we have a horse in front. If no horse were there, one would run the risk of having to make an explanation, but this way there is nothing to worry about and everything is under control: there is a horse up front. A wooden horse could be used just as well, but a horse there must be, lest the common man[824] become restless, begin to suspect something, and also so that the pastor may reassuringly say with a good conscience: We are advancing, we are on the move—after all, there is a horse up front.

XI¹ A 398   n.d.

« 4531   *Finitude—Infinitude, in Reverse*

The representation of the concerns of the spirit, of the idea, of Christianity, homogenized, please note, with finitude, has also contributed to the demoralization which is Christendom. Therefore what should have helped to lift society or at least to awaken a memory that there is something higher, now strengthens the finite and finite striving in its finitude, yes, in such a way that these very representatives of the idea and of Christianity villainously exploit the finite understanding of the common man[825] to oppose anything, if it did appear, which really bears the idea or is borne by the idea and is really related to Christianity.

Take a finite context: two merchants, one of whom buys and sells in such a way that he makes a lot of money and the other in such a way that he loses it. Finitude then says: one of the two is a merchant and the other is not a merchant.

Transfer this directly to the context of the spirit and of Christianity. There are two philosophers. One makes a lot of money and the other loses money. Well, finitude immediately concludes (and naturally swindling preachers and professors give encouragement in this) that the first is a philosopher and the second is not. Here are two teachers of Christianity. The one makes a lot of money and becomes something, and the other becomes nothing and loses money—surely the former is the true teacher of Christianity and the second is not.

But finitude and infinitude are related inversely. The true merchant is the one who makes money. But the true philosopher, not to mention the true teacher of Christianity, is precisely the one who does not make money, because to represent infinitude in such a way that it becomes finitude is still not infinitude.

How detestable to exploit the unclarity of the less-enlightened in order to stimulate him to what really is infinite striving while one himself under the guise of attending to the higher is really betraying it.

XI^1 A 431 n.d., 1854

« 4532 *"I am not that as yet, but I am trying"*

(Earlier than the end of 1854.)

"It really is very arbitrary and unjust and on top of that senseless to accost a man suddenly at four o'clock in the afternoon, confront him with the Christian requirement, and when it is discovered that his life does not express it, then conclude: Ergo, you are not a Christian. Good Lord, I certainly am not one, but I am trying, and after all—if we are not to go completely mad—this is the highest there can be any question of—an effort."

Well, well, fine words again. But when you yourself say: "I am not that as yet, but I am trying," you are, after all, saying "I am not that," and is it not remarkable that you think your statement that you are trying gives you the right to say that you are that, the right to call yourself Christian?

If someone aspiring to be a millionaire but as yet has managed to earn only three marks were to call himself a millionaire because, as he said, he was trying, I wonder if we men would be foolish enough to go along with his use of language, and I wonder if it really is not best for him—simply to keep him awake and alert for the exertion—to say to himself, "I am not a millionaire," so that by saying it and saying it to himself he would not contribute to his not becoming that.

Consequently we will not call someone a millionaire or take him seriously when he calls himself one, someone who has managed to acquire three marks but said himself that he was trying to get a million —and I wonder if we would be more inclined to call him a millionaire if we saw with amazement, precisely at the moment he once again was insisting he was a millionaire because he was trying—that he gave away one of the three marks, so that he now had but two marks but still said that he was trying?

The point is really this—if there is to be any meaning to it, if it is at all permissible to take the name of something simply because one is striving toward it, then one must at least resemble one who is striving.

Suppose the task is to run a race. If a man comes along walking at a leisurely pace, cane in hand and pipe in mouth, and carrying something under his arm to boot: well, now, is he running a race? No, but "he is trying; it will come, all right, little by little." Thereupon he calmly continues ambling along; then something else happens, a little boy comes running after him with an overcoat, and we see with amazement that he who already had on one overcoat (which certainly does not go with running a race) now puts on one more, and at the same time says: I may not be running, but it will come, all right. I am trying. Thus amid assurances about trying, what he is doing brings him more and more into a condition which is less and less appropriate to running a race.

The requirement of Christianity is to die to the world. The pastor declares emotionally (just to infuse truth into his discourse): I confess that I am not that as yet, but I am trying. This pastor has a public office, and that very same day he has applied for a promotion; furthermore, the same Sunday evening there is a party at the home of a prominent and powerful man, concerning which the pastor says to himself: "Strictly speaking, I do not need to go, but I know very well what it means if I don't—I will get no decoration this time, and it would be extremely beneficial to me right now, since I am seeking"—"I am not dead to the world, but I am trying; it will come, all right."

No, then I prefer to say straightforwardly to God: This matter of dying to the world—I am not striving for that and probably never will; I cannot get it out of my head that "by grace" I will probably manage to get into eternity without it. But in any case I simply cry out to you, O God, to grab me, get hold of me—I beseech you to do it!"—if this is what is required, if salvation depends on this. [*In margin:* But I will not attempt to make a fool of you, dupe you, men, and myself—no, I make an honest admission—there is still that much truth in me.]

XI^3 B 47 *n.d.*, 1854

« 4533 *"But He Is Trying"*

This is the phrase men use in seeking to hide the fact that Christianity simply does not exist;[826] they say: "I confess that in the strictest sense, in the New Testament sense, I am not a Christian, but I am trying." Having said that, or taking care to say it every Sunday year after year, or hearing it said, one reckons thereby to accomplish the same thing accomplished by the appointment of a committee: that one needs to do nothing.

Let me use an illustration. There is much talk these days about an expedition to the North Pole, an enterprise regarded as involving extreme exertion and danger.

Now suppose that in some way or other mankind has gotten the idea in its head that to have taken part in such an expedition to the North Pole is something which has significance for one's eternal salvation—and let us assume that the clergy have gotten into the affair and now are going to help men (out of love!).

It is sufficiently clear that in order to take part in such a North Pole expedition a person must first of all—if he lives in Europe—leave Europe, his home, and go to America; then travel a long way north before there can be any question of a North Pole expedition, which really must be assumed to begin with dangers and the initial exertion.

The pastors will now make use of this. They see, of course, that the number of those who will actually make the strenuous and dangerous North Pole expedition will be extremely small and that this number will by no means be able to justify a living for a legion of pastors with families. Consequently it is a matter of changing "North Pole expedition" to "an effort in the direction of such a North Pole expedition," and then to prattle something about it to men, thereby managing to delude everyone, the millions, into thinking that he, too, is striving in the direction of a North Pole expedition—for if there are not millions who strive, then thousands of pastors cannot possibly live with families—ergo, everyone must be deluded into thinking that he is striving.

How this may be done is clear enough. There is, for example, a man living in Copenhagen. He travels by ship to London and back in the greatest comfort and ease, "and," says the pastor, "this was his

North Pole expedition; true, he did not reach the North Pole, but he did try." "It is sufficiently clear," expounds the pastor, "that if one is going to make an expedition to the North Pole and lives in Copenhagen, he must first of all leave Copenhagen. This man did that. On the other hand, there is no one, after all, who has reached the North Pole; even the one who went the farthest only made an effort. But to travel to London is also an effort." Wonderful, tremendously popular! And to take a carriage to Deer Park on Sunday afternoon, leaving one's home, is also an effort aimed at discovering the North Pole: ergo, we are all striving.

This is the way the pastors have made Christians of all of us. The artistry they practice under the name of interpreting Scripture is to translate the words of the Bible into nonsense, and the better they succeed, the greater the number of believing, or, what is most important, paying Christians, who are naïvely consoled by the fact that the pastors, after all, have taken an oath upon the New Testament.

XI³ B 146 *n.d.*, 1855

SUBJECTIVITY/OBJECTIVITY

« **4534**

The objective reality [*Realitæt*] of Christ's Atonement, independent of the subjectivity appropriating this to itself, is very clearly indicated in the story about the ten lepers.[827] All of them were in fact healed, but "Your faith has made you well" is said only of the tenth one, who gratefully turned back to offer God the glory.

September 18, 1838

In margin: What was it, then, that made the others well?

II A 263 *n.d.*

« **4535**

There is, then, this diametrical contrast: between older times, when faith in God was greater, when the velvet on the pulpit was not as faded as it is now, when men appealed to the omnipotence of God, that nothing is impossible for God, in order to prove the resurrection of the body, etc.—and these modern times when men smile at this, since they interpret this thought in the most caricatured form possible and appeal to the deeply rooted need in man, to the demand, as it were, to the claim men make, in order to prove the immortality of the soul, etc., which can be caricatured just as much if this is to be understood in terms of man's merely subjective claim, for then every whim could make a similar fuss. Therefore these two sides need to be mediated.[828]

II A 433   May 17, 1839

« **4536**

There is a great difference between views on the forgiveness of sins—to forgive another person the same sin and to be convinced that God will forgive it, but when it comes to oneself, then it pinches. The philosophical talk which explains nothing and understands nothing, but simply goes further,[829] naturally does not halt at sin.[830] But the first condition for going further is that one becomes guilty in such a way that while all other men are able to find forgiveness, one cannot find it himself. One is willing to believe that there was very much which

345

served to excuse the others, but for himself there is no excuse. —All this is quite in order, and this emphasis on subjectivity is necessary in order that all existence may not be dissolved into utterly indifferent talk about Persia, China.[831]

VA 37 *n.d.*, 1844

« **4537**

Para. 3 [changed from 2].[832]

1. *What it means to treat a matter subjectively*
(infinitely interested).
2. To be subjective is regarded as something very easy. Of course, every human being is a subject, but [to be] a genuine subject, to comprehend infinite reality [*Realitet*] and infinite responsibility—only a few accomplish this, perhaps not ten in each generation.
3. The essential thing about subjectivity is that in resolution and the decision of choice one runs a risk. This is the absolute decision. And the risk ought to be equally great for the contemporary and for the most recent.
4. It is commonly believed that the task is to become more and more objective, to divest oneself of his subjectivity.
5. The poets say the opposite, that a lover is a great rarity. The pastors likewise, that a believer is a great rarity.
6. Of course, subjectivity must be thoroughly and intensively worked through in order to come to such a decision: to conceive of an eternal decision, of his *eternal* salvation (what enormous passion this takes). This is the art of subjectivity, which is infinitely more terrifying than the *summa summarum* of all the ¶¶ of the whole System, both internally and externally. Freely to make up one's mind concerning it and say: I will or I will not. Only such individuals have anything to do with God, either diabolically or as saints. (How many understand even the infinite decision of erotic love.)
7. Objective consideration does not accent *how* one is interested, that a person's eternal salvation depends on it, and that as a consequence it would be the greatest tragedy to be wrong.
8. Subjectivity is inwardness. Inwardness is spirit. To believe is not an *indifferent relation to something* which is true, but an *infinitely decisive relation to something*. The accent falls upon the relation.[833]

9. How many men have any idea of their eternal happiness. What energetic perseverance it takes not to relinquish [the idea of an eternal happiness] and to risk offering resistance under this responsibility; [what energetic perseverance it takes] to wrestle alone with God and to risk ruin.

10. Subjectivity, then, the requirement is that the point of departure for faith be just as original as it was for the apostles. The eternal decision that is sought is transformed into a continued striving by the synthetic factor of time in human existence. (There is a lot of careless talk about the solemnity of being in holy places—arising out of the fact that one goes there so seldom; otherwise the difficulties would be apparent.)

VI B 19:1–10 *n.d.*, 1844–45

« 4538

Modern theorizers are so foolishly objective that they completely forget that the thinker himself is like the flutist's instrument and that it is of utmost importance to know one's instrument (here is psychology), yes, of a quite different kind of importance, for the thinker has a relation of infinite inwardness to his object such as no flutist has to his instrument.

VI A 63 *n.d.*, 1845

« 4539

Objective thinking does not care at all about the thinker and finally becomes so objective that, like the customs clerk, it thinks that it merely has to do the writing, that the others have to do the reading.[834]

VI A 64 *n.d.*, 1845

« 4540

If a man does not become what he understands, then he does not understand it either. Only Themistocles[835] had an understanding of Miltiades; therefore he also became that.

VII¹ A 72 *n.d.*, 1846

« 4541

I am charged with inducing young people to rest satisfied in their subjectivity. Perhaps, for a moment. But how is it possible to get rid of all these illusions of objectivity, such as the public etc., without emphasizing the category of individuality.[836] Under the guise of objectivity people have wanted to sacrifice individualities completely. This is the whole question.

VIII¹ A 8 *n.d.*, 1847

« **4542**

Most men are subjective toward themselves and objective toward all others, frightfully objective sometimes—but the task is precisely to be objective toward oneself and subjective toward all others.[837]

VIII¹ A 165 *n.d.*, 1847

« **4543**

My view is not that God should love me more than anyone else, unconditionally anyone else, but that I think about God's loving me considerably more than others do. Let others find it great to reflect objectively that God loves all men; I find it blessed to reflect subjectively that God loves me and that this is open to everyone to think about.[838]

VIII¹ A 313 *n.d.*, 1847

« **4544**

During the initial period of Christianity, when it was introduced into the world, it was certainly doctrine that gave occasion for conflict more than anything else. In Christendom doctrine is really taken for granted, and if there is any conflict about doctrine it really turns out to be merely a sectarian movement. The conflict in Christendom ought to be about giving the doctrine the ethical power over one's life which Christianity demands. There is in fact something to it that we are all Christians. That means that Christianity's teaching cannot be alien to us as to the pagans. The calamity is that the doctrine has become a triviality to most people, is taken for granted by most of them as a triviality. Therefore, it is a matter of interiorizing the doctrine.

VIII¹ A 535 *n.d.*, 1848

« **4545**

The one and only consolation and absolute distraction in all one's suffering is to look to God, to think of him, submit everything to him, consider that it comes from him in that he allows it. In this way one becomes, rightly understood, objective and, rightly understood, subjective—objective toward others and subjective toward himself. In public meetings remarks are supposed to be addressed to the president, not to the individual person—why?—to avoid personalities.

And thus in the midst of all the persecutions one avoids all personalities. Someone spits in my face; I do not look at him but at God, address the remarks concerning it to God—that is, I remain personally on the outside, relate myself *personally* only to God. I do not talk *with* such a man but talk *about* him even in his presence.

This is the victory over all meanness. Any man would, I am sure, do this with respect to an animal, with respect to the elements etc., where he does not acknowledge any personal relationship. But the God-fearing man has really only one personal relationship: to God. He cannot relate himself to a representative of coarseness in any other way than he would to a dog that bit him.

This was the truth in the words of Socrates[839] when he reprimanded someone who wanted him to become angry because Xantippe did something unbecoming toward him—Socrates answered: If a hen did the same thing, you would not become angry.

But Socrates' mistake was that he did not have the inward turning of piety but only the outward turning of objectivity.

It is the opposite, however, with most men, as I have noted somewhere else [i.e., VIII¹ A 165]. They are objective in the wrong place, for they allow themselves everything, and subjective at the wrong place, for when the slightest thing happens to them they promptly become subjectively affected, sometimes even by a dog, which is the most bestial admission a man can make.

IX A 363 n.d., 1848

« **4546**

In the situation of actuality an expression of genuine piety sounds like utter madness. Take Christ's words:[840] Not a sparrow falls to the ground; the hairs of your head are numbered. But now forget that from childhood on you have learned it by rote so that it makes no impression upon you. And it must not be a minister (one of those fibbers) speaking from a pulpit and saying: This *every* man ought to believe just as it is, so strong *should* every man's faith be. No, let it be someone in daily life who declares that he believes it altogether literally, so that every second he feels surrounded by God, and when he goes for an autumn walk and the leaves fall from the trees, not one leaf falls except by God's will: just watch—he will be regarded as crazy.

But the fact of the matter is that men have hit upon so many tricks and equivocations in the way they say something that it actually is not to be reflected upon at all. They talk objectively.

X¹ A 30 n.d., 1849

« **4547**

To be an observer in the sense talked about so much is actually sin; the sin is to be objective, turned outward instead of inward.

x^1 A 223   *n.d.,* 1849

« **4548**

Christianity has been abolished by the ubiquitous relegating of personality into the background. People seem to fear that an *I* might be a kind of tyranny, and therefore every *I* might be a kind of tyranny, and therefore every *I* must be leveled and pushed behind some objectivity. I must not have the right to say: I believe there is a God—I must say: This is Christian doctrine and I believe it, but then this *I* is a more universal *I*, not my personal *I*.[841] There is doctrine, objectivity everywhere, and one is prevented everywhere from getting an impression that a person is in direct relation to God. If a pastor at times uses his *I* in the pulpit, it is forgiven, because his *I* in the pulpit is still not taken to be in the strictest sense his personal *I* but a kind of dramatic *I*, or an *I qua* public official.

Just as scholarly commentators often frustratingly come between the author and the readers he preferred, just as the daily press has frustratingly intervened between authentic literature and the reader, so objectivity has everywhere been slipped in frustratingly between God and actuality, has smuggled God far, far away. Instead of doctrine being the objective and my *I* a personal appropriating of it and that as a consequence I speak in the first person in actuality, I am supposed to get rid of my *I* and speak objectively. For that which should rule in the world must not be God, who acts upon the *I*, but should be an objectivity, an abstraction, to which the individual *I*'s relate like leaves to a tree, like animals to a species.

x^2 A 145   *n.d.,* 1849

« **4549**

[*In margin: The Difficulty of Essential Christianity and the Cunning of Our Age.*]

I have always maintained and Anti-Climacus[842] has expressly pointed up that the difficulty of essential Christianity really appears only when it is placed together with the single individual,[843] when the single individual, you and I, appropriates it in earnest, daring to say: It has to do with me, for essential Christianity is all too elevated and offense cannot be avoided.

Just as we nowadays avoid another difficulty in essential Christianity—contemporaneity—by changing it to the past, so we avoid the problem with the single individual by always slipping in some objectivity. If I say: As a bridegroom loves so Christ loves me—me, S. A. Kierkegaard, or me, H. Martensen, or me, J. P. Mynster—yes, then it pinches. What do we do then? We slip the Church in: As a bridegroom loves so Christ loves the Church, which is the bride. Now, you see, all goes well. Such an enormous thing as the Church, which has stood for 1,800 years, consisting of, as they say, millions and millions—according to human understanding such an enormous thing seems to be commensurable with Christ—and thus the offense disappears.

And now think of the confusion!

When I discourse on the single individual, it is supposed to be subjective *Liebhaberie*,[844] but the other—that is objective Christianity! O, you scoundrels! Or, more accurately, they themselves do not know how sly their tactics are for undermining all Christianity.

To my great joy I read in Luther[845] today (his sermon on the Twentieth Sunday after Trinity about the king who prepared a wedding feast for his son) his development of how "the old Adam," the blindness and obstinancy of flesh and blood, fights powerfully against this about Christ loving me and you as a bridegroom. I read these words on page 564, second column: . . . . . The world admits in a pinch that Christ is a handsome, noble, and faithful bridegroom and *his Church* a magnificent, glorious bride. But if *everyone for himself* shall believe that he also belongs to Christ and that Christ has such a fervent love for him—then everything comes to a halt.

Praise God for Luther! He is always a good help against the almost insanely inflated dogmatic and objective conceitedness which, by going further,[846] abolishes Christianity.

X^2 A 231 *n.d.*, 1849

« **4550**

[*In margin:* Joh. Climacus.]

In all the usual talk that Johannes Climacus[847] is mere subjectivity etc., it has been completely overlooked that in addition to all his other concretions he points out in one of the last sections[848] that the remarkable thing is that there is a How with the characteristic that when the How is scrupulously rendered the What is also given, that this is the How of "faith." Right here, at its very maximum, inwardness is shown to be objectivity. And this, then, is a turning of the subjectivity-principle, which, as far as I know, has never before been carried through or accomplished in this way.

x^2 A 299 *n.d.*, 1849

« **4551** *Dialectic*

There is a pious suspicion about subjectivity, that as soon as the least concession is made to it it will promptly become something meritorious—this is why objectivity must be emphasized.

Fine. In order to constrain subjectivity, we are quite properly taught that no one is saved by works, but by grace—and corresponding to that—by faith. Fine.

But am I therefore unable to do something myself with regard to becoming a believer? Either we must answer this with an unconditioned "no," and then we have fatalistic election by grace, or we must make a little concession. The point is this—subjectivity is always under suspicion, and when it is established that we are saved by faith, there is immediately the suspicion that too much has been conceded here. So an addition is made: But no one can give himself faith; it is a gift of God I must pray for.

Fine, but then I myself can pray, or must we go farther and say: No, praying (consequently praying for faith) is a gift of God which no man can give to himself; it must be given to him. And what then? Then to pray aright must again be given to me so that I may rightly pray for faith, etc.

There are many, many envelopes—but there must still be one point or another where there is a halt at subjectivity. Making the scale so large, so difficult, can be commendable as a majestic expression for God's infinity, but subjectivity cannot be excluded, unless we want to have fatalism.

x^2 A 301 *n.d.*, 1849

« **4552**

It is one of those foolish remarks which immediately identify one who does not understand man: "There are certain things which understandably can make a man insane—but others not"; it is a foolish attempt to explain insanity *in casu*[849] as if it were not insanity, since it is so very "understandable" that he became insane.

No, it is rather like this. As far as the more important, less common, more interesting factors in insanity are concerned, dwelling on a man's becoming insane is preoccupying and interesting; there is a kind of novelistic interest in it, and one's participation in it is quite accurately egotism. Where it is a matter of becoming insane over a trifle, as it is called, it is otherwise; and yet they forget what a psychologist would promptly think of, that this very trifle as a reflex had a part in constituting the insanity, so the man went out of his mind, became enraged "that such a trifle should have such power over him, that others would believe that such a trifle would have such power over him" and so on.

In regard to this whole side of psychiatry, it is so profoundly true that to be a physician is to be willing oneself to suffer. He who does not have this humble devotedness, patience, and love to be willing to endure the suffering, serving (like a servant, like the subordinate one, in the form of a servant), putting himself in the other's situation—he heals no one; and if the physician is in this way willing to suffer more than the patient—he heals many.

X^2 A 322 *n.d.*, 1849

« **4553**

It has happened in history that there have been whole periods during which by means of imagination alone men have been lost in Christian objectivity and have completely forgotten themselves while they profoundly developed doctrine, artistically painted Christ,[850] and the like—this still happens to the majority of those who nevertheless do have some relation to Christianity. They are not aware that the real problems first begin when all this objectivity is to be realized existentially in the individual's life. For safety's sake they continue to shout that the objective is the highest, the subjective the imperfect. And yet all Christianity is subjectivity. Christianity is no doctrine; it is a doctrine existentially realized in one single man, in the God-man.

But when will this confusion be controlled, this confusion which men do not want to get out of, for they really do not want the existential tasks—actual renunciation, to act Christianly, to have God and the prototype so close in life that it literally revolves solely around me, the single individual.

And these evasions of cowardice and secular-mindedness and effeminacy—these have been prettied up to be the highest—to be subjective is nothing, yes, an error. What profound cunning of evil there always is in the secular mentality! It is supposed to be modest and humble to be objective—at least it is the easiest.

X^2 A 336 *n.d.*, 1850

« **4554**

Fundamentally all understanding depends upon how one is disposed toward something.[851] If a misfortune happens on a day one is really trusting and full of faith—well, even if it were utterly calamitous—if he is trusting and full of faith, he can explain it in various ways in the context of his joy—that God is letting something happen to him simply because now he has the strength to bear it, that now he is to use the occasion to learn to know himself in surmounting it, etc. —If a person is despondent, broken-hearted, melancholy—the most insignificant matter is enough to make him suspect bad luck, the law of fatality, in what happens.

From this we see that a person's whole view of life actually is a confession of the state of his inner being.

X^2 A 355 *n.d.*, 1850

« **4555**

In this respect, too, I have not been understood at all. All the more profound thinkers (Hegel, Daub—and to name a less famous but very estimable one: Julius Müller*[852] et al.) are unanimous in locating evil in isolated subjectivity—objectivity is the saving factor.

For a long time now this has been a phrase; and every student knows, after all, that I am an isolated individuality—ergo, I am practically evil, "pure negativity, lacking earnestness, etc."

O, abysmal confusion. No, the whole concept of objectivity, which has been made into the way of deliverance, is merely a feeding of the sickness, and the fact that it is lauded as restoration to health shows precisely how fundamentally irreligious the period is, for the way of deliverance is really a turning back to paganism.

No, precisely in order to put an end to subjectivity in its untruth we must pass all the way through "to the single individual"—face to face with God.

But men have no idea of what religiousness is. They have no intimation that both Christ and all the heroes of faith were in one sense isolated individuals—*aber* they belonged absolutely to God.

Take Socrates! In those days one Sophist after the other came forward and showed that the trouble was a lack of adequate information, there must be more and better research, ignorance was the evil—and then comes old Father Socrates and says: No, ignorance is the restoration to health.

I wonder if it did not go with Socrates in his age as with me. He came to be regarded as representing evil, for in those days ignorance was looked upon as evil—and yet Socrates was in truth the physician.

It takes a rare genius (or infinite depth and an infinitely sensitive ear to get all the demonic phenomena themselves to proclaim, inversely understood, what they need) in order to get hold of things properly in these areas. I make no claims for myself.

It is absolutely true, isolated subjectivity as the age understands it is evil, but restoration to health by means of "objectivity" is not a hair better.

Subjectivity is the way of deliverance—that is, God, as the infinitely compelling subjectivity.

x^2 A 401   n.d., 1850

« 4556

* *Addition in margin of 4555* (x^2 A 401):

As far as J. Müller is concerned, it must always be stressed that he has a far deeper perception, even if he does not pursue its qualitative consequences and actually makes a $\mu\epsilon\tau\acute{a}\beta\alpha\sigma\iota s$ $\epsilon\grave{\iota}s$ $\overset{\text{\'}}{a}\lambda\lambda o$ $\gamma\acute{\epsilon}\nu os$.[853]

x^2 A 402   n.d.

« 4557

This I do not understand: to be able to be objective this way about the religious. On Saturday a person takes out the religious (about the way a lawyer takes out his law books) and "puts himself into it," works out a sermon which he delivers on Sunday—but otherwise has nothing to do with the religious; it does not overwhelm him, never grips him suddenly—no, it is a business like the merchant's, the attorney's, the administrator's.

x^3 A 22   n.d., 1850

« 4558 *What—and How*

In the relation between an established order and the new within Christianity, the rule is quite simply this: the new is not a new *what* but a new *how* of the old *what*.[854]

Yet serving a *how* cannot very easily become conspicuous or satisfy earthly passions which want to displace the old so that they themselves can rule, etc.: therefore for all impatient and secularly minded people it is important that the new becomes a *what* so that light can properly fall upon—the originators.

When such a new *how* is served by the originator in true self-renunciation—and a few men then attach themselves to him or adopt his ideas, then—if these few do not have the same self-renunciation—it will soon become impossible for him to satisfy their impatience. In their impatience it becomes important to them to get it altered to his having provided a new *what* and on that basis he can be proclaimed the ruler—to the advantage of those who have adopted his ideas. If he does not want to go along with this, his very adherents are likely to label it treason to the cause or weakness—well, this too is self-renunciation.

x^3 A 593 *n.d.*, 1850

« **4559 *The Modern Profitable Proclamation of Christianity***

Instruction in Prudence

or

in penciled parentheses: Quid pro quo

or

Maren's Secrets

How Christianity really ought to be proclaimed can be discovered even by a merely superficial reading of the New Testament.

This, however, is old-fashioned.

Here are examples of the modern approach to the relation between doctrine and existence.

Suppose, for example, you were to present the essentially Christian view that Christianity actually does favor the unmarried state—and you yourself are unmarried: no, *you* must not teach this; you would run the risk that the congregation might believe this should be taken seriously and they would shout: Exaggeration, exaggeration! No, you must wait until later in your life when you yourself are happily and well married—then you can successfully and profitably preach about it to the edification, contentment, and enjoyment of the congregation. If you are to present the essentially Christian view that so far as Christianity involves marriage it holds that a person marry only once—and you yourself are married but only for the first time: no, this is nothing for you; you run the risk that the congregation might believe that this is in earnest and they will shout: Exaggeration, exaggeration! No, wait until you have married a second time, and then you can successfully and profitably preach about it to the edification, contentment, and enjoyment of the congregation. If you are to present the essentially Christian view that the true Christian lives in need and poverty—and you yourself are a poor, paltry fellow—no, this is nothing for you, it will be interpreted as exaggeration. You must postpone preaching about it until you get a good appointment, and if you get a good fat appointment, then you can successfully and profitably preach about it to the edification, contentment, and enjoyment of the congregation. If you are a "nobody," you must not get involved in preaching that the true Christian repudiates the world's honors, medals, ribbons, and titles. The congregation would cry: What exaggeration! No, you must at least be a Knight of Denmark if you are to preach successfully and profitably about it to the edification, contentment, and enjoyment of the congregation.—And if you excel in this kind of preaching of Christianity, then you will become Your Excellency, which is, as the philosophers say, a necessary development.

The rule in original Christianity was: your life should guarantee what you say. The modern rule is: by expressing just the opposite of what you depict beautifully and picture fascinatingly, your life should guarantee that the whole thing is a game, a theatrical treat—then the congregation declares: By God, that was a lovely sermon.

x^3 A 720   *n.d.*, 1851

« 4560 *"Objective Doctrine, the Objective"*

Objective doctrine, the objective, this is what is clamored for, and subjectivity is sneered at. Quite naturally, for men want to be exempted from the inconvenience and sacrifice of being subjectivities.

Or was it perhaps objective doctrine, the objective, which triumphantly penetrated the whole world? What infinite nonsense! No, the objective has nothing to do with such things; it never moves from the spot. No, it was not doctrine, it was not the objective which conquered the world, but it was the blood of the martyrs and the sacrifices of the faithful in short, it was the subjectivities who triumphantly fought the doctrine through.

But to have to become subjective in this way is awkward, and this is why people allow it even to be sneered at instead of honestly admitting that they are incapable of it.

Now that doctrine has long since been treated as the objective and that being subjective has been abolished, what has happened to the doctrine? Well, what Schiller[855] said about money applies to it:

> *ein Wort*
> *es gehet vom Munde zu Munde*
> *das Herz giebt nicht davon Kunde.*

It was different in those times when there were subjectivities.

x³ A 756 n.d., 1851

« 4561 *The Objective*

It is this dreadful hypocrisy which has been promoted—that the objective, a doctrine, the cause is everything—the subject of no consequence—it is this which has helped put Christianity into utterly false categories.

Imagine two teachers with equal capabilities, equal gifts, teaching the same doctrine, but the one makes a brilliant career out of this proclamation, the other lives in poverty, persecuted—let us assume that it actually is the same doctrine (which, no doubt, No. 1 will maintain): the difference is infinite if what they are teaching is Christianity, for by this existence the one preaches Christianity right into an illusion, and the other makes it existentially clear what Christianity is.

x⁴ A 112 n.d., 1851

« 4562 *The Epistle of James: The Word Is a Mirror How To Look at Yourself in a Mirror with True Blessing*[856]

(1) You must not look at the mirror, the frame, for example (the blood-witness Savonarola[857] stresses this), but look at yourself in the mirror.

Yet this is precisely what has been done with God's Word as the mirror. This accounts for all those auxiliary sciences in connection with the Word which examine the mirror, the frame, etc., instead of looking at oneself in the mirror.

(2) You must in some measure know yourself in order to look at yourself in the mirror or to recognize your reflected image. It is common knowledge that if one happens to see himself, not knowing it is by means of a mirror (which he does not see), he does not recognize himself.

(3) You must be very sure to say to yourself: It is you; remember, it is you.

The mighty emperor[858] in the East had a slave to remind him to inflict vengeance on that little nation—such people were not worth remembering. No, then David was better served*[859]—although it was not the kind of service one was likely to volunteer for. He had Nathan,[860] who said: You are the man. And yet David himself certainly knew best what he had done and, generally speaking, how despicable it was, but nevertheless the proper transformation had not taken place —to You are the man. This is the difficult understanding of God's word —the learned, the colossally learned understanding is not nearly so difficult as this: You are the man.

(4) To look at yourself in a mirror is a feminine art. But a woman looks at herself in the mirror *in order to* see her beauty. It is true that she also sees unbeautiful features, but she does not look at herself in the mirror just to look at them but rather to camouflage them with a more attractive appearance.

But earnestness, masculinity, means to look at yourself—in God's Word—in order to see how you actually look.

Most people are afraid to look at themselves. It is, after all, a hazardous sight; once one has seen it, he does not get over it very easily.

(5) You must remember how you look in the mirror.

(6) Yet not despair, no matter how ugly you look, but neither let your appearance remain just a matter of memory—but begin with the most important, the decisive thing—to change before the mirror in accordance with the requirement of the mirror.

x^4 A 283   *n.d.*, 1851

« **4563**

* *In margin of 4562* (x^4 A 283):

The prophet Nathan[861] told him a story. But as happens when it is only a matter of history or doctrine etc., David listened quite calmly to the story. Who knows, the chosen poet perhaps was able to point out a few artistic defects in Nathan's story, that here and there the emphasis ought to have been different. But then the prophet gave the story another turn and said: You are the man. This made it personal.

x^4 A 284   *n.d.*

« **4564**

Christianity is simply not the objective,
is just the opposite, the subjective

This can also be seen in the way Christianity must be served.

Wherever there is something objective (for example, a government, a doctrine, an enterprise), someone working for a particular advantage (it could be money or rank or status) could also very well serve this objectivity. There is no self-contradiction in this whatsoever.

Not so with Christianity, which is pure reduplication. If someone insists on—for example, being made a baron—but also wants to devote everything to working for Christianity—Christianity simply cannot be served by this, yes, all his effort must be regarded as a counter-effort against Christianity.

As spirit Christianity is pure transparency,[862] infinite control, but we men would rather deal with something objective, for an objectivity is opaque, and all kinds of commerce and lunacy can go on behind its back.

x^4 A 346   *n.d.*, 1851

« **4565** *Objectivity—Hypocrisy*

Christianity is made into an objective doctrine; the objective is the main thing: in this way all checking, all existential exertion (the direction: to become subjective) are avoided.

Or an officeholder makes his position into something objective and thereby makes sure that his own person is kept out of it. Previously he was a completely unknown quantity, had carefully seen to it that he just passed his entrance examination and perhaps did some studying, but as a matter of fact he guarded against any kind of achievement, for he himself as a person would thereby become revealed; then he seeks an appointment, attaches himself to the establishment, makes sure of his career—and now everything is fine, for now he can continually hide himself under: "by virtue of my office," "in my official capacity," etc. The ensuing confusion can perhaps be illuminated by an illustration from another sphere—the criminal world. A criminal regards his situation face to face with the interrogator objectively; however wrong perjury is, every lie is permissible—in a way this is "by virtue of his office." Suppose now (Archdeacon Tryde[863] told me of just such an instance of a criminal out in the country) that a criminal has stood and told an out-and-out lie, and the interrogator knows very well that it is a lie and says to him: "Now tell the truth." He answers: "I have told the truth." "Will you shake hands on your having spoken the truth?" "No, that I will not." Curious! The criminal makes a clear distinction between the personal and the impersonal, the objective, this, so to speak, "in my official capacity." If the interrogator were to say to him: "Do you dare swear to that?" he would no doubt answer: "Yes." If the interrogator would say: "Do you dare shake hands on that?"—"No, that I will not do." For to the criminal this is a personal act.

O, is it not the case that hardly a pastor hesitates a moment to talk about Christianity and his faith in the strongest expressions and protestations in the pulpit—and if one were to say to him in private: "Will you shake hands on that?" he would perhaps say: "No, that I will not do." For the first is in an official capacity, the impersonal. We see how dangerous it is to have Christianity represented only by officeholders, how ambiguous it is, how this kind of proclamation can quietly undermine and enervate Christianity in a country, if in other ways there was any previously.

x^4 A 379   *n.d.,* 1851

« **4566** *"The Way is Narrow"*[864]

Is this a bit of historical information (that the way was narrow at the time of Christianity's coming into the world—in that case, we consequently must change the reading) or is it an eternal truth—in that case the person going along the easy way proclaiming that "the way" is narrow is making a fool of himself, for the *summa summarum* of his proclamation and his life yields at most: the way was narrow, historically.

Men have wanted to make this verse "the way is narrow" and others like it into an objective teaching—so objective that it does not apply to one single person, not even the one proclaiming it—no, it is purely objective. Utter rubbish!

"God has chosen the poor in this world."[865] Is this historical—or is it, from a Christian point of view, an eternal premise that is valid every moment and until the end of the world: God has chosen the poor in this world. Then it is indeed nonsense for someone to rig himself out in worldly splendor and preach—objectively—about God's having chosen the poor in this world. On the whole it is impossible to preach objectively, for to preach is gassing neither with the mouth nor with the r—— but is essentially one's existing; what my existing says is my sermon. But my existing is my subjectivity.

Luther was entirely correct in referring to the true Church as a despised little flock—the pope and all that are not the true Church.

Luther has been victorious for a long time now and the reduplication is forgotten—that it will now again hold true that the true Church is a despised little flock.

Either all the existential statements in Scripture become historical, so that all tenses in the New Testament must be changed to perfect or pluperfect, or they are eternal statements and existentially are just as valid as at the time Christianity entered the world. This nonsense about an objective doctrine is hypocrisy. For what will an objective existence-doctrine say? Shall it be an existence-doctrine which—objectively!—is indifferent to personal existing? But an existence-doctrine is, in fact, just the opposite, perhaps is indifferent to everything else but is not indifferent to—existences; otherwise it is no *existence*-doctrine.

X^4 A 407   n.d., 1851

« 4567 *Christianity in Christendom*

Christianity is taught objectively, it is heard objectively: in this way Christianity hovers over Christendom like a cloud but does not sink down into the individual, so the single individual says: It is talking about me, it is talking to me: ergo, Christianity is mythology, poetry.

All the protesting that Christianity is not mythology, is not poetry, is useless. As long as we relate to it only impersonally, we make it mythology, poetry.

X^4 A 667   n.d., 1852

« 4568 *Ordination*

A man binds himself by oath to teaching (objectively) the doctrine according to the N. T. and the symbolic books—but he does not bind himself sufficiently to living according to this doctrine personally, to expressing it existentially. Thus the fraud is made far too easily possible.

And yet Christianity is a doctrine in this very sense that if it is not existentially expressed by the teacher it becomes something else, does not become Christianity. The attention must be fixed precisely upon the existential; then the teacher at least makes himself aware of the fact that he does not express it existentially.

X^5 A 84   n.d., 1853

« 4569 *In a Peculiar Sense a Happy Coincidence with Christianity*

Christ[866] says: Judge not, that you be not judged. This is in the Sermon on the Mount. When the requirement for being a Christian is set as high as it is by Christ, when the Christian is supposed to strive to the uttermost—then the danger of judging others lies all too close. It is so very human to want to judge others rigorously when one himself must exert himself to the uttermost, to the point of hating his own life.

In our time, especially among us, it is part and parcel of the rascality that no one is inclined or cares to judge in any way. The smart thing is to leave judging alone, since everyone knows best for himself how the shoe fits. Therefore, especially among us, a rare Christianity prevails in which men refrain entirely from judging one another. Yes, I really believe it is so. The Christian life has just about died out—so above all things let us not put life and movement into it by judging others. This cannot be done without kicking up a bit of a row—and one never knows what this can lead to. This is how we follow Christ's command: "Judge not" —What rascality!

No, in our time, and especially among us, the concern of Christianity is to get men to judge—in order to get them out of their masks, to get a little personality into this objective rascality or this rascality with objectivity.

XI^1 A 201   n.d., 1854

« **4570** *At First-Hand——At Second-Hand*

In sensate matters the matter itself is one thing; whether or not one has it at first-hand is something else, often a matter of complete indifference, at most an inessential distinction of exclusiveness or favor.

In spiritual matters, however, the main point is to have it at first-hand; to have it at second-hand is not to have it. To be spirit at second-hand is to be devoid of spirit. To be a Christian at second-hand is not to be a Christian. The most unchristian and brutish invention of all is this: to be a Christian by virtue of belonging to a Christian society.

In Christendom, however, is it not apparent that what is said when a person speaks in this way of being a Christian is sheer nonsense, something like speaking of a yard of butter.

XI^1 A 380   n.d., 1854

« **4571** *Relating Objectively to One's Own Subjectivity*

The majority of men are truncated *I*'s; what was structured by nature as the possibility of being sharpened to an *I* is quickly truncated to a third person. [*In margin:* Like Münchhausen's dog,[867] a greyhound that wore down its legs and became a dachshund.]

It is something altogether different to relate objectively to one's own subjectivity.[868]

Take Socrates! He is not a third person in the sense that he avoids getting into danger, exposing himself or risking his life, as one usually does when he is third person, not an I. By no means. But in danger he himself relates objectively to his own person; in the moment he himself is condemned to death he talks about his sentence as if he were an entirely separate third party. He is subjectivity raised to the second power; his relationship is one of objectivity just like that of a true poet in relation to his poetic production; with this objectivity he relates to his own subjectivity. This is no mean achievement. Generally we get one of two things—either an objective something, an objective piece of furniture that is supposed to be a human being, or we get a jumble of accidental occurrences and arbitrariness. But the task is to relate objectively to one's own subjectivity.

The most any man has ever achieved in this respect can serve as an infinitely faint analogy to intimate how God is infinite subjectivity.

He has not an element of objectivity in his being, as I have indicated elsewhere [i.e., XI^2 A 54], but he relates objectively to his own subjectivity, but this again is simply a redoubling [*Fordoblelse*] of his subjectivity, for in his being subjective there is no imperfection at all that should be taken away, nor is there anything lacking that should be added, as is the case with human subjectivity and which explains why being related objectively to one's own subjectivity is also a corrective.

God is infinite redoubling, which, of course, no man can be; he can neither completely transcend himself in such a way that he relates perfectly objectively to himself, nor can he become subjective in such a way that he can bring to full consummation what he in his objective transcendence has understood about himself; he cannot look at himself with unconditioned and perfect objectivity; even if he could, he still cannot unconditionally achieve subjective reproduction of this view of himself.

XI^2 A 97 *n.d.*, 1854

« **4572** *Christianity*

relates to existence. The expression "Truth is naked" may also be interpreted in this way, for truly relating to truth means that all the inner and the outer garments of illusion have to be discarded, and you are brought into touch with truth so that this truth itself becomes your very own existential truth.

But in Christendom this business of millions of Christians is simply the outer garment of illusion, is distance; at most Christianity is for them a doctrine, but their existences are in completely different categories.

We human beings are so taken in by numbers, have such a hard time getting it into our heads that in relation to ideas numbers mean absolutely nothing. This is so difficult to comprehend because in this temporal and sensate world the numerical is all-powerful.

A million or ten million men who are not Christians believe numbers to be effective—what they effect in this world of numbers is in fact the reversal of the concept "Christian," and what these millions are is what it is to be Christian.

And men are strengthened more and more in this faith in the power of the numerical, everything trains them in this conviction, for everything, after all, is politics.

XI^2 A 196 *n.d.*, 1854

« 4573 *Public Official*

A public official cannot proclaim Christianity, because to be a public official means to thrust an objectivity (that it is "in an official capacity") between himself and the learner; but religion demands subjectivity, the teacher's relation to God.

XI^2 A 354 *n.d.*, 1854

« 4574 *The Objective Is Precisely What Christ Does Not Want*

Therefore his continual breaking of the Sabbath,[869] for according to Jewish concepts this was an objectivity, and therefore Christ wanted to worship God—by breaking the Sabbath.

XI^2 A 366 *n.d.*, 1854–55

SUFFERING

« **4575**

Adversity not only unites people but also brings about that beautiful inner communion, just as the winter cold draws figures on the windowpane which the warmth of the sun erases.

I A 85   September 14, 1835

« **4576**

Adversity binds men together and brings beauty and harmony into the relationships of life, just as the winter cold, working magic on the windowpanes, conjures up flowers which disappear with warmth.

I A 115   January, 1836

« **4577**

If a true and loyal friend were to say to one of us: Dear friend, you seem to be unhappy, come and see me, maybe my company will console you—would you not gratefully accept his invitation, would you not gratefully remember his loving invitation also when he had completed his time here on earth and was together with you only in the lightning flashes of thought—and yet there must have been moments when he, depressed or even weighed down, did not approach you in his usual friendly way, moments when you thought that he, too, was lost to you? Nevertheless you have felt the blessedness of particular moments and know what they signify. —And yet do you consider following a voice which is by no means strange to you but on the contrary has been familiar for a long time, a voice you heard from your childhood on, a voice which calls just as gently, just as warmly, just as freely: "Come to me, all you who suffer and are heavy laden"[870]—and arms are still open to you in which you can rest just as securely, just as sweetly as in your best friend's, although these arms encircle "all those who suffer and are heavy laden," encircle them all with equal tenderness, for it was only in our Savior's earthly life that John alone lay most intimately upon his breast. —"Come here, O, come here"—the servant of the Word must cry out in the same way, but is this his voice, then, the voice of that one in the desert who prepares the way of the Lord? Does not this also apply to us who have been brought closer to Christianity by our upbringing, family relationships, and whole development? Yes, indeed, to us, too, comes the beckoning voice which at any moment is prepared to console us and at any moment is prepared to lead us further: "Come here, O, come here"—until it discards all the melancholy which at times can be heard along with it and, filled with eternal love, sounds like the song of angels, familiar tones to all who have listened to it: "Come here, you blessed of my father, and inherit the kingdom prepared for you from the foundation of the world!"

II A 761 August 18, 1838

« 4578

..... For "sorrow" is an old word, almost as old as the world, but "the Comforter" is also an old word, yet still not quite as old, just as it does not become quite as old in the life of the individual even though he grew ever so old; there was always a night before the day, a night in which he visited Jesus[871] out of fear of the world, or a night when he doubted everything, when he found no stability between heaven and earth, a midnight—then Christ visited him, then Christ came as in days of old to the disciples through locked doors—[872]

II A 332 January 18, 1839

« 4579

..... For glasses conceal a great deal—also a tear in the eye.—

II A 417 May 11, 1839

« 4580

People are ready with a malicious helpfulness, for, as J. Paul says, they are always ready to help someone carry the cross if it is the cross he himself is to be hung upon[873] (like Simon of Cyrene).[874]

II A 458 n.d., 1839

« 4581

..... For tears are like rain, heaven's tears, at times a cloudburst from the pregnant heaven or from the massed clouds of despair, when the sluice gates of the eyes and of heaven are opened, at times a quiet, gentle spring rain—yet there is no rain so fruitful as tears.

II A 504 n.d., 1839

« 4582

We may, of course, regard it as rebellion against God to laugh when in the natural order of things one ought to cry. As I see it, to laugh is man's own invention; to cry is a divine gift of grace. This is why we also hear people say: God grant that I could really begin to cry.

III A 99   n.d., 1841

« **4583**

There truly is a fellowship of suffering with God, a pact of tears, which is intrinsically very beautiful.[875]

III A 181   n.d., 1841

« **4584**

..... the magnitude of suffering and pain cannot always be judged by the shriek and the noise.

III A 239   n.d., 1842

« **4585**

A deleted passage in an upbuilding discourse: about the thorn in the flesh.[876] *Too humorous.*

As it went in the case just mentioned, so it perhaps also happens at times in life, and since we are supposed to talk about sufferings, and since it seems to be characteristic of the times that one is not so likely to become self-important through honor, power, and superiority as by sufferings, and since there is a profound truth in regarding suffering as the true means of education, it would perhaps be helpful to bring to mind the untruth in this view. But since we do not have the authority to admonish, we choose another means. Smile only a little at what I will now tell you, my listener; it still is and continues to be an upbuilding discourse, and if by hearing it you are brought to smile at yourself, then the discourse has in fact induced you to admonish yourself. There was once a man who had a riding horse; every time he came home after having ridden, he was somewhat fatigued but was nevertheless pleased with the horse, pleased with riding. Then one day another man borrowed his horse and quickly turned back, explaining in the strongest terms that the horse jolted terribly. The owner answered: "Does it really? I never knew that, for since I have never ridden another horse, I believed that this was the way riding was supposed to be and that the rough motion was part of the fun." Yet from that moment on a change came over him; he never rode any more because he could not find a horse that was sufficiently smooth-riding, and because finally he wanted the impossible—that the horse should move without one's detecting it. In the same way, my listener, there are perhaps many who bear life's sorrows and tribulations in the belief that they are part of living and that living is like this, and for all that a joy—until someone tells him that living is dreadful, and he is never happy any more but becomes extremely self-important by not being happy and by being able to reject everything in life.

V A 43 *n.d.*, 1844

« 4586

It is and always will be the most difficult spiritual trial [*Anfægtelse*] not to know whether the cause of one's suffering is mental derangement or sin. Freedom, which is otherwise used for the struggle, in this case becomes dialectical with the most dreadful contrasts.

V A 49 *n.d.*, 1844

« 4587

Keeping a wound open can also be very beneficial: a healthy and open wound; sometimes it is worst when it skins over.

VI A 16 *n.d.*, 1845

« 4588

There is nothing more difficult to stop than the dialectical in the suffering of the God-relationship.[877] It is said that we must hope for the best, that when all is said and done we will thank God once again, after the rain comes the sun, etc. What does this mean? What is that something better for which we are to thank God—obviously that to which one attributes pleasantness or unpleasantness according to one's finite understanding. But then thanksgiving itself is a retrogression, since in giving thanks I move in the lower categories. I carry on with God just as Emmeline[878] did with her father. If the true and only expression for the God-relationship is that everything God does is good, then all talk about a stopping or a not-stopping, about good weather again, etc. (which is appropriate in the temporal world, where bad weather really is not good weather) is a retrogression. The dubiousness consists in this that one moment a person makes a show of wanting to make the prodigious movement of infinity and the next moment lacks the courage for it and hopes and gives thanks in the categories of finitude. It is just as with lovers. Satisfied with each other, they want to or are able to dispense with everything, but soon, soon they stop—well, they do not stop loving each other, but they give the whole thing a different turn, and when there is a pinch they hope for better times when love will be genuinely happy (consequently it is still not really complete) and will then give thanks again (consequently it was not really complete). With respect to this dialectical crisscrossing no guidance at all is to be found in most devotional literature. — Perhaps nothing from time immemorial has made such a deep impression on me these days as David's psalms, but, alas, he abandons one in the dialectical oscillations. It is like this: all the multiplicity—expressed deeply and gloriously, refreshing and alleviating when it shakes the inwards—is the content of his life, but now when I am going to begin and gather it together in an integral thought as lyrical as it is dialectical, it breaks to pieces. Now he hopes (now eternally, and now again for time, but these two qualifications of hope are separated by an eternity and it has to be clear which is which), now he consoles himself with his innocence, now he curses his enemies, etc. But the beginner, who has to begin uncertainly, is not helped by this; he needs the single thought, whether the eternal (that everything is good, equally good, and postponing giving thanks is stupid or deceitful) or whether it is to be the pleasant and the unpleasant; whether God is to be everything and man has nothing to say except that it is good—or man is to join the discussion.

VI A 46 *n.d.*, 1845

« **4589**

The dialectic of infinity in religious suffering[879] (for example, if we hoped only for this life we would be the most miserable of all[880]) must be halted in time (fear of God has promise for the life which now is[881]). But how are these two relations to be classified? The highest expression for the worth of earthly life (of temporality) is precisely the expectation of the eternal or its nearness. But at the same moment again I have given up the whole range of my earthly understanding, and the more concrete understanding of "promise for this life" is made difficult, since it really is identified with the latter, "promise for the life to come." If, then, fear of God has promise for the life to come and I know it, then my knowledge of it in time is the promise of the same fear of God for the present life.

A person would be regarded as mad if he really were to speak with the latent qualifications of religious infinitude in his conversation. Even such a statement as Socrates'[882] "that when the captain has brought the traveler across the sea to his destination, he (the captain) calmly walks back and forth on the beach, accepts his pay, and still he cannot know whether he has done a good deed by doing this or it would have been better if the traveler had lost his life at sea," even such a statement (if the reader has had adequate competence to discuss the dialectical profundity and did not slide over it or consider it to be just a manner of speaking) would be regarded as an expression of lunacy.

In this lies the deceptive lunacy of the dialectical presentation; only that the dialectician discovers it,[883] and he knows also that it is not simply lunacy (any more than it is lunacy to regard my eternal knowledge as more certain than sense knowledge, although it is usually stated the other way around, and if one dared to say God is just as certain as it is certain that I hold this cane in my hand—alas, it is a shabby certainty which even Greek skepticism could deprive one of—no, that God *is* is certain in a way entirely different from everything of sense perception); the inexperienced person, the systematically infatuated, discerns nothing, because it is not bellowed, and this is precisely the dialectical contradiction, because the immediate is conscious only when it shrieks, but the dialectical is itself certain.

VI A 48 *n.d.,* 1845

« **4590**

There is a strange psychological contradiction in the following:

It is well known that suffering and pain are a condition for many kinds of distinctiveness, such as with poets, artists, religious individualities, and the like.[884] Without these sufferings they would not have become great. Take away their sufferings, give them an easy life, grant them what they desire—and it is all over with greatness. If they had their desire satisfied and the suffering taken away, they would lose even more: ergo, they ought to be happy in their suffering, so happy that they would not wish it removed. But then again they are beyond suffering. I wonder if an individual so situated could really understand this. An individual could be held at the point of extremity where he constantly grasps for the highest in order to find out to what extent this could be done.

VI A 80 *n.d.,* 1845

« **4591**

When a person misguided to the point of being lost is about to go under, his last utterance and the signal is: Yet something better perishes with me. Like bubbles rising from a drowning man, this is the signal—then he sinks. Just as self-encapsulation can become a man's downfall because he will not articulate what is hidden, so the uttering of those words is ruination, because simply to say them expresses that he has become so objective about himself that he dares speak about his own ruin as one speaks about something which has been decided and may now be of psychological interest to a third party. The hope that there still might be something better in him which should have been used in silence to work for his salvation, this hope is expended and used as material for the funeral oration he delivers over himself.[885]

VII[1] A 22 *n.d.*, 1846

« 4592

All this talk about thanking God for not being involved in adversity, for having a comfortable life etc., can so very easily be fraudulent. This kind of talk actually transforms God into a shopkeeper who discriminates among his customers or does not have fixed prices, but to a few gives good, cheap deals under the counter. On the other hand one easily deceives himself by living in the conceit that he possesses the highest good even though he is exempted from the burdens. One who prays in this way has obviously not made up his mind concerning the extent to which the highest good is so good that it is the highest good at any price.

VII[1] A 213 *n.d.*, 1846

« 4593

N.B.

There is something very upbuilding in the thought that what is said of Christ[886] also holds true of all suffering: what he suffered he suffered once. One must suffer only once: the victory is eternal.[887] (In a worldly way one hears this talk often enough: Enjoy life—you live only once.[888])

VIII[1] A 31 *n.d.*, 1847

« 4594

N.B.

One suffers only once—but is victorious eternally.[889] Insofar as one is victorious, this is also only once. The difference, however, is that suffering's once is momentary (even though the moment were seventy years)—but the victory's once is eternity. Suffering's once (even though it lasted seventy years) can therefore not be pictured or portrayed in art. On the altar in Vor Frelsers Kirke there is a work which presents an angel who holds out to Christ the cup of suffering.[890] The error is that it lasts too long; a picture always endures for an eternity. It appears interminable; one does not see that the suffering is momentary, as all suffering is according to the concept or in the idea of victory. The victory, however, is eternal; this (insofar as it is not spiritual) can be portrayed, because it endures.

Meanwhile, the first impression of the upbuilding is *dismaying*—[891]if men take time to understand it properly, for in this case to suffer once is like being sick once—that is, for a whole lifetime. But the wisdom and impatience of this world must not demand, either, that one should be able to appeal to this consolation—if one is to speak of the essentially Christian, for the consolation of Christianity begins first of all where human impatience would simply despair. This is how deep the essentially Christian is—first of all one must scrupulously try to find the *dismaying* and then scrupulously once again—then one finds the *upbuilding*. Alas, as a rule we try scrupulously in neither the first instance nor the second.

VIII[1] A 32   *n.d.*, 1847

« 4595

To console others—yes, who would not gladly do that. However, if true consolation is dialectical in such a way that if men were to grasp the terror it posits—in order to console—they would rightfully prefer all their former troubles to being consoled in this way. Where does essential Christianity begin? It begins there where paganism ends.[892] Consolation for earthly sufferings etc. Christianity does not have; it assumes that in this respect the Christian fears nothing, and it posits the terror of sin and begins to console. To blather everything to each other and to console and console can very well be done, but here again is the difficulty: Do I have the right to do that.

VIII[1] A 85   *n.d.*, 1847

« 4596 *A Christian's Duty "To Beware of Men"*[893]

All striving of a more noble character always meets with opposition, either of misunderstanding or of envy. But do not be disturbed; it is a strange world. As long as you live, it will do everything to thwart you and to change you. If you give in, it will say of you when you are dead: It was, after all, a weakness on his part to give in. But if you do not give in, it will be furious with you as long as you live, but when you are dead it will say: He was right, after all. The objection against one living becomes his eulogy when he is dead—and the world remains the same. The world cannot admit that you are right as long as you can hear it (indeed, it struggles with you), but when you are dead the world thinks you can no longer hear, then comes the admission. In a certain sense this world cannot benefit you, and yet the attack cannot harm you, either, while you live—if you just do not let it get the power to change you. If you hold only to God, the attack and disparagement and the storm of opposition will help you discover things you otherwise would never discover; they will add new strings to your lyre. —Every man is like an instrument which no doubt can be disturbed and damaged by the world's wretchedness and rudeness—but if you hold to God, it can help you to ever new melody.

VIII¹ A 96 n.d., 1847

« **4597**

When a man has a toothache, the world says: Poor man; when a man has financial troubles, the world says: Poor man; when a man's wife dies, the world says: Poor man; when a man is arrested, the world says: Poor man. When Got lets himself be born and suffers for the world, the world says: Poor man; when an apostle of God is favored with the call to suffer persecution and death in the service of God, the world says of the apostle: Poor man. —Poor world!!!

VIII¹ A 113 n.d., 1847

« **4598**

N.B. Tauler:

> *Wem Leid ist wie Freud*
> *Und Freud wie Leid,*
> *Der danke Gott für solche Gleichheit.*[894]

VIII¹ A 117 n.d., 1847

« **4599**

To be designated this way as a sacrifice from birth or from his earliest years, to be so painfully set outside the universal so that everyone without exception would have pity on him (for although men usually are eager to complain about men's lack of compassion, such a person is only all too sure of it)—this is the beginning of the demonic. But now it depends upon whether such a person is evil—or good. If he is evil, then he becomes a Gloucester,[895] hating and cursing existence [*Tilværelsen*], revenging himself upon the universally human. If he is good, he will do everything for other men, his life as a self-sacrifice will mournfully gratify him; yet he also does have one condition, or even if he does not stipulate the condition to God, he nevertheless thanks him if he is successful—namely, to hide his wretchedness, to avoid becoming the object of pity. Of all sufferings there is perhaps none so martyring as to become an object of pity, nothing which so tempts one to rebel against God. People usually regard such a person as stupid and shallow, but it would not be difficult to show that precisely this is the hidden secret in the lives of many of the most eminent world-historical figures.[896] But this is kept in hiding, and it is possible to do this because it is as if God would say to such a man if he is to use his eminent gifts at all in the service of the good: I do not want you to be humiliated before men in such a way that you are forsaken in your guiltless wretchedness, but in relation to me it will help you to become aware of your nothingness.

VIII^1 A 161 *n.d.*, 1847

« 4600

The pathway of tribulation[897] remains just as long and just as dark to the end—the pathway that gradually becomes lighter must be a different one. Neither do we know when the change will come nor precisely whether we have reached it or how much nearer we have come (for such things cannot be determined in the dark). But we do believe that the change will come and then with the blessedness of eternity. When the child in the dark room is waiting for the door to be opened and all the anticipated glory to be revealed, at the last second before the door is opened it still is just as dark as at first. Insofar as there has been no arrangement between the parents and the child as to how long he has to wait, he still does not know whether or not he has a long time to wait. But one thing is sure, the second the door is open the glory will be revealed. The child may have the melancholy thought that they have forgotten that he stands there waiting. But then the child says to himself: How could I ever think that my parents could do a thing like that. So the child sees it through, for he well knows that to call out in fear of having been forgotten would upset everything. O, but it is hard for a man to have to stick it out this way, to stake everything on that last moment; we would far prefer to have it revealed gradually—that is, we prefer spoiling it for ourselves by receiving a little beforehand.

VIII^1 A 191 *n.d.*, 1847

« 4601

The duration or the fact that suffering is protracted in duration is always the hardest suffering. Daily worries, daily derision year in and year out are far worse than any catastrophe, also because to someone else they always appear to be nothing. Someone else always believes that for the particular person this is something for today or yesterday, which of course amounts to nothing—but duration—it is impossible to confront this every day with the same unconditionally fresh powers of the first encounter.

VIII¹ A 192 n.d., 1847

« 4602

To suffer patiently is not specifically Christian at all—but freely to choose the suffering which one could also avoid, freely to choose it in the interest of the good cause—this is Christian.[898] I wonder if many pagans did not also suffer patiently. Moreover, what similarity is there between suffering patiently (unavoidable suffering) and this, that Christ was God and yet chose to suffer?

VIII¹ A 259 n.d., 1847

« 4603

One must actually have suffered a great deal in the world and have been made very unhappy before there can even be any question of beginning to love the neighbor. The "neighbor" does not come into existence [bliver til] until in self-denial one has died to earthly happiness and joys and comforts. Therefore the spontaneous, immediate person cannot be censured for not loving the neighbor, because the spontaneous, immediate person is too happy for "the neighbor" to exist [være til] for him. Anyone who clings to earthly life does not love his neighbor—that is, for him the neighbor does not exist.[899]

VIII¹ A 269 n.d., 1847

« 4604

The suffering of Christ is really soul-suffering.[900]

VIII¹ A 275 n.d., 1847

« 4605

..... You lament your many sufferings. But consider this. Suppose a person walked among us who said: I know the consolation, all right, but the trouble is that I am never able to use my remedy. For when men send for me, I generally find it easy to convince myself that the case is not so dangerous—yes, and the hitch is precisely this, that the remedy I use is itself far more painful and agonizing than their slight suffering. Or think of a person who went around consoling men and who said: I must pretend to be happy and content and that I have always danced and still dance on roses, for if men get the slightest intimation of what a person has to suffer merely to be enabled to give consolation, they would despair.

VIII[1] A 463 n.d., 1847

« 4606

In margin of 4605 (VIII[1] A 463):
Or consider that the person who went around consoling others said to himself: "How deep and gaping is the wound I bear hidden, how demolished is every wish of mine for the future in the worldly sense, I myself am well aware, and therefore it is sometimes almost nauseating for me to console others. In the moment of pain and danger they snatch at consolation and it seems as if we two understood each other—O, soon it is apparent that their suffering is only momentary, and once again they live in altogether different categories. But I remain sick and need consolation as long as I live. If I were to speak from the bottom of my heart, at every moment I would be as if betrayed—for they soon get over their suffering and become entirely well again in a worldly sense—I, never."

VIII[1] A 464 n.d.

« 4607

Just as superstition prepared magic charms from the heart-blood of a child, so healing for another's pain is prepared in the inward agony of a deeply but secretly suffering man. Such a person consoles others, and even if he himself cannot be comforted in any way, he still has the consolation of consoling others.

VIII[1] A 468 n.d., 1847

« 4608

January 29, 1848

Christ drove out a devil, and he was dumb.[901] Have you ever been dumb or known what it is to be dumb. One can walk about and be dumb, not care to talk—but this is not it. One can act the man of mystery and be dumb—but this is not it. But have you ever been so unspeakably grieved that sorrow has dominated your whole existence, almost a force of nature—then you have experienced what it is to be dumb, that it was impossible, even if it meant your life, to express the anguish which brooded deep within and selfish of itself made you dumb—so that you might not get rid of it. For boundless sorrow is egotistical this way: it makes the person dumb in order to keep control over him.

VIII[1] A 514   January 29, 1848

« **4609**

Every sacrifice must be salted![902] For the one who is to be sacrificed the mockery and persecution which precede are the salt. On the other hand, the one who is not to be sacrificed is sugared (candied) in the "goody-good" of the secular mentality.

VIII[1] A 518   n.d., 1848

« **4610**

Christ's suffering naturally cannot be comprehended, since the divine and the human have to be *believed* together, something only faith is capable of doing.

Comprehending thought can be induced to be attentive up to the moment when the call must go out to it: Now believe, throw yourself down in adoration and believe.[903]

The intensity of suffering is greatest in the dialectical situation, when the suffering one has the power to free himself from the suffering and still chooses to suffer and does suffer, while those nearest to him, the sympathizers, may demand that he free himself from the suffering, that he spare himself, since he can. The suffering here is dialectical; it is enough to lose one's mind over. When the suffering is involuntary, I can use all my might to resist it, and, moreover, everyone will be able to understand me. But voluntary suffering is dialectical at two points: I must use my energy to force myself out into the suffering and then use it to endure the suffering.

And now Christ's suffering: to have everything divinely in his power—and then nevertheless to will freely to suffer humanly, every moment divinely capable of changing everything.

This is why he says to the disciples:[904] All of you will be offended in me this night. Where lies the possibility of offense? Quite simply, it is this: they must either despair of Christ's being the one he said he was, since he does not show himself to be the stronger one—or He is that, but then, indeed, humanly speaking, the whole thing is frightfully mad—that He, that God suffers in this way.

VIII[1] A 579   n.d., 1848

« **4611**

Continuation of 4610 (VIII¹ A 579) *with double crosshatching drawn over it:*

"My God, my God, why have you forsaken me"⁹⁰⁵ is freedom's ultimate spiritual trial [*Anfægtelse*]. The suffering which is not imposed but which is freely taken upon oneself has, at the ultimate point of the dialectic of responsibility, the pain that God lets the man feel that he has in fact freely taken it upon himself.

But it is impossible to comprehend these words of Christ's, for the divine is indeed present in Christ. I am accentuating the purely human side. But it would indeed be blasphemy if, after having explained something pertaining to this, I gave the impression of having comprehended Christ. Anything but. His person is only for faith and worship.

VIII¹ A 580 *n.d.*, 1848

« **4612**

It could be moving and upbuilding for me to go through the passion story sometime.⁹⁰⁶ For I am sure that Christ's sufferings should for the most part be discussed in such a way that I tremble: that is, his suffering is, after all, the Atonement–I, the sinner. But his suffering has another side also, where it is directly upbuilding for one who suffers.

VIII¹ A 581 *n.d.*, 1848

« **4613**

The infinite sorrow in finding the disciples sleeping⁹⁰⁷ three times—and then finally saying: Just go on sleeping, it is settled now. O–to struggle all alone—and the only sharing to be found is that the others are sleeping—as unconcerned as if it had nothing to do with them.

VIII¹ A 582 *n.d.*, 1848

« **4614**

Viewed from eternity, to enjoy is the same as to squander, to dissipate; to suffer is like accumulating savings—high-rate savings, although here in time one does not usually recognize this kind of currency or define its value.

VIII¹ A 597 *n.d.*, 1848

« 4615

There are many splendid stories in the fourth volume of *A Thousand and One Nights*⁹⁰⁸—for example, nights 759, 760, 763–765.[*] About the poor couple who prayed to God for a little help, and he let a ruby fall down. They rejoiced greatly. But that night the wife dreamed that she was in paradise and saw the countless pulpits and thrones. When she asked for whom they were, she was told that they were for the prophets, for the righteous and the God-fearing. She asked if there was one for her husband. It was shown to her—but she noticed a chink on one side, and it was explained to her that this chink signified the ruby which had fallen down to them. Then she became despondent, implored her husband to pray God to take the ruby back. "It is better to endure poverty these few days than to have to sit among the glorious ones on a throne which has a defect."

[*]*In margin:* All of these stories are excellent and ought to be remembered.

VIII¹ A 631   n.d., 1848

« 4616

Psalm 116:10. I kept my faith, even when I said, "I am greatly afflicted."

VIII¹ A 633   n.d., 1848

« 4617

Suppose a powerful emperor were to send an ambassador on an extremely important mission and chose a chamberlain to do it—how irritating this would be to the notables who would have liked to have the legation themselves. Let us imagine this. The ambassador departs. But it actually was not an attractive mission at all. The people he came to were enraged at his proposal and, disregarding international law and the powerful emperor he represented, attacked him, struck him, spit upon him, and drove him out of the city like a dog. Let us for a moment imagine his homecoming. He goes in to the emperor, bows before him deferentially—but before he begins reporting on his mission he says: Once again, Your Majesty, allow me to thank you for the indescribable graciousness you have shown me in entrusting me with this mission. This is the way an apostle thanks God for his flogging. He does not actually thank him for being flogged but for the graciousness of making him his apostle, and he completely forgets that this was why he has been flogged.⁹⁰⁹

IX A 17 *n.d.*, 1848

« 4618

This, you see, is the sadness: after having himself suffered every ignominy for the truth, finally the death of a criminal—then not to be able to say to his disciples: Now you shall have an easy life, but to have to say: Now go and suffer the same thing, begin where I left off.⁹¹⁰

IX A 162 *n.d.*, 1848

« 4619

The Lord Jesus Christ was not (O blasphemous misunderstanding!) in an earthly sense a happy man who proclaimed an earthly gospel about glorious, elevated things. But He (O equally blasphemous misunderstanding) was just as little an unhappy man in an earthly sense, someone who perhaps had other aspirations for his life, and when these were denied Him sadly decided to suffer for the truth.

IX A 270 *n.d.*, 1848

« 4620

It is a poor husband who would be jubilant during the time of his engagement and in the first days of his marriage but as soon as troubles come would complain about his position. These belong to the position. Similarly, it is a poor Christian who for reason of troubles complains about being a Christian; it is part of the position.

IX A 317 *n.d.*, 1848

« 4621

This is the situation. A sinner turns from his sins, from a culpable life, and becomes, humanly speaking, an honest, upright man. Now, as a matter of course, he expects to be rewarded with the esteem of good men etc. And this would be the case if we excluded Christianity. But it was through Christianity that he was converted—and now, as a Christian, he suffers much worse than he ever suffered when he was a lecher, a boozer, etc.

This is Christianity. But I wonder if it is proclaimed this way nowadays? And does it not take divine courage to preach conversion on these terms, for, humanly speaking, he is far better off by not being converted, or by merely having a kind of human conversion but without becoming a Christian.

Basically the world makes a lecher shift for himself, but the Christian it persecutes. The world itself is neither so very good, nor is it interested in persecuting someone because of his blameworthy conduct, either. But all (both the lechers and the respectable people) are united in persecuting the Christian.

IX A 330 *n.d.*, 1848

« 4622

Here as everywhere the sentimental pastors (who *in parenthesi*[911] also go farther than Christianity, since, despite the words: A disciple is not above his master,[912] they are far above the master; in the order of precedence they are honored and esteemed while the master was scorned) deceive men when they talk about Christ's praying for his enemies.[913] For one thing, they must first and foremost make it concrete, and in the situation of contemporaneity it is most inflammatory (so the contemporaries have judged) even to want to pray for one's enemies—instead of beseeching the enemies for mercy. There is nothing more exasperating to a man with whom you are struggling than to pray for him. For another thing, it must be remembered that as a voluntary sufferer Christ himself is partly responsible for his suffering; he denies them the sympathetic assistance of giving up his own and accommodating to them. To that extent this prayer for the enemy belongs to Christ's sacrifice in an entirely different sense. That is, from the beginning he has had them in his power, they think they are in control and yet they serve his will: therefore he prays for them.

IX A 336 *n.d.*, 1848

« 4623

It is always very natural and human, when one is suffering the opposition of the world, to start thinking this way: but I wonder if it is not your own fault; if you were gentler, humbler, meeker—then men would certainly be bound to think a lot of you. Yes, it is something quite literally to lose one's mind over, this Christian reply: no, the more gentle, humble, and meek you become, the worse it will go with you. Without this essentially Christian reply, one straightway commits blasphemy against Christ, saying in effect that he was not gentle and humble and meek enough, since he was mistreated when he was just that.

But note that this comes from the fact that one forgets that Christianity is never true except in the Christian situation. If I sit in a room and think: gentleness, humility, meekness, and in addition to this thought-about gentleness, meekness, etc., I then think a revelation of it in the world, it follows, *ipso facto,* that I think of it as being loved. But this thought-about world is certainly not the actual world.

The life of the true Christian is therefore always double. Over against God he must humbly confess that he is very far indeed from being sufficiently gentle and meek; he must thank God for the suffering, that it might help him to become meeker. But if over against men he were to say the same thing—that the reason he is persecuted is that he is not sufficiently gentle and meek—then this is nonsense, for if he were more so, he would simply be persecuted more.

O, what frightful strenuousness to have two such thoughts in one's head at the same time without confusing them and being rendered powerless. Before God it can be true that one suffers because he is not humble enough, and in respect to the world it is true that he suffers because he has some humility and would suffer more if he had more humility.

Here, lest we go wrong, we must keep the one infinitely separate from the other; always humble before God that one is not sufficiently humble, we must not confuse this with the relation to the world—and then, always humble before God that one is not sufficiently humble, we are to have the courage to go forward in humility, certain of being persecuted more.

O, many a time it is almost enough to lose one's mind over—to keep one's footing here and not confuse humility before God with the relationship to men.

IX A 349 *n.d.,* 1848

« 4624

This is how the human is related to the divine: the disciples sleep—while Christ suffers.[914] It is this craving to sleep which by its degree defines whether a man still has any spirit or he is altogether lacking in spirit.

Yet I do not suppose that the disciples slept because they were indolent—that is, that they were indifferent. No, they slept because of suffering. A man can become so exhausted by suffering that he falls asleep.

But the more spirit the more sleeplessness; therefore it is in and for itself already infinite, total suffering to be an individual human being if one is God, for spirit is sheer wakefulness and actuosity,[915] and man is more or less drowsiness.

IX A 367 n.d., 1848

« 4626

Eliminate the idea, say the Stoics, and the pain disappears, for the pain is simply the conception.[*]

Fine! But from a religious point of view, to eliminate the conception is actually to eliminate God, for the God-relationship begins in and with the conception. Piety means precisely to submit the pain to God (but then one must still have the conception), to understand that one is being brought up etc.

[*] *In margin:* Eliminate the conception and there is no "Alas and woe is me"; if there is no "Alas and woe is me," then there is no pain either. (Antoninus[916])

IX A 380 n.d., 1848

« 4626

All this sentimentality about placing oneself beside the cross of Christ in order to look out over the world from there is dreadful. In should be remembered that if this is going to be in earnest (and otherwise it is blasphemous pandering), it must be in the situation of contemporaneity, but then one would hardly have occasion to sit very long and look about, for then one more cross would probably be erected—and then it would depend on whether one, crucified alongside, would feel much like an observer in the one and only true situation.

IX A 407 n.d., 1848

« 4627

Christ[917] says: I myself have chosen them (the twelve), and yet one of you will betray me. These words could be interpreted in different ways, but there does seem to be here something of a suggestion of the voluntariness of suffering, that he himself has chosen for an apostle one who would betray him.

IX A 410 n.d., 1848

« 4628

This, too, is part and parcel of the world's meanness—that when someone in Christian self-denial submits to suffering, all those who cravenly and craftily refrain from coming to his help make capital of it, as if they had nothing to reproach themselves for. Meekness,[918] as I have pointed out, makes the others' guilt less; but it does not follow that the meek person does not very well perceive all their cowardliness and shabbiness. From the Christian point of view care must be taken that wrong be disclosed; otherwise the meek person only confirms the world in its evil, and the world could never find a better mask than the meekness of the meek.

IX A 425 *n.d.*, 1848

« 4629

The basis of the isolation in being made a laughingstock is that in the strictest sense there is no issue at stake but in the strictest sense it is all purely personal. It is impossible in this kind of an attack, therefore, for others to join with one, which is the case when there is a cause.

IX A 466 *n.d.*, 1848

« 4630

To know, and to be moved powerfully by it, that a person has a conception that the true can be found only in suffering, that the measure of truth is suffering—and then to be willing to accept privately the thoughts and expressions which are my life-blood and my sufferings—to be willing to receive this privately in order to give it again as one's own.

X^1 A 108 *n.d.*, 1849

« 4631

From the Christian point of view it is a plain duty to seek suffering in the same sense that from a purely human point of view it is a duty to seek pleasure.

X^1 A 319 *n.d.*, 1849

« 4632

I have often said that a person ought to do his utmost to appear benign and friendly, even if he is suffering inwardly, for the result is that others are benign, and sometimes this may also temper one's own suffering, but when a person looks annoyed he makes others annoyed. This is very true, but it should not be forgotten that the very feeling of impotence in not being able to appear benign and smiling when one is suffering, that just this can make a man look annoyed.

X^1 A 365 *n.d.*, 1849

« 4633

This, too, belongs to Christ's suffering—that from the beginning He[919] did not dare tell the apostles his true view, that there would be an attack, that there should be, had to be, that it was His intention that there should be an attack, that He should be persecuted, ridiculed, spit upon, and crucified. If He had told the apostles this at once, they too probably would have forsaken Him. What suffering of patience: To be "the truth" and then to be in the awkward position of having to use a few men, eventually find a few—and then to have to help Himself with a little untruth (reticence)—what suffering of patience! O "the truth" —and "men"—how do they fit together. What suffering, therefore, to be the truth, what suffering—not that of being put to death, no, the greater suffering of having to need a few men and then having to be a little untruthful! It is thought, however, that the apostles did provide Christ with some encouragement and a haven—well, if so, it was somewhat like moving out of the rain to the dripping eaves, because when he was together with the apostles his sadness was, if possible, even greater because He loved them and saw that they loved Him. But He has to use a few men—and this situation is a complete passion story by itself; He is like the most destitute of men, He who is the truth, He who nevertheless—cannot do without a few men (who consequently are almost able to name a high price), He who is unable to do without a few men (for otherwise the whole thing comes to nothing and Christianity returns into itself again), and He is the truth whom all need absolutely. What suffering of patience to educate the apostles, and even (to speak humanly), even if He had become impatient and thought: After all, I am not the one who needs them—yet in a certain sense He has to have a few men. He seeks the best and finally finds the best—and they misunderstand Him completely.

X^1 A 405   *n.d.*, 1849

« 4634

People cannot understand that a man would expose himself voluntarily to a danger with the idea that he will have to suffer. They think that when a man exposes himself to a danger it is with the idea that he will be victorious. When the one whose thought was that he would have to suffer actually does suffer, men busily talk about, saying: It is his own fault, his overweening pride, etc.

The life of Christ manifests this suffering also. The way they said: He wanted to tear down the temple and build it up in three days[920]—

SUFFERING 387

is reminiscent of the great things he said of himself. But they nevertheless made a mistake—for he did tear down the temple. His death on the cross was the downfall of Judaism, and consequently he did tear down the temple that very same moment, but he also built it up again in three days, for his resurrection (the third day) was indeed the beginning of Christianity, or the temple-structure of Christianity rests on it as on a foundation.

x^1 A 416 *n.d.*, 1849

« 4635

..... And when one distress or another, a pain, a suffering, seeks to gain a foothold and seems so dreadful to you that it would be a great thing if you could manage to drag yourself through life with it, but there can be no question of anything more—then look for some recreation, try to gain a new perspective on it all, for a new perspective revives. Reflect on one of our hymns in the authorized hymnal:[921]

> There (in eternity) I will bless you
> For the sufferings in time,
> What are they
> Compared to the bliss
> That is there.

Consequently it will be true of this suffering, too, if you do not yourself spoil everything, that you will even praise God for it; consequently it will not only prove to be far easier sometime in eternity, no, you will praise God for it. Think about that—it is the spirit's diversion and the spirit's recreation.

x^1 A 464 *n.d.*, 1849

« 4636

Since everything is ambiguous, what happens to a man can be just as much a test as a punishment, and only the individual can decide this for himself: it follows from this that with regard to another person I ought to interpret[922] everything as a test, and he ought to do the same for me. In any case the inclination to interpret the sufferings of other men as punishment is a very dubious matter.

x^1 A 603 *n.d.*, 1849

« 4637

Sometimes in a moment of despondency the notion occurs to me that Christ was not tested and tried in the suffering of illness, least of all in the most tormenting ones of all, where the psychic and the somatic dialectically touch each other—consequently it seems as if the prototype's life were easier in this respect. But then I say to myself: Do you believe, then, that if you were thoroughly healthy you would easily or more easily achieve perfection? Just the opposite: then you would yield easily to your passions, to pride if not to others, to an intensified self-esteem and the like. In that way sufferings, even though a burden, are a beneficial burden, like the braces used in the orthopedic institute.

To be thoroughly healthy physically and mentally and then to lead a truly spiritual life—that no man can do. The sense of spontaneous well-being immediately runs away with him. In one sense the life of the spirit is the death of immediacy. This is why sufferings are a help. If a person suffers every day, if he is so infirm that the thought of death is simply right at hand, then he may be somewhat successful in being continually conscious of needing God.

Physical health, the immediate sense of well-being, is a far greater danger than riches, power, and esteem.

Of course it has a deceptive appearance, as if it would still be a help to be physically, spontaneously strong. But if one is that, it is almost a superhuman task actually to live *qua* spirit. For that a consciousness of God is required, such as the God-man had. Usually a person fools himself very easily and confuses the sense of immediate well-being with—life of the spirit. Physical suffering, the infirm body, is a beneficial memento.

X^1 A 645 *n.d.*, 1849

« 4638

A pagan[923] has said: It is of no avail to try to ride away from sorrow; it sits behind on the horse. A pious man (Fenelon)[924] has said: Sorrow is like an arrow in the breast—the more vigorously the deer runs in order to run away from it, the more firmly the arrow becomes embedded in it.

N.B. Fenelon no doubt did not formulate it exactly this way; neither did he place it together with the lines by Horace, but the thought is from Fenelon.

X^1 A 662 *n.d.*, 1849

« 4639

In an otherwise really muddled funeral-pie on the Gospel story about the widow's son in Nain,[925] Visby[926] made a point which deserves attention. He said that "sorrow" κατεξόχην[927] is always sorrow for the dead, that to carry sorrow, walk in sorrow, etc. is always connected with sorrow for the dead. Therefore this sorrow is sorrow κα τεξόχην. Visby emphasized that for every other sorrow alleviation is understood to mean that the sorrow can still be changed to joy. But it is impossible to have the dead back again. In itself this is a very sound observation. However, I believe this should be used to show that there is yet a far deeper sorrow than the sorrow for the dead. The discourse ought to be developed to show that for the natural man sorrow for the dead is "the sorrow"; for the Christian sorrow for sin is the deepest sorrow. The loss of one dead is by no means irreparable; there is, in fact, an eternity; but the loss that sin entails is eternally irreparable.

Thus the sermon on the Gospel about the widow's son could be developed on the theme:

The Irreparable Loss.

To be sure, in order to describe a remarkable or remarkably lovable man we say: His loss is irreparable, but this is not true. Only the loss that sin entails is irreparable.

x^2 A 53   n.d., 1849

« **4640** *Inverted Suffering*

Ordinarily a person suffers because he did not become the great person he wished to become, etc.

But the reverse—to know, to know more surely than he knows anything else, to know the extraordinary[928] which is entrusted to him and dare not mention it to a single person, partly in order not to offend the supreme power, who does not want such loose talk, and partly because one is not sure of being even remotely understood even if he were to speak.

x^2 A 128   n.d., 1849

« **4641**

Religion is also used in a most shabby manner to flatter people.

Every person is eager to be flattered with the fancy that he has suffered something extraordinary. Nowadays the ministers help this along; if someone suffers the least little thing they find analogies between his suffering and that of the religious prototypes, Abraham who offers Isaac, Paul and the thorn in the flesh, between every suffering and these words—to enter the kingdom of God we must go through many tribulations.[929]

x^2 A 129   n.d., 1849

« 4642 *The Difference between Immediacy and Reflection in Relation to Religious Suffering*

The immediate or spontaneous person has also had his time of suffering, perhaps a frightful time—then suddenly everything is transfigured for him into bliss (this is immediate awakening). In this bliss he himself now forgets his sufferings; this can be quite appropriate. But then he begins to preach to others, and in a way he deceives them, for he completely forgets the suffering and thereby causes them either to take the whole thing in vain or, sometime later, to be almost enraged with him when they themselves experience suffering, enraged that he had not predicted it.

Reflection does not forget; it remembers backward; and reflection places suffering together with bliss.

In the moment immediacy produces a far greater effect; reflection works slowly but carefully.

What harm has been done to Christianity by taking mildness all by itself—and men have thereby been fooled into the fancy that they are Christians and Christianity has thereby been unmanned—instead of taking rigorousness along with it and gaining fewer but more genuine adherents.

X^2 A 131 *n.d.*, 1849

« 4643

> *In this way true consolation takes the shape of cruelty toward other men and reaps suffering instead of gratitude.*

The deeper the consolation and the deeper the sympathy, the more it goes beyond this or that trouble and suffering and searches out those suffering in the deepest sense, just as Christ searched out the demonic and looked for tax collectors and notorious sinners.

But then the contemporaries become embittered. For the generation as such has another tactic; it is so anxious about the demonic and such deep-seated suffering that it simply does not want to hear that there is consolation and healing for them—out of fear of being reminded that there are people who suffer in this way. Consequently such a "consoler" disturbs the happy society in life's various circles—indeed, it seems to be a kind of cruelty toward them that he, in order to heal them, searches out the demonic etc.—instead of doing as the public, Christendom, and the elite, Goethe and Mynster,[930] who in every way possible make sure they remain ignorant that such wretchedness exists.

So also with the wretchedness of sin. By wanting to save from sin and by laying the accent of eternity upon it, the rescuer brings to mind the consciousness of sin on a scale that disturbs the public, society, etc.; ergo, it is cruel of the consoler and rescuer, ergo, we are justified in hating and persecuting him.

And as it went with Christ, so it goes also on a smaller scale with anyone who more or less profoundly and sympathetically understands suffering and has a true Christian understanding of sin: his joyful, *si placet*,[931] speaking about an available consolation and salvation becomes a plague on society by reminding them of the frightful proportions of suffering in the world and of the horror of sin.

No, a consoler and rescuer must make the world happy; he must not dig too deeply, must produce cures for common ailments, and have advice for small calamities, and with respect to sin take grace in vain.

x^2 A 236   *n.d.*, 1849

« 4644 *"Be satisfied with my grace, for my power is made perfect in weakness."*[932]

(1) It is almost like a choice: Could you wish to be "strong and free" and thus exposed to the danger of forgetting me? The answer to that must be: No. Even if I am suffering pain and desire and pray that the thorn be taken away: O, if it should mean that I might forget God—no, let it remain! If by having the thorn removed I would come to feel my communion with God less intensely, then let it remain. And therefore when I pray that it may be taken away, it is in the thought that gratitude and joy might bind me even more strongly to God. But God alone really knows what binds best.

(2) Consider that this very weakness increases your strength, for when "God's power" "is made perfect" in weakness, then you are in fact stronger than in all your own power, as surely as God's power is the stronger.

x^2 A 246   *n.d.*, 1849

« 4645 *Christ's Entry into Jerusalem*[933] *from a Christian Viewpoint*

Just as he said of that woman who annointed him:[934] She did this for my burial (for he always had death in mind; indeed, he came into the world *in order* to die, his whole life aiming toward dying), so too the entry into Jerusalem is part of the whole by precipitating the catastrophe. But just as those who were present probably understood the woman differently and his burial was the last thing they thought of, so too the disciples and the people understood Christ upon his entry into Jerusalem even less. They thought: Now it is coming. He knew: Now my destruction is being prepared.

This loneliness belongs essentially to Christ's suffering as mental suffering, this solitary knowledge which understands all the signs inversely. He talks to his disciples in vain, tells it to them in advance; it does not help. If he had told them in advance that the entry was part of the whole by precipitating his death—yes, they perhaps would have understood him as long as he was talking. But then when he put this into action—and now they heard the people jubilating—it would promptly become reversed for them and they would think: Now he is triumphant. Only Jesus understood the jubilation as the sign of destruction.

But what use is it to explain such things to my generation. Perhaps they learn it by rote—and yet do not understand it. In order to understand it, one must be deeply initiated into sufferings—and a quiet man, quiet, alas, so very quiet from having long understood that chatter and foolishness and busyness infinitely[935] have the upper hand.

X^2 A 257 *n.d.*, 1849

« 4646

A human being can also experience a situation somewhat analogous to that of Christ before Pilate. Perhaps he is offered a recognition, which in itself people regard as somewhat extraordinary; and yet, loyal to truth, he must say: No, I will not accept it, it is false; I owe it to God and to truth to demand more. Then they become embittered—and now he must take the inverted expression of recognition—suffering.

X^2 A 272 *n.d.*, 1849

« 4647

The frightful thing one discovers when he stands outside of Christianity (the crucifixion of the understanding and the suffering consequent upon being a Christian, the unavoidable consequence in relation to the surrounding world), this frightful thing which could influence him so strongly that he would give up the hope and the resolution to become a Christian—this frightful thing is something quite different when seen from the inside. In the first place, suffering for a person in love is something quite different from what it is for the spectator who stands on the outside and looks at the same suffering, but a believer is more than a lover. In the next place, it becomes perfectly obvious to the believer that all these sufferings in relation to the world are not in the remotest manner the fault of Christianity, as if it were so rigorous or cruel—no, it is the world's fault because it is evil. But this is an enormous difference. If a girl were to suffer a great deal with a man because he was severe—well, she would put up with it if he were the beloved. But if it is infinitely clear to her that he is love itself, that the sufferings are not his fault but the fault of others, of evil men who hate him precisely because he is love itself: then it is a quite different matter.

This is correct. What is wrong is that Christianity has been made so mild that suffering has been completely removed. No, Christianity does not teach that there is no suffering; it teaches that there is enormous suffering, but that this enormous suffering nevertheless is light—not so light that it means that there is no suffering, no, light, although it is equally true that the suffering is enormous, consequently at one and the same time: enormous suffering—and yet light.

x^2 A 349   *n.d.*, 1850

« **4648**

"Pray for those who persecute you."[936]

Is this really possible? Think of it this way. Have you any idea of how blessed it is the more intimate your fellowship with God is. O, but the very moment this bliss passes beyond understanding—if you then honestly consider that it was the persecution by your enemy which helped you to perceive this blessedness: in a moment such as that is it not possible to bless them.

To bless them! Well, if I may put it this way, it is a festive expression of how indescribable the bliss is which you experience.

Just think of Socrates[937] when the poisoned cup was handed to him and he asked if it was permitted to make a libation to the gods: how festive! Now consider the Christian at the moment he is most blissfully aware of his fellowship with God and has to confess that he nevertheless owes a good share of it to his persecutors—then to say:

I will forgive them, I am not angry with them—how unfestive—no: I bless them.

It is like a fairy tale. A cruel stepmother throws a little child into a well—it is plucked out by elves and taken to enchantment's happy home and from here the child sees its stepmother and with the most blissful expression of childhood's innocent joy blows her a kiss—as if she were the fondest of mothers.

My friend, what does it matter, after all, that you basely did everything you could to hurt and embitter my life, since I nevertheless by its help—precisely by its help—came to know this bliss—what does it matter? Well, it does indeed matter, and I must bless you.

But be very careful about this "Never mind your persecutors"; rather be all the more sharply attentive to finding this bliss in your fellowship with God. Alas, but we men think most about our persecutors—less about using the persecution in connection with the God-relationship. Alas, and many end up cursing not only the persecutors but cursing God, too.

X^2 A 513 *n.d.*, 1850

« 4649 *Judaism——Christianity*

"It *sometimes* happens in this world that the righteous go through the same experience the unrighteous go through." This "sometimes" is characteristically Jewish. Christianly understood, it happens all the time, for Christianity is suffering truth.

But the preachers, of course, take care not to preach Christianity.

X^3 A 81 *n.d.*, 1850

« 4650

Abraham is an eternal prototype [*Forbillede*] of the religious man. Just as he had to leave the land of his fathers for a strange land, so the religious man must willingly leave, that is, forsake a whole generation of his contemporaries even though he remains among them, but isolated, *alien* to them. To be an alien, to be in exile, is precisely the characteristic suffering of the religious man.

X^3 A 114 *n.d.*, 1850

« 4651 *Just This One Conflict in Christ's Life
   —What Suffering!*

He who is himself a single human being is in need of a human being. He is God and as such is not in need of any man, all these millions who have lived, the hosts of angels. But he does not will to be God; he wills to be man. Ergo, he needs one man, he needs one he can use as an apostle. This other man, then, is infinitely important to him—of course, if he wills to be God, then this man is less than nothing to him, but he does not will to be God—consequently this man is infinitely important to him for the sake of the cause, and it is infinitely important that the apostle really remains faithful to the cause. Christ could plead with him in tears to remain faithful—to such a degree does he need him for the sake of the cause, and because he does not will to be God.

Christ does not will to be God. In an omnipotent decision he has forced himself into being a single human being and must now very concretely suffer the total impotence of wretchedness with the cause of humanity upon his heart, must suffer being a poor individual man —and at every moment it is his voluntary decision that constrains him; he does, after all, have the power to break through and be God.

This observation is no doubt true, but one ought to be cautious with even such observations, for what really pertains to him is the fact that it is also for his sake that Christ suffers and that Christ's suffering and death are Atonement for him also. And now consider the way speculation speaks about the God-man.

x^3 A 118   *n.d.*, 1850

« **4652** *Consolation*

In a sense it is certainly easier to console others if one is himself happy than to console others if one himself suffers, but in the first case the consolation is perhaps all the more insipid, and the person who is really suffering hardly dares have anything to do with it. —The proper relationship, therefore, is that the consoler be one who suffers and for whom it becomes a consolation to comfort another who is suffering. (See the discourse "The High Priest"[938] in the Friday discourses.)

x^3 A 131   *n.d.*, 1850

« **4653** *Effort*

O, when all are Christians and all who proclaim Christianity proclaim that it means to make life as easy and indulgent as possible and then on the other hand assume that God is merciful and wants you to be happy and satisfied, and that to want to make life somewhat more strenuous is to tempt God: how oppressive, then, to make life troublesome for oneself, almost as if one were getting into something meritorious.

396 SUFFERING

But, good Lord, what then is Christianity? I am supposed to make my life easy, be happy and satisfied. Consequently I really should not go where there is danger, God does not want it; where the truth is suffering, I really should hold back—this is what God wants, for he wants me to dance on roses. Consequently if a people is degenerating morally, if the existence of Christianity is becoming a pretense, a delusion, I really am supposed to keep still, it is the will of God.

O, impious worldliness, which has taken Christianity in vain.

No, I am supposed to suffer for the truth. When I see truth suffering along my way, I am to suffer even unto death; but despite this I am to feel most profoundly that I am saved by grace. I am supposed to be happy, always happy—"in God," which the suffering witness of truth knows best how to interpret.

Woe to you who have taken Christianity in vain, because you do so much harm this way, because you cause the witness to the truth so much trouble, which he could be free from had you not taken it upon yourself to explain what Christianity is, and now his flesh and blood look favorably upon your interpretation.

x^3 A 148 *n.d.*, 1850

« 4654 *God's Special Upbringing*

It probably goes something like this for a man who is the object of this special upbringing. At an early age he is bound to a suffering which is a thorn in the flesh to him, places him outside of the universally human. This hinders him from being able to enjoy life—and forces him into the God-relationship as the only consolation and salvation. It would be useless for him to pray and implore God that this thorn in the flesh be removed. Perhaps when at long last this man has died to the world in such a way that the secular and selfish enjoyment of life has lost its value for him as a God-fearing man, then perhaps the thorn in the flesh will also be taken away.

Men are often so crafty toward God that they readily pray to him and beseech him, and then very likely also thank him—for getting their own way.

Incidentally, this can also illuminate the forgiveness of sin. The crucial point is always this, to what kind of a life does a person want to return after having received the forgiveness of sins. What is the *integrum* to which there is a *restitutio*.[939] Many a person lives on determined essentially only by the urge to enjoy life. At the same time there is a guilt that oppresses him. So he very readily prays and implores for the forgiveness of sin—so that when his conscience is eased he can properly enjoy life. But here God may restrain him again. The man is unable really to find rest in the fact that his sin is actually forgiven. The thought continues to pursue him. Perhaps a year goes by, during which he is dying to the world—and then, then he also perceives that he now has the full forgiveness of sins.

x^3 A 182   n.d., 1850

« **4655 Why Do We See No Persecution At All?**

Because there is no Christianity. Let Christianity come, and persecution will come as well. And then passion will come again. He who has seen a man he regarded as devout, God-fearing, and, humanly speaking, righteous suffer mistreatment and persecution and finally death will acquire sufficient passion and hatred of this world—although not on the tremendous scale as did the apostles, who had seen the Holy One crucified, and then from that moment the world was crucified to them and they to the world.[940]

x^3 A 245   n.d., 1850

« **4656 Christianity—Baptism**

If Christianity were an obvious good like some earthly good—money, for example—then to put the child in possession of it as early as possible would be understandable.

But since Christianity is a good whose first obligation is willingness to suffer for truth, it is rather odd to be in such a hurry.

On the other hand there is also the question of what possible interest Christianity can have in our overloading it with millions of baptized Christians who otherwise have nothing to do with Christianity.

x^3 A 281   n.d., 1850

« **4657**

In a way Bürger's Lenore[941] is right:

O, Mutter, Mutter, was mir brennt
das lindert mir kein Sacrament.

Christianity recognizes only one suffering: that of sin. If Lenore will transform her suffering and, for example, no longer grieve over Wilhelm but over the fact that in her despair she has rebelled against God: then Christianity is able to help.

Incidentally, the mother's reply is characteristic of Christendom: immediately prescribing the sacrament for unhappy erotic love—why not also for a fever, etc.? Which no doubt has also been done.

x^3 A 305   n.d., 1850

« **4658** *The Life of an Apostle, What an Epitome of Suffering*

In the first place they understand Christ as wanting to establish an earthly kingdom. They jubilantly join up with him, no doubt have felt they would never be able to thank him enough for choosing them in particular, feel all the power such "that even the spirits are subject to them."[942]

Then the order is changed. Suffering is mentioned. It must almost seem to them as if Christ had treacherously lured them on.

Meanwhile they offer once again—they want to risk their lives with him.

Then it becomes clear that when things go to pieces they become frightened.

Then the pain of having denied him—and throughout the time he was dead.

Then the Resurrection, Ascension—and then begins this life filled with toil and trouble.

x^3 A 382   n.d., 1850

« **4659** *Concern for an Eternal Blessedness*

From the very beginning, however far I look back, nothing has been more sure to me than eternal salvation; all I would have to do when I died would be to mention Christ's name, this was the surest thing of all. —And so it is with everyone who is brought up from childhood in Christianity.

Does this assurance strengthen a person in the sufferings of this life? No, it actually makes him thinner-skinned. It is precisely the greater danger which helps venturing into the lesser one.

Here is the enormous illusion in Christendom, even where it is true that a child is really brought up in Christianity.

The same thing has happened in Christendom as with the person who inherits a fortune and has never had to earn a living; so also this illusory security comes from being coddled from childhood.

x^3 A 426   n.d., 1850

« 4660 *The Life-View of Early Christianity
—the Present Life-View*

In the early days people were almost surprised to find that life had a few joyful days (the same thing is expressed in one of the morning and evening prayers in the hymnal[943]), because they understood that this life was ordained to suffering, also suffering for Christianity.

Nowadays Christianity has come to mean gratifying oneself in a purely secular manner and clinging tightly to this life.

x^3 A 492   *n.d.*, 1850

« 4661 *"Christianity Is No Longer Persecuted"*

Well, no wonder, since men have completely abolished Christianity as a way of existing, a life of imitation, and have made it into nothing but doctrine. But a doctrine does not inconvenience, does not excite and arouse persecution. A doctrine makes no difference either way in the world; with regard to everything that merely wants to be doctrine, the world is as tolerant as the piety of the Romans: one god more or less, what difference does it make. The world is not in the least embarrassed to have someone teach the doctrine of self-renunciation and thereby make a secular living for himself; on the contrary, the world is pleased to have one more occupational category. But for someone to deny himself—this is embarrassing.

Let *imitation* come once again—and persecution will soon follow.

x^3 A 500   *n.d.*, 1850

« 4662 *The Official Proclamation of Christianity*

If we were to determine categorically where it is and how it relates to the proclamation of Christianity in the strictest sense, we could say: It gets up *to* Christianity but does not get *into* Christianity. It takes all the wretchedness of this earthly life etc.—and then Christianity is consolation.

But that this consolation is something very special, that there is the spiritual trial [*Anfægtelsen*] that the consolation is not entirely direct, that Christianity requires suffering for the doctrine, etc.—all this is completely suppressed.

x^3 A 671   *n.d.*, 1850

« 4663 *Ridicule and Misfortune Always Go Together*

says the proverb. But one must not automatically judge men so severely—as if they actually were so evil that they delighted in ridiculing misfortune. No, but when the misfortune supersedes a previous good fortune which perhaps was a source of envy, then especially do men retaliate by means of ridicule, insofar as they cannot do the slightly more dignified thing and retaliate—with sympathy.

x^3 A 731   *n.d.*, 1851

« 4664 *Unhappiness, Suffering Is Guilt; the Greatest Guilt Is To Be Unhappy*

Alas, yes, it is only all too true. But on second thought it ought not be judged so severely. There is a kind of instinct for self-preservation in men; they are afraid that knowing about another's unhappiness will disturb their enjoyment of their own happiness—and for their own security they would like very much to regard the fellow's unhappiness as guilt—for then it is something which cannot happen to them.

x^3 A 732   *n.d.*, 1851

« 4665 *Chrysostom*

also compromises.

He says somewhere that if a woman's child dies and she patiently accepts it, she ranks with Abraham, for in intention she was willing; likewise she ranks with a martyr, for in intention she was willing.

The words go something like this: Whoever endures sufferings and thanks God has earned himself a martyr's crown; for example, a child becomes ill and the mother thanks God—this is a martyr's crown. Are not her sufferings even greater than those of many martyrs? But she does not allow herself to be coerced. The child dies. She gives thanks anew. She has become a daughter of Abraham. Even if she has not sacrificed her son by her own hand, she was, however, willing to do it, was gladly prepared for it, etc.

Neander, *Chrysostomus*, part I, p. 249.[944]

Hom. 8 on Colossians IV, 133.[945]

x^3 A 774   *n.d.*, 1851

« 4666 *Christianly, the Ranking Is Reversed—*

that is, the higher the rank, the more suffering there is; this is also explicitly expressed in the New Testament[946] where Christ says to the disciples who aspired to sit on his right and on his left: You do not know what you are asking. Are you able to drink the cup that I am to drink?

You do not know what you are asking—no, the apostles did not notice the reversed ranking but understood it in the ordinary, direct way.

Everyone prefers to be ranked in the ordinary, direct way and to ascend higher and higher. In reversed ranking—yes, if one knows at all what he is asking for—hardly anyone asks to come under this ranking or for quick advancement to a higher level.

As soon as it is forgotten that Christianly the ranking is reversed, Christianity is abolished. From a Christian point of view, the direct scale ascending in honor and esteem is just like the calendar before Christ, a negative reckoning, a debit, which is accounted to a person.

O, how far God's thoughts are from man's! They compete to achieve a higher and higher status in honor and esteem and do not notice that they are sinking more and more deeply into debt. For this positive (honor, esteem, status, etc.) is a negative; and precisely this negative (to be insulted, ridiculed, persecuted, in short, suffering for the truth) is the positive. Likewise the world's earnestness is a joke, and in Christ-likeness to become a fool in the world is earnestness itself.

x^3 A 783   *n.d., 1851*

« 4667 *Suffering Combat*

That this, this alone, is the Christian way is expressed by the fact that this is what Christianity is intrinsically.

God does not use force to tear man out of the devil's power. No, Christ allowed himself to be born, to suffer, to die—to save man from the devil's power. Injustice also has its rights, and in considering injustice it is injustice to want to commit an injustice against it: it is simply unchristian. The essentially Christian is: in suffering to permit injustice to have all its rights down to the least detail—and thus to win, to conquer it.

At first glance the essentially Christian is always disappointing. This suffering combat appears so very weak. Seeing such a thing for the first time, many an unjust ruler has perhaps thought: "That man is not dangerous, he will not use force; yes, he is even more of a lunatic, he will help us against anyone who wants to use force against us, even if this force volunteered to help him. Such combat is then the most innocent private gratification." O, you shortsighted fool, precisely such a person is the most dangerous of all; yes, if you could inveigle him to use force, he would be less dangerous. True enough, the danger may be greater momentarily, but the downfall that is prepared with the aid of a suffering combatant is also completely and fundamentally different. What does it mean that, suffering, he battles? It means that he really transforms himself into something which makes you come to condemn yourself. You are not wronged in any way whatsoever—no, but it becomes absolutely clear how wrong you are.

But the world and Christendom have been sunk so deep and so long in the secular mentality that such tactics have been forgotten completely, and now, of course, it must look like pure madness. And is it not madness to believe that there is meaning in existence, justice at every single point, also that there is a God, also that one single individual who is in the truth, and as long as he is in the truth, is stronger than millions.

X^4 A 135 *n.d.*, 1851

« **4668** *Contrasts*

Consider these suffering figures: throughout a perhaps long life he has had to endure all the mistreatment of his contemporaries—and no one, not one, has concerned himself about his grief—except perhaps to increase it. No one took part in his agonies—for the sake of the truth—except with mockery and insult. Then he dies.

There also lives an altogether sensate man—ambitious, avaricious, self-indulgent, and on top of all that desperately eager to appear saintly: he makes a brilliant career of preaching about *how* the first man suffered! He has counted every single tear shed by the former one— I believe he gilds every tear! He has heard his every sigh—I really believe that the second man wallows in pleasure just thinking and talking about the first man's sighs!

How lofty is the divine, and how dignified, as it were! Indeed, anyone, even an apostle, could become unbalanced thinking about such things and grasp for worldly aid! But God in heaven sits calmly, keeps his price infinitely high, and says: But then the first one has had the relationship to me, and this is enough, even if he had suffered 10,000 times as much as he did suffer.

Yes, and it is so true! If such a suffering person seeks assistance in the external, then it is still because he does not value God highly enough; he would very much like to have the God-relationship on more lenient terms. Well, this is, after all, quite human, but on the other hand: God is still unconditionally right that the relationship to him is such a blessedness that it unconditionally and infinitely outweighs all suffering.

This is why an apostle, for example, has—if I dare say so—this aristocratic bearing on behalf of God. He is flogged, and the apostle says: I have the honor of being flogged, etc.

x^4 A 153   n.d., 1851

« 4669 *Ambrose:*

"The wounds which we get for Christ's sake are not wounds by which life is lost but by which life is propagated ..... I beseech you to let this battle take place—but you are only spectators! Bear in mind that when a city has an athlete it wants to see him contend. Why do you decline in greater things because of what you are doing in lesser things." (See Böhringer, I, pt. 3, p. 35.[947]) Well said. A Christian, after all, is like a strong man, and should we not wish to see him develop his strength by persecution or in persecution. This is strong talk, and since Ambrose himself is the one who is going to take over the obligations of the role, it is true strength.

x^4 A 156   n.d., 1851

« 4670 *Can This Hang Together Properly?*

Augustine, for example, says somewhere: "If you still consider that you have no affliction, then you have not even begun to be a Christian. This brief life is an affliction; if it is not an affliction, then it is no exile, but if it is an exile, then either you do not love your home very much, or you unquestionably have affliction (see Böhringer, I, pt. 3, p. 188[948]).

That is plain speaking. Indeed, the higher we come up in the definition of what it is to be a Christian (to God's chosen ones in the strictest sense, apostles) the more decisively and unequivocally it reads that it is sheer suffering—and the prototype himself!!

On the other side of the picture, things go on calmly and undisturbed from generation to generation—these thousands upon thousands who become pastors; they take their examination and think they have gotten through this tough bout; after this they long for an easier situation in order, after all, to be able to enjoy life somewhat; then they get married—and go out to proclaim the mild doctrine, Christianity. This mild doctrine which "sweetly soothes life's sorrows and for the first time gives joys their real flavor"—and this is Christianity.

x^4 A 158   n.d., 1851

« 4671 *The Donatist Thesis:*

The Church which persecutes is *eo ipso* the false Church; the

Church which is persecuted and counts its martyrs is *eo ipso* the true Church.

See Böhringer, I, pt. 3, p. 353.⁹⁴⁹

x⁴ A 169 *n.d.*, 1851

« 4672 *The Sufferings of the "Extraordinary"*

This alone, which is the whole alphabet of agony.

The extraordinary person is not vain about what has been granted him—for then he would definitely not be the extraordinary; moreover, he is far too exhausted by what has been granted him to be vain. But on the other hand it is nevertheless true that he is the extraordinary.

And then, yes, perhaps the extraordinary prefers to encourage men to believe that he is a fool, a nobody—but then the responsibility to God—does he dare, is it not deceiving God, since under the circumstances God has made him into the extraordinary.

O, so strenuous is the true God-relationship that it is always characterized by a tendency toward madness. To be the extraordinary, to know with God that one is that, to dare know that the future will reveal it more and more (yet here the future perhaps says: not until after one's death)—and then in his present life to have the most insignificant person among his contemporaries be more than the extraordinary, for the most insignificant person is in the previously given relativity, the extraordinary is the new—which is still nowhere at home.

x⁴ A 189 *n.d.*, 1851

« 4673 *Christianity as Consolation*

is all that is presented these days. Originally it was entirely different —one did not hear: Let yourself be talked into it, it is sheer consolation —no, one heard: If you have the courage and the mind to will to be in the truth—then become a Christian; it is sheer suffering.

x⁴ A 238 *n.d.*, 1851

« 4674

In margin of 4673 (x⁴ A 238):

As in Hebrews,⁹⁵⁰ from a Christian point of view it even holds true that in one sense they do not want to accept consolation—they want to go farther out in venturing for the truth.

x⁴ A 239 *n.d.*

« 4675

..... You suffering one, you are perhaps sighing: I have suffered so long now that a little encouragement simply has to come if I am going to be able to hold out—and then new sufferings come. O, do hold out then, simply believe that sufferings, these sufferings, too, and precisely at their most agonizing moment, are able to help you advance; as the coachman[951] uses the whip when the going is hardest for the horse, the horse, according to its ideas, must necessarily think that the only thing that could help would be permission to take a breather.

x^4 A 244   *n.d.*, 1851

« 4676 *Strenuousness*

Suffering is dreadfully intensified when it is voluntary. When, for example, a person has it in his power to make things easier for himself but for the sake of an idea or for the sake of truth voluntarily makes the greatest effort, and then, really suffering the pain, aware of the strenuousness, he still has it in his power to spare himself.

This is intensification. Let a horse be fagged out and tired—it is painful enough when it is required to go on pulling just the same—but suppose it is also required to cut capers while it is hauling.

x^4 A 256   *n.d.*, 1851

« 4677 *The Unhappy Failure*

When he eventually dies, God approaches him in eternity, caresses him, and says: "Poor child, that you had to suffer this way your whole life; O, I wanted so much to make it comfortable for you, too, but in the infinite plan of the world it was your destiny and that of many others to have to suffer this way. O, but I suffered with you; truly every undeserved suffering of yours has touched me deeply, even if I have not been able to alter it."

This is how God talks, for God in heaven—yes, how shall I say it! —God in heaven is the most loving person.

Just imagine an affectionate, loving person who in the service of a great plan has had to let another person suffer; O, how he suffers with him, how he remembers every detail, until the moment he can say to him: It could not be otherwise, but, O, I have perhaps suffered more because of it than you.

x^4 A 343   *n.d.*, 1851

« 4678 *Everything Depends upon the Conception*

Saul[952] is hurled to the ground, becomes blind—this means: you are an apostle. Simon Magus[953] is struck with blindness—this means: punishment.

Of Paul[954] it is written: "I (Christ) will show him what he will come to suffer for my name's sake, he, my chosen instrument." At this point must not a poor human being sigh: O my God, if this is what it means to have something to do with you, if this is the result, who dares get involved with you. Take a purely human situation. Let a man say of a woman: She is my heart's choice, I will show her what she will come to suffer for my sake—must not the girl rather decline the love with thanks.

Yet between man and man such a relation is false, perhaps frightful arrogance. But between God and man the relation cannot be otherwise: to be the chosen one is to be initiated into most terrible sufferings; God cannot love a man any other way.

x^4 A 386   *n.d.,* 1851

« **4679**

"The disciple is not above his master"[955]— Christ[956] says it this way: I have suffered, ergo you shall also suffer.

Humanly one could be tempted to turn it around and say: It is precisely a mark of distinction to be able to endure suffering that way, to be spirit that way. The disciple is incapable of it, because he is not spirit that way; being a frail human being, he must be allowed more lenient conditions, must be allowed to become loved, honored, esteemed, etc.

Well, in any case, it might be turned in such a way in order to be tolerable, for, from a Christian point of view, it is certainly intolerable if the disciple's distinction in the world is supposed to be a direct mark of earnestness and not the reverse, a frailty, an infirmity, an imperfection which can be tolerated if only the true situation is admitted.

x^4 A 420   *n.d.,* 1851

« **4680** *Suffering for the Doctrine—the Relationship of Absolute Majesty—the Positive Recognizable by the Negative*[957]

We know that Christianity is conscious of being the absolute, the divine, because it raises the tone so high that it defines a relationship to the absolute in terms of having to suffer—and that this nevertheless is the greatest grace and the highest blessedness. Nothing, nothing raises the tone so high. Neither in art nor in science does it happen that getting involved with it means suffering. This is the first thing. And then the second, that this is nevertheless sheer blessedness and sheer grace.

To suffer for the doctrine does not mean therefore to earn salvation—if it did, then the infinite, the absolute, would be finitized, because earning is finitizing. No, suffering means neither more nor less than the mark, the criterion, of my actually being involved with the absolute and of my relating myself to it.

The absolute, the highest good, is therefore heterogeneous to all other blessings—not a superlative of them. No, the very opposite, it is recognizable by a relationship of suffering.

Here as elsewhere the formula for essential Christianity is: the essentially Christian is always the positive which is recognizable by the negative—the highest blessedness, to relate oneself to it, is recognizable by the fact—that one comes to suffer in this world.

Here are the roots of the possibility of offense.

But the apostle always speaks out of this inverted dialectic: not only will he not be disturbed by suffering and opposition—no, no, he thereby proves the rightness of his course, that it is God's cause.

O matchless majesty!

X^4 A 456 *n.d.*, 1852

« **4681** *Suffering*

The purely human conception of suffering can never go farther than *either* to interpret suffering as ultimately teleological (one suffers for a time, a certain number of years, etc. in order to achieve this or that or become this or that etc.) *or*, if the suffering continues, then to bear it patiently, but it is an evil.

Christianity clearly considers suffering to be the mark of the God-relationship: if you do not suffer, you do not have anything to do with God. God is spirit and therefore a person (*qua* sensate being) can be involved with him only if he suffers. Furthermore, Christianity believes that it is out of love that God lets a man suffer—he spurns the ungodly, they have nothing to do with him; therefore they are exempted from suffering.

These, you see, are hard words for a poor human being to take. And what makes it doubly hard in "Christendom" is that from childhood one is brought up in all this mawkishness about God as a dear old grandfather and uncle, sensately understood; then, too, we live in a world of Christians who above all make a point of branding one's getting involved with God in this way as blasphemy, arrogance, pride —for if we had the integrity to admit that not becoming involved with God this way is cowardice, sensuousness, then one's life in the sensate world would have no safeguard, one would run the risk of being swept further out; but now we safeguard ourselves by regarding involvement of oneself with God in such a way as arrogance, blasphemy, etc.

x^4 A 481   *n.d.*, 1852

« **4682** *Christianity*

has been completely transposed into human egotism.

The truth is that Christianity really involves suffering (it invites those who suffer—and in becoming a true Christian you come to suffer).

But in "Christendom" it is actually the favored ones who have taken possession of Christianity, the rich and powerful who in addition to all their enjoyment of life also want all their power and might and wealth interpreted as proof of God's grace and a sign of their piety—and these are the ones the clergy would rather associate with, for here the pay is best, both in money and in dignity.

In a way those who suffer have actually been robbed of Christianity, and what is presented in the name of Christianity is the Jewish or pagan principle that having everything in life go well is a sign of one's piety.

But Christianity has the view that suffering is the mark of the God-relationship. It is the majestic expression of God's majesty that he is not like other majesties (a direct superlative) who give gifts, so that he is the one who gives the most—no, his grace is recognizable "in reverse"[958]—by suffering. Furthermore, God's relation to the world is not like ours, so that he looks upon it as a wonderful world. No, for him the world is immersed in evil. This being the case, it is also easy to see that it is his disfavor which allows these rich and powerful ones etc. to become more rich and powerful. No, he can express his grace and favor only by letting you suffer—in this evil world. Finally, God is indeed "spirit," and consequently a dialectical determinant has to be included in the relationship to him—namely, that the relationship is not directly indicated (by prosperity, for example) but by suffering, something the New Testament apostles, the witnesses of the truth, et al. also express.

To the extent that a man is unwilling to suffer and even rejoice in it, convinced that suffering is the mark of the relationship to God, this is an egotism which (perhaps in the most glowing adoration and thanksgiving) actually aims to drag God down so that he is not "spirit" but a god of good fortune, etc.

When I arrive at an understanding of this, I am moved to a willingness to suffer—and then, then it seems to me that this willingness on my part must move God to—watch out now!—reward me by sending me a few good things. O treacherous human heart!

Actually, to be able to endure "suffering as the sign of the relationship to God" is what Christianity is according to the New Testament. I am far from this height, but I understand it, and I understand it to my humiliation.

x^4 A 570   n.d., 1852

« **4683** *The Greatest Human Cruelty—Divine Love*

The greatest human cruelty—more terrible than anything the most terrible tyrant ever thought up or practiced, which we all practice, which the whole race practices—is that when someone is deeply unhappy and suffering enormously (dreadfully and protractedly) we shield ourselves (O, human sympathy!), we shield ourselves against him by making out that it is his own fault or that it is because of his sins. This is Job's situation. What really shocks Job most of all is that his friends want to explain his suffering as guilt. To the degree that we human beings love to enjoy life, to the same degree we shield ourselves against the unhappy and the wretched whose sufferings will disturb our zest for life and give us a different impression of God, that he is not the God of success, by saying: It is their own fault—and then we go on enjoying life and enjoying ourselves in the illusion that we have God on our side.

Then comes Christianity. Its thesis is: to suffer, to be unhappy, is precisely the sign that God loves you—and, no wonder, since God is love. Should not love especially love those who suffer? But this must not be misunderstood to mean that God is preoccupied with taking away suffering. No, the suffering remains, but Christianity means that to suffer is the mark of the God-relationship.

This thesis alone is enough to provoke persecution of Christianity. For the whole powerful secular mentality not only desires earthly goods but also wants its possession to be refined by having it regarded as the mark of piety and of the God-relationship.

x^4 A 573   n.d., 1852

« **4684**

In margin of 4683 (x^4 A 573):

How jolting the concise, terse truth of Seneca's account (*De ira,* III, chapter 17[959]) of the cruelty with which Lysimachus had his friend Telesphorus of Rhodes slashed, his nose and ears cut off, and then had him shut up in a cage like a wild animal, and when he became altogether unrecognizable because the cage was never cleaned of filth and because he had so little room that he could not stand erect or use his arms or legs—now it comes!—then sympathy for him also vanished. This is the way it is. Become really miserable and unfortunate—and compassion stops—at the proper point, no doubt!

x^4 A 574   *n.d.*

« **4685** *The Gospel Is Preached to the Poor*

A Brief

Christ[960] was not making a historical observation when he declared: The gospel is preached to the poor, no (and the word order itself emphasizes this), "the gospel" is preached to the poor, the accent is on the gospel, that the gospel is for the poor.

Here the word "poor" does not mean simply poverty but all who suffer, are unfortunate, wretched, wronged, crippled, lame, leprous, demonic.

The gospel is preached to them, that is, the gospel is for them. The gospel is good news for them.

What good news? Not: here is money, here is health, here is status, etc.—no, no, then it is no longer Christianity.

No, for the poor the gospel is the good news that to be unfortunate in this world (in such a way that one is abandoned by human sympathy, and the worldly zest for life even cruelly tries to make one's misfortune into guilt) is a sign of the God-relationship, that these poor from whom the generation divorces itself even more cruelly by making it a matter of their own guilt—that the good news is precisely for them.

So it was originally; this is the gospel in the New Testament. It is preached for "the poor," and it is preached by the poor who, if they in other respects were not suffering, would eventually suffer by proclaiming the gospel; since suffering is inseparable from Christianity, is presupposed in the hearers (it is, in fact, for the poor), accompanies the proclamation—the proclaimer must suffer for the doctrine.

But soon came the change, and secular confidence that this error is the gospel grew greater and greater.

In other words, when proclaiming Christianity is a livelihood, if possible even a lush livelihood, then, yes, then the gospel is preached best of all—for the rich—nothing is more obvious. When proclaiming Christianity means acquiring rank and title, if possible, a high rank and title, and medallions and ribbons—then, yes, then Christianity is proclaimed best of all for the mighty etc. (not only the preachers perceive this; I also perceive it).

This is the way in which the gospel has been thoroughly falsified.

(1) Christianity is no longer glad tidings for those who suffer, consequently joy in suffering, is no longer suffering transfigured by the hope of the gospel, but is *the enjoyment of life* intensified by the hope of eternity.

(2) Proclaiming Christianity no longer means suffering, suffering for the doctrine but happy in the hope of eternity—no, it is the most refined enjoyment of life (carried out with emphasis on the psychological) intensified by the hope of eternity.

(3) The gospel no longer benefits the poor essentially; no, it has even become a downright injustice to those who suffer (although one is not always conscious of this). Since proclamation of the gospel to the rich, the powerful, etc. has been discovered to be advantageous, we are right back again to the very things Christianity wanted to oppose. The rich and the powerful not only get to keep everything, but their success becomes the mark of their piety, the sign of the relationship to God. "Look," they say, "because this man is pious and God-fearing, everything goes well for him, this is why he amasses one barrel of gold after another, and when he responds to the proclaimers of Christianity with an appropriate contribution, they vouch for him that it is God's blessing, that it is because he is a true Christian, because this is most convenient both for him and for the preachers." But this prompts the old atrocity again—namely, the idea that the unfortunate, the poor are to blame for their condition, that it is because they are not pious, are not true Christians. Consequently they are supposed to have not only suffering but guilt as well, and the rich have not only pleasure but piety in addition.

This is supposed to be Christianity. Compare it with the New Testament, and you will see that this is as far from that as possible.

X^4 A 578   n.d., 1852

« **4686 Upside Down**

Those who personally enjoy honor and esteem, have medallions and ribbons, etc., preach about how blessed it is to be derided for the truth. And those who actually are suffering derision and for a good cause do not have the bold confidence of faith to say, "But it is blessed to suffer derision for the good"; they preach about the scurviness of the world etc., that is, they would prefer to be spared derision—so they themselves do not believe that it is blessed.

Therefore this preaching completely disappears; it is no longer heard. Only one who himself is actually being derided for some good cause can preach it. But if he does not have all the bold confidence of faith, he cannot do it either; if he prefers to be spared derision, he had better not preach about it, for one thing is sure, nothing incenses the world more than to have someone who is actually suffering indignities proclaim that it is a blessed thing. If the derision he suffered hitherto was minor, let him merely preach in this manner and the derision will mount to a raging passion.

x^4 A 579   *n.d.*, 1852

« **4687 *The Human—the Christian***

"If you do this and this, you will thereby make yourself and others unhappy, you will be hated, detested, cursed by men, who will prepare every suffering for you, fully convinced that you have richly deserved them—ergo it can never be God's will for you to take that path." In the New Testament[961] we read: You will be hated by all for my name's sake. Indeed, the hour is coming when whoever kills you will think he is offering service to God—ergo this is the path you should be taking! Amazing! And then we are all Christians.

"When your beloved, or your wife and children, and others beg and plead with you not to take that path, which will lead you away from them, then you can be sure that it is not God's will for you to take that path!" In the New Testament[962] we read: I have come to set at odds man and wife etc. etc.—therefore this is the way you ought to go. Amazing! And then we are all Christians and we have a thousand Christian pastors.

x^4 A 583   *n.d.*, 1852

« **4688 *The Two Theses of Christianity***

A.

Because you are a sufferer, therefore God loves you.

First: Come unto me all you who labor[963] etc. O, do not lose your bold confidence—as if to suffer, to be unfortunate, were a matter of guilt (a cruel invention of men in order to get rid of you)—no, it is precisely that God loves you; the fact that you suffer does not mean that you are abandoned by God, quite the contrary.

B.

Because you love God, therefore you must suffer.

This comes next and will happen if you have really involved yourself with Christianity: you must suffer, suffer for the doctrine, in short, you must suffer because God loves you, God is spirit and he cannot express his love except by requiring you to suffer; if you are not willing to suffer, you will then be free from God's love.

Be careful, however, for coming to this understanding will produce a deep and fervent mood within you, and in the same instant the sensate in you will slip in a deception; you will think that this emotion of yours must please God so much that he will now send you some good fortune or other—O, deceitful heart, then the whole thing is back on the old basis of the sensate and is no longer this: God's love expresses itself by your having to suffer.

Here, indeed, the last merely human consolation vanishes, for the last merely human consolation is this: when everything abandons me, I still have God and he will surely send good fortune and happiness —O, if God loves you, it is expressed by your having to suffer—otherwise he does not love you.

Does he not help you, then? Indeed he does, he helps you discover the inexpressible blessedness of suffering in this way. This is the witness of Spirit.

But watch out, now, lest an illusion slip in right then in the very moment of understanding. For this understanding will create a mood, and it will seem to you that this must be so pleasing to God that he will give you another chance—O, deceitful heart, then the whole thing has reverted to the sensate and is not the witness of the Spirit. No, take care, for perhaps God in that very moment will send you some painful mishap—so that you can immediately have practice, with the assistance of the witness of the Spirit, in finding this blessed.

Such is the complicated course of events before one finds consolation.

There is a God in heaven—is this not infinite consolation enough? Yes, indeed, if there were no sin.

There is a Redeemer—is this not sufficient consolation; after all, does he not make full satisfaction for all your sin? Yes, indeed, if only he, the Redeemer, did not require "imitation."

But the Spirit is "the Comforter"—there we come to a stop: be comforted!

Only one more thing. Just as the physician says to the one who has broken his leg and is about to use it again: Be extremely careful; the minute you feel the slightest pain, take it easy, rest a half hour, but then begin again; or if the pain is more severe, then put on the brace again for a day, use a cane, but then begin again the next day—and above all, do not be disturbed, do not become impatient and stamp the floor for pain, because then you will break the leg again; it will be "for pain" inasmuch as it will bring you the greatest possible pain—so it is here, too. Be careful—if it is too painful, relax a little, but then begin again. Above all, no impatience, that could be even fatal at this point.

Relax a little; there is and remains the eternal assurance that a man is saved by grace alone.

Relax a little, but then begin again. Ah, is it not true that the scurviest ingratitude would be for a man to spare himself all strenuousness because he is saved by grace. Or what would you think of a man who grew cold and indifferent to his wife because he knew that he was loved and would put forth effort only when he knew he was not loved and wished to earn her love.

X^4 A 593 *n.d.*, 1852

« 4689 *Suffering as a Sign of the God-Relationship, One Aspect of the Pain*

To suffer is a sign of the God-relationship.

If men, one's contemporaries, the outside world, understood a person's sufferings as the very expression of his clinging to God and being loved by him, then the pain would be half as great as it is, it would be like the self-denial which is understood by one's contemporaries to be God-fearing self-denial.

But this is not the case. It is precisely the contemporaries who regard the suffering as the sign of God's disfavor, and this suffering, the suffering of misunderstanding, is part of it.

Moreover, the suffering of the devout man is to a large measure based on his having to express the essentially Christian in this world, for it is precisely this that brings about his suffering—at the hands of men. That suffering is the mark of relationship to God is also seen in the fact that the more ardently one holds to God, the more authentically he expresses the essentially Christian in this world, this world will oppose him all the more.

X^4 A 611 *n.d.*, 1852

« 4690 *God Is Love—What It Means To Die to the World* 964

[*In margin:* See p. 181 etc. (i.e., x⁴ A 630).]

Believe it, be convinced of it (yet you cannot stick to it by yourself alone, but just persist and you will find that the Spirit is sure to come to your aid), and when everything goes against you and there is continual suffering and new suffering, be assured that this is God's love, and that it is because God is love.

How can this be and why? Because God in infinite love wants to help you so that you may be able to love him.

Therefore you must die to the world, and this is his aim with suffering, because without dying to the world you can never love God. It will be sheer agony for you—but consider what infinite love, that God in love wants to help you to love him so that you can be genuinely blessed in this love, which is possible only when you die to the world!

The fact of the matter is that man does not love spontaneously, naturally. Even though one perhaps speaks in flaming words about loving God, upon closer examination you will find that his relationship to God is essentially egotistic—he loves God because he sends him good earthly gifts or because he still hopes that he will send them soon. He loves God because he hopes that God will steer sufferings away from him or soon end them. But is this loving God, or is God in this sense love? When suffering comes in earnest, the natural man must despair and come to the conclusion: God is not love.

So everything goes well. At first a person lives in the spontaneous, natural condition. Perhaps God showers him with benefactions; he is successful in everything, etc. He feels so happy and fortunate that he as yet merely needs the joy of thanking God, of saying to himself: It is God's love; yes, God is love.

Then there awakens in him an urge to love God anew, something God also requires in the Law.

God, who sees into the heart, looks to see whether he honestly means this. Let us suppose that God finds this integrity. Then God, infinite love, says: Well, now I shall in infinite love help this man to love me. Alas, the man himself, however genuine his urge to love God, hardly understood himself; otherwise he would hardly have dared venture out, for what must happen, without which he cannot come to love God, is the change from the natural man to spirit, and this path goes through dying to the world, and to die to the world is prodigiously painful.

Let us suppose that by searching Scripture this man gradually becomes aware that to love God cannot be done except through dying to the world. He makes one attempt after the other, but the pain is so great that he cannot.

But God, who is infinite love, has compassion for him and says to himself: Very well, I shall help him.

See, this is the purpose of suffering! O, he does not understand it this way immediately, for if he understood it this way immediately he would not begin to die to the world.

But then comes the Spirit and witnesses with him that it is all intended to help him be able to love God. For only one who is dead to the world can become happy by loving God. If you have not died to the world, your relationship to God will be sheer suffering, the suffering of a bad conscience. The Spirit will prompt you to do this, now that, out of love to God, in order to serve his cause, to witness to his kingdom. O, but you cannot, for you are not dead to the world and therefore are bound in all earthly respects: you do not dare break with that influential man, and you do not dare relinquish this or that, and you do not dare expose yourself to the possibility of suffering want, etc. And this will press upon you continually as a bad conscience. Frightful suffering—you will have become involved with God but only in such a way that he has become a burden to you. You will feel unceasingly a prompting to express your love—but you cannot; you dare not venture either this or that, for you are bound by earthly considerations.

So God in infinite love has compassion for you—because he loves you!—and he presses down heavily with suffering in order that you may go through, through death.

Why would he do this? Yes, while it lasts you are almost inclined to doubt that God is love—but only hold on—then comes the Spirit and witnesses with your spirit that it was love, that it was intended to make you able to have genuine joy in your relationship to God.

But take care that you do not get all mixed up, that now that you have come through such a radical cure you do not revert again to recognizing God's love by the earthly goods he sends and the sufferings he averts. No, no, then it would not be a spirit-relationship, then loving God would not amount to anything, that which out of infinite love he had intended for you.

Believe, then, that it is so, that suffering is love, that its intention is to help you to die to the world—and that you then can come to a blessed understanding with God as love.

That suffering is supposed to be punishment is, after all, both a cowardly and a conceited idea. Even if you were such a great sinner, do you think that you are so important to God that he would have a kind of satisfaction in punishing you? No, no, the situation is completely different. God punishes the ungodly simply by ignoring them. This is why they have success in the world—the most frightful punishment, because in God's view this world is immersed in evil, because this time is the time of grace, something the ungodly, because of their sheer prosperity, never become aware of. But God sends suffering to those whom he loves, as assistance to enable them to become happy by loving him.

X^4 A 620 *n.d.*, 1852

« 4691 *An Eternal Blessedness*

An author[965] has declared that to expect punishment is to suffer punishment; but is it also true that to expect blessedness is to be blessed?

This is what Christianity believes; in spite of the fact that the life of the true Christian in this world is sheer suffering, yet the expectation of an eternal blessedness is already a blessing.

X^4 A 623 *n.d.*, 1852

« 4692 *Suffering as the Mark of the God-Relationship or of God's Love*

[*In margin:* See p. 159 etc. (i.e., X^4 A 120).]

This thought—Christianity's really essential thought—which in a certain sense is also the most fearful of all to a poor human being (consequently it is also the thought by which one dies to the world)[966] is in another sense so extremely glorious that as a kind of intoxication it has also had a very corrupting influence. Therefore it is true here as everywhere in practicing Christianity: caution, but always return to the same.

It is easy to see that this thought can be dangerous. If suffering is the token of the God-relationship, then the individual could (stoically) want to dare God, so to speak, to send suffering so that he could prove to God that he would manage to love God just the same. This is presumptuous and is as remote as possible from being the fear of God, for it is an egotism which impudently wants to compete, as it were, with God. —On the other hand, one could become so anxious and afraid because suffering is the sign of the God-relationship that he would not dare let himself become involved in the relationship, since it would seem as if he would be daring God to continue the suffering. Therefore a person could become so anxious and afraid that he would scramble back from this thought (which is still truly Christian) to that which is really not Christianity but only an approximation of Christianity.

Therefore the following ought to be noted. (1) One must never ask for suffering. No, just keep on in the sphere of praying for good days in the earthly sense. If one asks for suffering, then it is as if he succeeded all by himself in resolving this fearful thing—that suffering is the very token of God's love. And this is precisely what he cannot do; it is "the Spirit" which witnesses with him that it is true; consequently he must not himself have asked for the suffering. In any case, to ask for suffering has to be understood in such a way that one also asks for "the Spirit," so that he does not ask for suffering in and for itself but for suffering as the condition for discerning the witness of the Spirit. Yet this also is so high that caution must be used, and there must be frequent resting in lower forms.

(2) You most certainly ought to venture, for to venture (for truth, etc.) is specifically Christian. But nevertheless you shall not for the present venture in such a way that it is not humanly possible for you to see it through, humanly speaking. This means that there is the possibility of coming to grief as well as the possibility of seeing it through.

But if, humanly speaking and understood, suffering is not to be avoided and you understand yourself before God in wanting to and being obliged to venture—yet suffering must never itself be the τέλος —you must not venture in order to get suffering, for this is presumptuously tempting God. To want to lay yourself open to suffering for the sake of suffering is presumptuous personal indiscretion and impertinence toward God, as if you would challenge God to a competition. No, but when it is a cause—even though you see that the suffering is, humanly speaking, unavoidable—go on venturing. You are not venturing in order to get suffering; you are venturing in order not to betray the cause.

X^4 A 630 *n.d.*, 1852

« 4693 *Leniency—Rigorousness*

The leniency we show others is often but a reflex of self-coddling. We dare not think of a single other person's going to hell—how lenient —but perhaps this is to avoid applying this terrifying thought to ourselves.—We do not have the heart to blurt out: To be Christian means to suffer; no one has been a true Christian who has not suffered for the doctrine—how lenient, but perhaps this is to save ourselves, for if we blurted it out our contemporaries would think and act accordingly: Well, whether or not being a Christian means to suffer, as far as you are concerned we will certainly see to it that you get to suffer—and perhaps (if it is to be taken so literally!) one would not be quite so ready to admit that to be a Christian is to suffer.

x^4 A 643   *n.d.*, 1852

« 4694 *Suffering as the Sign of the God-Relationship*

It is impossible to avoid suffering if you choose not to be prudent and practical, if you choose to take your stand with God, and then there is the added suffering that men utilize this very suffering to prove that you are in God's disfavor, that you are being punished for your pride, as they say, because good luck and prosperity are usually considered to be proofs of the God-relationship.

In a certain sense this is dreadful. But do not ask yourself if you have courage for this, for then you will not be able to do it. You must say to yourself: The question is not whether I have the courage or not, as if it were left up to me to decide—no, I *must;* and then the Spirit witnesses with my spirit.

x^4 A 660   *n.d.*, 1852

« 4695 *It Is Blessed To Suffer*

This is how the world reasons: When a man ventures out so far that he comes to suffer and does not have the courage to say truthfully: It is blessed to suffer, the world says of him: It is a crazy thing for him to do. Or it says: Maybe it is because he is so afraid of God, he does not dare do anything else—and then the world scoffs at it.

If, however, someone comes along who with personal truth dares say: It is blessed to suffer, the world goes stark raving mad; nothing, nothing incites a world so much as this. For the fact that there are those who come to suffer that is, against their will, and then find it anything but blessed to suffer—this the world is able to understand and have sympathy for, because this, after all, is how the world itself interprets enjoying life—since the one who suffers against his will and finds it an unhappy experience actually is a hedonist, in agreement with the world. But that "suffering is supposed to be blessed" is, after all, a shocking thing, says the world. It is mutiny against the world's whole theory of enjoyment. This is why the world becomes so embittered that it says: Well, in any case we will surely see to it that he gets to suffer.

Nothing upsets the world so frightfully as this ultimate in bold confidence, this inversion, that it is blessed to suffer.

A witness to the truth who does walk into danger (and therefore is really a witness), but reluctantly, does not embitter the world so much and is let off on easier terms.

Luther really gives the impression of being a bit reluctant; he says he dares not do otherwise, but he does not say: It is blessed to suffer. In a quite different way Socrates[967] creates bitterness, for he expresses complete tranquillity, complete disinterest in whether it pleases the people to condemn him or not. As for the apostles! They went away rejoicing—because they had been flogged, because they had enjoyed the honor of being whipped—nothing more is really needed to know in advance that they are certain to die—it is a shocking shame, says the world, in fact, this means a rejection of the solidarity and community of language and ideas with us: ergo, let them die.

x^4 A 670   *n.d.,* 1852

« 4696 *The Christian Formula*

The Christian formula is: to relate to something higher in such a way that the relation becomes suffering.

Everyone who relates himself to something or other that is higher (even if this is not Christianity) in such a way that he suffers for it has something similar to Christianity, but, of course, it is not Christianity, because for Christianity it is required that the higher something is marked by suffering for it, not in such a way that a person accidentally, against his will, comes to suffer for it, but in such a way that a person himself freely understands that the relation is and is only a suffering for it, that otherwise one is not related to it.

The secular mentality (the opposite of Christianity) reverses the relation: one relates to a higher something—to get profit from it, or one relates to something higher in order *also* to have profit from it. This is the secular mentality. It is easy to see that this turns the relation around, that the higher actually becomes the lower, for when the lower relates to the higher in order to profit from the relation, then the lower is actually higher than the higher from which one wishes to profit, consequently higher than the higher. It is the same when a person relates to a higher in such a way that he wants to profit *also.*

The essentially Christian is *the* higher which continually reflects itself *inversely.* Any higher which reflects itself directly is not Christian. The reason that the essentially Christian must reflect itself inversely is that finitude and infinitude, time and eternity, from a Christian point of view, are qualitatively heterogeneous; the infinite is anything but a superlative or the most superlative superlative of the finite.

But all the sophistry in the Christian domain—and right at present everything in the Christian domain is sophistry—consists of substituting directness for inversion. Thus the essentially Christian becomes a *direct* development of the natural, the human, and all the existential qualifications which express inversion and make it fast—namely, dying to the world, renunciation, rebirth, suffering for the doctrine, etc.—disappear, and so we get secular formulas: to relate to Christianity in order to profit from it or in such a way that one has profit from it *also;* yes, we not only get these formulas, but they become Christianity, and the good old Christianity becomes—a ridiculous, awkward exaggeration.

X^5 A 11 *n.d.,* 1852

« **4697** *The Proportions of Christianity*

Klædeboderne[968]
October 7, 1852

Christianity is the glad news for those who suffer, not that the suffering will stop but that suffering is the mark of the God-relationship. (But Christianity is not an accompaniment to the enjoyment of life.)

Consequently those who suffer are the ones to whom the glad news is to be proclaimed.

In order, then, that "the teachers" in Christianity may have authority, in conformity with those who suffer they should have *voluntarily* risked suffering. (Thus the voluntary is not required of those to whom the gospel is proclaimed but of the teachers.)

This is not observed at all, and therefore Christianity (the glad news for those who suffer) has really reached the point that the sufferers are not benefitted at all, but rather that one ingratiates himself with the fortunate and the powerful by preaching to them a cozy Christianity. This is what the "teachers" are doing since preaching Christianity is their career.

$X^5 A 28$ October 7, 1852

« 4698 *The Christian—The Human*

According to purely human conceptions it is quite natural to think that being beloved of God would just have to mean that everything comes your way. But this is precisely the view the devil in the story of the temptation [*Fristelsens*][969] wants to entice Jesus with, "that God will give his angels charge of him, and he will not strike his foot on any stone." But Christ rejects this as a temptation.

The Christian view is this: to be God's beloved means to suffer most of all.

Consequently the essentially Christian is ranked according to the God-relationship: the closer to God the more suffering.

$X^5 A 30$ *n.d.*, 1852

« 4699 *The Last Battle*

To those magnificent men there came the final suffering, the most terrible of all: strength ebbs away and God, too, forsakes them. It now becomes quite obvious to every contemporary pharisee, every grocery clerk, that is, to all contemporaries, that the man was a fool, "as the outcome of his life shows," and he himself is devoid of strength and forsaken by God and must suffer this final humiliation, the last, in which God puts him to the test to see whether he will still hold fast to God.

So it has been with all of them, beginning with him who on the cross, surrounded by the scorn and mockery of his gloating-in-victory contemporaries, in a way had to admit they were right and say: My God, my God, why hast thou forsaken me.[970] So it has been with them all. If one wants to cite Luther, it must be pointed out that Luther, after all, turned off into worldliness and really was victorious in a secular sense and consequently did not reach the point of running the last lap, something for which at the very end of his life he upbraided himself, wondering whether he should not have gone to Rome and been put to death instead of permitting himself to be a protégé of secularity. If he had done that, this final suffering would have come to him, also. But honest Luther, in spite of all his integrity, nevertheless perhaps became an occasion for the prodigious confusion which has confounded Protestantism: mistaking secular victory for godly victory.

Terrible suffering! I just cannot conceive of it otherwise than that such a sufferer is with God's help still able to hold fast, that this suffering is not the truth, that it is the last spiritual trial [*Anfægtelse*], that it is just one last suffering hour to go through and then he has God again forever, eternally victorious, so that this very suffering also belongs to the consummate victory. But, nevertheless, nevertheless terrible!

If one has no other notion of Christianity than that it is related to the enjoyment of life, he can of course very easily be communicative, zealous in winning others. To invite others [971] when there is something to be gained is just as easy as falling off a log. But if one understands that it is suffering, sheer suffering—then divine authority and faith are needed to be able quite calmly to invite others. It can be hard enough for me to stay with the suffering and not jump out of the way—but I really do not have the strength then to invite others. My situation is such that I really do not dare have anyone understand what suffering there must be, how I am suffering (I, who compared with the magnificent men, suffer only in a childish way), for then I think that everyone will be afraid of me and anxious. But how divine—to invite men to sheer suffering and agony—truly this assures one of the rightness of his cause —it is divine!

x^5 A 38 *n.d.*, 1852

« **4700** *The Christian Difficulty,* ANGUSTIAE[972]

As a Christian you do want to refer everything to God; it is truly your deep desire to be loved by God and to love God.

Pick up the New Testament, especially the gospels. What does it say? It teaches: the more you devote yourself to God the more certain it is that you will come to suffer in this world; this is how it went with his beloved son, so also with the apostles, and so, it is prophesied, will it go with all true Christians.

You are suffering. Alas, to whom shall a person flee but to God? O, but here it comes: the more you become involved with God, the more certain is the suffering. You wanted God's help to get rid of suffering—and suffering came right along with the God-relationship.

Without concerning ourselves with how it happened, let us assume that you did get rid of the suffering, that you conquered—is it not true that your deepest, most inward need would be to turn to God in gratitude, overflowing with thankfulness. Alas, and here it comes again, according to the New Testament God might answer you: Well, my friend, you are not to thank me for this, because you know that according to the New Testament victory in this world is to be understood as a sign that I have not had a hand in it.

For according to the New Testament the relationship is thus: the pagan will not suffer at all; the Jew will endure a few years of it but will nevertheless be victorious in this world and enjoy this life; the Christian will suffer all his life.

Then, true enough, the New Testament teaches that the Christian will receive a spirit which will make the suffering a blessing to him.

As I have noted earlier in this journal [i.e., x^5 A 72], I am brought to a stop by this difficulty; my praying is not as before but is more a quiet surrendering to God, that it might become clear to me in what sense "grace" is to apply.

According to the New Testament to be genuinely a Christian means to be sacrificed. The apostle rushes forward in order to halt; there is, he witnesses, one sacrifice, once and for all; no more sacrifices are needed—and in order to proclaim this properly he is—sacrificed. Thereupon thousands and thousands of martyrs are sacrificed in order to get this properly proclaimed, that no further sacrifices are needed. The New Testament even prophesies that every true Christian will be sacrificed in one way or another.

If Christ has been sacrificed once and for all in the sense that I now —instead of imitating, for then I would also become sacrificed—have the right to plunge aggressively into preoccupation with finite interests and enjoying life—then the apostle existentially has made a big mistake and so have all the early Christians—and only the Christendom of our age has hit upon the right way.

To repeat, I am brought to a stop right here. At present I can only say: Imitation must nevertheless at least be introduced, brought to mind, so that a person can rightly feel how much he needs "grace." The fact that we are completely silent about the requirement of "imitation" has altogether demoralized Christendom. We go on living as if a respectable life, a social morality were the requirement. And to this we apply "grace"! What wonder, then, that men finally get tired of this drivel about grace, for they regard themselves—and some of them legitimately so—as righteous already.

Furthermore, is it honest to apply "grace" as a round figure without prompting men to become genuinely aware of what is being given them by "grace." If someone were deeply in debt—suppose that a family had inherited an enormous debt and therefore did not really know how large it was—and someone else paid the whole thing—would it not be ungrateful not to want to have the slightest interest in knowing the size of the debt in order at least to be properly grateful, would it be a fine thing to prefer slipping out of it, the sooner the better, with a conventional "thank you" to the other person for having paid the entire debt. Is there no distinction between a debt of four shillings and one of millions? In a situation where one has no idea of how he can possibly make repayment, is it not genuine gratitude to bear in mind the size of the debt as honestly as possible?

Alas, but we do not dare dwell upon the idea of "imitation" even enough to become conscious of what we have been exempted from—if it is true—"by grace." No, no, away with every thought and reminder of "imitation"—we have grace.

Strangely enough, however, men have finally become quite bored by all the drivel about grace so that they really long for a little rigor.

Yet here we have the same difficulty—that it does not reverse itself or change.

x^5 A 81   n.d., 1853

« **4701** *To Be the Extraordinary—The Collision of Sympathy*

This is usually given the following turn: it must be wonderful to be the extraordinary, in any case sometime in eternity after having endured all the sufferings—therefore one merely has to warn against the conceitedness and arrogance which want to be the extraordinary without truly being that.

Here is another turn, in the direction of the collision of sympathy.

Think of someone granted the extraordinary. Now for the first time comes the moment when, after having first comprehended the fascination of being the extraordinary, he understands that it is not quite so simple, that it gets to be sheer and utter suffering for this life.

Let us now assume that he holds out, that he has seen it through. What then? Then eternity opens up before him, the reward awaits, the prize of victory.

Here, it seems to me, comes the collision. It simply cannot be denied that the N.T., especially the gospels, pictures the true followers of Christ as being unlike all the others in eternity. Is this not an excruciating pain? Let him have sympathy, really love being man, really love men just as they are generally, and perhaps a particular individual in a very special way—what an excruciating agony to become unlike them in the eternalness of eternity—and in such a way that a greater blessing falls upon him!

With what dreadful accuracy Christianity knows how to describe the loving God! For here the collision will appear in its most painful form, so that it is almost as if the very blessedness, Christianity's supreme promise, must necessarily be ruined for a person, because to love God seems to mean to hate father, mother, to hate being a human being.

Allow me to speak quite humanly about it. I do not make myself out to be better than I am; I am, after all, a paltry poet, but perhaps, perhaps—it is still not impossible that a transformation could take place in me so that I would find the courage and enthusiasm actually to endure sufferings in this world, to venture out into sufferings as do those who measure up to being the extraordinary—what then? As I see it now, be that a bias or whatever, the next thing, that which Christianity promises as a reward, that is the very thing I would be most afraid of—that for a whole eternity I would be blessed *differently* than other men are.

The New Testament, especially the gospels, clearly promises a more exalted blessedness to both the apostles and the disciples, and above all to those who suffer for the teaching—but men do not ordinarily live in this way, and suppose now that I humanly loved men as they ordinarily are and that there was one among them I loved in particular, loved as much as I loved myself—then I could not wish to become blessed *differently* than he is throughout eternity!

What I have observed earlier someplace in a journal [i.e., VIII¹ A 271, X² A 279] is nevertheless true—that the last leg of the race always has the characteristic mark that all the collisions are in the area of sympathy. In the earlier stage the collisions are in the area of danger to oneself.

x^5 A 85   *n.d.,* 1853

« 4702 *To Be Willing To Suffer—To Want To Have the Assistance of Men*

Is this not really the meaning of Christianity: to live is to be examined, in eternity comes the judgment, and in the judgment there will be among other things the question: Have you suffered for the teaching—but why all the bustle to get the assistance of men;[973] I must rather take care to prevent it, lest it possibly result in my scoring a success with the help of men instead of suffering and thereby place me in an awkward situation on judgment day when I am asked the question: Have you suffered for the teaching?

The first Christians understood it in this way, and therefore they actually did come to suffer and were able to carry Christianity through. But the person who says, even though he says it honestly: I am willing to suffer, and then adds: But I will not disdain the help of men, will end up, you will see, without having suffered—in order not to disdain human assistance, or, as they will soon say, in order not to be guilty of responsibility for disdaining the help of men, or as they will soon say, in order not to be guilty of the ungodliness of disdaining the help of men; he will eventually, perhaps without really knowing himself how it happens, alter his cause somewhat (to get the help of men more readily), and when his cause thus becomes less true, he of course wins the support of men, and thus becomes less and less true, and he naturally wins the support of men to an ever greater degree, he scores a victory, hurrah—and the whole thing gets to be even worse than if it fizzled out.

No, as the first Christians understood it, they saw it through. And the very moment such a person came to be humanly discouraged because he was obliged to say to himself—if you go that far out, you will not get the help of men, precisely then he was strengthened by the thought: the cause is such that if human help is offered to you, you had better think twice about accepting it, for suffering has value in and for itself, and this is what the question will be about.

This is how the first Christians understood it. For us today, coddled as we are by being Christians and spoiled from childhood by Christian sweets, it would be ever so hard, and the person who has set himself to it seriously would acquire the enormous burden that he in a sense makes the others into hypocrites because they call themselves Christians (this was not the situation in the first period of Christianity, since the others were pagans)—therefore I believe that God, at least for the present, will not call us to account more severely than to demand that it be recognized.

X^5 A 114   *n.d.*, 1853

« **4703** *A Rough Estimate*

..... You are now thirty years old; you still have perhaps forty years to live, perhaps only ten, perhaps only a day.

You can fill up this time with becoming just like the others, nice, amiable people, above all with whatever counts in having advantages in life, with whatever suggests pleasure, and also with whatever danger frightens the others away—that is, with flight together—let us assume that you succeed in making this kind of life for yourself (for it is of course possible that in spite of all your zeal and effort you could fail): and then you die.

You desire, of course, to be saved. Far be it from me, who am without authority,[974] to doubt it. Consequently I take it for granted. But have you ever pondered this—I wonder if it is really true what the gushing preachers assure us, that "in eternity there is sheer joy and happiness"—I can go along with the pastor on that, but do you believe that "every suffering and pain is forgotten"? I do not. The New Testament makes the very specific exception of one suffering: having suffered for the truth. Or do you believe that Christ's suffering is forgotten in eternity. Neither is the suffering of his witnesses forgotten (a terrible injustice if it were!). No, the very memory and the remembering of this (divine justice!) is precisely the glory of these magnificent ones.

And you are going to live together with these glorious ones for eternity, you who, I dare say, were put to the test in buying and selling, were experienced in desire and indulgences, deftly avoiding danger and loss (something your contemporaries could not admire enough) —and thereby avoiding suffering, even so much as a little bit, for the truth!

Consequently an eternity in this heavenly company and seventy years at the most, perhaps only ten, perhaps only a day in this earthly company. Was it by judicious calculation, then, that you decided to choose to conform to this earthly company in order not to be conspicuous here—thereby making sure of being conspicuous for all eternity?

XI^2 A 297 *n.d.*, 1853–54

« **4704** *Persecution*

In our times there is no persecution at all—for Christianity has been made so completely devoid of character that there is really nothing to persecute.

In the Middle Ages persecution was prevented by making genuine renunciation the extraordinary which found satisfaction in letting itself be admired. But then again there is nothing to persecute. Only when unconditioned renunciation is quite simply made the ordinary, that which is required of everyone, only then does it goad to persecution. For the world wishes to be rid of the unconditioned, but it can achieve this in two ways: by admiring or by persecuting. When unconditioned renunciation makes a compromise—whereby, as a matter of fact, it ceases to be unconditioned renunciation—and accepts admiration, persecution falls by the wayside.

XI^1 A 8 *n.d.*, 1854

« **4705 *Increasing Villainy***

With the increase of villainy in the use of poisons, powerfully acting poisons were discarded and slow-acting poisons were cowardly invented; so, too, the world has now discovered how to kill men by a kind of mistreatment which destroys gradually, as if it were nothing. O, depth of villainy!

XI^1 A 9 *n.d.*, 1854

« **4706 *An Error in Judgment***

This is the way we men conceive of it (I know this from my own experience).

Even if a man is himself conscious of being a great sinner, he is told: Just believe that you are forgiven, be absolutely sure of this, God is so kind and loving; this is precisely what Christianity is. Yes, he will rejoice in the very fact that you try to enjoy life without a care, because everything, everything is forgotten, and the more you are able to express this, the more it pleases God.

And when someone is successful and everything comes his way, then we are absolutely sure that this pleases God—this Christian confidence.

O, and in Holy Scripture it is continually pointed out that those whom God loves always become unhappy, must suffer, and everything falls through for them.

XI^1 A 66 *n.d.*, 1854

« **4707 *Consolation from Others***

The Christian, of course, cannot really be consoled by anyone other than one who himself is just as tried in suffering or even more.

It is quite simple. If suffering stood in an accidental relation to the higher life, then one person leading a higher life would be spared sufferings, another would be tried in them—this is how the sophists picture it, the late lamented liar Bishop Mynster,[975] for example—well, then there would be some meaning in the Christian's letting himself be consoled by a happy man who has it easy and is pleased slap-happy about life.

But the relation is as follows: to have it easy in this world, to have no suffering, and thereby to be happy and satisfied, is achieved quite simply by—mediocrity, by avoiding every relation to spirit.

But from a Christian point of view to be consoled by such a person is nonsense; the Christian could also be consoled by a cow, which has it easy. To be consoled in this way would tend to let the higher life die out—but that would be the most tragic of all.

Consequently the Christian has consolation in only these two ways: either by consoling other sufferers himself or [through consolation by another] if there perhaps is someone tried in the same or even greater suffering, in whom the spiritual is so much stronger that he can console—console, of course, not in the direction of becoming a cow but of becoming spirit.

XI^1 A 208 n.d., 1854

« **4708** *Christianity Is So Very Elevated*

that in a certain sense it could be a mitigation to dare interpret all suffering and anguish as punishment for one's sins. For if it is punishment for one's sins—well, then it is deserved and in this there is no definitional difference between what it is to be God and what it is to be man. Furthermore, there is, after all, a chance, yes, a certainty, that it may be changed, especially and perhaps all the more quickly the more patiently one suffers the punishment.

But from a Christian point of view the anguish signifies that one is loved by God—consequently there can be no thought or mention here of any change, any termination in time. From a Christian point of view there is a definitional difference between what it is to be God and what it is to be man. What frightful exertion and sharpening, which in one sense intensifies the agony.

XI^1 A 311 n.d., 1854

« **4709** *The Christian Requirement*

What Christianity continually points toward is this: to suffer for the teaching, to suffer at the hands of men.

When fasting and the like are universal (consequently something rated high by men), then, strictly speaking, it is not essentially Christian to fast etc.

No, the characteristically Christian suffering is to suffer at the hands of men. This is consistent with the Christian view that to love

God is to hate the world or that there is hostility between God and men.⁹⁷⁶

xi¹ A 340   n.d., 1854

« 4710 *If Your Righteousness Does Not Exceed That of the Scribes and the Pharisees*⁹⁷⁷

I understand "the more" here to mean suffering for the teaching, suffering for the good one does, suffering at the hands of men.

Consequently one perceives that the asceticism of the Middle Ages, with its direct recognizability, is not the Christian requirement. Christianity constantly points toward suffering at the hands of men, doing the good and then suffering at the hands of men, because Christianity breathes in this context—there is hatred between God and men.⁹⁷⁸

xi¹ A 350   n.d., 1854

« 4711 *The Turn Which Leads Away from Christianity*

As soon as this variation makes its appearance: he (Christ) has suffered and now the rest of us will have it easy, Christianity is *eo ipso* altered and is transposed from what it is in the New Testament (to be a Christian is to suffer, is to be martyred) into this human villainy: to let one person or a few be martyred agonizingly—in order that the others can have it easy. The animal nature, the bestiality of man really sticks out clearly in this invention.

Consequently as soon as we get this variation: he has suffered—and now the rest of us will have it easy, Christianity is altered. Seen this way, it becomes a question to what extent even what is commonly understood about the martyrs and blood-witnesses was in the strictest sense essentially Christian suffering. For one thing it must be remembered, as I have often emphasized [i.e., xi¹ A 340, 350, 352], that when one lives surrounded by men who sanction, yes, admiringly acknowledge this going to one's death, then it really is not Christian suffering; Christian suffering always involves the unfavorable judgment of men; thus, for example, it would be Christian suffering to go to one's death ridiculed by the surrounding world, which regards it as foolishness to risk one's life for such things. For another thing, the question must be asked: What was these martyrs' last thought? If it was that they wanted to have it easy in this world and believed that to be Christian meant to have it easy in this world but a hostile outside world would not permit it but persecuted them—if this was how they understood martyrdom, then this was really not Christian suffering.

No, New Testament Christianity (it is the Christianity of Jesus Christ, for the apostle has already altered it somewhat) is pervaded with the thought: there is a life and death battle between God and man; God hates man just as man hates God.[979] Consequently if you want to be loved by God and to love God (and this is what it is to be a Christian), you must come to be despised, cursed, etc. (see the New Testament). And God hates this whole existence [*Tivœrelse*], a sinful falling away from him and insurrection against him—to be Christian will therefore mean that you will be tortured in every way possible. The best would be that you yourself voluntarily be inexhaustibly imaginative in inventing means of torturing yourself, but should you not be that strong—assuming that there is some truth in you, that you hate yourself—then you dare hope that God will have mercy on you and help you to come to suffer.

This, then, is Christianity. We humans are fooled by having no idea of the scale on which God squanders millions and trillions.

But man—O, if you want to learn to know infamy, then study man! —man takes delight in the brutish cruelty of one person being martyred agonizingly in order that all the rest of us will have it easy.

No, no, no! To be Christian is to be martyred—this enormous annex of trillions and quadrillions who unblushingly eat, drink, beget children, clink their glasses etc., all cheerfully in the understanding that others have had to groan in extreme agony—this annex, from a Christian point of view, is a mistake.

XI¹ A 357 *n.d.*, 1854

« **4712** *The Christian Meaning of Life*

is—to suffer. Yes, whether it pleases men or not, the meaning of life, in the Christian view, is neither to amass money nor to beget children nor to become somebody, and so on—but it is to suffer.

This can easily be seen: only in suffering can the eternal come in contact with the temporal in time: only in suffering can spirit come in contact with worldliness in worldliness.

What there is of the eternal in a human being or whether there is any of the eternal in him is known by his desire or willingness to suffer. Just as one knows that an insect wants to become a butterfly when it begins to spin a cocoon, and a physician can tell that a woman is pregnant by what she requires of food and drink, so, too, whether and to what extent the eternal is within a person is known by—willingness to suffer. The spouting of the swindlers is, of course, only a new swindle. But how odd to want to make oneself and others believe something regarding the eternal when there is an eternity in which to regret that one fooled himself by not earnestly making use of time.

XI^1 A 377 *n.d.*, 1854

« 4713 *Suffering——and Suffering*

What is commonly understood by suffering is one thing; the kind of suffering which means that a man has to do with God is something else.

Yet the religious person must put up with the humiliation of having the surrounding world take pity on him because of his suffering without suspecting that this kind of suffering is a distinction which kings and majesties do not have.

Yes, O God, you certainly are able to play a game with a poor man! You take him captive as no one else can—but you are, after all, invisible, and any practical man readily understands that one is a fool to involve himself with an invisible person who cannot, in case of need, be forced to appear in court and from whom one has nothing in writing.

But away with that—the testimony, your testimony in the inward self easily counterbalances all that. Alas, but you go further. You take a man captive unto yourself—and then, then you actually trick him, you bring him to the point where everything demonstrates that you have tricked him and he is loudly ridiculed for having been tricked—yes, so that he himself—the final humiliation!—must say: God has abandoned me.

True, it is only a transition, infinite love, infinite love, it is only a transition, you eternally faithful one, but nevertheless it is bitter and full of anxiety—who knows this better than you, infinite love, you who thereby suffer still more in love than this suffering one, although you cannot for that reason be changed.

XI^1 A 404 *n.d.*, 1854

« 4714 *Speaking in Tongues*

To have understood and at all times to have to experience the truth that to be loved by God and to love God is sheer torment and suffering—and then still be able to keep up one's courage so that with full voice one can say *ex animi sententia*:[980] It is blessed, which it is in fact in the highest sense—yes, this is what it is to speak in tongues.

This is how the apostle speaks. The whole prevailing confusion comes from taking these words literally, leaping over the dialectical aspect, that it is sheer torment and suffering.

XI^1 A 413 *n.d.*, 1854

« **4715** *Another Way of Looking at Christianity*

Christianity is what God has to suffer with us human beings.

This is to be understood in the following way. The beloved naturally understands that being loved means that the lover is changed according to the beloved's will and conception; a lover understands that loving means being changed into likeness to the beloved, becoming what the beloved wishes or wants him to be.

If it may be put this way, there is a contradiction in God which is the source of all the agony. He is love and yet he is eternally unchangeable. Consequently he cannot be changed—and yet he is love. Consequently in a sense he must make the beloved unhappy—and yet he is love.

To be love and at the same time to be unchangeable in such a way that there is no possibility of sparing the beloved—no, unchanged—seeing everything pile up against him, seeing him forsaken, hated, persecuted, without helping him—and still to be love.

When Christ cried out, "My God, my God, why have you forsaken me,"[981] it was terrible for Christ, and this is the way it is usually presented. But it seems to me it would have been still more terrible for God to hear it. To be unchangeable in this way—terrible! But, no, this is not what is terrible, but to be unchangeable this way and still to be love—what infinitely deep, inscrutable grief!

Alas, what I, a wretched human being, have experienced in this respect, this contradiction of not being able to change and yet to love—alas, what I have experienced helps me in a very remote way to get a faint notion of this suffering of divine love.

XI^1 A 422 *n.d.*, 1854

« **4716** *Sympathy*

If the law is: the highest can be achieved only in the utmost suffering, then it follows as a matter of course that sympathy for such a sufferer is a mistake. For if such a sympathizer is suffering less, then the one who is suffering more ought to sympathize with him, who as the one suffering less consequently only achieves less.

XI^1 A 433 *n.d.*, 1854

« 4717 *The Apostle——Propagation*

The reason the apostles could intensify propagation [of Christianity] and without Christian risk [*Risico*] was that there were so few of them and the world had such enormously superior power that suffering for the doctrine (which is indeed part of Christianity) was unavoidable.

"Christendom" is rubbish. The method must be changed; offense and repulsion must be used continuously.

XI^1 A 493 *n.d.*, 1854

« 4718 *Prudence——Christianity*

Christianity has come to a stop and is stuck fast in "prudence." This is what we have to get through.

Christianity puts it this way: Suffering belongs to being a Christian —eternity judges.

The prudence of the human race has discovered the possibility of teaching Christianity objectively, having Christianity, being Christian —and also prudently avoiding suffering. And man is not just a little proud of this prudence—an enormous advance has been made.

And so it will continue—until man learns that since eternity has given a certain shape to being a Christian and suffering is part of the condition of salvation—then the most prudent thing may just be to get a chance to suffer.

O, shortsighted human prudence—everlastingly fooling itself. No, when God has decreed something, the smartest thing to do is to do what he wants.

XI^1 A 494 *n.d.*, 1854

« 4719 *The Extraordinary*

It is one thing to be a so-called extraordinary with *direct* recognizability (that is, the spurious extraordinary), getting along fine with all the relativities that participate in that which is merely the maximum of their range and on that basis interpret the extraordinary's behavior as the extraordinary.

It is something quite different to be the true extraordinary, who relates *inversely*, explodes the relativities, which therefore defend themselves with all their might against him—the true extraordinary who explodes existence [*Tilværelsen*], so that in this case the extraordinary is inversely recognizable by being that which is ridiculed, cast off etc., and the life of the extraordinary one is sheer wretchedness and suffering. When this is so, it actually would be a relief quite simply to be allowed to be merely the most miserable and wretched of all—exempted from being the most extraordinary, for under such conditions to have to sustain being the extraordinary is merely a new sharpening of the suffering,[*] since it must, after all, make an impact on him when he lets himself for a moment actually be affected by his surroundings as if he were a buck private and consequently could harbor the desire of daring to keep it secret that he was the extraordinary. Furthermore, to be declared a madman has an overwhelming effect upon him.

Take the supreme example, take Christ![982] To stand as he did—and then to say: I am indeed a king! Truly those are the proudest words ever spoken, and the very situation makes them so; but looked at from another side I believe that it took a kind of surmounting of the situation to say it, that it would have been easier to remain silent, resting in his own consciousness of himself; therefore I assume it was said because he owed it to the idea to say it. But it is easy to overlook how loathsome it must be for someone to have to say of himself: I am indeed a king, when the world of appearances (the phenomenal world) is against one in this way. But the idea requires it.

What child's play is everything one generally reads about human misery and suffering compared to the horrible combination of intense agonies bound up with having to be the extraordinary!

XI^1 A 541   *n.d., 1854*

« 4720

[*] *In margin of 4719* (XI^1 A 541):
It is a sharpening such as being in extreme poverty—and yet possessing substantial securities which, unrecognized in that region, are literally worthless; it is a sharpening, for it is easier simply to be very poor and free from possessing these securities, free from this demented kind of agony of also being enormously rich.

XI^1 A 542   *n.d.*

« 4721 *Theme: "Show me clearly my miseries and troubles"*[983]

—that is, show me how meaningless and empty are all those things I call my miseries and troubles

—and show me what my miseries and troubles truly are.

But here it is again. It is evident that Christianity does not fit us human beings very neatly. For we imagine (and this is Christianity in

Christendom) that we very readily know what our own miseries and troubles are—and that Christianity, then, should help us. Christianity thinks that we must first of all get to know what our miseries and troubles are. And when Christianity then begins to talk about poverty, sickness, not being appreciated by other men, etc.—that these are not the real miseries and troubles at all, but on the contrary they are even helpful—well, then we men, humanly speaking, are not helped much.

The whole tragedy and confusion is connected with this whole scaffolding of high-ranking and highly paid clergymen and public officials, for they must, after all, proclaim Christianity to be something other than it is, for if to be a Christian is to suffer, then it does not follow that to proclaim it can become a fat living.

XI^1 A 561 *n.d.*, 1854

« **4722** *Religious Suffering*

If a brewery horse or a farm horse could only see the instruments of torture used on a circus rider's horse, it would shudder. In the same way the natural man would shudder to see the instruments of torture used for the religious suffering which goes along with becoming saved.

How thoroughly nauseating and revolting, then, the dishonesty of this brood of jovial professors and preachers who make a living—by presenting this, and then this comes to be regarded as being religious, yes, unusually deep religiousness, for the religiousness of the congregation, after all, consists of hearing this presented once in a while. Charming religiousness—just as authentic as tea made from a piece of paper which once lay in a drawer together with another piece of paper in which a few dried tea leaves had been kept, leaves which had already been used three times.[*]

Yet it is not right to complain about it, for when eternity is at stake —these professors certainly will not lie themselves into eternity, so it seems only fair to demand that they have it all the better in this world.

XI^1 A 579 *n.d.*, 1854

« **4723**

[*] *In margin of 4722* (XI^1 A 579):
Note. But if one wanted to point out the difference, it is that with respect to the tea men would say: Thank you for this, but if you have stronger tea I would be grateful for it. But with respect to Christianity man's interest is precisely in getting it as thin as possible; he is not grateful for getting it stronger but shields himself against this.

XI^1 A 580 *n.d.*

« 4724 *God-Relationship*

The sophists, of course, teach that being involved with God is sheer blessedness. In fact, the world believes that for the sake of security the best thing for it to do is to take God along in its own way —for he is a great power, and it could be dangerous to bypass him altogether. But that to be involved with God should be suffering (of which, incidentally, the sophists have a secret intimation, which accounts for their bad conscience over their syrupy lies about God) the world does not want to be aware; there are enough things to torment one in this world, and it would be crazy to get involved with God if this were the case.

It is the apostle who speaks most sublimely about the relationship to God. He is so perfect that he proclaims being involved with God to be sheer blessedness—although the apostle's life is sheer suffering.

Authentic speech about the relationship to God is that which proclaims it to be suffering.

The sophists concoct for men a syrupy nonsense about sheer and utter blessedness, make it pay handsomely—the whole thing, of course, is a lie and a swindle.

But the screams from the torture chamber (the operating room) where the religious man experiences the suffering of dying to the world—this the world does not wish to hear, it curses such a religious person. The sophist makes it over into sheer sweetness, and this is especially pleasing to the world.

XI^2 A 66   *n.d.,* 1854

« 4725 *The True Christian Collision*

occurs very simply this way: the world by no means wants to eliminate Christianity, no, the world is not that straightforward, nor does it have that much character (understood this way the atheist is a dangerous man compared with official Christianity)—no, it wants it proclaimed falsely, proclaimed as epicureanism, a refined epicureanism, using eternity to give a flavor to the enjoyment of life.

The truly religious person, of course, dares not do this at any price.

He must first of all himself learn that Christianity is suffering, anguish, a death struggle.

And then he is commanded to proclaim this, and the world becomes enraged as if he were the greatest criminal.

Thus he is forced into this double collision: God, who constrains or moves him—and the world which mistreats him because he is obedient to God.

XI² A 67 n.d., 1854

« 4726 *The Change Which Has Taken Place in Christianity Within Christendom; To Enjoy —To Suffer*

An illustration. Once upon a time learning to read was a rigorous matter for a child; it took a lot of hard work. But eventually the theory was devised that everything ought to be enjoyable. So they introduced the practice of having a little party after each quarter hour of reading, and the A, B, C's were decked out with pictures etc. Ultimately that quarter hour was also dropped, and the A, B, C's became simply a picture book. But still they went on talking about learning to read—although the child did not learn to read at all; but learning to read was understood to mean eating cookies and looking at pictures, which became an even more pleasant experience just because it was called: learning to read.

So also with the transformation of Christianity in Christendom, except that here (which is not the case in the illustration) "the teacher" is also interested in this transformation, it suits him best of all.

Christianity has been transformed from suffering to enjoying—and then this enjoyment is refined by the pretense that it is Christianity and by giving it a tinge of sanctity and earnestness.

Christianity has been transformed into the artistic—into artistic enjoyment for the listeners. And "the teacher" has transformed the proclamation into an artistic performance (in art-buildings—theaters—that is, churches) and into profit.

But in suffering to think of God, that this can be loving God, cannot be understood. But in pleasure to think of God, that this is supposed to be loving him—is actually to make a fool of him. To enjoy is to think of oneself, to dwell upon oneself, is selfishness—and to do it claiming that it is to the glory of God either degrades God to a man who must be lionized with lavish fetes and banquets, or it makes a fool of God, if one assumes that he is spirit.

XI² A 72 n.d., 1854

« 4727 *Human Sympathy*

A sufferer may perhaps have such a thought as this: My torments and sufferings are so frightful that if people were to learn about them everybody would sympathize with me. O my friend, beware of men. If it is true that your torments and sufferings are of such a nature, then see to it that people do not find out; you are in such a situation that men would become so apprehensive and so afraid of you that instead of sympathizing they would turn against you, cruelly seek to get rid of you in every way; in order not to be made apprehensive by such things they would cruelly make your sufferings your own fault, so that perhaps it would even be a "duty" to be severe with you.

Yes, Anti-Climacus[984] is right in what he says about human sympathy.

Human sympathy! Subtract from this rubric "human sympathy," subtract everything that perhaps is not actually sympathy but egotism, sympathy for what one is egotistically interested in or egotistically interested in relieving, preventing establishing, supporting; subtract from this rubric everything that perhaps is not sympathy but disguised envy; place an enormous *NB* alongside this rubric to indicate that precisely at the point of the greatest agony and torture sympathy changes even into cruelty—and now see how much sympathy there is in the world.

XI^2 A 82   n.d., 1854

« 4728 *Suffering*

To imitate is to have an authentic impression that the truth must suffer. To be able to present this or to hear or read this presented is so far removed from being an authentic impression that it is just the opposite, is epicureanism. In a much quoted passage Lucretius[985] says quite correctly that it is a pleasure to see another in the sufferings from which he himself is free.

XI^2 A 136   n.d., 1854

« 4729 *The God-Relationship as Sheer Joy, the Apostle, First-Order Christians*

When the apostle and what I would call first-order Christians picture the God-relationship or relating oneself to God as sheer joy, this is due presumably, as has often been noted, to their being so advanced, to their being masters in the art of translating suffering into bliss, masters in the art of looking away from the suffering in order to see the blessedness of its being the relationship to God and so on, but perhaps it has another basis as well. Perhaps what led them to talk this way was also a prudent solicitude for men; perhaps they were afraid of frightening men away by talking about the God-relationship as suffering.

But my question is this: Does not the history of Christendom adequately show the end results of such accommodation? No, when it is proclaimed that the relationship to God is suffering, men are more readily prompted to become aware of their own condition; on the other hand, it is far too easy to get this matter of sheer joy changed into a phrase which millions of liars declaim while not a single person becomes involved with God.

No, proclaim that Christianity is suffering—if anyone advances to the point where he actually perceives that it is sheer joy—well, then he has nothing to complain about. But proclaim that Christianity is suffering, and do not forget that only twelve apostles were found; men do not feel particularly qualified to be apostles (ambassadors), while on the other hand they all feel very well qualified to get something to gad about with, a piece of nonsense, a phrase. That Christianity is suffering can, of course, also become a phrase, but not as readily as the bit about sheer joy, which by its very rhetorical lilt is altogether suitable for falsification by those who love phrases, and if it becomes a phrase this phrase is not nearly so dangerous; to speak incessantly about Christianity as suffering and yet not to become involved with Christianity is not nearly so dangerous as talking incessantly about Christianity as sheer joy and bliss and not becoming involved with it. The former is constantly closer to an actual beginning than the latter, which is twice-removed from actually beginning.

XI^2 A 208 *n.d.*, 1854

« **4730** *The Clash (the Collision) with:*
The Others
The Specifically Christian Suffering

The suffering which the New Testament Christianity refers to specifically is suffering at the hands of men.

God wills to be loved—but conversely, loving God must come to mean that you thereby collide with men.

All the asceticism of the Middle Ages is by no means Christian suffering. This whole matter of fasting etc. as something in and for itself is of no consequence. And when the admiration of men is accepted for fasting, and therefore according to an understanding with them—this simply is not Christianity.

No, the collision man shrinks from the most, the collision with the others, not to be like the others, having to suffer because by loving God one becomes unlike the others (not the opposite—becoming honored because one loves God as the others, which is a fraudulent trick): this collision, which actually is the animal-creature's greatest suffering, is the very one Christianity heads toward.

Consequently Christianity is opposed to nothing so much as to a Christian nation, a Christian world, where inevitably all conditions for becoming a Christian are changed and the formula always remains the same: to be just like the others.

Tranquillity, an animal slothfulness in being just like the others—this is what man loves and precisely what Christianity hates.

If someone says that this idea of loving God in contrast to others cannot, after all, be carried out if we are all Christians, I reply: Do you actually believe that you can fool God with this rubbish; he knows best what the world is like and that even if he has Christianity proclaimed to all, it is pretty certain that not everybody will become Christian.

Furthermore, every man is created unique, so that if he actually loves God he will nevertheless come to a point of collision with "the others," even if all were Christians.

Finally, if you doubt that you will be kept from loving God in a contrasting way because all are Christians, then become a missionary, which every Christian really is, after all.

XI^2 A 396   *n.d., 1855*

SUICIDE

« 4731

Ewald's poem, "Advice against Suicide," is magnificent. One verse in particular:

> I wonder if the ocean waves expunge?
> I wonder if poison eats away the stamp of God?
>   Can the dagger slaughter thoughts?

See vol. I, p. 299.[986]

                              IV A 48   *n.d.*, 1843

« 4732 *A Suspicion*

Why is it that although Holy Scripture does not actually contain a definite prohibition against suicide, although significant character-philosophers allow, yes, praise it, although as far as I know no pagan religion forbids it—why, then, is it that in common daily exchange in the market and on the street suicide is spoken of again and again as cowardice.

Once more my explanation of it is that human language is thieves' slang, that what is said means something else. There is scarcely any doubt that it is precisely cowardice which restrains a goodly number of men from suicide; this is then expressed in thieves' slang: It is cowardly to take one's own life. Perhaps it is also because man snatches after every fragment of compensation—so he consoles himself by thinking that he displays courage by living—for to take one's own life is cowardly.

                              XI[1] A 269   *n.d.*, 1854

« 4733 *Suicide*

For the very reason that this life, from a Christian point of view, is a suffering of punishment and for the very reason that Christianity promises a blessed, an eternally blessed, existence when the last suffering, that of death, has been endured, it displeases God if someone arbitrarily breaks out of this existence.

443

That this life is supposed to be a great good and that consequently suicide should be regarded as reprehensible because it is ingratitude is, of course, a lie and rubbish, the swindle which the prison has invented for mutual support in the notion that it is a splendid world.

No, but for the simple reason that this life is a suffering and for the simple reason that eternal salvation awaits the one who patiently endures it, Governance is opposed to suicide.

It is the same here as when the children must wait in a dark room on Christmas Eve—precisely because the parents know how much has been done to increase their happiness and that the time is used for that purpose—for that very reason impatience is frowned upon.

XI^1 A 292   *n.d.*, 1854

SUPERIORITY

« 4734

In the intellectual sense, the benefaction and the benediction one feels in talking with someone genuinely superior intellectually, when through his observations every expression becomes enlarged, underlined, and spaced out in a competent thought, are the same as the benediction which in the religious sense made a great gift of the widow's mite in the temple offering-box.[987]

II A 477   July 14, 1839

« 4735

The plain citizen who, when he presented his poor gift (he could not afford more) to a needy person, always took off his hat and bowed as deeply as if he were his superior, as warmly as if he were his best friend.

VI A 23   n.d., 1845

« 4736

There is a certain superiority which in the situation of contemporaneity scarcely can avoid becoming the object of a certain kind of sympathy, even from those who recognize this superiority. They feel his superiority, but they also perceive that it is so totally unlike all temporal and worldly superiority that his superiority is really like impotence. Therefore they do not venture to acknowledge his superiority openly (this would set them at odds with life), but in a quiet hour they are uplifted by it.

X^3 A 61   n.d., 1850

« 4737 *Superiority's Suffering*

When a superior person uses his superiority to slacken off, or even to profit from the less clear concepts of others by deceiving them, then there is no suffering; it is natural. The suffering comes when the superior one remains faithful to the idea and has to put up with their misunderstanding—which he could so easily avoid by deceiving them.

X^3 A 429   n.d., 1850

« 4738 *The essentially Christian always has, first, lowliness—and then, second, a paradoxical expression for loftiness.*

Christ is born in a manger: how lowly—but then the star shines over it, and the kings come to worship, yet the lowliness is not removed. It is a strange expression for the impotence of these kings: they bring these costly gifts, they themselves worship the child—but the crib and the poverty are unchanged. Precisely this is the divine.

Christ does not have a place where he can lay his head—how lowly! and yet a woman anoints his feet—and as a reward is immortalized in history—what eminence beyond all regality! Yet lowliness remains, without change, in first place; he goes on being the poor man of humble birth. You see, it is an incognito.[988] On the other hand, the instant there is a glint of splendor concealed in this incognito, it can almost blind a person—so powerful is the effect of the light.

The disciples were sent out poor and without owning the least thing—how lowly! And yet "Whoever gives to one of these little ones even a cup of cold water because he is a disciple shall not lose his reward." (Matthew 10:42.) How lofty! What rank above all kings and emperors! Yet lowliness remains literally in first place. The two spheres are kept absolutely separate; their elevation does not find any expression through the removal of lowliness—no, it remains.

An apostle achieves the extraordinary, even doing miracles! How impressive! But look, he is bound in one or another perhaps accidental suffering which makes him more wretched and impotent than the most wretched and impotent man. And he must go on living this way; his power as an apostle does not find its expression in his being able to take this suffering away now.

This is why the essentially Christian eminence is really something to lose one's mind over. It is almost enough to lose one's mind over —to be elevated to such a degree—and still be lowly to that degree. And there are security measures against taking this elevation in vain—the divine knows very well how to secure itself.

x^4 A 86 *n.d.*, 1851

SUPERSTITION

« **4739**

There is something curious about superstition—we would expect the person who has once seen that his morbid daydreams have not been fulfilled would be all the more ready to give them up in the future, but on the contrary they get stronger, just as the desire to gamble increases in one who has once lost in the lottery.

I A 116   January, 1836

« **4740**

The Socratic experience "that people became so angry when he wanted to take one or another of their stupidities away from them that they almost wanted to bite him"[989] one can experience for himself.

Every man is likely to have a goodly sum of superstitions, habits, and the like. He perhaps willingly confesses that they are a weakness, but he does everything to keep them, to make sure that nothing affects him in this respect because it would disturb him too much.

If it happens just the same, it promptly seems to him as if he were in the power of a hostile force which tricks him, instead of humbly understanding that this perhaps is happening to him in order that he might become master over such things.

But this true "good behavior" of faith is extremely rare.

Yet the one who is really aware of such things—no wonder that in many a weak moment he is afraid really to get involved with God, since it may very well amount to a complete transformation of even the most minor aspects of a person, even more rigorously than when a girl is loved by a definitely superior mind, so that she must go completely beyond her whole range of ideas, not merely to love as she understands it but as he understands it.

X^2 A 562   n.d., 1850

« **4741** *Superstition*

No wonder that geniuses, also criminals (as Vidocq points out in *Pariser-Geheimnisse,* part II[990]), in short, everyone who in one way or another is set outside the universal, are so superstitious. They have no *impressa vestigia*[991] for their feet, push forward on unfamiliar and forbidden paths; therefore they are aware on a quite different scale than others and of quite different things than others. The majority of people do not really *live;* they are only repetitious, center their lives within the security of probability, and therefore are not superstitious—that is, they are not aware that this, their faith in probability and their security within probability, is in another sense a prodigious superstition.

x^3 A 727   *n.d.*, 1851

« 4742 *A Church Father Warns against a Superstitious Faith in an Externally Established Church*

Hilarius contra Auxentium: For one thing I warn you to beware of the anti-Christ. A fanatic love for walls deceives you. You fanatically do honor to God's Church in beautiful architecture. You ridiculously seek God's peace there. Is there any doubt that the anti-Christ will enthrone himself there sometime. Mountains, forests, seas, prisons, and deserts are more secure places . . . . . Why does the world today admire these powerful bishops, for what reason does it honor them as religious, saintly teachers—only because they rule over great places.
  See *Henry Calvins Leben,* I, pp. 91–92.[992]

x^4 A 312   *n.d.*, 1851

« 4743 *Superstition—Superstition*

We cross ourselves when we read, for example, that the Finns pray to God or sacrifice to him—so that he will provide them a good catch.

But we, we—anyone who looks to God for the sake of success—are, after all, just as superstitious.

x^4 A 477   *n.d.*, 1852

TELEOLOGICAL SUSPENSION

« **4744** *The Highest as the Abnormal*

This form (that the abnormal is the highest, often even the abnormal, with the teleological suspension of the ethical the absolute) is, ethically, what miracle is in nature.

X^4 A 182 *n.d.*, 1851

TEMPTATION

« **4745**

..... But where in the world does one find this deep sympathy?*
  *See Hebrews 4:15:⁹⁹³ Οὐ γὰρ ἔχομεν ἀρχιερέα μὴ δυνάμενον συμπαθῆσαι ταῖς ἀσθενείαις ἡμῶν.— This is a sympathy which is of greater worth than all the sensitivities of the world.
                                                II A 366   February 12, 1839

« **4746**

..... and then when the temptations [*Fristelserne*] approach, we shall not avoid them, because we know that they are not overcome in this way but rather come again all the stronger. We shall not slip into an impotent drowsiness which almost makes it possible to say that things happen to us rather than that we act, and then if the temptation does not carry us away to our downfall, we need not stand disgraced like those who must say it was through no responsibility of ours that we did not fall but that rather it was fate which saved us. We do not say this as if we in any sense wish to nourish the vain thought that it was we ourselves who saved us by our own strength, for we know that without God we achieve nothing, but everything if God is with us. Therefore we deliberately said that it was as if fate saved us, for how could we have dared to call it Governance and thereby elevate the thought to God, if at the same time we were conscious of not having been active ourselves, for just as God must be with us if something is to be accomplished, we, too, so to speak, must be with God, be awake, Christ's coworkers, and not dozing and dreaming, because the removal of temptation without our cooperation gives no assurance against new struggle, no battle-strengthened and renewed confidence in God's help.

The second attack of the temptation is always worse, whether it finds us arrogant over having conquered the first temptation or troubled because of having withdrawn from it.

And God will make the temptation and its ending such that we can bear it. You, my listener, you who have been tried in great temptations and perhaps have often fought the good fight[994] and conquered—but, alas, when at times you buckled under it and you stood there when it won over you, and then you stood there with a consciousness of having lost the battle and looked out upon the desolation which was your soul, and it seemed to you as if everything were lost and despair beckoned to you, its passion already intoxicating you, then perhaps these words came to mind: God will make the ending of the temptation such that we can bear it, for the ending of temptation is not always victory, but in any case God will make the ending such that we can bear it, and your soul will again become sober and awake.

III C 14   n.d., 1840–41

« 4747

It is very curious: a small trifle naturally leads a very disdained life and is disregarded by all the clever; in return the small trifle sometimes avenges itself, for when a person goes insane, it is almost always over a small trifle.

VI A 116   n.d., 1845

« 4748

It is true of "temptation" [*Fristelse*] also: it is only a brief hour. Temptation has its power in "the moment." It has frightful power for making one anxious and, as it were, for concentrating everything in a moment—the next moment it is impotent.

X^2 A 161   n.d., 1849

« 4749 *The Temptation of Christ*[995]

It is not only a universally human temptation [*Fristelse*]—but what an intensification: when a person is hungry and then has the power of being able to perform a miracle and in that way to obtain bread. This is something different from merely being hungry; it is a superhuman agony simultaneously to have the power of miracle and not dare use it.

X^4 A 181   n.d., 1851

TERSTEEGEN

« **4750**

It is a beautiful thought Tersteegen[996] had (in his sermon on the thief on the cross) that Christ's prayer:[997] Father, forgive them, they know not what they do, that this sermon or that these words had converted the thief, that he was gripped by Christ's love which prayed for his enemies.

And in the same sermon he makes good use of the fact that the thief's faith was promptly tested. For the very next moment the one who had promised that he would be with him in paradise sighs:[998] My God, my God, why have you forsaken me. And this, indeed, was the one on whom the thief had built his hope.

It is rightly noted that one cannot use the example of the thief to justify postponement of one's conversion until the end, for the thief presumably had not heard a word about Christ before.

x¹ A 484   n.d., 1849

« **4751** *A Superb Expression by Tersteegen*

"Die Gelehrten sind meist Schuld daran (in disputes about terms and distinctions), die doch bedenken sollten, dass nicht der Tausendste unter wahren Gläubigen einen völligen Begriff von verschiedenen ihrer Ausdrücke und Distinktionen habe, gleichwie hingegen tausend Andere *die Worte der Wahrheit, nicht aber die Wahrheit der Worte haben.*"

In a little essay, "Von dem Glauben und
der Rechtfertigung," p. 474 in my edition.[999]

x¹ A 486   n.d., 1849

« **4752**

Tersteegen's observation (p. 378)[1000] is very penetrating, but he himself does not seem to have grasped it properly, namely, it does not say that Mary has chosen the best part—but the good part, that is, the best part beyond all comparison.

That is to say, the positive is more than the superlative. It is something I have also pointed out in other connections. The highest expression for erotic love or the expression for the highest erotic love is: I love this particular person. If one says, I love more than everybody else,[1001] or I love as no one has ever loved his beloved, then one says less; the superlative subtracts and demonstrates that there is an unerotic comparison in the erotic love.

This is why, as I have shown someplace in this journal [i.e., X^1 A 481], "reasons" in connection with faith are a subtraction. I believe—not one word more—is the maximum; if I have seventeen reasons, my faith is less, and still less if I have eighteen.

X^1 A 490   n.d., 1849

« 4753

Tersteegen's sermon *am Erscheinungsfeste*, 1755, on Matthew 2:1–12 (pp. 117ff. in my edition[1002]) is superb. The second point especially is true in the deepest and most inward sense, so rooted in experience and life. Truly in him there is inward truth.

X^1 A 492   n.d., 1849

« 4754

This by Tersteegen is superb—in a little essay, *Von dem Unterschied und Fortgang in der Gottseligkeit,* para. 24, p. 443 in my edition:[1003] "Aber woher kommt es, dass solche theure Schriften (the mystics) insgemein so wenig geachtet und gebraucht werden? Ist es nicht deswegen, weil die neugierige Vernunft solche Nahrung nicht darin findet, auch der alte Sinn des Fleisches und der tiefe Grund des eignen Lebens zu scharf darin angegriffen wird, und sie nicht, wie andere, nach dem Geschmack des alten Adams und der Vernunft ein wenig mehr accommodirte Bücher, ein *Raisonniren und Speculiren, sondern ein Mortificiren und Verlaügnen erfordern?*"

X^1 A 572   n.d., 1849

« 4755

What Tersteegen says in *"Stimme aus dem Heiligthum"* is very true. V. 63 (p. 515 in my edition of Tersteegen's works by George Rapp, Essen, 1841).

Untreu und Trägheit zu verhehlen,
Lässt man sich zu den Schwachen zählen;
Man scheut, zum Schein, den frommen Schein,
Wenn man nicht Lust hat, fromm zu sein.[1004]

x¹ A 607   n.d., 1849

« **4756**

Tersteegen (*Auswahl seiner Schriften*, v. Georg Rapp; Essen: 1841) p. 370, quotes from Psalm 77:3:[1005] *"Meine Seele soll sich weigern sich trösten zu lassen."* This is in contrast to being consoled by God alone.

This could indeed be regarded as tempting God, just as in those verses from the Letter to the Hebrews[1006] which speak about those who "would not accept consolation," that is, human consolation, again in contrast to being consoled by God alone.

x³ A 185   n.d., 1850

« **4757**

Tersteegen made an excellent point (in a sermon *am Erscheinungsfeste*, p. 131 in Rapp's selections from his writings[1007]): The scribes knew enough to say where the Messiah was to be born—but they remained passively in Jerusalem and did not go along to look for him.

Alas, in similar fashion a person can know all about Christianity, but it does not *move* him. This power which moved heaven and earth —simply does not move him.

On the whole Tersteegen is incomparable. In him I find genuine and noble piety and simple wisdom.

Alas, what a difference—the three kings had only a rumor to go on —but it moved them to travel that great distance. The scribes were informed in a quite different way; they sat and studied scripture as professors—but it did not move them. Where was there more truth— in the three kings who pursued a rumor or in the scribes who remained sitting with all their knowledge.

Tersteegen did not use the circumstance[*] in this way; he uses it —and splendidly—as the spiritual trial [*Anfægtelse*] it must have been for the kings when the scribes, who gave them the information, remained passively in Jerusalem—"We certainly have been fooled, the kings must have thought"; for it is indeed a suspicious self-contradiction that the scribes should actually know this and yet remain passive. It is just as suspicious when someone knows about Christianity—and his own life expresses the opposite; we are tempted to assume that he wants to make a fool of us, unless we assume that he is merely making a fool of himself.

x^3 A 202   n.d., 1850

« 4758

* In margin of 4757 (x^3 A 202):
Incidentally, in reading an earlier passage[1008] in the same sermon I see now that Tersteegen was also aware of what I was about to point out.

x^3 A 203   n.d.

« 4759

Tersteegen declares somewhere[1009] that Jesus arises from the love-feast and goes out—to Gethsemane. So it is always—Gethsemane lies closest to the highest bliss.

x^3 A 205   n.d., 1850

« 4760

Tersteegen says it beautifully somewhere in a Christmas sermon (p. 108 in Rapp's selections[1010]): *"Ja, Seelen raümet eure Herzen aus von euren Lünden, von der Welt, und von allen ihren Eitelkeiten; denn Christus will kommen und in uns geboren werden. O, dass es nicht auch heisse: Er fand keinen Raum in der Herberge!"*

x^3 A 229   n.d., 1850

« 4761

Tersteegen is correct in saying somewhere:[1011] If a sick person were to say, I believe there is a physician living there or there who is perfectly able to cure me—how does he then demonstrate that he has this faith? By seeing to it that he gets in touch with this physician. It is the same with any faith: if it does not *move* a man to act according to it, his having faith is imaginary, just as anyone would see that the sick man's faith was imaginary if he quite passively refrained from making the slightest move to get in touch with that physician he fully and firmly believed and maintained was perfectly able to cure him.

x^3 A 240   n.d., 1850

« 4762

By Tersteegen.[1012]

*Wer glaubet, der ist gross und reich,
Er hat Gott und das Himmelreich.*

> *Wer glaubet, der ist klein und arm,*
> *Er schreiet nur: Herr Dich erbarm.*
>
> x³ A 259   *n.d.*, 1850

« **4763**

A hymn for Ascension Day is beautiful if the first two and the last two lines are dropped and it is punctuated differently to read:

> *Lehr' mich nur im Geiste leben,*
> *Als vor Deinen Augen da:*
> *Fremd der Welt, der Zeit, den Sinnen,*
> *Bei Dir abgeschieden drinnen.*

Instead, Tersteegen[1013] has a period, and then two more lines, whereby the beauty is lost.

x³ A 287   *n.d.*, 1850

TERTULLIAN

« **4764 *Christianity—Tertullian*[1014]**

I have often pointed out that Christianity can be presented in two ways: either in man's interest (mitigating accommodation) or in God's interest (true Christianity). And then I have suggested that if I do not or dare not present Christianity in the latter way, I must then make an admission and keep the space open.

Hardly any Church Father has presented Christianity in God's interest so powerfully as Tertullian has.

Here Christianity is not a bit of morality and a few propositions of faith; here Christianity is an accounting between God—and the world. This is why Tertullian takes such a decisive look at its opposite—idolatry.

And now that Christianity has for a long time been victorious, as they say, and has left a mark on the shape of culture, Christianity and the world have actually changed in such a way that the matter must once again, on a higher level, be brought to a head with the question: Does Christianity belong to God or to man?

In its early beginnings, the Church was on fire because Christians literally felt that the struggle was about God's cause—not a few dogmatic propositions—but about whether God shall be God.

My very subordinate task[1015] is continually to make aware. I make the admission: I do not dare risk more—but yet I am like a shout of alarm.

X^4 A 137 *n.d.*, 1851

« **4765 *I Cannot Do Otherwise***

The expression is as old as Tertullian. The sentence reads: "He who has known the truth cannot do otherwise, he must cling to it."

See Böhringer, *Die Kirche und ihre Zeugen,* I, pt. 1, pp. 285, 286.[1016]

Here we must again credit old Father Socrates[1017] a little, for he advances a similar meaning of "to understand," maintains that the person who has truly understood something also does it, that to do the truth is the criterion for having understood it. This is also acknowledged in all finite matters. If someone were to praise a medical remedy as the only sure preventive and not use it himself, one would conclude that it is not his conviction. It is the same everywhere, except that we have concocted the strange idea that in the realm of the spirit it is supposed to be like this: a person asserts that he has a faith—while his life expresses the opposite, and then the assertion is supposed to be sufficient. No one acts that way in finite matters; one is not satisfied with assertions but tries to find out about the other's actions. A financier who is undecided about what stocks he should buy consults another financier. Let us assume that the latter in a spellbinding lecture assures him that 3% bonds are the only safe security. Perhaps the other financier believes him, but he says: I would still rather know in what securities you yourself invest your money. If he finds out that the financier had just bought 4% bonds, he thinks: Hang what he says, I'll stick to what he does, for what he himself *does* is his conviction.

X^4 A 138 *n.d.*, 1851

« **4766** *Tertullian*

in the doctrine of the means of grace advances the unity (*die Einfachheit der Erscheinung*) of inferior externality and interior divine power as the characteristic mark of the divine, whereas paganism is interior emptiness supported by external ostentation.

(See Böhringer, *Die Kirche und ihre Zeugen*, I, pt. 1, p. 343.)

This is what I maintain in the distinction between *direct* recognizability and *indirect* recognizability.[1018]

X^4 A 139 *n.d.*, 1851

« **4767** *Tertullian*

stresses the difference between faith and non-Christian wisdom. He declares among other things that the difference is in range. "Christianity is the completed revelation and has a definite goal. We do not need to speculate further after we have found the gospel. *Since we believe, we do not need to go further than to believe,* for above all we believe that *there is nothing more that we have to believe.*" This is the boundary, otherwise we would have to go on seeking in the infinite. Philosophy, on the other hand, has no boundary and therefore goes on into the infinite. And why? Because philosophy gives *unconditioned* freedom of inquiry. "Since a person has to be everywhere in order to seek and find, he is unable to be anywhere . . . . . No doubt it is only because a person cannot find that he seeks constantly, for he seeks there where there is nothing to be found. Someone knocks constantly only because the door is never opened, for he knocks where no one is within. A person asks constantly only because he is not heard, for he asks the one who does not hear."

Böhringer, I, pt. 1, p. 313.[1019]
x⁴ A 140   n.d., 1851

« 4768 *Tertullian*

"What God has commanded is always good and always the best. *What are you hesitating about—God has commanded it!*"

Böhringer, I, pt. 1, p. 295.[1020]
x⁴ A 141   n.d., 1851

« 4769 *Tertullian*

in his consolatory writing to martyrs actually sets Christian freedom so high that he establishes the paradox that one really does not become free until he becomes a prisoner for the sake of Christianity. "Prison gives the Christian what the desert gave the prophet. The Lord himself often went into solitude in order to be *more free* to pray. Let us take away the name prison and put solitude in its place."

A little earlier he says: "The world itself is a prison; therefore by being imprisoned you get out of prison rather than into prison. Regard prison as a place of asylum. Certainly it is dark in prison, but you have *the light;* there are chains in the prison, but you are free. The Christian outside of the prison has in fact renounced the world and in prison has also renounced the prison. No matter where you are in the world, you are still outside the world."

See Böhringer, I, pt. 1, p. 294.[1021]
x⁴ A 142   n.d., 1851

« 4770 *Tertullian*

in his book on the Lord's Prayer declares somewhere: "Formerly *prayer* called down scourges, killed the warlords, withheld the fruitful rain. But Christ has given prayer power only for *good.* The evangelical prayer heals the sick, drives out demons, opens prisons, loosens the chains of the innocent; wipes out sins, drives away temptations, halts persecutions, comforts the forsaken, strengthens the fallen . . . . ."

See Böhringer, I, pt. 1, p. 348.[1022]
x⁴ A 143   n.d., 1851

« 4771 *Tertullian*

declares somewhere that since the birth of Christ astronomy has acquired a new content: Christ—his star, which the wise men saw in the east, is now the only one.

I read this quoted in Böhringer.[1023]

I think it is also Tertullian who states somewhere:[1024] He who himself does not wish to suffer cannot love Him who has suffered.

I read this in Böhringer. Yet it must be remembered that with respect to Christ this thesis could be pressed so audaciously that one would arrive at the opposite extreme: an almost unseemly fraternization with the God-man, forgetting that there is also the human truth in the fact that Christ did not suffer in order that I should also suffer, but that I should be saved and thank him, except that this again must not be interpreted as meaning a purely secular existence which merely seeks what belongs to this world dressed up as a prescriptive right.

x^4 A 144   *n.d.,* 1851

« 4772 *Tertullian*

De præscript., no. 23: *dum verisimilia mentiuntur, veritatem frustrantur.*[1025]

See Wessenberg, I, p. 65 note.[1026]

x^4 A 402   *n.d.,* 1851

THEOLOGIANS, THEOLOGY

« **4773**

A remark for theologians: *King Lear,* act IV, sc. 6 (in Tieck's translation, volume VIII, p. 362, bottom[1027]). Lear: . . . . . *Ja und Nein zugleich, das war keine gute Theologie.—*

II A 34   n.d., 1837

« **4774**

The old Christian dogmatic terminology is like an enchanted castle where the most beautiful princes and princesses rest in a deep sleep—it needs only to be awakened, brought to life, in order to stand in its full glory.

II A 110   July 8, 1837

« **4775**

Scholasticism achieved its own parody (it is my theory[1028] that this happens to every development) in the attempt of Paulus Cortesius[1029] not so much to paraphrase the scholastics but rather to make a new copy of them in classical Latin. "Christ died" became "Christ crossed over the river Acheron" etc.

II A 291   November 3, 1838

« **4776**

Rationalist theology ought to formulate all its teaching about God around this one passage in the gospel:[1030] "He made his sun rise on the evil and on the good, he sends rain on the just and on the unjust," because the unchangeableness contained therein becomes the point of departure for all such speculation.

II A 543   August 28, 1839

« **4777**

In margin of 4776 (II A 543):
or the unchangeableness which Isaac's blessing had despite the mistake.[1031]

II A 544   n.d.

« 4778

Have a *summa cum laude* in theology, on top of that be the smartest of all the *summa cum laude's*, stand at the cultural peak of the times—and then at some time read one of those old theological works by an authentic spiritual guide—and learn to be nauseated by all your knowledge *qua* theological knowledge—learn to be nauseated by this pious bosh on Sunday, this dissertation nonsense, which proves nothing, except one thing, that the one who stands there stringing out words is a chicken thief, especially when he sweats and wipes away tears.

VIII^1 A 433   *n.d.*, 1847

« 4779   *N.B.*

What is needed is a new theological science of arms[1032]—a new maneuver—with the help of the double-dialectic. It is pitiful to observe orthodox theology these days; it holds the weapons (and thinks they are weapons of defense instead of weapons of attack) as if one were holding a cane by the tip and reaching it out to the attacker—so that he can hit him with it. Somewhere Jean Paul makes a proposal to give clubs to the town militia to defend themselves with (for they do not know how to use guns, and the enemy can simply take those away from them): the same with theology in our day, the only virtuosity it has is in suffering defeat.

VIII^1 A 480   *n.d.*, 1847

« 4780

The saying that Councillor H. C. Ørsted[1033] told me is a good one: When a lark wants to fart like an elephant, it has to blow up.

And in the same way all scholarly theology must blow up, because it has wanted to be the supreme wisdom instead of remaining what it is, an unassuming triviality.

X^1 A 397   *n.d.*, 1849

« 4781 *Bible Interpretation*

Earlier the Bible was reflected imaginatively in imagination: here is the whole range of allegorical interpretation. It is really an expression of the inability to comprehend how the infinite descends to the ordinary, the historical. Allegory as the primary interpretation is really an indirect attack upon Christianity, that Christ was a particular human being, the apostle a particular human being who amid prodigious activity tossed a few words on a scrap of paper for a congregation.

Then came the Reformation and affirmed something which in principle had been partially affirmed (but not in decisive opposition to the established order, but rather "in agreement with the Catholic Church," although there was as little agreement as possible, but those involved [for example, an Erasmus] did not dare to venture decisively; they were interested only in having it articulated) and introduced a sounder philological interpretation.

But now we are veritably drowning again in sound scientific philology. It is readily forgotten that the Bible is Holy Scripture; whereas at first, in the period of imaginative interpretation, the position that the Bible is Holy Scripture was everything.

Above all, it is quite naturally overlooked that the apostle is an existing person who with matchless agility tosses off a few words to keep a congregation on the move.

At first the apostle's "letters in haste" were imaginatively changed into God knows what. Now they are evaporated into teachings, doctrine. They are incitements. Where everything is invested, where every day it is a matter of winning more believers and caring for those won, there is time neither for fantasies nor for doctrinal treatises. Preoccupied with the piece of paper Paul sent out, we completely forget Paul, and we treat it now in a most un-Pauline way.

x^2 A 548 *n.d., 1850*

« **4782**

In margin of 4781 (x^2 A 548):

In the Seventeenth Century, which in a strict sense began to conceive of Holy Scriptures as doctrine, there arose, parallel to allegory in its time when each word, each letter was allegorical, an equally imaginary[1034] concept of inspiration. But here, too, as always: the imaginary is an indirect attack upon Christianity. Christianity is not allowed to be the paradox—this is not regarded as sufficient—so the imaginary is to be substituted, which, however, it should be noted, is not Christianity, which always has an inverted dialectic; whereas the imaginary is the most superlative superlative of a direct dialectic. This is a fundamental confusion which appears again and again. Men simply refuse to be satisfied with acknowledging the absurd; so they substitute the most profound profundity and the most sublime sublimity—well, thanks, then Christianity is still paganism, and in the meantime it is thought that with the new approach Christianity has been raised much higher. But this is a lack of respect for the qualitative dialectic. The most superlative superlative of superlatives *within* the direct dialectic is still qualitatively different from the inverted dialectic.

x^2 A 549   *n.d.*

THOMAS À KEMPIS

« **4783**

Thomas à Kempis[1035] expresses it very well.
Adversities do not make a man weak, but they do reveal what strength he has.

Book I, chapter 16.
x^1 A 550 *n.d.*, 1849

« **4784**

Thomas à Kempis[1036] says: Man has two wings with which he rises to God: simplicity and faithfulness.

x^2 A 42 *n.d.*, 1849

« **4785** *Kn. and Ethical-Rel. Kn.*

How true what Thomas à Kempis[1037] says (in *The Imitation of Christ*, bk. I, ch. 2): "Therefore be not lifted up on account of any skill or knowledge, but rather fear on account of the knowledge that is given you. For the more you know and the better you understand it, the more rigorously you will be judged if you have not lived more holily."

See, this is another story. One seeks after knowledge, stretches all his thoughts, achieves it—and, see, he has captured himself.[1038] It must, however, be kept in mind that this holds true only of ethical and ethical-religious knowing.

x^2 A 93 *n.d.*, 1849

« **4786**

Thomas à Kempis[1039] says: Practice (of evil) is overcome by practice (of good).

x^2 A 122 *n.d.*, 1849

« **4787**

Thomas à Kempis[1040] (bk. IV, ch. 6) quotes Ezekiel 33:16 this way: None of his sins shall remember him. Usually it reads differently: None of his sins shall be remembered against him. It would be remarkable if the first translation is correct, for it is a far stronger expression of the forgiveness of sins.

x^2 A 282 *n.d.*, 1849

TIME

« 4788

The Jews continually worked themselves backward into the past (they wrote from right to left not only in the physical but also in the spiritual sense), but the more they leaned backward in this way, the greater was the necessity for the soul to seek a hereafter, which was a result, as it were, of the light particles the eyes had absorbed staring at the past, which now shone all the brighter in the empty and dark present in which they felt themselves bound. Thus they lacked the calm security of a genuine evolution.

II A 372   February 21, 1839

« 4789

Eternity is the fullness of time[1041] (these words are also taken in the sense in which they are used when it is said that Christ came in the fullness of time).

II A 437   May 21, 1839

« 4790

..... for time is the most dangerous of all to combat; it wounds like the Parthian archer[1042] in that it takes flight and always assaults worst from behind.[1043]

IV A 184   n.d., 1844

« 4791

..... the day today is a bird-in-the-hand, which will fly, and the day tomorrow is a bird on the roof.

IV A 186   n.d., 1844

« 4792

That time (succession, one after the other) is or can be man's worst enemy[1044] is curiously expressed in many suggestive turns of speech: to kill time, to slay time—and conversely, that time drags out in a *deadly* way.

It could be a psychologically proper
line for a man committing suicide
to say the moment before he shoots
himself: With this shot I kill time,
I put time to death.

VII¹ A 237 *n.d.*, 1845–47

« 4793

Time¹⁰⁴⁵ is not merely appalling to a human being but is also mitigating, not merely that which makes life so strenuous (for what strenuousness can be compared to this: an eternal spirit living for years, for weeks, and for hours¹⁰⁴⁶) but also that which alleviates. If you have ever broken God's commandments, you certainly did not dare at the time to think about God, not even penitently. But after an interval of time in which you again did not sin, you gained the courage; it was as if your guilt had diminished somewhat because it was some time ago and during that time you had not sinned very often. For an eternal spirit this specious semblance does not exist.

VIII¹ A 75 *n.d.*, 1847

« 4794

In connection with the trend of historical thinking, it is very significant that what preoccupied the ancients so much—pre-existence¹⁰⁴⁷—has become post-existence in Christianity. The pagans turned to pre-existence to explain existence; the Christians turn to post-existence. This is in harmony with the futurism in Christianity and the presentism in paganism.

VIII¹ A 147 *n.d.*, 1847

« 4795

Somewhere in the second installment of his reminiscences of the South, Magister Ussing¹⁰⁴⁸ calls time "the galloping ghost." God knows if this is his own expression; in any case it is very descriptive. But the dialectical task here is simply to get to see the ghost, and to that extent time itself cannot be called a ghost, for the sophistry of time is precisely that one cannot see it.

VIII¹ A 193 *n.d.*, 1847

« 4796

This is a remarkable characterization of the Furies: μνήμονες Ἐρινύες.¹⁰⁴⁹

See Solger: *Über den Ursprung der Lehre von Dæmonen und Schutzgeistern in der Religion der alten Griechen.* *Nachg. W.,* II, no. XI, p. 655.[1050]

It makes me think of the common phrase: to remind someone of something [*at huske En Noget*]. What one would like to say emphatically is: Don't forget, don't forget justice! In the passage just quoted Solger calls attention to the common German expression *ahnden,* in the sense of "to punish." Fate, the Greeks say, pursues: μοῖρα ἕπεται or, also, it sees all. "Dieses begleitende Bewusstsein ist auch die *Zeit,* in einem höheren göttlichen Sinne gedacht, und daher ist auch χρονος eine Schicksalsgottheit, welche alles Einzelne als eine und dieselbe anschaut..... Dieses unbekannte dunkle, alles anschauende Wesen erkennt also vorzüglich auch die Vergehungen der Menschen, und straft sie, wenngleich noch so spät; denn dasselbe begleitet in ununterbrochener Einheit wie die Gegenwart so die fernste Zukunft."[1051]

On the whole, it is indeed a qualification of time to make manifest.

How profound the Greeks were; I am thinking specifically of Plutarch's treatise[1052] on the slowness of divine justice, a gripping ethical treatise.

X^1 A 261 *n.d.,* 1849

« 4797

In temporality's "actual" moment things appear so deceptive. One sees a crowd of men around him and thinks that he is just as good a Christian as they are.

But in eternity! All these millions who have lived! Just think of the incalculable host of—blood-witnesses. And what if this were now to be the standard. And yet there is one even greater: the standard of the ideal.

Reverse the experiment. Let earthly honor and esteem be the standard, and take just the present generation of the whole world. Being a bishop in Denmark—Your Excellency—yes, that is something if Denmark is the standard. But it almost disappears out in the world.

And in eternity sufferings are the standard.

X^1 A 581 *n.d.,* 1849

« 4798 *"Stopping"*[1053] *as Necessary in Order To Become Aware of Christianity and To Become a Christian*

The majority of men live from the cradle to the grave constantly on the go and never stopping, in the medium of ceaselessness (temporality, the merely quantified, etc.). Then finally death comes along and stops them—and now they become aware of Christianity, repent of not having availed themselves of it earlier, by means of this repentance achieve a relationship to Christianity, and then die.

While he is alive, the natural man does not fear death more than he fears stopping. Well, death and stopping have much in common. Stopping is comparable to a fish's being taken out of water and having to breathe in the air. The natural man shudders at this other element, at the enormous power residing in "the stop," and he understands very well that as soon as it gets the least power over him, there is no limit to the power it can get over him. And again the natural man fears this limitlessness as he fears death. To a person whose element is "up to a point," the limitlessness, the infinitude, the stationariness of the eternal in the stopping is just like being killed.

Christianity changed into doctrine can do a capital job of flowing along with the busyness and quantifying of temporality and ceaselessness: it does not lead one to Christianity. On the other hand, "the stopping" can also become a paragraph in Christianity's doctrine—it is just as useless.

In the story about the thief on the cross there is something typical from one side which is not stressed. All, all have fallen away, even the apostle[1054] has denied Christ—the one and only contemporary Christian with Christ was the thief on the cross—if I may put it this way, Christianity is so infinitely much too high for men that during their lifetime (when the situation is most strenuous, namely, contemporary with Christ) not even the apostles can stick it out with Christ. Only a thief, a dying thief, only him does the consciousness of sin and the situation of death help to hold fast to Christ.

What is it that makes death "the situation" for becoming a Christian? It is the finalizing and the finality of the fact that now it is all over; it helps one to make an absolute bid on the absolute. If the dying person is not told that this is death but is put off by being told that he will come out of it all right, then death is not "the situation" either.

Even for the truest and most earnest Christian who ever lived, it will still be true; I believe that it will not be absolutely true that he is a Christian until the time of death. We are all related to Christianity in this way; we have, so to speak, made a bid on it. But the higher one has bid in life, the more true will be his final bid in death, the nearer he will be to bidding absolutely in that moment. In life only one has made an absolute bid on it and persevered (although he went on living) at all times in expressing and standing by the one and the same absolute bid: he who himself was the absolute. We men need support, and in the moment of death a man is helped by the situation to become the truest he can become.

x^3 A 47   n.d., 1850

« 4799 *The Disparity between Christianity and the Christianity in Christendom*

[*In margin:* See p. 38 in margin (i.e., x^3 A 282)]. is that Christianity continually speaks about eternity, constantly thinks about the eternal—and then Christendom repeats the same thing and thinks about this earthly life.

The apostle says:[1055] Rejoice always—that is, at the thought of eternity, for here in the world you will have misery enough. Christendom also says: A Christian is always joyful, and understands that to mean the earthly joy of being hale and hearty and full of zest for life etc.—Christianity declares that we are given everything by grace—success, happiness, blessing—it is thinking all the time of eternity, of which it has such a tremendous conception. Christendom repeats what it says and applies it to this life. So it is with everything.

x^3 A 286   n.d., 1850

« 4800 *The Merely Human—the Essentially Christian*

The merely human thinks something like this: If I just get through time all right, I can manage eternity all right.

The essentially Christian is: If only I am certain of eternal happiness, I shall no doubt manage time all right, even if my life should become difficult and burdensome.

But we have made the certainty of eternal happiness too easy or *wohlfeil*[1056]—that is, we have transformed it into something imaginary.

x^3 A 320   n.d., 1850

« 4801 *"No One Can Serve Two Masters"*—[1057]

but just look around once in the world of men, but do not forget to include yourself, and you will perhaps not find a single one about whom it is even approximately true that he serves only one master. It seems, therefore, that it might be possible to serve two masters, since everyone is doing it.

And yet the Gospel says: No one can serve two masters.

[*In margin:* But even if there were not one single human being alive who would serve only one master—the Gospel is not impressed by these millions, does not give a discount, but repeats: No one can serve two masters.]

The meaning of the Gospel is: to do so is the person's downfall.

The temporal and the eternal stand opposed to each other in this way. In time it holds true that if you want to succeed and become somebody and all that in this world, then you simply must manage to serve two masters, for you do not get very far in this world by willing one thing[1058]—precisely this is the road to failure in this world. But in eternity willing to serve two masters is the road to perdition.

x^3 A 390   n.d., 1850

« **4802** *Theme for a Sermon*

Suddenly of a Sunday make out as if it were New Year's Day, which in a certain sense is the truth, in order to gain a proper impression of the vanishing of time. On the stated New Year's Day people are perhaps too well prepared.

x^3 A 699   n.d., 1851

« **4803** *Eternity—The Official Proclamation of Christianity—Epicureanism*

Christianity teaches that this life is a life of suffering—but then comes eternity. Here Christianity is different from Judaism and paganism, which taught essentially that this life is a life of enjoyment, but then also lacked eternity.

"Christendom" has invented a refinement: Christianity is to enjoy this life, raised to a higher power because there is an eternity.

In a book by Thomas Moore[1059] (*The Epicurean,* right at the beginning) I find this very fittingly expressed, which is a credit to the author, since it is an Epicurean who says it. The Epicurean declares: "The disturbing thing about enjoying life is that there is no eternity; if there were, how I should enjoy it!" Great! All he needs to do is become a Christian in Christendom today.

It is dreadful how "the proclamation" has been distorted! The parable of the unfaithful steward[1060] really applies to the preachers.

There was a time when those who proclaimed Christianity either knew how to work, to dig (in order to make a living) or to live on charity: then Christianity was not diminished. But then came that swarm of unfaithful stewards who did not know how to dig and refused to beg since they knew what to do. Just as the unfaithful steward in the gospel sat down and wrote false evidence, they distorted Christianity and got it to be something which provided excellent opportunities to earn money and earthly advantages. And with this kind of Christianity they won friends for themselves in this world (just like the steward in the gospel)—and like the steward in the gospel they were smarter than the children of light who worked with their own hands in order to be able to proclaim the gospel *gratis* or lived in poverty and on charity in order to do it as cheaply as possible.

x^5 A 65   *n.d.*, 1853

« **4804**

Christ[1061] says to the man who wanted him to divide an inheritance between himself and another: Who has made me a judge and divider—

and yet did not Christ come to the world precisely in order to judge and divide. Yes, he judged and divided between time and eternity: either/or. On the other hand, he certainly did not want to be a judge and divider of all the nonsense and paltriness within the temporal.

XI^1 A 3   *n.d.*, 1854

« **4805**

The amazing ingenuity with which even the most stupid person knows how to talk about the infinite and—hypocritically—acquire the finite.

Understood in this way, even the most stupid person is frightfully clever.

XI^1 A 20   *n.d.*, 1854

« **4806** *"Time" Is the Sophistical*

Can an eternal happiness be decided in a moment of time, or can something eternal be decided in time?[1062] Philosophically this question may properly be addressed to Christianity and answered in the negative. It does not follow, of course, that Christianity is obliged to relinquish its position, because Christianity itself declares itself to be against the understanding, to be a paradox—a view one does well to cling to in the face of all the mythological conceptions about Christianity, that it is a mythology, and one might ask these conceptions if they are able to point to any mythology which declares itself to be against the understanding. On the whole all objections to Christianity are by virtue of the understanding but without sufficient understanding to halt at this sign, that Christianity itself proclaims itself to be against the understanding. The *summa summarum* of all objections is a ludicrous waste of time and trouble.

Consequently, philosophy can deny that something eternal can be decided in time.

The common version of this issue has been that it is much too audacious of philosophy to deny this thesis out of hand and thereby deny Christianity, that seventy years was too short a time and that it takes a long, long series of years.

Here the rubbish begins by means of the sophistical.

If something eternal can be decided in time, then seventy years and ten years and five minutes are equally adequate, and nothing is gained by 170,000 years—the only gain is a way out for those who are unable to think.

If something eternal can be decided in time, then seventy years is more than enough. And there will be no decision if a man in his thirtieth year solemnly says to himself: Now you have forty years ahead of you and it is up to you to use them for an eternal decision. No, it cannot be done that way. Neither is it true, for existence [*Tilværelsen*] knows very well what it wants and has planned things in such a way that no one can know if he will be alive the next hour—and Christianity believes this unrest helps lead to an eternal decision.

For an eternal decision in time is the most intensive intensity, the most intensive leap.

But men are continually looking for a way out, they continually want to practice sophistry with the aid of sophistry in time. With the help of time, that is, by taking more time and making it seem that the longer the time the closer one comes to an eternal decision, they understand very well that they evade the decision, that this is achieved precisely by intensively denying time—indeed, the shorter the time the closer to the possibility of an eternal decision; this is why death is so encouraging for an eternal decision, because here time is so short.

But a human being is naturally afraid of an eternal decision, just as of death, and therefore the matter always gets twisted around—a long series of years is needed, even seventy years are too little, and perhaps a million years are insufficient. No, just as surely as the man who reserved the right to find the tree on which he should be hung was unable to find an appropriate tree, just as sure can one be that a million years would only place more distance between men and an eternal decision.

When someone presents this popular plausibility that seventy years are too short a time, that a long series of years is needed, he could be answered with the words of Abraham[1063] to the rich man:

They have Moses and the prophets; if they do not believe them, neither will they believe if someone should rise from the dead. Nothing is more certain. Someone rising from the dead might very well give them a superstitious scare, but this is not faith. And it must also be said that the person who believes that seventy years are insufficient time, that the trouble lies there and not in himself, will never get any closer to an eternal decision if he were to live 170,000 years.

This is evident if one pays attention to how men live: their so-called striving as the years pass is nothing more nor less than a steady retrogression.

XI[1] A 329 *n.d.*, 1854

« **4807** *Restlessness——Tranquilizing*

This is how Christianity presents it. Before you lies an eternity—your fate is decided in this life, by how you use it. You have perhaps thirty years left, perhaps ten, perhaps five, perhaps one, perhaps, perhaps only one month, one day: frightful restlessness.

Christendom arranges things differently. The pastor assures us (that is, if you make his income secure for him, otherwise you do not get a word out of him) that before us lies an eternity of millions, billions, and trillions of years. It is an endless striving. This life is only the beginning; what is seventy years to an eternity, not so much as five minutes—what does it matter if you waste them! Amen!

XI[1] A 399 *n.d.*, 1854

« **4808** *"Just Like the Others"*

Just as a ship may be said to be trading with China or the West Indies, so the ship "just like the others" may be said to be trading with temporality; one sails on it comfortably, cozily, securely——but it does not sail to eternity.

XI[1] A 419 *n.d.*, 1854

« **4809**

In margin of 4808 (XI[1] A 419):

Although in the external world small ships are used for short distances and no one dares sail to distant lands except on large ships, it is the reverse in the world of spirit. The ship which trades with temporality ("just like the others") is an enormously large ship. For sailing to eternity, on the other hand, only a few very small boats are used, boats for one person, nutshells. Yet it goes without saying that there is an enormous distance to cover before eternity is discovered and taken possession of, and it is frightful to sail alone on an ocean greater than the world's oceans, since it is not one of the oceans of this world but one that separates two worlds, yet for the person for whom eternity has come into existence it is no distance at all, and thus a nutshell is more than sufficient.

XI^1 A 420   n.d.

« 4810 *The Temporal——The Eternal*

The temporal is the retardation which spreads out in time and space; the eternal is the intensity which hastens toward death.

XI^1 A 468   n.d., 1854

« 4811 *Ridiculous Earnestness*

From what I learn, the tax on rank and titles[1064] is not levied by the year or half year, no—for each day! What profound earnestness! Now for the first time I understand how infinitely full of meaning each day is!

XI^1 A 535   n.d., 1854

« 4812 *To Deceive in Relation to the Temporal*
——in Relation to the Eternal

In a certain sense the former is understandable—that is, there is some point to it. For one thing, earthly goods are such that if the deception succeeds, one actually gets possession of them, and for another, it is indeed possible that the deception will succeed.

There is no point at all to the second. For it is impossible to get possession of the eternal by means of cheating. True enough, the eternal does not have policemen and guards but is considerably better protected; the eternal is not indifferent about who the possessor is— no, the eternal can be present to and be possessed only by the proper possessor. Therefore to cheat here unconditionally means simply to cheat oneself. Furthermore, any cheating here will be discovered in eternity—consequently, just when a man should reap (if it were at all possible) the benefits of the cheating.

Thus cheating in relation to the eternal is impossible, the cheating cannot actually take place; if it could, it would be discovered precisely at the crucial moment.

Yet, strange to say, men have so little understanding of the eternal, are so spiritlessly ignorant of what spirit is, so far from being spirit, that no doubt the majority of men are of the opinion that it is far better to cheat in relation to the eternal than in relation to the temporal—alas, because the eternal is so infinitely elevated that it does not raise an alarm, does not run after the police, etc.—but with infinite subtlety punishes so dreadfully that the one punished does not even notice that judgment has overtaken him—dreadful punishment!

A very weak analogy to the eternal's mode of punishment in time can be seen in the relation of a man of superior intellect to a thick-skinned lout. His method of slaying, his irony, will be so subtle that the lout will be completely oblivious—yes, will even be tempted to regard him as a weak man easy to fool.

No, the law is this: the more distinctive and superior, the easier to fool him—for his punishment essentially consists of knowing very well that the others are fooled by wanting to fool him. It is this inner security which makes it appear as if he were easy to fool. A person lacking superiority is promptly eager to assert his rights—and therefore people think him difficult to fool.

Therefore, instead of thundering away as the preachers do and twisting the matter by shouting that it is impossible to fool God, one should, for the sake of arousing attention, reverse things and say: My dear friend, watch out, wake up and fight and struggle and pray and shout to God—for it is ever so easy to fool him. Precisely because he is so infinitely elevated it is so very easy to get him—to ignore you. Reflect on this and you will come to shudder at the thought of wanting to fool him, you will come to understand that even if you prayed and implored every moment of your whole life, it would nevertheless be indescribable mercy if he were to be aware for one moment that you exist [*er til*].

But who understands how to speak about the majority of God these days. Those scoundrels, the preachers, demoralize men more and more because they themselves have no intimation at all of the meaning of the majesty of God and therefore force men on him in such a way that it almost turns out that God, like any other earthly king, stands in need of men.

XI^1 A 554   *n.d.*, 1854

« **4813** *Temporality—Eternity*

Temporality is the procrastinating, the extending [category], therefore is related essentially to *talk;* eternity is sheer urgency, the intensive, is related essentially to *action, the transformation of character.*

The main thing in the world of temporality is to be able to talk, to have a regular devil's gift of gab. —This is the case all down the line, right from the merchant talking up his wares, and someone buttering up the women, and the agitator soft-soaping the public, right up to the poet, speaker, and scholar—for this, too, is talking, not character-transformation.

But eternity has an eye for action, character-transformation. Every change along the line of talk is no assistance into eternity. If someone who has indulged in lewd talk now talks piously, it does not help, there is no essential difference.

From the point of view of temporality the primary deficiency in action is that it is so brief—there really is nothing to talk about, no procrastination. This is why temporality loves the poetic, for it is a lingering which does not become action—and scholarship, which helps in sneaking out of action. If eternity were allowed to rule, there would be no verbosity, which is just what temporality loves—it loves appearance, procrastination, and talk.

XI^2 A 76   *n.d.*, 1854

« 4814   *Time—Eternity*

(Reversed)

In a higher sense becoming nothing in this world is the condition for being able to become something in the other world.

Thus they are inversely related to each other. But ideals are completely abolished—particularly in Protestantism, particularly in Denmark. Catholicism, however, is somewhat less lacking in ideas and spirit than Protestantism. Catholicism still has a concept and impression of Christian ideality: to become nothing in this world. Protestantism is finiteness from one end to the other, everything revolves around finite objectives for finite purposes, and at best Christianity is fitted in as a mood, a mood one has only on Sunday, lest he overdo it, or perhaps, in order not to overdo it, only every other Sunday. Protestantism, particularly in Denmark, is afraid of nothing more than of overdoing. Well, it can hardly be said to be guilty of this, unless it should be that in exaggerated fear of overdoing it extravagates.

XI^2 A 123   *n.d.*, 1854

« 4815

Christianity's view is: These seventy years, or thirty years, in short, temporal life, is the critical time, the crisis, when the decision is made whether you are Christian or not and thereby, again, your situation for an eternity is determined.

In "Christendom" the matter is turned this way—as early as possible it is said, and if it could be said to the child still in its mother's womb it would be done: Take it easy, you are a Christian, and these seventy years are but the first very little bit of an eternity lying before you, an infinite process; therefore these seventy years are scarcely more than five minutes—therefore do not strain yourself; if you waste these seventy years, what are five minutes more or less.

XI^2 A 318   *n.d.*, 1854

« 4816

Christianity does not exist,[1065] at least not in "Christendom," where we are all Christians and all are saved.

―――――

Just as the statement "Everything is true" means that nothing is true, so to say that all are Christians means that no one is a Christian.

In "Christendom" we are all Christians. Being a Christian has been made synonymous with being human. Just as by being human I share in everything universally human, so we also share in the universally human with respect to becoming eternally saved and we are all saved.

Christianity in the New Testament maintains specifically that this is determined in temporal life, that temporal life is for this decision.

But in "Christendom" this is decided simply by being born; since it is determined that we are all saved, temporal life can be used for something else entirely. Eternal salvation is something we share as a matter of course by being human—in the New Testament eternal salvation is that least of all.

XI^2 A 382   *n.d.*, 1854–55

TOLERATION

« 4817 *Freedom of Religion*

The concept of freedom of religion today is so remote from expressing that Christianity has been victorious that, on the contrary, it expresses that Christianity has abandoned all hope of being victorious over the world and is willing to be satisfied with getting freedom to shift for itself. Indeed, if Christianity had had that attitude originally, it would never have come into the world. It came into the world through its desire to suffer to the death for the faith; precisely for this reason it was victorious over the world. This urge to martyrdom was its "suffering" intolerance. Now it has lost the desire and the need to suffer, lost martyrdom's intolerance, and is well satisfied with being a religion just like any other religion, on equal footing with Judaism, paganism, and irreligion.

Christianity detests the intolerance which wants to put others to death because of their faith. But to be personally willing to be put to death for one's faith—well, let us not overlook this—it, too, is intolerance, it is suffering intolerance. Modern religion is indifferentism and thus does not so much express that Christianity has abandoned the world as that Christianity has abandoned itself, or, more correctly, that Christendom has abandoned Christianity.

X^4 A 10 *n.d.*, 1851

« 4818 *The Old Orthodox*

actually want to separate from us and live by themselves, yet maintaining the position that they are the only true Christians.

How tolerant! So tolerant that they want to abandon us! I am not that tolerant. I do not want to separate from the others, because the good I possess in Christianity, in fact, only through a relation to Christianity, I will continue to call to the attention of others, even though exposing myself to misunderstanding.

The Old Orthodox have really become old and lethargic.

X^4 A 48 *n.d.*, 1851

« 4819 *Prosit!*

Grundtvig[1066] does not perceive at all that the concept of toleration which flourishes at present is indifferentism, the most extreme falling away from Christianity—and he wants to go along and vote together with this.[1067] [*In margin:* the kind of secularism in which the clergy are "Your Excellency" and all that is not nearly so dangerous as drinking *Du's* with the executioner.][1068]

In Franklin's little essay on the passion for persecution in earlier times, on dissenters and the like (his *Life and Works* by Binzer, pt. II, p. 165 etc.[1069]), he says that gradually toleration came to be accepted (that is, people became more and more indifferent).

This toleration is commended as follows. In an ingenuous footnote to the text (p. 167) he says: Obvious as this toleration appears to sound human intelligence, it was not originally a fruit of reason but—of commercialism. [*In margin:* Any shopkeeper is able to understand that toleration is an asset to business. And when the world sank so low that we had no higher concept than the mercenary concept, toleration emerged—and this was the improved Christianity.] The Portuguese had already perceived what a great asset toleration was to business—congratulations! I really believe that this is the explanation: business and shipping and railways and the whole secular social amity—tolerance is an asset to all this. Long may it live!

x^4 A 66 *n.d.,* 1851

« 4820 *The Fall from Christianity*

Through the rigorousness with which Christianity was adhered to originally, through the unyieldingness of the blood-witnesses, Christianity pressed on victoriously, transformed the world, tempered the morals, etc.

Now there exists a Christian tradition (volatilized Christianity, but yet a fruit of Christianity), and it is this which at present in the name of tolerance, but essentially as indifferentism, wants to have freedom of religion and freedom from Christianity—this is how Christianity is rewarded. And the Old Orthodox walk into the trap and think that this is great.

x^4 A 70 *n.d.,* 1851

« 4821 *Christianity as It Was in the Beginning
—and Now*

It is well known that Tiberius was willing to take Christ in among the gods. Indeed, the situation was as favorable as possible. The Christians could have said: We few men, how in all the world will we ever be able to convert a whole world; no, let us live quietly with our religion, a tolerated religion; Christ is taken in among the other gods.

And now! Now Christianity is such a lost cause that they who insist they are the only Christians are slap-happy if they simply get permission to live for themselves, if their religion is tolerated or recognized like the other religions—while at the same time the whole world gets the right to call itself Christian, consequently the world which they themselves deny is Christian. Who recognizes in this sniveling that fearfully (in the suffering sense) domineering, divinely domineering religion—Christianity.

x^4 A 328   *n.d.*, 1851

TRAGEDY/COMEDY

« 4822

Would *Jacob v. Thyboe*,[1070] if we were to think of Jacob dying because of stumbling over his spurs in the fifth act, or *Lenore*[1071] (considered as a play), if Wilhelm were really to come and she were to die of joy—become tragedies?

I A 25   October 5, 1834

« 4823

The proximity of the tragic to the comic (an observation particularly attributable to Holberg's use of comedy—for example, his *Jeppe paa Bjerget, Erasmus Montanus, den Stundesløse,* etc.)—seems to account also for the fact that a person *can laugh until he begins to cry*.

January 19, 1835

On the other hand, the comic lies so close to the tragic that, for example, in Goethe's *Egmont*, act 5, scene 1, we are inclined to smile at the Hollanders.

I A 34   n.d.

« 4824

Would a play in which the hero or heroine dies of joy (for example, if *Lenore*[1072] were adapted as a drama), or a play such as *Jacob v. Thyboe*,[1073] if Leander is made to pick up a loaded pistol and accidently shoot Jacob, would these plays, I ask, be tragedies.

I A 209   n.d., 1836

« 4825

A possible theme for a tragedy would be to have a hero carry out a genuinely prodigious exploit but without discovering the collision at the moment of the action, only afterward, and with this the play would begin. He would become bewildered over whether or not it was defensible, whether or not one dares violate universal law etc. Thus, for example, have Queen Elizabeth regret that she had had sufficient courage to have Essex executed, had not followed the judgment of the heart but the command of the political situation. Or Brutus repent having the son executed.

III A 199 *n.d.*, 1842

« 4826

δι' ἐλέου καὶ φόβου περαίνουσα τὴν τῶν τοιούτων παθημάτων κάθαρσιν. Aristotle, ch. 6.[1074] The controversy over these words. (Lessing, *Hamburgische Dramaturgie*[1075]—correspondence with Nicolai and Moses M.[1076]) I believe this to mean that by means of pity and fear (the medium—the necessity and the esthetic significance of these) tragedy effects the purification of these by ennobling the sympathies. As egotistical determinants ἔλεος and φόβος are the condition for making an esthetic impression; the effect is that ἔλεος and φόβος become purely sympathetic, that I forget myself in esthetic, purely sympathetic ἔλεος καὶ φόβος.[1077] Generally speaking, this is the calming effect produced by the esthetic, not through the thought that others suffer more but through the loss [of oneself] in contemplation of the esthetic itself, of the esthetic suffering.

IV C 110 *n.d.*, 1842-43

« 4827

Poetry softens. This was even Plato's view.[1078]

IV C 111 *n.d.*, 1842-43

« 4828

Tragedy seeks to elevate; comedy seeks to reform. (The usual rubbish about satire and drama. —Significance of the theater—Lessing, Rahbek. —Its significance in antiquity. A national institution, therefore gratis, now paid. —The Church.)

IV C 112 *n.d.*, 1842-43

« 4829

In tragedy the hero succumbs. This is supposed to reconcile me with actuality [*Virkelighed*]. Is it through grasping how greatness consists precisely in succumbing that I am supposed to be inspired to a similar heroism? But in that case I am, in fact, at loggerheads with actuality, inasmuch as I assume actuality to be such that the fate of greatness is that it must succumb.[1079]

IV C 113 *n.d.*, 1842-43

« 4830

Kant:[1080] "disinterested satisfaction."
Is it the poet who wins this reconciliation by his production or the reader and the viewer through the poet's production? An unhappy individual is a poet, a corresponding sympathy.

IV C 114 n.d., 1842-43

« 4831

If the aim of poetry were solely ethical, then reward and punishment would have to follow as quickly as possible, because the ethical demands to see this consequence as quickly as possible. What then would become of the five acts and the ascending complication, for the complication is precisely unethical.[1081]

IV C 115 n.d., 1842-43

« 4832

If all poetry is imitation, what then is the source of the verse form itself?
  Imitating — Creating
The joy every man has in imitating, even that which generally dismays him. See chapter 4.[1082] Is not this the basis of a characterization of the restlessness (terror and compassion)[1083] which poetry arouses and also of the soothing effect it produces.

IV C 116 n.d., 1842-43

« 4833

The esthetic reconciles the imagination.
Boethius minimizes the reconciliation of poetry for this reason (see bk. I, p. 9)[1084]: "quis, inquit, has scenicas meretriculas ad hunc ægrum permisit accedere? quæ dolores ejus non modo nullis foverent remediis, verum dulcibus insuper alerent venenis? Hæ sunt enim quæ infructuosis affectuum spinis uberem[1085] rationis segetem necant, hominumque mentes assuefaciunt morbo, non liberant."

IV C 117 n.d., 1842-43

« 4834

Homer is the first inventor of comedy: ..... Οὕτω καὶ τῆς κωμῳδίας σχήματα πρῶτος 'ὑπέδειξεν οὐ ψόγον ἀλλὰ τὸ γελοῖον δραματοποιήσας. Aristotle, ch. 4.[1086] Here already there is an element of the metaphysical; instead of invective there is laughter.

IV C 118 *n.d.*, 1842-43

« **4835** *Curtius's Translation of Aristotle's* **Poetics,**
  p. 101[1087]

Solon[1088] refused to let Thespis perform tragedy in Athens lest the Athenians be seduced into untruth. Thespis introduced one person. Phrynichus brought feminine masks onto the stage; women never appeared. Aeschylus, two persons. (Dialogue?) Sophocles, three. (Situation?)

IV C 119 *n.d.*, 1842-43

« **4836**

That comedy approaches the metaphysical is seen also in this that it has the universal as its object in a sense different than tragedy. Comedy developed out of the purely personal. —Epicharmus, Magnetes, Chionnides lived between the 70 and 80 Olympiads; Krates around 450 B.C. He developed the comedy which ancient comedy had begun. Aristophanes lived 436 B.C. Lamachus's decree comes in the year 400 and *comoedia media* begins. With Menander the new comedy begins in 333. (See Curtius, p. 110.[1089])

IV C 120 *n.d.*, 1842-43

« **4837**

In margin of 4836 (IV C 120):
The relation between the time of the play and the time in the play —the problem.—The category of time.

Why does tragedy require history more than comedy?[1090] Because tragedy is less probable. Comedy justifies itself metaphysically. It is a strange contradiction that tragedy seeks to depict the extraordinary and then, in order to make me believe it, links it to history. Is historical certainty a stronger argument than the certainty immanent in tragedy? Why are there so few wholly imaginary tragedies? (Riccobini's tragedy *Arcagambis.*)[1091] (Lessing, *Emilie Galloti*—its origin. His correspondence with Nicolai.)[1092] —What an indirect evidence against the absolute reconciliation of poetry and art, that I do not believe them in and for themselves when they show the extraordinary but demand external proof; on the other hand, I believe the comic and demand no historical proof. If I am depicting a fool, I do not need to give him a historical name, because if I do, I weaken the effect; if I want to depict a hero, I must try to find a historical person, otherwise no one believes it.

IV C 121   n.d.

« 4838

In ancient drama love was not the motivating force. Now in modern drama, however, it is always the case.

IV C 122   n.d., 1842–43

« 4839

In the fourteenth chapter[1093] [of *Poetics*] Aristotle classifies tragic actions according to their tragic value as follows: (1) Someone deliberately is about to commit a crime but is prevented from doing it. (2) Someone deliberately and knowingly commits a crime. (3) Someone unknowingly commits a crime and discovers it later. (4) Someone unknowingly is about to commit a crime but is prevented from doing it. The last has the highest tragic value. He cites examples.

In order to understand properly Aristotle's theory of the different values of these actions, one must know his *Ethics*,[1094] especially Book III, where he develops the distinction between the voluntary and the involuntary, acting through ignorance and in ignorance. This becomes especially important with respect to the distinction he makes between a voluntary act and a premeditated act.

IV C 125   n.d., 1842–43

« 4840

The Sophist Gorgias[1095] is supposed to have said: *die Tragödie sei eine Taüschung, bei welcher der Taüschende gerechter erscheine als der Nichttaüschende; und der Getaüschte weiser als der Nichtgetaüschte.* —This is said about acting, that it is and always will be a deception. —Rötscher quotes the words in his *die Kunst der dramatischen Darstellung,*[1096] Berlin, 1841, p. 20, note, and quotes this passage from Bode, *Geschichte der hellenischen Kunst.*

V A 80   n.d., 1844

« 4841

In margin of 4840 (V A 80):
and this holds for many things—that the one deceived, i.e., the one who lets himself be deceived, is wiser than one not deceived—for example, with respect to illusion and enthusiasm.

V A 81   n.d.

TRUTH

« 4842

The trouble with our age is that all men speak the truth—how much better it might be to live in an age in which all men would lie but the stones would speak the truth.

II A 178   October 10, 1837

« 4843

Just as the Quakers refrained on moral grounds from taking an oath, so eighteenth-century scientificity on intellectual grounds never dared to call upon God as witness to its truth.

II A 296   November 11, 1838

« 4844

Sextus points out that the Academicians as a rule got too involved in detail, instead of sticking to the main issues, as did the skeptics.

See Tennemann, p. 102.[1097]
IV C 52   n.d., 1842–43

« 4845

Sextus Empiricus:[1098] No science is possible; *discere et docere disciplinam* presupposes four conditions: an object for the scientific-scholarly discourse, one who teaches another, one who learns, and finally, a method.[1099]

IV C 53   n.d., 1842–43

« 4846

How are the ideas of beauty, goodness, truth related to each other?[1100] Are they coordinated? Are they united in one that is higher? Which one? Truth? Then would truth not be a coordinated idea?

IV C 95   n.d., 1842–43

« 4847

When I had *Either/Or*[1101] end with the clause:[1102] "Only the truth that builds up is truth for you," only a few, I regret, perceived the outlook involved. There was considerable argument among Greek philosophers about the criterion of truth[1103] (see, for example, Tennemann, *Geschichte d. Philos.*, V, p. 301[1104]); it would be very interesting to pursue this matter further. Meanwhile I doubt very much that a more concrete expression will be found. Probably people think that these words stand there in *Either/Or* as a phrase, that another expression could also be used. Indeed, the words are not even italicized. Good Lord, then they probably are not very significant.

IV A 42 *n.d.*, 1843

« **4848**

Nicodemus[1105] did in fact come by night but did not leave by day. To seek the truth at night is like seeking the living among the dead.

V A 22 *n.d.*, 1844

« **4849**

If things have to go wrong (for the best would be *latere, bene latuit*)[1106], it is always preferable for the general run of men to tear a person down than to admire him, for the general run of men has an essential sameness. Whether they do the one or the other, they are just as stupid, just as foolish. But if they do the former, the relationship is less lunatic than if they do the latter. They do not understand the truth—so they tear it down; there is still some meaning in this. But if they do not understand the truth—and then admire it—that is lunacy.

VII^1 A 32 *n.d.*, 1846

« **4850**

If the law for truth were that truth is what the majority[1107] are able to understand, then *eo ipso* the truth is betrayed; for the condition of most people is such that they will need a rather extended period of transformation before being able to comprehend the truth. It follows that what the majority can understand is *eo ipso* nonsense. Therefore something like this should be said: what most people immediately and directly understand is, a priori, rubbish and nonsense. Then comes the next thought: what most people regard as nonsense may be nonsense, but it may also be the truth. Truth is always found only in the minority, but it does not necessarily follow that the minority is always in the truth.

VIII^1 A 141 *n.d.*, 1847

« 4851

When a truth conquers with the help of 10,000 buzzing men[1108]—assuming also that which conquers, such as it is, to be a truth: by the form and method of the victory a far greater untruth is victorious.

VIII[1] A 605   n.d., 1848

« 4852

Balloting (which actually is the life-principle of the people's government, number) is the downfall of all that is great, honorable, holy, and lovable, and above all of Christianity, since it is a deification of the secular mentality and an infatuation with this world.

Christianity is diametrically opposed. (1) Purely formally. For Christianity is eternal truth, and balloting abolishes this altogether. As eternal truth Christianity is completely indifferent to whether or not something has the majority.[1109] But in the abracadabra of balloting the majority is the proof of truth; whatever does not have the majority is not truth, and whatever has the majority is truth. What a dreadful absence of spirit! (2) Christianity is diametrically opposed to actual conditions. For Christianity is militant truth, assumes that here in this wretched world truth is always in the minority. Consequently from a Christian point of view truth is in the minority; according to balloting the majority is truth: splendid!

IX A 4   n.d., 1848

« 4853

The real trouble in the communication of truth is that one must be anxious and fearful about expressing the truth, about showing what constituted the previous error—for there are ten to one ready to repeat the same error with a little modification—that is, a new and still more dangerous untruth arises—for the closer untruth lies to truth the more dangerous is the untruth.

IX A 278   n.d., 1848

« 4854

So far, so infinitely far is the modern age (compared to the Middle Ages and antiquity) from having even the faintest intimation of truth that it believes that the only validity [*Realitet*] solitude has is as punishment (see an earlier comment [i.e., VIII[1] A 40]) and that to walk the streets,[1110] to be seen by everybody, and to associate with everybody signifies merely that one is a gadabout. Alas, that this, too, is a qualification of truth, that truth, even though otherwise present, if it is not present in this form, is an illusion or is undergirded by an illusion.

IX A 287 *n.d.*, 1848

« **4855**

If the distinctive mark of the true is the opposition it suffers, if I am to prove the rightness of my view by the opposition it finds—how then shall I order things; then all the distinctive marks will have become completely dialectical. Quite so, for precisely thereby and therefore faith is what it is, if it is preceded by an absolute dialectic which has made everything dialectical. That the distinctive mark is opposition is really the expression for the inwardness of the conviction; indeed, it is hoping against hope, believing against the understanding etc.

IX A 304 *n.d.*, 1848

« **4856**

Who, after all, ever said that the truth will be victorious *in this world?* Certainly not Christ. No, the truth will suffer or must suffer in this world, yes, it will suffer, for this whole life is meant to be an examination.

This is the view of eternity. Anything else is rubbish. It is also an illusion that the presumed truth will be victorious after a man's death. No, when the man is dead there develops a delusion that it is accepted as true now when there is no danger and no tension—this delusion is victorious, not the truth.

It will always be the case that truth declared creates hundreds and hundreds of possibilities for untruth, and this is what triumphs. Alongside the one who in truth proclaims the true there often stands one or more sophists who get a sniff of what it is he intends and teaches. These are victorious—and why? Precisely because they are not the truth. But the witness to the truth becomes a martyr.

Or is there any meaning in saying that Christianity has now triumphed or has triumphed more than when it began? Well, the delusion that all are Christians has triumphed. Now when every advantage is bound up with being a Christian, now everybody is a Christian or everybody says that he is a Christian: is this the victory of Christianity? Merciful God, what an appalling way to be victorious. No, some deformed something which is not Christian, which resembles Christianity no more than blather resembles wisdom, but even less—this has been victorious.

But the fact of the matter is that man always wants to pull God's nose and does not want to think the thought all the way through as God wants it done. God intends Christianity to remain embattled to the end, oriented not to victory in time but to eternity. Man turns this around.

O, but this is hard, hard. A person battles for the truth, suffers persecution etc.—during this time he does not, humanly speaking, have joy from it, but toil and trouble (although always joy in a deeper sense). And then when he is dead, then he is victorious—alas, and then the situation is even more to be despaired over, for then a delusion has triumphed, and his name is put to it.

Yes, only the person with some finite end can be victorious, but this certainty is not the truth. A reformation of the lighting system—yes, this can be said to be victorious. The person who opposes a king can perhaps win and get a republic instead—but such foolishness, is this the truth.

Right here is the satire on Luther. The good that was in Luther certainly has not been victorious, although to a certain degree he won over the pope. Good God, this puts him in with the analogies of reforms in the fire department and the like.

IX A 326 *n.d.*, 1848

« **4857**

Instead of all this rubbish about mediation, it would be better to establish a doctrine about the media: *The medium of imagination—actuality* or the various modes of being in which truth is and which alter all the relations of truth, that in one medium everything relates directly (the good is held in honor, etc.) and in another everything is reversed, that the truth is to be identified by the very fact that it suffers.

IX A 487 *n.d.*, 1848

« **4858**

The words of Pilate,[1111] "What is truth?" say essentially the same as his "Behold what a man,"[1112] for Christ, who is the truth, does indeed stand before Pilate and consequently this (What is truth?) means: *Here* (in Christ right before me) you can see what truth is, that is, [truth] in the world.

Christ before Pilate: who is the judge, who the judged?—certainly an inversion of the immediate. Kolthoff[1113] said something like this today (in a sermon on the words from the passion story), although perhaps not expressed as precisely.

x^1 A 159   n.d., 1849

« 4859

Christ[1114] forbids those he has healed to talk about it, but the more he forbade it the more they did it. —That he did not desire sensation and ostentation was truth in Christ; it was truth also in the others, precisely because there was danger attached to spreading his praise. If those who had been healed (or to take an example, this was the case with nine of the lepers[1115]) had been cowardly and clever, they would have said: The Lord himself forbids it—ergo we will be silent, for that, after all, is his will.

Such collisions still happen continually in life. It may be the one party's duty and self-denial to renounce—but it does not follow that it is not contemptible to take advantage of it and say that it is his own will.

x^1 A 347   n.d., 1849

« 4860

In margin of 4859 (x^1 A 347):
In this way Christ makes them completely free—it is as remote as possible from his demanding that they praise him; on the contrary he even opens up for them the opposite recourse so that they may avoid the danger attached to praising him and say, "He himself orders us to be silent": thus it becomes really clear what resides in them.

x^1 A 348   n.d.

« 4861

The "established" is, after all, an altogether unchristian concept. But it is still more ridiculous to hear the established boasting in comparing itself with "the sects"—since there is infinitely more Christian truth in the fallacies of the sects than in the torpor and drowsiness and sluggishness of the established. And it is even more ridiculous that the established appeals to the New Testament. Yes, when Christianity itself was "a sect" (indeed, was called that at the time) and itself had an *awakening* (and here also, of "truth"): then it was a matter of warning against the sects. But nowadays a sect always has the advantage over the established of having the awakening of truth—that is, the truth contained in the "awakening," even if what the sect regards as truth is untruth and error.

X¹ A 407 *n.d.*, 1849

« **4862** *"Concerned Truth"*

is the truth which, eternally certain itself of being the truth, is essentially occupied with communicating it to others, concerned that they accept it for their own benefit, although the truth does not in fact need them.

This is the dialectic. Dabblers and half-men need to communicate in order to become convinced themselves. Purely intellectual striving is occupied solely with discovering the truth. Concerned truth is sufficiently certain of being the truth but is concerned about communicating it, because it knows how the others need the truth. This is Christianity.

It goes without saying that as long as a person struggles to find the truth for himself, his life cannot express concerned truth, for his one and only concern is to find the truth.

This is the case with my striving, which in great part is also purely intellectual but has not been able to concern itself with communicating to others because I myself was striving and readily perceived what is only all too true—that getting a few others along simply means delay. To want to have the others along[1116] in order to find the truth betrays a muddlehead. In Christianity the relationship is altogether different: out of concern for the others to be willing to endure the suffering and torment of communicating the truth to them.

X¹ A 410 *n.d.*, 1849

« **4863**

There is something in the inverted syllogism that Fenelon[1117] draws up somewhere. It is said: There are so many false miracles, all pagan religions have miracles, also etc.: ergo, the Christian miracles are also false. He turns it about: from all this he concludes that the Christian miracles are miracles. The point is that underneath such a universally human error there must be something true; this truth of miracle is the Christian miracle. In the same way, *ni fallor*,[1118] Frantz Baader[1119] has concluded from all the incarnations of paganism: ergo, the Christian incarnation is true.

And in this there is also the truth that untruth is a striving of truth, a *nisus*.

As I have pointed out somewhere else [i.e., x^1 A 325], it is consoling that there are so many words in the language which signify nonsense, rubbish, drivel, etc.—otherwise we might fear that everything is drivel; now there is still hope that there is something in which there is meaning. From the fact that there are so many words for nonsense, drivel, etc. we could also conclude: ergo, everything is drivel. But the other conclusion is more correct.

x^1 A 448 *n.d.*, 1849

« 4864

That "the single individual" is the truth is really expressed also in the word "demagogue," for he is always one who operates with the help of the crowd.

x^2 A 409 *n.d.*, 1850

« 4865

There is something very suggestive in the story about Sibylla and Tarquinius Superbus.[1120] Lying and deceit always begin with a sham loftiness which, however, is quite willing to lower the price when the buyer will not pay such a high one. Truth always begins with the lowest possible yet true price; if the buyer will not buy, the price the next time is a little higher, and thus it ascends. Sham superiority always begins on the highest key—if this is not accepted, very well, it comes down. True superiority always begins as low as is possible with integrity; if it is rejected, it goes up.

x^2 A 435 *n.d.*, 1850

« 4866 *Poetic Lines by an Individuality*

"Instead of voting by ballot—where there can so easily be further questions, which makes the decision doubtful—I propose that there be elected in addition to the president, secretary, etc. one more official: the counter. He ought to be analogous to *Notarius publicus*—that is, he ought to be a specific person chosen for this function, one who could be brought to every place where there is a meeting, or arranged for a day in advance. His task would be to count the buttons. As soon as an issue has been debated, the president says to the counter: Will you please count the buttons. The idea is that whatever wins is the truth. The whole assemblage falls down adoringly and says: It is the will of God. The counter also ought to be a holy person, since the state intuits in him its principle; consequently he is a kind of deity, or at least a mythological person who in Oriental style could be worshiped, and a yearly festival could be held in his honor."

x^2 A 463   *n.d.*, 1850

« 4867

What is Christianity? Christianity is suffering truth, or the teaching that the truth must suffer in this world.

It is conceivable that you, solely concerned for the salvation of your soul, turn to Christ. He says: Be assured of your salvation. I am your Savior and Redeemer. But now in this life (for I guarantee you the other life) you must be my imitator in being willing to suffer for the truth.

This, you see, is Christianity.

Suppose now that I am a proclaimer of Christianity—but also that I am a clergyman. A man sends a message, or he comes himself to talk with me. What does he want? Is it an anxious conscience—well, that is a task for me. But no, it is a slap-happy, jolly man who has gotten engaged to an enormously rich and beautiful girl, with whom he intends to set out on a European journey the day after the wedding—and I am supposed to marry them. But the lines I must speak as a proclaimer of Christianity are actually this one statement: I declare unto you the gracious forgiveness of your sins in the name of the Father, etc. If I say this—and then: Since your sins are now forgiven and your eternal salvation thus assured, pledge to your Savior and Redeemer to live in this life as his imitator, suffering for the truth. And this ought not be a sacrifice for you, for it is true that you are truly concerned for the salvation of your soul (and without this you in fact take the forgiveness of sin in vain, a guilt which will be sufficient to plunge you once again into the deepest torment of an anguished conscience) and therefore to you every earthly thing is nothing, yes, your only desire must be to suffer for the truth in order to express some gratitude for what Christ is for you.

This, you see, is Christianity. And the man is supposed to pay me for saying this to him. One of two things: either this man understands what I say, and then he is an altogether different man who has something else to think about than the girl's money and beauty and the foreign travel, or he does not understand it, and so it is still unreasonable that he is supposed to give me money for this kind of talk, so disagreeable and fatal to him. Yes, it is a crime on the part of the state, by bringing him in contact with the preacher, either to tempt the clergyman to speak quite differently or to tempt him to take sacred things in vain.

x^2 A 635   n.d., 1850

« 4868

In this world truth is always suffering and always defenseless. To find coworkers and to secure power are not so difficult, but in choosing coworkers the truth must use truth's infinite caution and therefore require few, perhaps none; thus it is contented with a verification of the words I read yesterday or the day before in one of Seneca's letters[1121] (which curiously reminded me of Frater Taciturnus's lines[1122] in the first article in *Fædrelandet,* which in a certain sense seem even more felicitous, because in addition to a polemical quality they also have a sadness in the expression of inner satisfaction, "I am content with being an author"): I am content with few, with one, with none. (I have just begun to read Seneca.[1123])

The truth is incessantly subject to fraud, particularly on the part of those closest to it. Since the outcome is never decided by *what* but by *how,* it is clear that it is possible at all times to have false editions of the same truth. Take a person with whom the teacher has most carefully shared the truth—this very person will have the power to apply apparently the identical truth but with another *how*—and make a big hit in the world, while the teacher must suffer. And the fraud will not be discovered; of this he can feel quite secure, for simply because he is the closest of all, he consequently is closest to having understood the teacher. If, then, he found no one who was closer by understanding him, how would he be able to find someone capable of understanding how there could be this deception, the understanding of which would require an even better understanding of the teacher than the deceiver had, he who was closest to him of all.

x^3 A 25   n.d., 1850

« 4869 *A Queer Sort of Evidence for Truth*

Although the clergy have done everything to make Christianity into sheer human sympathy, leaving out altogether its requirements, or in any case if they are mentioned making them by means of "grace" into something merely a bit embarrassing or into nothing, they still are unable to get men to embrace Christianity. Why? Because there is still enough truth in men to have a suspicion that this simply is not Christianity and that Christianity is a dangerous power with which to come in contact.

Here it comes again—if men are to be persuaded to embrace Christianity, it must be presented in all its rigorousness.

x³ A 85   n.d., 1850

« **4870** *Always Illusion,*

the world always wants to be deceived, yes, so passionately that the martyrs always are put to death because they will not deceive, as the world *partout* wants them to do.

Here is an example of illusion. A person who wants the world to regard him as earnest must withdraw and rarely be seen etc.—but the earnestness of truth is to take this illusion (which so many have utilized in a paltry way, so that one was a celebrity because he was seen so seldom) and to live in the streets[1124] until he is regarded as a loafer, until men grow weary of him, until there is no astonishment at all upon seeing him etc.

x³ A 432   n.d., 1850

« **4871** *Greatness Humanly Understood and Divinely Understood*

Greatness, humanly understood, is a matter of coming as close to the truth as possible but continually holding one's own, thus becoming the victor, self-consciously standing above the whole.

Greatness, divinely understood, is to commit oneself in such a way that one sinks under the truth, happy only to help the truth get ahead. It means leading truth forward in triumph and then, as it were, in order to expedite it, throwing oneself under the carriage, happy to succumb in this way, happy that the glory of God is advanced in this way.

This I understand. But then it seems too lofty for me; I sink back to a lower level—but call attention to it, make a place for the glorious men who accomplished it—O my God, you will surely help me do this.

x³ A 478   n.d., 1850

« **4872**

..... No, instead of wanting to tear the veil from divinity, as that young man[1125] did, I want to tear the veil from all the human prattle and the conceited human smugness which fools itself and others into thinking that man is so eager to know the truth. No, every man is more or less afraid of the truth; and this is being human, for the truth is related to being "spirit"—and this is very hard for human nature and the sensate thirst for knowledge. Between man and truth lies dying to the world[1126]—this, you see, is why we are all more or less afraid.

x^3 A 614   n.d., 1850

« 4873 *The Majority—the Minority*[1127]

The truth is always in the minority; and the minority is always stronger than the majority, because the minority is ordinarily composed of those who do actually have an opinion, whereas the strength of the majority is illusory, composed of the crowd which has no opinion—and which therefore the next minute (when it becomes apparent that the minority was the stronger) embraces the opinion of the minority, which now becomes the majority, that is, the opinion becomes rubbish by having statistics and the whole crowd on its side, while truth is again a new minority.

As far as truth is concerned, the same thing happens to this awkward monster, the majority, the public etc. as we say happens to the person traveling for his health: he always arrives one station too late.

x^3 A 652   n.d., 1850

« 4874 *A Duty of Conscience*

The Quakers make it a matter of conscience for the Christian not to participate in war. I would like to ask if voting on what constitutes truth is not a matter of conscience for the true Christian. Is not this (voting with regard to "truth") the old idolatry, a worship of the human race or of statistics, based on the idea that "truth" has no higher origin, no higher authority.

x^3 A 664   n.d., 1850

« 4875 *Voting*

The more insignificant a matter is, the more suitable it is to make a decision by voting; the more significant, the less suitable.

Truth and everything connected with it cannot be decided by ballot.

Someone who believes that there is a God cannot participate in any voting on whether there is a God. The outcome—which cannot be known in advance—makes no difference in the case. For even if our Lord got an absolute majority in the voting, yes, unanimity, it is blasphemy to vote; and even if the voting took only five minutes, God's name is taken in vain for that time, and also by the kind of sanction that voting can furnish.

x^4 A 35   n.d., 1851

« 4876 *For "Thinkers"*

If someone believes that there is a God before it is decided affirmatively by voting, after it has been decided by voting does he believe it for a different reason than before? And someone who did not believe before, is there any reason for him to believe because it has been decided affirmatively by voting that there is a God?

x^4 A 42   *n.d.*, 1851

« 4877 *Augustine*[1128]

"There is a truth which remains even if the world disappears ..... This truth is not *subordinate* to the human spirit (if it were, the human spirit then could not judge according to it but must exercise judgment *over* it), not *coordinate* (for then it would be inconstant like the human spirit), but the human spirit is *subordinate* to it—and this is to be truly free, when a person is the subordinate one."

x^4 A 161   *n.d.*, 1851

« 4878 *The New Proverb*

" 'I really believe that the lie is a science,' said the devil; he had attended lectures at Kiel."

This was what so delighted Bishop Mynster[1129] yesterday when I talked with him. I was about to say—but did not, for then Mynster will most likely not put the proverb into circulation, which I do want him to do—I was about to say: That is what I have always said: The lie is a science, the truth a paradox.

x^4 A 337   *n.d.*, 1851

« 4879 *Truth Is a Power,*

yet this is rarely seen, for as long as it is truth, it suffers, must get the worst of it. As soon as it has triumphed, everyone adopts it. Why? Because it is the truth? No, in that case they would have adopted it when it was suffering. They adopt it because the others are doing so; consequently they do not adopt it because it is in and for itself power, but because it is power through its adoption by the others.

x^4 A 342   *n.d.*, 1851

« 4880 *The Negative Mark of True Communication of Truth*

At the top stands Christianity with its thesis: the world is immersed in evil.

Then comes the more clever paganism with its thesis: the world wants to be deceived.

Then comes nonsense with its thesis: this is a wonderful world, and the crowd is the truth. Lowest of all in this nonsense is the daily press, which has transformed the human race into "a crowd"[1130] of nonsense.

x^4 A 391   *n.d.*, 1851

« 4881 *Character-Service——Counterfeiting*

Truth suffers in the world. The witness to the truth expresses this thesis in character: he suffers for the truth. Upon seeing this, the person who still wants to appear to be of the truth should be motivated to want to suffer in like manner.

But no. Here comes the counterfeiting—instead of personally suffering for the truth, he chooses the task of presenting, depicting how truth must suffer and does suffer in this world. It is easy to see that this is an undertaking which will not bring suffering but is a way to make a brilliant success in the world. In fact, this is a poetic task, a theatrical entertainment, *absolutely, absolutely* the same as when Nielsen[1131] *acts* the Nordic hero and Dame Heiberg[1132] *acts* the innocent sufferer.

The closer the poet—or what he could just as well be called, the theater-actor—is to the one who suffers in character for the truth, the more revolting it is. If he is a contemporary, then it is as base as it could possibly be. For the suffering of one who suffers for the truth puts the greatest possible claim on anyone who wants to appear to be on the side of truth; it demands that he come to the aid of the suffering truth, step out in character, that he suffer—instead of pretending to help and even turning another's suffering into money and other advantages. — Generally speaking, this can hardly be done in the situation of contemporaneity, for the truth is still so embattled that first the witness to the truth must have lost his life. But in another sense it would be extremely comical to imagine that when Paul was being persecuted, flogged, etc. there lived an orator who traveled around to other places and made a big hit presenting and acting out (in pastoral gown): how Paul was suffering for the truth.

Presenting and depicting how the truth suffers does not incite persecution but brings profit—why? Because it makes demands on a person no different from any other esthetic performance; it does not put the audience under any obligation (and it has not put the orator, the eminent or most reverend artist, under obligation, either), but intends merely to divert (edify) them for an hour, merely helps people pass a pleasant hour.

This treachery would be most loathsome in the situation of contemporaneity, just like being at a fire and, instead of helping, taking it all in quite calmly in order to travel around later and describe the horrors of this fire, how dreadful the shrieks of the man who burned to death inside—and whom one could have rescued had one not been occupied canvassing the whole situation with the aim of describing it.

This treachery is most loathsome in the situation of contemporaneity. But now, aided by imagination, everyone should be able to bring this sacred history so close that he becomes contemporary with it—and then he will really see how loathsome this treachery is which makes a hit (instead of suffering like those glorious ones) by describing, presenting Christianity, or by *playing* at it, yes, *playing* at Christianity just as children play soldier—for the fact that it takes place in a church, in God's house in the sight of God, the fact that it is supported by organs and trumpets, does not make it more earnest—it only makes the game more accountable.

Incidentally, this game is played especially by the effeminate, the cowardly, etc.—the wicked still have enough power to go gunning for the truth.

x^4 A 609   *n.d., 1852*

« **4882 *A Deceiver——The World Wants To Be Deceived***

From a Christian point of view, this one and that one is a deceiver —the world wants to be deceived: ergo, he must make a tremendous hit in this world, they suit each other.

It is extremely easy to show that from a Christian point of view he is a deceiver, *aber*, it must be demonstrated in this world, and this world wishes to be deceived: ergo, the deceiver will be victorious.

It certainly does happen in this world that a deceiver is discovered to be a deceiver, but usually this happens when he is old and decrepit and no longer really equipped to be a deceiver, or perhaps there has appeared on the scene an even greater deceiver who takes the wind out of his sails and while he unmasks the former deceiver he himself *qua* deceiver, amid the jubilation and acclamation of the world, draws the world into a new swindle, something for which the world is utterly ready and willing, for the world wants to be deceived.

Never has the truth been victorious in this world. No, as long as it was the truth, it was suffered for. Then came the moment when the deceivers became aware of it, that it had—as businessmen say—possibilities: and then it was victorious—that is, it became a deception. People thought it was the same cause—yes, this is precisely the point, and the important thing for the deceivers is to trick men into believing it is the same cause—and precisely this is the deception. The swindlers steal the firm away from those who suffer and have fabulous success, for *mundus vult decipi.*[1133]

This is something for deceivers! Why should I conceal the fact that if a deceiver were to read this he would say: Wait a minute, there is something to this idea of deceiving by means of unmasking a deception. He would then explain and describe (so authentically, so very authentically!) how one can deceive and deceive—and he would make such a profound impression on men that he would have fabulous success in the world with his harrowing description—for the world wants to be deceived.

No, if you yourself do not really come to suffer, then it still is and remains a deception, a bit of sophistry.

X^4 A 653   *n.d., 1852*

« 4883 *A Quotation from Bacon*

which I see Ritter[1134] has used as a motto (his *Erdkunde*, the volume which is in the *Athenæum*,[1135] most likely volume 17) has struck me; I believe I have more use for it than Ritter. It runs something like this:

Ex errore citius emergit veritas quam ex confusione.[1136]

[*In margin: Ex errore citius emergit veritas quam ex confusione.*]

XI^1 A 57   *n.d., 1854*

« 4884 *An Age Demoralized by Prudence*

naturally has sufficient prudence to be able to discern what is more true, is the truth. But it defends itself against that which is more true and the truth, not by rebellion etc.—no, by shrewdly taking a certain dose of the truth, by letting the truth be true to a certain degree and then conjuring up the appearance that, after all, what one teaches and declares and expresses is indeed the same as the true, although in a tricky way it is the very opposite; for example, enjoyment is the very opposite of renunciation, and yet Christianity has been conveniently reversed in such a way that enjoyment is actually gotten out of it.

The exact opposite of the truth, unconditioned truth, the unconditioned, is everything that is called: to a certain degree.

The unconditioned does not consist of an approximation, but it is a point of repulsion. That which lies nearest to the truth is not, if you please, closest to the truth—no, this is the most dangerous delusion of all, the most dangerous simply because it lies so near to the truth without being the truth.

XI^1 A 146 *n.d.*, 1854

« **4885 The Truth**

Every man is more afraid of the truth than of death—this is the truth about all the rubbish and hypocrisy about loving the truth and being so willing if one were only able to understand it, etc.

No, man is by nature more afraid of the truth than of death—and this is quite natural, for in essence the natural man is even more opposed to the truth than to death. No wonder, then, that he is so afraid of it.

In order to become aware of the truth it is necessary to have *apartness* ("Christ took him aside"[1137]), apartness from the crowd. And this alone is sufficient to make a man anxious and more afraid than he is of death. For man is a social animal[1138]—only in the herd is he happy. Whether it is the most abysmal nonsense or the worst villainy is *ganz egal*[1139] to him; he is perfectly at home with it if it is the crowd opinion, what the crowd does—and he can be along with the crowd. For man is an animal who can become spirit, something he *qua* animal fears even more than to die. He is animal—and apartness aims at making him spirit.

If a man enters into the truth, this apartness comes to mean more particularly the apartness of being ridiculed, despised, and mistreated by the others, by the crowd—an apartness which is far greater than the first.

This, you see, is why men change the concept of "truth." Truth is to run with the herd, and this is also said to be love. And this has now become Christianity.

XI^1 A 352 *n.d.*, 1854

« **4886 The Truth**

is a snare: you cannot get it without being caught yourself; you cannot get the truth by catching it yourself but only by its catching you.

XI^1 A 355 *n.d.*, 1854

« 4887 *Truth*

Quite naturally it always seems best to try to get the help of a few others in order to strive together for the truth; and the constant cry is: Let us unite to strive for the truth!

No, no, no, it does not work that way. Truth is truly anything but a result of a unified effort. The truth is simply that every single one of us is a scoundrel; therefore the only way there can be any possibility of coming to the truth is for us—like the seventy interpreters[1140] who were shut up, each one in his cell, like the criminals who nowadays are put in solitary confinement—to become single individuals—joining together is nothing but untruth.

To become a single individual, to continue as a single individual, is the way to the truth. The longer a man can endure being a single individual and, in fact, the more profoundly he is a single individual —even so far from being united with others that he is mistreated by them—the closer he is to the truth.

But the animal quality makes life cozy, comfortable, secure. Hence: Let us join together. And in the course of time this has become more and more dominant, so that man has more and more become more animal-creature.

XI^1 A 438 *n.d.*, 1854

« 4888 *Wisdom's Discourse*

admired by the contemporary age as the discourse of wisdom—watch out, it is nonsense; no human being is such a giant. This is why truth (which is always dialectical and needs the tension of opposition) manages things in such a way that wisdom's discourse is regarded as foolishness by the contemporary age—wisdom's discourse is not entrusted to any man on any other condition, something for which he personally should be glad if he is most afraid of becoming a driveler.

Afterward, in the course of generations, that discourse of wisdom comes to be admired—but then it has been changed, is no longer wisdom's discourse but a kind of nonsense.

XI^1 A 508 *n.d.*, 1854

« 4889 *The Truth Is Naked*

In order to swim, one strips naked—in order to seek the truth, one must strip in a far more inward sense, must take off a much more internal attire of thoughts, opinions, selfishness, etc. before one is sufficiently naked.

XI^2 A 227 *n.d.*, 1854

UNCHANGEABLENESS

« **4890** *God's Faithfulness*

This was actually written as a conclusion to the sermon [*Prædiken*]¹¹⁴¹ on God's unchangeableness,¹¹⁴² but it is more appropriate to the theme of God's faithfulness.

..... But have you personally experienced God's unchangeableness, does it perhaps seem as if you have experienced rather the opposite? When you were a child, did you not have a conception of God different from the one you have now as an adult? Has not your experience with God been the same as with a man—on closer contact you find him to be different from what you had pictured to yourself and in the course of years you find him changed?

Let us talk purely humanly about it. The unchangeableness of God is sometimes talked about so positively that the positiveness itself is a kind of swindle. In every situation it seems to be true that what the inexperienced say is likely to have a dubious positiveness and assurance, while at first glance what the experienced say appears to be less positive, but it is more durable.

What is said about God's unchangeableness and faithfulness is like this. Even one word suggesting that he would be able to change or at times even want virtually to deceive a man—O, the very thought of saying anything like that makes one shudder. But what about Luther —he certainly was a man of experience! He says: If I am to be deceived, I would rather be deceived by God than by men. There is a devout man —and not merely a devout man, but a blood-witness—and he says in a sermon: You deceived me, O God, etc. (It is Savonarola, quotation found on page 18 in this journal [i.e., x^4 A 264].)

So it is with every man who truly gets involved with God; there comes a moment when he must say: You deceived me, O God—and he is unable to say right away—but for my own good; you deceived me, O God—but into the truth.

That God is obliged to use deception does not mean he is not faithful or has changed—no, he is eternal, unchanged, educating love.

But it is inherent in us to be very reluctant to venture out. We want very much to put God off by assuring him that we really do want to profess the truth; at the same time we assure him that if we only understood the right thing to do, we would surely do it. This is the swindle. This is why God, like any other pedagogue, has to use cunning.

And you deceived me in the same way, O God! You showed me those lovely pictures. You did not say to me: Just watch out, be smart, use the intelligence with which I have so richly endowed you, never get involved in anything like this. No, you beckoned to me, so to speak. I cannot say that I followed recklessly, for early in life fear and trembling were a part of my nature. So I followed. Sometimes it was as if you frightened me back: then I gave up everything. But there were signals again and I followed. O, it is horrible to be deceived, to be deceived by God—dreadful! As the swimmer grabs at something to hang onto and, not finding it, sinks, so it is with the one who is deceived. For the thing which in possibility looks so very inviting is dreadfully forbidding in actuality. And yet even if one were deceived, there would still be nothing to regret, to become deceived in having ventured out in order to seek the eternal is still always preferable to being worldly wise. O, but you only deceive one into the truth. And this pain of seeming to have been deceived is part of it all before the eternal is reached—alas, but soon it will again be necessary for you to deceive me, for otherwise I will doze off into secular security.

But who glorifies you most truly, consequently the best: the one who merely cries out for your faithfulness—and perhaps does not say a thing, or the one who says: You faithful one, you deceived me—into the truth. You were too loving and faithful not to deceive me, for then I would have gone on living with an imaginary notion of your faithfulness but without ever becoming involved with you.

X^4 A 297   n.d., 1851

« **4891** *Everything Moves Him—Nothing Changes Him*

New themes for sermons on God's unchangeableness[1143]

Your sigh, your prayer, etc. are heard; O, in grace they have touched him, moved him deeply, him who is infinite love. But it does not follow from this that your desire is fulfilled. He has so infinitely much to take care of, and one thought is to be maintained throughout the whole, and thus it may well be that he must deny you this. But it touches and moves him, both your prayer and that he must deny it—for nothing changes him.

* *

God is unchangeable—could you wish it otherwise.

X^4 A 305 *n.d.,* 1851

« **4892** *The Error in Judgment Resulting in Christendom*

———

This is the way we men always are. When we hear that someone is supposed to be a loving person, very kind and loving, this means that we no doubt will have our way with him—for, after all, he is such a kind, loving person. [*In margin:* This is how men have treated God.]

But this is not the way the New Testament puts it.

In the New Testament God is love, infinite love; yes, this is a certainty, eternally certain. He knows best of all what an agony it is if a man is to become spirit, is to love God in truth. To that end he is willing enough to suffer with the beloved in infinite love, he will hear your every sigh, sorrow with you, weep with you, count your tears——but change him——no, that you cannot do. Be assured that he suffers much more than you do——but change him——no, that you cannot do. Be assured that he suffers much more than you——for he cannot change.

The whole thing rests on the fact that one can be love personified without implying thereby that he can be changed according to the beloved's will.

But God cannot be changed. If he could be changed—and you really meant you wanted to love him, him who is so loving, then on other grounds it would be impossible for you to love him—for if he could be changed in this way, then he would not be God but a phantom, an unreality.

Thus it is easy to see that Christendom has fallen away from Christianity, for Christendom is: God changed according to mankind's will. It is this old familiar human way of thinking that one can order the loving one to do anything—he is, after all, the kind, loving soul.

XI^1 A 418 *n.d.,* 1854

THE UNCONDITIONED

« **4893**

Christianity's primary aspect is and must be so appalling that only an absolute *shall* is able to drive a man into it. But this primary aspect has been abolished, and Christianity's other aspect has now been taken: mildness—and this is recommended for various reasons, is defended, and so on.

But this will cost the race dearly. Just as a spoiled child manipulates his parents into being lenient to his own ruin, so also the race, to its own ruin, has fooled and intimidated those who should command and use authority into not daring to say: You shall.

What the world needs most of all right now is this *You shall,* pronounced with authority. This is the only thing that can give impetus, and he who implores another, "Just speak rigorously to me!" understands what is best for him.

"You shall" has been abolished. In every relationship, even in preaching, the contemporaries are made the authority; the speaker or the individual recommends his cause, his wares, be it raisins or Christianity—but there is no teacher and no assembly of learners—far from it—every assembly is the master, and the individual is the candidate up for examination.

X^1 A 625   *n.d., 1849*

« **4894** *Unconditional Commitment*

You must commit yourself unconditionally to Christ; nothing, neither the most trifling nor the most important thing, must stand between you and him in such a way that it is a condition and signifies that in a certain situation you cannot commit yourself. No, the commitment must be unconditioned. Then—and this is something else—you can pray that you will not be treated too severely.

The mistake of the man in the gospel story[1144] who wanted to be a disciple but wanted to bury his father first is that he wanted to do it *first,* consequently that he made it a condition; therefore if this condition was not granted, he would not commit himself—that is, he would commit himself only conditionally. He should have committed himself unconditionally, should have said: Even if I am asked to give up doing what I want so very much to do—bury my father—all right, I will give it up. I commit myself unconditionally; I do not make burying my father a prior condition—no, after I have unconditionally committed myself I request of you that this may be permitted.

It is most certainly true that committing yourself absolutely to Christ, which is absolute spirit and a dying to the world, means that you run the risk of Christ's making things so tangled for you that you must almost despair. This is what—and so must it be—is appalling for flesh and blood in unconditioned commitment. So must it be, but at the same time remember that he is indeed grace, that it is to grace that you commit yourself.

x^3 A 393   *n.d.*, 1850

« 4895 *The Unconditioned—"Reasons"*

The unconditioned cannot be assisted by reasons—for whatever needs to be supported by reasons is *eo ipso* not the unconditioned.

It is not a matter of there being, so to speak, no reasons—no, but the proclaimer dares not give reasons at any price; he must say: This is a betrayal of the unconditioned.

As far as the unconditioned is concerned, reasons, the fact that there are reasons, is not a plus—no, no, it is a minus, a subtracting which changes the unconditioned into the conditioned.

x^4 A 350   *n.d.*, 1851

« 4896 *Faith—"Reasons"*

Just as the statement must read: faith cannot be comprehended; the maximum is, it can be comprehended that it cannot be comprehended—so also: reasons cannot be given for an unconditioned; the maximum is, reasons can be given for the impossibility of giving reasons for an unconditioned.

x^4 A 356   *n d*, 1851

« 4897 *Dimensions*

A.

When someone wishes to win men[1145] to a cause or has a cause he wants to win them to, what does he do? He gives them reasons and reasons, shows them the advantages, etc.—since he (not being daft himself, as they say) is not unconditionally convinced of the unconditioned rightness of his cause, and he (as the saying goes, he does not consider men to be daft either) knows very well that this is the way it has to be if men are going to accept something. He needs men—therefore he makes every effort—how nice!—to win them, and wins them—yes, *mit Speck fangt man Maüse!*—[1146]with reasons and visions of conquering etc. etc.

B.

The ultimate purely human dimension is Socrates. He is so unconditionally established in his unconditioned relation to what he has to communicate that he—utterly consistent!—places irony between himself and those he wants to win for his cause; he ironically repels them; he has a cause to which he sacrifices everything, life itself; he wants to win men to it—but precisely because he himself is unconditionally related to it he ironically repels them, saying something like this: I do not know if I am doing anyone a service by getting him to accept my cause. Quite right, for willingness to accept an unconditional signifies willingness to suffer, and that is not everybody's cup of tea. But the very fact that he manages to repel men, even though he wants to win them, indicates that he himself is related to an unconditional. The common zeal for winning men merely expresses that one does not have an unconditional himself or is not unconditionally related to an unconditional.

C.
The God-man

He says: I am God, follow me, believe in me—and you will then be persecuted, cursed, loathed, thrown out of the synagogues, put to death.

This is divine. With these lines alone I prove that the God-man is the God-man—no human being has ever talked like this. Many a man prior to this and afterward had the audacity to pass himself off as being divine and has then also sought to win men—but *ad modum* A. It is a finite way; what does this mean? It means that he himself is not unconditionally convinced that he is the divine; he is eager to have people, a great number of them, accept his cause—for then, you see, he would even acquire palpable power (the fact that they are numerous) to help him coerce others into accepting his cause, and in any event he would be reassured himself. Consequently he passes himself off as being the divine; indeed, he says it himself, he claims and goes on claiming it—yes, but he still does not dare to say, for he does not dare to say: The result will be that you will be scourged, persecuted, etc. This he does not dare to say. Why should he? Indeed, he would run the risk that no one accepts his cause—aha!—that means he does not himself believe that he is the divine; in saying this about himself he does not dare let himself go and establish the criterion—no, he clings to men and palms himself off on them as being the divine—dreadful!

But Christ says: Come to me,[1147] all of you—the result of following me will be that you will be scourged, will lose everything, etc.—in other words, they all flee. It is doubly divine (no man has ever spoken thus) to say: Come to me, all of you, because as God he knows that he is concerned about all and there is no question here of any esoteric relation to a few individuals—and then to make the next statement. A human being with the stamina to say the latter would not then have the divinity to say, nevertheless, the former: Come to me, all of you.

This, you see, is the unconditioned. This is spirit, and this is the proof that Christ is the God-man, for in willing to win all, unconditionally, he frightens everybody away.

x^4 A 468   n.d., 1852

« 4898   *"I Am Who I Am"*[1148]

This is an analogy to the metaphysical point that the highest principles for all thought cannot be proved but only tautologically paraphrased: introverted infinity.

As everywhere else, here also the highest and the lowest have a similarity, for tautology is the lowest kind of communication, is rubbish —and tautology again is infinitely the highest; in this case, then, anything other than tautology would be rubbish.

x^4 A 480   n.d., 1852

« 4899   *"Prudence" Has Abolished Christianity;*
What It Means To Be "Sacrificed,"
Its Difficulties

For the longest time, from generation to generation, the law for every individual's striving has been this: Will only the possible; if a person ventures in such a way that he goes under, he has made a mistake, has not waited for the opportune moment, etc.; "to be victorious in such a way that one goes under" (the essentially Christian) is madness, and neither is it pleasing to God, the dear loving God.

Wait a minute! The idea is that each one should venture a little like that, and then the next generation a little, etc.—and then in the end it will come.

Can the unconditioned, Christianity, come into the world in that way? It is merely a quantitative trick. The continued effort of 70,000 generations, in which the venture is only so far out that there is a cautious victory, will not bring the unconditioned into the world; the striving of these 70,000 generations does not express drawing near to the unconditioned, but expresses: the unconditioned does not exist.

Or would it be possible to get this "forsaking everything" into the world by having everyone, for 70,000 generations, venture only so much that he forsook nothing but simply profited from it. Why then this rubbish about history and the historical process? Yes, it is hypocrisy, a subterfuge.

Prudence turns the whole thing around, selfishly makes the individual the τέλος:[1149] "I must, after all, enjoy life"; ergo, I shall not venture more than it will pay in the end, ergo, it is I who am the unconditioned, and the unconditioned is not the concern.

No, the unconditioned can be served only in such a way that he who serves defines it as the τέλος and himself as the sacrificed; he must endure going under, must find victory in going under.

So it is with being "sacrificed," and this is the way Christianity was served in the beginning.

The difficulty is that the one who serves in this way not only endures, suffers, does not only suffer patiently, no, the difficulty is to look to God in such a way that he maintains the elevation to insist that it is out of love on God's part, infinite love on God's part, that he assists him in entering into this suffering; thus he does not know God's love through God's prevention of his suffering, but—O blessed sublimity! —through God's sending suffering, keeping him in suffering, allowing him to suffer—something to which the purely human mentality is diametrically opposed.

The next problem is that spiritual trial [*Anfægtelse*] comes, spiritual trial which distresses him with men's judgment upon him, that it is arrogance and that his suffering is punishment for his arrogance.

The final difficulty is to avoid becoming self-important before God (meritoriousness). For if one is conscious that he looks to God egotistically only in order to profit from him, it is easy to protect oneself from presumptuously wanting to have merit before God. This is how meritoriousness is prevented these days. This is why "the sermon" has become sheer flattery of God. "You are the infinite, I am nothing, nothing, less than a sparrow." Well, this may be all right as humility, but it may also be a clever trick to get out of "imitation," which goes along with being somewhat more than a sparrow before God. Perhaps a crafty child could hit upon the idea of minimizing himself before his father, of being as insignificant as a little bird—thus getting out of the earnestness of being disciplined.

x⁴ A 509   n.d., 1852

« 4900 *An "Unconditioned" Served—by "Reasons"!*

Can an unconditioned be praised, commended, served by reasons? No. Anyone who does this reveals that he is a blockhead who cannot think two thoughts together, for "reasons" by means of the reasons transpose into relativity precisely that to which they are added, put it on the same level as that which is such only to a certain degree, like a pasha with seven reasons,[1150] another with only three reasons, etc.

No, the unconditioned, or that this is the unconditioned, is the unconditioned truth or unconditionally is the truth—the "unconditioned" is this: *abgemacht,*[1151] period—and therefore μετάβασις εἰς ἄλλο γένος,[1152] since a messenger is sent out with this unconditioned. This unconditioned must not be intellectually speculated about in the remotest way, researched, chattered about—no, it is the unconditioned, so hold your tongue.

How, then, is the unconditioned to be served? With utter simplicity, as can be seen in the New Testament.

"The unconditioned" is entrusted (as a king sends a servant on a mission) to "the apostle." He goes out, then, with the unconditioned truth to proclaim it unconditionally. If anyone were to ask him: For what reason should we assume this to be unconditioned truth, are you able to state some reasons, he would be obliged to answer: No, I shall certainly beware of that. Woe is me if I dared to do that; it is a dreadful thing to fall into the hands of the living God, and to give reasons would, in fact, change the unconditioned into the conditioned.

Consequently the apostle serves the unconditioned *in character;* this is the only way in which one can relate himself to the unconditioned. He proclaims this unconditioned early and late—and thereby comes to be declared mad by his contemporaries—but he sticks to his position, that it is unconditioned truth, and continues to proclaim it. Then he is persecuted, but he does not change; neither does he risk making a fool of God by giving reasons—no, he suffers but sticks to his position and goes on proclaiming it, continues to the end, until he is put to death. This is character: service—the proof, the only possible proof, that this man was entirely clear that what he had to proclaim was unconditioned truth, was from God.

The person who supplies reasons manifestly has greater fear of those to whom he comes to proclaim than of him from whom he comes (for reasons are relativity itself), but as a consequence he does not come from God, neither does he have any unconditioned to proclaim, no matter how much he gives "assurances."

But the Christianity "the pastors" represent is also a very curious kind of unconditioned, it is an unconditioned which—assuming an appropriate waiting period of at least a half dozen years (before the unconditioned!)—supports a man with family, and as the years advance gives him rank, etc. Well, an unconditioned truth like that can be served very well by—"reasons."

x^4 A 569   *n.d.*, 1852

« **4901** *Only the Unconditioned Can Carry a Man*

Let a man willingly work for the good—diligently, strenuously—yet with the expectation that he will derive joy from it and see the fruits of it: well, done this way it will not amount to much, for if he is not willing to venture beyond the calculable fruits of his labor during his lifetime, that is, fruits visible in his contemporaries, then he is obliged to accommodate to a certain degree and to make concessions now here and now there, so that his willing the good actually becomes an illusion.

Well, then, let a man more resignedly stake his whole life—but still in such a way that he wants to have the satisfaction that the next generation will improve: done this way it will not amount to much either. For soon he will come to understand existence so profoundly that he will see that the world never gets better, that if he actually ventured his life for the good in this way, the next generation would merely make him the subject of lectures and actually would become only worse. Consequently this idea (that his life would benefit posterity) will not motivate a man really to stake his life for the good.

Thus there is but one view left, but it is adequate—it is that a person says to himself: As far as venturing everything is concerned, I have no "Why" at all; I am controlled simply and solely by this unconditional; I must do it, I cannot do otherwise. Why? Well, that is up to God.

That is to say: with the intellectual awareness which a more eminent individual may have these days, no consideration of ends-in-view can get him actually to venture everything.

We urgently need the unconditioned again. In the unconditioned all teleology vanishes.

We have been living in the inversion that the more "Why's" there are the easier it is for a man to be able to venture everything—no, every "Why" simply subtracts. Only when every "Why" vanishes in the night of the unconditioned and becomes silent in the silence of the unconditioned, only then can a man venture everything; if he dimly glimpses one "Why," something is impaired, he sees 1,000 "Why's"—watch out, he will never venture a thing but will become a professor of the 1,000 "Why's."

X^4 A 613   *n.d.*, 1852

« 4902 *Being-in-and-for-Itself*——*"Faith"*

Is there a being-in-and-for-itself? Christianity answers: Yes, that is what I am.

How is it known whether or not someone is related to a being-in-and-for-itself, a relationship which certainly must be in the form of the unconditioned?

It is known by this, that he holds fast to this being-in-and-for-itself, even though he *suffers* because of the relationship (thus the relationship is the occasion and cause of suffering).

If someone wants to relate himself to a being-in-and-for-itself and also have the things of this world, then this is a duplicity.

But how does one live in Christendom these days? One lives in such a way that he imagines that he is relating in faith to the being-in-and-for-itself, but stays as far away from it as possible (probably so that he does not discover his delusion) and on the whole is mainly occupied with making his earthly life as comfortable as possible, getting through life satisfactorily—yes, he even thinks that the relationship to the being-in-and-for-itself is supposed to help him—what nonsense! —to get through this world satisfactorily, to have a good life of it.

But what is Christianity's intention for this life? That it shall be used to help one out into—and to let God help us out into—such decisions that it becomes clear to one whether or not he has faith or imagines himself to have it.

This is why the scriptures prescribe means you are to use to tighten up your life in such a way that this life may become an examination as to whether or not you have the faith.

But it is not so that strenuous exertion and suffering prove that you are truly relating in faith to the being-in-and-for-itself (for then pride and arrogance as well could venture out in this way)—no, faith is the assurance, there is no other assurance. But strenuous exertion and suffering are there so that you do not have to reproach yourself for evading the means of intensification which Christianity recommends—yes, commands—in Holy Scripture.

Therefore unconditioned faith is not present wherever this suffering is found, but wherever this suffering is not, unconditioned faith is not—there faith is merely something imaginary.

But this is how we men have conducted ourselves. We have introduced "grace" to release us from all strenuous exertion (authentic dying to the world, renouncing this world, suffering for the doctrine, etc.) and then we make the faith something imaginary and go on living totally occupied with enjoying this life—and this is how we approach eternity, where the decision is: relate your life to a being-in-and-for-itself. Was Christianity this being-in-and-for-itself for you?

x^4 A 636   *n.d.*, 1852

« **4903** *Serving the Unconditioned*

All who have served the unconditioned have first received a blow that seemed to crush them, yet without slaying them, a blow that infinitely elevated them again but under which their entire lives remained and by virtue of which their lives were what they were. So it was with Paul[1153] when he was thrown to the ground, so also with Luther[1154] when the lightning struck him and killed his friend, so also with Pascal[1155] when the horse ran away with him.

This blow is like a sunstroke directly on the brain. It is the infinite concentrated intensively in one single blow and one single moment.

The rest of us cannot bear to come this close to the unconditioned; therefore we continually put it at some distance, just as one covers himself to guard against sunstroke. Our relationship to the unconditioned therefore becomes only a relation of reflection or in reflection.

Moreover no man can bring himself this close to the unconditioned, he cannot do it, and no man dares venture it since this blow, this sunstroke, is like the deadliest danger, something every man must shrink from as more horrible than death.

It is Governance itself which brings a man so close to the unconditioned or strikes him this way with the sunstroke of the unconditioned. This being the case, it is the greatest favor which can be shown to a man.

It is the concentration of the infinite in one single blow and one single moment; as soon as it is divided in such a way that it, for example, strikes in two places and acts in two successive moments, it is not the unconditioned.

To be sure, the blow of the unconditioned also takes the form of sin-consciousness; there is a concentration of sin or past sins in one single blow, in one single moment, and this falls on a man's conscience. This is again a form of the unconditioned which can give momentum, compared to which any movement in reflection is a remaining-on-the-spot or a no-moving-off-the-spot.

X^5 A 17 *n.d.*, 1852

« 4904 *The Basic Confusion in Christendom, or That Christianity Has Its Center of Gravity in the Wrong Place, or That It Is Standing on Its Head, or That It Does Not Exist*[1156]

The misrelation (in relation to the original) can be categorically and precisely expressed with two clauses: Christianity was originally represented (by the preachers) in the fear of God; nowadays it is represented (by the preachers) in the fear of man—but this is also turning everything upside down.

Christianity was originally proclaimed by someone who came with direct orders from God, yes, with God directly behind him—this was discerned in his fear and trembling, something we are scarcely ever able to get a conception of. You see, he feared God—but he did not fear men, although he knew very well that they had the power to put him to death. But he feared God; therefore there cannot even remotely be any question of giving reasons, or of scientific scholarship—O, infinite abyss of nonsense, that where God joins in the game in this way there should be time for scientific scholarship.

But how different in Christendom's later times, in our time. The impression one gets is that God had pulled himself millions of miles away from actuality, pulled himself back into seclusion. But he has given something in writing, something we call God's Word—and although we call it God's Word, we treat it as calmly as the papers of someone dead for 1,800 years; no one notices, if I may put it this way, that the whip is burning.[1157]

Then the preacher begins. But naturally he is not at all afraid of God; for him God is infinitely far, far away. What the preacher fears is—men, so he is careful to preach Christianity in such a way that they do not deny him his career, offerings, and incidentals. Thus the art of preaching consists of seeing how the wind blows, how men really want to be talked to—this he studies, and then he preaches Christianity. This is Christianity!

Then come the "reasons," and then "scientific scholarship" appears, whole sciences and professors etc., all these enterprises which, themselves dependent on men by needing their money etc., are supposed to help men into—the unconditioned! If someone who was going to run a race came rolling up dressed in seven overcoats, five pairs of trousers, and enormous boots and an open umbrella, everyone would find it ridiculous, but scientific scholarship and professors and reasons which are supposed to help men into the unconditioned are fundamentally just as ridiculous.

No, only the fear of God can help a man into the unconditioned ("help" is here used in the sense old Professor Nielsen[1158] used it when he said: Boy, I will help you). This business of scientific scholarship and reasons and men who together with their families live by preaching reasons and with the help of reasons help men after a fashion *to a certain degree* into the unconditioned (how masterly topsy-turvy!) shows how infinitely far away God must be from us, how infinitely distanced.

It is idyllic that in the virgin forests of America a whole family of frogs lives in the rain water collected on a single palm leaf—but it is still strangely topsy-turvy that in relation to what in the eminent sense is the catastrophe of existence, Christianity's entry into the world, that in relation to this a man and his family live by preaching "reasons"; it is strangely topsy-turvy that what was the catastrophe of existence ended by being almost the surest thing to get married on.

X^5 A 40   *n.d.*, 1852

« 4905 *"Something Is Better Than Nothing"*

Of course this holds true of everything finite, temporal, and earthly—and why? Because the finite is not itself the unconditioned but the relative. No wealth is unconditioned wealth, wealth is a relativity—therefore something is always better than nothing, for the nature of all finite things is to be something, not to be all or not to be.

It is otherwise with the unconditioned. The relation here is a matter of either/or, either unconditioned or not. Here it is very far from something being better than nothing. No, no, if the unconditioned does not exist unconditionally for a person, one is still always closer to it by unconditionally not relating to it than by having muddled and garbled even the unconditioned with the nonsense that something is better than nothing.

This is what has confused all Christianity. Rather than that Christianity is to be served as the unconditioned, it has been treated as something finite, where it holds true that something is better than nothing. The movement is in the wrong direction altogether. One thousand clergymen, not one of whom serves the essentially Christian unconditionally, are always considered to be something, after all, and better than nothing; if they could get 10,000 clergymen of this sort they would no doubt think this was something still more and consequently a good deal better than nothing. Abysmal depth of nonsense, thoroughly adulterating Christianity!

* *

Strangely enough, this thought has occupied me a good deal; more than once I have picked up the pen, wanting to write it down, but it would not clarify itself to me in such a way that I believed everyone could grasp it. Last night (May 10), at a time I was not thinking about this even in the remotest way, it suddenly occurred to me in all its clarity that only finitely is it true that something is better than nothing, where the infinite is concerned, the opposite holds—nothing is better than something.

x^5 A 118   May 11, 1853

« 4906 *According to the New Testament To Be a Christian Is To Be Sacrificed*

By this, however, is not meant all instances of being a martyr to men but to be sacrificed in the context of and in connection with relating oneself to the unconditioned, for Christianity is the unconditioned and to relate oneself unconditionally to the unconditioned is *eo ipso* to be sacrificed to the conditioned.

I refer here to Mark 9: 42–50, which presents the unconditioned requirement in terms of *unconditionally* avoiding offense. And then it reads (consequently with reference to those who unconditionally avoid offense): "For everyone will be salted with fire, and every sacrifice will be salted with salt." Therefore the unconditioned means to be sacrificed, to become a sacrifice. Then it reads further, "Have salt within yourselves," so that even without becoming a sacrifice to others the Christian becomes a sacrifice by being sacrificed in the unconditional relation to the unconditioned.

That he is a sacrifice is expressed by the metaphor which Christ continually uses and is here repeated: to be salt. To be salt means not to exist for oneself but to exist for others, that is, to be sacrificed. "Salt" has no being in itself but is purely teleological, and to be qualified wholly in a teleological way means to be sacrificed.

Yes, as mentioned, Christ presents sacrifice in such a way that unconditionally relating oneself to the unconditioned also means to be sacrificed; therefore not only the martyr is a sacrifice but also one who unconditionally relates himself to the unconditioned, even though he is not persecuted.

Understood in this way there is no objection to the unconditioned renunciation of the Middle Ages. The fault, as I have pointed out elsewhere (in the journals [i.e., x^4 A 531]), lay in conformity to the world by wanting to enjoy prestige as the extraordinary instead of simply expressing that it was merely the simple requirement. In this way the unconditioned relation to the unconditioned was further hindered, since a finitizing middle term of this sort was interpolated.

xi^1 A 7   n.d., 1854

« 4907 *Rejoinder*

Let an apostle or a witness to the truth proclaim Christianity in character and with authority and let me be a heathen—and I believe I could become a Christian!

But to be a Christian, to be brought up in this interminable nonsense, in this interminable nonsense with millions of preachers and trillions of Christians: O, my God, how is it possible to get an impression of the unconditioned!

xi^1 A 29   n.d., 1854

« 4908 *The Night of the Unconditioned*

By nature man dreads walking in the dark—no wonder, then, that he by nature dreads the unconditioned, getting involved with the unconditioned, of which it holds true that no night and "no darkness is half so black" as this darkness and this night in which all relative goals (the ordinary milestones and road markers), in which all considerations (the lights we generally use to help ourselves), in which even the most sensitive and warmest feelings of devotion—are extinguished, for otherwise it is not unconditionally the unconditioned.

xi^1 A 95   n.d., 1854

« 4909 *The Human Is the Relative, and Man Is a Social Animal*[1159]

To become or to be the only unfortunate person is a hard thing. But is it not just as hard for a man to be the only one who comes to be blessed, can this be a blessed thought for a man.

Here we see how elevated Christianity is and what dreadful collisions it therefore points to: to be blessed in contradistinction to others, in contradistinction to the people one loves most of all, father, mother, wife, children—what a dreadful thought!

But such is the unconditioned, and Christianity is the unconditioned.

Is it too much to ask, then, as I propose, that we at least admit that what we are living in is not New Testament Christianity at all.

XI[1] A 351 *n.d.*, 1854

« 4910 *"Let Me First Say Farewell"*[1160] *etc.*

All those portions in which Christ unconditionally accentuates the unconditioned this way must be interpreted in relation to the making of conditions by the persons concerned, expressing thereby that they did not unconditionally will to seek the kingdom of God *first.*

It would have been a different matter altogether if the person concerned had said, "I make no conditions, there is nothing I desire *first,* but you know how much I would like to say farewell to my family." Or if he did not say this but still thought it, thus did not hesitate to choose the unconditioned unconditionally, it was certainly possible for him who knew all things, and consequently what he was thinking, to have said: "Good, follow me, but first go and say farewell to your family."

In other words, Christ's concern is the sovereignty of the unconditioned, that there must not be any condition, a first; if it is to be "first," then any concession is unconditionally excluded. On the other hand, it cannot mean that Christ was unable to sympathize with this human wish to want to bury his father, to want to say farewell to his family, he who himself wept at the grave of Lazarus,[1161] he who himself with a son's solicitude entrusted his mother.[1162]

XI[1] A 427 *n.d.*, 1854

« 4911 *The Divine——The Human*

are related to each other as polemically as possible, according to Christian teaching.

When Peter,[1163] with every good intention, *humanely* wants to hold Christ back, Christ says as categorically as possible: You perceive only what is human; this is Satan's impulse. Get behind me, Satan.

On the other hand, when Christ talks to the Jews about God and himself (for example, John 8),[1164] the Jews cry: He has Satan, the devil; he is a Samaritan. And Christ declares the Jews to be the children of the devil.

The human as such is the relative, the mediocre, the bliss-producing "to a certain degree." Seen from this point of view, the unconditioned is the devil, for the unconditioned is a real plague for this human mediocrity, which egotistically wants an easy life of sensate enjoyment and does not want to learn from the unconditioned to say —the unconditioned is indeed sheer restlessness, strenuousness, and torment.

That the unconditioned can be the divine, that what occasions so much torment and trouble can be the divine, cannot be grasped by a man before he has surrendered to it and learned from the unconditioned itself that it is the divine. If a man continues with this purely human outlook, then the unconditioned is the devil, or God is the evil, as modern French philosophy[1165] maintains, God is the evil in the sense that he is guilty of all man's unhappiness; if we could only eliminate the unconditioned, knock all ideals out of our heads, everything would go well—but God makes us unhappy, he is the evil.

On the other hand, from God's point of view it is this very mediocrity, seeking a life of sensate enjoyment, which is demonic possession, is of the devil. From God's point of view the worst we say of the wildest sins—that they are devil-inspired—is very likely more true of mediocrity's sensate enjoyment of life, because, ideally, this mediocrity is much farther from higher things than the greatest sins. Where there is restlessness[1166]—and this is present where there are great sins—there is still a possibility of a higher life, but this passivity is as far as possible from "spirit."

Mediocrity is the principle which forms the human race's *compact mass*. And what the unconditioned and thus also God must demand as the first condition for entering into relation with men is that they be split apart. This, again, is why great crimes make the relation more possible than does mediocrity, for great crimes isolate.

Instinctively "man" has a tactic he uses against "spirit" (just as the cuttlefish stirs up mud and the skunk spreads a stench and the porcupine raises quills): Let us form a crowd; this is man's tactic, his mode of defense.* Just as the ostrich sticks its head into the ground and thinks it is invisible, so man forms a crowd and thinks no one can see him. We speak of not being able to see the woods for the trees; by his tactic man hopes that one cannot see the trees for the woods. Just like the person who says he is not at home to visitors, man is not at home by becoming a third person—that is, in the crowd—instead of being an *I.*

As a crowd, man is physical power; he carries on *en masse* as an animal-creature and is very happy and pleased to be protected as mass against God, the unconditioned, idea, spirit, the ideals. What a tragic kind of well-being, for whatever is mass is always that which goes to waste in every generation, and is itself to blame for it.

XI^1 A 516   *n.d.*, 1854

« **4912**

* *In margin of 4911* (XI^1 A 516):
It is done cunningly this way: Let us join together, form a crowd, in order to strive toward the ideals—because to form crowds is precisely the way to get rid of the ideals.

XI^1 A 517   *n.d.*

« **4913** *A Tactical Discretion*

When the unconditioned is to be introduced—and the contemporary age excels on the most dreadful scale in vapidly agreeing to everything, everything to a certain degree, then discretion invites one not to do what one otherwise would prefer doing both for his own sake and the sake of others—before making the crucial charge, to go and speak to the powers that be, to see if this possibly could lead them to yield a little bit. No, this one dares not do, because—yes, the tragedy is simply the certainty that however strongly one expressed himself, they would go along with it up to a certain degree—and thus one would simply have defeated his purpose: to introduce the unconditioned [*in margin:* the heterogeneity of the unconditioned would promptly or soon be made unrecognizable in the homogeneity of characterless-ness]. No, in the face of this characterless "to a certain degree" the unconditioned should be introduced with something of the beast of prey's lunging leap and the bird of prey's plunging attack.

It is this which has been long overlooked in Christendom. Christianity is the unconditioned—millions have been persuaded to enter into it from generation to generation, but it has not been observed that they went along with it to a certain degree, whereby in the course of time what is now called Christianity has come to be something unconditioned in only one sense—namely, it is unconditionally the opposite of New Testament Christianity.

XI^1 A 526   *n.d.*, 1854

« 4914 *Making Distinctions*

Basically, all *upbringing* is a matter of making distinctions, learning to make distinctions. The child is continually admonished to make distinctions. The farm boy who becomes a soldier has it pounded into him: You must make distinctions! The person from the country offends constantly in the metropolis because he does not know how to make distinctions. It is the same in more serious situations. A stupid prank by an adolescent is counted as nothing, but if it is an older person, they say: He should know how to make distinctions.

Now apply this to Christendom, particularly Protestantism, particularly in Denmark, and you will see that it can be quite simply understood as a lack of upbringing, a boorish attitude toward the divine. This wanting to have an eternal salvation and—ALSO—the lack of upbringing lies in this *also;* it is obvious that one who talks this way has not been brought up, lacks upbringing, has not learned to make distinctions. For there are many things in relation to which it is suitable, very suitable, to say that one wants them and *also;* yes, actually it holds for all things—with one exception, the unconditioned, but the unconditioned is precisely what Christianity is. To want to have an eternal salvation and—also—is just like the behavior of a country bumpkin who, having just arrived by cattle-boat from Jutland, goes up to the full-uniformed general in the barracks and says: Listen here, my good man. But the corporal will no doubt teach him something else, teach him to make distinctions.

Christendom has removed the expressions of respect from Christianity, the expressions of respect which are related to divine majesty —Christendom needs upbringing. The time of the prophets, both major and minor, is long past; our age no longer believes in prophets:

thus there is only one kind of prophet left—the club-prophets, who have always known how to make sure they are believed, for even the worst infidel has never doubted a good thrashing.

Christendom lacks upbringing. It does not help much that magnificent houses have been built to God, that both his Word and his priests have been bound up in velvet, this is of no interest whatsoever to God, but this *also* has to go. God has a particular language for addressing him—the language of action, the transformation of the mind, the expression in one's life; it is no good for us to bow and scrape before him in words and phrases and in such activities as building churches and binding Bibles in velvet.

How epigrammatic: if any man has had any pretensions of being a cultured, cultivated person and been very satisfied that he is that, it is Bishop Mynster.[1167] And yet I maintain that from a Christian point of view he was as ill-bred a churl as any country bumpkin.

XI^1 A 568   *n.d.*, 1854

« 4915 *The Unconditioned—The Relative*

The law for introducing a relativity is: Look around, look around; the law for introducing an unconditional is: Close your eyes, become blind in faith, for heaven's sake do not look around; just as the fox lost the cheese because he listened to what was being said, so you will personally lose the unconditioned if you look around, regardless of whether your circumspection signifies looking around in anxiety for your own welfare or looking around out of so-called sympathy.

Christianity has totally vanished[1168] because what little Christianity has been introduced has always followed the law: Look around.

But, after all, the world is so wretched, lies immersed in evil—as Christianity teaches[1169]—so if you want to look around, you must say every time: Just to get people to live a little more decently than they do would be a great thing in itself—and so you slacken off and do not introduce the unconditioned. Or it would be a great thing in itself just to get a few people to adopt to some degree a toned-down Christianity —and so you slacken off and do not introduce the unconditioned.

XI^2 A 2   *n.d.*, 1854

« 4916 *The Unconditioned Beginning*

It is indeed most strenuous and exhausting for a poor human being to begin unconditionally, which is the case with everything related to the unconditioned; but then again there is the consolation which only the *unconditioned* beginning has—namely, that one can begin at any and every moment. What torments men, what they use, in part faintheartedly and in part probably also villainously and cunningly, to torment themselves or to excuse themselves is that one says: Yes, a year ago, or a month ago, if this or that had not happened, I could have begun, but now I cannot. And this is partially true when the beginning involves conditions. But just as the ostrich is able to digest iron and stone, the unconditioned has the power to assimilate everything—and then begin. Whatever it is you think may prevent you—begin unconditionally; then this belongs to the beginning, is no longer that which prevents a beginning but is that with which you begin. The unconditioned does not blink an eye, does not make mistakes about anything, but transforms whatever it is into the beginning, if you will begin unconditionally.

What I have pointed out elsewhere [i.e., XI^1 A 456] holds true of this unconditioned beginning: always to see the task. The person who practices this art sees the very hindrance to be the task. And assuredly this is how it is, the hindrance and the task are one and the same, only seen from different sides.

XI^2 A 60   *n.d.*, 1854

« 4917 *The Christian*

Here is a definition, somewhat modernized. Christians are pages of the unconditioned majesty.

The only art they practice is also unconditionally the only art: unconditionally to worship—not with words and chatter, hyperbolical prose or sonorous verse—no, with action in unconditioned obedience.

Just as the back and muscles of the tightrope-walker's child are made lithe and supple from earliest childhood, and this daily exercise results in his becoming thoroughly limber, able to make any movement, unconditionally every movement, take positions that would be murder for an adult, yet always with ease and with a smile, just so it is to worship the unconditioned majesty, to worship him unconditionally, with no thought of any why and wherefore, to worship him unconditionally in everything, always happy, grateful, smiling. Now we understand what the ancient Church meant when it talked about the Christians being taken up among the angels after death—this [worship] is indeed a kind of schooling for that.

But what has happened is that the concept of the unconditioned and the idea of the unconditioned majesty disappeared long ago from

Christendom. God has been downgraded, dragged down into the abjectness of relativities and finite teleology; we have foisted upon God the ideal that he, too, humanly speaking, has a cause and needs men, should be glad that anyone would want to serve him. We have foisted on him the idea that world history is a mighty important cause to him, so that he probably has his hands full taking care of and coping with it and thus is obliged to keep his wits properly about him, as they say.

No, heaven's majesty is not such a majesty. This is why one single Christian life—if there were such a one—concerns him more than all four world-historical monarchies, and all the hullabaloo we humans have contrived and contrived to attribute importance to.

Just as an eminent "thinker" looks simply and solely at the thought-determinants and calmly puts aside masses of manuscripts even though these contain most interesting knowledge, saying: *Finaliter* from all this I learn nothing; and just as "the mathematician" imperturbably says of the poet's tragedy, "What does it prove?"[1170] just so does God look unmoved at only one thing, the unconditioned worship, and of the four monarchies and all the bravado of professors and assistant professors, who by talking about them seek themselves to become the subject of discussion, with the help of history to become history themselves—of them he says: What does it prove anyway?

XI^2 A 204   *n.d.*, 1854

« 4918 *Christendom (Protestantism) without God*

One of two things must be said: either Christendom worships a muddlehead or Christendom, in spite of all its Christian preaching and preaching, has no God at all.

This is the situation. In the course of generations, the race has degenerated more and more, has become less and less significant and more and more finds consolation in extensity and numbers to make up for what has been lost of the intensive. In a certain sense this also holds true for animals. In animal species, since there are no individuals [*Individer*] but only specimens [*Exemplarer*] the extensive has significance and in a sense an animal species becomes more significant in proportion to numerical extension. But since the whole point about the human race is precisely that the individual is higher than the race, the despair underlying forfeiture of the intensive for the extensive becomes apparent.

In the course of generations the race has become less significant.

This is consistent with saying that in another sense it has made progress. It has grown in the direction of common sense, finite common sense. But this advance is in a deeper sense so ambiguous that it is retrogression, it is retrogression from the unconditioned, from the impression of, a conception of the unconditioned, and an advance in the direction of getting to know the relative more and more, the mediocre, the "up-to-a-point." Thus it is easy to see that this progress is a falling away from the eternal, for the life of this world consists in: "up-to-a-point," everything "up-to-a-point." When this has been achieved, when everything is only up to a point, then the world will have managed to free itself from all association with the eternal, which is what this world naturally tends to do and which takes place amid the rejoicing of men, who admire themselves and the race for the matchless progress that is made.

The unconditioned, the being-in-and-for-itself—yes, show me if you can, but I doubt that there is a single person living who has the remotest impression of such a being or who could entertain the thought of wanting to relate himself to such a being, which of course can be done only by unconditionally obeying, by being willing to let oneself be reduced to nothing, if you please, for the unconditioned is fatal to relative being and only through this fatality can it be given life.

But when the unconditioned does not exist [*ikke er til*] for men, what good is it to have something called God but which is only a name, since God is indeed unconditioned being.

Consequently, one of two things: Christianity is without God or it has a muddlehead for its God.

The latter is surely the truth. Take the New Testament. There is no Christian qualification that does not bear the mark of the unconditioned. Place alongside this the customary preaching of Christianity or, instead, the existential proclamation (for a little oratory is of no importance and incidentally the oratory itself is not exactly marked by the unconditioned), and you will see that everything is "up-to-a-point" or, what amounts to the same thing, that there are reasons everywhere, everywhere a *what for*, which is answered—in other words, there is no unconditioned.

Take just one example which I have frequently used [i.e., XI^2 A 47 and 161], take the idea of martyrdom. Imagine that there is someone who commits himself to becoming a martyr (incidentally, this is far too flattering to the general run in Christendom)—you will see that he does not rest in the unconditioned conception of martyrdom's unconditioned validity—no, he has reasons—in short, he is basically a politician, basically still homogeneous with this world of relativities.

XI² A 205   n.d., 1854

« 4919 *Religious Guarantees*

Surely there is no guarantee for the unconditioned; this is implicit, for whatever is not the unconditioned itself is *eo ipso* inferior and consequently the guarantee is inferior—thus there is no guarantee.

But there is a difference. When a man renounces all earthly rewards, advantages, and enjoyment in order to proclaim that there is something higher—well, everyone knows it does not necessarily follow that this is true, for it can, after all, be arrogance etc.; but still it is a kind of guarantee, for the very thing he does is certainly superior, consequently a guarantee at least that there is something higher.

But when someone wants to guarantee that there is something higher by the fact that his proclamation of the existence of this something higher makes him some altogether trivial earthly profit, etc., if possible even more trivial than that of the most insignificant tradesman who is never so assured of a profit, then this is nonsense, is really ridiculous, if anything at all, yes, the ultimately ridiculous, among grown men an obscenity.

One of two things, either/or: either give up the things of this earth or confess that this is what you want—we are only poets, orators, or, however you want to express it, not preachers—but not this confusing, meaningless talk, to say nothing of hypocrisy, that it is the highest one wants but also the things of this earth, for this, after all, is a downright self-contradiction; if you *also* desire the things of this earth, it is, after all, *eo ipso,* not the highest that you want.

XI² A 320   n.d., 1854

UNIVERSALISM

« **4920**

They argue about whether God intends the salvation of all or only of some—almost forgetting the far more important theme: You, O God, intend my salvation; would that I myself might intend it also.

X^1 A 516 *n.d.*, 1849

« **4921** *We Are All Saved*

It is pure and simple shyster-talk to recommend taking this as a sign of humility, true Christian love, noble humaneness, etc.

The fact is that the statement is man's own invention to avoid the pressure of being saved in *contradistinction* to others. But hypocritical man also wants to be honored for humility, truly noble humaneness, etc. O, you rogue, and to think that you were created in the image of God.

XI^1 A 261 *n.d.*, 1854

« **4922** *For Orientation on Christian Issues*

As soon as the question of a man's eternal salvation is made commensurable with a decision in time by a relation to something historical occurring in time, the nightmare comes at once, the torments of sympathy, that there will be countless millions who will not be eternally saved.

If one thinks with regard to the countless millions who lived before this historical event and the countless millions who live after it but in complete ignorance of it, if one assumes that they could not possibly be eternally damned for this reason—if one assumes this and finds a sympathetic relief in it, the matter still remains painful with respect to the millions who lived afterwards, or for every individual in relation to the countless many who are his contemporaries and to whom that historical event is proclaimed but upon whom it does not make a decisive impression.

UNIVERSALISM

The more exactly the terms of salvation are stipulated, the fewer there always are who one can believe will be saved. But sympathy finds it tormenting to be saved in contradistinction to others.

So I have interpreted it as follows: the terms of salvation differ for every individual, for every single solitary human being. There is a universal proclamation of Christianity, but with respect to the conditions of salvation every single individual must relate to God as a single individual.

This is undeniably a sympathetic relief; that which to me is so crucial that for me the terms of salvation are bound up with it—I understand this to pertain only to me and that the terms of salvation for every other individual are different.

Yet this sympathetic relief (which makes me dare exert myself without being anxious for the others) has a sad note to it—namely, that one person cannot help another at all, cannot reassure him in a more profound sense or himself gain reassurance from another person.

I must accept the fact that this is the way it is. But how do I interpret it? I interpret it as a forward step and as a punishment, as a judgment upon Christendom.

What was it that men wanted? They wanted to throw out all authority. Fine! Here, then, is the punishment, and as always the punishment fits the sin. You shall be free! And when you are lying on your deathbed, perhaps in despair, and would give anything to have a person with authority reassure you—no, my friend, it is too late now, you did not want to have authority, and therefore there is none, either.

In this way it is a punishment, but it is also easy to see that it is a step forward: from now on mankind is established in its rights, every single person is suitable for the highest.

This formula, if I may say so, from now on will simultaneously stand as a judgment upon Christendom and as a forward step.

Note. Compare this with the conclusion of my "literary review" of *Two Ages*.[1171]

XI[1] A 296 *n.d.*, 1854

THE UPBUILDING

« **4923**

And so it is no longer devotional literature which teaches us to despise the present and hasten to eternity, but the tales of everyday authors.[1172]

I A 201   July 2, 1836

« **4924**

Only that which is upbuilding truly unites jest and earnestness. Consequently it is a jest—more priceless than the whole world—that God in heaven is the only great one whom one unceremoniously addresses with *Du*,[1173] even though one is ever so insignificant; but this jest is also the deepest earnestness, simply because every human being does it. On the other hand, it is a very mediocre, cheap, and human joke when a particular favorite addresses an earthly majesty with the familiar *Du;* therefore there is no earnestness at all in this jest.

IV A 80   *n.d.*, 1843

« **4925**

To exchange the temporal for the eternal (usually said about death) can be used with great effect in the upbuilding [discourse].

V A 67   *n.d.*, 1844

« **4926** *An Upbuilding Observation*

In an old devotional book[1174] (Arndt) it says that God sleeps as lightly with those who suffer as the mother with a sick child, that she awakens the instant it moves. A masterpiece of pathos, skirting the boundary of distraction.

* *

In one of the morning or evening prayers in *The Evangelical Hymnbook*[1175] is the line: "While we are sleeping, you keep watch, O God" —alas, as if we could help ourselves if only we were awake. No, there should be added: But when we are awake, we understand our own welfare no better than if we lay in a deep sleep—thus, O God, you must keep watch just the same.

This remark may well be in an earlier journal, for I remember that it occurred to me earlier.

x^3 A 83   *n.d.*, 1850

VENTURE, RISK

« 4927

..... However different the knights and scholastics were, they nevertheless had this in common—they went in search of adventure; for thought, too, has a certain setting-out-on-an-adventure about it which is just as invigorating, just as noble, and just as heaven-born as the knights!.

II A 428   May 16, 1839

« 4928

Aladdin[1176] is so very refreshing because of the genial, childlike audacity of the wildest wishes. For how many are there in our day who truly dare wish, dare desire, dare demand, dare address nature either with a *polite* child's *"bitte, bitte"* or with the raging frenzy of one damned; how many are there who, inspired by what our age talks about so much, that man is created in God's image, are his natural representatives, have the authentic voice of command, the authentic, divinely official style, or do we not all stand like Nourredin, bowing and scraping, worrying about asking too much or too little; or does not this magnificent demanding gradually diminish to morbid reflecting over the *I,* from insisting to inquiring, which from the outset the child is indeed *brought up* to do.

II A 451   June 10, 1839

« 4929

One of those servants who each received his pound[1177] when the master went away on a journey immediately went and buried it. The error at the very outset was that he fabricated a semblance, an illusion. The one who puts his pound to work risks it at that very moment; not until the next moment does it become apparent whether he won anything or has even lost his pound. The one who buries it immediately seems to have done something, seems to have accomplished something—has he not protected himself? And when one has already done something, then, to be sure, one can have an easy time. Ah, precisely that is the pitfall—and that servant was cast into uttermost darkness by the master.[1178]

VIII[1] A 66   n.d., 1847

« 4930

A person can distress the spirit[1179] by venturing too much. True it is, but in such a case there is the consolation that punishment will surely come and will help him if he honestly humbles himself under it. But a person can also distress the spirit by venturing too little. Alas, but this comes home to him only after a long time, perhaps after many years when he is living in the security he sought by avoiding danger, and now he must experience the truth that he was untrue to himself; perhaps it does not come until old age, perhaps not until eternity. But in any case the thing to do about venturing too little is, while doing it, to admit humbly before God that he is coddling himself, that he weakly, perhaps cowardly, coddles himself; this he does lest he begin to imagine that what he is doing is mighty clever—alas, for then a man is lost forever. At that very moment the eternal in a man goes out, the God-relationship closes up, the truth in him dies, and he becomes loathsome untruth. If, on the other hand, he makes the humble admission—perhaps he was sick and therefore despondent, perhaps he was too hard on himself in judging himself, but in any case he keeps his God-relationship. The admission will keep him awake and alert, will not permit him to become happy in a dearly purchased security and distance from danger, and perhaps tomorrow, perhaps in a year, faith and confident boldness will rise up in him and he will be able to venture.

IX A 351   n.d., 1848

« 4931

Shrewdness promptly uses the means of the moment; the good renounces using them. When the good has triumphed in spite of everything, people sometimes, on the basis of results, explain the good as a kind of shrewdness and say: After all, it was the smartest thing to do. It [the means] must be looked at together [with the envisioned result] in "the beginning." For when the result is at hand, people forget the "risk," forget that there actually was a risk involved in giving up the means of the moment. If shrewdness and willing the good were one and the same, then they must be seen as one and the same in "the beginning." "The beginning" is the crucial, the decisive point.

X^2 A 144   n.d., 1849

« 4932

In the first lap of a man's life the greatest danger is *not to venture.* However, when he has been profoundly venturesome, then the greatest danger in the second lap is to venture too much. In the first lap by not venturing one swings off into the service of trivialities; in the second, by venturing too much one swings into the visionary, perhaps into presumption.

X^2 A 531   *n.d.,* 1850

« 4933 *How Does a Person Become a Christian?*

It is very simple. Take any Christian rule for action—venture to act in accordance with it. The action whereby you become engaged in actuality will be branded with the unconditioned, for this is the brand of everything truly Christian.

At the same moment through this action you will collide with the environing world, which has its life essentially in "up to a point."

It may be put this way: the collisions will be such that in a certain sense you will come to discover the essentially Christian and the collisions of the essentially Christian, while you will also come to discover that you need Christianity in order to persevere in these collisions, since you will come to suffer for the good that you did, but you will also discover in the tension that face to face with the ideal you yourself are a poor wretch, so that you unconditionally need grace.

Without situation, without this situation which isolates him almost unto despair and always in inverted proportions, a person never comes to believe.

This is also what Christ[1180] says, and this is the only proof possible for the truth of Christianity: if any one will act according to what I say, he will experience whether I am speaking on my own.

But a genuinely Christian action, an action branded by the unconditioned, Christianly branded by the unconditioned, is a great rarity—and yet in no other way can one enter into the situation where faith can come into existence [*blive til*]. Venture giving all your possessions to the poor and you will certainly experience the truth of the teaching simply by experiencing the scale on which you need the teaching in order to persevere in what you ventured. Venture once to make yourself completely vulnerable for the sake of the truth, and you will certainly experience the truth of the teaching, experience how it alone can save you from despairing or from succumbing, for you will need Christianity both to protect yourself against others and to maintain yourself upright when the thought of your own imperfection would weigh you down. In solidarity with others one can very well go about babbling nonsense about his imperfection, but the person who by an unconditioned act has broken with everything so that now the others do everything to label him as mad or as an egotist or as a hypocrite, etc. —in inner spiritual struggle he will discover his own imperfection on a dreadful scale, even though he was right ten times over in what he did, right in relation to the others; he will discover his imperfection before God and will therefore need Christianity.[*]

But this has been completely abolished; such things are never mentioned in sermons; instead, this mass of reasons and proofs and God knows what has been heaped up.

Christ, who never engaged in proving, demanded unconditioned action: break with everybody in order to commit yourself to me. When a person did this, it is true he became a Christian by way of the relation to Christ, but it was also by way of the break with everything, by coming out into this enormous tension, so that he could persevere only by adhering to Christ. Even though a person, without breaking with everything, without being unconditioned, had chased around all day after Christ, talked with him day in and day out, had been an observer of all his miracles—despite all this he would never in all eternity have become a Christian.

x^3 A 470   n.d., 1850

« **4934**

[*]*In margin of 4933* (x^3 A 470):

Venture unconditionally to break with everything in order to get a clear idea of what Christianity is, and you will find out that you yourself will become a Christian; you will experience such collisions and become so inwardly aware, simply in the consciousness of your imperfection, that you will learn to need Christianity in order to hold out—so you become a Christian, even though you were not one from the outset. On the other hand, one who begins with the idea that he is something of a Christian, even though, if it were possible, he presents Christianity quite accurately without venturing anything himself, will hardly ever become a Christian himself.

x^3 A 471   n.d.

« **4935** *The Constraint of Conscience*

As far as earnestness is concerned, there is no phrase as subtly cunning as this one, because it is so enormously obligating.

It is so very easy—and so pompous—to appeal to conscience and to lament the pressure of conscience.

But watch out—lamenting the pressure of conscience can so easily be self-revelation.

I can, for example, lament that my shoes pinch without giving myself away as the guilty one—for, after all, the shoemaker is the one who is guilty.

But if I feel a twinge of conscience and do nothing more than complain, there may well have been an external pressure, it is true. But on the other hand, the freedom in me did not respond strongly enough to will to venture the utmost. If I had done that, unconditionally ventured everything, I would once again have been at peace with my conscience.

The trouble is that a person feels some pressure or other but is not willing to risk everything—and so he laments; but he thereby gives himself away, confesses that it actually is not a matter of conscience for him.

X^4 A 18 *n.d.*, 1851

« 4936 *A Matter of Conscience Cannot Be Represented by Occasioning a Discussion,*

for the person who introduces the discussion is throwing out a feeler to see if it will go through or not. The person who has a matter of conscience ought to express that it *must* go through; if not, he falls—otherwise he actually does not have the right to say that for him it is a matter of conscience.

X^4 A 19 *n.d.*, 1851

« 4937 *To Give Oneself Completely to Christ*

One can belong to him only by giving oneself completely. The person who has not given himself completely has not really given himself to Christ, either, for the one corresponds to the other.

But you do not necessarily become a martyr by giving yourself completely. No, the result of this is only that you are no longer the master of your own life, you do not know how it will end. Just as when the child about to go into the water flings its arms about the adult's neck and from that moment on it is completely up to the adult whether they shall merely go wading or go out upon 70,000 fathoms[1181] of water —so it is with giving oneself to Christ.

The secular mentality is the callousness with which a man willfully hardens himself in advance and says: I will venture only so far; I dare not, I cannot go farther; the instant there is a move in that direction, I use prudence to protect myself from arriving at a decision.

x⁴ A 290   n.d, 1851

« 4938 *Not To Venture*

This is characterized in the Gospel¹¹⁸² by the servant who buried his pound—he was cautious and prudent: yet the Lord casts him out.

Imagine one more incident in that Gospel, imagine that someone came and said: Lord, I was so eager to acquire more with the help of the pound you entrusted to me—I took a risk, perhaps too much of a risk, for I won nothing and even lost the one pound—I wonder if he would not be forgiven more readily than the cautious, prudent servant.

x⁴ A 501   n.d., 1852

« 4939 *Venturing Christianly*

It is the nature of all prudence never to venture more than my understanding tells me I am capable of doing or more than it reckons I will be able to endure in terms of suffering. Seneca¹¹⁸³ has correctly stated it thus: I should not venture that which I would be amazed to see accomplished—it is too high.

But as for renouncing the world and the things of the world (which is Christianity's demand), how in the world will I ever come to attempt such a thing if prudence and understanding are to decide if I will and can or cannot! Take Christ's prophecy about what would happen to him and his followers and explain how in the world any man could think of getting involved in such a thing on the basis of understanding and prudence.

But the point is that Christianity is the unconditioned—period. If something is the unconditioned and is God's will and command—then for the second party all responsibility with regard to using prudence ceases—he simply has to obey. It is nonsense: God's will for a man, the unconditioned—and then for the person concerned to ponder prudently whether he dares to get involved in such a thing, something which does not need to be pondered, since understanding, prudence, everything vociferously shout: It is foolish to get involved with such a thing!

This is why Christ promised his apostles a Spirit. Now everything is in order: the disciples are simply to obey, venture—God will take care of the rest, his being able to achieve it, achieve it victoriously, or manage to endure it if he sinks exhausted while venturing.

But we men have pulled Christianity down to our level, and we are brought up in a Christianity which does not place upon us in any way the pressure of the unconditioned, of "God's will for us." We relate to it and its demands as we do to every other enterprise in life; we believe that we must calculate prudently how far we dare to venture—rather than that we must venture. This is why dying to the world and renunciation[1184] are completely abolished, for, after all, on the basis of understanding and prudence it is impossible to decide to will to die to the world; prudence and understanding are diametrically opposed to that.

X^4 A 538 *n.d.*, 1852

« 4940 *Eternity—Venturing*

So often the matter looked to me like this: if you do not venture now, you will perhaps regret it sometime later in your life.

O, the matter is much more earnest: if you do not venture—an eternity to repent; a moment to enjoy—and an eternity to repent this moment's enjoyment; or a whole life of time to enjoy because one did not venture—and an eternity to repent that one did not venture.

Alas, but it must also be remembered that one can venture wrongly, and so there is suffering in time because one ventured wrongly, and an eternity to repent that one ventured wrongly. Yet if there was integrity in one's wrong venturing, he dares hope to God that the temporal suffering itself will help him into the truth; whereas not to venture always carries the danger of avoiding Governance somehow, of not coming out so that it can grab hold of a person.

X^5 A 41 *n.d.*, 1852

« 4941 *To Want To Be The First One*

No matter how well a dog is trained there is always something that momentarily breaks through whereby one recognizes the animal, the animal nature.

Also in relation to being a man, the animal nature is recognizable by something which is even praised: "I do not want to be the first; I am not crazy enough to want to be the first one."

You do not want to be the first one. That means you need something ahead of you; you need "the herd," don't you? That is, you want to be animal.

But God will not change the condition, the condition of grace in

Christianity: first the kingdom of God, and only he who comes first is saved—as at the pool of Bethesda.[1185]

You do not want to be the first one. Quite right, because you do not want to venture. When you simply take care to have the others ahead of you, the more the better, the less you venture, or, more accurately, you finally do not venture at all, or, rather, you do the very opposite of venturing. But God wants you, wants every single individual to venture. God will not let himself be fooled. When in infinite grace he almost jests with his divine majesty and offers every single individual the infinitely highest—to be involved with God, he will not let himself be mocked by the cravenly prudent foolery of men who prefer aping and brutishness and yet expect to get the same.

You do not want to be the first one. But this is the condition, otherwise it cannot be. Just as God must love every single individual in order to love (for loving cannot be done *en masse*), so he also demands, in order to be loved, that you, each one, become the first one. Anyone who has even the slightest idea of what it means to love must know that wanting to love someone in common with others is an insult, is false modesty and humility, disgusting to the object of the love. Therefore, if you want to be loathsome to God, just run with the herd, yonder where the journalists (certainly not divine servants) are beckoning to you, and where the public guarantees you security and certainty.

* *

Here I stand again at the conclusion of the review of *Two Ages*,[1186] the picture which has been sketched of the future.

XI^1 A 453 *n.d.*, 1854

« **4942** *To Be the First*

To win the eternal without venturing is just impossible.

But to venture means quite simply not to have others out in front.

O, Socrates,[1187] when a person becomes solitary in this way, then we encounter this "if"!

"To venture everything on an if," you say. My friend, if you do not venture on an if, you do not venture; when you take away the if, you take away the venturing. You cannot truly object to venturing on an if, for this is precisely what it is to venture; therefore when you have some objection to make it must be to venturing. Watch out that you do not fool yourself by making it seem as though you had nothing against venturing, that you would surely do it were it not for an if, which is just like saying: I have nothing against swimming; on the contrary, I am very eager to go swimming—but not in water.

Then the man shudders, clutches at the others; I must be sure, he says, before I venture. Once again backside front, to be sure before one ventures is like wanting to have a prologue at the end or wanting to fill one's mouth with flour before one talks. No, it is exactly the opposite: if your mouth is full of flour you must remove it before you begin to talk. It is the same with venturing. What a person is sure about he cannot venture. If he is going to venture, he must first remove the positive assurance, just as if one has been sure in a childish way or thought he was sure and now has to remove this positive assurance in order to be able to venture. Consequently first of all away with the positive assurance in order to venture—so far from the truth is this idea: I must first of all be sure before I can venture.

But he shudders, he must have positive assurance first of all; he clutches at the others.

The others! And even if these others grow to millions, trillions x billions through the centuries—well, then a person no doubt thinks that he dares to venture. O, my friend, nothing is more sure than that you will be cheated of the eternal if you rely on this positive assurance.

Existence [*Tilværelsen*] is so cunning, if you please (yet "spirit" cannot possibly be otherwise), that the greatest, the utterly, utterly greatest human certainty is precisely what most assuredly cheats us of the eternal—and in the least possible human certainty there is the possibility of the eternal.

Security, indolence, dearth of spirit want to be sure before they venture—and this is why secure, indolent, and spiritually impoverished pastors villainously played the yes-man and supplied proofs and proofs and positive assurances. These villains who have murdered millions—spiritually—with their false Christianity, have caused the abortion of possibilities (as one speaks of inducing abortions), possibilities of becoming spirit, possibilities which were in every single one of these countless millions whom the clergy murdered by playing the yes-man and giving them proofs.

Christianity wants the opposite of what indolence and the sensate want—it wants to rouse up.

As far as being a teacher is concerned, the special point is that the teacher can remain calm and not let himself be disturbed by shrieks and whines or immediacy's most cunning insinuations, that he knows that all these things are part of teaching. Good Lord, a surgeon certainly knows that screaming is a part of surgery; he does not stop operating because the patient screams. Similarly, a swimming instructor knows that a person is afraid the first time he goes out into the current, and the corporal knows that the recruit is afraid, etc. But in all these situations everything has not been indulgently altered because of the shrieking.

Only with respect to the one thing important, the eternal, Christianity, only there has it been found proper to change everything to please the patient. What they have done, alas, is to cheat themselves and millions of the one thing important.

XI^1 A 458 *n.d.*, 1854

« 4943 *Politics——Christianity*

Politics is: never venturing more than is possible at any moment, never beyond human probability.

Christianity is: wherever there is no venturing beyond the probable, God is unconditionally not along; this, of course, does not mean that he is along wherever and whenever there is venturing beyond the probable.

XI^1 A 502 *n.d.*, 1854

« 4944 *To Will the Good in Truth*

It will never be any different in this world: to will the good in truth is regarded as a kind of bigotry and stupidity; to will the earthly and bungle is not regarded as nearly so stupid.

Nothing is likely to be pitied more than willing the good in truth, for nothing is more feared than to be stirred by or to enter into even the remotest relation with willing the good in truth, and feeling sorry for it is reckoned to be the very best way to insure oneself against it, because to confess that the task is to will the good in truth but one is unable to bring himself to do it is not as safe, for it might end in coming to grips with the good, in making a start at it—no, but when one commiserates with willing the good in truth, then one is personally perfectly safe and secure.

XI^1 A 521 *n.d.*, 1854

« 4945 *To Venture*

We delude outselves into thinking that to refrain from venturing is modesty, and that it must please God as humility. No, no, not to venture means to make a fool of God—because all he is waiting for is that you venture. In fact, this is what he has had proclaimed to you by means of Christianity—that he is waiting.

XI^2 A 104 *n.d.*, 1854

VOCATION

« **4946**

It is all very well to say that the ethical expression is to transmute one's talent into one's calling. But the issue here is far more difficult. To what extent is the individual obligated not to overlook the religious consideration in his choice?[1188] My own life is an example. If I had followed my inclination, chosen that for which I apparently have had a definite talent: becoming a police official, I would have been far happier than I came to be later, even though everything is better now. My acuteness would have been turned outward. The religious would have become a qualification of inwardness which would not have been pursued further, even though I would have turned back to it frequently. By going through the religious to my proper task, I turned my acuteness against myself. If this so-called actuality is supreme, I ought to have chosen otherwise. Here a new difficulty is apparent.

IV A 160   n.d., 1843

« **4947**

And there is in fact an opportunity for that, there is in fact a need in man which is a call from God, for God's call is issued to a man in many places and at many times, but the call to seek him in the confession of sins is always at the eleventh hour. Whether he is young or old, whether he has sinned much or little, it is the eleventh hour—repentance understands this.[1189]

VII^1 B 145   n.d., 1846

« **4948**

In margin of 4947 (VII^1 B 145):
First of all comes lightly armed desire wanting to capture the world—but retreats in terror. Then comes the manly strength wanting to venture battle—but must fall back. Now it is the eleventh hour—then comes repentance.

VII^1 B 146   n.d.

« 4949 *The God-Relationship*

When a person dares appeal to God, speak in God's name, then —yes, it is human to think this way—then one would think that everything must go his way, yield to him, that he must be capable of everything—ergo, it is wonderful to be such a person. Yes, this is the human way of thinking, which at its maximum always wants to make the divine the superlative of the human.

No, to speak in God's name means to suffer, to come up against all possible opposition, the hatred and curses of men. If things were the way the purely human imagines them to be, everyone would no doubt appeal to God and speak in God's name, and on the other hand God would have no control, whether someone looked to God in order to gain earthly benefits or looked to God in and for himself.

Therefore, to speak in God's name (even if it is true that the one who speaks has a vocation as such) means to meet all possible opposition, to become the most wretched of men, hated, persecuted, etc. And not only this, it also means that the one called must submit to this, that in the world of phenomena God lets it seem as if he testified against him with all his might.

Frightful! But it cannot be otherwise, for God is spirit, and if God helped him directly and bore witness directly with the one called, he would be prevented from becoming spirit and consequently from becoming or being the one who is truly called.

But in the spirit God witnesses with the one who is called; this is faith's secret.

When a person called in this way goes out to run errands for God, when they, God and he, part as it were, I imagine that God says to him at the very last: Be sure to remember what it means, that you will ultimately suffer; above all do not forget that I must in fact also witness against you, my child, my little friend; it cannot be any other way, for otherwise I am not God, and you will not become spirit. But simply have faith, do not be shocked at me for letting it seem as if I, the faithful God, were faithless and left you in the lurch: it cannot be otherwise—if you want it to be different, then this means that you no longer have a relationship to me.

It is clear that much of what Luther explained (an explanation which actually needs its own explanation) as the work of the devil—quite as if the devil were actually able to set limits upon God—may be explained by the discrepancy between God's infinite majesty and man.

If a man is really going to have anything to do with God, it must become suffering—the discrepancy between these two qualities in the relationship must needs bring suffering; but, but despite all this, the relationship is still blessedness.

x^4 A 487   *n.d., 1852*

THE VOLUNTARY

« 4950 *The Voluntary*

There is a curious unclarity about this subject in Luther's sermon[1190] on the temptation of Christ.

Luther uses the gospel as an occasion to warn against self-chosen sufferings. He says we are not to choose sufferings ourselves if the spirit does not drive us.

But if the spirit drives us to it, it is still the voluntary.

As far as suffering is concerned, what is the difference between the voluntary and the involuntary? Involuntary suffering is that suffering which is factually present without my collaboration in any way. If in spite of all my efforts to make a living I am unable to do it—this is involuntary. If I am assaulted just as I am walking along the street, this is involuntary. But if I step forth witnessing as Luther himself did, witnessing against the pope, this is voluntary; he could, indeed, have refrained from doing it. To declare that he could not do otherwise is quite correct, but it is sham if he in this way makes the prompting of the spirit identical with external necessity.

Consequently the voluntary still remains. It cannot be otherwise, either, for if the voluntary goes, Christianity is abolished—and so it is. When the voluntary disappears, "spiritual trial" [*Anfægtelse*] disappears, and when spiritual trials disappear, Christianity disappears—as it has disappeared in Christendom.

Christ's whole life is voluntary suffering, just as his coming in order to suffer is voluntary. Yes, even in the story of the temptation and specifically in the first instance (the occasion for Luther's observation), the voluntary is apparent. If I am hungry and have no bread, this is involuntary; but if I have bread or have it in my power to get bread and will not use it—this is voluntary—and Christ certainly had it in his power to obtain bread. The voluntary is suffering in faith's struggle with God.[1191] I have it in my power to get out of it, but there is something in me which tells me God would rather have me keep on —but this can also be pride, can also be tempting God. Clever as usual, the world, by stressing the concept "tempting God" has abolished Christianity.

x³ A 43   n.d., 1850

« **4951** *Concerning "the Voluntary"*

It stands to reason that a man cannot involve himself with "the voluntary" (the requirement of which is higher than the universal requirement) unless he has a *direct, immediate* assurance that it is demanded of him *specifically*. Otherwise he is unable to get started, for if he does not have this *direct,* immediate assurance the voluntary will continually change into presumptuous arrogance, which he must repent of. From the point of view of the universal requirement, the voluntary is in fact presumptuous arrogance; consequently, in order to be able to venture it, one must have a spontaneous, immediate assurance of its being specifically required of him.

The voluntary therefore cannot possibly be that which is required of all, since it is a specific requirement.

In order to prove that the voluntary is the universal requirement (which, as has been shown, is a contradiction), one cannot appeal to the examples found in the New Testament, where Christ requires it of those who wanted to be disciples (the rich young man,[1192] the one who wanted to bury his father first,[1193] etc.), for these examples prove the very opposite, since the requirement was laid specifically upon each of them, so that each one of them had Christ's own word for it that it was required of him.

When Christ[1194] says: Everyone who has left father and mother etc. will receive a hundredfold—this does not at all prove that the voluntary is the universal requirement; it merely shows what reward would be received by the one who was placed under the requirement of the voluntary and who fulfilled it.

The universal is: purely and simply to admit before God that one is human, to desire both this and that, to work by permissible means to achieve these things, leaving it up to Governance whether or not they are achieved, since fulfillment is at all times in the power of Governance. The universal is to leave it up to God whether or not he will prevent one from achieving what is desired or will take it away—but not to give it up voluntarily, humbly recognizing, however, that one is incapable of it and that one does not have the direct, immediate assurance of a specific one [called to the voluntary]—and as for the rest, to rest in "grace."

X³ A 617 *n.d.*, 1850

« 4952 *The "Voluntary"*

Actually the voluntary is the knot in essential Christianity which is able to hold.[1195] But precisely because this knot has been untied for a long time now, essential Christianity has become meaninglessly unraveled.

1. The voluntary, as everyone knows, is 1,000 times more difficult than situations created by conditions and external forces, in which, without any responsibility, one may use all his powers merely to endure.

2. The voluntary genuinely expresses the true fear and trembling and respect for the divine majesty—compulsory poverty, for example, expresses nothing.

3. The voluntary provides the double collision which is the mark of everything essentially Christian: to become hated, cursed, detested, to have to suffer for—one's willingness to suffer. No one ever thinks of persecuting someone because he is in poverty against his will, but no one, no one, no one is as hated as the one who voluntarily renounces that in which men naturally center their lives.

4. Only one who is marked by the voluntary can be entrusted with a command in the Christian sense. One who lives in compulsory poverty and suffering etc. is not tough enough, far from it, does not stand firmly enough; indeed, he expresses that if he could only get out of it, he would certainly prefer it.

But is it not dreadful, dreadful, dreadful that men have pulled Christianity down to their level so that for generations life is lived in such a way that good, decent, and otherwise competent men, even with a public reputation for their Christianity, have *bona fide* taken for granted that the voluntary is childish and immature. What the heroes of mankind have squirmed under like worms, but endured, what another troop of distinguished men have despaired over, is now taken for granted to be childish, something to smile at. Christianly, is this not more dreadful than if life were such that the good, decent people themselves *bona fide* took being upright for childishness.

XI¹ A 327 *n.d.*, 1854

« 4953 *Will—Knowledge*
           (*Christendom*)

Christianity as it is in the New Testament is concerned with man's will, changing the will; everything touches this, all the phrases (renouncing the world, denying one's self, dying to the world, etc., also, to hate oneself, to love God, etc.) are connected with this fundamental idea in Christianity, that which makes it what it is: transformation of the will.

In Christendom all Christianity has been transposed into the sphere of the intellectual; then it becomes doctrine and tends to be wholly occupied with intellectual matters.

If this is not a fraudulent trick, then I do not know what is! Anyone with the slightest human knowledge as well as self-knowledge knows very well that what puts the squeeze on a man is a change of will, and this is where Christianity aims its deadly blow. But Christendom deftly dodges the blow—and transposes everything into intellectuality.

How nauseating! And to think that millions are doing this, that children are being brought up this way, so that in Christendom a father lies to his child about the highest and the holiest.

It is dreadful! When one who is not a surgeon is present at the dissection of a body, he becomes ill; likewise the student the first time he himself has to do the dissecting—but nothing like this happens to the old anatomist! And yet at times it can happen that a corpse is so loathsome that he also gets sick. If the average man were to learn the details of a crime that a police detective knows, he would be upset—the old police detective has no uneasiness about crime, and yet at times it can happen that the case is so frightful and so dreadfully encompassing that he also feels upset. —I can truthfully say that I have an innate genius for criminality; I too am old and hardened, but all this about Christendom truly overwhelms me with its horror. The corruption in Russia where every official was bribed is but a faint image of this dreadful situation where the lie that we are Christians, that we have Christianity, is mixed into everything, while we mendaciously give the name Christianity to the very opposite of the New Testament.

How abominable that it must be this way—if a man in Christendom actually is going to become a Christian, he must first of all take the blow of having it seem for a time almost as if God in heaven were the most abominable deceiver—just because he has been brought up from childhood in the lie about what Christianity is. This is how the child is sent out into life: God in heaven will surely help you; whatever happens, God will surely help you. But in the New Testament the matter is presented this way: What God wants is that you love him, and this means that you will, humanly speaking, come to suffer frightfully —just because you have involved yourself with God. What is the New Testament? A handbook for those who are to be sacrificed. What villainy, then, to bring up a child in the brand of Christianity that prevails in Christendom and thereby to cause the child either to dribble away his life in the same nonsense, or go through the horrible experience of having God seem to be a deceiver who in the moment of crisis, just when a man needs him most, changes, and becomes the very opposite of what was palmed off on the child.

But, to repeat, I am sickened, to such a degree I am overwhelmed by the impression that in the most committed relationship, the relationship between oathbound teachers and the congregation, in the most intimate relationship, the relationship between parent and child, that everywhere, everywhere this lie is present. I am not talking of a few scoundrel preachers, no, no, but of those whom I both wish to call and must call upright and earnest parents; they are involved in this story of crime, for the kind of Christianity drilled into the child is a lie, and the parents cannot be entirely without guilt; as a matter of fact, anyone who truly learned to know New Testament Christianity would not even let himself get married. In many ways the false concept of Christianity is connected with our wanting to have this world again, in the earthly sense.

But if the kind of Christianity in which a child is brought up were New Testament Christianity, then it would say in the New Testament that Christ talked about his death primarily as a sacrifice, sparing others, and spoke most sparingly and circumspectly about imitation [*Efterfølgelse*]. But instead Christ mentions his death as a sacrifice only once, and then only with qualifications; what he really teaches is: imitation.

XI^2 A 86   *n.d.*, 1854

WIT

« **4954**

To what extent is it true that I should not laugh at my own witticisms?

I A 163   n.d., 1836

« **4955**

The ubiquity of wit.

I A 164   April, 1836

« **4956**

The pursuit of brilliant wittiness, which is so characteristic of our age, has gradually infected even the most sacred matters, and little by little prayer, by means of an emptying reflection, has become a played-out witty conversation. There certainly need be no fear that our prayers will become too long, like the Pharisees', but on the contrary a morbid reflection seems to lead to finding more and more piquant things to pray about; we are ashamed, so to speak, of our earthly existence, as if God had not placed us in it. Everything is supposed to be so brilliantly witty, so facile, that it forms a characteristic contrast to the simple artlessness which pervades the May Song[1196] that we used to sing in this country.

II A 455   June 14, 1839

« **4957**

Every time I note the appearance of a new "humor" magazine, I always have the melancholy thought: Good Lord, here is another one who was at the point of jumping into the ocean but prior to that wanted to take the desperate risk of attempting to be a hack journalist of the witty, the satirical.

VII[1] A 16   n.d., 1846

WITNESS

« **4958**

On its own the universally human position writes uncertainly and unsteadily; the Christian position writes with *guided** pen, witnesses to the accuracy (this in the subjective sense), but does not produce. This explains the profound significance the word "witness" has in Christianity. They are neither firsthand inventors nor improvers of the given, but witnesses, partly because Christianity is an objective act which realizes itself in the world, partly because they assimilate it.

II A 452 June 11, 1839

« **4959**

In margin of 4958 (II A 452):
* for what man does on his own never becomes more than a fig leaf.[1197]

II A 453 *n.d.*

« **4960** *To Confess Christ to the World*

(1) It must not be forgotten that we are challenged to confess Christ in truth, a confession which even if it is silent is more eloquent than all verbosity, a confession which to the rest of the world is just as secret as the high priest's sacrifice before the ark of the covenant, the secrecy we have with God in Christ.

(2) The outward confession. Here we must remember that Christ is not a vain worldly lord who asked us to proclaim him to the world for his own sake or for the glorification of his name, because the heavenly host proclaims his power; he is not a sovereign who anxiously watches over his rights, jealously safeguards them, for he does not regard it as robbery to be like God.[1198]—A true confession of this kind is necessary* since it is the spontaneous expression of what is alive in us. And you who in your hour of impotence perhaps implored his assistance and felt his help, you who perhaps in many a quiet moment look up to heaven when you feel in astonishment how wonderfully he has helped you, how powerfully he is present to you, and yet you would rather have the world not know where the spring has its secret source,

554

the spring which refreshes you in the hour of need, you no doubt will thank your benefactor quietly and often with heartfelt emotion, but you think it is too much to ask that you confess to the world that you are his debtor. O, ask yourself what awakens thoughts like these; is it perhaps the continual prompting of your benefactor, or is it rather some good within you, a truthfulness toward yourself and toward the world. O, test yourself and decide; at some time you will bless the hour. Do we not see how children whose birth and parentage are a secret try to find their parents, and you know who they are and maybe think they are so poor that you cannot be associated with them—no, that is not your thought, but you yourself feel so poor and insignificant before them and perhaps so great in the world's eyes that it is a difficult choice for you. O, come to a decision; such a decision will open your eyes to search yourself to see whether you actually belong to Christ, and if after such a testing you dare say to yourself as you leave the judgment to him who searches hearts, dare to say as Peter[1199] did: Lord, you know that I love you—if after such a testing of yourself you really experience at the root of your soul that you are seized by Christ, have you then not won, won that for which, if lost, the whole world could not compensate or make amends, won the heavenly possession, the heavenly citizenship papers, which the whole world cannot take away from you, the devil cannot render invalid for you. And if you did not find yourself up to it, if you perhaps had to hang back from letting the word's penetrating double-edged sword sever way down to the marrow and joints—O, you will nevertheless rejoice over really having had the opportunity to feel how much you lack, and with God's help you will make up for it. —Such a confession is important for you, for it will place you in the right relation of his true confessors, for Christianity is not a cloaked and masked freemasonry but an open and revealed kingdom.

In margin: *and not even a mistaken concern for the good of Christianity dares hold it back, as when Abraham,[1200] out of concern for Sarah, said that *she was his sister—not his wife,* as, indeed, we often see people who certainly admit a family relationship with Christianity but not the indissoluble union of marriage.

II A 466 July 3, 1839

« 4961

Matthew 10:41–42. The point is to do something *in contemporaneity* for the witness to the truth—instead of this hypocrisy of building tombs to the prophets; but in contemporaneity danger is always involved, so that such a person is himself also something of a witness to the truth.

VIII² C 3:5   *n.d.,* 1847–48

« **4962**

Every time a witness to the truth suffers innocent death or suffering, the final judgment of his contemporaries is always that he is himself guilty. Naturally. For if he had been cowardly and weak and not eternally convinced he was right and had truth on his side, if he had yielded, the age would in fact have gotten the power to change him, and his life would actually have expressed: It is a wonderful age I live in. But he stood his ground and made it clear that the times were wretched. In the language of the times (which of course cannot see its own wretchedness) it goes like this: He is himself guilty in this.

O, it is so old and so easy, this erroneous switch-about "that it is better that one suffers than that a whole nation suffers."[1201] In the same way it is far better, it is advantageous to infinitely more people, that all the others are right and are wonderful people—only one, the witness to the truth, is a bad person.

Here we encounter Socrates[1202] with his excellent question: I wonder if it is also true in connection with horses—that everyone knows how to ride and there is only one who does not.

Here is the battle or the conflict between the human and the divine truth. If God is the source of truth, then we have the essentially Christian position: only a few are of the truth. If man is the source, well, then the truth is where the majority is and is what the majority believes.

IX A 124   *n.d.,* 1848

« **4963**

Mynster really takes the view that there is an established Christendom, and he must be judged from that point of view.

He declares (in *Prædiken,* I, no. 17, on the Covenant of Baptism) that we are not appointed to propagate Christianity.

This may well be true, but it is only half true, and here is where the tasks really begin.

IX A 138   *n.d.,* 1848

« **4964**

Rats are trained to eradicate rats: in the same way every generation brings up the one or the ones who are to proclaim Christianity in earnest to them. The more they persecute and abuse him, the more his mind turns away from the world so that he has only God to cling to. And not until a man is unhappily tormented in the world to the degree that his suffering is like misanthropy, not until then does Christianity come into being for him. All this beer-hall enthusiasm about living *gemütligt*[1203] and having such a good life in animal-human categories and then putting the name of Christ on top of the cake every Sunday —that this cowardice is Christianity is, of course, a pure lie.

The words: Come to me all you who labor and are heavy laden[1204] —must either have been said by Christ early in his life, so it is only the first invitation—and at first glance the truth is indeed attractive to all —or the words must be understood, as I have explained someplace else [i.e., IX A 16], as the divine elevation which, although it knows how few will follow, still, in consideration of who it is who speaks, says: All of you. That is, Christ knows that all *should* follow, that he is the Lord of all; therefore he says: All of you, although he knows there will only be a few. No man could talk so divinely if he had the same prior knowledge; there would come to be something humanly polemical in his invitation, because he would be suffering in the knowledge that there would be only a few. But God, who is "the truth," can address himself only to all—even if only one accepts the invitation, yes, even if no one at all accepts it and he knew that in advance. About himself and about the truth he can speak in no other way than that it pertains to all.

X^1 A 209   *n.d.*, 1849

« **4965**

A martyr who gesticulates with his daily existence cannot concentrate in the moment the way these delicate speakers can who are coddled all week long until they dress up and make protestations for one hour on Sunday. A martyr who gesticulates with his daily existence cannot sensuously draw esthetic attention to his melodious voice and his mighty gestures, for inasmuch as all his gesticulating is basically a translating into action, it escapes that fleeting attention of the moment.

Merely to understand this takes patience. But of course the impostors, who stick to the sensuous in man, naturally have absolute dominance.

This difference alone: what I have to say requires quiet almost like that of an individual in the confessional—what the others say is better off the more thousands there are to hear.

The actor is really an honest man: he advertises in advance by poster that tonight, between 7 o'clock and 10, he will play the noble father, the chief forester, the suffering witness to the truth, the glorified hero, etc.; he is honest, he prompts no one into the fatal confusion that he himself is what he is acting.

There has been a lot of comment about placing the theater under the minister of culture;[1205] to me it would seem better for the minister of culture to have the theater and Church under him, but to take the title of theater-director.

From the standpoint of Christianity, I really do not see how there can be any objection to the theater with respect to truth; the simple truth is that the actor admits that he is an actor.

Nothing disturbs me more than a man who misuses his imagination and eloquence to depict suffering truth when his life expresses just the opposite—and then fraudulently even becomes the object of admiration, affection, sympathy—instead of suffering the derision and mistreatment of the actual witness to the truth.

What is an actual seducer compared to a seducer like that? He infatuates a girl, heightens her desires, all right, but in the deepest sense he does not actually confuse her concepts as does that other seducer, whose forgery is instrumental in hardening our hearts still more against the witness to the truth, because his existence only becomes still more incongruous in comparison with that delusive image.

x^2 A 143   *n.d.*, 1849

« 4966

This is how it should be, and this is how it once was: the proclaimer of Christianity (not "the teacher," which he therefore is not called at all, but "the witness") was the sonorous figure[1206] of what was said. The sound patterns which the vibrations of the air produce is the sonorous figure, consequently that which is heard made visible—in this way "the witness" was the sonorous figure, the existential visible demonstration of that which was proclaimed.

x^2 A 557   *n.d.*, 1850

« 4967 *Christendom*

The fact that Christianity is not proclaimed by witnesses but by teachers is another result of the basic confusion.

What is a witness? A witness is a person who directly demonstrates the truth of the doctrine he proclaims—directly, yes, in part by its being truth in him and blessedness, in part by volunteering his personal self and saying: Now see if you can force me to deny this doctrine. By means of this struggle, in which the witness perhaps gets the worst of it physically—may die—the doctrine is victorious. The opposing side has no such view for which it would risk dying. This is the continuing practical proof of the truth of the doctrine.

But a teacher! He has proofs and arguments—but he stands outside, and the whole thing becomes ridiculous, all the objections triumphant.

X^3 A 5 *n.d.*, 1850

« **4968**

The person who is to provide the criterion has the task, as long as he functions as such, to keep as close to men as possible, like a gadfly, and to be recognized and continually seen by them.

This gives rise to the almost insane confusion: they know or have a sort of general opinion that he is supposed to be something extraordinary, but as for his ideas and thoughts, they have neither the time nor the opportunity to inform themselves about them or do anything with them—so they interest themselves in his accidental characteristics. Every person has plenty of these, but his promptly become eccentricities. How does this happen? From the fact that instead of concentrating their attention on his teaching and his mission (which is the proper relation) people concentrate their attention on his accidental characteristics, as if they were the extraordinary. The attention has an inverse relation to what has become its object—and in their language it is expressed this way: He is peculiar. No wonder, then, if it is something close to madness that they direct their attention this way.

Thus there is a kind of skirmish between the extraordinary person and men—they defend themselves against him.

Why do they do it? Actually because they want to have him withdraw. They feel strongly that his life is a demand, but they do not wish to be reminded of it, and so they want him to withdraw and live a secluded life so that they do not get to see him and feel the memento in his life—and then they will honor him.

X^3 A 15 *n.d.*, 1850

« **4969** *Christianity—Man*

"But if Christianity is going to make a man unhappy—humanly speaking—for his whole life, if Christianity is to be taken in its most rigorous form, it is almost too much to ask that a man involve himself with it." To this Christianity must answer: The fact that you talk this way gives evidence that you have neither God's idea of how dreadful sin is nor God's idea of the blessedness of eternity; if you had this counter-balance you would find that even on these terms Christianity is still absolute, infinite gain.

Incidentally, it is usually true that those who have proclaimed Christianity in its strictest terms (assuming that it has been truth in them) have been constrained to do so. Through specific acts of providence they are brought to such an extremity that they must go forward.

x^3 A 301   n.d., 1850

« 4970 *The Theater—the Church*

Richard Rothe (*Anfänge der christliche Kirke*[1207]) merges the Church into the state and quite consistently makes out that the theater stage will come to be the divine service (as in paganism).

This has already been achieved in a singularly satirical manner: the clergy are not much more than stage players.

On the whole it would be extremely helpful if someone would really illuminate the difference between a pastor, a poet, and an actor. Christianity has demanded "witnesses," and therefore the distinction is sufficiently conspicuous, but the present-day concept of the pastor has much in common with a composite of poets and stage players.

x^3 A 561   n.d., 1850

« 4971 *The Christian Order of Precedence*

I

The Apostles
with a special quality.

II

The Witnesses
whose lives express what they teach
and are marked by sufferings "for the
sake of the Word."

III

What could be called teachers of religion, or what are presently called pastors
   whose conception of Christianity essentially is that it is a doctrine.

These are again ranked among themselves

according to their true rendering of the doctrine (orthodoxy), a certain imaginative fervor in respect to conviction (this fervor is nevertheless esthetic, for if it were existential, "witnesses" would necessarily result), according to penetration and depth in reflecting on the doctrine, according to imagination, feeling, artistry in presenting the doctrine eloquently, etc.

But all these differences among them are still only esthetic differences.

x^3 A 570 *n.d.*, 1850

« 4972 *Speech Fraud*

The moment someone speaks emotionally about the believer's finding a joy in suffering contempt, a pleasure in poverty, etc., at that very moment (especially if he is speaking to an audience) he is about to be carried away by the impression he is making on his listeners, how he is rising in their esteem, etc.: that is, in the very opposite categories.

The question is: Is a person really able to find a joy in suffering contempt at the time he suffers it. If it is done this way, is it not almost superhuman not to gain by some guile a little honor for having to suffer contempt in this way.

Let this venturing to preach that there is joy in suffering insult be met with insults, and then we will see what becomes of the speaker.

The trouble is that what makes "the speaker" is imagination—but this relationship is by no means essentially Christian.

The essentially Christian makes witnesses, and so good night to eloquence; a "witness" is far too earnest a man to be eloquent in the sense in which a speaker is eloquent. No, a speaker, like a poet, needs coddling.

This relationship shifts Christianity into categories completely different from the essentially Christian.

x^3 A 677 *n.d.*, 1850

« 4973 *The Contemporary Age—The Future*

A contemporary age persecutes, puts to death a witness to the truth.

Then a future age comes along and makes a big fuss about him, and now it is eager to give the appearance of being far superior to that contemporary age.

But this hypocrisy is just as great as the contemporary age's guilt of putting him to death.

This is what Christ says to the Pharisees in Matthew[1208] as well as in Luke 11:48.

x⁴ A 178   n.d., 1851

« **4974 *The Witness of the Truth Is Put to Death***

In a certain sense one of the reasons for this is that he is so great that he simply does not need men; if he did, he would have given an explanation which would have helped him, men would have had sympathy for him and with him.

x⁴ A 341   n.d., 1851

« **4975 *The Sacrificed Ones***

. . . . . And when such a witness of the truth has endured all the mistreatment of his contemporary age for a whole lifetime and now finally has witnessed with his death—then comes the admiration, and then it is that the orators make a regular business of presenting and presenting and enjoying the profit of it both in money and in esteem, almost as if they were the one who had died.

This is the falsity of it all. The one who has died ought to be talked about in such a way as to make vividly present how he had suffered, how he suffered, and how he would actually suffer in the very same way if he were living now. But woe to the person who would dare to be true even in this minimal way; he would come to suffer just as much as the one who died.

For what the generation wants is to flatter itself through this admiration of—one who has died, as if this generation were far superior to the one that put him to death. And the orators flatter this generation's conceit.

It is generally true that all historical knowledge is demoralizing if one does not understand how to make the past ethically present so that the past judges the present just as it judges the past. Thus one generation should actually have as little knowledge as possible of the other, for along with this knowledge come, for one thing, evasions and excuses, and for another—illusions.

x⁴ A 381   n.d., 1851

« **4976 *The Alteration of the World, the Alteration of Christianity; To Witness for Truth, To Witness against Untruth***

One could say that to witness for truth is enough, that one could confine himself to this; to witness against untruth could be too much, a tempting of God and plunging oneself into danger. Consequently one ought to wait until the untruth appears and seeks to force me into untruth—then I must resist it, witnessing for the truth.

There is something to this, but the question is whether the shape of the world has not altered significantly.

There was a time when untruth was conscious of being a power; stronger by far, it reigned despotically—in such times one can be quite certain that untruth keeps a sharp lookout for everyone who is of the truth and attacks him; thus he can witness for the truth.

But in our age everything has been transformed into shrewdness. On its own behalf there is nothing untruth wants more than that nothing will happen, that everything will remain peaceful; it avoids decision in every way, desires only that everything stay just as it is, and shrewdly guards against being affected by anything or anybody. In this way untruth shrewdly hopes to be able to put everything off. Now if in such a time one is prepared only to witness for truth (not against untruth) and only in case I am coerced into untruth do I oppose it—then it is a question whether one has not really been tricked.

The situation in Luther's time was entirely different (and incidentally, he still witnessed against untruth). The pope was a power, a domineering power, and his administration was not too bad. But when power is administered slyly and shrewdly there must be witness against untruth. In times like these the first battle is simply to force the untruth out into battle, because it shrewdly prefers peace. But when this is the case there is the usual nonsense, the squawking about what was appropriate at other times.

Suppose someone in Luther's time stepped forth and said: Christianity does not exist.[1209] He could be sure that the rulers would hear it and use force against him. But in our age it is different. The government will say: Let us merely pretend that we did not hear it; it is too dangerous to touch. Consequently, to flush them out, one must fight to get them to please be so good as to be the government. This is the alteration in these times; whereas in an earlier period the government defended itself by using force against the truth, it now defends itself by avoiding the attack and by giving the avoidance the appearance of the spirit of peace.

X^4 A 406 *n.d.*, 1851

« 4977 *Results*

..... And when a witness to the truth sinks in death, executed as a criminal, the wisdom of the contemporary age proves thereby that he is wrong, indeed, the results prove it. And there is not one contemporary who is able to maintain that he was right, because to be able to do that in contemporaneity 2/3 of a witness to the truth is required. Therefore there is no one, at most a couple of women who, womanlike, cannot relinquish the thought that he was right after all.

And now the life of the witness to the truth begins to take effect —and the wisdom of the whole generation proves that he had been right, and this generation now imagines itself to be better than the previous one, although it is just the same, a conclusion by virtue of a result.

And if the world were to continue for 170,000 years, it would be the same everlasting nonsense.

In order to endure to the end, some witnesses to the truth have needed the illusion that their death would benefit the world.

Such people are also witnesses to the truth, to be sure, but not in the deepest sense; if they had understood this matter—and to have grasped the truth is also part of being a witness of the truth—they perhaps would have lost their enthusiasm.

Most people would surely say that if a man can understand that by his death he benefits the world in no way whatsoever, how in the world can he decide to sacrifice his life, what can possibly inspire him to do it?

Answer: the most inspiring thought of all, actually the only truly inspiring thought—this unconditioned thought that there is no reason, no "Why."

Yet, as I have often told myself, it is clear that no teleology is capable of enduring this final skepticism and consequently cannot inspire the final venture either. No, the final, the unconditioned venture—yes, here it comes so very consistently!—only the unconditioned can inspire to this, this unconditioned which is unconditioned obedience to God: I take my life's examination, submit obediently to the final test, to be sacrificed—it is a matter between God and me, not at all to benefit the world, for the world remains just the same.

Such is the boundless consistency of the essentially Christian. Instead of this busyness in wanting to benefit the world, wanting to risk one's life to benefit the world—which has certainly inspired many a man because he did not in the deepest sense understand the truth—there is this simple instruction: Just take your life-examination in the unconditioned obedience which leads to your being sacrificed. All this honorarium you want to arrange for yourself, that your death should bring some benefit, is an illusion. You benefit men just as little by becoming unconditionally obedient as by taking a theological examination—and in this respect there is no one so confused that he would demand to have any other advantage from having taken his final university examination than the fact that he has taken his examination. The most he can be said to benefit others is that he proves thereby that this examination can be taken.

O, but it is a cunning compromise between the conceitedness of certain martyrs and the world's craftiness—to understand that by taking his examination he acquired the great merit of having benefited the world—and the world profited by being excused from having to take its final examination. How mixed up! It is just as if someone were to think that by taking his theological examination he benefited others, and then others would avail themselves of the fact that he has taken his examination to excuse themselves from submitting to the examination and yet be theological candidates by virtue of his having taken his examination.

Consequently this comes first in Christianity—life is an examination. All this about benefiting others is rubbish. And the next thing that comes—and here we see the consistency of Christianity—is judgment, judgment for all—each one individually.

———

Furthermore, this cannot be taught. If an assistant professor could steal my ideas from me, he would be a tremendous hit. I know it very well and understand that this is part of the intensification of the examination. For I am a long way from trumpeting about a better future, although I know full well that posterity will judge me differently than my contemporaries, but I do deny that it will therefore be better. No, if I were able to reach into the future as I would like, it would be to frustrate if possible that lying assistant professor who wants to live off me. But this is not possible; indeed, if it were, life's examination would be altered. No, it cannot be done. No, the envy and mediocrity of the contemporary age will eat you up, and after your death the assistant professor will just as nauseatingly live off you.

Many a one has perhaps pondered unto despair whether or not it is possible to expel the vermin of the contemporary age; it cannot be done if you are unwilling to relinquish the truth and join the vermin yourself. The majority of them, to repeat, have consoled themselves with the thought of a better future. Less frequently it has occurred to someone to wonder if he could take steps to get at the assistant professors in the next generation, but this cannot be done.

So there is only one thing left: see to it that you take your examination—and then comes the judgment, both for you who have loved the truth and for the assistant professors, those nauseating vermin that hypocritically live off the sufferings of the dead.

Hypocritically. Yes, this is why Christ[1210] also says that there is the same guilt—to murder the prophets—and that the next generation build their bombs and say: If we had lived together with them, it would not have happened this way.

When a person suffers in his own age, it is human to lean on the next generation, which will let him have his due, but it is stupidity and delusion to be unable to perceive that the next generation, the assistant professors, are just as disgusting as the bestiality of the contemporary age.

No, no, forget it, do not think about the mistreatment by your contemporaries or of the loathsomeness of the assistant professors—no, just take your examination.

If you take it, this is eternally and infinitely decisive. It may or may not happen that an individual in the next generation will be inspired by your life to want to take his life's examination, too. It will go with him just as with you—the examination neither can nor should be altered, but it will still perhaps encourage him many times to think of you, as you have done in relation to someone who is dead.[1211]

X^5 A 18 *n.d.*, 1852

« 4978 *The Man of God—and the Man of God*

According to New Testament Christianity the man of God is the person who is hated by men, of whom it therefore is said: Upon him will fall the troubles of the whole country and the world.

In "Christendom" the man of God is the person of whom it is said: The man of God—he is really supposed to have the best cut of the roast, the tenderest, and the chief seat at the table, etc.

When this point is reached, has not Christianity become exactly the opposite of what it is in the New Testament? Is it then Christianity? Or is it not rather the case that *Christianity simply does not exist?*[1212] Or perhaps more correctly: Christianity simply does not exist, but what does exist is the very opposite of Christianity—is as far removed from Christianity as possible.

XI^2 A 282 *n.d.*, 1853–54

« 4979 *The Witness to the Truth and the Liars*

..... And when a witness to the truth breathes his last in death by torture, then these liars who are going to make a living out of presenting his sufferings get moving as soon as possible.* Indeed, the whole thing is so upside-down that they not only understand how true it is that for the sake of effect and profit it is best to come first, but they even imagine that being the first to present him will benefit them eventually in eternity's accounting, where the question will be about imitation [*Efterfølgelse*]. You fools, the closer you have been to him, the greater your guilt because you did not imitate him but made a living by presenting him.

[*] *In margin:* It is a kind of superstition, just as when the common people at the place of execution catch the blood of the one who is being executed and use it as a medical remedy.

XI^1 A 103   *n.d.*, 1854

« 4980

My God, my God, why have you forsaken me.[1213]

Perhaps it is not so (as it stands in *For Self-Examination*,[1214] where I all too hastily made it into a theory) that every martyr will experience in a minimal way something similar.

The point here is that there is this difference between the God-man and the witness to the truth: the God-man voluntarily undertook to suffer unconditionally—consequently this last, most horrible suffering.

The witness to the truth is a whole quality lower; even though he is willing, God must still constrain him in many ways—thus he is perhaps spared also this suffering.

XI^1 A 115   *n.d.*, 1854

« 4981 *The Future*

There will no doubt come to be a great change, like a world revolution, in the way in which Christianity will be served in the future.

In former times the teacher,* designated by God to be that, was one of those deeply religious natures who no doubt could also be very severe if necessary, but everything was simple and direct with him; he was not at all designed for, nor did he have any eye for, the criminal, the cunning, etc.

But in the course of centuries, little by little as the human race moved more and more into reflection, Christianity underwent a complete change in so-called Christendom; it became a matter of cunning tricks—there is no defiance, no mutiny against Christianity, no, but sheer knavish trickery, criminal affairs, forgeries.

But Governance is in no hurry, always takes time, until the moment arrives. Then Governance takes a look at the whole matter and says: Well, now, knavish trickery is really rampant; all right, we will change the method.

In the future, then, the teacher will be of entirely different cast, will be a completely different person, designed for dealing, not with raw passions, but with subtle crimes and forgeries.

This is what the teacher will be like. He will be anything but one of these originally deep religious natures; on the contrary, he will have a most refined and intense sensuous nature, with an imaginative energy for enjoying life, so that ten seducers and ten poets could be made out of him. Furthermore, he will be extremely intellectual, so that several sets of professors could live off him; finally, he will have a decided sense for intrigue. This will be his make-up, and he must have at his personal disposal the most opulent, the most interesting, the most complete secularity ever seen.

But he may not use all this. Governance will give this man a blow (somewhat as one clips the wings of a decoy). This blow will make it impossible for him to enjoy life. This being the case, everything that has been granted him will now be almost a torment, at least in the beginning. The blow will place him unconditionally in the power of Governance, who desires to control this very endowment of talents and qualifications. Perhaps the blow will be administered in such a way that no one else will know about it; it will be his own secret with God —and he will be attached to God all the more firmly.

Such a character is designed to deal with criminality.

Really and truly, the human race is not progressing, except in knavish trickery. In earlier times it was almost as if being a human being was something worthy—which accounts for "teachers" being those pious, spontaneously deep religious natures. Now it is otherwise. Now everything is trickery—so the police agents come—those simple, pious natures would only be deceived. No, it will be police agents, and even they will be controlled to such a degree that by means of a blow they will be so directly in the hands of Governance that they will be able to feel the pressure and pull every second.

It was a bloody business fighting against raw passions, but the operation against forgeries will perhaps be more strenuous and will perhaps end in a life-and-death struggle; therefore the difference between the earlier witnesses to the truth and these later ones will be that the latter will have a very important exhausting task at the beginning to get this shrewd and wily age, the falsifier, out of its shrewdness and into a passion.

* Note. Naturally I am not thinking of the foolish human invention involving these thousands of state-appointed officials who play at Christianity in the role of preachers and professors. Their whole activity and *Wirtschaften*[1215] amounts not merely to nothing but less than nothing, since what they have undertaken is an altogether superfluous inconvenience.

XI^1 A 185   n.d., 1854

« 4982 *Swindles*

Rigorousness is what they want to be free of. And if there is someone who, like it or not, has to venture out because God makes him, people defend themselves against him by calling it arrogance. "Pfui, how should I be so arrogant."

It is no doubt pure drivel or, more correctly, it is hypocrisy as well, this rubbish about a teacher of religion having to be such a mild and kind-hearted and nice man. No, the best thing would be for him to make preliminary studies in a penitentiary—but even this is hardly adequate.

XI^1 A 191   n.d., 1854

« 4983 *A World Change*

—and for this one single man, one solitary human being is used! My friend, were this not so, there would be no world change.

Disaster lies in sociality—two people, and it becomes change up to a point, within the old setup.

Governance is too good a dialectician not to see this.

But in a certain sense what sufferings are in store for the poor (in a certain sense) man who is to be used in this way, continually suspended in the infinite weakness of nothing—O, infinite, infinite love!

But no more of this. Yet in a wonderful way, O God, just as you create everything from nothing, you also hang everything, to use the words of the pious, upon nothing—something men only mendaciously delude themselves into thinking they are able to do (the system)!

XI¹ A 544   *n.d.*, 1854

« 4984 *A Thought-Experiment:*[1216] *Imagine That a King Has Turned to Christ and Wants To Be His Disciple*

From the moment the divinely appointed teachers ceased and Christianity was entrusted to men in order to see how upright they would be—from that moment everything was transposed into the purely human idea of extension, dissemination.

To get a king, an emperor, to want to be a Christian—this was considered of prime importance, although it meant forgetting that Christ's kingdom is not of this world and serving Christianity quite as if Christ's kingdom were a kingdom in and of this world. There was no pause to reflect whether making a king a Christian would turn the whole relation around—no, they went ahead ferociously, with great—Christian!—eagerness and zeal—well, or with Jewish eagerness and zeal.

Let us imagine the situation in contemporaneity with Christ; this is the true reply to all questions. As Nicodemus[1217] came at night, so a king comes to Christ at night and wants to be a disciple. I wonder what Christ might say to him. If you want to continue being what you are—a king—then fear nothing from me; my kingdom is not of this world.[1218] I will be your subject like anyone else, will be your humble and loyal subject, and I will teach my disciples to be the same. But if you want to be a disciple—O, man, then I am the king—consequently, take off your crown, give everything away, follow me in poverty.

This, you see—does it even need to be said—this is what it is to proclaim Christianity: the imperturbability of divine majesty which does not—O, human nonsense—make a mistake and get slaphappy over a king's wanting to be a disciple.

But the point is, as soon as the proclamation of Christianity is attended to in purely human ways—that is, with human shrewdness and not in hatred of self, the whole relation is reversed. Christianity then becomes a doctrine and the proclaimer is not sufficiently strong in the character of being a Christian to express by his personal existence that the kingdom of Christ is not of this world.

Thus the whole thing is reversed; we get kings and emperors to be Christians, get Christian states and countries, a Christian world—that is, everything reverts to the old groove, and Christianity is pushed aside; "my kingdom is not of this world" becomes a meaningless platitude, except that in one sense it says a great deal, for, inasmuch as Christianity does not exist at all,[1219] Christendom does in fact express that Christ's kingdom is not of this world.

XI^1 A 555 *n.d.*, 1854

« 4985 *To Confess Christ*

in Christendom is, after all, impossible. What Christ understands by confessing is certainly clear enough (Matthew 10:32, 33). There is always a relationship of contrast, to confess Christ in opposition to men—this is intrinsic, and this is how it must be if there is to be any question of confessing someone.

But in "Christendom" to confess Christ has come to mean to be a yes-man, to play up to all the others—and this is called confessing Christ.

XI^1 A 563 *n.d.*, 1854

« 4986 *The Nourishing—The Consuming*

When a witness to the truth proclaims Christianity, this is a consuming—of illusions—it subtracts from them, and yet it is nourishing by providing nourishment, nourishment of the spirit.

When one of the instruments of illusions proclaims Christianity, this is a consuming—of that which Christianity once was, and a nourishing in the realm of illusions.

There are witnesses to the truth who are so intensive that entire legions of professors and pastors, together with their families, are able to live by consuming them. On the other hand there are those among the instruments of illusion who are generally able to devour a half dozen witnesses to the truth, to such a degree are they virtuosos in consuming, virtuosos in transposing spirit into illusion, suffering into enjoyment, etc. The late Bishop Mynster[1220] was not bad along these lines.

XI^2 A 57 *n.d.*, 1854

WOMAN/MAN

« 4987

On man's relation to woman in the light of its historical origin—"It is not good for man to be alone"; the Oriental point of view resulting in several women over one man, as it were (man, denominator—woman, numerator)—woman's slavery—the Scandinavian—the Christian view—modern emancipation.

II A 246　August 13, 1838

« 4988

The more a body is organically developed, the more dreadful is the decay. When grass rots, there is a fragrance. When an animal rots, it stinks. A man's perdition is dreadful, more dreadful even than a woman's. Is this a proof that man is superior to woman?

III A 206　n.d., 1842

« 4989

..... she is more sensate than man; for were she more spiritual she could never have her culmination point in another. Spirit is the true independent.

Of course every religious view, like every more profound philosophical view, sees women, despite this difference, as essentially identical with man; but it is not foolish enough to forget for that reason the truth of the difference, esthetically and ethically understood.[1221]

V B 23:25　n.d., 1844

« 4990

The whole plan of *A Thousand and One Nights*[1222] is very profound. This battle between masculinity and femininity, the fact that femininity conquers by means of her storytelling, her persuasiveness. In the future the Sultan, who has discovered the basic unfaithfulness of all women, intends to have every woman put to death after one single night. Then Scheherazade offers to save the sex (since the Sultan demands one every night it must end rather soon with the eradication of the women) and she saves the sex by telling stories, which means:

never listen to a woman. Once she gets permission to tell stories you never get rid of her. Fundamentally there is a terrible tenacity. No man could go on living this way for three years facing the possibility of death—but a woman can—if only she gets permission to tell stories. A woman does not have the strength for a break or finds it difficult to make such a decision, but she is able to conquer by means of your not being able to get rid of her.

VIII[1] A 485   n.d., 1847

« 4991

Woman's reflection is almost overpowering to her; this is why it is so dangerous for a woman to reflect. A woman's reflection usually goes like this: if she has won on one point or another, she is so overcome herself that she cannot avoid gazing at her victory—and then she stumbles.

The man is more essentially character; and character consists not so much in winning as in continuing after having won, keeping in character. The woman endures something and counts on the approaching moment when she can take a deep breath. This moment is precisely the danger. Character is essentially continuity.

X[1] A 436   n.d., 1849

« 4992

The few contemporaries who might be said to be remotely capable of evaluating my case see very well that I have nothing at my disposition which has practical value at the moment, that I have no patronage to distribute, etc. Or on the other hand they see very well that already I possess a historical renown which is unusual, but they also understand that they cannot derive any profit from it, for history does not summarily take the likes of them along: ergo, they work against me even quite pettily.

O, human egotism! And then we all weep on Sunday when the pastor weeps and preaches about the truth.

There is really something to it that in the last resort women are a bit more self-sacrificing. It is probably because they live more quietly and withdrawn and thus a bit closer to ideality. They are not as likely to acquire the market-price standard the way a man does, who from the outset is on the go in life. The saving factor for women (which is why one still sees in them the traces and expressions of individuality, the boldness to grasp a single thought and to dare hold on to it) is the distance from life which is granted her for a period. This quieter life sometimes has the result that she becomes somewhat more herself than does a man, who already even as a lad is demoralized by having to be like the others, and as a youth, to say nothing of the adult, is completely demoralized by learning how things go in practical life, in actuality. This very knowledge is the ruination of him. If girls were brought up the same way—then good night to the whole human race. And no doubt the emancipation of women, which tends toward this kind of upbringing, is the invention of the devil.

X^1 A 459   *n.d., 1849*

« **4993**

There is a fine parallel in Lavater:[1223] as Paul had to have a thorn in the flesh, Mary had a sword through her heart. The difference between the masculine and the feminine is very significant.

X^2 A 321   *n.d., 1849*

« **4994**

In Richard Rothe's *Ethics*[1224] I find this reason adduced, among others, for Christ's not being married: because he could find *"keine ebenbürtige Person."* Superb!

X^3 A 554   *n.d., 1850*

« **4995** *Men—Women*

..... Compared to men, women always have essentially more of that which no doubt is calculated to cause a person troubles and make him unhappy in this world, but from which, however, in a different sense, life issues: she has more heart.

X^3 A 562   *n.d., 1850*

« **4996** *Strangely enough,*

it was Eve who seduced the man—in compensation there is no undertaking more appealing to a woman than to become loved by someone who has gone astray and who now, in loving her, will let himself be led along the right path. This appeals to a woman so much that she is not infrequently deceived, because such a person puts everything over on her—and she believes everything—perhaps also because the thought of being the man's savior is so very satisfying to her.

X^3 A 718   *n.d., 1851*

« **4997** *Man—Woman*

For woman the temptation to misuse cunning (for example, to deceive) corresponds to man's temptation to misuse power.

The fact that the woman's guilt is always more strongly emphasized than the man's is basically an indirect compliment to the woman, an admission of the degree to which she is the stronger sex in cunning.

x⁴ A 106   n.d., 1851

« 4998 *The Christianity of Our Time*

In the New Testament the matter is put this way: "Let all those trivialities, those egotistical trivialities with which men generally fill their lives—job, marriage, having children, getting to be somebody in the world—let them all go, break with them completely, and let your life be dedicated to loving God, to being sacrificed for the human race. Be salt!" This what our Lord Jesus Christ calls Christianity. When a man is intending to get married, the invitation (see the Gospel)[1225] comes to him: Let it go—and become a Christian, etc.

Now Christianity has become the very opposite. It has become a divine blessing upon all the trivialities and putterings of finitude and the temporal enjoyment of life. The lovers summon the clergyman—he blesses them—this is Christianity, in spite of Luke 20:34-35 (which is a suitable text for a wedding). If the buyer of the six pairs of oxen were to summon a clergyman and pay him ten dollars to bless him and the oxen before he went out to test them, he would be considered an extraordinary, incomparable Christian worthy of adoration.

Of course it is Protestantism in particular which is total nonsense.

This is why Protestantism has elevated woman so high, more accurately, to first place. Everything revolves around woman. Charming, but then one can also be sure that everything revolves around chatter, trivialities, and in a refined way, around sexual relations. To some extent woman may be said to have ennobled social life in that we do not fight any more or drink and swear as did the old heroes—but refined lust or a carefully concealed, refined allusion to sexual relations—that is what has ennobled social life—Christianity!!

This is how some of my pseudonyms have portrayed it and which I now also find Schopenhauer[1226] rages against in his own way. Woman is not to blame, but she is determined to humble man and to make him mediocre. Existence is also a sovereign and like every sovereign knows very well how best to maintain its regime—specifically by humbling and breaking those over whom they rule.

A woman is proficient along this line when a man gets involved with her too seriously. She contributes the first and the most to his humbling. Generally it can be assumed that every married man is secretly mortified because he feels that he has been made a fool of when all this ravishing talk from the courting days, all this about Julie being the paragon of loveliness and beauty, and getting to possess her is the highest bliss turns out to be—a false alarm. This is the first knock the husband gets, but this in itself is not insignificant, because it is hard for a man to admit that he has been fooled, that both he and Julie must have been crazy. The next undermining is that the husband and Julie (who incidentally has had the same experience on her side) agree to keep a stiff upper lip and to hide things from others; they agree to tell the lie that marriage is the true happiness and that they especially are happy.

When we have settled all this, providence knows that this fellow is easy to control, that he is one of those who will make no conquests in the world of ideas. Constantly lying like this is extremely degrading to the man. It is different for a woman; she is once and for all a born virtuoso in lying, is really never happy without a little lying, just as it is *a priori* certain that wherever a woman is there is a little lying. In a sense she is innocent in this; she cannot help it. It is not possible to get angry about it: on the contrary, we find it very attractive. She is in the power of a natural disposition which uses her with extreme cunning to weaken the man.

Thus in the forward march of history—I mean of marriage—there come along with woman all the follies of finitude, this puttering around, and an egotism peculiar to woman. As wife, as mother—well, here is an egotism of which the man has no intimation. Society has licensed it under the name of love—good heavens, no, it is the most powerful egotism in which woman most certainly does not love herself foremost but through (egotistically) loving her own she loves herself. From then on ideas, and every higher infinite striving likewise, whistle in vain for the man—yes, even if our Lord and his angels tried to move him, it would do no good, because the egotism of the mother is such an enormous power that she can hold him fast.

Woman has a dangerous rapport with finitude in a way quite different from man. She is, as the seducer says, a mystification;[1227] there is a moment in her life when she deceptively appears to be infinitude itself—and that is when man is captured. And as a wife she is quite simply—finitude.

This is why the Church has laid more emphasis upon the preservation of the woman's virginity than upon the man's and has honored the nun more than the monk, for the woman gives up more than the man when she renounces this life and marriage.

XI¹ A 141 n.d., 1854

« 4999 *Woman*

What the judge in the second part of *Either/Or* ¹²²⁸ says in his way about women is to be expected from a married man who, ethically inspired, champions marriage.

Woman could be called "the lust for life." There is undoubtedly lust for life in man, but essentially he is structured [*lagt an paa*] to be spirit, and if he were alone, left all alone to himself, he would not know (here the judge is right) how to begin, and he would never really get around to beginning.

But then "the lust for life," which is within him indefinitely, becomes manifest to him externally in another form, in the form of woman, who is the lust for life: and now the lust for life awakens.

Likewise, what is said in "The Seducer" (in *Stages*)¹²²⁹ about woman being bait is very true. And strange as it may seem, it is nevertheless a fact that the very thing which makes the seducer so demonic and makes it hard for any poet to contrive such a character is that in the form of knowledge he has at his disposal the whole Christian ascetic view of woman—except that he employs it in his own way. He has knowledge in common with the ascetic, the hermit, but they take off from this knowledge in a completely different direction.

XI¹ A 164 n.d., 1854

« 5000 *Woman—Man*

Woman is personified egotism. Her fervent, burning devotion to man is neither more nor less than her egotism.

But His Honor, Man, has no inkling of this; he considers himself very lucky and feels highly flattered to be the object of such fervent devotion, which always takes the form of submission perhaps because woman has a bad conscience about it, wondering if it is not really egotism; man, however, as mentioned, does not see this but feels enhanced by the devotion of this other I.

Woman herself does not know that it is egotism; she is always a riddle to herself, and by a subtlety of nature the whole mystification of egotism manifesting itself as devotion is concealed from her. If woman could understand what an enormous egotist she is, she would not be that, for in another sense she is too good to be an egotist.

This whole business of man and woman is a very intricate plot or a practical joke intended to destroy man *qua* spirit.

Man is not originally an egotist; not until he is lucky enough to be united with a woman does he become that, and then completely. In contrast to a loose-jointed framework egotism, this union, commonly known as marriage, could be called a stone-wall egotism, egotism's proper enterprise.

Having once entered this company enterprise, egotism really begins to hum—and this is also why there are two, a company, in order to have someone to blame and to share the telling of lies (just as in the practical world it is recommended to have an associate who can be blamed for everything).

And it follows as a matter of course that once man enters this company he is essentially lost for everything higher.

This is the reason that Christianity and all more profound views of life take a dim view of the relation to the other sex, for they assume that getting involved with the other sex is the demotion of man.

And this is precisely why it is said (in the thieves' slang we humans use) that everyone is duty-bound to marry and that marriage is the genuinely ennobling life.

In this context it is distressing to me that an eminent person like Luther[1230] came to such an erroneous position. He should have understood that his marriage was an exceptional act, a corrective; therefore, as I have pointed out somewhere in my journal [i.e., X^4 A 324], he should rather have married an ironing board. I mean that he simply should have taken pains to stress the fact: Although I am a monk, I have married—the woman is not at all the important factor here; what was needed was an awakening, and it would have been just as awakening if it had been an ironing board, which naturally would have had to be kept secret. This would have been a way of being salt! But instead Luther became the commander-in-chief of that whole swarm of prolific people or breeders who, inspired by Luther, assume that getting married belongs to true Christianity.

As far as I am concerned, I will not claim to have understood everything at first as I later came to understand it; if I had not once and for all run aground on the exceptional, I too would have been married.

Something very exceptional held me back—and now at long last I see that the exceptional for me is what Christianity would call the universal, the normal, that Christianity insists on the single state and rather makes marriage the exception.

Here again a Governance has been with me. But it really had to be done this way, for how could a man born and brought up in this Danish-Protestant eudaemonism have his eyes opened to what is essentially Christian if a Governance, through exceptional collisions, did not help him by always having him first experience formally the essentially Christian, even though he did not perceive this to be Christianity but believed it to be something quite uncommon—and subsequently let him see that it is in fact the essentially Christian, the truly Christian—which, incidentally, has come to be something very uncommon, particularly in Protestantism, particularly in Denmark.

XI^1 A 226   n.d., 1854

« 5001 *Woman*

Intellectually, in the realm of ideas, thought, etc., woman as compared to man is usually pictured as being something of a little goose.

But in the realm of what could be called instinctive sagacity, man is a big clod compared to woman.

In an idle moment as I walked today it occurred to me that if for the sake of curiosity one were to imagine momentarily that the man could bear children—I am convinced that the births would be extremely difficult, and why? Among other reasons because he would not scream. He would say to himself: You are a man; it is inappropriate to scream—and would force back the scream. The woman, on the other hand, screams immediately—and it is well known that this screaming assists the birth.

There is something of genius about this instinctive sagacity in every woman; with a stroke of genius she takes a radical shortcut, whereas the man, who is weighed down by a thousand reflections, is also weighed down by an occasional but all too pompous idea of his own dignity in being a man.

XI^1 A 231   n.d., 1854

« 5002 *The Weaker Sex*

can wail and scream etc.; this is perhaps why the woman suffers much less than the silent, enclosed man.

In this context one could be tempted to say that woman is the stronger sex, for if it is strength to defend oneself against suffering, then woman defends herself far better than man.

But the main point is this: it is strength to be able to accept suffering, to be able to enter into suffering, to bear up under it; and it is weakness to ward off suffering by every means possible. Woman's weakness lies in the very fact that she immediately has entreaties, tears, and sighs at her disposal to ward off suffering; her weakness is simply her propensity to wail and scream and thus mitigate her suffering. Man's strength is that he has no means of defense, no way to mitigate suffering; therefore his strength—yes, it is a paradox—his strength makes him suffer more than the weaker sex. It is paradoxical, but no more paradoxical than something equally true, that it takes health to become ill; there are sickly people who lack the health to become ill.

XI^1 A 233   n.d., 1854

« 5003 *Woman*

In the Bible it is woman (Eve) who seduces man.

Perhaps as repayment or compensation it is factually the case that feminine love is by no means predilected to the thought that the beloved man should be the epitome of virtue and perfection. On the contrary, there is not a single girl who would be bothered if her beloved had gone somewhat astray, for then the significance of her relation to him is that she saves him (this is in contrast to the Bible, where she seduces him).[*] Yes, woman is, after all, a lovable egotist —but an innocent one, she does not know it herself. But just the same it is an egotistical thought to wish that the beloved had gone somewhat astray so that her love can save him.

Incidentally, it cannot be denied that her wish often comes true and a man is saved from previous excesses by a woman's love and by loving a woman.

But despite this the Bible is right in yet another and higher sense; it is right from a Christian point of view. Maybe she saves a man or two from excesses and makes a proper man of him, but she corrupts all men who get married by finitizing and mediocritizing them.

When a youth or young man goes astray in his passions, there are two powers alert to save him: a loving woman—and God in heaven. If he is saved by the former, he will still be finitized. If, however, he is not saved by woman's love, if he does not find a harbor here—but he is saved nevertheless, consequently by God, then his life becomes meaningful.

XI^1 A 281   n.d., 1854

« 5004

[*] *In margin of 5003* (XI¹ A 281):

A similar inversion of the Bible is repeatedly this—in life the man is always said to seduce the woman. But this is not the case but is rather an expression for the cunning of woman; she seduces so cunningly that the nice fellow, man, always takes on the appearance of being the seducer.

XI¹ A 282   *n.d.*

« 5005   *Man——Woman*

Woman was taken from the man's side—but Christianly understood, may not man's relation to woman be compared to what is called making a side remark.

Man was structured for eternity; woman leads him into a side remark.

In this world man without woman is weaker; he has a weak side which woman protects, and united they have strength for this life. But Christianly this weakness, the weakness of the solitary, weakness for this life, is a part of being strong for eternity.

XI¹ A 426   *n.d.*, 1854

« 5006   *Man and Woman in Relation to the Religious*

In a certain sense woman is by nature better suited for essentially religious service, for it is a woman's nature wholly to give herself. — But on the other hand she does not explain anything. —An eminently masculine intellectuality joined to a feminine submissiveness—this is the truly religious. Woman's devotedness is essentially limited to interjections, and if it is more than that it is unfeminine. But on the other hand an eminent masculine intellectuality is directly related to an enormous selfishness which must be slain in submissiveness.

XI² A 70   *n.d.*, 1854

« 5007   *Man—Woman—Child*
Christianity

Basically it is terrible but true, and it expresses the dreadful extent to which it is true—Christianity simply does not exist.[1231]

This is the real situation in Christendom, especially in Protestantism.

The men—and that means the miserable weaklings and clods that are called men these days, compared to the Oriental idea of what it is to be a man—men turn away from religion with a certain pride and egotism and say: Religion (Christianity) is something for women and children.

But the truth of the matter is that Christianity as it is found in the New Testament has such prodigious aims that, strictly speaking, it cannot be a religion for women, at most secondhand, and is impossible for children.

As a psychologist I maintain that no woman can endure a dialectical redoubling [*Fordoblelse*], and everything that is essentially Christian is intrinsically dialectical.

The essentially Christian task requires a man, it takes a man's toughness and strength simply to be able to bear the pressure of the task.

A good which is identified by its hurting, a deliverance which is identified by its making me unhappy, a grace which is identified by suffering, etc.—all this, and everything essentially Christian is like this, no woman can bear, she will lose her mind if she is to be put under the tension of this strenuousness.

As far as children are concerned, it is sheer nonsense that they are supposed to be Christians.

A woman and, above all, a child relate to things directly and breathe the air of directness and immediacy. If something is a good, well, then it must be recognizable by its doing good; there is no use in forcing a woman (I will not even mention the child) into a good that hurts—it would break her.

Just notice why it is that a woman cannot tolerate irony, that as far as her emotions are concerned irony is fatal. Is this not because she cannot bear the dialectical?

In this respect I have really taken the comprehensive philosophy examination. Try it: make a girl unhappy, and then tell her: I did it all out of love for you—and you break her, her mind snaps. Adapt yourself to her and say: I am a thoughtless scoundrel—that she will be able to bear, and she will heartily forgive you. But then she also escapes the dialectical redoubling.

So it is with everything essentially Christian. Only man has from the hand of Governance the toughness to be able to endure the dialectical.

Having to endure the dialectical is the most intense agony there is. A child, the little rascal, is completely safeguarded against it; he can never even get close enough to lose his mind over it, even if you were to pour as much of it into him as you can. A woman can come so close that she collapses under it, or her mind, in order to get her out of this, slips away—that is, she loses her mind.

To have to endure the dialectical is the most intense agony possible. It is also easy to see that far more intense than, for example, becoming unhappy, is the suffering of becoming unhappy and in addition having to take this as one's very happiness—and in every respect. Thus anyone who comprehends this (if there is such a person), when he thinks of the figure of speech, a dialectical redoubling, and imagines a woman in such a situation, will (just as when one sees the instruments of torture for the martyrs, he involuntarily hears, as it were, a martyr's shriek) involuntarily hear this scream: O, save me, save my sanity!

What has really happened in Christianity, then, is that this sublimity, which is the essentially Christian position, this sublimity which no man has reached, not even when to be man was an ideal and not even one of those with highest ideality even attempted it or felt its weight without its bringing him to his knees, this sublimity under which (to put it as strongly as possible) even the Savior of the world sinks—that God who is love yet can abandon him and do it out of love—this sublimity Christendom has so flatly and heartily jabbered down into the vulgar gossip which is characteristic of the ordinary human mentality, that this sublimity has even become too light and easy for the kind of creatures dressed up to look like and whom we nowadays call men, and it is turned over to women and children, for whom religion really is intended, after all.

In the New Testament it is aimed at the man, religion is related to the man; woman participates in religion at second hand, through the man; she cannot herself endure a dialectic, but by seeing how the man feels the weight of the task she gets an impression of something more than the immediate pure and simple; the child shifts for himself until his time comes. To want to pour true Christianity into a child (if it were at all possible, for the child's nature makes it impossible to appropriate this) is just as crude as wanting to pour brandy into a child (which happens too often), because the parents themselves drink brandy, and the sweet lassie has to have it as well as her parents. And in the name of Christianity to want to pour something into the child which is not Christianity is, after all, indefensible.

But, as stated, Christendom has gotten everything transposed over into the immediate and direct—and therefore, quite right, "the child" has become the measure of what it is to be Christian! Christendom does not seem to be at all aware that all this about "the child" has raised an ironic problem, a question which has been kindly answered, the problem of what shall we do with the child, can the child become a Christian—a question to which the New Testament gives no answer since it assumed that the Christian does not get married. Christendom's enrichment of Christianity with all this great and profound learning about children, the Christianity of children, the baptism of children, their faith, etc., is just as ironical as what Peer Degn[1232] says about Saxo Grammaticus' enrichment of the Latin language with a host of expressions. Have a third-party relationship to a child, and you will see that everything is just as the New Testament presents it. But then the nice Christians hit upon the very thing Christianity put a stop to, even wanting to start all over afresh—so children got another significance. And thus, quite logically, by means of the child Christianity was turned upside-down, became exactly the opposite of what it is in the New Testament, got to be sugar candy for children, even to the point that the kind of men we have nowadays were right in turning away from it and regarding it as something that was only for women and children, something which disgusts a man just like gossip, chit-chat, and the temperature in the nursery.

No, let it become again what it once was, let it bring the man to his knees to pick up and carry the task, let woman shudder to see how heavy it is. And the child? Yes, let it become as it once was, let us be free from this child-begetting by Christians: then it is possible that Christianity may be seen again. Otherwise it is impossible, and I for my part cannot see how it is possible that anyone with an impression of Christ's life and what the evangelists understood it was to be Christian and with an idea of Christ's demand for discipleship and imitation [*Efterfølgelse*] can think of getting married.

XI^2 A 192   *n.d.*, 1854

« 5008 *Woman*

To say that Christianity makes man and woman equal, and therefore the woman must relate to Christianity the same way as the man, is baseless talk. Christianity does indeed make man and woman equal, but it still does not change their natural qualifications; otherwise by the same logic one could conclude that Christianity must cause women to grow just as tall and muscular as men, or even (if Christianity normally had this result) have the effect of making the business of childbirth in

Christendom so confusing and indiscriminating that sometimes it would be the woman, sometimes the man, who bore the child.

To say that women relate to Christianity even more essentially than men is a fraudulent trick to get Christianity redrafted in terms of the immediate and direct. No, on the scale of the immediate and direct women certainly have the advantage both in delicacy and depth and inwardness, but as soon as there is a dialectic, women are in the same situation as people in the southern countries when they have to pronounce a Slavic word with five or six consonants before a vowel.—XI^2 A 193 *n.d.*, 1854

WORK

« 5009

The situation is this: in an eternal sense there is nothing that cannot wait, and yet I ought to be as diligent as the most diligent. I ought to be as diligent as the most diligent, as scrupulous and economical with time as a beggar with a penny, and then every little iota ought to engage my greatest and most deliberate solicitude. But as a rule people do not remember that there is a God and an eternity; if they are diligent, then they are also usually hurried and bustling, for, of course, "this is what the world is waiting for" *or* "a little misconduct does not make much difference when one is doing big things."—

VIII^1 A 104   *n.d.*, 1847

« 5010

In margin of 5009 (VIII^1 A 104):
An excellent statement by Jacob Boehme:[1233]

Wem Zeit ist wie Ewigkeit,
Und Ewigkeit wie Zeit,
Der ist befreit
Von allem Streit.

VIII^1 A 105   *n.d.*

« 5011

In margin of 5009 (VIII^1 A 104):
Goethe:[1234]

Nicht Kunst und Wissenschaft allein,
Geduld will bei dem Werke sein;
Ein stiller Geist ist Jahre lang geschäftig,
Die Zeit nur macht die feine Gährung kräftig.

VIII^1 A 106   *n.d.*

« 5012

In the worldly sense a man works—and then gets his wages, and if he does not get them, he still needs them; for in the worldly sense work is enervating and wages are nourishing. But to work Christianly is nourishing; as Christ[1235] says: My food is to do my father's will. Thus it is not: The more I do my father's will, the more exhausted I become and, as it were, hungry for wages—no, the more satisfied I am. —Here again it holds true that out of the eater came something to eat.[1236]

IX A 399 *n.d.*, 1848

« 5013

See, here we have Bishop Mynster.[1237] In the sermon about John the Baptizer (it is definitely this one or the one about the power of prayer or one of the first five in the first sermons) he says that before God we should deliberate upon our choice of occupation [*Opgave*] and work [*Gjerning*], "and if you cannot understand how you will succeed along some line—you can be quite sure that it is not the occupation for you." According to this procedure there is no place for the essentially religious: venturing with confidence in God. [*In margin:* Moses, for example, could not understand how he was going to manage, he who was unable to speak; he said: No, send someone else.] It becomes purely and simply a matter of intellectual deliberation; there is no religious action whatsoever. A person uses his little bit of understanding and then perhaps ornamentally adds God's name to it or for the sake of ornamentation uses the name of God.

IX A 430 *n.d.*, 1848

« 5014 *"How, then, is the Christian life to be expressed at all?"*

is the question I am obliged to ask the established order of Christendom. The expression which the Middle Ages insisted upon—going into the monastery, fasting, praying, asceticism, and the like, has been thrown out. The Christian must remain in the world, it is said. But then he must express that he is a Christian in his occupation, etc. Take a merchant. He is a Christian. Consequently he ought to express that he is a Christian by not getting mixed up in this gray dishonesty which is the normal thing in the commercial world but ought to strive for the kind of conscientiousness which is truly Christian. Fine, but then after a time he will also shut up shop and will be branded a traitor by the other merchants. But, they say, he is carrying it too far, he must be like the others—aha, there the expression for what it is to be a Christian disappeared.

If Bishop Mynster[1238] had expressed the kind of conscientiousness which is specifically Christian, he would never have become bishop. By remaining among men, the Christian would rather have the achievement of being persecuted.

x^3 A 401 *n.d.,* 1850

« **5015** *Bernhard*

He said it beautifully—"Let us not forget that Martha and Mary still were sisters" (meaning the other side of life should also be included).

I read this in Neander's *Bernhard,* second edition, p. 68.[1239]

x^3 A 589 *n.d.,* 1850

WORLD

« 5016

An enthusiastic youth will make many mistakes until he learns to remodel his conception of the world. If the world works against him, he will believe it is because he is not acting unselfishly and nobly enough. He will then exert himself enthusiastically in the noblest and most unselfish self-sacrifice—and the world will oppose him even more. The misunderstanding lies in this—to win the world's approval and love he must do exactly the opposite and manage to become a bit scoundrelly. How could the world, which in its very being is little more than scoundrelly, admire unselfishness—no, it ridicules it or hates it.

VIII^1 A 150   *n.d.*, 1847

« 5017

It is all very well to preach about the world being fine and wonderful—and then personally live under a cheese-bell,[1240] far removed from people and any contact with the fine world, and live in this way out of prudence and precaution, because one knows well enough what contact with this fine world would lead to.

VIII^1 A 409   *n.d.*, 1847

« 5018

Would you not consider it to be a fine world, really a moral world, when signs on the street corners (as is the case today) declare: "The world wants to be deceived."[1241] Alas, just this brash, superficial knowledge is the deepest degradation.

X^2 A 24   *n.d.*, 1849

« 5019

"The world wants to be deceived"[1242] can be said in several different ways—(1) by a shrewd person who takes advantage of it and says: The world wants to be deceived; (2) by a shrewd person who hypocritically defends himself with it, saying: It cannot be any different in practical life; the world wants to be deceived; (3) by someone who has mystified in reverse, pretended to be far worse than he is, a villain, a heartless fellow, when he was just a very kind person and now, convinced that the world actually likes the scoundrel best, cries out in fright: But, my God, the world does in fact want to be deceived; (4) by a witness of the truth, who sadly declares: It wants to be deceived; it is not merely deceived, it *wants* to be deceived; I patiently suffer the consequences of not wanting to deceive them, all the persecution, contempt, ridicule, etc.

x^2 A 31 *n.d.*, 1849

« **5020**

This too is part of the hypocrisy of the world, the sham which is maintained when it is said: If only a man's character is not attacked, then the rest is nothing.

O, the hypocrisy! The dangerous thing for a man in this world is by no means to be regarded as being somewhat morally corrupt at the very core of his being—no, no, just so one is not stupid and clumsy enough to do something so bad that he is liable under the law. And in that event it is the stupidity, the clumsiness which the world detests.

The judgment of the world is not *moral* at all (naturally, for then the world would not be the world) but *esthetic:* the world admires everything that has power, cunning, selfishness etc.—successfully—that is, so that it wins money, honor, esteem.

This is why the world has actually substituted as the most dreadful of fates: ridicule, being laughed to scorn, which quite rightly is an esthetic judgment. This is why no one dreads in the least having a wrong opinion—not if he is in the majority, but he is afraid—even though it be truth itself—of standing alone.

x^2 A 568 *n.d.*, 1849

« **5021**

I wonder if Bishop Mynster[1243] actually dares maintain that the world has become a better world now? But he does not do that either; on the contrary, he depicts it in rather dark colors.

How does he explain, then, that Christianity today is not persecuted? Alas, he does not get involved in such things; he is too cautious for that. For that matter, the explanation is easy enough: because Christianity has become nothing.

Incidentally, there is satire in the fact that the world gets worse but Christianity is no longer persecuted—one might take this to be proof that the world has become better. Christianity is no longer persecuted

—well, I have an idea that in a certain sense one would have some difficulty in persecuting it since it does not exist.

x^3 A 273   n.d., 1850

« 5022 *When the Doors Were Locked, Christ Came to the Disciples*[1244]

So must the doors be locked, locked to the world—then Christ comes, in through the locked doors; in fact, he also comes from the inside.

When Christianity struggled, the doors were always locked—the heterogeneity of the essentially Christian.

In Christendom the doors have been left wide open (homogeneity with the world), but then Christ does not come, either.

x^4 A 524   n.d., 1852

« 5023 *Service to God above Service to the King*

Service to God ranks highest of all, that is certain. Obviously nothing, then, is too good for it—neither silk nor velvet nor gold nor medallions, and obviously, since it is service to God, God will also provide on the greatest possible scale—that is certain, if there were not an even higher level of distinction: that service to God is marked by poverty and insignificance.

All deception in Christendom, from the first to the last, involves substituting the secular concept of rank for the divine.

x^4 A 672   n.d., 1852

« 5024 *To Live Quietly and Go Happily through the World*

Perhaps you say: It probably is the case that the world is immersed in evil, but up till now I have managed to live quietly and to slip through happily.

To this the reply must be: Watch out lest this happen. It is no good for you to say verbally that the world is immersed in evil; by slipping through easily your life expresses that it is really a very good world. No, if the world is immersed in evil and if you live in a demoralized generation, then you do not have permission to slip through easily, that is, it cannot be done without your being an accomplice in one way or another.

And on the other hand, when God's judgment falls upon a generation, it spares none who has not suffered evil in the evil world, that is, it treats the others as accomplices, and their guilt is not that they have done something but that they have not done anything. Or is it your opinion that literally all were lechers, etc.? Is it not your opinion that there was a great number of respectable people—but none was spared except him who had suffered evil. For to be a respectable man in an evil world in such a way that the evil world considers one a respectable man means *eo ipso* to be an unrespectable man in one way or another, and to hide as well as possible so as to be permitted to live well in an evil world is to be an accomplice and to evade the service of the good.

XI^1 A 84 *n.d.*, 1854

« 5025 *The Best World*

Anyone with a little experience knows that it is a trashy world. But just as in a penitentiary it is *bon ton*[1245] to keep a stiff upper lip, as well as the smartest thing to do, and to pretend that everything is fine, and just as it is therefore customary in penitentiaries to make it rough for the person who lets his suffering show, so it is with the whole world or with the human race. In fact, anyone who wants to understand human life as a whole would do best to study the criminal world—there is the analogy, the only genuinely trustworthy one.

XI^1 A 243 *n.d.*, 1854

« 5026 *That This World Is a Vale of Tears, a Prison, a Penitentiary*

There is a certain kind of indirect proof which I value almost more than the direct proofs.

So it is in this case. How does it happen that all the expressions and figures of speech related to suicide are along the line of "breaking out," which is used about breaking out of prison, a penitentiary?

Or I wonder if during the world's 6,000 years there has ever lived among all the happy people one single person so happy that, confronted by a suicide, he found it natural to say: This man must have been insane, taking his own life and thereby making it impossible for him to enjoy the indescribable happiness of living in this glorious world any longer?

XI^1 A 254 *n.d.*, 1854

« 5027 *It Is a Splendid World*

Imagine a penitentiary: all the prisoners are assembled—and a man steps forward to address them, saying: Worthy gentlemen, may

I have the cordial attention and considered judgment of this esteemed audience, etc.—is it not true that all the prisoners would burst out laughing and regard as mad anyone who calls them an esteemed audience.

The ludicrous aspect is quite simply contained in the contradiction: penitentiary inmates—this esteemed audience.

They would laugh at the ridiculousness of it, get a kick out of the speaker—nothing else would enter their heads.

And why would nothing else cross their minds? Because as prison inmates they are surrounded and far outnumbered by an environment which has the power to express: You are a bunch of thieves etc.

But now imagine this assembly of prison inmates as a world by itself where there consequently is no outside world to drive home the truth that they are thieves—imagine this audience of prison inmates as a world by itself: do you still believe that they would burst out laughing if someone stepped up to address them, saying: This esteemed audience? No, by no means. On the contrary, they would interpret it thus: We are, in fact, the world. Consequently we have the power to impose the idea that we are splendid, worthy, virtuous men; how could it ever enter our minds to laugh if someone calls us worthy gentlemen? No, this is just exactly what we demand; to address us thus shows that one is an earnest and even a worthy gentleman; to talk any other way is ludicrous, is lunacy.

It is the same with the world. If this world were surrounded by another world, if it were a little world within a far more powerful world which drove home to us the truth about ourselves, that we are scoundrels, we would then all laugh every time a man stepped forward and addressed us: This esteemed audience, etc. But this world is itself the superior power and this explains why we are not lunatic and laugh— no, we have the power to impose the idea that we are a splendid world.

XI^1 A 286   n.d., 1854

« 5028 *This World Is a Prison*

———

From a Christian point of view, this picture gives the best understanding of existence [*Tilværelsen*].

And here is a new aspect. What is the situation in a prison? It is a continual conspiracy; just as we speak of living on the edge of a volcano, so also deep down in any person there is a conspiracy. Perhaps it never reaches the point of eruption, but it is there nevertheless.

Similarly, from a Christian point of view, this whole existence is a conspiracy against God, a monstrous swindle aimed at falsifying the concepts in such a way that we get something quite different out of them than God has in mind. In this way we make out that this is a very splendid world and, in addition, that to enjoy it is true worship of God and the meaning of life—yes, this is true Christianity.

XI^1 A 291 *n.d.*, 1854

« 5029 *The World Is What You Take It For: A Splendid World——A Trashy World*

This phrase or proverb, "The world is what you take it for," means more than it is perhaps thought to mean; it contains a Christian truth and therefore is perhaps the only proverb of this kind,[*] for the usual connection between proverbs and Christianity is this: Comply with the proverb, and in all probability everything will go well with you in the world but you will be doing the exact opposite of Christianity.

"This is a splendid world." That means—bow and scrape to the world, express in every way that it is a splendid world—and it will be a splendid world—that is, it will go with you as it usually goes with such craven, wretched, hypocritical, characterless, spineless fellows in this world—that is, you will get along fine, will be successful, etc.

Now along comes Christianity and declares: It is a trashy world. Christianity offends. If someone were to say to Christianity, "But how do you know that it is a trashy world?" Christianity would no doubt answer, "Prove it yourself—tell the world that it is a trashy world, and you will see that it is."

But then the objection could be made: "In a way is it not Christianity's fault that it becomes a trashy world, inasmuch as it is precisely this judgment upon the world which makes it apparent that it is a trashy world; whereas the world is generally like other scoundrels who are quite decent fellows when one bows and scrapes before them but really become what they basically are when one tells them what they basically are." This may be answered by saying that it is by virtue of its police intelligence that Christianity knows the true condition of the world, and it is in the character of a policeman that it says it—in order to get the truth out in the open.

Incidentally, here one sees what it leads to when Christianity is not served in character, when cowardice is hypocritically dressed up in this sentimental rubbish that those being addressed are splendid men. When this is done, thereby expressing that it is a splendid world, when Christianity is proclaimed in this way (quite meaninglessly, for Christianity definitely says it is a trashy world, and this proclamation as much as says: You, world, to whom I am speaking, you are a splendid world), in all probability it will go well for one in this world, but in recompense Christianity takes its leave. As soon as the proclaimer expresses that the world he addresses is a splendid world, the world has conquered, has conquered Christianity.

But men become more and more clever in an evil sense, and if they become so clever as to proclaim objectively the objective principle "that it is a trashy world," they will proclaim it in such a way that they flatter the world, the audience they are addressing.

XI^1 A 301   *n.d.*, 1854

« **5030**

[*] *In margin of 5029* (XI^1 A 301):
Nevertheless this proverb is still no different than other proverbs, for its meaning is clear: Treat the world as if it were a splendid world.

XI^1 A 302   *n.d.*

« **5031** *That This World Is a Vale of Tears*

This is life in "Christendom": everyone no doubt privately feels that this world has various and sundry drawbacks and suffering—but believes that the task is to manage to make his life as enjoyable and happy as possible—and this is supposed to be Christianity.

Christianity, on the contrary, holds that the task is really to discover that this world is a vale of tears, to venture out in such a manner that it becomes that, to understand that its being a vale of tears this way is our punishment and that it is but little help eternally to pretend fraudulently that we are unable to see what God wants us to see, or actually are not able to see it because we have made life easy—by making it meaningless, devoid of spirit, abandoned by idea, and brutish for men.

Christianity is so far from making this life easy for us that, on the contrary, it wants to make it terribly hard—for the sake of eternal life.

But to understand this already means to be spirit and is just as difficult to get into men's heads as the principle that men are not spiritually strengthened by joining together and uniting but are weakened, that a million is less than one, which is the case, just as certain as it is certain that the laws of "spirit" are directly opposite to laws in the sensate and finite sphere.

But in "Christendom" Christianity is revised according to the natural notions of the natural man. This is why public worship in Christendom is nothing more nor less than blasphemy, making a fool of God.

XI^1 A 519   n.d., 1854

« 5032 *Christianity*

It goes like this: for God, seen from his point of view, the world is immersed in evil, lost, every one of these individuals eternally lost.

I will show mercy, he declares; I will have salvation, an eternal salvation, proclaimed.

But, he says, the result of that, again, will be that your temporal life will become a time of suffering. And anyone who is able to entertain God's idea of how brief these seventy years are and how dreadful eternal perdition is would understand that it could never occur to God that there could be any hesitation on man's part, as if this condition were too severe.

Christianity in Christendom has become nonsense, a continual attempt to make a fine world out of it, instead of firmly acknowledging that this world is immersed in evil, your life is lost, eternal salvation is possible only on the condition that this life becomes a time of suffering.

XI^1 A 545   n.d., 1854

« 5033 *The World*

..... "But the world is so beautiful," you say. Well, yes, so it is. Beautiful—who could invent or imagine anything more beautiful? Beautiful—when after long, quiet preparation suddenly one day it is ready to surprise you, dressed in nature's summer frock. Beautiful—indescribably beautiful—when the moonlit winter night is strangely like a fairy tale, a poem, or when the stars on a dark night twinkle in the enormous arch of the sky, or when echo waits in the still night for something to break the silence so that it can have the joy of echoing! Beautiful—rapturously beautiful, who can keep from surrendering to it—beautiful, to gaze out over the ocean, far, far into the distance, this distance which continually, captivatingly remains distance and continually seems to beckon you, so close that it invites you to let your gaze follow—into the distance.

Yes, indeed, the world is beautiful when looked at in this way.

But is this Christianity, is this looking at the world from a Christian point of view. Look now at the world, the human world—is it not a beautiful world, a splendid world. A splendid world, where man, created in the image of God, essentially lives to eat, drink, accumulate money—in short, occupies himself with the things which make him forget that he is created in the image of God. A splendid world, where there is nothing but dishonesty, and so much so that restricting one's thievery to one's trade is praised as honesty. A splendid world, where there is nothing but faithlessness, and so much so that faithfulness to a party in dealing faithlessly with all the others is praised as faithfulness. A splendid world, where a man, a real man, is a wonder which is not only not to be seen but is not even missed, and where every eighth female in a large city is a prostitute, and all the rest more or less corrupted by social life, so that feminine virtue is a wonder which is not only not to be seen but is not even missed, and if it did appear would be extremely inconvenient. A splendid world, where despite all the police injunctions against disguises,[1246] everything—police included—is a disguise, is not what it pretends to be, where envy deceitfully disguises itself as concern, sympathy, that is, sympathy with the overthrown, the fallen, where malice disguised as concern comes and gazes solicitously at the suffering one, where slander lays a finger on its mouth as if it were silence and perhaps by this gesture manages to say just exactly what it wanted to say, where the thing to watch out for most is the openness which has craftily become the hiding place for the most subtle kind of concealment, where the person who wants to deceive you comes to warn you, warn you against being deceived, where the person who wants to betray you comes in the guise of alerting you to the snares laid for you, where you can depend least of all on the one who reassures you that you can depend on him and least of all when he says that he well knows that others make a habit of assuring that they can be depended on precisely when they want to deceive. Yes, a splendid world, where the only truth to be heard either has to do with the most trivial things, such as, for example, that the weather today is fine, or is the kind of truth which is a lie (as, for example, politeness), and yet all are witness to the fact that it is a lie, etc.[*]

XI¹ A 566   *n.d.*, 1854

« 5034

[*] *In margin of 5033* (XI¹ A 566):
Where one never gets to know the truth as long as it is important but only when it has become a matter of indifference, consequently only when it is absolutely clear and certain that it is not worth the trouble, not in the least, of lying.

XI¹ A 567   n.d.

« 5035 *World History*
A Question

We humans flatter ourselves that world history is enormously important, something which therefore must also attract considerable attention from God.

Question—I do not undertake to answer it, I merely raise it, and again I am doing so only because Christianity does in fact teach that the propagation of the race is a false step, but the personnel of history, these millions, are, after all, produced in this manner—the question: I wonder if this whole matter of world history, the four monarchies, Hegel, Grundtvig,[1247] Gert Westphaler[1248] (note—he also posits four monarchies), the railways and telegraphs, is of any concern to God or pleases him more than all the noise and fun children can make in the playroom instead of sitting still and studying their lessons, which would please their parents. Is not this faith in the immense importance of history one of the human delusions which aim to sustain and enliven a zest for life, the desire to join the hubbub stirred up by the stories of the devilish uproar and hullabaloo all these various emperors and kings made while they lived?

When his mother is about to curse him, Richard III,[1249] in order not to hear her curses, turns to the drummers and says, "Strike up the drums!" Is this not the case with all of us—there is something we do not wish to hear and therefore we want noise, and world history is just such a noise; but is it anything more than a self-gratifying illusion that such things are supposed to concern God, is it not attributing our own misinterpretations to him? Is it not a "mistake" when wise seers think that by extreme effort they are able to perceive dimly that God is involved, also how he is involved in this history, and is it not even a greater mistake when they believe that sometime in the hereafter they will be able to see with perfect clarity how God was involved in all this historical hullabaloo?

Does not mankind itself seem to tend more and more to show that this whole matter of history is meaningless, is nothing more than the grownups' noise and fun and uproar? As long as there was a certain separateness, as long as only the more important, the more outstanding matters were preserved for history, while the whole mass of trivialities sank into forgetfulness, then it could seem as if this were an object of God's attention, however much he is a friend of stillness, but nowadays everything is working toward a level of indifference, everything is preserved for history, the enormous mass of insignificant material is dragged in so that what once inspired men to want to become more significant now no longer inspires them, with the result that no one becomes anything more significant, so that the concept of history is completely abolished, for the whole mass of information down to the most trivial about what triviality's mass has done for a mass of trivialities—does not produce history, to say nothing of history which must be able to draw God's attention to itself.

XI^2 A 203 *n.d.*, 1854

« 5036 *Drivel*

When a child is born, it is said: What joy that a world citizen has come into existence, and so on. And when a man dies, it is said: He is well off; he is released from this world.

As Professor M. Nielsen[1250] said, this is stuff and nonsense.

XI^2 A 219 *n.d.*, 1854

« 5037 *This World a Penitentiary*

As I have pointed out elsewhere [i.e., XI^1 A 243], this whole world is like a penitentiary, where it is both most prudent and also most audaciously satisfying to give the appearance that one is having a very good time of it, and if there happen to be any prisoners who prefer to humble themselves under the point of view of the authorities and admit that it is not good to be here, and after all it should not be, since we are here to be punished—these prisoners would be badly treated and ridiculed by the others.

Christianity holds that this world is a penitentiary. The world, of course, devotes itself to carrying on as if it were a fine world, both because it is the most prudent thing to do and because it satisfies its refractory nature. If there are any individuals (these are the Christians) who humble themselves under God's point of view and say, "It is not good to be here, but, after all, it should not be, since it is a punishment," they would be hated and abominated by the world.

According to Christian doctrine all men are condemned. But the heavenly authority does not intervene; in a way he leaves us to ourselves. Those who voluntarily report to suffer their punishment are the Christians. Grace, then, is to suffer punishment in this life and be saved eternally. Grace is not an epicurean life. When a person condemned for life receives a reduction of sentence to imprisonment for five years, this in fact is grace, but grace does not mean that he is promptly set free.

This is the essentially Christian view of existence—test it out and see if this harmonizes with begetting children.

To change Christianity into the enjoyment of this life is animalistic.

XI² A 223 n.d., 1854

« 5038 *Two Wills in the World*

cannot be tolerated. God is the one and only.

To be sure, God has given man and the human world the power of having a will. But as punishment for willing its own will the world must take the consequences of its not really existing for God, of his handing it over.

However, as soon as a will wills to become involved with God, this will must go. This is the meaning of dying to the world.[1251] That a will wills to involve itself with him is precisely what God wants, but the next comes as a matter of course if God and this will are to be bound together.

The God-forsaken world seems to have freedom, although different from that of the Christian—this is because God has handed over the God-forsaken world, it is free from God.

XI² A 239 n.d., 1854

WORSHIP

« **5039**

Richard d. St. Victore[1252] says it superbly. He points out that one is not to be as busy as Martha but as "unoccupied" as Mary. Then he adds that there nevertheless are many for whom this is not helpful since they lack the busyness of work, are not employed, "but still do not know how to make a Sabbath of the Sabbath."

x^2 A 373   *n.d.*, 1850

« **5040** *Theater Review*

An Imaginary Piece

Yesterday Dean John Doe, Knight of Denmark, appeared as guest at the Church of Our Lady.

The house was sold out, filled to overflowing. Probably no one who was there will ever forget it—on the other hand, many will perhaps regret not having been there, if it had been possible at all to get in; for the sake of that multitude we hope that Dean John Doe will let himself be heard again sometime.

Dean John Doe is a genuine artist—his manner is impressive, his appearance noble, his carriage dignified, his gestures fitting, his facial expressions unforgettable. Without exaggerating, I dare assert that neither Director Nielsen nor even the late Dr. Ryge could put on a performance such as this.

He presented the well-known number about faith; he has great resources at his disposal. He has horror when this is required, ingratiation when this is necessary, tears when they are needed—in short, he has everything. Director Nielsen may have a more beautiful voice, but then again Dean Doe knows how to use his voice in all its nuances with matchless virtuosity.

[*Bracketed in margin: this is inverted;* sketch does not fit here. If someone says: Yes, but Dean Doe—he weeps, he practically sobs Director Nielsen is able to do this also.]

I was entranced. Nevertheless, as I sat there in the best seat, it occurred to me—but where is the prompter?[1253] Indeed, there is no prompter! There is no prompter—therefore this is in earnest, this must be in earnest! This thought made me so uneasy that I almost fainted.

Curious? In a theater the illusion is disturbed if one becomes aware of the prompter; in church the illusion would be perfect only if the prompter were there.

x^4 A 90   *n.d.*, 1851

« 5041 *The Quiet Hours*

in the church are really not the ultimate in religiousness. On the contrary, they are school exercises—to enable you to put religion into actuality, and to that extent the church's true meaning or the significance of the quiet hours in the church is to make the church superfluous, even if we never get that far, even if we want to benefit from going to church just the same.

Imagine a violinist. If, without having learned the least bit of music, he were to take his seat in the orchestra right away and begin playing, he would himself be disturbed and would disturb others. No, for a long time he practices in quiet hours. As far as possible not a thing disturbs him there; he sits and beats time etc. there. But he is supposed to play with the orchestra; he must be able to tolerate the profusion of all the most varied instruments, this interweaving of sounds, and yet must be able to attend to his violin and play along just as calmly and confidently as if he were home alone in his room. O, this again makes it necessary for him to utilize quiet hours to learn to be able to do this—but the objective ($\tau\acute{\epsilon}\lambda$os) is always that he is to play in the orchestra.

It is the same with the religious.

x^4 A 306   *n.d.*, 1851

« 5042 *The Worship of God*

In these days when action, character-transformation etc. as media for the worship of God have been abolished, the worship of God has become a kind of compliment, a sort of court service, a matter of the pastors' competing to see who can say the most affable things, the most subtle flatteries, to our Father.

Is this not worshiping idols—to worship (the true God) in this manner?

x^4 A 475   *n.d.*, 1852

« 5043 *A Curious Glimpse*

into Christianity is provided in Christendom! God is a spirit; consequently worship of God should be in spirit and in truth. The customary

Sunday service these days is perhaps already rather strongly designed for a sensate effect. But wait a minute: on the great festival days of the Church, on precisely those days the worship service moves even farther from the spiritual. Trumpets and every possible appeal to the sensate are used—and this is because it is one of the great festival days of the Church. What nonsense, what an anticlimax! Christianly speaking, this would perhaps be appropriate for an ordinary church service, but on the great festival days not even the organ should be used (if an essentially Christian climax is wanted). Thus (if an essentially Christian climax is wanted) the great festival days should be observed by abstinence—but in Christendom they are celebrated with roast goose and punch, and what is so confusing is that this is supposed to be a climax, because it is such a great Christian festival.

Therefore we perhaps come closer to worshiping God in spirit and in truth on the lesser festival days, but on the great festival days, when we wish to give full expression to truly authentic Christianity, then we really see what people think Christianity means, and we also find out that the reason why the lesser festivals are not celebrated just as—Christianly!—is no doubt because it would be so expensive!

It is not the roast goose, the punch, the trumpets and all the sensate tumult that is curious, but that this, Christianly, is supposed to be a climax, that this is how the Christian worships God only on the great festival days, so that this is the truest expression of Christianity, and perfection would be achieved if God were worshiped in this way every blessed day.

x^4 A 654 *n.d.*, 1852

« **5044** *Man's Worship of God*

The New Testament holds the view: Venture as a single individual to become involved with God. We men say: Let us join together to worship God; the more we are, the more blessed, the more true—indeed, the more pleasing to God.

O, you fools and scoundrels—for you are both.

As Christianity definitely puts it: as a single individual to become involved with God—yes, that is a piece of daring which takes the courage of despair and the most exhausting effort.

But when we join together ("Let us join together") to worship God, pay close attention and you will see that every one of these united thousands continually interjects between himself and God the middle term: the others, society, the human race—aha! in this way venturing and exerting oneself are both evaded. [*In margin.* Note: Of course, they also defraud themselves of the highest of all—as a single individual to relate oneself to God; they continually take cover under: the others, just like the others.]

But God's self-affirmation, if I dare say it that way, requires that he keep an eye on all human efforts to become the mass, the crowd, etc. For God is the being for whom to be is to be the concept; man is the being for whom the numerical is the way to power. This, you see, is why God confused Babel and why he is always suspicious of organizations.

When men say: Let us join together to worship God, they craftily mean (perhaps not consciously but by natural instinct): Let us revolt against God, let us manage to become powerful over against God. O, but man is instinctively a crafty scoundrel—and has an anxiety about God which leads him to use every human technique and trick in the bag.

In Christianity God has involved himself with men on the largest possible scale: it is made possible for the single individual to be related to God.

Precisely in this enormous concession we find once again God's self-affirmation: I will involve myself only with the single individual.

He wants to involve himself with the single individual, with every single individual. This is the enormous MORE than all paganism and Judaism, in which God always permits the single individual to relate to him only through an abstraction.

And this is how we live (aided by deep, impenetrably deep thinkers like Hegel and no less impenetrably deep prophets like Grundtvig) in Christendom (also here in Denmark, for example)—so that this business of nationality and the state and the single individual's relation through them to the idea or to God is supposed to be higher than New Testament Christianity. You asses!

XI^1 A 248 n.d., 1854

« 5045 *The Faith of the Thousands and Millions*

This is how it all hangs together. One impresses upon the child: You are immortal—and then says: Never pay attention to it any more; never think about it, now get on with the busy activity of life (which, frivolously, is called being earnest), get married, have children, make something of yourself, be active early and late, but for heaven's sake see to it that you never give immortality another thought, for you are immortal, this is absolutely certain—this is called having faith.

This means that instead of using life to arrive at faith, one uses life to prevent himself from arriving at faith—this is called having faith.

It is the same with the worship of God by these thousands and millions, for if you look a little more closely at their worship, you will see that it does not consist of involving themselves with God but of defending themselves against God under the name of worshiping him; there is nothing they fear more than becoming involved with God; therefore they worship him in order to be rid of him: Abracadabra, Amen, Hallelujah!

XI^1 A 251   n.d., 1854

« 5046 *The Unconditioned*

Every man has an idea that if a person is going to involve himself with God as a single individual, he must unconditionally submit in everything—this is why they prefer to worship God in association with others; they calculate that the exertion will not be as great, which is the case, but the blessedness is also less.

XI^1 A 257   n.d., 1854

« 5047 *The Sacraments*

Actually Christianity has been taken back to Judaism with the help of the position given to and the use made of the sacraments—and what Pascal[1254] says about Christianity is entirely true, the truest words ever spoken about Christianity: that it is a society of men who, with the help of a few sacraments, exempt themselves from the duty of loving God.

Through baptism men are—objectively—the people of God and, in addition, by infant baptism——just as men are the people of God through circumcision.

Thus the imitation [*Efterfølgelse*] of Christ has been completely abolished. The sacrament is an objectivity, and every earnest person must feel the need of an objectivity—thanks for that. And the whole matter of eternity is decided once and for all in the easiest and cheapest way possible with the help of this objectivity—and now we have a whole lifetime for being happy and enjoying ourselves and indulging in this life—and then after that an eternity, so our pleasure can continue into infinity.

The sacrament of the Lord's Supper is used just as the sacrificial offering is used in Judaism—everything is designed to reassure us about eternity speedily and objectively, and then we have a lifetime ahead of us for enjoying existence, propagating, and filling the earth

This is Christianity. And that it is New Testament Christianity is proved by—Christ's being present at a wedding in Cana. All honor to Christendom!

XI¹ A 556 n.d., 1854

« **5048** *Talking Obscure Nonsense*

An example of this is all the solemn talk in Christendom about quiet, deep quiet, festive quiet, quiet festivity, etc. as the condition for true religiousness.

This is completely ridiculous, just as ridiculous as for a birdcatcher to sally forth with kettledrums and trumpets and, when he had set his snares, to play as loudly as possible: the more zealous he is in making noise in the hope of trapping more birds, the more ridiculous. Similarly, the more artistically proper and dramatically perfect both the setting and His Right Reverend are, the more everything expresses artistic quiet, which His Right Reverend sets forth as the condition for true religiousness—the more ridiculous.

Well, quiet does indeed pertain to the religiousness which is a matter of *enjoyment.* But essentially Christian religiousness is *suffering,* and therefore it is a matter of bringing about restlessness—in fact, the more restlessness there is, the more profound it is, the more essentially Christian religiousness is possible. For this reason it is not at home in theatrical churches where theatrical preachers declaim—but in actuality and the restlessness of actuality. But as with everything, so also with this: men are *höchstens* so advanced that they know a little bit about art —and since we, of course, are all Christians, the clergymen utilize this and shift Christianity over into the domain of art—and with enormous pretensions. The result is that the artistic is regarded as superior to simple Christianity. Otherwise the swindle would not be properly secured. Remaining in the artistic but confessing that it is something far inferior to the essentially Christian would not be sufficiently secure; perhaps it would end with the essentially Christian getting hold of one. But when one remains in the artistic in such a way that it is the superior —well, then one is completely secured against the essentially Christian.

XI² A 35 n.d., 1854

« **5049** *The Forgery*

At times the alarm has been raised that the doctrine has been falsified on some points, on many points, practically all points. This is no doubt possible. But Christendom's forgery is far more dangerous, is on a deeper level; what has been falsified is the concept of "Christian."

In the New Testament a Christian is understood to be a swimmer[1255] who in order to express the divine requirement proclaimed to him leaps out into the depths—that is, right out into the middle of actuality, so that he may then find out whether or not he has faith, and so that he may practice learning to be a Christian. This is what God wants. As soon as someone does it, God in heaven says: Fine, this is just what I am waiting for, and just trust me, I shall not abandon you.

But in Christendom, from generation to generation in mounting millions, to be a Christian means to be a sissy swimmer, the kind who does not want to go out into the water, a society of such swimmers who on dry land make each other believe that they are swimmers but that to leap out would be frightfully presumptuous, would be tempting God, something the pastors din into their ears with all their might, which is natural since it is, after all, important to their trade that no one leaps out into the depths.

Meanwhile God sits and waits in heaven; he neither can nor will involve himself with anyone who does not leap out into the depths, he does not involve himself with anyone who, very solemnly, plays Christianity.

Christendom's guilt is really to make a fool of God, to consider him a fool, to let him sit and wait in heaven and then play Christianity in public or in theaters built for that purpose and called houses of God, and quite appropriately, if it is in the same sense as calling a house designed to keep out storms, a storm-house.

No, God needs no house—he wants to be present in the world of actuality where, even the New Testament notwithstanding, the law is: One must take the world as it is.

This forgery, you see, is by far the most dangerous, far more dangerous than the falsification of doctrine. And this again is why no one wants to interfere with it; they would rather deal with doctrinal falsifications, for here the controversy is objective, and the objective always conceals the subjective.

No, the falsification is the subjective.

XI^2 A 50   *n.d.*, 1854

ZACHAEUS

« **5050**

It is a very ingenious idea of Z. Werner (*Werke,* XIII, p. 34)[1256] to conceive of Zachaeus this way: he has really made himself ridiculous because of his zeal to see Christ. Werner says that the wild fig tree in the text really means the ridiculous fig tree, with reference to its shape, which prompted derision and a proverb; it was a little crooked, with stunted leaves, wrongly shaped, "so that little Zachaeus surely must have looked ridiculous in the tree."

There is the phrase "Zacharias in the pear tree";[1257] it would be curious if it were really Zachaeus in the fig tree. There is also the expression: Did you get the pear, Zacharias.

X^1 A 294   *n.d.,* 1849

Bibliography
Collation of Entries
Notes

Bibliography

KIERKEGAARD'S WORKS IN ENGLISH

Editions referred to in the notes.
Listed according to the original order of publication or the time of writing.

The Concept of Irony, tr. Lee Capel. New York: Harper and Row, 1966; Bloomington: Indiana University Press, 1968. (*Om Begrebet Ironi,* by S. A. Kierkegaard, 1841.)

Either/Or, I, tr. David F. Swenson and Lillian Marvin Swenson; II, tr. Walter Lowrie; 2 ed. rev. Howard A. Johnson. Princeton: Princeton University Press, 1971. (*Enten-Eller,* I–II, ed. Victor Eremita, 1843.)

Johannes Climacus or De omnibus dubitandum est, and *A Sermon,* tr. T. H. Croxall. London: Adam and Charles Black, 1958. ("Johannes Climacus eller *De omnibus dubitandum est,*" written 1842–43, unpubl., *Papirer* IV B 1; "*Demis-Prædiken,*" 1844, unpubl., *Papirer* IV C 1.)

Upbuilding [Edifying] Discourses, I–IV, tr. David F. Swenson and Lillian Marvin Swenson. Minneapolis: Augsburg Publishing House, 1943–46. (*Opbyggelige Taler,* by S. Kierkegaard, 1843, 1844.)

Fear and Trembling (with *The Sickness unto Death*), tr. Walter Lowrie. Princeton: Princeton University Press, 1968. (*Frygt og Bæven,* by Johannes de Silentio, 1843.)

Repetition, tr. Walter Lowrie. Princeton: Princeton University Press, 1941. (*Gjentagelsen,* by Constantin Constantius, 1843.)

Philosophical Fragments, tr. David Swenson, 2 ed. rev. Howard Hong. Princeton: Princeton University Press, 1962. (*Philosophiske Smuler,* by Johannes Climacus, ed. S. Kierkegaard, 1844.)

The Concept of Anxiety [Dread], tr. Walter Lowrie. 2 ed., Princeton: Princeton University Press, 1957. (*Begrebet Angest,* by Vigilius Haufniensis, ed. S. Kierkegaard, 1844.)

Three Discourses on Imagined Occasions [*Thoughts on Crucial Situations in Human Life*], tr. David F. Swenson, ed. Lillian Marvin Swenson. Minneapolis: Augsburg Publishing House, 1941. (*Tre Taler ved tænkte Leiligheder,* by S. Kierkegaard, 1845.)

Stages on Life's Way, tr. Walter Lowrie. Princeton: Princeton University Press, 1940. (*Stadier paa Livets Vej,* ed. Hilarius Bogbinder, 1845.)

Concluding Unscientific Postscript, tr. David F. Swenson and Walter Lowrie.

Princeton: Princeton University Press for American-Scandinavian Foundation, 1941. (*Afsluttende uvidenskabelig Efterskrift,* by Johannes Climacus, ed. S. Kierkegaard, 1846.)

The Present Age [part of *Two Ages: the Age of Revolution and the Present Age. A Literary Review*] and *Two Minor Ethical-Religious Essays* [*Treatises*], tr. Alexander Dru and Walter Lowrie. London and New York: Oxford University Press, 1940. (*En literair Anmeldelse. To Tidsaldre,* by S. Kierkegaard, 1846; *Tvende ethisk-religieuse Smaa-Afhandlinger,* by H. H., 1849.)

On Authority and Revelation, The Book on Adler, tr. Walter Lowrie. Princeton: Princeton University Press, 1955. (*Bogen om Adler,* written 1846–47, unpubl., *Papirer* VII² B 235; VIII² B 1–27.)

Upbuilding Discourses in Various Spirits. (*Opbyggelige Taler i forskjellig Aand,* by S. Kierkegaard, 1847.) Part One, *Purity of Heart* ["*En Leiligheds-Tale*"], tr. Douglas Steere. New York: Harper, 2 ed., 1948. Part Three and Part Two, *The Gospel of Suffering* and *The Lilies of the Field* ["*Lidelsernes Evangelium*" and "*Lilierne paa Marken og Himlens Fugle*"], tr. David F. Swenson and Lillian Marvin Swenson. Minneapolis: Augsburg Publishing House, 1948.

Works of Love, tr. Howard and Edna Hong. New York: Harper and Row, 1962. (*Kjerlighedens Gjerninger,* by S. Kierkegaard, 1847.)

The Crisis [*and a Crisis*] *in the Life of an Actress,* tr. Stephen Crites. New York: Harper and Row, 1967. (*Krisen og en Krise i en Skuespillerindes Liv,* by Inter et Inter, *Fædrelandet,* 188–91, July 24–27, 1848.)

Christian Discourses, including *The Lily of the Field and the Bird of the Air* and *Three Discourses at the Communion on Fridays,* tr. Walter Lowrie. London and New York: Oxford University Press, 1940. (*Christelige Taler,* by S. Kierkegaard, 1848; *Lilien paa Marken og Fuglen under Himlen,* by S. Kierkegaard, 1849; *Tre Taler ved Altergangen om Fredagen,* by S. Kierkegaard, 1849.)

The Sickness unto Death (with *Fear and Trembling*), tr. Walter Lowrie. Princeton: Princeton University Press, 1968. (*Sygdommen til Døden,* by Anti-Climacus, ed. S. Kierkegaard, 1849.)

Practice [*Training*] *in Christianity,* including "The Woman Who was a Sinner," tr. Walter Lowrie. London and New York: Oxford University Press, 1941; repr. Princeton: Princeton University Press, 1944. (*Indøvelse i Christendom,* by Anti-Climacus, ed. S. Kierkegaard, 1850; *En opbyggelig Tale,* by S. Kierkegaard, 1850.)

Armed Neutrality and *An Open Letter,* tr. Howard V. Hong and Edna H. Hong. Bloomington and London: Indiana University Press, 1968. (*Den bevæbnede Neutralitet,* written 1848–49, publ. 1965; *Foranledigt ved en Yttring af Dr. Rudelbach mig betræffende, Fædrelandet,* no. 26, January 31, 1851.)

The Point of View for My Work as an Author, including the Appendix " 'The Single Individual' Two 'Notes' Concerning My Work as an Author" and *On My Work as an Author,* tr. Walter Lowrie. London and New York: Oxford University Press, 1939. (*Synspunktet for min Forfatter-Virksomhed*, by S. Kierkegaard, posthumously published, 1859; *Om min Forfatter-Virksomhed*, by S. Kierkegaard, 1851.)

For Self-Examination, tr. Edna and Howard Hong. Minneapolis: Augsburg Publishing House, 1940. (*Til Selvprøvelse*, by S. Kierkegaard, 1851.)

Judge for Yourselves!, including *For Self-Examination, Two Discourses at the Communion on Fridays*, and *The Unchangeableness of God* (tr. David Swenson), tr. Walter Lowrie. Princeton: Princeton University Press, 1944. (*Dommer Selv!* by S. Kierkegaard, 1852; *To Taler ved Altergangen om Fredagen*, by S. Kierkegaard, 1851; *Guds Uforanderlighed*, by S. Kierkegaard, 1855.)

Kierkegaard's Attack upon "Christendom," 1854–1855, tr. Walter Lowrie. Princeton: Princeton University Press, 1944. (*Bladartikler* I–XXI, by S. Kierkegaard, *Fædrelandet*, 1854–55; *Dette skal siges; saa være det da sagt*, by S. Kierkegaard, 1855; *Øieblikket*, by S. Kierkegaard, 1–9, 1855; 10, 1905; *Hvad Christus dømmer om officiel Christendom*, by S. Kierkegaard, 1855.)

The Journals of Søren Kierkegaard, tr. Alexander Dru. London and New York: Oxford University Press, 1938. (From *Søren Kierkegaards Papirer*, I–XI[1] in 18 volumes, 1909–1936.)

The Last Years, tr. Ronald C. Smith. New York: Harper and Row, 1965. (From *Papirer* XI[1]–XI[3], 1936–48.)

Søren Kierkegaard's Journals and Papers, tr. Howard V. Hong and Edna H. Hong, assisted by Gregor Malantschuk. Bloomington and London: Indiana University Press, I, 1967; II, 1970; III–IV, 1975; V–VII in preparation. (From *Papirer* I–XI[3] and XII–XIII, 2 ed., and *Breve og Akstykker vedrørende Søren Kierkegaard*, ed Niels Thulstrup, I–II, 1953–54.)

At various times in recent years over twenty-five paperback editions of twenty Kierkegaard titles have appeared in English translation. For paperback editions currently available, see the latest issue of *Paperback Books in Print*, published by R. R. Bowker Co., 1180 Avenue of the Americas, New York, N.Y.

General works on Kierkegaard are listed in the bibliography, *Søren Kierkegaard's Journals and Papers*, I, pp. 482–88. Studies of a more limited and specific nature are listed in the appropriate section of topical notes in each volume of *Søren Kierkegaard's Journals and Papers*.

Collation of Entries in this Volume With the Danish Edition of the *Papirer*

Numbers in the left-hand column are the standard international references to the *Papirer*. Numbers in parentheses are the serially ordered references in the present edition.

Volume I A		Volume I A		Volume II A		Volume II A	
3	(3989)	305	(3848)	66	(3997)	296	(4843)
25	(4822)	307	(4070)	90	(3998)	297	(3888)
34	(4823)	308	(4071)	91	(3849)	310	(4001)
42	(4060)	309	(4072)	110	(4774)	311	(4002)
52	(4385)	310	(4073)	117	(3993)	321	(4407)
85	(4575)	313	(4392)	122	(3855)	323	(4091)
92	(3991)	314	(4393)	123	(3856)	331	(4510)
93	(4061)	319	(4394)	152	(4399)	332	(4578)
115	(4576)	321	(4395)	153	(3904)	337	(3889)
116	(4739)	322	(4396)	163	(4400)	339	(4408)
121	(4386)	Volume I C		169	(4401)	343	(4409)
122	(4387)	20	(3843)	170	(4402)	357	(4410)
133	(4062)	23 in XI³,		178	(4842)	358	(4411)
139	(4063)	p. xxxiv, and in		186	(4243)	359	(4412)
163	(4954)	XII	(3844)	188	(3857)	366	(4745)
164	(4955)	31	(3990)	199	(3850)	372	(4788)
167	(4388)	56	(3845)	218	(4403)	378	(4092)
180	(4064)	69	(3846)	219	(4080)	417	(4579)
183	(4389)	70	(3847)	242	(3851)	427	(3960)
201	(4923)	125	(4397)	246	(4987)	428	(4927)
209	(4824)	126	(4398)	248	(3887)	433	(4535)
246	(4065)			257	(4081)	436	(4093)
255	(3854)	Volume II A		263	(4534)	437	(4789)
279	(4390)	1	(3913)	272	(4082)	446	(4003)
282	(4391)	19	(3992)	274	(4083)	451	(4928)
285	(4066)	34	(4773)	279	(4406)	452	(4958)
288	(4067)	63	(3994)	286	(3914)	453	(4959)
289	(4068)	64	(3995)	290	(4084)	455	(4956)
304	(4069)	65	(3996)	291	(4775)	458	(4580)

COLLATION

Volume II A		Volume III A		Volume IV A		Volume V A	
459	(4413)	139	(3891)	205	(4252)	61	(4305)
460	(4094)	181	(4583)	206	(4253)	67	(4925)
464	(3890)	189	(4416)	207	(4254)	76	(4424)
466	(4960)	199	(4825)	208	(4255)	77	(4106)
467	(4095)	206	(4988)	209	(4256)	80	(4840)
477	(4734)	226	(4005)	210	(4257)	81	(4841)
478	(3961)	239	(4584)	211	(4258)	96	(3980)
481	(4096)	Volume III B		212	(4259)	113	(4261)
500	(4414)	8	(4244)	Volume IV B		Volume V B	
504	(4581)	27	(4245)	57	(4423)	4:3	(4262)
515	(4415)	30	(4246)	Volume IV C		23:1	(4263)
531	(4097)	41:2	(4101)	1	(3916)	53:25	(4989)
532	(4098)	41:18	(4102)	26	(3892)	53:27	(3962)
543	(4776)	Volume III C		52	(4844)	53:28	(3963)
544	(4777)	1	(3915)	53	(4845)	53:38	(3964)
563	(3859)	14	(4746)	54	(4511)	Volume VI A	
573	(4099)	Volume IV A		69	(4316)	1	(4107)
584	(3999)	4	(4417)	77	(3893)	2	(4364)
604	(4000)	7	(4103)	93	(4420)	16	(4587)
619	(4074)	9	(4104)	94	(4421)	23	(4735)
668	(4075)	10	(4418)	95	(4846)	26	(4108)
669	(4076)	13	(4105)	110	(4826)	30	(4008)
680	(4077)	18	(4419)	111	(4827)	46	(4588)
703	(4078)	28	(3978)	112	(4828)	48	(4589)
705	(4079)	42	(4847)	113	(4829)	52	(4426)
710	(4085)	44	(4512)	114	(4830)	63	(4538)
721	(4404)	48	(4731)	115	(4831)	64	(4539)
735	(4086)	50	(3972)	116	(4832)	67	(3973)
754	(4087)	52	(4422)	117	(4833)	68	(3974)
756	(4405)	80	(4924)	118	(4834)	71	(4427)
761	(4577)	124	(4260)	119	(4835)	80	(4590)
774	(4088)	160	(4946)	120	(4836)	105	(4009)
775	(4089)	166	(3894)	121	(4837)	112	(4428)
783	(4090)	184	(4790)	122	(4838)	114	(4429)
796	(3858)	186	(4791)	125	(4839)	116	(4747)
797	(3959)	189	(4006)	Volume V A		123	(4430)
Volume III A		194	(3971)	22	(4848)	124	(3975)
		199	(4247)	37	(4536)	132	(3895)
99	(4582)	200	(4248)	43	(4585)		
100	(3977)	202	(4249)	49	(4586)	Volume VI B	
106	(4100)	203	(4250)	51	(3979)	19:1–10	(4537)
118	(4004)	204	(4251)	59	(4007)	175	(4425)

COLLATION

Volume VII¹ A		Volume VIII¹ A		Volume VIII¹ A		Volume VIII¹ A	
16	(4957)	8	(4541)	261	(3918)	581	(4612)
17	(4109)	17	(4439)	265	(3919)	582	(4613)
20	(4110)	22	(4440)	266	(3920)	597	(4614)
22	(4591)	31	(4593)	269	(4603)	598	(4131)
32	(4849)	32	(4594)	275	(4604)	599	(4132)
39	(4317)	40	(4306)	279	(4122)	600	(4133)
45	(4431)	47	(4365)	280	(4123)	605	(4851)
47	(3896)	48	(4366)	281	(4269)	606	(4134)
54	(4111)	64	(4010)	284	(4011)	607	(4135)
57	(4432)	66	(4929)	285	(3921)	608	(4136)
63	(4112)	67	(4441)	287	(3922)	609	(4137)
65	(4264)	75	(4793)	299	(4124)	613	(4138)
68	(4433)	78	(4442)	306	(4446)	614	(4139)
69	(4265)	79	(4115)	313	(4543)	615	(4140)
72	(4540)	85	(4595)	321	(4125)	618	(4141)
74	(4266)	93	(4367)	324	(3923)	624	(4142)
163	(4113)	95	(4443)	334	(4324)	625	(3897)
168	(4323)	96	(4596)	382	(4126)	631	(4615)
193	(4267)	104	(5009)	386	(3924)	633	(4616)
212	(4114)	105	(5010)	409	(5017)	635	(3927)
213	(4592)	106	(5011)	433	(4778)	636	(4143)
235	(4308)	108	(4116)	463	(4605)	662	(4014)
237	(4792)	109	(4117)	464	(4606)	667	(4144)
250	(4318)	113	(4597)	468	(4607)	Volume VIII² B	
Volume VII¹ B		117	(4598)	473	(4012)	71:6,7,9,	
145	(4947)	123	(4118)	480	(4779)	10,12	(4447)
146	(4948)	134	(4119)	485	(4990)	Volume VIII² C	
192:12	(4434)	141	(4850)	490	(4270)	3:5	(4961)
192:13	(4435)	147	(4794)	491	(4271)	Volume IX A	
192:15	(4436)	150	(5016)	497	(4013)	4	(4852)
Volume VII¹ C		154	(4268)	498	(3925)	17	(4617)
1	(4319)	160	(4444)	506	(3926)	29	(4145)
2	(4320)	161	(4599)	514	(4608)	31	(4146)
3	(4321)	165	(4542)	518	(4609)	37	(4448)
4	(4322)	191	(4600)	520	(4272)	38	(4325)
Volume VII² B		192	(4601)	531	(4127)	40	(3976)
256:19,20	(4437)	193	(4795)	535	(4544)	61	(4147)
261:18	(3981)	208	(4445)	551	(4128)	117	(4148)
266:26	(4438)	222	(4120)	552	(4129)	124	(4962)
Volume VIII¹ A		245	(4121)	556	(4130)	138	(4963)
3	(3982)	259	(4602)	579	(4610)	162	(4618)
		260	(3917)	580	(4611)	194	(4449)

COLLATION

Volume IX A		Volume IX A		Volume X¹ A		Volume X² A	
204	(4450)	487	(4857)	436	(4991)	53	(4639)
266	(3928)	494	(4452)	448	(4863)	65	(4328)
267	(3929)	Volume X¹ A		452	(4373)	67	(4274)
268	(3930)			459	(4992)	74	(4025)
269	(3931)	17	(4052)	464	(4635)	80	(4456)
270	(4619)	22	(4372)	477	(4374)	87	(3901)
272	(3932)	30	(4546)	478	(4375)	93	(4785)
278	(4853)	50	(4453)	484	(4750)	103	(4329)
287	(4854)	65	(3899)	486	(4751)	122	(4786)
295	(3838)	96	(4156)	490	(4752)	128	(4640)
303	(4149)	108	(4630)	492	(4753)	129	(4641)
304	(4855)	124	(3983)	493	(3905)	131	(4642)
309	(4150)	133	(4018)	516	(4920)	143	(4965)
313	(4015)	134	(4454)	522	(4162)	144	(4931)
317	(4620)	159	(4858)	550	(4783)	145	(4548)
326	(4856)	171	(4157)	572	(4754)	161	(4748)
330	(4621)	195	(4019)	581	(4797)	182	(4376)
331	(4368)	209	(4964)	591	(4273)	229	(4275)
332	(4369)	223	(4547)	603	(4636)	231	(4549)
333	(4370)	255	(3900)	607	(4755)	236	(4643)
334	(4371)	261	(4796)	625	(4893)	240	(4168)
336	(4622)	269	(4158)	627	(4022)	246	(4644)
339	(5012)	294	(5050)	632	(4163)	248	(4276)
341	(4016)	319	(4631)	637	(4023)	257	(4645)
342	(4451)	347	(4859)	645	(4637)	272	(4646)
349	(4623)	348	(4860)	652	(4327)	274	(3938)
351	(4930)	350	(4159)	662	(4638)	279	(4457)
353	(4151)	356	(4160)	669	(4164)	282	(4787)
363	(4545)	365	(4632)	682	(4165)	292	(4169)
364	(4152)	369	(4161)	Volume X² A		299	(4550)
367	(4624)	383	(4455)	7	(4166)	301	(4551)
373	(3898)	384	(4020)	13	(4053)	313	(4458)
380	(4625)	394	(3984)	24	(5018)	318	(4459)
407	(4626)	397	(4780)	26	(3934)	321	(4993)
410	(4627)	405	(4633)	28	(3935)	322	(4552)
425	(4628)	407	(4861)	29	(4024)	325	(3939)
429	(4017)	410	(4862)	31	(5019)	327	(4330)
430	(5013)	416	(4634)	42	(4784)	333	(3940)
445	(4153)	417	(4326)	43	(3985)	336	(4553)
449	(4154)	428	(3933)	50	(3936)	349	(4647)
453	(4155)	429	(4519)	51	(3937)	350	(3941)
466	(4629)	433	(4021)	52	(4167)	351	(4170)

COLLATION

Volume X²	A	Volume X²	A	Volume X³	A	Volume X³	A
355	(4554)	557	(4966)	199	(4041)	529	(4186)
356	(4171)	562	(4740)	202	(4757)	554	(4994)
373	(5039)	568	(5020)	203	(4758)	561	(4970)
379	(4331)	571	(4182)	205	(4759)	562	(4995)
391	(4172)	590	(4377)	213	(3949)	566	(4044)
394	(4173)	597	(3942)	229	(4760)	570	(4971)
395	(4174)	598	(4278)	240	(4761)	575	(4187)
400	(4026)	635	(4867)	241	(4334)	579	(4336)
401	(4555)	642	(4460)	245	(4655)	587	(4188)
402	(4556)	643	(4183)	253	(4279)	589	(5015)
403	(4027)	Volume X³	A	259	(4762)	593	(4558)
404	(4028)	5	(4967)	273	(5021)	596	(4337)
409	(4864)	14	(4513)	281	(4656)	597	(4338)
416	(3852)	15	(4968)	286	(4799)	601	(3912)
417	(3853)	22	(4557)	287	(4763)	603	(4189)
424	(4332)	25	(4868)	301	(4969)	607	(4190)
429	(4029)	26	(4184)	305	(4657)	614	(4872)
435	(4865)	29	(3906)	315	(4280)	617	(4951)
436	(4030)	31	(3907)	320	(4800)	643	(4514)
437	(4031)	35	(3908)	341	(4042)	652	(4873)
445	(4333)	36	(3909)	346	(4185)	654	(3829)
449	(4277)	43	(4950)	376	(4043)	662	(4465)
456	(4032)	47	(4798)	382	(4658)	664	(4874)
463	(4866)	61	(4736)	390	(4801)	671	(4662)
467	(4033)	79	(4461)	393	(4894)	677	(4972)
472	(4034)	81	(4649)	394	(4462)	679	(4191)
473	(4035)	83	(4926)	396	(4463)	684	(4520)
477	(4036)	85	(4869)	401	(5014)	685	(4521)
478	(4175)	107	(3943)	425	(4307)	686	(4522)
479	(4176)	108	(3944)	426	(4659)	688	(4045)
482	(4037)	109	(3945)	429	(4737)	690	(4192)
483	(4038)	110	(3946)	432	(4870)	695	(3950)
486	(4177)	111	(3947)	452	(3910)	699	(4802)
490	(4178)	114	(4650)	470	(4933)	702	(3860)
497	(4179)	118	(4651)	471	(4934)	705	(4339)
498	(4180)	131	(4652)	477	(4281)	706	(3951)
506	(4181)	148	(4653)	478	(4871)	707	(3952)
513	(4648)	155	(3948)	481	(3911)	708	(3953)
531	(4932)	180	(4039)	492	(4660)	709	(3954)
536	(3965)	181	(4040)	493	(4335)	711	(3955)
548	(4781)	182	(4654)	500	(4661)	718	(4996)
549	(4782)	185	(4756)	512	(4464)	720	(4559)

Volume X³ A		Volume X⁴ A		Volume X⁴ A		Volume X⁴ A	
727	(4741)	119	(3830)	276	(3840)	447	(4217)
731	(4663)	120	(3831)	277	(3841)	456	(4680)
732	(4664)	125	(4469)	279	(3842)	461	(4476)
736	(4340)	126	(4209)	280	(3862)	462	(4381)
745	(4466)	129	(3832)	283	(4562)	463	(4287)
746	(4193)	133	(4046)	284	(4563)	464	(4515)
754	(4194)	135	(4667)	290	(4937)	466	(4309)
756	(4560)	137	(4764)	291	(4473)	467	(4288)
773	(4195)	138	(4765)	297	(4890)	468	(4897)
774	(4665)	139	(4766)	305	(4891)	469	(4310)
777	(3956)	140	(4767)	306	(5041)	475	(5042)
783	(4666)	141	(4768)	312	(4742)	476	(4311)
791	(4467)	142	(4769)	314	(4283)	477	(4743)
Volume X⁴ A		143	(4770)	319	(4284)	480	(4898)
10	(4817)	144	(4771)	328	(4821)	481	(4681)
16	(3986)	153	(4668)	333	(4285)	484	(4312)
18	(4935)	155	(4210)	334	(4286)	486	(4342)
19	(4936)	156	(4669)	335	(4474)	487	(4949)
31	(4196)	158	(4670)	337	(4878)	490	(4289)
35	(4875)	160	(4470)	341	(4974)	497	(4290)
40	(4197)	161	(4877)	342	(4879)	501	(4938)
41	(4198)	169	(4671)	343	(4677)	508	(4343)
42	(4876)	173	(4047)	346	(4564)	509	(4899)
43	(4199)	178	(4973)	350	(4895)	523	(3957)
47	(4200)	181	(4749)	356	(4896)	524	(5022)
48	(4818)	182	(4744)	379	(4565)	530	(4291)
51	(4201)	185	(4211)	381	(4975)	534	(4048)
59	(4468)	186	(4212)	386	(4678)	538	(4939)
63	(4202)	187	(4213)	391	(4880)	555	(4313)
65	(4203)	189	(4672)	397	(4054)	569	(4900)
66	(4819)	191	(4523)	402	(4772)	570	(4682)
68	(4204)	209	(4214)	406	(4976)	573	(4683)
70	(4820)	226	(4341)	407	(4566)	574	(4684)
72	(4205)	235	(4471)	409	(3863)	575	(4219)
83	(4206)	238	(4673)	411	(4379)	576	(4516)
86	(4738)	239	(4674)	412	(3902)	577	(4517)
90	(5040)	244	(4675)	420	(4679)	578	(4685)
95	(4378)	249	(4215)	430	(4475)	579	(4686)
97	(4207)	250	(4282)	431	(4380)	583	(4687)
102	(4208)	251	(4472)	434	(4506)	593	(4688)
106	(4997)	256	(4676)	435	(4507)	598	(4292)
110	(3861)	264	(3839)	436	(4508)	599	(4293)
112	(4561)	268	(4216)	438	(4509)	608	(4314)

COLLATION

Volume X⁴ A		Volume X⁵ A		Volume XI¹ A		Volume XI¹ A	
609	(4881)	136	(4221)	178	(3879)	350	(4710)
611	(4689)	Volume X⁶ B		179	(3880)	351	(4909)
613	(4901)	257	(4218)	181	(3881)	352	(4885)
617	(4344)	Volume XI¹ A		182	(3882)	355	(4886)
620	(4690)	3	(4804)	185	(4981)	357	(4711)
623	(4691)	7	(4906)	191	(4982)	363	(4349)
630	(4692)	8	(4704)	201	(4569)	366	(4232)
632	(4345)	9	(4705)	208	(4707)	371	(4299)
636	(4902)	15	(4296)	211	(4348)	377	(4712)
639	(4524)	17	(4223)	212	(4527)	380	(4570)
643	(4693)	18	(4224)	219	(3966)	397	(4529)
653	(4882)	20	(4805)	220	(3967)	398	(4530)
654	(5043)	29	(4907)	221	(3968)	399	(4807)
660	(4694)	30	(4225)	226	(5000)	404	(4713)
667	(4567)	34	(4347)	231	(5001)	413	(4714)
670	(4695)	54	(4226)	233	(5002)	418	(4892)
672	(5023)	57	(4883)	243	(5025)	419	(4808)
Volume X⁵ A		63	(4495)	248	(5044)	420	(4809)
5	(4525)	66	(4706)	251	(5045)	422	(4715)
11	(4696)	74	(4496)	254	(5026)	426	(5005)
17	(4903)	75	(3872)	257	(5046)	427	(4910)
18	(4977)	78	(3873)	259	(3969)	428	(4300)
24	(4477)	83	(3958)	261	(4921)	430	(4301)
28	(4697)	84	(5024)	266	(4528)	431	(4531)
30	(4698)	93	(4227)	269	(4732)	433	(4716)
35	(4315)	95	(4908)	271	(3834)	438	(4887)
37	(4346)	98	(4228)	281	(5003)	440	(3835)
38	(4699)	99	(4229)	282	(5004)	448	(4302)
40	(4904)	102	(4497)	285	(3903)	449	(4303)
41	(4940)	103	(4979)	286	(5027)	453	(4941)
63	(4518)	105	(4498)	291	(5028)	456	(4480)
65	(5803)	111	(3874)	292	(4733)	457	(4481)
69	(4294)	112	(3875)	296	(4922)	458	(4942)
81	(4700)	115	(4980)	301	(5029)	461	(3865)
82	(4478)	118	(4230)	302	(5030)	465	(3866)
84	(4568)	140	(3876)	311	(4708)	468	(4810)
85	(4701)	141	(4998)	318	(4297)	472	(4482)
95	(4479)	144	(3877)	327	(4952)	475	(4483)
114	(4702)	146	(4884)	329	(4806)	478	(4484)
115	(4220)	159	(3833)	330	(4231)	481	(4485)
118	(4905)	164	(4999)	334	(4298)	487	(4350)
133	(4295)	165	(3878)	340	(4709)	493	(4717)
134	(3864)	167	(4526)	348	(4499)	494	(4718)

Volume XI¹ A		Volume XI¹ A		Volume XI² A		Volume XI² A	
498	(4351)	574	(4487)	85	(4237)	239	(5038)
502	(4943)	575	(4488)	86	(4953)	242	(4051)
507	(4233)	579	(4722)	94	(3869)	246	(4359)
508	(4888)	580	(4723)	97	(4571)	279	(4360)
516	(4911)	583	(3868)	104	(4945)	282	(4978)
517	(4912)	Volume XI² A		106	(4056)	291	(4222)
519	(5031)	2	(4915)	108	(4238)	292	(4239)
521	(4944)	6	(4049)	111	(4501)	297	(4703)
524	(4352)	10	(3836)	112	(4502)	317	(4361)
526	(4913)	14	(4050)	117	(3870)	318	(4815)
527	(4304)	20	(3884)	123	(4814)	319	(4058)
534	(4500)	23	(4235)	132	(4384)	320	(4919)
535	(4811)	24	(4236)	136	(4728)	343	(4059)
536	(4234)	29	(4489)	142	(3987)	352	(4240)
537	(3883)	30	(4382)	143	(3988)	353	(4362)
538	(4353)	33	(4383)	161	(4057)	354	(4573)
541	(4719)	35	(5048)	192	(5007)	356	(4241)
542	(4720)	41	(4355)	193	(5008)	362	(3871)
544	(4983)	42	(4490)	196	(4572)	366	(4574)
545	(5032)	50	(5049)	198	(4357)	373	(4503)
554	(4812)	57	(4986)	202	(3970)	378	(4363)
555	(4984)	58	(3885)	203	(5035)	382	(4816)
556	(5047)	59	(3886)	204	(4917)	396	(4730)
557	(3867)	60	(4916)	205	(4918)	410	(4504)
558	(4354)	62	(4356)	208	(4729)	416	(4505)
561	(4721)	66	(4724)	219	(5036)	Volume XI³ B	
562	(4055)	67	(4725)	223	(5037)	45	(3837)
563	(4985)	70	(5006)	225	(4492)	47	(4532)
564	(4486)	72	(4726)	227	(4889)	126	(4242)
566	(5033)	73	(4491)	228	(4358)	146	(4533)
567	(5034)	76	(4813)	232	(4493)	148	(4494)
568	(4914)	82	(4727)				

Notes, Commentary, and Topical Bibliography

The summary presentation of basic concepts is by Gregor Malantschuk and the notes and bibliography are by the editors.

The following abbreviations have been used throughout the notes:

> *S.V.* *Samlede Værker* by Søren Kierkegaard, I–XIV (Copenhagen: Gyldendal, 1901–1906).
>
> *Pap.* *Papirer* by Søren Kierkegaard, edited by P. A. Heiberg, V. Kuhr, and E. Torsting, I–XI^3 (20 vols.) (Copenhagen: Gyldendal, 1909–1948); 2 ed., ed. Niels Thulstrup, I–XI^3 and suppl. vols. XII–XIII (Copenhagen: Gyldendal, 1968–70). References to the *Papirer* and the appropriate serial number in *J. and P.* will usually be in the form of I A 1; 2240.
>
> *ASKB* *Auktionsprotokol over Søren Kierkegaards Bogsamling* (Auction-catalog of Søren Kierkegaard's Book-collection), ed. H. P. Rohde (Copenhagen: Det Kongelige Bibliotek, 1967). This enlarged edition of the auction-catalog contains the basic serially numbered list of books indicated by number (*ASKB* 200), two appendices designated by I and II (*ASKB* II 200), and a section on books otherwise unlisted but in various ways known to have belonged to Kierkegaard, designated by U (*ASKB* U 100).

Titles of studies pertinent to a particular theme are given under the appropriate heading. The editions of Kierkegaard's works referred to in the notes are listed in the bibliography.

SACRIFICE

For Kierkegaard the concept "sacrifice" holds a central position within Christianity, and in numerous utterances he concurs completely with the view that Christ's death is a sacrificial death. In one place he says that even as a child he had the devout belief "that the sin of the world required this sacrifice" and that he continued to believe this "unswervingly" ("Has a Man the Right . . . ," with *The Present Age*, p. 81). In *Christian Discourses* he speaks of Christ and "the sacrifice he made" (p. 278) and of "the sacrifice of Atonement" (p. 288, ed. tr.), and in a number of passages in *Practice* [*Training*] *in Christianity* and "The Woman Who Was a Sinner" he refers to Christ's sacrifice (see, for example, pp. 195, 270–71).

According to Kierkegaard, Christ chose a sacrificial death in order to save man. He expresses the significance of Christ's sacrifice for man by saying "that Christ died to save him, that Christ's death is the Atonement, is the full satisfaction " (p. 270, ed. tr.). The sacrifice means simultaneously that in this world, which is immersed in evil, the good can be victorious only by being sacrificed.

Also on the human level "precisely this is the highest that can be said of any human being: he is sacrificed. The question, however, is this, whether that for which one is sacrificed is the highest" (*Works of Love,* p. 288). For example a person can sacrifice himself for his country or out of love sacrifice himself to another person (p. 286). But the highest sacrifice takes place on the religious level, as illustrated by Abraham, who in the sacrifice of Isaac sacrificed more than if he had sacrificed himself.

According to Kierkegaard a sacrifice presupposes two movements, one inward and the second outward. The first is the movement of self-renunciation whereby one becomes an instrument for God, and the second is a willingness to be used outwardly, therefore in the world. "In self-renunciation one achieves the ability to be the instrument of God by inwardly making himself nothing before God; in sacrificial disinterestedness he externally makes himself nothing, an unprofitable servant" (p. 336). The first movement is the condition for the eventuation of the second. How close together they are is expressed in this way: "This sacrificial disinterestedness is in a certain sense, inwardly understood, a consequence of self-renunciation or one with self-renunciation" (p. 336). Even though Christ's sacrifice is on an altogether different level than everything human, it also has this double aspect: self-renunciation, the eternal resolve, that is, "consecrated from all eternity to be the sacrifice" (*The Moment,* no. 7, in *Attack,* p. 207), and then the concrete, to suffer the sacrifice of death in this world.

The thought of sacrifice came to play a special role in Kierkegaard's own life. He mentions this in various places in *The Point of View for My Work as an Author:* "the thought goes very far back in my memory that in every generation there are two or three who are sacrificed for others, are led by frightful sufferings to discover what redounds to the good of others; so it was that I melancholically understood myself, that I had been singled out for that" (p. 79, ed. tr.).

For references in the works to sacrifice, see, for example, *The Concept of Irony,* pp. 277–78, 328; *Fear and Trembling,* passim; *The Concept of Anxiety* [*Dread*], p. 93; *Stages,* pp. 373–74, 411; *Works of Love,* pp. 19, 116–19, 123–24, 132–34, 247–60, 286, 288, 336–43; *Christian Discourses,* pp. 278–80, 283–88, 307; "Has a Man the Right To Be Put to Death for the Truth?" together with *The Point of*

View, pp. 81, 86; *The Sickness unto Death*, p. 258; *Practice* [*Training*] *in Christianity*, pp. 12, 64, 119–20, 195, 246, 270–71; *For Self-Examination*, pp. 12–13, 100–101; *Judge for Yourselves!*, pp. 143–49, 202, 206–7; *Armed Neutrality*, p. 41; *The Point of View*, pp. 100, 133; *Attack*, pp. 34–35, 65, 103, 187, 203, 207, 271, 286.

1. See Laurids Kruse, *Don Juan* (Copenhagen: 1807), p. 33.
2. See X^3 A 478.

SAVONAROLA

Apparently Kierkegaard had not read anything by Savonarola (1452–98) other than what he found in A. G. Rudelbach's *Hieronymus Savonarola und seine Zeit* (Hamburg: 1835). Yet he did also know Nicolaus Lenau's poem *Savonarola* (Stuttgart: 1837). It is quite possible that Kierkegaard wrote his first journal entry on Savonarola (IX A 295) while reading this poem, in which Savonarola characterizes himself as an instrument or a small candle God can put out when he no longer has use for it (pp. 224–25). In the entry Kierkegaard is revolted by the view that God would use a man as an instrument and then cast him aside. According to Kierkegaard, a person is always under God's care and God does not abandon him.

During the reading of Rudelbach's book, Kierkegaard made a number of entries that referred particularly to Savonarola's sermons, which Rudelbach had included. Kierkegaard was especially impressed by Savonarola's telling how step by step God had "deceived" him into his work. Seeing the similarity to his own situation, he then went on to make observations on this question, carefully describing how God had also deceived him "into the truth" (X^4 A 297). He had already touched on this idea earlier, although not as directly, in *Practice* [*Training*] *in Christianity*, where Anti-Climacus describes a youth who gradually is led into greater and greater suffering. With regard to Governance's solicitous procedure with the youth, the writer says: "it has not the heart to let him understand at the outset that there is a disappointment here, that he does not reckon with his host" (p. 189, ed. tr.).

There are other expressions of Savonarola's that Kierkegaard adopts in his journals. For Kierkegaard, Savonarola was an example of a man whose convictions found expression in his action and in his readiness to suffer for the truth, and therefore he calls him "the blood-witness Savonarola" (X^4 A 283).

There are no direct references to Savonarola in Kierkegaard's published works.

3. See Nicolaus Lenau, *Savonarola, Ein Gedicht* (Stuttgart, Tübingen: 1837), pp. 224–25. *ASKB* 1743.
4. Andreas G. Rudelbach, *Hieronymus Savonarola und seine Zeit* (Hamburg: 1835). This volume is not listed in *ASKB* or in supplemental lists of Kierkegaard's books, which indicates that his reading ranged beyond his own collection and that his collection was larger than the auction catalog indicates.

5. See note 4.
6. Ibid.
7. Ibid.

SCHLEIERMACHER

In his reading of the works of the German theologian Friedrich Schleiermacher (1768–1834), Kierkegaard received considerable stimulation for the solution of issues important to him. In the well-known dogmatics *Der Christliche Glaube* (Berlin: 2 ed., 1830) Kierkegaard was particularly preoccupied with the conceptions of predestination and original sin. During the spring of 1834 he received tutoring from H. L. Martensen on the main themes in Schleiermacher's dogmatics with emphasis on the problems of predestination. Kierkegaard's earliest journal entries (I A 2, 3 and others) lay the groundwork for his later work on these issues and show his opposition to an absolute predestination and his attempt to maintain the possibility of man's free determination (see PREDESTINATION). Kierkegaard sees a similarity between Schleiermacher and Hegel in that they both assert a "necessary development" (I A 170). As early as 1836 Kierkegaard thought he had found the "solution of the problem of predestination" (I A 295), which in one respect, according to Kierkegaard, could be united with "Schleiermacher's relative predestination" (see *Der Christliche Glaube*, p. 288), which predicates that only when a person encounters Christianity can there be any question of a decision either unto salvation or unto perdition. Consequently this decision takes place in time and is not something that, as in Calvin, is determined from all eternity; however, Christianity, its manifestation in its wholeness, was determined from eternity (I C 40). But at the same time Schleiermacher considers that every human being will be led finally from condemnation to salvation through a necessary development. Kierkegaard calls this idea in Schleiermacher "the modification of infinite sin and infinite atonement" (II A 31). Here Kierkegaard disagrees entirely with Schleiermacher, because he regards a necessary development as unjustifiable, since with respect to sin as well as to acceptance of forgiveness he wants to maintain unconditionally the significance of the individual's freedom.

Kierkegaard also was deeply absorbed in Schleiermacher's extensive deliberations on original sin, and he considers Schleiermacher right on an essential point: that in relation to original sin all men are in the same position as Adam (see *Der Christliche Glaube*, p. 442). When Vigilius Haufniensis, Kierkegaard's pseudonym in *The Concept of Anxiety* [*Dread*], which deals primarily with the question of original sin, speaks of "Schleiermacher's immortal service to this science" (p. 18), no doubt it is because Schleiermacher has presented a position that is also very important to Vigilius Haufniensis.

Despite his acknowledgment of Schleiermacher's service in this area of dogmatics, Kierkegaard was obliged to take a critical position against the place of necessity in Schleiermacher's thought, because it seemed to him that Schleiermacher did not succeed in presenting Christianity in proper relation to human existence, where freedom and appropriation are essential elements. Therefore, he speaks of Schleiermacher's position as "remaining in pantheism" (II A 91). He later sharpens this criticism; Kierkegaard points out that the defect in Schleiermacher's dogmatics is that "he treats religiousness in the sphere of being" (X^2 A 416), and it is interesting that here he compares Schleiermacher with Spinoza. If religiousness is treated as being, no regard at all is given to the religious and ethical difficulties that arise when the individual seeks to practice Christianity in his existence. This transformation of the individual's existence Kierkegaard calls "becoming," and he thinks that "as soon as this is understood, every single Christian qualification is characterized differently than in S." (X^2 A 417). Kierkegaard's objections to the use of the expression "the Christian consciousness (X^4 A 232) must also be understood as an extension of this criticism. For Schleiermacher "the Christian consciousness" is synonymous with Christianity, but for Kierkegaard this is a volatilization of Christianity, because it is regarded as equivalent to the cultural layer that Christianity deposits. For Kierkegaard what is primary in true Christianity is the transformation of the individual's existence.

Finally, it must be added that it was Schleiermacher who gave Kierkegaard the idea of using persons as representatives for various life-views instead of presenting them in an abstract way. Schleiermacher uses this procedure in *Vertraute Briefe uber die Lucinde*, which is a review of Friedrich Schlegel's book *Lucinde*, in which he has persons with various life-views express their thoughts on the book (see I C 69).

O'Connor, D. Thomas. "Schleiermacher and Kierkegaard: 'The Odd Couple' of Modern Theology." *Religion in Life*, 41, 1, 1972, pp. 8–17.

For references in the works to Schleiermacher, see *The Concept of Irony*, pp. 90–92, 95, 99–100, 115–16, 141–42, 148, 150–52, 196, 201, 207, 237, 241–43; *The Concept of Anxiety* [*Dread*], p. 18; "Public Confession," *S.V.*, XIII, p. 401; "A Fleeting Observation Concerning a Detail in *Don Juan*," *S.V.*, XIII, p. 445.

8. In 1834 Kierkegaard had tutoring in Schleiermacher's *Der christliche Glaube* with Prof. H. L. Martensen. See H. L. Martensen, *Af mit Levnet* (Copenhagen: 1882), I, 78.

9. Scholarly disciplines.

10. The feeling of absolute dependence, in which the antithesis again disappears. Friederich Schleiermacher, *The Christian Faith*, ed. H. R. Mackintosh and J. S. Stewart (Edinburgh: Clark, 1960), para. 5, 1, pp. 19–20 (in portion tr. D. M. Baillie).

11. The fact that man allowed himself to be tempted. Ibid., para. 44, 2, p. 163 (tr. H. R. Mackintosh).

12. The title of this entry is from the catalog made by Hans P. Barfod; the text itself is missing.

13. Vol. XV.

14. A review of *Nye Fortællinger af Forfatteren* [Thomasine Gyllembourg] *til en Hverdagshistorie, Andet Bind, "Extremerne." Efterladte Skrifter* (2 ed., Copenhagen: 1850), VI, p. 49.

15. Because of concern with being rather than with becoming. See X^2 A 416.

16. *De Principiis, On First Principles.*

17. Schleiermacher, *Der christliche Glaube*, I–II (Berlin: 2 ed., 1830). *ASKB* 258 lists the third edition (Berlin: 1835), but the second edition is used in the *Papirer* (see I C 20).

SCHOLARSHIP AND SCIENCE

In Danish *Videnskab* means science in the broad sense, just as does the German *Wissenschaft*, not only the natural sciences and social sciences, but the humanistic intellectual disciplines as well.

Kierkegaard, who during his student years had devoted himself to various areas of scholarly work, had great respect for science, but in contrast to many others of his time he also saw clearly that it had its limits. The essential sphere of scholarship and science lies, according to Kierkegaard's view, within "immanence," the finite world, but it cannot cope with "transcendence," the world beyond the finite, and where faith belongs. Kierkegaard deals with the relation between faith and knowledge again and again in his writings, and it is precisely one of Kierkegaard's great contributions that he is able to show exactly where the border should be traced between the sphere of scholarship and science and the sphere of faith. (See PHILOSOPHY.)

Kierkegaard criticizes Hegel's philosophy in particular for not sharply distinguishing these two spheres. In *The Concept of Anxiety* [*Dread*] the pseudonymous author Vigilius Haufniensis shows how Hegelian thought mixes concepts from logic with ethical and dogmatic concepts. Thus Hegel mixes concepts from two qualitatively different spheres, the concepts that belong to scholarship and science in an ordinary sense, consequently lying within immanence, and concepts from dogmatics, a science built on presuppositions with which logic cannot cope because they are "absurd" and must be believed. For example, that man is a sinner, that God became man, etc., which constitute the point of departure for dogmatics. That Haufniensis regards dogmatics as a science, even though it is based on transcendent presuppositions, Haufniensis expresses as follows: "Every science has its province either in immanental logic or in an immanence within a transcendence which it cannot explain" (p. 45). But for Kierkegaard the principle also holds everywhere, as Haufniensis says, that "every concept must be used within the terms of the science to which it belongs" (p. 32, ed. tr.). When in the same work Haufniensis acknowledges

Schleiermacher, it is for the very reason that he had discerned that theology as a science is based on transcendent presuppositions. (See SCHLEIERMACHER.)

The relation of scholarship and science to faith is presented extensively in *Concluding Unscientific Postscript,* in which are treated all the essential aspects of the problems pertaining to the relation of thought to existence. In particular an accounting is made with the position in Hegel's philosophy that philosophy as a science is a higher form of truth than Christian faith and with the theological position holding that a scholarly-scientific approach can yield a direct proof of the truth of Christianity. (See PROOFS.)

Kierkegaard extends his critique of the misuse of scholarship and science to apply also to theological research, because it distinguishes sharply between an objective knowledge of and a subjective appropriation of Christianity. Johannes Climacus says: "the present author yields to none in profound respect for that which science regards as holy. But one does not get any unalloyed impression from learned critical theology. All its efforts suffer from a certain conscious or unconscious duplicity. It constantly appears as if something for faith should result from this criticism, something pertinent to faith; therein lies its dubious character" (p. 27, ed. tr.). Climacus' complaint against contemporary learned theologians is essentially that in their uncritical enthusiasm for the philological and the new historical-critical methods of investigating the Bible they create a hindrance to the practical exercise of Christianity, because there is a continual wait for the latest research results as to what Christianity is.

Later Kierkegaard takes to task his contemporaries for their scholarly interpretations of the Bible. In *For Self-Examination* he speaks of the way "God's Word" ought to be read: "All this interpretation and interpretation and science and new science is produced on the solemn, grave principle that it is for rightly understanding God's Word. Look more closely and you will see that it is to defend itself against God's Word" (p. 37). And in a journal entry from 1854 he writes that "scholarly research is given the appearance of Christian zeal, it is lauded for seeking to penetrate the mass of 1,800 years of history— and thus we do not see that it is a man-made swindle that continually places God at a distance of 1,800 years . . ." (XI^1 A 465). In another entry he even goes so far as to say: "To treat Christianity as a science means . . . to express that it is no longer something present" (XI^1 A 557).

In his later writings and journal entries Kierkegaard ironizes even more sharply over the way scholarship and science have been made direct substitutes for faith and imitation. "But sin, that you and I are sinners (the single individual), has been abolished" (*Practice [Training] in Christianity,* p. 71, ed. tr.) and scholarship and science "have invented the *doctrine* of sin in general" (p. 65, ed. tr.). In a journal entry he writes: "Take a child. Instead of ordering him to say "no" to himself in a particular instance, give him a lecture about self-denial, perhaps a historical survey of the different conceptions of self-denial, etc.—the child would go mad" (X³ A 702). And further: "In former days they wrote apologies; this was in the situation of actuality against the pagans. Nowadays we have a scientific scholarship which is called apologetics, a science of writing apologies (X⁴ A 280).

Kierkegaard also saw clearly the danger created for "the ordinary Christian" by the enthusiasm of his age for a scholarly, scientific view of Christianity. Either he will entirely give up a relation to Christianity or, if he tries "to immerse himself first of all in scholarship," it will prevent him from practicing Christianity and he "perishes in the scholarly nonsense" (XI² A 295).

For references in the works to scholarship and science, see, for example, *The Concept of Irony*, pp. 60–61, 76–77, 150–51, 189, 199–200, 202; "Public Confession," *S.V.*, XIII, pp. 399–402; *Either/Or*, I, p. 89; II, pp. 271, 342–43; *Fear and Trembling*, pp. 22–24, 93, 107, 108, 116–17; *Repetition*, pp. 8–9, 128–29; *Fragments*, pp. 3, 96; *The Concept of Anxiety* [*Dread*], pp. 9–21, 32–37, 43–46, 52fn., 55, 56–57; "Prefaces," *S.V.*, V, pp. 5–6, 28, 36, 40, 45–46, 54–55, 57–59, 61, 65; *Three Discourses on Imagined Occasions* [*Thoughts on Crucial Situations*], p. 21; *Stages*, pp. 29, 97, 99–100, 128–29, 181–82, 184, 263, 377, 440; *Postscript*, pp. 15–18, 25–32, 39–43, 54–55, 117–19, 134–47, 178–82, 192–93, 232, 255, 260–61, 266–82, 307–14, 415, 494, 501, 509–11, 549; *Two Ages* [*The Present Age*, pp. 6–7, 58–59]; *Upbuilding Discourses in Various Spirits*, Part Two [*What We Learn from the Lilies of the Field and the Birds of the Air*, with *The Gospel of Suffering*, pp. 200, 209–10]; Part Three [*The Gospel of Suffering*, pp. 59–64]; *Works of Love*, p. 335; *Christian Discourses*, pp. 206–8, 250; "The Difference between a Genius and an Apostle," with *The Present Age*, pp. 139–41; *The Sickness unto Death*, pp. 142–43; *Practice* [*Training*] *in Christianity*, pp. 33–34, 71–72, 205; *For Self-Examination*, pp. 23–45; *Judge for Yourselves!*, pp. 131, 169–70, 203–5, 216–17; articles in *Fædrelandet*, no. 10, January 12, no. 81, April 17, 1855, in *Attack*, pp. 16 fn., 40–41; *The Moment*, no. 7, ibid., p. 219.

18. Georg C. Lichtenberg, *Ideen, Maximen und Einfälle*, I–II (Leipzig: 1830–31), I, p. 117. *ASKB* 1773–74.

19. Ibid., pp. 119–20. It is much like reading out of a cookbook when one is hungry.

20. A reference to Hegel's concept of *"schlechten Unendlichkeit,"* infinity as merely unqualified prolongation of time.

21. On title-page: "Translated by N.M." (i.e., Niels Mygind).

22. If you do not know Christ, it matters not what else you know. If you learn to know Christ, that is sufficient, even if you do not know the other matters.

23. N.C. Ditlevsen, bookdealer at Store Kjøbmagergade 49, was the librarian for the *Christelige Læsebibliothek*.

24. See *The Concept of Irony*, p. 47.

25. See Matthew 5:28.

26. A play on *forrykt* (demented, mad) and *forryket* (dislocated, shifted).

27. See X³ A 425.

28. See Friedrich Böhringer, *Die Kirche Christi und ihre Zeugen*, I, 1–4–II, 1–4¹⁻² (Zurich: 1842–58), I, 1, p. 82. *ASKB* 173–77.

29. See "The Difference between a Genius and an Apostle," with *The Present Age*, pp. 137–63.

30. The kind forbearance ... and from judges who still have a heart in their breast, after this true performance I may expect consideration.

31. See *The Concept of Anxiety* [*Dread*], p. 2; *Postscript*, p. 34fn.

32. See various articles and issues of *The Moment* in *Attack*, pp. 29, 32, 35, 83, 149, 166, 182, 191, 272, 277.

33. Ludvig Holberg. *Erasmus Montanus*, I, 4 (see also sc. 2).

34. See *An Open Letter* and *Armed Neutrality*, pp. 47–55, and Introduction, pp. 30–31.

35. See *Stages*, p. 312.

36. See Matthew 23:13.

37. The scholar's students. The repetition and the diminution suggest nonprogress or even retrogression (see *Fear and Trembling*, p. 132), and the use of a German phrase is an obvious poke at ponderous, interminable German academic writing.

SCHOPENHAUER

Kierkegaard has most of Schopenhauer's (1788–1860) writings. The most important, *Die Welt als Wille und Vorstellung*, he had in the second edition (Leipzig: 1844). But he must have heard of Schopenhauer as early as 1837, inasmuch as his teacher and close friend Professor Poul M. Møller in his treatise *On Immortality*, which Kierkegaard read thoroughly, mentions Schopenhauer as the philosopher who had drawn most clearly the implications of the "nihilistic aspect of modern pantheism" (*Efterladte Skrifter*, Copenhagen: 1856, V, p. 99). Although Schopenhauer was not well known at the time, not even in his homeland, where he was still trying his hand as a university lecturer, it is amazing that Kierkegaard does not mention Schopenhauer's name a single time before 1854, and then only in his journals. Therefore it is possible that he read him for the first time then.

On the whole, Kierkegaard is very critical of Schopenhauer, even though he must acknowledge that he is "a significant author" (XI¹ A 537). What Kierkegaard values and enjoys is his unimpressed, even coarse, criticism of Hegel's philosophy and of "professor-philosophy" generally, as well as his telling polemical mode of expression, so much like Kierkegaard's own. Just as Schopenhauer ruthlessly exposes the "wretchedness" of human life and the miserableness and pettiness of men, so Kierkegaard lays bare the character of life in Christendom, particularly the unchristian optimism of Protestantism and the falsification of Christianity by pastors and professors. Kierkegaard even says that it could be "expedient" to recommend that theological students "take a daily dose of Schopenhauer's *Ethics*" as a counterpoison against "eudaemonistic Protestantism, especially Danish epicureanism" (XI^1 A 165).

But otherwise there is "total disagreement." Kierkegaard himself uses this expression in a journal entry (XI^1 A 144), in which, possibly under the impression of the similarity mentioned above, he makes a comparison from an ethical angle between Schopenhauer's misanthropic life-view more closely inspected and his own Christianly-oriented attitude. According to Kierkegaard's conception, the motivation for asceticism is of decisive significance. When Schopenhauer gives the recommendation to "mortify the desire for life," consequently asceticism, the presupposition is that "to exist is to suffer" (XI^1 A 182), and therefore one should be engaged as little as possible in this life, should assume the "contemplating" position of a spectator of the drama in which one himself plays. Kierkegaard objects that this attitude is really only a shrewd pessimism, in fact a kind of eudaemonism, and therefore it is meaningless to speak of asceticism. "Christian asceticism," however, is true asceticism, because "Christianity proclaims itself to be suffering, to be a Christian is to suffer" (XI^1 A 181); the Christian gives up claims to joys in this life in order to prepare for eternal life. On the whole, Kierkegaard thinks the question is "whether or not this kind of asceticism and mortification" which Schopenhauer advises "is actually possible for a man if he does not respect 'You shall' and is not qualified by the motif of an eternity" (XI^1 A 144).

With regard to the individual's practice of asceticism, according to Kierkegaard's view it must be made clear "that suffering is a voluntary choice" (ibid.). But "Schopenhauer is not a man who possessed the power to be successful, to win recognition.... But then to choose pessimism can easily be a kind of optimism—from a temporal point of view the smartest thing to do" (XI^1 A 537). Kierkegaard, however, was able to decline renown and admiration for the sake of a higher task.

Kierkegaard's most essential objection to Schopenhauer is that he himself does not carry through the ascetic conduct of life that he recommends, but "relates contemplatively to that asceticism" (XI^1 A 144) and thereby himself adopts the sophistic life-attitude of other philosophers and professors that he ironizes over so sharply. Such an attitude may even approach the demonic, because "the most dreadful kind, a corrupting kind, of melancholic voluptuousness may be concealed here, also a profound hatred of men and the like." Kierkegaard considers that the decisive difference between Schopenhauer and himself lies here, because Kierkegaard personally drew the implications of his "protest" against the Christianity of the official Church and even exposed himself voluntarily "to being caricatured and laughed at by the whole rabble, the ordinary people and the elite...."

Schutz, Alfred. "Mozart and the Philosophers." *Social Research*, 23, Summer 1956, pp. 219–42.

Stack, George, J. "Kierkegaard and Nihilism." *Philosophy Today,* 14, Winter 1970, pp. 274–92.

In the works there are no direct references to Schopenhauer.

38. Arthur Schopenhauer, *Die Welt als Wille und Vorstellung,* I–II (Leipzig: 2 ed. 1844), II, ch. 44. *ASKB* 773–773a.

39. Goethe, *Torquato Tasso,* 5, 5, *Werke,* I–LV (Stuttgart, Tübingen: 1828–33), IX, p. 244. *ASKB* 1641–69.

> And when in agony the man was dumb
> A god gave me the power to tell my suffering.

40. Diels, *Fragmente der Vorsokratiker,* 12 B 48: Life has the name of life, but in reality it is death.

41. See note 38; ibid., II, ch. 46.

42. By teaching others one himself learns.

43. Schopenhauer, *Die beiden Grundprobleme der Ethik* (Frankfurt am Main: 1841), para. 6. *ASKB* 772.

44. Ibid., para. 4, 13, 15.

45. See Schopenhauer, *Parerga und Paralipomena,* I–II (Berlin: 1851), II, ch. VIII, para. 115, also ch. XXVI, para. 356. *ASKB* 774–77.

46. See note 38; ibid., I, bk. 4, esp. para. 67–68.

47. After Kierkegaard's attack on *The Corsair,* a satire and scandal tabloid, caricatures of him in *The Corsair* were picked up even by children, so that he became the object of taunts and derision as he tried to continue his customary strolls on Copenhagen streets (see note 1110).

48. See note 42.

49. Ye gods! as in, for example, Plautus, *Amphitryon,* II, 2, 190 (l. 822).

50. See note 48.

51. For edition see note 38.

52. Ibid.

53. "... like the costly phial of poison to be found among the magnificent ornaments and apparel of Oriental despots...."

54. See *Postscript,* pp. 360, 386, 516–19.

55. See note 38; ibid., II, ch. 17, also ch. 46, 48 and I, bk. 4, para. 59, 70.

56. Ibid., I, bk. 1, para. 16; ch. 16.

57. Schopenhauer, *Die Welt als Wille und Vorstellung,* I–II (Leipzig: 2 ed. 1844), I, bk. 4, para. 68; *Parerga und Paralipomena,* I–II (Berlin: 1851), "*Fragmente zur Geschichte der Philosophie,*" I, para, 14. *ASKB* 773–73a and 774–75.

58. At best, at most.

59. Schopenhauer, *Parerga* (see note 45), II, ch. 9, para. 128.

60. Schopenhauer, *Die Welt als Wille und Vorstellung* (see note 38), II, ch. 7, end.

SELF

The self, according to Kierkegaard, constitutes the highest form of being, namely, conscious, personal, and altogether independent being. Understood this way, only God is a self in the genuine sense. Of all created beings, only man has the possibility of becoming a self, which is the very goal of human existence. But man can never become an independent self, only a "derived self" (*The Sickness unto Death*, p. 202), consequently a self indebted to God for its being. There will always be an eternal, essential "qualitative difference" between God and man. This difference does not disappear even in eternity ("The Difference between a Genius and an Apostle," with *The Present Age*, p. 151).

In his writings Kierkegaard has accurately described the becoming, the coming into existence, of the human self and has shown that this becoming is a protracted process. For even though man is created with the possibility of becoming a self, he must go through many developmental levels before he can become this self. Every human being begins as an individual (see INDIVIDUAL), essentially dependent upon the race and the milieu. In *The Concept of Anxiety* [*Dread*] Vigilius Haufniensis discusses extensively the individual's primary dependence on the race, saying among other things: "at every moment the individual is himself and the race" (p. 26). Another of Kierkegaard's pseudonymous writers, Anti-Climacus, says of the self on this level: "Thus the self is bound up in immediacy with the other, wishing, desiring, enjoying, etc., but passively; even as desiring, this self is in the dative, like the child's "me." Its dialectic is the pleasant and the unpleasant; its categories: fortune, misfortune, fate" (*The Sickness unto Death*, p. 184, ed. tr.).

The first step to the becoming of the self is made only when a person becomes aware of the eternal within himself and becomes conscious by relating himself to this. (See CONSCIENCE.) "The more consciousness, the more self ..." (p. 162). The next step begins with the person's relating himself to God as the personal "eternal power" (*Either/Or*, II, p. 181; see also VII[1] A 10), whereby the consciousness of one's eternal destiny is also raised to a higher power. This is emphasized particularly by Judge William in part II of *Either/Or*, where he says that through the relation to God the person chooses his "Self according to its absolute validity" (p. 223, ed. tr.). Here it holds true, as Anti-Climacus says later: "The more conception of God, the more self ..." (*The Sickness unto Death*, p. 211). This relationship is characterized particularly by Anti-Climacus in *The Sickness unto Death* and *Practice* [*Training*] *in Christianity*. In this forward movement the person learns to know himself in the true way in that he discovers his impotence and dependence upon God. Thus the person is prepared to receive God's forgiveness, whereby he becomes a true self, "grounded transparently in the power that established it" (pp. 147 and 262, ed. tr.).

The becoming of the self takes place through continuing choice. There is potentially not only the above-described movement toward a clearer consciousness of the self, and toward acknowledgement of one's own sinfulness and need of forgiveness, but also the opposite movement: that the person abstains from relating himself to the eternal or even consciously sets himself against the good, understood as God's command and God's offer of forgiveness. In the latter case there is also a potentiation of the self, but in a negative sense, whereby the self becomes selfishness (ibid., p. 211). In *The Sickness unto Death*, Anti-Climacus has delineated the negative way of the self by going, step by step, through the steadily more potentiated forms of the self's opposition to becoming the self to which God has destined every man, an opposition whereby the person moves into deeper and deeper despair, which finally is changed into offense in the encounter with Christ.

The positive movement of the self, ultimately marked by faith as a healed relation to the eternal, Kierkegaard has delineated especially in *Practice* [*Training*] *in Christianity*, as well as in the various upbuilding discourses.

Allen, K. R. "Identity and the Individual: Personhood in the Thought of Erik Erikson and of Søren Kierkegaard." Ph.D. dissertation, Boston University, 1967.

Bertman, Martin A. "Kierkegaard: A Sole Possibility for Individual Unity." *Philosophy Today*, 16, Winter 1972, pp. 306–11.

Cole, J. Preston, "Kierkegaard's Concept of Dread: with Constant Reference to Sigmund Freud." Ph.D. dissertation, Drew, 1964.

———. "The Existential Reality of God." *Christian Scholar*, 48, 1965, pp. 224–35.

———. *The Problematic Self in Kierkegaard and Freud.* New Haven and London: Yale University Press, 1971.

Copp, John Dixon. "The Concept of the Soul in Kierkegaard and Freud." Ph.D. dissertation, Boston University, 1953.

Croxall, T. H. " 'Border Conflicts': Secretiveness," in *Kierkegaard Commentary*, ch. 11. London: James Nisbet & Co., Ltd., 1956.

Dietrichson, Paul. "Kierkegaard's Concept of the Self." *Inquiry* (Oslo), 8, 1, 1965, pp. 1–32.

Dupré, Louis. "The Constitution of the Self in Kierkegaard's Philosophy." *International Philosophical Quarterly*, 3, December 1963, pp. 506–26.

Elhard, Leland. "Faith and Identity." Ph.D. dissertation, Chicago, 1965.

Elrod, John W. *Being and Existence in Kierkegaard's Pseudonymous Works.* Princeton: Princeton University Press, 1975.

Glicksberg, Charles I. *The Self in World Literature.* University Park, Pa.: Pennsylvania State University Press, 1963.

Grene, Marjorie. "Søren Kierkegaard: 'The Self against the System,' " in *Dreadful Freedom*, ch. 2. Chicago: University of Chicago Press, 1948.

Hansen, Olaf, "The Problem of Alienation and Reconciliation: A Comparative Study of Marx and Kierkegaard in the Light of Hegel's Formulation of the Problem." Ph.D. dissertation, Princeton Theological Seminary, 1956.

Hartman, Robert S. "The Self in Kierkegaard." *The Journal of Existential Psychiatry*, 2, Spring 1962, pp. 409-36.

Khan, Theodore A. R. "A Critique of Kierkegaard's Category of the Individual Based on His Philosophico-religious View of Man." Ph.D. dissertation, New York University, 1962.

Likins, Marjorie Huvjes. "The Concept of Selfhood in Freud and Kierkegaard." Ph.D. dissertation, Columbia, 1963.

Madden, M. C. "The Contribution of Søren Kierkegaard to a Christian Psychology." Ph.D. dissertation, Southern Baptist Theological Seminary, 1940.

———. "Kierkegaard on Self-acceptance." *Review and Expositor*, 48, July 1951, pp. 302-9.

Malantschuk, Gregor. "The Problem of Self and Immortality," in *Kierkegaard's Way to the Truth*, ch. 6. Minneapolis: Augsburg, 1963.

May, Rollo. *Man's Search for Himself.* New York: Norton, 1953.

May, Rollo et al. *Existence,* particularly pp. 20-29. New York: Basic Books, 1958.

Miller, Libuse Lukas. *In Search of the Self.* Philadelphia: Muhlenberg Press, 1962.

Nagley, Winfield E. "Kierkegaard on Liberation." *Ethics*, 70, 1, 1959-60, pp. 47-58.

Price, George. *The Narrow Pass: A Study of Kierkegaard's Concept of Man.* London: Hutchinson, 1963.

Schrag, Calvin O. "The Problem of Existence: Kierkegaard's Descriptive Analysis of the Self and Heidegger's Phenomenological Ontology of *Dasein.*" Ph.D. dissertation, Harvard, 1957.

Schwandt, Jack Allan. "Alienation and Reconciliation in the works of Søren Kierkegaard." M. A. thesis, University of Minnesota, 1959.

Shmüeli, Adi. "The Alienation of Consciousness," in *Kierkegaard and Consciousness,* ch. 6. Princeton: Princeton University Press, 1971.

Skorper, Erling. "The Philosophy of Renunciation East and West." *Philosophy East and West*, 21, July 1971, pp. 282-302.

Sontag, Frederick. "Kierkegaard and the Search for a Self." *Journal of Existentialism*, VII, Spring 1967, pp. 443-57. Reprinted in *Essays on Kierkegaard,* ed. Jerry Gill. Minneapolis: Burgess, 1969, ch. 9.

———. "Existentialism: Greek Ethics and the Way Back to the Future: a Note." *The Thomist,* 34, April 1970, pp. 306-10.

Soper, W. W. "The Self and its World in Ralph Burton Perry, Edgar Sheffield Brightman, Jean Paul Sartre, and Søren Kierkegaard." Ph.D. dissertation, Boston University, 1962.

Stack, George J. "Kierkegaard's Analysis of Choice: the Aristotelian Model." *Personalist,* 52, Autumn 1971, pp. 643–62.

―――. "Kierkegaard: The Self as Ethical Possibility." *Southwestern Journal of Philosophy,* 3, Winter 1972, pp. 35–61.

―――. "Kierkegaard: the Self and Ethical Existence." *Ethics,* 83, January 1973, pp. 108–125.

Sugerman, Shirley G. "Sin and Madness: A Study of the Self in Søren Kierkegaard and Ronald Laing." Ph.D. dissertation, Drew, 1970.

Taylor, Mark. "Time and Self in Kierkegaard's Pseudonymous Writings." Ph.D. dissertation, Harvard, 1972.

―――. *Kierkegaard's Pseudonymous Authorship.* Princeton: Princeton University Press, 1975.

For references in the works to the self, see *The Concept of Irony,* pp. 202–3, 234–35, 248–54, 314; *Either/Or,* I, p. 147; II, pp. 137–47, 173, 178–82, 210, 218, 236, 252, 270, 275–76, 279, 322, 338; *Repetition,* pp. 26–27, 42–48, 57, 144–46; *Upbuilding* [*Edifying*] *Discourses,* II, pp. 121–22; IV, pp. 22–47, 84–85, 106, 109, 116; *Fragments,* pp. 14, 46–48, 58–59, 60; *The Concept of Anxiety* [*Dread*], pp. 69–71, 121–37; *Three Discourses on Imagined Occasions* [*Thoughts on Crucial Situations*], pp. 33–34; *Stages,* pp. 56, 392, 420–28; *Postscript,* pp. 55, 67–68, 112, 223, 230–33, 277–78, 284, 293–95, 305–6, 314–19, 365–67, 414, 421–22, 438, 470, 484–89; *Upbuilding Discourses in Various Spirits,* Part One [*Purity of Heart,* pp. 61–62, 99–103, 122–23, 140, 182–219]; *Works of Love,* pp. 34–40, 53, 65–72, 105, 113, 119, 123, 149, 150, 188–90, 217, 247–60, 261–62, 332, 341–42; *Christian Discourses,* pp. 43–44, 73–82, 91–92, 134, 199; *The Sickness unto Death,* pp. 146–213, 231, 236–38, 241, 244–45, 248–55, 262; *Three Discourses at the Communion on Fridays,* with *Christian Discourses,* p. 384; *Practice* [*Training*] *in Christianity,* pp. 159–60, 194–95; *For Self-Examination,* pp. 39–51; *Judge for Yourselves!,* pp. 120–22, 130–35.

61. See, for example, *Either/Or,* II, p. 181; *Postscript,* pp. 277–78, 450 fn.

62. Matthew 12:36.

63. See *The Concept of Irony,* pp. 234–35; *The Sickness unto Death,* pp. 147, 213, 262.

64. Kierkegaard uses the Danish translation of Matthew 16:25: *"tager Skade paa sin sjæl,"* which has been translated literally here.

65. See Luke 9:25.

66. *Nicomachean Ethics,* 1168a, 1177a.

67. Ibid., X, 7, 1177a, 27–28; 1178a, 5 ff. Translation here is of the text as given in Kierkegaard's Danish version.

68. Ibid., X, 7, 1177a, 16 ff.

69. Ibid., X, 6, 1176b, 30–31.

70. Ibid., 1176b, 4–5.

71. Ibid., 1178b, 7 ff.

72. See Matthew 16:26; Mark 8:36.

73. See *Stages,* p. 62.

74. See *Repetition,* p. 138.

75. Heinrich Ritter, *Geschichte der Philosophie alter Zeit,* I–IV (Hamburg: 1836). *ASKB* 735-38.

76. Correctly quoted and spelled from Ritter; reference is to Caelius Aurelianus, physician in Sicca, Numidia, around the fifth century A.D., author of *De morbis acutis* and *De morbis chronicis* (*The Time of Death*), which is quoted: They say, according to Empedocles, that one insanity results from the cleansing of the soul, that another with a loss of mind is from a physical source or, if you please, from unrighteousness.

77. See Luke 15:3-10.

78. Marcus Aurelius Antoninus, *Meditations,* XI, 3; *M. Antoninus Commentarii libri XII,* ed. J. M. Schultz (Leipzig: 1829), p. 160. *ASKB* 1218.

79. See "Has a Man the Right to Let Himself Be put to Death for the Truth?" with *The Present Age* [part of *Two Ages*], pp. 102-4.

80. See X^4 A 283; *For Self-Examination,* pp. 23-61.

SENECA

Kierkegaard had the collected works of Seneca (ca. 4 B.C.–65 A.D.) in both Latin and German translation in his own library (*ASKB* 1274-80c.). Yet as late as 1850 he wrote in his journal: "I have just begun to read Seneca" (X^3 A 25), although there are earlier references in the journals to him. In the published works there appears only one quotation from Seneca, the well-known statement that there was never a great genius without a touch of madness (*Fear and Trembling,* p. 116; see also IV A 148 and VIII^1 A 161), essentially a compaction of Aristotle's theory based on the idea that in recompense for their genius the great geniuses must bear the suffering of melancholy (*Problemata,* 30:1). In his journals of 1850 Kierkegaard made several notations of sayings from Seneca, especially while reading Seneca's letters, which he says are "pithy" (X^3 A 35). A characteristic of these few quotations is that Kierkegaard seems to cite them because each one corresponds in a different way to some aspect of his own difficult situation at the time. Thus when he mentions Seneca's advice "to learn to die," the link to his own thought at the time about "death as imminent" (X^3 A 3) seems obvious. In the same way his hesitation and uncertainty at the time about seeking a pastoral position (see X^2 A 619 and 636) are mirrored in the quotation: "From the most difficult of situations there is hopefully a way out, if one does not hurry before it is time or procrastinate when it is time" (X^3 A 29). The same is true of the twice-cited passage "He is not a man of courage if his courage does not increase under difficulties" (X^3 A 31 and 601). Kierkegaard saw that he would need more courage if he were to meet the increased difficulties he would be exposed to in the future, for example, because of the publication of *Practice in Christianity,* which was an indirect, penetrating criticism of official Christianity. Another thought that naturally suggests itself is that Kierkegaard had his own suffering and unhappy position in mind when he twice (X^3 A 48 and X^4 A 574) refers to Seneca's account in *De ira* of the unhappy man whose sufferings are so dreadful that finally people ceased even to pity him.

Despite his acknowledgment of Seneca, Kierkegaard nevertheless regarded the Stoic life-view as "a false edition of the essentially Christian" and its pride as altogether foreign to his own attitude, which was marked by Christian humility (X^3 A 14). (See also STOICISM and X^3 A 13.)

For references in the works to Seneca, see *Either/Or*, II, p. 71; *Fear and Trembling*, p. 116.

81. Seneca, *Ad Lucilium Epistulae Morales*, Epistle 87, para. 4: "What hiding-place is there where the fear of death does not enter?" Kierkegaard's books included: *Annæi Senecæ tum rhetoris tum philosophi Opera omnia*, ed. A. Schotto (Geneva: 1626), *ASKB* 1274; L. Annæi Senecæ, *Philosophi, Opera omnia*, I-V (Leipzig: 1832), *ASKB* 1275-79; *L. Annæus Seneca's Werke*, tr. J. Moser, I-XV in 4 vols. (Stuttgart: 1828-35). The passages from Seneca in the *Papirer* are in Danish, presumably Kierkegaard's own translation from Latin or German. The English versions in *J. and P.* are translations from the Danish.

82. Seneca, *Moralia*, *"De cohibenda ira"* ("On the Control of Anger"), bk. I, ch. 5. See note 81.

83. Epistle 22, para. 6.

84. Para. 27.

85. Para. 8-9.

86. Para. 8.

87. Epistle 98, para. 8. He suffers more than is necessary who suffers before it is necessary.

88. See Epistle 53, para. 8. Why will no man confess his faults? Because he is still in their grasp. Only he who is awake can recount his dream. (Loeb. ed., tr. R. M. Gummere.)

89. Epistle 22, para. 7.

SERMONS

Only once in his life did Kierkegaard preach at a regular service in a church: Sunday, May 18, 1851, in Citadelskirken (See PREACHING, PROCLAMATION.) As a theological candidate he preached twice, a practice sermon on January 12, 1841, at noon in Holmens Kirke (see III C 1), and a trial sermon in Trinitatis Kirke on February 24, 1844 (see IV C 1). In addition he spoke a few times at Communion on Fridays in Frue Kirke: August 27, 1847 (see *Three Discourses at the Communion on Fridays*, with *Christian Discourses*, pp. 275-81), September 1, 1848 (see IX A 266 and 271; also *Practice [Training] in Christianity*, pp. 151-56), and at least once earlier, since the second of *Three Discourses at the*

Communion on Fridays (see pp. 157–66) was given in Frue Kirke, but Kierkegaard does not say when (see VIII² B 107).

In the journals from the beginning (1837–38), we find entries which indicate that Kierkegaard had sermon themes in mind, and many of these were used later in his upbuilding and religious writings. It is striking, however, that although in the journals he frequently designates his draft as intended for a sermon, in publication he always calls them "discourses." The most important reason for this terminology is that in his upbuilding writings, just as in the pseudonymous writings, he uses his dialectical method and begins by addressing men in the esthetic stage in order later to lead them further through the ethical-religious to the essentially Christian. (See Gregor Malantschuk, *Kierkegaard's Thought*, pp. 307 ff.) Therefore in the early upbuilding discourses he omits entirely the purely Christian categories, which appear in the drafts. In *Concluding Unscientific Postscript* Climacus says of this: "Presumably Magister Kierkegaard knew well enough what he was doing when he called the upbuilding discourses Upbuilding Discourses and also why he refrained from employing Christian-dogmatic categories, from mentioning Christ's name, etc., which is generally done copiously in our day, and instead the categories, the ideas, the dialectic of presentation are solely those of immanence" (p. 243, ed. tr.). The sermon pertains only to the essentially Christian; therefore, as Climacus says, "the sermon is reserved for the religious-Christian existence" (ibid., p. 229, ed. tr.). Later, when Kierkegaard does not call his Christian discourses sermons (see, for example *Upbuilding Discourses in Various Spirits*, Part Three [*The Gospel of Suffering*, p. 3], and *Christian Discourses*), it is because they are too dialectically constructed to qualify as sermons. The Christian discourse deals to a certain extent with doubt—a sermon operates absolutely and solely on the basis of authority, that of scripture and of Christ's apostles (VIII¹ A 6). At the end the same entry reads: "A sermon presupposes a pastor (ordination); Christian discourse can be by a layman." This is another important reason why Kierkegaard never published sermons—he was not ordained and therefore did not have the authority that is the presupposition for the sermon. In later years Kierkegaard's view was that it was not so much ordination that gives authority to preach as the correspondence of the preacher's life to his preaching. (See PREACHING, PROCLAMATION.)

The explanation of Kierkegaard's not using the term "sermons" for the published versions of what were sermons is that proclamation from a pulpit does indeed contain "some truth," inasmuch as "to preach from the pulpit means to bring charges against oneself" (X⁴ A 287), but the same situation does not obtain when the sermon is published. In addition, after his sermon in 1851, Kierkegaard became entirely convinced that it was not his task to preach (see X⁴ A 323) and consequently that he could not publish sermons either.

Kierkegaard's practice sermon and trial sermon were naturally given in the form required by the pastoral seminary, but already the special tone of inwardness characteristic of all of Kierkegaard's later sermons or discourses is detectable. Kierkegaard's form of communication in these sermons is in precise agreement with his carefully considered dialectic of communication, a subject on which he later (1847) prepared some lectures, possibly intended for instructional use in the pastoral seminary (see VIII² B 79-89, X⁴ A 299, and A 300).

Kierkegaard's "discourses" are intended to be read (preferably aloud) rather than to be delivered, except for the few that were given as sermons. (See *Three Discourses at the Communion on Fridays*, with *Christian Discourses*, p. 257.)

Instead of giving a description of the historical situation of the sermon text, as is commonly done, Kierkegaard seeks to bring his reader into the situation of contemporaneity with what is recounted (see II A 1), and in concentrating on a single specific thought he illuminates it from all sides, considers together with his reader all the difficulties a person may encounter when he acts accordingly, and finally places him in a position for a personal decision. Through constant repetition, poetic and picturesque metaphors, and vivid examples, the tone appropriate to the central thought of the discourse is maintained, and by a frequently complicated sentence structure and an indirect mode of expression Kierkegaard constrains his reader to read carefully.

Kierkegaard spoke preferably to the distressed, the suffering, the penitent, and those in spiritual trial. Therefore he also preferred discourses at the Communion on Fridays to Sunday sermons (VIII¹ A 285 and A 560). Even when he thought he was at the end of his work as an author, he still continued to consider publication of Friday discourses (X² A 39); yet after 1849 it amounted to only one more publication, *Two Discourses at the Communion on Fridays* (1851). Instead he came more and more to see his task to be writing for the "awakening" of his contemporaries. (See *The Sickness unto Death* and *Practice [Training] in Christiantiy*, title pages.)

The last discourse Kierkegaard published (September 3, 1855) was the sermon "God's Unchangeableness," which he had given in Citadelskirke in 1851. The text, which according to the pericope was for the Fourth Sunday after Easter, was James 1:17-25, which he had used earlier in *Two Upbuilding Discourses* (1843). In the preface he had Regine particularly in mind (see X¹ A 266). The discourse of 1851 does not have a specifically Christian content but a universally upbuilding content. One of the reasons for choosing this particular text, Kierkegaard admits, was "the thought of 'her' " (X⁴ A 323); manifestly he had considered the possibility that Regine would be there. But surely the deeper reason was that by that time, especially through the publication of *Practice [Training] in Christianity*, Kierkegaard had already settled accounts with Mynster and official Christianity and now wanted to make a new beginning by again pointing to the power that stands fast when everything totters—God's unchangeableness.

Holmer, Paul L. "Kierkegaard and the Sermon." *Journal of Religion*, 37, 1957, pp. 1–9.

Stanley, Clifford L. *Søren Kierkegaard: Preacher to Christendom*. Alexandria, Va.: Lectern Press, 1972.

For references in the works to sermons and preaching, see, for example, *Either/Or*, I, p. 37; II, pp. 71–72, 103, 318–19, 341–56; "A Little Explanation," *S.V.*, XIII, pp. 416–17; *Upbuilding [Edifying] Discourses*, I, pp. 5, 59; II, p. 5, III, pp. 5, 69; IV, pp. 5, 83; *Fear and Trembling*, pp. 39–40, 63; *Repetition*, pp. 36–37; *The Concept of Anxiety [Dread]*, pp. 14, 60; "Prefaces," *S.V.*, XIII, pp. 35–38; *Three Discourses on Imagined Occasions [Thoughts on Crucial Situations]*, p. vii; *Stages*, pp. 139–40, 168, 211, 237, 282, 214–15 417–20; *Postscript*, pp. 229–30, 242–44, 306, 334, 361–62, 371–75, 383, 389–400, 418–36, 472, 478–79, 499; *Upbuilding Discourses in Various Spirits*, Part Three [*The Gospel of Suffering*, pp. 3, 73–75]; *Works of Love*, pp. 191, 292–93; *Christian Discourses*, pp. 171–73, 195, 201–4, 257, 277–78; "Has a Man the Right . . . ?" with *The Present Age*, pp. 100, 120–22; "The Difference between a Genius and an Apostle," with *The Present Age*, pp. 149, 154–57; *The Sickness unto Death*, pp. 235, 259–60; *Practice [Training] in Christianity*, pp. 110, 112, 115–16, 134–35, 173, 222–23, 227–31, 240, 250; *Two Discourses at the Communion on Fridays*, with *Judge for Yourselves!*, pp. 127–28, 179, 197–99; articles in *Fædrelandet*, in *Attack*, pp. 6–7, 10–15, 16–17; *The Moment*, nos. 5, 7, in *Attack*, pp. 119–20, 172–73, 202, 209–10.

90. See *Christian Discourses*, pp. 239–50.

91. See II A 285.

92. Given in Holmens Kirke, Tuesday, January 12, 1841. The seminary records contain the following account: " 'On the same day Mr. S. K.'s first sermon, given at noon in Holmens Kirke on the text Philippians 1:19–25, was criticized. The critics were Messrs. Fenger and Linnemann. Presentation: the sermon was very well memorized, the voice clear, the tone dignified and vigorous. The sermon as a whole was written with great thoughtfulness and sharp logic, but it was quite difficult and probably pitched too high for the ordinary person.' " From note by H. P. Barfod, ed., *Søren Kierkegaards Efterladte Papirer 1833–43* (Copenhagen: 1869), p. 273.

93. See Luke 12:34.

94. See Philippians 3:20.

95. See Matthew 25:13.

96. See Romans 14:8.

97. See Philippians 1:7, 13; 4:22.

98. See Philippians 1:20; 4:1.

99. See Philippians 1:8.

100. See Deuteronomy 32:52; 34:4.

101. See Philippians 1:19.
102. See Philippians 1:23.
103. See Philippians 2:16; I Corinthians 9:26.
104. See Philippians 1:25.
105. See Philippians 3:14.
106. See Philippians 3:18.
107. See Romans 1:14.
108. See Romans 15:9–11.
109. See I Corinthians 9:19–22.
110. See I Corinthians 15:19.
111. See Philippians 1:22.
112. See Colossians 4:5.
113. See Colossians 1:26–27.
114. See Jude, v. 12.
115. See Philippians 1:21.
116. See Philippians 1:23.
117. Ibid.
118. Ibid.
119. See Ephesians 2:12.
120. See Philippians 1:21.
121. See Acts 3:15.
122. See Romans 12:15.
123. See Job 1:5.
124. See Ephesians 6:11.
125. I Corinthians 15:26.
126. See II Timothy 4:7–8; James 1:12; I Corinthians 9:24; Philippians 3:14; 4:1.
127. See Luke 15:32.
128. See John 3:8.
129. See Acts 17:28.
130. See Ephesians 2:4–7; John 3:16.
131. See John 14:6.
132. See Luke 23:43.
133. See Job 7:10.
134. See *Works of Love* in its entirety and especially pp. 73–98 for a development of this intimation of Kierkegaard's social ethics and expressive-indicative ethics.
135. See I Peter 4:8; *Works of Love,* pp. 261–78; *Upbuilding [Edifying] Discourses,* I, pp. 61–90.
136. See Acts 9:3 ff.
137. See II Corinthians 11:26 ff.
138. See Matthew 6:27.
139. See II Timothy 1:9; VOCATION.

140. See I Corinthians 12:4.
141. See I Corinthians 3:9.
142. See II Corinthians 12:4–5.
143. See Colossians 1:27.
144. See I Peter 3:4.
145. See I John 4:19.
146. See Matthew 5:44.
147. See John 1:27.
148. See Luke 18:22; Matthew 19:21.
149. See Acts 3:6.
150. See Mark 15:46.
151. See *Works of Love,* pp. 306–16.
152. See Philippians 4:7.
153. See I John 5:7; Hebrews 10:15.
154. See II Corinthians 4:7.
155. See I Corinthians 4:9, 11, 13, 16; IMITATION.
156. See Genesis 50:20.
157. See Romans 12:4–5; I Corinthians 12:12 ff.
158. See II Corinthians 5:11; *For Self-Examination,* p. i.
159. See Colossians 3:3–4.
160. See Romans 8:26–27.
161. See I Corinthians 12:11.
162. See Matthew 19:6.
163. See Hebrews 11:1.
164. See Romans 5:3 ff.
165. See I John 3:1–2.
166. See Ephesians 4:13.
167. See II Corinthians 4:16.
168. See I Corinthians 13:9 ff.
169. See Matthew 6:6.
170. The text of Kierkegaard's trial sermon at the pastoral seminary, given in Trinitatis Kirke, December 24, 1844. See IV C 1; *Pap.,* XIII, pp. 353–55.
171. See I Corinthians 1:12 ff.
172. See I Corinthians 15:9.
173. See I Corinthians 4:13.
174. See Philippians 3:12–14.
175. See Philippians 3:8.
176. See II Corinthians 12:2.
177. See Philippians 2:12.
178. See Acts 26:29.
179. See Acts 17:28.
180. See Acts 17:23.

181. See I Corinthians 1:23.
182. See Matthew 27:24.
183. See II Corinthians 11:27.
184. See I Timothy 3:16.
185. See *Christian Discourses,* pp. 239 ff.
186. See I Corinthians 2:9.
187. *Practice [Training] in Christianity,* pp. 96–144; *The Sickness unto Death,* pp. 244–62.
188. See Genesis 18:12.
189. See Luke 10:23.
190. See Luke 24:13 ff.
191. See John 20:14.
192. See Luke 10:24.
193. See *Fragments,* ch. V, pp. 111–38.
194. See *Fragments,* pp. 32–42.
195. See Luke 12:3.
196. See, for example, Matthew 11:15.
197. See Matthew 13:13.
198. See Deuteronomy 30:11 ff.
199. Required addition suggested by the Danish editors of the *Papirer*.
200. See Kierkegaard's later use of "contemporaneity" in the works, for example, *Fragments,* pp. 28–88, 111–38; *Postscript,* pp. 88–89.
201. See *Fragments,* pp. 9, 45.
202. See ibid., pp. 46–48.
203. See SUBJECTIVITY and references.
204. See *Fragments,* pp. 61–62.
205. See Romans 8:38.
206. See *Christian Discourses,* p. 305.
207. Johann Gerhard, *Meditationes sacrae,* ed. S. Guenther (Leipzig: 1842). *ASKB* 518. *The mystery of Holy Communion:* to wonder, not to pry into, is true wisdom.
208. See Philippians 3:20.
209. See I Corinthians 11:23; see *Christian Discourses,* pp. 286–88.
210. See *Christian Discourses,* pp. 298–99.
211. Ibid., pp. 259–60.
212. Ibid., pp. 260–68.
213. Ibid., pp. 259–60.
214. The Danish *"Opløb"* (*"Oprør"* in the 1754 Danish translation of the New Testament) can be translated as "uproar" or "disturbance" or "crowd," or "multitude" as it is in the King James and the Revised Standard Version.
215. See Luke 22:19.
216. See Luke 18:9–14; *Three Discourses at the Communion on Fridays,* with *Christian Discourses,* pp. 371–77.

217. Ibid., see pp. 361-29.
218. On Friday, September 1, 1848, Kierkegaard preached in Frue Kirke.
219. See Hebrews 4:15.
220. See note 216; ibid., pp. 371-77; Luke 18:9-14, in 1848 the text on September 3.
221. See note 216.
222. Zacharias Werner, *Poetische Werke*, I-XIII (Grimma: n.d. [1835-41]). *ASKB* 1851-54.
223. See note 222.
224. See Luke 17:21.
225. See John 20:26.
226. See *Three Discourses at the Communion on Fridays*, With *Christian Discourses*, pp. 276-81.
227. Hymn by Bernhard S. Ingemann in *Tillæg til den evangelisk-christelige Psalmebog* (Copenhagen: 1845), no. 596.
228. See I Corinthians 11:24.
229. December 23 in 1849.
230. See John 1:19-28.
231. See Philippians 4:4-7.
232. See Luke 15:11-32.
233. See Matthew 21:28-30.
234. Usually, as can be noted in the latter portion of this section of *J. and P.*, the term "discourse" (Danish: *Tale*) is used. In this entry the word is *Prædiken* (sermon). For a discussion of Kierkegaard's distinctions, see the commentary above and also Translators' Introduction to *Works of Love*, pp. 11-13. Kierkegaard makes distinctions in kind among sermons, discourses, and reflections, and he also distinguishes between those with authority (ordination) and those "without authority," such as he was. On the basis of his own terms there is nothing to justify Kierkegaard's use of "sermon" here. In terms of kind, however, most of the "discourses" developed or sketched in the *Papirer* may be regarded as sermons.
235. *Evangelisk christelig Psalmebog* (Copenhagen: 1845), no. 5, stanza 6. *ASKB* 197.
236. The first two lines of the eight o'clock stanza sung by Copenhagen watchmen for decades from 1784. There were eight lines per stanza and a stanza for each hour from eight o'clock at night to five o'clock in the morning (this one with two extra lines: "Praise be to God our Lord; to him be praise, glory, and honor.") See J. Davidsen, *Fra det gamle Kongens Kjøbenhavn*, I-II (Copenhagen: 1880-81), II, pp. 107-9.
237. Adolf Helfferich, *Die christiche Mystik in ihrer Entwickelung und in ihren Denkmalen*, I-II (Gotha: 1842). *ASKB* 571-72.
238. See Luke 14:16-24.

239. See Matthew 22:2.
240. Ibid., 22:7.
241. See Luke 14:16-24.
242. See Matthew 22:2-14.
243. Ibid., 14:16-24.
244. Ibid.
245. Ibid., 22:7.
246. See Luke 15. In the Danish there is some play on the common root (*tabe*, to lose) in the three modifying words: *Den tabte Penning—Det fortabte Faar —Den forlorne (forlore, forlire*, German *verlieren*, to lose) *Søn*, quite commonly called *Den fortabte Søn.*
247. Just H. V. Paulli (1809-65), in 1850 pastor of Christiansborg Slotskirke.
248. *Mensch! Wie du glaubst so lebst du,*
Wie du lebst, so stirbst du,
Wie du stirbst, so fährst du,
Wie du fährst, so bleibst du.
See *The Sickness unto Death*, p. 224.
249. See Matthew 7:20.
250. Refers to X³ A 706, point (3).
251. See, for example, *Postscript*, pp. 152-58; IMMORTALITY.
252. See, for example, *The Sickness unto Death*, pp. 147, 262.
253. See Philippians 3:12.
254. See Matthew 11:28; *Practice [Training] in Christianity*, pp. 6-72.
255. See Matthew 8:22.

SEX

Kierkegaard's view of the sexual is determined by his understanding of man: "a synthesis of mind and body, which is sustained by spirit," as stated in *The Concept of Anxiety [Dread]* (p. 44, ed. tr.). This work provides a coherent exposition of Kierkegaard's view of the sexual in the context of an analysis of the biblical account of the fall. Man, precisely because he is a synthesis of the corporeal and the mental, in the fall not only learns the distinction between good and evil but also becomes conscious as a sexual being, or, stated in a different way, when spirit begins to affirm itself in man, even though it occurs negatively through sin, man begins to be ashamed of being also animal, therefore modesty is the first reaction of spirit to the presence of sexuality in man. The pseudonymous Vigilius Haufniensis stipulates, however, that the sensate, the extreme range of which is the sexual, is not in itself sin; it is sin only when "the drive at some moment manifests itself simply as drive in all its nakedness, for this can occur only through an arbitrary abstraction from the spirit" (V B 53:38). This means, then, that "by sin the sensate became sinfulness" (*The

Concept of Anxiety [*Dread*], p. 57, ed. tr.). It now becomes the task for man to join these two extreme points of the synthesis, the sexual and the spiritual, which may take place first through the interpretation of the sensate by the mental component and gradually by the spiritual. Consequently there must occur in man a development away from the sheerly sexual relation between the sexes, in which the sensate factor is dominant, in the direction of a relation qualified more by mind, in which a higher form of love is primary. Within paganism love reaches its highest form in erotic love. (See *Works of Love*, pp. 58–59, 65–66.)

Christianity brings a new factor into man's relation to the sexual, first and foremost because it posits a further cleft between spirit and the physical-mental, but secondly because it presents a demand for a love that is higher than the erotic, namely, love to the neighbor. But this demand involves God as the middle term in all human relations, consequently also in the love of man and woman for each other.

Confronted by Christianity's demand that the entire sphere of sexuality be interpreted by spirit, man can respond in three different ways. As was the case in the Middle Ages, man can seek to solve the issue by denying the sensate and wholly consecrating himself to the spiritual by entering the monastery. The opposite can be chosen: revolting against spirit and affirming the sensate as the central principle. This position, represented by the Don Juan type, is conceivable only within Christianity as a protest against the ascetic ideal. The sound position is continually to seek to join the two contrasting components in the synthesis, so that spirit interpenetrates all relations. But this development is long and must proceed through various phases; it applies also to married love. Of this Judge William says: "But also within Christianity love has had to undergo many fates before a vision was gained of the depth the beauty and the truth contained in marriage" (*Either/Or*, II, p. 29, ed. tr.). But since "it is the tendency of Christianity to lead the spirit further," the religious will gradually suspend the sexual, not "as the sinful but as the indifferent, because in spirit there is no difference between man and woman" (*The Concept of Anxiety* [*Dread*], p. 63). Therefore, the highest goal Christianity posits in relation to the sexual is "the triumph of love in a person in whom the spirit has triumphed in such a way that the sexual is forgotten and remembered only in forgetfulness. When this has taken place, then the sensate is transfigured into spirit and anxiety cast out" (p. 72, ed. tr.).

In *The Concept of Anxiety*, and especially in the journal entries for the book, Haufniensis-Kierkegaard directs a sharp critique against his contemporaries for their ambiguous position on the question of the place of the sexual within the Christian life-form. Although in church the sexual is generally treated as sin or there is more or less silence about the fact that marriage also signifies a sexual relation, one can "of an evening go to the theater with the permission of the Church and hear erotic love praised" (V B 53:29). Instead of admitting an awareness of the sexual and seeking to place it more and more under love and responsibility, one pretends an intellectual superiority transcending such things or an "immorality that wants permission to talk naïvely about them" (see also X² A 536). It is important especially in the upbringing of children that the sexual be treated neither frivolously nor narrowly but with an understanding of how "to speak right humanly about it" (V B 53:29) and above all that the child not be given the idea that everything about the sexual is sinful. Apparently Kierkegaard had been exposed to such a negative influence (see VI A 105), which may have contributed to his melancholy.

From the very beginning of his authorship Kierkegaard perceived that in his time there was a reluctance to think through either humanly or Christianly the basic questions related to the sexual. It was only after he had deepened the requirements for being a Christian that he expressed condemnation. For example, in one of the latest journal entries he says: "the one and only thing which preoccupies men is sex, sexual desire, propagation, and the like" (XI¹ A 219), and in *The Moment* he says: "Christianly it is egotism in the highest degree that, because a man and a woman cannot control their burning, another being must therefore sigh, perhaps for seventy years, in this vale of tears—and perhaps be eternally lost" (in *Attack on Christendom*, p. 223, ed. tr.; see also p. 213).

Through such expressions Kierkegaard wanted to point out the great gulf between the life-form within official Christianity and the goal Christianity sets for human life.

For references in the works to sex, sexuality, see, for example, *The Concept of Irony*, pp. 79–81; *Either/Or*, I, pp. 297–440, passim; II, pp. 3–157, passim; *The Concept of Anxiety* [*Dread*], pp. 44, 47, 52–72; *Stages*, pp. 95–178, passim.

256. ... in any event after his own degradation from the spiritual to the corporeal, from the eternal to the temporal, from the incorruptible to the transitory, from the loftiest to the lowest, from that of a spiritual man to that of an animal, from simple nature to a complex sex, from the status of an angel and such a host to the insolent and disgraceful herd which perishes miserably in body in their own generation, concerning such consequence he has been admonished.

257. Christian F. Wadskiær, *Poetiske Reflexioner...* (Copenhagen: 1747), p. 12.

258. From draft of *The Concept of Anxiety* [*Dread*], p. 60, ll. 23 ff.

259. Ibid., ll. 27 ff.

260. Ibid.

261. See Plato, *Symposium*, 209–11, also 181 ff.

262. See *Stages*, p. 126, an interpretation of Thales' declaration that out of love for children he will have no children.

263. See *Either/Or*, I, pp. 63–89.

264. Oliver Goldsmith, *Præsten i Wakefield*, tr. S. S. Blicher (Copenhagen:

1737), p. 5. Blicher has added "the states"; otherwise the Danish translation is quite literal.

265. Do not laugh, my friends!

266. Schopenhauer, *Die Welt als Wille und Vorstellung,* I–II (Leipzig: 2. ed., 1844), II, bk. 4, ch. 49. *ASKB* 773–773a.

SHAKESPEARE

In his own library Kierkegaard had various editions of the dramatic works of Shakespeare (1564–1616), a Danish translation and two German translations (*ASKB* 1889–96, 1874–81, 1883–88). The edition he used most was *Shakespeare's dramatische Werke,* tr. A.W. von Schlegel and L. Tieck (Berlin: 1839).

Kierkegaard had a thorough acquaintance with most of Shakespeare's dramas; he uses the expression, "studied my Shakespeare" (VII^1 A 105). As testimony to the deep impression made upon him especially by Shakespeare's tragedies, in his despair at the time he wrote the entry "the great earthquake" (II A 805) under the superscriptions "25 Years Old" he quotes a long passage from *King Lear* (II A 804). Overall, Shakespeare is one of the poets most frequently quoted in Kierkegaard's works. Apparently many scenes and lines found such a permanent place in his consciousness that he had them ready for illustrative purposes in the pseudonymous writings. By the pseudonymous writers Shakespeare is called "the great Shakespeare" (*Fear and Trembling,* p. 72), "immortal Shakespeare" (*Stages,* p. 209), "the most profound poet" (*Purity of Heart,* p. 140), and "the poet's poet" (*The Sickness unto Death,* p. 171).

What Kierkegaard admired particularly in Shakespeare was his capacity for delineating human passions in their pure, undialectical form, that is, in their immediacy and magnitude. For example, the pseudonymous author Frater Taciturnus says in *Stages on Life's Way* (p. 210): "Shakespeare knows how to speak fluently the language of passion," and of Shakespeare's characterization of Romeo and Juliet's love it is said that "his definitive pathos makes him just as unerring as Romeo and Juliet are undialectical in their passion" (ed. tr.). In this connection, Frater Taciturnus reproaches his contemporaries for having no sense for such true passion but at the theater feeling they are "in an almost painful situation" (p. 371) when it is presented to them.*

Kierkegaard was quite in agreement with the well-known passage in *Either/Or* (I, p. 27, ed. tr.): "Let others complain that the age is evil; I complain that it is wretched, for it has no passion. ... That is why my soul always returns to the Old Testament and to Shakespeare." In the Old Testament and in Shake-

---

* *Romeo and Juliet* was staged for the first time in Denmark on December 2, 1828, with the scarcely sixteen-year-old Johanne Luise Pätges as Juliet. In 1845 the play was again included in the repertoire with the sixteen-year-old Emma Mayer in the leading female role. In January 1847 the now thirty-four-year-old Johanne Luise (Pätges) Heiberg assumed her old role again. On this occasion Kierkegaard wrote *The Crisis and a Crisis in the Life of an Actress.*

speare he found depicted the collisions that powerful passions lead men into and that can lead to their destruction in a human sense.

Shakespeare's capacity for dramatic protrayal of such collisions in his tragedies was the object of great admiration by Kierkegaard, but no less did he admire Shakespeare's profound insight into men and his capacity for delineating motives and responses. Kierkegaard repeatedly returned to characters such as King Lear, Richard III, Macbeth and Lady Macbeth, as well as Hamlet. Of "the most demonic character Shakespeare has portrayed and portrayed incomparably, Gloucester (later Richard III)," who could not bear the pity that surrounded him from childhood, Johannes de Silentio says: "His monologue in the first act of *Richard III* is more valuable than whole moral systems that have no intuition of the horrors of existence or of the explanation" (*Fear and Trembling*, p. 114, ed. tr.). The reason for Kierkegaard's unusual interest in Richard III was undoubtedly that he felt himself overtaken by peculiar fate so that the demonic had been a possibility also for him.

In *Macbeth* what struck Kierkegaard was Shakespeare's unusual insight into the mentality of crime and sin, particularly a person's despair over sin. The pseudonymous writer Anti-Climacus says in *The Sickness unto Death* (p. 241, ed. tr.): "Psychologically it is a masterful speech by Macbeth (II, 2):
> For from this instant,
> There's nothing serious in mortality:
> All is but toys: renown and grace are dead.

... he is just as remote from being able to enjoy himself in ambition as he is from laying hold of grace." (See also pp. 237–38.)

Kierkegaard had a special relation to *Hamlet*. Some of the earliest journal entries regarding Shakespeare center on this tragedy, which obviously touched Kierkegaard very personally (see II A 454 and 584). No doubt this underlies a comparison of the Hamlet character and Kierkegaard (see Denis de Rougemont, "Kierkegaard and Hamlet: Two Danish Princes," *The Anchor Review*, no. 1, 1955). *Hamlet* is also the only one of Shakespeare's tragedies that received somewhat more extensive treatment in the authorship and the only one to which in one respect Kierkegaard took a critical position. He has Frater Taciturnus say that a character like Hamlet, who gives himself to reflection instead of acting, ought to be treated comically rather than tragically if there is no religious motivation for his procrastination, but in that case the theme would not be at all appropriate for dramatic treatment (*Stages*, pp. 409–11).

Moreover, Kierkegaard does not find genuinely religious collisions depicted in Shakespeare. For example, Johannes de Silentio, in his deliberations on Abraham's journey to Mt. Moriah to sacrifice his son, exclaims: "Thanks be to you, great Shakespeare, you who can say everything, everything, everything, just as it is—and yet why did you never give expression to this anguish"

(*Fear and Trembling*, p. 72, ed. tr.)? Anti-Climacus says: "But it seems that even Shakespeare recoiled from the genuinely religious collisions. Perhaps these can be expressed only in the language of the gods. And this language no human being is able to speak, for, as a Greek has already said so beautifully: 'From men one learns to speak, from the gods to remain silent!' " (*The Sickness unto Death*, p. 258, ed. tr.).

Consequently, Shakespeare's significance and greatness, according to Kierkegaard's view, lie on the esthetic and human levels, but it is possible, Johannes de Silentio suggests, that Shakespeare as poet purchased "this power of the word to express the heavy secrets of all others at the price of a small secret which he cannot express, and a poet is not an apostle—he drives out devils only with the devil's power" (*Fear and Trembling*, p. 72, ed. tr.; see also VIII[1] A 161). As poet and genius Shakespeare is rarely surpassed. In these respects not even a Paul can measure up to him, according to the pseudonymous writer H. H. But in the religious sphere another criterion applies, "for an apostle is what he is by divine authority," which is the case with Paul, whereas for Shakespeare it holds true that "a genius is what he is by himself, that is, by that which he is in himself" ("The Difference between a Genius and an Apostle," with *The Present Age*, p. 141, ed. tr.).

Rougemont, Denis de. "Two Danish Princes: Kierkegaard and Hamlet," In *Love Declared: Essays on the Myths of Love*. New York: Pantheon Books, 1963. "Kierkegaard and Hamlet: Two Danish Princes." *The Anchor Review*, I, 1955, pp. 109–27.

Ruoff, James E. "Kierkegaard and Shakespeare." *Comparative Literature*, 20, Fall 1968, pp. 342–54.

For references in the works to Shakespeare and quotations from the plays, see *The Concept of Irony*, p. 336; "Literary Quicksilver," *S.V.*, XIII, p. 475 (see ed. note p. 396); *Either/Or*, I, pp. 27, 332; *Fear and Trembling*, pp. 72, 144–15; *Repetition*, p. 76; *Fragments*, pp. 2, 67; *The Concept of Anxiety* [*Dread*], pp. 117, 130; "Prefaces," *S.V.*, V, pp. 23, 43; *Stages*, pp. 62, 136, 141, 142, 209–10, 248, 250, 271, 296, 323–24, 328, 370, 371, 384, 409–11; *Postscript*, pp. 3, 90, 93, 136, 148, 214–15, 234, 254 fn., 394–95, 400; *Upbuilding Discourses in Various Spirits*, Part One [*Purity of Heart*, p. 140]; *The Crisis and a Crisis in the Life of an Actress*, p. 81; *Two Minor Ethical-Religious Essays*, with *The Point of View*, pp. 237–38, 241, 256, 258; *The Point of View*, pp. 2, 67; article in *Fædrelandet*, no. 83, 1855, in *Attack*, p. 59; *The Moment*, no. 7, ibid., p. 203.

267. *Shakespeares dramatische Werke*, tr. A. W. Schlegel and L. Tieck, I-XII (Berlin: 1839–40), III. *ASKB* 1883–88.

268. . . . . . love-in-idleness.
    Fetch me that flower; the herb I show'd thee once:
    The juice of it on sleeping eye-lids laid

Will make or man or woman madly dote
Upon the next live creature that it sees.
ll. 168–72

269. Presented at the Royal Theater in Copenhagen, March 5, 9, and 25, 1843.

270. V, 1.

271. The "gentlewoman attending on Lady Macbeth" is not named and there is no character in *Macbeth* named Lady Seymour; the "officer attending on Macbeth" is named Seyton.

272. See *Postscript*, p. 459 fn.

273. *Othello*, V, 2; *William Shakespeares Tragiske Værker*, tr. Peter Foersom and P. F. Wulff, I-IX (Copenhagen: 1807–25), VII, p. 181. *ASKB* 1889–96.

SILENCE

In the first of the "Three Godly Discourses" composing *The Lily of the Field and the Bird of the Air* (with *Christian Discourses*), Kierkegaard says: ". . . simply because man can speak, for that very reason it is an art to be able to remain silent" (p. 322, ed. tr.). For Kierkegaard "to speak" is an expression for the open, the immediate, whereas silence presupposes reflection. By silence Kierkegaard rarely means silence in the literal sense (on the contrary, just by talking a person can in actuality keep silent about the essential), but rather that a person consciously cuts himself off from the multitudinous impressions from the world of relativities surrounding him, or from communication with others, in order to concentrate on something of ideal or eternal value. Therefore by silence the person undertakes a form of the movement of infinity, which is the condition for inwardness, or, as Kierkegaard puts it: "The idea of silence, the whole conception of silence as inwardness, is the way of inward deepening to the highest for every man . . ." (VII^2 B 235, p. 153; *On Authority and Revelation*, p. 122, ed. tr.).

Thus silence as inwardness becomes the condition for all genuine creation and action; this holds true in the esthetic, ethical, and religious. The poet, for example, seeks the "silence of nature" (*The Lily of the Field and the Bird of the Air*, with *Christian Discourses*, p. 324) in order to listen to the voice in his own inner being. It is also true in the esthetic sphere, particularly when action is at stake, that "secrecy and silence really make a man great for the very reason that they are the qualifications of inwardness" (*Fear and Trembling*, p. 97, ed. tr.). That a man "by virtue of the absurd wills to be higher than the universal" is due to this silence (ibid., 102, ed. tr.). But here is the paradox that his silence can be either the divine or the demonic. If silence is due to the "snare of the demons," it means that through silence one shuts himself up with the idea and avoids communication with others; whereas silence as the divine means "Deity's understanding with the single individual" (ibid., p. 97, ed. tr.) and is, as it is called in *The Concept of Anxiety* [*Dread*] (p. 110, ed. tr.), "identical with expansion, and there is no individuality expanded in the more beautiful and nobler sense than one who is enclosed in the womb of a great idea." But thereby collisions can arise between the single individual and the universal as representing the ethical. In *Fear and Trembling*, Johannes de Silentio gives many examples of such collisions, but they are examples subordinate to the main issue of the book, that it is God who requires an action that is in conflict with the ethical, namely, that Abraham must sacrifice his own son. Abraham is thereby placed *outside* the universal, and his silence is due to the fact that, in contrast to the persons in the other examples, he *cannot* speak, for even if he were to speak, he would not be understood. He is placed as the single individual "in an absolute relation to the absolute" (p. 103), that is, he stands in a direct relation of obedience to God.

According to Kierkegaard, authentic ethical action presupposes silence, since it contains a relation to the eternal that cannot be expressed directly in words. Particularly in the upbuilding discourses Kierkegaard points out how silence is the beginning of the ethical-religious, of obedience to God. In the above-mentioned "Three Godly Discourses," which treat of the way man can learn from "the lily of the field and the bird of the air as teachers," Kierkegaard says that "to become silent in the deepest sense, silent before God, is the beginning of the fear of God" (p. 323, ed. tr.) and that "this silence ... is the first condition for being truly able to obey." The marvelous thing happens that the more inwardly a person prays, the less he has to say, until finally he becomes silent, he finally becomes what is even more contrasted to speaking than silence, if that is possible—a "hearer" (p. 323).

But it is especially true that silence is an indispensable presupposition if a person is chosen by God for a particular task. "If God has favored him with his confidence, ... he will at least not insult God by making his confidence loose talk and town gossip," Kierkegaard says in his *The Book on Adler* (VII^2 B 235, p. 67; *On Authority and Revelation*, p. 52, ed. tr.), and in one of his latest journal entries he writes: "Silence in the relationship to God is invigorating; absolute silence would be like a jail or the point outside the world Archimedes speaks of" (XI^2 A 143).

However, when it is a matter of witnessing to the truth, the Christian cannot remain silent. Kierkegaard took as a clear sign that the clergy of his time were not "witnesses to the truth" (article in *Fædrelandet*, April 23, 1855, in *Attack*, p. 48) the fact that they kept silent during his attack on official Christianity in 1855. For if it were true, Kierkegaard said, then it was wrong of the clergy to use silence as a way "to slink away from any truth," and if he had been wrong, then as witnesses to the truth they ought not in silence have allowed "any untruth to stand" (p. 49).

Silence came to play a decisive role in Kierkegaard's own life. His use of pseudonyms was a form of silence (see VIII^2 B 7:10) whereby for a time he could conceal the real aim of his authorship. But silence about a particular relationship in his life also came to be of essential importance for the course of his life. Kierkegaard writes in a letter of 1847 to his brother Peter Christian: "Silence is necessary for my life, and precisely through silence it gains its power. Even if I wanted to speak, I would have to keep silent about that which is most important to me and most deeply determines my life" (*Breve og Aktstykker*, no. 149, p. 167). Therefore, among other things, he may be thinking of himself when he writes in *The Book on Adler*: "And yet something extraordinary has happened, and there lives a man who with a life devoted in holy resolution works in all silence" (VII² A 235, p. 67; *On Authority and Revelation*, p. 52, ed. tr.).

By silence (*Taushed*), which is a form of the double movement of infinity, a person consciously shuts himself away from the relativities of the world and seeks to enter into himself. Thus silence is a presupposition for a person's achieving the attitude of openness, receptivity, and responsiveness, which Kierkegaard calls quiet or stillness (*Stilhed*).

Quiet is the condition for all spiritual life. It is, as the pseudonymous writer Quidam says, "an infinite nothing and precisely thereby possibility's capacious form of an infinite content" (*Stages on Life's Way*, p. 307, ed. tr.). He also has the experience that "the testing quietness of responsibility teaches one to have to help himself through the power of the spirit" (p. 334, ed. tr.).

Especially in the first of *Three Discourses on Imagined Occasions*, "On the Occasion of a Confessional Service," Kierkegaard speaks of how important it is for a person to seek quiet in order to be able to listen to the voice of conscience, to "God's voice of judgment in solitude" (*Thoughts on Crucial Situations in Human Life*, p. 4), and he points out how this quietness becomes the transition to life, because through it a person learns that he himself "can do nothing" (p. 40) but in all that he undertakes he needs God's help and that in the fulfilling of even the slightest duty he has infinite responsibility before God. In *Upbuilding Discourses in Various Spirits*, Part One [*Purity of Heart*] Kierkegaard develops in detail the significance of quiet for the penitent who prepares himself for confession. "He is in quietness," says Kierkegaard because he "in truth has come to be at one with himself" and desires to be "concealed in quietness in order to become open" (pp. 47–48, ed. tr.). "The quietness grips" him with the "earnestness of eternity" because he stands before "the omniscient One" (pp. 49–50, ed. tr.). Toward the end of the discourses Kierkegaard reminds us that one day "eternity's accounting" will be made in the "infinite quietness" of eternity in which the conscience speaks with the single individual only about whether he as an individual has done good or evil (p. 186, ed. tr.).

But the person who understands how to seek quiet this way by making every relation "a matter of conscience" will also experience that "Christianity makes the transformation of infinity in all quietness as if it were nothing!" (*Works of Love*, p. 132).

Yet Kierkegaard perceived that most of his contemporaries knew only the quiet that constitutes the external frame for religious enjoyment or "vegetating quietness" (*Stages*, p. 308), in which there is no spiritual life and which ends as "the quietness of death, extinction" (*For Self-Examination*, p. 17). Therefore in one of his last journal entries, he ironizes over "all the solemn talk in Christendom about quiet, deep quiet, festive quiet, quiet festivity, etc.," and he continues: "Well, quiet does indeed pertain to the religiousness which is a matter of enjoyment. But essentially Christian religiousness is *suffering*, and therefore it is a matter of bringing about a restlessness ... " (XI^2 A 35). Kierkegaard regarded it as his own task to point men to the quiet in which conscience is disquieted and, as he expresses it in *For Self-Examination* (p. 17), to work "to awaken unrest in the direction of inward deepening."

For references in the works to silence (*Taushed*), see, for example, *The Concept of Irony*, pp. 49, 53, 63, 67, 188, 232, 237, 275; *Either/Or*, I, pp. 155-56; *Fear and Trembling*, pp. 91-129, *Repetition*, pp. 123-24; *Fragments*, pp. 30, 45; *The Concept of Anxiety* [*Dread*], pp. 50, 110-17; *Upbuilding* [*Edifying*] *Discourses*, IV, p. 108; *Three Discourses on Imagined Occasions* [*Thoughts on Crucial Situations*], pp. 30, 94; *Stages*, pp. 207, 210, 346, 387-89; *Postscript*, pp. 5, 61, 437, 487-88; *The Present Age*, pp. 49-53; *Upbuilding Discourses in Various Spirits*, Part One [*Purity of Heart*, pp. 62, 213-14]; Part Two [*What We Learn from the Lilies of the Field and the Birds of the Air*, with *The Gospel of Suffering*, pp. 170-72, 176]; ibid., pp. 12-14; *Works of Love*, pp. 268-71; *The Lily of the Field and the Bird of the Air*, with *Christian Discourses*, pp. 315, 322-32, 349, 354-55; *Two Minor Ethical-Religious Essays*, with *The Present Age*, pp. 80-84; *The Sickness unto Death*, p. 200; "The Woman Who Was a Sinner," with *Christian Discourses*, p. 381; *Practice* [*Training*] *in Christianity*, p. 251; *The Point of View*, pp. 5, 21, 64, 85, 91; articles in *Fædrelandet*, no. 295, December 18, 1854, no. 107, May 10, 1855, no. 120, May 26, 1855; in *Attack*, pp. 9, 47-49, 67-70; *The Moment*, no. 3, no. 6, no. 9, ibid., pp. 135, 184, 259.

For references in the works to quiet, stillness (*Stilhed*), see *The Concept of Irony*, p. 176, 222; *Either/Or*, I, pp. 31, 33, 374-75; II, pp. 32, 146, 181; *Fear and Trembling*, pp. 21, 91-129; *Repetition*, p. 145; *Three Discourses on Imagined Occasions* [*Thoughts on Crucial Situations*], pp. 2-5, 25, 30, 36-40; *Upbuilding* [*Edifying*] *Discourses*, IV, pp. 104-5; *Stages*, pp. 33-35, 182, 191-92, 259, 307-8, 439, 443-44; *Postscript*, pp. 210-11, 234, 366, 373, 478-88; *Upbuilding Discourses in Various Spirits*, Part One [*Purity of Heart*, pp. 47-51, 106-8, 142, 184-86, 213-14]; Part Two [*What We Learn from the Lilies and the Birds*, with *The Gospel of Suffering*, p. 202]; *Works of Love*, pp. 88, 138; *Christian Discourses*, pp. 171, 277; *For Self-Examination*, pp. 54-61; *Judge for Yourselves!*, pp. 143, 153, 169, 198; articles in *Fædrelandet*, no. 295, December 18, 1854, no. 97, April 27, 1855, in *Attack*, pp. 6, 45; *The Moment*, no. 1, no. 7, ibid., pp. 87, 202.

274. See *Fear and Trembling*, p. 97.
275. See *Postscript*, p. 80 fn.

276. Entry is from a draft of *The Book on Adler* (English translation under the title *On Authority and Revelation*, p. 121).

277. Adolph P. Adler, *Studier og Exempler* (Copenhagen: 1846). *ASKB* U 11.

278. *Patrum apostolicorum opera,* ed. C. J. Hefele (Tübingen: 3 ed., 1847), p. 169. *ASKB* 152.

279. Exodus 14:15.

280. Martin Luther, *En christelig Postille,* tr. Jørgen Thisted, I–II (Copenhagen: 1828), I, p. 322 (Fifth Sunday after Easter, in 1849 on May 13). *ASKB* 283.

281. See VI A 55–59 and VII^1 A 6, 22.

282. See Plutarch, *Marcellus* 14, *Levnetsbeskrivelser,* tr. Stephan Tetens, I–IV (Copenhagen: 1800–1811), III, p. 272. *ASKB* 1197–1200.

SIN

Sin is disobedience against God, and only in relation to God can one properly speak of sin. The most pregnant "definition" of sin is given by Anti-Climacus in *The Sickness unto Death:* "Sin is, before God or with the conception of God, in despair not to will to be oneself or in despair to will to be oneself" (p. 208, ed. tr.). In essence this definition says that under sin a man in divided against himself (in despair) and that he clings to this condition at the same time that he has the conception of God.

But Kierkegaard and his pseudonyms realize that before man in his existential movements can come under this stringent qualification of sin there are forms of disobedience against the eternal which are not sin in the stricter sense. For instance, Vigilius Haufniensis (*The Concept of Anxiety*) gives a lengthy description of the sin Christian dogmatics calls original sin. Original sin is the individual's first transgression, which as such forms the transition from innocence to guilt, and by which the individual comes to share in the sinfulness of the race, which in this way reproduces itself in the history of the race. The burden of original sin is thereby quantitatively increased through the generations. The distinctive mark of original sin is that even though it increases quantitatively within the history of the race, it can never become absolute guilt. To be able to come within the sphere of absolute guilt, a person must have arrived at an awareness of his eternal validity. Therefore it is anxiety and, along with it, feeling which are dominant within the sphere of original sin—and not self-knowledge. Here the strongest expression for the reality of sin is the demonic as anxiety over the good.

In *The Sickness unto Death* Anti-Climacus continues the characterization of sin as it shows itself on a higher level of development, since it is assumed that man has an awareness of the eternal (infinity) and that the task consists of bringing the eternal into proper relation to the temporal in this life. When a person resists this task, despair supersedes anxiety. Anti-Climacus describes the steadily more pronounced stages of this condition down to its most extreme forms. At its greatest intensity, despair expresses itself as defiance, which revolts against the demands of the eternal and wants to be its own master.

But all these forms of disobedience against the eternal described in *The Concept of Anxiety* and in the first part of *The Sickness unto Death* still are not sin in the proper sense. Not until a person in his disobedience (despair) meets God is it qualified as sin. In this relationship despair is intensified to sin as defined earlier.

A qualitatively new intensification of sin occurs when God through his revelation in Christ enlightens man as to the depth of his immersion in despair and disobedience. "The definition of sin" now becomes: "Sin is, after being enlightened as to the nature of sin by a revelation from God, in despair before God not to will to be oneself or in despair to will to be oneself" (p. 227, ed. tr.). According to this interpretation of sin, an intensification of sin is also possible, namely, when a person rejects the invitation to reconciliation which Christ offers. Anti-Climacus calls "the sin of despairing of the forgiveness of sin" an offense (p. 244). Sin in the form of offense reaches its climax when a person consciously turns against Christianity, declares it untrue, and begins to attack it. This is the gravest form of sin, and Anti-Climacus says that this "form of offense is sin against the Holy Spirit" (p. 255).

In his authorship Kierkegaard has given a detailed description of the progressive forms of sin on various existential levels, emphasizing its special seriousness in Christianity; consequently he has given us a kind of "dialectic of sin" (pp. 236-37, 250-51). He has also stressed that sin is not merely the specific sins but that as an expression of man's disobedience toward God they "have an inner coherence." At the same time, however, Kierkegaard is opposed to an abstract view of sin, to "talking about the universality of sin" (*Three Discourses on Imagined Occasions* [*Thoughts on Crucial Situations*], p. 27). What Anti-Climacus says applies here: "For the earnestness is simply that you and I are sinners; the earnestness is not sin in general, but the accent of earnestness falls upon the sinner, who is the single individual" (p. 250, ed. tr.).

Hamilton, Kenneth. "Kierkegaard on Sin." *Scottish Journal of Theology*, 17, 1964, pp. 289-302.

Swenson, David. "Kierkegaard's Treatment of the Doctrine of Sin," in *Something about Kierkegaard*, ch. 6. Minneapolis: Augsburg, 1951.

For references in the works to sin and original sin, see, for example, *The Concept of Irony*, pp. 112-13, 250, 307; *Either/Or*, I, pp. 19, 20, 27, 88, 142, 146-47; II, pp. 55, 92-93, 193, 253; *Fear and Trembling*, pp. 64-65, 108; *Repetition*, pp. 152-53; *Upbuilding* [*Edifying*] *Discourses*, I, pp. 61-90; IV, pp. 77-78; *Fragments*, pp. 19-24, 64, 139; *The Concept of Anxiety* [*Dread*], passim; *Three Discourses on Imagined Occasions* [*Thoughts on Crucial Situations*], pp. 24-35; *Stages*, pp. 428-

36; *Postscript,* pp. 186, 192, 201-4, 239-43, 248, 303, 458, 467, 474-93, 516-18; *Upbuilding Discourses in Various Spirits,* Part One [*Purity of Heart,*pp. 40, 63]; Part Three [*The Gospel of Suffering,* pp. 41-43, 67-96]; *Works of Love,* pp. 39, 106, 149, 193, 261-78, 351-56; *Christian Discourses,* pp. 108, 111-12, 118, 128, 138, 141, 153, 163, 180, 189, 265, 271-73, 287, 297; *Three Discourses at the Communion on Fridays,* with ibid., pp. 379-86; *The Sickness unto Death,* pp. 208-62; *Practice [Training] in Christianity,* pp. 64-65, 71-72, 155; *An Upbuilding Discourse,* with ibid., pp. 261-71; *Two Discourses at the Communion on Fridays,* with *Judge for Yourselves!,* pp. 9-25; *For Self-Examination,* pp. 77-78.

283. Franz von Baader, *Vorlesungen über speculative Dogmatik,* I-V (I, Stuttgart, Tübingen: 1828; II-V, Münster: 1830-38), II. *ASKB* 396.

284. Gotthilf H. Schubert, *Die Symbolik des Traumes* (Bamberg: 1821), p. 155. *ASKB* 776.

285. With this not therefore because of this . . . with this and because of this.

286. The problems of individual and race, heredity and environment, are treated compactly but thoroughly in *The Concept of Anxiety [Dread],* especially pp. 24-72.

287. Anton Günther, ed., *Süd- und Nordlichter am Horizonte spekulativer Theologie* (Vienna: 1832). *ASKB* 520.

288. Justus Kerner, *Eine Erscheinung aus dem Nachtgebiete der Natur, durch eine Reihe von Zeugen gerichtlich bestätigt und den Naturforschern zum Bedenken mitgeheilt* (Stuttgart, Tübingen: 1836).

289. Vicarious satisfaction.

290. See F. L. F. v. Dobeneck, *Des deutschen mittelalters Volksglauben und Heroensagen,* ed. Jean Paul (Berlin: 1825), p. 150 (quoted from a report on a repentant thief, p. 171 of Luther, *Tischreden;* Leipzig: 1700). See II A 145. In his punishment he died with a joyous heart.

291. See *Mythologie der Feen und Elfen . . . aus dem Englischchen übersetzt,* tr. Oskar L. B. Wolff, I-II (Wiemar: 1828), I, p. 153. Not listed in *ASKB.*

292. See Luke 15:3-7; Matthew 18:12-14.

293. "Ueber den Begriff des Sünderfalls und des Bösen. Ein Versuch von Dr. [J.E.] Erdmann "*Zeitschrift für spekulative Theologie,* ed. Bruno Bauer, II, pt. 1, pp. 192 ff. *ASKB* 354-357.

294. See *Johannes Climacus,* p. 166.

295. See *Either/Or,* I, p. 153.

296. Robert, first duke of Normandy. See G. Schwab, *Buch der schönsten Geschichten und Sagen,* I-II (Stuttgart: 1836), I, p. 347, *ASKB* 1407; *Either/Or,* I, p. 153.

297. Ibid.

298. Carl C. Rafn, tr., *Nordiske Kæmpe-Historier, efter islandske Haandskrifter,* I-III (Copenhagen: 1821-26). *ASKB* 1993-1995.

299. See James 1:13; *Upbuilding [Edifying] Discourses,* I, pp. 42-43.

300. See note 297.

301. Ibid.

302. See John 11:4.

303. See *The Concept of Anxiety* [*Dread*], p. 23; Karl Hase, *Hutterus redivivus*, I–II (Leipzig: 4 ed., 1839), I, pp. 194–95. *ASKB* 437–38.

304. Original righteousness.

305. See *Fragments*, p. 58.

306. Greek fire is a combustible material capable of burning under water and was used by the ancient Greek navy. Old books on fireworks have formulae for Greek fire. See VI B 173.

307. See *Postscript*, pp. 521–22.

308. See *The Sickness unto Death*, p. 213.

309. See *Either/Or*, I, p. 20.

310. See *The Sickness unto Death*, p. 213.

311. Ibid., p. 211.

312. This line is a slightly altered quotation of Lamentations 3:39 as given in the so-called Kalkar's *Bible*. See *Bibelen*, tr. C. H. Kalkar et al., I–III (Copenhagen: 1847), II, p. 924. *ASKB* 8–10.

313. *Ludovici Blosii Opera omnia* (Louvain: 1568). *ASKB* 429. "He questions sufficiently who recognizes death (sin) for what it is; he who weeps over it and firmly believes in it begs the question excessively."

314. See note 280; ibid., I, p. 28; II, p. 46; *Works of Love*, p. 193.

315. See John 16:8–9 (in 1849 the text on May 6).

316. Pp. 208–62.

317. See Luke 19:41 ff.

318. See *The Concept of Anxiety* [*Dread*], pp. 103–4.

319. See Luke 7:36 ff.

320. See John 3:2, 7:50, 19:39.

321. See note 222.

322. Johann Arndt, *Fire Bøger om den sande Christendom* (Christiania: 1829), p. 251. *ASKB* 277.

323. *Theodicy*, para. 20–27; *Theodicee* (Hannover, Leipzig: 5 ed., 1763), pp. 271 ff. *ASKB* 619.

324. *Republic*, X, 610 e: . . . [Plato characterizes] injustice [as] liveliness; (injustice) renders its possessor very lively indeed, and not only lively but wakeful.

325. See Julius Müller, *Die christliche Lehre von der Sünde*, I–II (Breslau: 3 ed., 1849), I, p. 381 fn. *ASKB* 689–90. The page number given in the text is for the first edition (Marburg: 1839).

326. Hans P. Kofoed-Hansen, a pastor of Vor Frelsers Kirke, Christianshavn, September 9, 1849–November 3, 1850, then pastor in Haderslev. In *For Literatur og Kritik* (1843) he wrote a review of *Either/Or* and later claimed to

have been the first to give a sound interpretation of the most important authorship in all Danish literature.

327. See *The Sickness unto Death*, pp. 240–44.

328. See note 325.

329. Carl Daub, *Darstellung und Beurtheilung der Hypothesen in Betreff der Willensfreiheit* (Altona: 1834), pp. 309 ff., in *Carl Daubs philosophische und theologische Vorlesungen*, I–VII (Berlin: 1838–44). *ASKB* 472–472g. Daub is quoted by J. Muller (see note above), II, p. 237.

330. See *The Sickness unto Death*, pp. 147–50.

331. See *Postscript*, pp. 284–92.

332. In a particular instance.

333. See note 325; ibid., II, p. 419.

334. As a whole.

335. See *Fragments*, pp. 27, 44–45, 57–58.

336. See *Augsburg Confession*, articles II, V, pp. 46, 48–49, and Philipp Melanchton, *Apologie*, pp. 148–50, in *Den rette uforandrede augsburgske Troesbekjendelse*, tr. A. G. Rudelbach (Copenhagen: 1825), *ASKB* 386. Other editions Kierkegaard had were: *Confessio augustana invariata* (Copenhagen: 1817), *ASKB* 469; *Libri Symbolici* (Leipzig: 1837), *ASKB* 624; *Den augsburgske Confession*, tr. Henrik N. Clausen (Copenhagen: 1851), *ASKB* 387.

337. The "second" refers to God's forgiveness (the "first" is sin), which again is according to God's standards ("it") and not man's. See *The Sickness unto Death*, p. 231.

338. See note 325, ibid., II, pp. 310 ff., esp. p. 335.

339. See Immanuel H. Fichte, *Sätze zur Vorschule der Theologie* (Stuttgart, Tübingen), p. 214. *ASKB* 501.

340. See *Fragments*, pp. 92–94.

341. See *Postscript*, pp. 127, 131, 280–81, 284–92.

342. The reference is to Peter in particular, who explicitly denied Christ; see Matthew 26:69–75.

343. See Luke 23:40–43.

344. See Luke 24:42–43.

345. See Matthew 27:46; Mark 15:34.

346. Georg Rapp, *Auswahl aus Gerhard Tersteegens Schriften* (Essen: 1841), p. 169. *ASKB* 229. See Note 1005.

347. Luke 7:37–38. See *Three Discourses at the Communion on Fridays*, together with *Christian Discourses*, pp. 379–86; *An Upbuilding Discourse*, with *Practice [Training] in Christianity*, pp. 255–76. The Danish has a feminine ending for nouns which usually cannot be duplicated in English.

348. See note 28.

349. Ibid.

350. That without which nothing; the necessary condition.

SITUATION

By situation (Danish: *Situation* or *Bestedelse*) Kierkegaard means the background of contemporaneously present external conditions which are determinative for the way a person's conduct (speaking or acting) is to be understood. In the authorship there are numerous examples of the significance Kierkegaard attributed to the contemporary situation for an understanding of a person's expressions, moods, feelings, and actions.

As early as in *The Concept of Irony* (p. 54) Kierkegaard criticizes Xenonphon's conception of Socrates because of the *"total absence of situation"* (ed. tr.), but on the other hand points out that Plato had a sense of the significance of the situation, even though his presentation is "purely poetical." In *Either/Or*, I (for example, pp. 245-46, 264-65), the esthete, Mr. A, emphasizes that situation plays an essential role in all poetry, but especially in drama. Thus he shows, for example, how the comic effect in comedy stands or falls with the appropriateness of the situation-background of the lines.

But not only the poet needs to know about the contrasts of "moods, situations, and environments" (*Stages*, p. 31); essentially it holds true for every man that a sense of situation is of crucial importance in understanding oneself. Quidam in *Stages* puts it this way: "But to understand oneself ultimately requires being in the right situation. She has helped me into the situation of responsibility" (*Stages*, p. 334, ed. tr.).

Likewise the two life-attitudes of irony and humor presuppose that a person has given up his first immediacy and can see himself in relation to the situation, namely as one whose striving corresponds all too little to the ideal. But although the ironic reply is understandable when taken against the background of the situation, one will not be in a position to understand the humorist's mode of expression unless one has the same life-outlook; on the contrary, frequently his utterances will be taken as irony and this will "make the situation ironical" (see *Postscript*, pp. 401 and 490).

Undoubtedly it was this insight into and experience of the crucial importance of situation that led Kierkegaard to the thought that Christ's words and the ethical claim upon a person can be understood only in a situation corresponding to the original—in short, the situation of contemporaneity (see CONTEMPORANEITY). This idea is suggested by Climacus in *Concluding Unscientific Postscript* (p. 333) and in a journal entry from 1849: "only in the situation of actuality is it possible to get the true impression of the essentially Christian" (X^2 A 13). The idea is developed in *Practice [Training] in Christianity*, where it is pointed out that in "the situation of contemporaneity" it will be manifest that "to become a Christian (to be transformed into likeness to God) is, humanly speaking, an even greater anguish and wretchedness and pain than the greatest human auguish" (p. 67, ed. tr.), just as everyone will become aware of the possibility of offense when the situation is "that an individual human being standing at your side is the God-man" (p. 84, ed. tr.). But Kierkegaard also perceived that even though an identification in a situation of contemporaneity is a presupposition for understanding Christ's claim upon one, it is not adequate to enable the individual to have faith. The person himself must create a situation which in a genuine sense makes him contemporary with Christ, that is, by venturing an action "branded by the unconditional," whereby he will come to discover "the collisions of the essentially Christian;" "without this situation, which isolates him almost into despair, . . . a person never comes to believe" (X^3 A 470; see also *Judge for Yourselves!*, pp. 199–200).

It became increasingly clear to Kierkegaard that although in the early times of Christianity the difficulties of becoming a Christian arose directly out of the situation, in Christendom, where there is no danger involved in calling oneself a Christian, all relations have been "transformed into reflection," and an entirely new tactic must be used in order to make men aware of what it really means to be a Christian. He treats of this in *The Point of View* (p. 42) and also in *On My Work as an Author* (together with the above): "The *situation* (of becoming a 'Christian' in Christendom, where of course one is a Christian) . . . also makes an indirect method necessary, because the task here must be an operation directed at an illusion . . ." (p. 149 fn., ed. tr.). Kierkegaard had used this indirect method in his pseudonymous authorship from the very beginning, and therefore he can justifiably say that in his presentation of how a person becomes a Christian there is no absence of what usually is lacking in preaching: "a crucial categorical qualification and a crucial expression of the situation: proclaiming Christianity—in Christendom" (*The Point of View*, p. 43, ed. tr.).

For references in the works to situation in various forms see, for example, CONTEMPORANEITY; *The Concept of Irony*, pp. 54, 56–57; *Either/Or*, I, pp. 245–46, 264–65; *Stages*, pp. 31, 334; *Postscript*, pp. 401, 490; *Christian Discourses*, pp. 171–73; *Practice* [*Training*] *in Christianity*, pp. 162–64, 171, 233–34; *Judge for Yourselves!*, pp. 200 and 203 (*Bestedelse* translated as "predicament"); *The Point of View*, pp. 149–50; article in *Fædrelandet*, no. 68, March 21, 1855, in *Attack*, pp. 26–27; *The Moment*, no. 2, ibid, p. 97.

351. Plato, *Republic*, bk. VII, 520 d, 521 b.

352. See Exodus 4:10; 6:12, 30.

353. See *Fragments*, p. 79; *Postscript*, pp. 367, 530; *Practice* [*Training*] *in Christianity*, pp. 27, 127. For other uses of *incognito*, see *The Concept of Irony*, 301; *The Concept of Anxiety* [*Dread*], pp. 83, 114; *Postscript*, pp. 3, 386, 447, 449, 452–53, 455, 464, 473; *The Sickness unto Death*, pp. 199, 229.

354. See OFFENSE.

355. That is something else.

356. Matthew 10:32–33.

357. *Ugeskrift for den evangeliske Kirke i Danmark*, ed. J. L. M. Hjort, 1854, pp. 117 ff.

358. But, but.

SOCIAL-POLITICAL THOUGHT

Kierkegaard's teacher and friend, Professor Poul Martin Møller, wrote in his essay *"Tanker over Muligheden af Beviser for Menneskets Udødelighed"* (*Efterladte Skrifter*, København: 1855–56, V, p. 52) that because Christianity has lost its meaning for most men, "catastrophes" will occur that will once again bring men along another road to a "full conviction" of the truth of Christianity. Kierkegaard and Poul Martin Møller may well have discussed this question; in any case it is a fact that Kierkegaard began writing early about the various signs of disintegration due to the abandonment or the distortion of central Christian truths (see I A 328). Moreover, in 1838 in "From the Papers of One Still Living" Kierkegaard mentions the disintegration in the social and political life and likewise "Protestantism's life-view, now sharply and inwardly reduced *in absurdum zum Gebrauch für Jedermann*" (*S.V.*, XIII, pp. 63–64).

It was entirely clear to Kierkegaard that social and political renewal could come only through religious renewal. To find the way to such a religious renewal Kierkegaard advanced step by step toward what became his central concept, "the single individual," and he became more and more convinced that only by leading men to be responsible "single individuals" could a basis for a new beginning be laid. As he saw it, the essential development takes place solely in the interior of the individual person through his entering as a single individual into relationship to the eternal outside the world and outside the person himself. Kierkegaard calls this development a qualitative movement because a person thereby comes into an absolute relation to the absolute.

But through such a relation the single individual also influences the laws of external, relative actuality—that is, social and political life. On this point Judge William declares that a person must always translate himself from the personal and the religious to the civic and social, because the self is not only "a personal self but also a social and civic self" (*Either/Or*, II, p. 267). But the social and political can never have absolute importance, because they lie within the world of relativities. Thus a person can practice love and self-denial to his neighbor, but in the world as an external actuality his action will be judged as good or bad by a relative criterion, because the world and thereby the social and the political have other criteria. But although the interior life of the single individual is on another and higher plane than that of the social and the political, there is always interaction between the individual and society. If many single individuals are on a high spiritual level, social conditions will be elevated (see XI^1 A 431). But when men lose their religious foundation, there is a constant erosion and leveling of values in the social and political spheres, which Kierkegaard observed on a large scale.

In *Two Ages* (1846) Kierkegaard stresses that only the single individual can halt the leveling and demoralization of the age by "obeying the order of divinity" (*The Present Age*, p. 65) and "without authority" by helping others in a suffering and indirect way. Only in this way can one assist others to "gain the specific gravity of religiousness, gain its essentiality, first-hand from God" (p. 65, ed. tr.). Not only will the single individual's absolute relation to God help others to a relationship to God, but it will also secondarily influence social and political life.

In pondering this question, Kierkegaard also came to see that completely opposite tendencies characterized the age—namely, to make the political and social central, to the exclusion of all religious influences. The unruly mass-man was on the march, and Kierkegaard realized that these political directions would exploit him. "Bread-uprisings" in 1847 only strengthened his conviction (VIII[1] A 108 and 172). When writing *Works of Love* from January to August of 1847, Kierkegaard was aware that while the book advanced Christian-ethical points of view, it also indirectly attacked the leveling and the political, social tendencies of the age (pp. 119–22). In a journal entry (VIII[1] A 299) he says of *Works of Love* "Reflection no. VII in part two about mercifulness is also rightly turned against communism." To Kierkegaard the outbreak of the February revolution in France in 1849 and the workers' revolt in Paris completely confirmed his view that when Christianity is abolished, the crowd enters the political arena and can be used for all sorts of experiments (IX B 10, 24).

The world-historical "catastrophe" in 1848, which Kierkegaard regarded only as a "beginning" (IX B 10), made a strong impact on him, and he frequently comments on it in his journals (for example, IX B 8, 10, 22, 24 and X[6] B 40, 41). He sharply attacks particularly the revolutionists' idea of trying, "through the introduction of the 4th estate, i.e., all men, to solve the problem of human equality in the medium of secularity—that is, in the medium whose essence is dissimilarity" (IX B 10). In *Works of Love,* especially, Kierkegaard had pointed out that there is an *essential* equality among all men, and that secular, external equality can never be accomplished (see, for example, pp. 81–83). In 1851 Kierkegaard points this out again in his book *On My Work as an Author.* Here he calls 1848 the year when "the shrill sound, announcing chaos, was heard" and goes on to say that under the slogan "Liberty, Equality, Fraternity" men felt themselves released from all bonds. The relationship to the unconditioned was lost, but only this relationship can save men (with *The Point of View*, p. 163, ed. tr.). The relation between the political and the religious is even more precisely delineated in *The Point of View for My Work as an Author,* which was not published until after Kierkegaard's death. Here he declares: "Politics begins on earth and remains on earth, whereas the religious, taking its beginning from above, seeks to transfigure and thereby elevate the earthly to heaven." Kierkegaard was aware that to a politician Christianity must seem extremely impractical, and he says: "But although 'impractical' the religious is nevertheless eternity's transfigured rendition of politics' most beautiful dream." He goes on to point out the primary reason for the impossibility of achieving equality among men: "Only the religious, with the help of eternity, can achieve human equality in its ultimacy, the godly, the essential, the non-worldly, the true, the only possible human equality . . ." (pp. 109–10, ed. tr.).

Many entries on the subject in his later journals reveal Kierkegaard's concern with these problems. However, in 1851 he objected that people such as Dr. Rudelbach used his ideas to attack the state church (see *An Open Letter*, with *Armed Neutrality*, pp. 47–55), even though Kierkegaard himself believed that it can be "dangerous when the state and Church grow together and are identified." For "the Church" should really represent " 'becoming' [*vorden*]"; "the state, on the other hand, 'the established' [*Bestaaen*]" (X^1 A 552). Only after Mynster's death did Kierkegaard in several numbers of *The Moment* directly make a sharp attack on "the merging of Christianity and the state" (no. 3, in *Attack*, p. 127, ed. tr.) in Denmark and all the unfortunate consequences thereof for state and church alike. By means of this merger the state became the determining force in Church affairs as well. Kierkegaard believed that the movement in Christendom from the religious toward the political began with the Reformation, but in our day, when everything up until now has had a political aspect, the movement will be from the political to the religious. He writes of this: "The future will correspond inversely to the Reformation: then everything appeared to be a religious movement and became politics; now everything appears to be politics and will become a religious movement" (IX B 63:7; see also X^6 B 40, X^5 A 115, and X^3 A 696).

For Kierkegaard the central issue in the relation between Christianity and politics is that a person, while continually relating absolutely to the absolute, is to practice his love within the relative world of the social and political. But there can never be absolute solutions (chiliasm) in these relative situations, because they belong to finitude and have their limitations. Similarly, neither race nor state nor party may be set up as an absolute authority, since this leads to a demonic religiousness. The only authority man shall obey absolutely is the eternal (God).

Arendt, Hannah. "Tradition and the Modern Age." *Partisan Review*, 21, 1, 1954, pp. 53–75.

Berdyaev, Nicholas. *Solitude and Society*. New York: Scribner, 1839.

Buber, Martin. *Between Man and Man*. Boston: Beacon Press, 1955.

De George, Richard T. "Solitude and Communion: a Study of their Meaning and Relation in Human Existence." Ph.D. dissertation, Yale, 1959.

Demson, David. "Kierkegaard's Sociology." *Religion in Life*, 27, 1958, pp. 257–65.

Diem, Hermann. "Church and State," in *Kierkegaard's Dialectic of Existence*, trans. Harold Knight, ch. 16. Edinburgh and London: Oliver and Boyd, 1959.

Fackre, Gabriel Joseph. "A Comparison and Critique of the Interpretation of Dehumanization in the Thought of Søren Kierkegaard and Karl Marx." Ph.D. dissertation, University of Chicago, 1962.

Grene, Marjorie. "Søren Kierkegaard: 'The Self against the System,' " in *Dreadful Freedom*, ch. 2. Chicago: University of Chicago Press, 1948.

Halevi, Jacob. "A Critique of Martin Buber's Interpretation of Søren Kierkegaard." Ph.D. dissertation, Hebrew Union College, 1960.

Hansen, Olaf. "The Problem of Alienation and Reconciliation: a Comparative Study of Marx and Kierkegaard." Ph.D. dissertation, Princeton Theological Seminary, 1956.

Harper, Ralph. *The Seventh Solitude: Man's Isolation in Kierkegaard, Dostoevsky, and Nietzsche*. Baltimore: Johns Hopkins University Press, 1965.

Hartt, Julian N. "The Philosopher, the Prophet, and the Church: Some Reflections on Their Roles as Critics of Culture." *Journal of Religion*, 35, July 1955, pp. 147–59.

Heiss, Robert. *Hegel, Kierkegaard, Marx*, tr. E. B. Garside. Boston: Seymour Lawrence, 1971.

Hopper, S. R. "Modern Diogenes: a Kierkegaardian Crochet," in W. Leibrecht, *Religion and Culture*. New York: Harper, 1959.

Jaspers, Karl. "The Importance of Nietzsche, Marx and Kierkegaard in the History of Philosophy." *Hibbert Journal*, 49, 1950–51, pp. 226–34.

Johnson, Howard A. "Kierkegaard and Politics." *Anglican Theological Review*, 38, January 1956, pp. 32–41. *A Kierkegaard Critique*, ch. 5. New York: Harper, 1962. *American Scandinavian Review*, 43, 1955, pp. 246–54.

Lowry, Charles W. *Communism and Christ*. New York: Morehouse-Gorham, 1953.

Lønning, Per. "Salvation and Politics." *Lutheran World*, 18, November 3, 1971, pp. 268–71.

McFadden, Robert "Nuclear Dilemma with a Nod to Kierkegaard." *Theology Today*, 17, January 1961, pp. 505–18.

McLaughlin, Wayman B. "The Relation between Hegel and Kierkegaard." Ph.D. dissertation, Boston, 1957.

Malantschuk, Gregor. "Kierkegaard and the Totalitarians." *American-Scandinavian Review*, 34, 3, 1946, pp. 246–48.

Marcuse, Herbert. *Reason and Revolution*, pp. 262–67. London, New York, and Toronto: Oxford University Press, 1941.

Moore, Stanley R. "The Social Implications of the Category of the Single One in the Thought of Kierkegaard." Ph.D. dissertation, Drew, 1964.

———. "Religion as the True Humanism: Reflections on Kierkegaard's Social Philosophy." *Journal of American Academy of Religion*, 37, 1, 1969, pp. 15–25.

———. "Kierkegaard's Politics." *Perspective,* 10, Winter 1969, pp. 235-51.

Nauman, St. Elmo H. "The Social Philosophies of Søren Kierkegaard and Nikolai Frederik Severin Grundtvig." Ph.D. dissertation, Boston, 1968.

Neumann, Harry. "Kierkegaard and Socrates on the Dignity of Man." *Personalist,* 48, Fall 1967, pp. 453-60.

Odajnyk, Walter. *Marxism and Existentialism.* Garden City, N.Y.: Doubleday (Anchor), 1965.

Perkins, Frances. *The Roosevelt I Knew,* pp. 147-48. New York: Viking, 1946.

Petras, John W. "God, Man, and Society; the Perspectives of Buber and Kierkegaard." *Journal of Religious Thought,* 23, 2, 1966-67, pp. 119-28.

Rasmussen, David M. "Between Autonomy and Sociality." *Cultural Hermeneutics,* 1, April 1973, pp. 3-45.

Rasmussen, Knud. "Søren Kierkegaard's Political Ideas." Ph.D. dissertation, Rutgers, 1964.

Schwandt, Jack Allan. "Alienation and Reconciliation in the Works of Søren Kierkegaard." M.A. thesis, University of Minnesota, 1959.

Smith, Constance J. "Single One and the Other." *Hibbert Journal,* 4, 1947-48.

Sontag, Frederick. "Existentialism: Greek Ethics and the Way Back to the Future: a Note." *The Thomist,* 34, April 1970, pp. 306-10.

Spahr, C. "Therapy for an Envious Age: The Age of Faithlessness." *Dialogue* (Phi Sigma Tau), 14, October 1971.

Stark, Werner. "Kierkegaard on Capitalism." *Sociological Review* (Manchester), 42, 1950, pp. 87-114.

———. "Søren Kierkegaard," in *Social Theory and Christian Thought,* ch. 3. London: Routledge and Kegan Paul, 1959.

Tillich, Paul. "The Breakdown of the Universal Synthesis," in *P. Tillich, Perspectives on 19th and 20th Century Protestant Theology,* ed. Carl E. Braaten, pp. 136-207. N.Y.: Harper & Row, 1967.

Tiryakian, Edward A. "The Individual and Society," in *Sociologism and Existentialism,* ch. 7. Englewood Cliffs, N.J.: Prentice-Hall, 1962.

Underwood, Byron E. "Kierkegaard's Category of the Concrete Individual." Ph.D. dissertation, Harvard, 1965.

Whittemore, Robert C. "The Levelling Process as a Function of the Masses in the View of Kierkegaard and Ortega y Gasset," *Kentucky Foreign Language Quarterly,* 7, 1960, pp. 27-36.

Wild, John. *Human Freedom and the Social Order.* Durham, N.C.: Duke University Press, 1959.

Wolf, William. "Alienation and Reconciliation in the Writings of Søren Kierkegaard." Ph.D. dissertation, Union Theological Seminary, 1945.

For references in the works to social-political issues see, for example, articles in *Københavns flyvende Post*, no. 76, February, 18, 1836, no. 87, April 10, 1836, *S.V.*, XIII, pp. 9–15, 28–39; "From the Papers of One Still Living," ibid., pp. 55–56, 59–64; article in *Fædrelandet*, ibid., p. 401; *The Concept of Irony*, pp. 146, 188, 195, 204–8, 210, 217–21, 223–25, 249–50, 252–53, 277–78, 287–88, 318–19; *Either/Or*, I, pp. 33, 86, 138–40, 147; II, 7, 19–20, 70, 91, 154–55, 244–45, 259–61, 266, 295, 309, 327, 333–34, 342, 356; *Fear and Trembling*, pp. 65–69, 72–73, 78–81, 84–85, 103; *Upbuilding* [*Edifying*] *Discourses*, I, pp. 98–99; III, pp. 97–98; IV, pp. 17–18; *The Concept of Anxiety* [*Dread*], p. 99; *Stages*, pp. 121, 167, 346, 373–74; *Postscript*, pp. 49, 277–78, 444, 281–82, 484–85, 486, 536–37, 543, 548; *Two Ages* [of which *The Present Age* is a part], passim; *Upbuilding Discourses in Various Spirits*, Part One [*Purity of Heart*], pp. 66, 130, 205–6; *Works of Love*, pp. 137–38, 255–56, 273, 350, 352; *Christian Discourses*, pp. 17, 22, 47–48; *Two Minor Ethical-Religious Essays* [*Treatises*], with *The Present Age*, pp. 92–94, 102, 150–53; *The Sickness unto Death*, pp. 179, 210, 249; *Practice* [*Training*] *in Christianity*, pp. 49–51, 52–53; *An Open Letter* and *Armed Neutrality*, 49–51, 53; *Judge for Yourselves!*, pp. 9–15; *On My Work as an Author*, with *The Point of View*, pp. 162–64; ibid., pp. 55–56, 60–62, 109–10, 112–22, 128–32; articles in *Fædrelandet*, no. 76, March 30, 1855, no. 83, April 11, 1855, in *Attack*, pp. 34, 43–44; *This Has To Be Said*, ibid., pp. 63–64; *The Moment*, no. 1, no. 2, no. 3, ibid., pp. 79, 83–86, 97, 99–100, 102–4, 127.

359. *Tidsskrift for udenlandsk theologisk Litteratur*, ed. H. N. Clausen and M. H. Hohlenberg, 1835.

360. 1834.

361. In Norse mythology the "tree of the world" was an ash tree named Ygdrasill, the top of which is the heavens and the three roots the realms of men, giants, and the dead.

362. See Suetonius, *The Lives of the Caesars*, IV, "Caligula," XXX: "Angered at the rabble for applauding a faction which he opposed, he cried, 'I wish the Roman people had but a single neck.' " See *Either/Or*, II, p. 192.

363. Presumably Kierkegaard has in mind Henrich Steffens' *Karikaturen des Heiligisten* (*ASKB* 793–94), in which political ideas are interpreted as caricatures of religious and Christian ideas.

364. Chiliasm or millennialism, the expectation of Christ's return to reign for 1,000 years; therefore here a political utopianism.

365. In Norse mythology, Balder, whom all loved, was killed by a spur of mistletoe hurled by the blind god Høder, who had been deceived by Loki.

366. See *Justinus Martyrs Apologier eller Forsvarsskrifter for Christendommen*, tr. C. H. Muus (Copenhagen: 1836), "The First Apology," ch. 26, p. 36. *ASKB* 141. Simon Magus, early first century A.D., a Samaritan worker of magical wonders and reputed to be a god. "And they call a certain Helena, who was his traveling companion at that time, and had formerly been a prostitute, the first idea generated from him."

367. Belonging to constitutional law, also belonging to the public domain, commonly known. This entry is Kierkegaard's first critical note against "the public," "the crowd." Later in the *Corsair* affair he likens *The Corsair* to a public prostitute (see "The Dialectical Result of a Literary Police-Operation," *Fædrelandet*, no. 9, January 10, 1846; *S.V.*, XIII, p. 434.

368. Walter von Have-nothing.

369. T. C. Croker, *Irische Elfenmärchen*, tr. J. and W. Grimm (Leipzig: 1826), p. xxxvii. *ASKB* 1423. See *The Concept of Irony*, p. 180.

370. *"Die kluge Else"* ("Clever Else"), J. and W. Grimm, *Kinder- und Haus-Märchen*, I-III (Berlin: 2 ed., 1819-22), I, pp. 173 ff. *ASKB* 1425-27. The story centers around the consequences of a series of imagined conditions or "if" clauses. Except for a reference in *The Concept of Anxiety* [*Dread*], p. 45, no use of the story is found in the works or the papers.

371. See article *"Om Almeenaand"* ("On Public Spirit") in *Kjøbenhavns Posten*, 239-40, August 28, September 1, 1838.

372. See *"Aabenbart Skriftemaal,"* *Fædrelandet*, no. 904, June 12, 1842; *S.V.*, XIII, p. 403; *Repetition*, p. 137.

373. *"Der Schneider im Himmel,"* J. and W. Grimm, *Kinder-und Haus-Märchen*, I-III (2 ed., Berlin: 1819), I, pp. 177 ff. *ASKB* 1425-27. See *Fear and Trembling*, p. 131.

374. See *Fragments*, pp. 65, 67; TERTULLIAN.

375. Wilhelm M. L. de Wette, *Lærebog i den Christelige Sædelære og Sammes Historie*, tr. Carl E. Scharling (Copenhagen: 1835), p. 215. *ASKB* 871. The quotation is from Lactantius but it comes right after a reference to Tertullian.

376. From draft of *Either/Or*. See II, p. 7.

377. From draft of *Either/Or*. See II, pp. 87-88. This omitted portion preceded the first sentence on p. 88.

378. Flavious Philostratus *des Aeltern*, *Werke*, tr. F. Jakobs, books I-V in one vol. (Stuttgart: 1821-32). *ASKB* 1143.

379. C. Suetonii Tranquilli, *Tolv første romerske Keiseres Levnets Beskrivelse*, tr. J. Baden (Copenhagen: 1802). *ASKB* 1281. A collapsing of elements has taken place here. Suetonius, "Tiberius," *The Lives of the Caesars*, III, p. 58, reads: ". . . this kind of accusation gradually went so far that even such acts as these were regarded as capital crimes: to beat a slave near a statue of Augustus, or to change one's clothes there; to carry a ring or a coin stamped with this image into a privy or a brothel. . . ."

380. Should be *Politics*, bk. V, ch. 10; *Die Politik Aristoteles*, tr. Christian Garve, I-II (Breslau: 1799), I, pp. 460 ff. *ASKB* 1088-89.

381. See note 378.

382. On January 1, 1843, Kierkegaard bought *Cassius Dios Romische Geschichte*, tr. L. Tafel, I-XIII in 3 vols. (Stuttgart: 1831-38). *ASKB* 1098-1100.

383. See note 379.
384. See *Fragments*, p. 5.
385. See *Theologiske Tidsskrift. Ny Række*, ed. Scharling and Engelstoft, II, 2, 1844, pp. 350 ff.; *Fædrelandet*, 1666, August 27, 1844; *Prefaces, S.V.*, V. p. 17.
386. "*Det astronomiske Aar,*" *Urania Aarbog for 1844*, ed. J. L. Heiberg (Copenhagen: 1843), p. 122.
387. See, for example, Aristotle, *Categories* I, 5, 2 a, b.
388. See Aristotle, *Rhetoric*, I, 1, 1354 a, b, 1355 a; *Postscript*, p. 185 n.
389. See *Two Ages* [*The Present Age*], p. 28.
390. This triangular relational pattern is the central theme of *Works of Love*.
391. See *Postscript*, p. 383.
392. *Zeitschrift für Philosophie und spekulative Philosophie*, ed. J. H. Fichte (Tübingen). Relation, reference, unity.
393. *Kiøbenhavnsposten*, no. 122, May 30, 1846; see also ibid., no. 124, June 2, no. 126, June 4, and no. 134, June 13, 1846.
394. Henrich Steffens, *Nachgelassene Schriften. Mit einem Vorworte von Schelling* (Berlin: 1846), p. xivii. *ASKB* 799.
395. Possibly a reference to *Fædrelandet*, no. 97, April 26, 1847; see also ibid., no. 82, April 9, 1847, and *Berlingske Tidende*, no. 94, April 24, 1847.
396. On the disturbances because of food scarcity and high prices, see *Fædrelandet*, no. 96, April 24, 1847 (about Berlin), no. 99, April 28 (about Paris), no. 100, April 29 (about a number of Prussian cities), no. 102, May 3 (about Odense, Denmark), no. 109, May 11 (the expression "bread-riots" used in connection with a number of German cities), no. 113, May 17 (about Flensborg, a Danish city at that time), no. 121, May 27 (about "bread-riots" in Ghent).
397. Menenius (Menius) Agrippa, Roman consul in 502 B.C., was sent by the senate to the plebeians who had "seceded" and had gone up the "sacred mountain." He persuaded them to return by telling the parable of "The Belly and the Limbs." See Livy, II, 32 (l. 2: "*in sacrum montem secessisse*").
398. Kierkegaard's criticism of Grundtvig's cultural nationalism centering upon the mother-tongue does not preclude his own praise of the Danish language (see *Stages*, pp. 440–41; *Two Discourses at the Communion on Fridays*, with *Judge For Yourselves!*, Preface, p. 5).
399. R. T. Fenger, "*Religionsunderviisningen og Folkeskolen,*" *Dansk Kirketidende*, ed. R. T. Fenger and C. J. Brandt, II, no. 95, July 18, 1847. *ASKB* 321–25.
400. See *Works of Love*, pp. 306–8.
401. Ibid., pp. 292–305.
402. See Rasmus T. Fenger, "*En Udflugt til Skaane,*" *Dansk Kirke-*

tidende, ed. R. T. Fenger and C. J. Brandt, III, no. 4, October 24, 1847. *ASKB* 321-25.

403. A drinking song by Zetliz in *Seidelins Visebog eller Danske Selskabssange* (Copenhagen: 1821).

404. The reference here is to the fear and hysteria aroused by the German nationalist threat in Slesvig (German: Schleswig) and Holsten (German: Holstein), which were Danish dukedoms. See note 411.

405. Part 3 of *Upbuilding Discourses in Various Spirits.* See *The Gospel of Suffering,* pp. 144-46.

406. See pp. 237-38.

407. The allusion is presumably to a crowd-demonstration before Christiansborg on March 21, 1848, followed by a change in the form of government.

408. The crowd. See note 407.

409. See note 407.

410. See note 407.

411. "Nationality" refers to the "Slesvig (German: Schleswig) question." The National Liberals in Denmark (Hvidt, Lehmann) wanted the Duchy of Slesvig separated from the Duchy of Holsten (German: Holstein), which was German-oriented, and placed directly under Denmark through a new constitution. This move led to warfare (1848-50). See VIII[1] A 531, 609, 618.

412. Anton F. Tscherning (1795-1874), who became Minister of War, March 24, 1848, as part of the new government.

413. See notes 404, 411.

414. Ibid.

415. See note 407.

416. Ibid.

417. See note 407.

418. Peter Jacob Mynster, Bishop of Sjælland.

419. Ditlev G. Monrad (1811-87), theologian and liberal journalist, became head of the ministry of education and church affairs in March, 1848.

420. See notes 404, 411.

421. See *Tausend und eine Nacht,* tr. Gustav Weil, I-IV (Stuttgart, Pforzheim, 1838-41), III, p. 924. *ASKB* 1414-17.

422. The text is not clear, but it seems to read *"M. ell.,"* i.e., *"Menneske eller"* (man or).

423. Kierkegaard has in mind here a monarch who is tyrannical, not the ancient and modern tyrant who has gained power through demagoguery.

424. See Genesis 37 and 46.

425. See Plato, *Apology,* 28, 29, 74.

426. See Revelation 13:18.

427. See John 19:6, 15.

428. See Luke 23:46.

429. On Easter day, April 23, 1848, the Prussians made a successful attack on the Danes in the Danish Duchy of Holsten.

430. May 19, 1848, in Frelserens Kirke.

431. See note 407.

432. See *Two Ages* [*The Present Age*], pp. 21–28.

433. Meïr Goldschmidt, editor of *Corsaren (The Corsair)*, an intimidating, satirical, rumor-mongering periodical which only Kierkegaard dared call to account (see XI^2 A 85; and *Journals and Papers,* V).

434. See *Fædrelandet,* no. 272, October 25, 1848.

435. This curious phrase is drawn from Holberg's comedy, *Erasmus Montanus,* act III, sc. 3, in which Peer Degn, thinking that *Imprimatur* is a person rather than the third person passive form of a verb, asks "Who is *Imprimatur?*" See *The Concept of Anxiety* [*Dread*], p. 6; *Postscript,* p. 34.

436. See Matthew 22:20.

437. See Luke 14:26.

438. See Isaiah 53:5.

439. Most likely a reference to the *Corsair* affair. See note 433.

440. See John 11:50.

441. One might have expected Kierkegaard to use "subject" here rather than "object" [*Gjenstand*]. Objectively viewed, each human being is an object, but Kierkegaard maintains that each one is a "prodigious object," because he is intended to become an authentic subject and is not simply an object in the "appalling objectivity" with which men are customarily viewed by others and sometimes also by themselves.

442. See Plato, *Apology,* 34.

443. See Matthew 19:21.

444. See Genesis 2:18; for the expression as given here, see S.B. Hersleb, *Lærebog i Bibelhistorien* (Copenhagen: 3 ed., 1826), p. 3. *ASKB* 186.

445. The world wants to be deceived. See note 1241.

446. Andreas G. Rudelbach, *Den evangeliske Kirkeforfatnings Oprindelse og Princip* . . . (Copenhagen: 1849). *ASKB* 171. See *An Open Letter* and *Armed Neutrality,* pp. 30–32 (introduction), 47–55 (text), 104–25 (entries from the *Papirer* pertaining to Dr. Rudelbach) and 137–42 (commentary).

447. See Luke 18:11.

448. Christ is not a "preformation" or exemplar of collectives but rather of authentic individual persons.

449. The reference is presumably to Rasmus Nielsen, professor of philosophy, University of Copenhagen. His book *Evangelietroen og den moderne Bevidsthed* (*ASKB* 700) was published in May, 1849.

450. See *Dansk Kirketidende,* November 19, 1848, May 13, 1849, July 8, 1849, IV, col. 132 ff. 537 ff., 562–63, 688.

451. *S.V.,* VIII, pp. 98–102; *The Present Age* (part of *Two Ages, A Literary Review*), pp. 69–70, omits all but one paragraph of the concluding portion.

452. See *The Concept of Anxiety* [*Dread*], pp. 135–37, on artistic and intellectual approaches to the eternal.

453. Nicolai F. S. Grundtvig, contemporary poet, pastor, and politician of great influence.

454. See I Corinthians 9:25.

455. See *The Sickness unto Death*, p. 249.

456. See *Two Ages* [*The Present Age*], pp. 27–47.

457. See *Berlingske Tidende*, no. 31, 1850 (on the meeting of February 6), no. 36, 1850 (on the meeting of February 12).

458. Peter Christian Kierkegaard (1805–88), pastor, elected to Parliament December, 1849, named Bishop of Aalborg in 1856 and Minister of Ecclesiastical Affairs and Public Instruction in 1867.

459. Outside of oneself, beside oneself.

460. Brocken, a peak in the Harz Mountains, the site of *Walpurgisnacht*, the Witches' Sabbath. See, for example, Goethe's *Faust*, I, 21.

461. Unconnected members, fragments.

462. Johan L. Heiberg (1791–1860), poet, dramatist, esthetician, philosopher, foremost Danish exponent of Hegelian philosophy, and the leading Danish intellectual in the 1840's and 1850's.

463. A Copenhagen newspaper founded in 1834 as a weekly, changed to a daily in 1840 with Professor C. N. David, J. F. Giødvad, and Orla Lehman as editors, strong proponent of Danish nationalism and the National Liberal Party politics.

464. See notes 404, 411, 429.

465. A Copenhagen newspaper founded in 1854 by E. Meyer with the support of political conservatives and other opponents of the National Liberal Party policies.

466. See note 432.

467. Ibid., pp. 88–89.

468. Ibid., pp. 91–93.

469. Kierkegaard most likely has in mind his experience in the *Corsair* affair.

470. See Numbers 11:11–17.

471. Relating what is told [to them].

472. See, for example, *Fragments*, pp. 30–42.

473. See Matthew 22:21.

474. Peter Michael Stilling (1812–69), assistant professor (*Privat Docent*) in philosophy, University of Copenhagen.

475. Published September 27, 1850.

476. François Guizot, French politician and historian. In 1850 his *Discourse sur la Révolution d'Angleterre* appeared. See *Berlingske Tidende*, no. 294. December 16, 1850.

477. See Romans 13:1.

478. Eggert Christopher Tryde (1781–1860), pastor (including Glumsø-Bavelse), Dean of Vor Frue Kirke, 1838–60, considerably involved in ecclesiastical-political affairs along with H. N. Clausen, A. S. Ørsted, N. F. S. Grundtvig, and others.
479. See *Armed Neutrality* and *An Open Letter*, pp. 37–38, 51.
480. See *Two Ages* [*The Present Age*], pp. 63–66.
481. By concession; on the basis of what has been conceded by the opponent.
482. See *Fragments*, p. 7.
483. *Benjamin Franklin's Leben und Schriften*, tr. ed. A. Binzer, I-IV (Kiel: 1829). *ASKB* 1871–72.
484. Ibid., I, p. 94, freely rendered by Kierkegaard.
485. Ibid., I, p. 103.
486. Immanuel H. Fichte, *System der Ethik*, I-II$^{1-2}$ (Leipzig: 1850–53), I, p. 608. *ASKB* 510–11. Fraternal love is suddenly proclaimed as an equalizing, revolutionary force: a strange self-contradiction!
487. See Hans Christian Andersen, *"Lykkens Galoscher"* ("The Galoshes of Fortune"), V, in which Kierkegaard is satirized as a parrot: "The only human sounds that the parrot could bawl out were, 'Come, let us be men!' Everything else that he said was as unintelligible to everybody as the chirping of the canary. . . ."
488. J. P. Mynster, Bishop of Sjælland and thereby primate of the Church in Denmark. Kierkegaard's chief criticism of this old family friend was that he represented and fostered an accommodation of Christianity and the Church to the current cultural and also political interests.
489. See note 446.
490. See note 28.
491. Alexander R. Vinet, *Der Sozialismus in seinem Princip betrachtet*, tr. D. Hofmeister (Berlin: 1849). *ASKB* 874.
492. Andreas G. Rudelbach, *Om det Borgerlige Ægteskab* (Copenhagen: 1851), p. 70. *ASKB* 752. See *An Open Letter* and *Armed Neutrality*, pp. 47–55.
493. Professor Hans L. Martensen, later Bishop Mynster's successor.
494. See note 491.
495. Wilhelm Carl E. Sponneck (1815–88), financier and politician, minister of finance November 16, 1848–December 12, 1854.
496. See *Berlingske Tidende*, no. 276, November 26, 1851.
497. Restoration to an earlier state. See note 939.
498. *Friedrich Schlegel's sämmtliche Werke*, I-X (Vienna: 1822). *ASKB* 1816–25.
499. Euripides, *The Phoenician Women*, ll. 524–25.
500. See Hebrews 12:5.
501. *For Self-Examination*, p. [i].
502. See *Upbuilding Discourses in Various Spirits*, Part Three [*The Gospel of*

Suffering, pp. 145-46]; "Has a Man the Right to Let Himself Be Put to Death for the Truth?" with *The Present Age*, p. 129; *On My Work as an Author*, with *The Point of View*, p. 164.

503. Push, preoccupation.

504. Jacob Peter Mynster (1775-1854), Bishop of Sjælland (including Copenhagen) 1834-54 and friend of the M. P. Kierkegaard family.

505. See note 456.

506. See *Either/Or*, I, p. 284; Aristotle, *Politics*, I, 1, 9.

507. For similar metaphors, see *For Self-Examination*, pp. 101-3; *Judge for Yourselves!*, pp. 123-25.

508. Plato, *Republic*, VII, 520 d, 521 b.

509. See *Fædrelandet*, no. 232, October 5, 1854.

510. Literally, cat-yowling; the morning-after misery.

511. On a large scale.

512. On the idea that one is not a number, that counting and number begin with two, see IV A 38, 57.

513. Yes, that is something else.

514. As much as nothing; [amounts] to nothing.

515. If it so pleases, or if it may be put this way, or if it may be called that.

516. See Judges 15:3-5.

517. See G. W. F. Hegel, *Grundlinien der Philosophie des Rechts* (Berlin: 1833), para. 105-360, especially 257-58. *ASKB* 551.

518. *The Concept of Irony*, pp. 249-50.

519. Plato, *Republic*, II, 368 c-e; *Platons Stat*, I-III, tr. Carl J. Heise (Copenhagen: 1831), I, pp. 94-95. *ASKB* 1167.

520. See *Fragments*, p. 5.

521. See note 515.

SOCRATES

In a journal entry from 1843 (IV A 43) Søren Kierkegaard tells about "a young man, as favorably endowed as an Alcibiades," who "lost his way in the world" and in distress looked around for a Socrates, but when he found none among his contemporaries "he implored the gods to change him into one." No doubt this story refers to Kierkegaard's own situation; in any case Socrates (469-399 B.C.) was the man to whom Kierkegaard felt most closely related intellectually-spiritually and with whom he had an "inexplicable rapport" at "a very early age" (X^5 A 104).

There are similarities between Kierkegaard and Socrates at several essential points. Both made their appearance in an "age of disintegration," which impelled them to seek the true point of departure for human existence. Both concentrated on self-knowledge and introspection rather than on the external, physical world. Both were very interested in conversing with their fellow men in order to gain insight into the deepest motives for men's actions. Kierkegaard also tried to realize in his own thinking what he says of Socrates—that he knew how to think "one thought all the way through" (VI A 15). He also believed that Socrates in particular could teach him something about the art of communication (see, for example, VIII^2 B 89), an art Kierkegaard subsequently developed to perfection. And just as he called Socrates "the only world-historical philosopher of life" who ever lived, so for a later age Kierkegaard became the thinker who concentrated most of all on the life-problems of man. These similarities justify calling Kierkegaard Christianity's Socrates, for just as Socrates tried to make men aware of the highest truth in paganism, Kierkegaard tried to make men aware of Christianity.

It is also significant that just as Kierkegaard used the stages to describe his own intellectual-spiritual development, he also attempted to apply the same pattern to Socrates. With this in mind, in *The Concept of Irony* he painstakingly and one-sidedly depicts only Socrates' first position, the standpoint of irony. Climacus later comments that Magister Kierkegaard consciously or unconsciously brings out only "the one side" (*Postscript*, p. 449).

The next stage is mentioned in *Either/Or*, where Judge William speaks of Socrates' "ethical view" (II, p. 244) and his attempt to develop "the personal virtues" by which he becomes an ethicist.

In *Philosophical Fragments* Socrates is used as an example of the highest human knowledge, inasmuch as through introspection he arrives at "recollection" and "knowledge of God" (p. 14). With this the religious factor emerges as basis for the ethical in addition to recollection.

In *Concluding Unscientific Postscript* Socrates is represented as the supreme example within a human philosophy of life. His "inward passion to exist," that is, his attempt to actualize the ethical truth he discovered, is seen as an "analogue to faith" (p. 185 fn.).

In addition to a depiction of Socrates' various positions in Kierkegaard's doctoral dissertation and pseudonymous works, we find that he has used Socrates many places in his upbuilding literature, where he is most frequently called "that simple wise man of antiquity" or something similar. Here Socrates as the representative of the highest form of ethical internalizing in paganism is considered in relation to Christianity's ethical and religious demand. This is frequently done to show that in Christendom men can learn much from Socrates' understanding of existence. But throughout all his writings, the upbuilding literature as well, Kierkegaard affirms the qualitative difference between what we can learn from Socrates and what Christ gives to the individual. He mentions this distinction as early as the first thesis in his dissertation: "The similarity between Christ and Socrates consists essentially in dissimilarity" (p. 349). In his *Christian Discourses* (p. 245) he describes in a poignant and personal way this dissimilarity between the two figures. First of all Kierkegaard says of his own relation to Socrates: "I have admired—to pick out one who most certainly, humanly speaking, stands second to none in the world, and is usually brought into the closest relation to Christianity—that noble, simple wise man of antiquity. While reading about him my heart has beat as violently as the heart of that young man when he spoke with him; the thought of him has been my youthful inspiration and has imbued my soul. . . ." But in comparison with Christ, Socrates must take a back seat, and Kierkegaard says, among other things: "As soon as I consider the matter of my salvation, then that simple wise man is to me a person of utmost indifference, a sheer negligibility, a mere nothing" (pp. 245-46, ed. tr.).

Croxall, T. H. "Christ, Socrates, and Hegel," in *Kierkegaard Commentary*, ch. 12–13. London, New York: Harper, 1956.

Diem, Hermann. "The Socratic Paradox: Preliminary Provisional Account of the Dialectical Method," in *Kierkegaard's Dialectic of Existence*, trans. Harold Knight, ch. 10. Edinburgh and London: Oliver and Boyd, 1959.

Dunne, Mary R. "Kierkegaard and Socratic Ignorance: a Study of a Philosophy in Relation to Christianity." Ph.D. dissertation, Notre Dame, 1969.

Hess, M. Whitcomb. "Kierkegaard and Socrates." *The Christian Century*, 82, 1965, pp. 736–38.

Holder, F. L. "Advance Beyond Socrates." *Encounter*, 31, Summer 1970, pp. 235–40.

Levi, A. W. "Socrates in the Nineteenth Century." *Journal of the History of Ideas*, 17, January 1956, pp. 104–6.

Neumann, Harry. "Kierkegaard and Socrates on the Dignity of Man." *Personalist*, 48, 1967, pp. 453–60.

Perkins, Robert L. "Two Nineteenth Century Interpretations of Socrates: Hegel and Kierkegaard." *Kierkegaard-Studiet*, International Edition (Osaka, Japan), 5, 1968, pp. 9–14.

Sontag, Frederick. "Existentialism: Greek Ethics and the Way Back to the Future: a Note." *The Thomist*, 34, April 1970, pp. 306–10.

Swenson, David. "Søren Kierkegaard—a Danish Socrates," in *Something about Kierkegaard*, ch. 2. Minneapolis: Augsburg, 1951.

Trentman, John Allen. "Kierkegaard's Interpretation, on the Socratic-ethical Theory." M.A. thesis, Minnesota, 1958.

Warner, D. H. J. "The Dialectic of Existence in Kierkegaard, with Particular Reference to Socrates." B. Litt. thesis, Oxford, Magdalen, 1956.

Weiss, Raymond L. "Kierkegaard's 'Return' to Socrates." *The New Scholasticism*, 45, Autumn 1971, pp. 573–83.

For references in the works to Socrates, see *From the Papers of One Still Living, S.V.*, XIII, pp. 6, 89; *The Concept of Irony, with constant Reference to Socrates*, passim; *Fear and Trembling*, pp. 79, 92, 110, 126–27; *Repetition*, p. 67; *The Concept of Anxiety* [*Dread*], pp. 2–3, 15, 61, 63, 74–75, 85, 99, 120, 143, 145; *Prefaces, S.V.*, XIII, pp. 45–46, 48; *Upbuilding* [*Edifying*] *Discourses*, IV, p. 60; *Three Discourses on Imagined Occasions* [*Thoughts on Crucial Situations*], p. 40; *Stages*, pp. 63, 65, 67, 75, 122, 154–55, 157, 210, 292, 335, 377, 379, 398, 426, 427, 434–35; *Postscript*, pp.

2, 34, 37, 50, 65, 74, 76–77, 81–83, 85, 95, 131–32, 144, 163, 180, 183–88, 197, 221–22, 242, 247, 253–54, 276, 281, 291, 297, 329, 342, 409, 419, 449, 450 fn., 464 fn., 491 fn., 495, 502, 543; *Two Ages, S.V.* XIII, pp. 32 [*The Present Age*], 20, 48–49, 68; *Upbuilding Discourses in Various Spirits*, Part One [*Purity of Heart*, pp. 70, 144–45, 191–92, 212]; *Works of Love*, pp. 103, 131, 171, 219, 257–58, 338, 341–42; *Christian Discourses*, pp. 19, 29, 108, 225, 245–46, 264; "Has a Man the Right to Let Himself Be Put to Death for the Truth?" with *The Present Age*, pp. 114, 122; *The Sickness unto Death*, pp. 193, 218–27, 230; *Practice* [*Training*] *in Christianity*, pp. 11, 68, 89; *For Self-Examination*, pp. 1–2; "A Passing Comment on a Detail in *Don Juan*," with *The Crisis* [*and a Crisis*] *in the Life of an Actress*, p. 95; *The Point of View*, pp.109, 138, 139–40; *The Moment*, no. 6, no. 10, in *Attack*, pp. 186, 188, 283–84; *The Unchangeableness of God*, with *Judge for Yourselves!*, p. 229.

522. *Tidsskrift for udenlandsk theologisk Litteratur*, ed. H. N. Clausen and M. H. Hohlenberg, V, 1837. *ASKB* 429.

523. Ferdinand C. Baur, *Das Christliche des Platonismus oder Sokrates und Christus* (Tübingen: 1837). *ASKB* 422. See *The Concept of Irony*, pp. 51–52.

524. See note 522, ibid., p. 485.

525. See HUMOR, especially II A 75, 78, 102.

526. Entry is from papers related to *The Concept of Irony*.

527. The principle of the excluded middle between two contradictories.

528. The page reference to the *Phaedrus* (265 e–266 b) is to *Platonis quæ exstant Opera*, tr. F. Ast, I–IX (Leipzig: 1819–32). *ASKB* 1144–54.

529. The page reference to the *Protagoras* (322 a-c) is to *Udvalgte Dialoger af Platon*, tr. C. J. Heise, I–III (Copenhagen: 1830–38), II. *ASKB* 1164–66.

530. The page references to the *Republic* (436 b ff.) are to *Platons Werke*, tr. F. Schleiermacher, I$^{1-2}$, II$^{1-3}$, III^{1} (Berlin: 1817–28), III. *ASKB* 1158–63.

531. See note 526.

532. The page reference to the *Crito* (52 b) is to Heyse's translation, volume I. See note 529 for edition.

533. The page reference to the *Phædrus* (230 c-d) is to Ast's translation. See note 529 for edition.

534. H. T. Rötscher, *Aristophanes und sein Zeitalter* (Berlin: 1826).

535. J. W. Suvern, *Ueber Aristophanes Wolken* (Berlin: 1826).

536. See note 534.

537. P. W. Forchammer, *Die Athener und Sokrates, die Gesetzlichen und der Revolutionär* (Berlin: 1837).

538. See Plutarch, *Moralia, De cohibenda ira*, 461 d-e; IX A 363. Kierkegaard had a number of Plutarch editions: *Plutarchi varia scripta*, I–VI (Leipzig: 1829), *ASKB* 1172–77; *Plutarchs Werke*, tr. J. C. F. Baur (Stuttgart: 1828), *ASKB* 1178–80; *Plutarchi vitæ parallelæ*, I–IX (Leipzig: 1829), *ASKB* 1181–89; *Plutarchs Werke*, tr. J. G. Klaiber and C. F. Baur, I–II (Stuttgart: 2 ed., 1828–30), *ASKB* 1190–91; *Plutarchs moralische Abhandlungen*, tr. J. F. S. Kaltwasser, I–V (Frankfurt am

Main: 1783–93), *ASKB* 1192–96; *Plutarks Levnetsbeskrivelser,* tr. S. Tetens, I-IV (Copenhagen: 1800–11). Kierkegaard's reference presumably is to one of these editions, not all of which have been available to the editors.

539. Theodor Heinsius, *Sokrates nach dem Grade seiner Schuld zum Schutz gegen neuere Verunglimpfung* (Leipzig: 1839).

540. *Diogin Laertses filosofiske Historie,* tr. B. Riisbrigh, I-II (Copenhagen: 1811–12), I, p. 71. *ASKB* 1110–11.

541. Prattler, babbler.

542. *Plutarks Levnetbeskrivelser,* tr. Stephan Tetens, I-IV (Copenhagen: 1800–1811). *ASKB* 1197–1200. Entries IV A 199–212 are Kierkegaard's handwritten notations in a copy of *The Concept of Irony* (Copenhagen: 1841).

543. Plutarch, *Moralia,* "On the Sign of Socrates," 589 e; *Postscript,* p. 131 fn.

544. Wilhelm G. Tennemann, *Geschichte der Philosophie,* I-VIII$^{1-2}$, XI (Leipzig: 1798–1819). *ASKB* 815–26.

545. D. *Imperatoris M. Antonin: Commentariorum qvos sibi ispsi scripsit libri* XII (Leipzig: facsc. ed., 1820). *ASKB* 1218. German translation by J. M. Schultz, *Marc. Aurel. Antonin's Unterhaltungen mit sich selbst* (Schleswig: 1799). *ASKB* 1219.

546. See note 540.

547. Presumably "Agesilaus II," note J, in Bayle, *Historisches und Kritisches Wörterbuch,* tr. J. C. Gottscheden, I-IV (Leipzig: 1741–44), I, p. 95. *ASKB* 1961–64.

548. See note 530; ibid., II^3, p. 292. On the interpretation see ibid., pp. 296–97.

549. Carl F. Flögel, *Geschichte der komischen Literatur,* I-IV (Liegnitz, Leipzig: 1784–87). *ASKB* 1396–99.

550. Aristotle, *Rhetorik,* tr. K. L. Roth (Stuttgart: 1833). *ASKB* 1092. This constitutes vols. 1 and 2 of *Aristoteles Werke,* tr. von Zell, Roth, and Walz [and Sprengel], I-X (Stuttgart: 1833–41).

551. Kierkegaard usually omits an "e" in the spelling of Trendelenburg.

552. *ASKB* 845.

553. 107 d, 108 c.

554. See note 550.

555. See note 545. "This volume" refers to the copy of *The Concept of Irony* in which this entry and others are found. See note 542.

556. See note 549.

557. *The Frogs,* ll. 1491–94. The quotation is a translation of the Danish version by J. Krag, *Aristophanes's Komedier,* I (Odense: 1825), p. 118. *ASKB* 1055.

558. Ibid., p. 271. Kierkegaard quotes Krag's translation directly. Lines 1075–79 in the Loeb edition of Aristophanes' *The Wasps* do not refer to these evils; however, in the section referring to *The Clouds* mention is made

(l. 1039) of "the Agues and Fevers that plagued our land" and thereafter specifics such as "welding together proofs and writs and oath against oath" (l. 1042), "idle knaves" (l. 1119).

559. Ameipsias, Athenian comic writer, was the author of *Konnos* (423 B.C.), which placed second in competition and above *The Clouds*. Socrates is a character in the play. Konnos was a harpist who taught Socrates (see *Euthydemus*, 272 c) and is the name of a dissolute musician in Aristophanes' *The Knights* and *The Wasps*. Eupolis, a tragic poet mentioned in Aristophanes' *The Frogs*, l. 14, and in *The Clouds*, ll. 553-54, was regarded in antiquity as one of the three greatest Old Comedy writers.

560. See note 558.
561. Plutarch, *Lives*, "Marcus Cato," ch. 23. See note 542.
562. See note 542; ibid., III, p. 327.
563. See note 530; *The Concept of Irony*, p. 143.
564. See Plato, *Apology*, 28 d.
565. Entry written in a copy of *Fire Opbyggelige Taler* (1844), bottom of p. 60 (p. 127 in *S.V.*, V and p. 79 in *Upbuilding [Edifying] Discourses*, IV).
566. Marginal note in draft of *Fragments*, p. 29, ll. 25 ff.
567. From draft of *Fragments*, p. 127, ll. 25 ff.
568. See Christian Bredahl, "*Fragmenter af 4. og 5. Act af Sokrates,*" in *Gæa* 1846, ed. P. L. Møller, pp. 51 ff.
569. See Plato, *Apology*, 30 e; *Works of Love*, p. 131.
570. See *Fragments*, p. 14.
571. Ibid., pp. 28-30.
572. See *The Concept of Irony*, pp. 91-94.
573. See *Two Ages, S.V.*, VIII, p. 10.
574. See note 569.
575. Ibid.
576. See Plato, *Phaedo*, 115 c.
577. See Plato, *Symposium*, 216 d; *The Sickness unto Death*, pp. 192-93.
578. See note 504.
579. See note 222.
580. See Plato, *Republic*, 600 e, 605 a-c, 608 a; *Gorgias* 502 b-e.
581. The source of this dialogue has not been located.
582. See Plato, *Apology*, 83-89.
583. See Plato, *Apology*, the entire dialogue, particularly 34-38.
584. Totality.
585. *C. M. Wielands sämmtliche Werke*, I-XLIX, 6 supp. vols. (Leipzig: 1784-1802), XXXIV.
586. See note 765.
587. See *The Sickness unto Death*, pp. 218-27.
588. See Galatians 6:14.
589. See *The Concept of Irony*, pp. 251-53.

590. Danish: *numerisk*. In *The Concept of Irony* (p. 251) the issue is the universal "in opposition to the particular" or the individual, which is the meaning here of "numerically," individuals who as particular persons are integers in their individuality.

591. Plato, *Republic*, 487 c ff., especially 489 d; *Platons Stat*, tr. C. J. Heise, I–III (Copenhagen: 1831), II, p. 86 ff., especially p. 91. *ASKB* 1167.

592. See *For Self-Examination*, pp. 1–2; Diogenes Laertius, *The Lives and Opinions of Eminent Philosophers*, II, 40–41; see note 540, ibid., I, p. 74.

593. Plato, *Phaedrus* 230 d.

594. Wherefore we ought to fly away from earth to heaven as quickly as we can; and to fly away is to become like God, as far as this is possible ... *Theaetetus*, 176 a.

595. Christoph Meiners, *Allgemeine kritische Geschicte der ältern Ethik und neuern Ethik*, I-II (Göttingen: 1800–1801). *ASKB* 675–76.

596. *Apologia Socratis*, especially para. 5 ff.

597. *Tusculanæ Disputationes*, I, 96; reference is to Theramenes, but see also 71 and 97 ff.

598. Plato, *Phaedo* 117 b-c.

599. Claudius Aelianus, *Werke*, I-IX, in *Griechische Prosaiker* (Stuttgart: 1839–42), III, pp. 318–19. *ASKB* 1043. The painter was Pauson.

600. See Plato, *Apology*, 24 b, 26 b–27; *Crito* 54 b.

601. See Plato, *Apology*, 37 a–b.

602. Plato, *Apology*, 23 b–c; see 31 b–c.

603. See note 504.

604. See note 28; ibid II^1, p. 527.

605. The Danish for "crusade" is *Korstog* and for "cross" is *Kors;* the two English words have the same Latin root *crux*, but this is obscured in the English spellings.

606. See note 587.

607. See Luke 23:34.

608. See note 587.

609. See note 28; ibid., I^3, pp. 322–24.

610. See Plato, *Symposium* 215 d-e. See *Fragments*, p. 29; *Christian Discourses*, p. 245. The translation here is from the Danish, which is close to but not precisely the same as C. J. Heise's translation. See Platon, *Udvalgte Dialoger*, I-VIII (Copenhagen: 1830–1859), II, pp. 104–5. *ASKB* 1164–66 lists vols. I-III (1830–38). Kierkegaard also had Plato in Greek: *Platonis quae exstant opera*, ed. F. Astius, I-IX (Leipzig: 1819–32). *ASKB* 1144–54.

611. Adam Oehlenschläger, *Sokrates* (Copenhagen: 1836).

612. See *Postscript*, pp. 16, 46–47, 219 fn., 222, 361, 389–99.

613. "*Über eine zeitige Aufgabe,*" Gotthold Ephraim Lessing's *Sämmtliche Schriften*, I-XXXII (Berlin: 1825–28), IV, pp. 293–94. *ASKB* 1747–62.

614. Plato, *Symposium* 221 e-f.

615. Legendary last king of Assyria, noted for his sensual indulgence.
616. Aristotle. See Cicero, *De finibus*, 2, 106.
617. See IV A 200.

SOLITUDE

For Kierkegaard not only has the word "solitude" the literal meaning of being alone, but it also means a state of mental isolation which, like quiet and silence (see SILENCE), is an expression of a person's withdrawal from the external world in order to concentrate within himself. "On the whole the desire for solitude is a sign that there is still spirit in a person and the measure of what spirit is there," says Anti-Climacus in *The Sickness unto Death* (p. 198, ed. tr.).

However, the desire for solitude in an esthetically oriented person can take on an unjustified form, an egotistical withdrawal from others in order to maintain or cultivate one's own singularity in proud isolation (see, for example, *Either/Or*, II, pp. 333-34). For although "everyman is the universally human and also an exception," he is still first and foremost the "universally human" (ibid., p. 333, ed tr.), and his essential task, as Judge William says, is that "of expressing the universally human in his individual life" (p. 333), even though it is not possible for any man to do this to perfection. The ethical task, then, as Climacus says later in *Concluding Unscientific Postscript*, is "a breathing of the eternal and in the midst of solitude the reconciling fellowship with every human being" (p. 136, ed. tr.; see *Three Discourses on Imagined Occasions* [*Thoughts on Crucial Situations*], pp. 39-41).

Thus solitude is a presupposition for the ethical and is thereby also of decisive significance in a person's God-relationship. In his upbuilding discourses Kierkegaard reminds us again and again that in the God-relationship a person is always alone; here "the path of the solitary" is the right one, even though it is "narrow and shut in" (p. 30, ed. tr.). A person must be alone before God in the sense that every comparison with others must drop away (pp. 29-30, and *Postscript*, p. 477). In *Works of Love*, which treats primarily of the Christian's relations to other men, Kierkegaard concludes by emphasizing how important it is for a person to become "truly solitary" in order to hear God's "echo," that is, to listen to "the word of grace or of judgment" (p. 355, ed. tr.). In other works we find similar thoughts: ". . . within every man's heart lives his penitential preacher," his conscience, which "takes care to be heard in the moment . . . when quiet makes you completely solitary" (*Christian Discourses*, p. 201, ed. tr.). But conscience, like a "secret-sharing preacher," can also keep one from "feeling solitary even in the most solitary place" (*Two Discourses at the Communion on Fridays*, with *Judge For Yourselves!*, pp. 19-20, ed. tr.).

Although, as mentioned above, every person is in a certain sense an exception and therefore solitary, there are the genuine exceptions, those for whom it is impossible to realize the universally human in some essential point, either because they are themselves "responsible for this imperfection" or because they are "without responsibilities" as a result of fate (*Either/Or*, II, p. 334, ed. tr.). Now the question is whether being an exception also signifies being selected (*Upbuilding* [*Edifying*] *Discourses*, IV, p. 139; see also *Stages*, pp. 175–76, 322–23). Concerning the solitude of such a person the strongest expressions are used, for example, "abandoned by all existence" (p. 175, ed. tr.), or "alone in the whole vast world" (*The Point of View*, p. 70), an expression similar to what is said of the knight of faith, that he is "absolute isolation" (*Fear and Trembling*, p. 89) or that he "in the solitude of the universe never hears any human voice but walks alone with his dreadful responsibility" (p. 90). Kierkegaard regarded himself as such an exception and knew that in this anguish of solitariness the demonic was a constant temptation (see *Stages*, p. 363), but also that through this a person can be helped to become more and more dependent upon God (IX A 116) and to learn "true *Christian* self-denial" (*The Point of View*, p. 8). Kierkegaard finally thought it had become clear that his solitariness was a result of his having been entrusted with something "extraordinary" (p. 69). He writes: "The turn things take depends upon a person's distinguishing characteristics, whether this solitary inner anguish demonically finds its expression and satisfaction in hating men and cursing God or the very opposite. In my case it was the latter" (p. 79, ed. tr.). But he also knew that day after day over the years he needed God's help in order to be able to persevere and to find blessing in the terrifying forms of solitude bound up with being such an exception (pp. 70–72).

For references in the works to solitude, see *Either/Or*, I, pp. 149, 157, 182; II, pp. 332–34, 336; *Fear and Trembling*, pp. 89–91, 122–24; *Upbuilding* [*Edifying*] *Discourses*, IV, p. 139; *Three Discourses on Imagined Occasions* [*Thoughts on Crucial Situations*], pp. 2–12, 29–30, 39–41, 98–99; *Stages*, pp. 33–35, 175–76, 320, 346, 420; *Postscript*, pp. 136, 163, 283–84, 373, 477; *Upbuilding Discourses in Various Spirits*, Part One [*Purity Of Heart*, pp. 47–50]; *Works of Love*, pp. 152, 239, 355; *Christian Discourses*, pp. 201, 264–65; *The Lily of the Field and the Bird of the Air*, with *Christian Discourses*, p. 354; *The Sickness unto Death*, pp. 197–98. See also SILENCE.

618. The Danish for "hysterical" is *hysterisk*. In *Politivenner*, 1495, August 16, 1844, p. 524, the word was spelled with *hyl*, meaning "howl."

619. See *The Sickness unto Death*, p. 198; see also *Works of Love*, pp. 135–36.

620. The translation here is from the Danish version in the text. See Diogenes Laertius, *The Lives and Opinions of Eminent Philosophers*, II, 117; *Diogen Laertses filosofiske Historie*, tr. B. Riisbrigh, I–II (Copenhagen: 1811–12), I, p. 106. *ASKB* 1110–11.

621. Jens Finsteen Giødwad (1811–91), political journalist on *Kjøbenhavnsposten* 1834 (the so-called birth year of the Danish political press) –1837, editor

1837-39, and an editor, together with Orla Lehman and others, of the newspaper *Fædrelandet* when it became a daily in 1840.

622. Martin Hammerich (1811-81), literary historian and rector of Borgerdydskolen (which Kierkegaard had attended) from 1842.

623. See VIII¹ A 204.

624. *Sämmtliche Werke,* I-XXII (Lindau: 1845), XV, pp. 54-55. *ASKB* 294-311.

SOPHISTRY, SOPHISTS

While working on his doctoral dissertation, *The Concept of Irony, with constant Reference to Socrates,* during which time he had to immerse himself particularly in the Platonic dialogues, Kierkegaard could not avoid getting involved with the Sophists and Socrates' and Plato's criticisms of them. On the basis of this acquaintance with the Sophists and sophistry Kierkegaard describes their essential characteristics in *The Concept of Irony.*

Kierkegaard makes a sharp distinction between the ironist and the Sophist, who is on a lower level and remains within the world of phenomena, where sophistry is "the perpetual life-and-death struggle of knowledge with the phenomenon in the service of egotism . . ." (p. 63). The Sophist clings to the "empirical I" and does not know the "ideal I" (p. 158, ed. tr.). Therefore the Sophist falls "under the concept of species, genus, etc., whereas the ironist is always singular and comes within the category of personality" (p. 176, ed. tr.). The Sophists remain within relativities, but Socrates as an ironist approaches infinity.

Kierkegaard also refers in a few places to Socrates' charge that the Sophists earned money by their instruction (see, for example, pp. 211-12). Later, while reading Tennemann's *Geschichte der Philosophie,* Kierkegaard, thinking of himself, remarks apropos this question: "If anyone wants to call my fragment of wisdom sophistic, I must point out that it lacks at least one characteristic which belongs, according to both Plato's and Aristotle's definitions: that one makes money by it" (IV A 63). On the page (I, p. 355) in Tennemann's book that Kierkegaard cites in his entry, Tennemann refers to critical comments about the Sophists made by Socrates, Plato, and Aristotle.

As time passed Kierkegaard felt himself placed in a position vis-à-vis his age similar to that of Socrates, for, just as they had done in Socrates' day, men were beginning—only on a higher plane—to lose the specified criteria for their lives because of the increasing knowledge and reflection that made everything relative. As Socrates before him had done, Kierkegaard fought to awaken men to a consciousness of the eternal. He discovered "Modern Sophistry" (X⁴ A 472) and in another entry says of it: "In the sphere of the ethical and the ethical-religious, anyone who does not himself existentially express what he teaches, or at least call attention to this, inform against himself, and explain his own position in the matter—every such person is a sophist, and all such communication is sophistry" (X^4 A 484). Thus the sophists do not think about the cause or about sacrificing anything for it, but think about the advantage to be gained (X^4 A 608). When toward the end of his life Kierkegaard became convinced that clergymen also thought more about advantages than about serving the cause of Christianity, he was forced to designate them as sophists. In the final number of *The Moment,* published after his death, he writes of the Sophists in Christendom: "These legions of clergy and Christian assistant professors are all sophists, making a living (following the pattern of the Sophists of antiquity) by getting those who understand nothing to imagine they understand something and then using these human numbers as the criterion for what truth, Christianity, is" (in *Attack,* p. 284, ed. tr.).

For references in the works to the Sophists and to sophistry, see *The Concept of Irony,* pp. 55, 58, 63, 70, 73–74, 89–98, 128–29, 143–48, 158, 163–65, 167–68, 174–76, 211–12, 224–40, 251–52; *Either/Or,* I, p. 4; II, p. 257; *Fragments,* pp. 4, 11, 32, 48, 113; *The Concept of Anxiety* [*Dread*], pp. 15, 28, 74; *Stages,* pp. 96, 122–23, 435, 437–38; *Postscript,* pp. 34, 119, 127, 132, 265, 466, 468; *Works of Love,* p. 338; *The Crisis* [*and a Crisis*] *in the Life of an Actress,* p. 81; *The Moment,* no. 10, in *Attack,* pp. 283–84.

625. See Plato, *Theaetetus,* 152 a, *Cratyllus,* 385 e; Diogenes Laertius, IX, 51 (see note 540); *Fragments,* p. 48; *Works of Love,* p. 338.

626. *Fortgangs und Verfalls der Wissenschaften in Griechenland und Rom,* I–II (Lemgo: 1782), II, pp. 194 ff.

627. Plato, *Republic,* 343 d–344 c.

628. See note 626; ibid., p. 221.

629. See Matthew 7:16.

630. See I Timothy 5:18.

631. X^4 A 466.

632. See *Armed Neutrality* and *An Open Letter,* pp. 33–46.

SPINOZA

Kierkegaard first mentions Spinoza in the draft of his ironical drama *The Battle between the Old and the New Soap-Cellars* (II B 1–21), declaring that his philosophy was so objective that "all existence became undulations of the absolute" (II B 19, p. 299). In *Either/Or* the pseudonymous writer A says similarly that Spinoza views everything "*æterno modo*" (p. 38). This formulation is only a paraphrase of the familiar phrase "*sub specie æterni,*" which especially characterizes Spinoza's philosophy and which Climacus in particular later uses again and again in *Concluding Unscientific Postscript.* Interestingly, however, there the expression is used concerning Hegel's philosophy (see, for example, pp. 75, 153, 172, 195, 203, 267, 271), whereby Climacus equates the philosophical methods of Hegel and Spinoza. Thus Climacus regards Spinoza's philosophy also as a system, and "all systematic thinking is '*sub specie æterni*' " (p. 153).

With respect to Hegel, Climacus goes on to point out in *Concluding Unscientific Postscript* that "precisely because abstract thinking is *sub specie æterni*, it does not consider the concrete, the temporal, the becoming of existence . . ." (p. 267, ed. tr.). The same applies to Spinoza's thought. As early as *Philosophical Fragments*, Climacus demonstrates Spinoza's overrating of abstract thought when it comes to the concept of God, whereby "a distinction between factual being and ideal being" (p. 51 fn.) is overlooked (see also VII[1] C 3, 4).

The criticism is intensified after the publication of *Concluding Unscientific Postscript*, during Kierkegaard's reading of Spinoza's books, especially his *Ethica more geometrico demonstrata* (see VII[1] A 35), very likely in order to confront this whole immanental and rationally grounded ethics with his reflections on Christian ethics, which he was ready to publish at that time under the title *Works of Love*.

In the journal entries Kierkegaard made while reading Spinoza's *Ethics*, he reproached Spinoza for remaining within immanence, even though Spinoza at the same time speaks of "the transition, the movement" (VII[1] C 1) which actually breaks through this immanence (VII[1] A 31, 34, and 35, but especially VII[1] C 1 and 2). In making his criticism Kierkegaard points out that in *Concluding Unscientific Postscript* Climacus tried to solve these problems. On the basis of his philosophy of immanence Spinoza would have to exclude miracles and also the possibility of a transcendence. This draws sharp criticism from Kierkegaard (IV A 190; see *Upbuilding [Edifying] Discourses*, III, pp. 83-85). Johannes Climacus also points out that man in his thought encounters "the supreme paradox of all thought" which points beyond immanence (*Fragments*, pp. 46, 49).

However, Kierkegaard commends Spinoza for saying that before commencing one's scientific-scholarly pursuits a person ought to clarify his relation to the ethical (VII[1] A 28, 29). Kierkegaard also jots down Spinoza's remark that he realizes that his book *Tractatus theologico-politicus* is not for the mass (VII[1] A 39), and he likewise evidences understanding of Spinoza's doubt about how much the adherents of various religions practice their faith in any but an external way (VII[1] A 250; see also VIII[1] A 315).

Kierkegaard also notes that from a "scientific-scholarly point of view Spinoza is and remains the only consistent one" (X[2] A 128). But thereby he also says that Spinoza's system cannot help the single individual in the questions pertaining to freedom and the central ethical and existential issues.

Čapek, Milič. "Professor Blanshard on Kierkegaard." *The Modern Schoolman*, 48, November 1970, pp. 44-53.

Muska, Rudolph C. "Antithetical Religious Conceptions in Kierkegaard and Spinoza." Ph.D. dissertation, Michigan State, 1961.

For references in the works to Spinoza, see *The Concept of Irony*, p. 326;

Either/Or, I, p. 38; *Upbuilding* [*Edifying*] *Discourses*, III, p. 83; *Fragments*, pp. 51–52 fn., 76; *Prefaces*, *S.V.*, XIV, p. 62; *Postscript*, p. 92.

633. B. Spinoza, *Tractatus theologico-politicus*, *Opera philosophica omnia*, ed. A. Gfroerer (Stuttgart: 1810). *ASKB* 788.

634. Ibid. "To the rest of mankind I care not to commend my treatise, for I cannot expect that it contains anything to please them: I know how deeply rooted are the prejudices embraced under the name of religion; I am aware that in the mind of the masses superstition is no less deeply rooted than fear; I recognize that their constancy is mere obstinacy, and that they are led to praise or blame by impulse rather than reason. Therefore the multitude, and those of like passions with the multitude, I ask not to read my book; nay, I would rather that they should utterly neglect it, than that they should misinterpret it after their wont. They would gain no good themselves, and might prove a stumbling-block to others." B. Spinoza, *A Theologico-Political Treatise*, tr. R. H. M. Elwes (London: Bell, 1909), p. 11.

635. For edition, see note 633. "Matters have long since come to such a pass, that one can only pronounce a man Christian, Turk, Jew, or Heathen, by his general appearance and attire, by his frequenting this or that place of worship, or employing the phraseology of a particular sect—" (tr. R. H. M. Elwes, see note 634).

636. See *Ethica*, I, Appendix; def. 7, prop. 17, 20, 26, 28, in *Opera philosophica omnia*, ed. A. Gfroerer (Stuttgart: 1830). *ASKB* 788.

637. See *Ethica*, III, prop. 6 ff.; IV, prop. 8. Persist in its own being.

638. See *Postscript*, pp. 30, 208–9, 510, 535.

639. See *Ethica*, III, def. 2, 3, and explanation (in Appendix to III).

640. See note 636 for edition. *Pars* I, VI. Why some have insisted upon a metaphysical good.

641. ... a thing itself and the tendency which is in it to conserve its own being.

642. *Pars* I, III. Reconciliation of our freedom of choice with God's predestination exceeds human grasp.

643. *Principia philosophiæ Cartesianæ*, *Pars* I, *proleg.* For edition of *Opera omnia*, see note 633.

644. Ibid.

645. Ibid.

SPIRIT

According to Kierkegaard only God is spirit in the proper sense, and here he is in agreement with the New Testament: "God is spirit" (John 4:24), where spirit means a conscious personal power which has created the world and rules it. In the created order it is only man who can also come under the category of spirit, but man is always "derived spirit," that is, the actuated spirit in relation to God as "the eternal spirit" (*Postscript*, pp. 218, 220; see also *Two*

... *Essays*, with *The Present Age*, pp. 151-52, and *On Authority and Revelation*, p. 112). But man is spirit only in the sense that he is created with the possibility of becoming spirit, and he must traverse several stages of development before he can be called a spiritual being or a self, to use one of Kierkegaard's parallel expressions. (See SELF.)

In addition Kierkegaard uses the definition of man as a synthesis of the two factors, time and eternity, and his pseudonyms also use the trilogy (trichotomy) body, mind, and spirit, especially when depicting the spirit's movement from its possibility to its actuality. This trichotomy, which is also found in Paul (I Corinthians 2:14-16 and 15:38-49), enables Kierkegaard to describe very precisely a person's stages of spiritual development. At the outset a man lives only in the composite of body-mind; the psychical component dominates, and the spiritual is present only as possibility. As psyche, man is bound to the temporal, and all his activity is expended upon relative, finite goals; The spiritual, which always represents the eternal, is only present as "dreaming spirit" (*The Concept of Anxiety* [*Dread*], p. 37), and therefore is not yet something actual. The domain of human life in which a man lives only under the qualification body-soul is very comprehensive, and it constitutes the whole esthetic stage. Kierkegaard expresses the view that most men never get beyond this stage; for them the possibility of spirit never becomes actuality. "The majority, who just live out the factors of the mind-body synthesis, never attain the qualification: spirit" (*The Point of View*, p. 82, ed. tr.).

A man first becomes a spiritual being through a relationship to the eternal, or, more correctly, through a relationship to God. It is worth noting that Kierkegaard, in line with the New Testament, uses the expression "soul" in referring to the beginning of one's spiritual development, as in the two discourses "To Acquire One's Soul in Patience," (*Edifying Discourses*, II, pp. 67-87) and "To Preserve One's Soul in Patience" (III, pp. 7-35). Here the ground is broken for the transition from man as a psychic being to man as a spiritual being, since a person must learn to free himself from his dependence on finitude through patience in the reverses of life.

In the ethical and religious books, Kierkegaard and the pseudonymous writers continue to sketch the line of development in which the spiritual in a person steadily becomes a greater actuality in him through his relationship to God and Christ as the revealed truth. The highest the spiritual man can reach is the impregnation of his life by his knowledge of the eternal requirement, or as Kierkegaard says: "*Spirit* is the power a person's understanding exercises over his life" (X^3 A 736). "Spirit is restlessness," Kierkegaard says elsewhere (XI^2 A 317). To express that spirit penetrates the psychic-physical synthesis like a fire, Kierkegaard uses the poet Baggesen's phrase: "burned out to spirit" (XI^7 A 41; see *Stages*, p. 272). The strongest expression Kierkegaard uses, predominantly in the later books and journal entries, to describe the condition of the spirit in this world when a person allows himself to be led by Christianity's requirement is that "Spirit is to live as if dead (to die to the world)" (XI² A 279).

Besides this positive description of the actuality of spirit in a person's life, Kierkegaard also provides a sketch of what happens to a man when the actuality of spirit does not get power in his life and when man is in flight from it (see SIN).

Kierkegaard is sharply opposed to the volatilization of the meaning of spirit which results from regarding spirit only as mental activity—that is, as the mere cogitating on the eternal, which prevents spirit from getting an existential meaning for the individual. This applies especially to philosophers with their talk about "the objective spirit" (see VI A 26), a situation which Climacus criticizes in particular in *Concluding Unscientific Postscript*, where he points out the error of being satisfied with remaining within the objective side of spirit and forgetting the earnestness of ethical commitment in existence.

Cole, J. Preston. "The Function of Choice in Human Existence." *Journal of Religion,* 45, July 1965, pp. 196–210.

Cruickschank, Andrew. "Wittgenstein and the Language of the Gospels." *The Church Quarterly,* 3, 1, 1970, pp. 40–51.

Fabro, Cornelio. "The Problem of Desperation and Christian Spirituality in Kierkegaard." *Kierkegaardiana,* 4, 1962, pp. 63–69.

Hamilton, Kenneth. "Created Soul—Eternal Spirit; a Continuing Theological Thorn." *Scottish Journal of Theology,* 19, March 1966, pp. 23–24.

Kainz, Howard P. "The Relationship of Dread to Spirit in Man and Woman, according to Kierkegaard." *The Modern Schoolman,* 47, November 1966, pp. 1–13.

Smith, Kenneth R. "Dialectical Conceptions of Spirit: Hegel, Kierkegaard, and Nietzsche." Ph.D. dissertation, Yale, 1972.

For references in the works to spirit, see, for example, *The Concept of Irony,* pp. 189–93, 305–6; *Either/Or,* I, pp. 60, 62, 65–69, 71–72, 87–89; II, pp. 61, 190–91, 193, 208–9, 214; *Fear and Trembling,* pp. 38, 56, 58; *The Concept of Anxiety* [*Dread*], pp. 21, 37–41, 58–66, 71–72, 79–81, 84–86, 92–93, 96, 104, 134; *Stages,* pp. 244, 335–36, 303, 398–402; *Postscript,* pp. 79–80, 108, 160, 169–73, 216–17, 220–21, 227, 233, 250, 286–87, 307–22, 481, 492 fn.; *Two Ages, S.V.,* XIII, pp. 20–21; *Upbuilding Discourses in Various Spirits,* Part Two [*What We Learn from the Lilies of the Field and the Birds of the Air,* with *The Gospel of Suffering,* pp. 211–13]; Part Three, pp. 54–57, 97–100; *Works of Love,* pp. 42, 59, 65, 68–70, 199–202, 204–5, 332; *Christian Discourses,* pp. 57, 68–69, 121–25; *The Sickness unto Death,* pp. 146–213, especially pp. 146–50, 224–25, 232–35, 244–45; *For Self-Examination,* pp. 83–87; *Judge for Yourselves!,* pp. 115, 126, 154–56, 201–2; "The Single Individual," with *The Point of View,* p. 134; *This Must Be Said,* in *Attack,* p. 65; *The Moment,* no. 5, no. 7, no. 10, ibid., pp. 162–63, 201, 286.

646. See Acts 2:1–13.

647. See John 16:7.

648. In the *Papirer* Kierkegaard is not consistent in capitalizing certain pronouns. All nouns in Danish at that time were capitalized, so there is no way of knowing his particular intention.

649. *Von dem Zwecke Jesu und seiner Jünger. Noch ein Fragment des Wolfenbüttelschen Ungenannten*, ed. G. E. Lessing (Braunschweig: 1778), pp. 120–27, particularly pp. 126–27. Same pages in Berlin edition of 1784.

650. See I Corinthians 15:32.

651. See Matthew 6:33.

652. See Luke 17:12–19, in 1849 the text on September 9.

653. Rasmus Nielsen (1809–1884), Professor of Philosophy, University of Copenhagen, from 1841, and Kierkegaard's potential confidant.

654. A whole heaven, heaven-wide; completely, diametrically.

655. See Matthew 11:28; *Practice [Training] in Christianity*, pp. 3–12.

656. By classifying on the basis of the dominant or the majority.

657. Martin Luther, *En christelig Postille*, tr. J. Thisted, I–II (Copenhagen: 1828), I, pp. 296, 300–301.

658. The condition without which nothing; the indispensable or necessary condition.

659. See note 507.

660. See *The Concept of Anxiety [Dread]*, p. 123.

661. See Richard Rothe, *Die Anfänge der christlichen Kirche und ihrer verfassung. Ein geschichtlichen Versuch*, I–II (Wittenberg: 1837), I, pp. 1 ff., 18 ff.

662. Aristotle in *Politics* (1278 c–d) distinguishes three kinds of association characterized by the ends of the good life, of social life, and of life itself, just as he also distinguishes *demos* (Athenian assembly), *plethos* (plurality) and *ochlos* (crowd or mob). Kierkegaard has in mind the crowd and may have recalled portions from the *Politics* such as 1281 c (para. 5) rather than most of the work, which is based on Aristotle's ideal view of man's telic nature and the state as an organic unity expressive of man's nature.

663. See Matthew 25:29.

664. See Matthew 10:22; John 16:2.

665. The two terms ("egotism" and "egoity") express respectively: arbitrary, aggressive self-centeredness and selfhood. Kierkegaard continually makes the crucial distinction between being selfish and becoming and being a self. The latter is proper self-love and the other eccentric self-aggrandizement. See SELF and, for example, X^4 A 509.

666. See Ephesians 6:12.

667. See Romans 6:6.

668. See Romans 14:23.

669. See Isaiah 3:4.

670. See *Stages*, p. 209.

671. See Luke 12:49–53; *For Self-Examination*, pp. 71–72.
672. Laurids Kruse, *Don Juan* (Copenhagen: 1807); see *Either/Or*, I, p. 96.
673. Jens Baggesen, *Min Gjenganger-spøg, Danske Værker*, I–XII (Copenhagen: 1827–32), VI, p. 135. *ASKB* 1509–20.
674. See Ecclesiastes 1:18.
675. See, for example, *For Self-Examination*, pp. 87–98.
676. Nymphomania.
677. See, for example, *For Self-Examination*, pp. 12–21.
678. No happiness without quiet. Cicero uses the expression *"nisi quietum nihil beatum est"* in a discussion of Epicurus' conception of God in *De natura deorum*, I, 20, 52.
679. See note 677.
680. See note 675.
681. Matthew 11:6. See, for example, *Practice [Training] in Christianity*, pp. 73–144.

SPIRITUAL TRIAL

In a journal entry from 1844–45 Kierkegaard says: "If one puts on the religious for common everyday use, then spiritual trials [*Anfægtelser*] are bound to come (VI A 2), and in 1849 he writes: "Because religion is not taken seriously nowadays in Christendom, there is never a hint of a word about spiritual trials" (X^1 A 22). In the same vein Kierkegaard's pseudonym Johannes Climacus declares that "one almost never hears spiritual trial mentioned these days, or if it is mentioned at all, it is automatically lumped together with temptations, in fact, even with adversities" (*Postscript*, p. 410, ed. tr.). This observation illustrates for Climacus the relation of the age to the religious, since to his mind spiritual trial belongs "to the sphere of the essentially religious" and increases "in proportion to religiousness."

Kierkegaard's view is that as long as a person has his life within the ethical sphere in such a way that fulfilling the universally valid ethical requirement is supreme, he will meet temptations but not spiritual trial. Spiritual trial will not manifest itself until a man successfully renounces the relative goals in life in order as the single individual to endeavor to relate himself to the absolute. The pseudonymous writer Johannes de Silentio describes this situation in *Fear and Trembling*. Abraham, as the single individual in submission to God, is led to a teleological suspension of the ethical, inasmuch as he was prepared to sacrifice his own son at God's command (see also *Postscript*, p. 234). Consequently spiritual trial begins when a man "who has had inwardness enough to lay hold of the ethical with infinite passion" (p. 231) discovers that there is something still higher than the universally valid ethical.

But real spiritual trial is in the sphere of the Christian-religious, when a person is faced with Christianity's absolute demand for perfection and with

Christ as the prototype. Thus spiritual trial is one of the forms of religious suffering a man meets when, with all his limitations (see X¹ A 22), he endeavors to relate to God and takes this demand in earnest.

At the end of *Concluding Unscientific Postscript*, Johannes Climacus elaborates on what he understands by spiritual trial and how it is different from temptation [*Fristelse*] (see TEMPTATION). He says among other things: "Spiritual trial lies within the sphere of religious suffering and can be defined only there." He says further: "In temptation it is the lower which tempts, in spiritual trial it is the higher; in temptation it is the lower which lures the individual, in spiritual trial it is the higher which, seemingly envious of the individual, wants to frighten him back . . . spiritual trial expresses the boundary's reaction to the finite individual" (p. 410, ed. tr.). Kierkegaard says the same thing himself, only more simply, in the previously mentioned entry from 1849: ". . . it is spiritual trial because it seems to the person himself as if the relationship were stretched too tightly, as if he were venturing too boldly in literally involving himself personally with God and Christ" (X¹ A 22).

Kierkegaard struggled with spiritual trials all his life, but according to his journals most of all in his later years. In later journal entries he emphasizes that "spiritual trial is really associated only with the voluntary" (X⁴ A 459), making it extremely difficult for a person to clarify whether he is acting out of the daring courage of faith, consequently according to God's will, or is making himself guilty of presumption (X⁴ A 411). Thus for Kierkegaard the way one best relates to spiritual trial is a deeply personal problem. In *Fear and Trembling* it is shown that Abraham escaped spiritual trial because he acted in obedience and never wavered in his faith (see, for example, pp. 35 and 124). What could have been for him a spiritual trial proved to be a testing [*Prøvelse*], and he became "the father of faith" (pp. 31–33). Kierkegaard describes the parallel to this in the discourses on "Strengthened in the Inner Man," which was published the same year, telling how he "who is tested in the distress of spiritual trial" must learn in stillness and humility "to wait for the explanation," and how his testing eventually leads him to "the full assurance of faith" (*Upbuilding* [*Edifying*] *Discourses*, I, pp. 114–15, ed. tr.). Through the years Kierkegaard had to remind himself continually that the only thing to do with a spiritual trial is to "be silent and wait in prayer and faith" (IX A 333), to "go straight toward it, trusting in God and Christ" (X¹ A 637), and that spiritual trial "can be fought only with the rashness of faith" (X⁴ A 95). But on the other hand he also perceived clearly that what "the old devotional literature" teaches is right—namely, that "the individual is completely innocent" in spiritual trial, and that "these thoughts which try the spirit prove that he has really become thoroughly involved and engaged" (XI² A 132).

Wood, Forrest E. "Kierkegaardian Light on Ibsen's *Brand*." *Personalist*, 51, Summer 1970, pp. 393–400.

For references in the works to spiritual trial (*Anfægtelse*; German, *Anfech-*

tung), see, for example, *The Concept of Irony*, p. 249 (tr. "tribulations"); *Either/Or*, II, pp. 126, 142 (tr. "trials"), 291 (tr. "temptation"), 328 (tr. "terrors"), 337 (tr. "temptations"); *Upbuilding* [*Edifying*] *Discourses*, I, pp. 6 (tr. "trials"), 22 (tr. "exertion"), 24 (tr. "temptations"), 33 (tr. "anxieties"); II, pp. 98 (tr. "tempted"), 112 (tr. "temptation"), 114–16 (tr. "temptation"); III, p. 106 (tr. "temptation"); IV, pp. 44 (tr. "temptation"), 54 (do.); *Fear and Trembling*, pp. 42 (tr. "base temptation"), 65–67 (tr. "temptation"), 79–80 (do.), 88–89 (do.), 91 (do.), 96 (do.), 120 (do.), 124 (do.), 127 (do.); *Fragments*, pp. 52 (do.), 60 (do.); *The Concept of Anxiety* [*Dread*], pp. 104 (tr. "assaults of the spirit"), 107 (tr. "temptations"), 127 fn. (tr. "assault of doubt," "temptation of doubt," "temptations of religious scruples and doubts," "assaults of temptation"); *Three Discourses on Imagined Occasions* [*Thoughts on Crucial Situations*], p. 54 (tr. "temptation"); *Stages*, pp. 59 (tr. "trying doubts"), 114 (tr. "temptation"), 121 (do.), 155 (do.), 160 (do.), 166 (do.), 169 (do.), 176 (tr. "trial and temptation"), 215 (tr. "trials of temptation"), 285 (tr. "temptation"), 289 (do.); *Postscript*, pp. 15 (do.), 27 (do.), 30 (do.), 32 (tr. "doubts and temptations"), 33 (tr. "temptations to doubt"), 120 (tr. "temptation"), 123 (do.), 124 (do.), 202 fn. (tr. "evil temptation"), 231 (tr. "temptation"), 234 (do.), 238–39 (do., *Fristelse* also tr. "temptation"), 292 (do.), 304 (do.), 372 (tr. "trials and temptations"), 386 (tr. "temptation"), 410–12 (do.), 444 (tr. *Anfechtung*); *Works of Love*, p. 145 (tr. "temptation"); *Christian Discourses*, p. 173 (tr. "alarms"), 198 (tr. "temptations"), 244 (do.); *Three Discourses at the Communion on Fridays*, with ibid., p. 366 (tr. "trial"; see fn.); *An Open Letter* (tr. "spiritual trials"); *For Self-Examination*, pp. 15 (tr. "temptations"), 21 (tr. "torments of anxiety"), article in *Fædrelandet*, 295, December 18, 1854, in *Attack*, p. 7 (tr. "trepidation"); *The Moment*, no. 9, ibid. (tr. "temptations"), p. 265.

682. Presumably a reference to Minna's saying that a single grateful thought heavenward is the most perfect prayer. *Minna von Barnhelm*, II, 7, *Gotthold Ephraim Lessing's sämmtliche Schriften*, I–XXXII (Berlin: 1825–28), XX, p. 241. *ASKB* 1747–62.

683. The state of siege or being bitten by serpents must precede the second (Atonement). "First the first and then the next" (VIII^1 A 49).

684. See Numbers 21:6 ff.

685. See II Corinthians 12:7; *Upbuilding* [*Edifying*] *Discourses*, IV, pp. 49–74; *The Sickness unto Death*, pp. 204, 209.

686. In this case.

687. See *For Self-Examination*, pp. 96–98.

688. Too much.

689. Johan Christian Lund (1799–1875), married to Kierkegaard's sister, Nicoline Kristine (1799–1832).

690. See note 314; ibid, I, pp. 168 ff.

691. See *Postscript*, pp. 49–50.

692. A very significant term in Kierkegaard's thought. See, for example, *The Concept of Irony*, p. 162; *Either/Or*, p. 146; II, pp. 164, 183, 262; *Postscript*, pp. 228, 462; *Upbuilding Discourses in Various Spirits*, Part One [*Purity of Heart*, pp. 108, 136, 176–77, 183]; *Works of Love*, pp. 218, 232; *The Sickness unto Death*, pp. 147, 179, 262.

693. See, for example, *Fear and Trembling*, pp. 22, 129–32.

694. See *Postscript*, pp. 97–98.

695. *Geist aus Luthers Schriften oder Concordanz der Ansichten und Urtheile des grossen Reformators* . . . , ed. F. W. Lomler et al. I–IV (Darmstadt: 1828–31), "Kirche," entry no. 5780. *ASKB* 317-20.

696. Apuleius, *Amor und Psyche*, tr. J. Kehrein (Giessen: 1834). *ASKB* 1216.

697. Holberg, *Barselstuen*, III, 5.

698. See note 675.

699. See *Upbuilding* [*Edifying*] *Discourses*, IV, pp. 31–37.

700. See note 692.

STAGES

Through his concentration on the various levels of spiritual development in human existence, Kierkegaard formed an integrated view of man expressed in his conception of the three stages of life. He thereafter used this view consistently in structuring his authorship, all the way from *Either/Or* at the beginning of the authorship proper (See *Postscript*, pp. 226–29; for the plan of the stages see p. 448, 475 fn., and Gregor Malantschuk, *Kierkegaard's Thought*, pp. 143–50).

The point of departure and basis for this view of man was Christianity's presupposition that in addition to being a temporal creation man also has an eternal constituent or, as it frequently is formulated in Kierkegaard's writings, that man is a synthesis of the temporal and the eternal. In other words, even though man is primarily a temporal being, eternity is the goal of his existence. According to Kierkegaard's interpretation, the qualitatively different elements of the synthesis explain the essential conflicts and struggles during man's spiritual development.

The ideal movement in this development would be that a person seeks to subordinate the temporal to the eternal. After the first primitive mythological level, man finds this eternal constituent in himself, as Socrates, for example, did. On a higher level man encounters the eternal as God's personal requirement and later as God's revelation in time. But the movement can also take a negative course, because man has the possibility of choice and a person can resist the requirement of the eternal and thereby become guilty over against the power to which he is responsible. Each man must begin his development from the very beginning and must go through the spiritual stages which have been traversed in human history (see *Three Discourses on Imagined*

Occasions [*Thoughts on Crucial Situations*], pp. 14-15, 183; on the genius, *The Concept of Anxiety* [*Dread,*], pp. 93-94).

The course of this movement is briefly described as follows. A human being begins his life as a natural entity, inasmuch as he is completely bound by the givens of nature that constitute him. He lives in the now and reacts altogether spontaneously, ignorant of good and evil. This is man's innocent condition. By reflection he rises above the now and begins to form a concept of past and future. It is on this level that anxiety awakens in a man; it is a sign that he is about to lose his secure anchoring in nature and find the first intimations of his freedom. This is the beginning of the *esthetic stage.* Characteristic of this stage, he still hangs on continually to the external, to the temporal. Man is living in what the pseudonymous writer Vigilius Haufniensis calls "a synthesis of the psychic and the physical" (*The Concept of Anxiety* [*Dread*], p. 39, ed. tr.); the spiritual is still present only as possibility. In the esthetic stage heredity and milieu play the important roles, because on that level the individual lacks spirit as the guiding factor. The esthetic stage is actually the stage of paganism; but, as Kierkegaard and his pseudonyms often stress, there is also paganism in Christianity, insofar as every individual is born a pagan and can very well remain in this stage if he continually lets himself be bound by finitude. Generally speaking, all the philosophies of life and religions which stay within finitude and do not have a relation to a transcendent power are in the esthetic stage. The highest one can go in this stage is the attempt of metaphysics to explain existence. According to Kierkegaard, ethics proper is not found in the esthetic stage, but custom and habit constitute the norms for man's mode of life.

The crucial transition to the next stage, the ethical, is made in paganism by Socrates, who having with irony seen through the vanity of finitude comes to the eternal ideas of the beautiful, the true, and the good by way of recollection. The idea of the good, or of how man ought to act in conformity with intrinsic good, becomes the point of departure for Socrates' ethical philosophy of life, with which he penetrates paganism's esthetic philosophy of life. The ethical stage is also found in Judaism, inasmuch as the Jewish people are addressed by a personal transcendent power who communicates his message to the people. Thus the spiritual (the eternal) reveals itself in two ways: in Socrates as the eternal in man himself, with absolute requirements upon man, and in Judaism as a personal God (Spirit) who places his ethical requirements upon man and to whom man is responsible. This is the beginning of the ethical stage, and with the qualifications that have been given to him man can attempt to actualize the possibility of spirit in his life. Kierkegaard gives ample evidence in his writings of how man's attempt to honor the requirement of the eternal ends in a realization of his incapability. At this point man has arrived, existentially speaking, at the position of humor, which is "the confinium between the ethical and the religious" (*Postscript,* p. 448, ed. tr.).

The collapse of the ethical domain leads a person to the realization of absolute guilt, to "the eternal recollection of guilt" (*Postscript*, p. 492), preparing him to listen attentively to the message Christ brings—namely, that he is a sinner and needs redemption. Kierkegaard has described this religious stage very carefully in his writings.

This positive movement through the stages, which is also the movement toward faith, is described by Anti-Climacus as follows: "in relating itself to itself and in willing to be itself, the self is grounded transparently in the power that established it" (*The Sickness unto Death*, pp. 147, 262, ed. tr.). But by resisting the external, a person can go steadily deeper into guilt through anxiety, despair, and offense—the guilt which is intensified as sin when it stands before God and the revealed truth. In the two books *The Concept of Anxiety* and *The Sickness unto Death*, Kierkegaard's pseudonymous writers have described at length how man's guilt and sin continually assume more conscious (intensified) forms the more he tries to put distance between himself and God's eternal purpose for man.

Allison, Henry E. "Kierkegaard's Dialectic of the Religious Consciousness." *Union Seminary Quarterly Review*, 20, March 1965, pp. 225-33.

Amore, Roy, and John Elrod. "From Ignorance to Knowledge: in the Kierkegaardian and Theravada Buddhist Notions of Freedom." *Union Seminary Quarterly Review*, 26, 1970, pp. 59-79.

Anshen, Ruth Nanda. "Accents of Humanism in Søren Kierkegaard." *Religious Humanism*, 5, Spring 1971, pp. 54-58.

Bedell, George C. "The Three Stages," in *Kierkegaard and Faulkner: Modalities of Existence*, ch. 8. Baton Rouge: Louisiana State University Press, 1971.

Brophy, Liam. "Kierkegaard: the Hamlet in Search of Holiness." *Social Justice Review*, 9, 1955, pp. 291-92.

Brontl, George E. "The Tragic Commitment: an Essay in Existentialist Metaphysics." Ph.D. dissertation, Columbia, 1957.

Broudy, Harry S. "The Artist and the Future." *Journal of Aesthetic Education*, 4, January 1970, pp. 11-22.

———. "Kierkegaard's Levels of Existence." *Philosophy and Phenomenological Research*, 1, 1940-41, pp. 294-312.

Chervin, Ronda de Sola. "The Process of Conversion in the Philosophy of Religion of Søren Kierkegaard." Ph.D. dissertation, Fordham, 1967.

Clive, Geoffrey H. "The Connection between Ethics and Religion in Kant, Kierkegaard and Bradley." Ph.D. dissertation, Harvard, 1953.

Cole, J. Preston. "The Function of Choice in Human Existence." *Journal of Religion*, 45, July 1965, pp. 196-210.

Colette, Jacques. *Kierkegaard*, tr. Ralph M. McInerny and Leo Turcotte. Notre Dame: University of Notre Dame Press, 1968.

Collins, James. "The Meaning of Existence." *New Scholasticism*, 22, 1948, pp. 371–416.

Comstock, W. Richard "Aspects of Aesthetic Existence: Kierkegaard and Santayana." *International Philosophical Quarterly*, 6, June 1966, pp. 189–213.

Dewey, Bradley R. "Kierkegaard on Suffering: Promise and Lack of Fulfillment in Life's Stages." *Humanitas*, 9, February 1972, pp. 21–45.

De Young, Quintin R. "A Study of Contemporary Christian Existential Theology (Kierkegaard and Tillich) and Modern Dynamic Psychology (Freud and Sullivan) concerning Guilt Feelings." Ph.D. dissertation, Southern California, 1959.

Diem, Hermann. *Kierkegaard's Dialectic of Existence*, tr. Harold Knight. Edinburgh: Oliver and Boyd, 1959.

Doubleday, Kathleen "Søren Kierkegaard's Concept of Faith." M.A. thesis, Illinois, 1961.

Duncan, Elmer H. "Kierkegaard's Value Theory: a Study of the Three Spheres of Existence." Ph.D. dissertation, Cincinnati, 1962.

Dupré, Louis K. *Kierkegaard as Theologian: The Dialectics of Christian Existence.* New York: Sheed and Ward, 1963.

———. "The Philosophical Stages of Self-Discovery." *Thought*, 39, 154, 1964, pp. 411–28. 154, 1964, pp. 411–28.

Fabro, Cornelio. "The Problem of Desperation and Christian Spirituality in Kierkegaard." *Kierkegaardiana*, 4, 1962, pp. 63–69.

Forrest, William. "A Problem in Values: The Faustian Motivation in Kierkegaard and Goethe." *International Journal of Ethics*, 63, 4, 1953, pp. 251–61.

George, Arapara G. *The First Sphere. A Study in Kierkegaardian Aesthetics.* London, New York: Asia Publishing House, 1966.

Gerry, Rev. Joseph. "Kierkegaard: The Problem of Transcendence; an Interpretation of the Stages." Ph.D. dissertation, Fordham, 1959.

Glicksberg, Charles I. "Aesthetics of Nihilism." *University of Kansas City Review*, 27, December 1960, pp. 127–30.

Goulet, Denis A. "Kierkegaard, Aquinas, and the Dilemma of Abraham." *Thought*, 32, 1957, pp. 165–88.

Grieve, Alexander. "Søren Kierkegaard: A Study of the Third Section of His 'Stadia upon Life's Way.'" *Expository Times*, 19, 5, 1907–1908, pp. 206–9.

Hamilton, Kenneth. "Man: Anxious or Guilty? A Second Look at Kierkegaard's *The Concept of Dread.*" *Christian Scholar*, 46, Winter 1963, pp. 293–99.

———. *The Promise of Kierkegaard.* New York: Lippincott, 1969.

Hamilton, Lester I. "The Existential Dialectic in the Writings of Søren Aabye Kierkegaard." M.A. thesis, Kentucky, 1951.

Harper, Ralph. *Existentialism. A Theory of Man.* Cambridge: Harvard University Press, 1948.

Holmer, Paul L. "Kierkegaard and Ethical Theory." *Ethics*, 63, 3, April 1953, pp. 157–70.

Hong, Howard. "On Kierkegaard's Philosophical Anthropology." *Memorias del XIII Congreso Internacional de Filosofia*, I–X, vol. VIII, pp. 173–78. Mexico City: University of Mexico, 1963–66.

Jones, Jere J. "On the Distinction between Religiousness 'A' and Religiousness 'B' in the *Concluding Unscientific Postscript* of Søren Kierkegaard." Ph.D. dissertation, Nebraska, 1971.

Humphries, Hugh W. "Søren Kierkegaard's Conception of Sanctification." Ph.D. dissertation, New York University, 1962.

Jung, Hwa Y. "Confucianism and Existentialism: Intersubjectivity as the Way of Life." *Philosophy and Phenomenological Research*, 30, December 1969, pp. 186–202.

Kainz, Howard P. "Ambiguities and Paradoxes in Kierkegaard's Existential Categories." *Philosophy Today*, 13, Summer 1969, pp. 138–45.

Kean, Charles Duell. *The Meaning of Existence*. New York: Harper, 1947.

Johnson, David. "Søren Kierkegaard's View of the Aesthetic Existence." M.A. thesis, Columbia, 1947.

Klemke, E. D. "Some Insights for Ethical Theory from Kierkegaard." *Philosophical Quarterly* (St. Andrews) 10, 41, 1960, pp. 322–30.

Kroner, Richard. "Existentialism and Christianity." *Encounter*, 17, 3, Summer 1956, pp. 219–44.

Kuhn, Helmut. "Existentialism, Christian and anti-Christian." *Theology Today*, 6, 3, 1949, pp. 311–23.

Larson, W. R. Curtis. "Kierkegaard and Sartre." *Personalist*, 35, 1954, pp. 128–36.

Lowrie, Walter. "*Existence* as Understood by Kierkegaard and/or Sartre." *Sewanee Review*, 48, 1950, pp. 379–401.

MacCallum, Henry Reid. "Kierkegaard and Levels of Existence." *University of Toronto Quarterly*, 13, April 1944, pp. 258–75.

McInerny, Ralph. "Ethics and Persuasion: Kierkegaard's Existential Dialectic." *The Modern Schoolman*, 33, 1956, pp. 19–39.

Mackey, Louis H. "The Nature and the End of the Ethical Life according to Kierkegaard." Ph.D. dissertation, Yale, 1954.

———. "The Poetry of Inwardness," in *The Existential Philosophers*, ed. George Schrader, pp. 45–107. New York: McGraw-Hill, 1967.

Malantschuk, Gregor. *Kierkegaard's Way to the Truth*, tr. Mary Michelsen. Minneapolis: Augsburg, 1963.

May, Rollo. *Man's Search for Himself.* New York: Norton, 1953.

May, Rollo, et al. *Existence*, particularly pp. 20–29. New York: Basic Books, 1958.

Miller, Libuse. *In Serach of the Self.* Philadelphia: Muhlenberg, 1962.

Minear, Paul S. "Thanksgiving as a Synthesis of the Temporal and the

Eternal." *Anglican Theological Review*, 38, January 1956, pp. 4–14. In *A Kierkegaard Critique*, ed. Howard Johnson and Niels Thulstrup, ch. 17. New York: Harper, 1962.

Mourant, John A. "The Limitations of Religious Existentialism." *International Philosophy Quarterly*, 1, 1961, pp. 437–52.

Nelson, C. A. "The Dimension of Inwardness in Christianity." *Augustana Quarterly*, 2, 1941, pp. 125–40.

Norborg, Sverre. *Varieties of Christian Experience*, particularly pp. 113–15. Minneapolis: Augsburg, 1937.

Noxon, James. "Kierkegaard's Stages and [Greene's] A Burnt-out Case." *A Review of English Literature*, 3, 1, 1962, pp. 90–101.

Otani, Hidehito. "The Concept of a Christian in Kierkegaard." *Inquiry* (Oslo), 8, 1, Spring 1965, pp. 74–83.

Otani, Masuru. "Self-manifestation of Freedom in 'Anxiety' by Kierkegaard." *Orbis Litterarum* (Copenhagen) 22, pp. 393–98.

Perkins, Robert. "Existence and Aesthetics: Some Kierkegaardian Themes." M.A. thesis, Indiana, 1959.

Price, George H. *The Narrow Pass, a Study of Kierkegaard's Concept of Man*. New York: McGraw-Hill, 1963.

Rappoport, Angelo S. "Ibsen, Nietzsche and Kierkegaard." *New Age* (London), 3, 21–22, 1908, pp. 408–9, 428–29.

Schmitt, Richard. "The Paradox in Kierkegaard's Religiousness A." *Inquiry* (Oslo), 8, 1, 1965, pp. 118–35.

Schrag, Calvin O. "The Problem of Existence: Kierkegaard's Descriptive Analysis of the Self and Heidegger's Phenomenological Ontology of *Dasein*." Ph.D. dissertation, Harvard, 1957.

———. "The Structure of Moral Experience . . ." *Ethics*, 73, 4, July 1963, pp. 255–65.

Schwandt, Jack Allan. "Alienation and Reconciliation in the Works of Søren Kierkegaard." M.A. thesis, Minnesota, 1959.

Shearson, William A. "The Notion of Encounter in Existential Metaphysics: an Inquiry into the Nature and Structure of Existential Knowledge in Kierkegaard, Sartre, and Buber." Ph.D. dissertation, Toronto, 1970.

Shmuëli, Adi. *Kierkegaard and Consciousness*, tr. Naomi Handelman. Princeton: Princeton University Press, 1971.

Smit, Harvey. *Kierkegaard's Pilgrimage of Man*. Grand Rapids: Erdmans, 1965.

Smith III, J. Weldon. "Religion A–Religion B: A Kierkegaard Study." *Scottish Journal of Theology*, 15, 1962, pp. 245-65.

Stack, George J. "Kierkegaard and the Phenomenology of Repetition." *Journal of Existentialism*, 7, 1966–67, pp. 111–28.

———. "Kierkegaard's Ironic Stage of Existence." *Laval Theologique et Philosophique*, 25, 1969, pp. 192–207.

———. "Kierkegaard's Concept of Possibility." *Journal of Thought*, 5, April 1970, pp. 80–92.

———. "Kierkegaard and Romantic Aestheticism." *Philosophy Today*, 14, Spring 1970, pp. 57–74.

Stavrides, Maria M. "The Concept of Existence in Kierkegaard and Heidegger." Ph.D. dissertation, Columbia, 1952.

Stein, Waltraut J. "Truth as Subjectivity: The Thought of Søren Kierkegaard." *Religious Humanism*, 4, Spring 1970, pp. 78–82.

Stevens, Eldon L. "Kierkegaard's Categories of Existence." Ph.D. dissertation, Colorado, 1964.

Swenson, David F. "The Existential Dialectic of Søren Kierkegaard." *Ethics*, 49, 3, 1938–39, pp. 309–28.

———. "Objective Uncertainty and Human Faith," "Supernaturalism—Source of Moral Power," "The Transforming Power of Other Worldliness," in *The Faith of a Scholar*, ch. 5, 6, 7. Philadelphia: Westminster, 1949.

———. "The Existential Dialectic of Søren Kierkegaard," "Kierkegaard's Doctrine of the Three Stages on the Way of Life," in *Something about Kierkegaard*, ch. 3, 5. Minneapolis: Augsburg, 1951.

Thielicke, Helmut. "Nihilism and Anxiety." *Theology Today*, 12, 3, October 1955, pp. 342–45.

Thompson, Hugo Wilfred. "Ethics and Religion in the Philosophy of Kierkegaard." Ph.D. dissertation, Yale, 1935.

Thomte, Reidar. *Kierkegaard's Philosophy of Religion*. Princeton: Princeton University Press, 1948.

Thulstrup, Marie M. "Kierkegaard's Dialectic of Imitation," in *A Kierkegaard Critique*, ed. Howard Johnson and Niels Thulstrup, ch. 15. New York: Harper, 1962.

Tweedie, Donald F., Jr. "The Significance of Dread in the Thought of Kierkegaard and Heidegger." Ph.D. dissertation, Boston, 1954.

Ussher, Arland. *Journey through Dread*. New York: Devin-Adair, 1955.

White, Willie. "Faith and Existence: A Study in Aquinas and Kierkegaard." Ph.D. dissertation, Chicago, 1965.

Wilburn, Ralph G. "The Philosophy of Existence and the Faith-Relation." *Religion in Life*, 30, 1961, pp. 497–517.

Wild, John D. *Existence and the World of Freedom*. Englewood Cliffs, N.J.: Prentice-Hall, 1963.

Wilde, Jean T., and William Kimmel. *The Search for Being; Essays from Kierkegaard to Sartre on the Problem of Existence."* New York: Twayne, 1962.

Williams, Forrest. "A Problem in Values: the Faustian Motivation in Kierkegaard and Goethe." *Ethics*, 63, 4, July 1952–53, pp. 251–61.

Wolf, W. J. "Alienation and Reconciliation in the Writings of Søren Kierkegaard." Ph.D. dissertation, Union Theological Seminary, 1945.

Wood, Forrest E. "Kierkegaardian Light on Ibsen's *Brand.*" *Personalist,* 51, Summer 1970, pp. 393–400.

Wyschogrod, Michael. *Kierkegaard and Heidegger; the Ontology of Existence.* New York: Humanities Press, 1954.

Zeigler, Leslie. "Personal Existence: A Study of Buber and Kierkegaard." *Journal of Religion,* 40, April 1960, pp. 80–94.

Yonezawa, N. "The Problem about the Ethical Existence in Kierkegaard." *Journal of Religious Studies,* 33, 162, 1960, pp. 84–85.

The entire authorship is concerned with the stages of personal and relational becoming. For particular references in the works to the stages, see, for example, *The Concept of Irony,* pp. 190, 199–200, 248–51, 253–55, 279, 312–14, 317–22, 338–42; *Either/Or,* I, pp. 37–39, 43–134, 220–24, 236, 279–96, 301–2; II, pp. 36–44, 57–63, 95–100, 135–44, 149–50, 167–97, 212–36, 255–67, 309, 337; *Fear and Trembling,* pp. 21–23, 46–64, 66, 78–80, 91–92, 107–11, 130–32; *Repetition,* pp. 33–35, 104–20, 125–27, 134–37; *Fragments,* pp. 11–26; *The Concept of Anxiety* [*Dread*], pp. 16–17, 42, 43, 45, 48, 49, 54–55, 57, 66–67, 69–71, 74–80, 96–100, 102, 108, 123, 126–28, 130–36, 139–45; *Stages,* pp. 15, 157–61, 162–63, 335–36, 350–51, 387–89, 391, 394–95, 399–400, 404–36, especially p. 430; *Postscript,* pp. 37–38; 79, 84, 107–13, 115–47, 169–91, 221–23, 226–66, 273–97, 305–22, 340–43, 345–415, 448–68, 473–77, 489–99, 505–8, 512–19; *Works of Love,* p. 235; *The Sickness unto Death,* pp. 146–47, 162–213, 262; *The Point of View,* pp. 27, 75.

701. Lines 1–2 of *"Vanitas! Vanitatum Vanitas!"* ["Vanity! Vanity of Vanities!"], ll. 1–2, *Gesellige Lieder, Werke,* I–LV (Stuttgart, Tübingen: 1828–33), I, pp. 145–47. *ASKB* 1641–68. "I don't trouble myself about anything. Hurrah!"

702. Thomas Kingo, *Psalmer og aandelige Sange af Thomas Kingo,* ed. P. A. Fenger (Copenhagen: 1827), no. 93, ll. 1 and 9. *ASKB* 203.

703. Johann G. von Herder, *"Der Gewinn des Leben. Nach dem Englischen," Sämmtliche Werke. Zur schönen Litteratur und Kunst,* I–XX (Stuttgart, Tübingen: 1827–30), I, p. 34. *ASKB* 1685–94.

704. F. Schleiermacher, *Monologen* (Berlin: 1800), no. V, end.

705. Ludwig Tieck, *Novellen,* I–XII (Berlin: 1852–54), XII, pp. 14 ff.

706. The Carpocratians, a Gnostic sect of the second century.

707. See I C 125.

708. In Norse mythology the daughters of Aeger and Ran.

709. W. Vollmer, *Völlstandiges Wörterbuch der Mythologie aller Nationen,* I–II (Stuttgart: 1836), II (Abbildungen); for text see I, p. 1537. *ASKB* 1942–43.

710. Jonah 4:6 ff.

711. See *Either/Or,* I, pp. 45–134.

712. See I A 319.

713. In love, infatuated.

714. Stephani the Younger, *Apothekeren og Doctoren*, music by Ditters von Dittersdorf, tr. Lars Knudsen (Copehagen: 1789).

715. In Norse mythology Thor was challenged in various ways by King Utgard-Loki; each challenge involved an enormous deception, such as in the drinking bout. See "Thor's Unlucky Journey to Jotunheim."

716. Simpler.

717. See I C 125; note 712.

718. See notes 708 and 709.

719. See *Either/Or*, I, p. 26; Friederich Heimrich von der Hagen, *Erzählungen und Märchen*, I–II (Prenzlau: 1825), I, pp. 147–52, 156–209 (see I C 82, 83).

720. Anon. [T. C. Croker], *Irische Elfenmärchen*, tr. J. and W. Grimm (Leipzig: 1826). *ASKB* 1423.

721. The exact words.

722. *The Cleric's Meal:* Those who understand such things say that the quiet people are a part of those angels banished from heaven, who are now established on earth, whereas another part have sunk still deeper in a much worse place because of greater sins. . . . *The Bottle:* In the good old days, when the quiet people still appeared more often than now in this unbelieving time.

723. Ibid. That may be left undecided.

724. See Galatians 4:19.

725. Still life.

726. Matthias Claudius, *Der Besuch im St. Hiob zu***, *Werke*, I–II 1–4, (Hamburg: 1838), II, pt. 4, pp. 123 ff., including an etching of the four brothers. *ASKB* 163–32.

727. *Upbuilding [Edifying] Discourses*, II, pp. 67–87.

728. A reference presumably to Diderot's *Encyclopedia*, I–XXVIII (1751–72), with five supplementary volumes (1176–77) and two volumes of index (1780). See Kierkegaard's "Open Confession" in *Fædrelandet*, no. 904, June 12, 1842; *S.V.*, XIII, p. 400.

729. See Luke 16:25.

730. Opposites become clearer when they are placed side by side.

731. *Die Politik des Aristoteles*, tr. Christian Garve, I–II (Breslau: 1799), I. *ASKB* 1088–89.

732. Lines spoken to the audience at the end of a well-acted play.

733. *The Lives of the Caesars*, "The Deified Augustus," bk. II, XCIX.

734. Applaud loudly, all of you, and show genuine enthusiasm.

735. Gottfried W. Leibniz, *Theodicee*, rev. J. C. Goftscheden (Hannover, Leipzig: 5 ed., 1763), pp. 459–60. *ASKB* 619. The lines in Suetonius and Leibniz do not correspond fully. Kierkegaard has followed Leibniz.

736. See *Stages*, p. 122; *Postscript*, p. 253 fn.

737. P. A. Wolff, *Preciosa*, tr. C. J. Boye (Copenhagen: 1822), p. 25. See *Stages*, p. 122.

738. Seneca, *De Beneficiis*, V, 6, 2.

739. See *Postscript,* p. 157.

740. Plutarch, *Moralia,* "The E at Delphi"; *"Ueber die Inschrift Ei im Tempel zu Delphi," Plutarchs moralische Abhandlungen,* tr. J. F. S. Kaltwasser, I–IX (Frankfurt am Main: 1786), III, pp. 508–9. *ASKB* 1192–96.

741. See *Two Ages, S.V.,* VIII, p. 47 (omitted in partial English translation under the title *The Present Age*).

742. Ammianus Marcellinus, XXIII, 6, 85–86; *Ammian Marcellin, aus dem Lateinischen übersetzt und mit Anmerkungen begleitet,* tr. J. A. Wagner, I–III (Frankfurt am Main: 1792–94), II, p. 213. *ASKB* 1257–59. "Among the Indians and the Persians pearls are found in strong, white sea-shells, being conceived at a definite time of the year by mixture with dew. For at that time they desire, as it were, a kind of copulation, and by often opening and shutting quickly they take in moisture by sprinkling with moonlight. . . . And it is a proof that they are of ethereal origin, rather than that they are conceived and fed from nourishment derived from the sea, that when drops of morning dew fall upon these gems, they make them brilliant and round, but the dew of evening, on the contrary, makes them irregular, red, and sometimes spotted; and they become large or small under varying conditions, according to the quality of what they have taken in." Ammianus Marcellinus, *The Surviving Books of the History of Ammianus Marcellinus,* XXIII, 6, 85–86. (Loeb ed., tr. J. C. Rolfe.)

743. See *Postscript,* pp. 195, 369, 439; "The Difference between a Genius and an Apostle," with *The Present Age,* p. 151; *The Sickness unto Death,* pp. 230, 248, 253, 257, 258; *Practice [Training] in Christianity,* p. 67.

744. See *Works of Love,* p. 318.

745. From draft of *Upbuilding Discourses in Various Spirits,* Part One [*Purity of Heart,* p. 60 end, also p. 177].

746. Ibid.; see p. 66, ll. 7 ff., also pp. 176–77.

747. Ibid., see p. 78 end, also p. 176.

748. Entry is from a draft of *The Book on Adler* (English translation under the title *On Authority and Revelation,* which does not include this portion).

749. Ibid.

750. See *Works of Love,* p. 160; L. Achim von Arnim and Clemens Brentano, *"Der Tannhäuser," Des Knaben Wunderhorn,* I–III (Heidelberg: 1819), I, pp. 86 ff. *ASKB* 1494–96.

751. See *Works of Love,* pp. 129–30, 150–52.

752. Ibid., pp. 330, 332, 335.

753. A marginal addition very similar to this entry is found in the final manuscript of *Works of Love* (p. 237, l. 10), but it was not used in the published work.

754. No doubt a reference to Kierkegaard's father. See *Works of Love,* pp. 317–29.

755. Entry is a deleted portion in manuscript of *Works of Love,* p. 36, ll. 6 ff.

756. See note 755; ibid., p. 36, ll. 19 ff; ibid., pp. 34-57.
757. See note 755; ibid., p. 37, ll. 31 ff.
758. See note 755; ibid., p. 38, ll. 4 ff.
759. See note 755; ibid., p. 40, ll. 17 ff.
760. See J. P. Mynster, *Prædikener holdte i Aaret* 1848 (Copenhagen: 1849), pp. 72, 74. *ASKB* 232.
761. Meïer Goldschmidt, novelist and editor of *Corsaren*. See note 433.
762. See *Postscript*, p. 226, 320, 480 fn.; "The Difference between a Genius and an Apostle," with *The Present Age*, p. 139.
763. See note 915.
764. On this note of criticism of Paul, see *The Moment*, no. 5 and no. 7, in *Attack*, pp. 159-61 and 213; see also note 69 and note on pp. 282-83.
765. H. H., the pseudonymous author of the two small but very important treatises, "Has a Man the Right to Let Himself Be Put to Death for the Truth?" and "The Difference between a Genius and an Apostle," in English translation with the first edition of *The Present Age* [part of *Two Ages*] (London, New York: Oxford, 1940), pp. 77-163.
766. See *Fear and Trembling*, pp. 22-25.
767. Exodus 33:23.
768. See, for example, *Either/Or*, II, pp. 343-56.
769. See note 280; ibid., II, p. 397.
770. Hatred of the whole human race.
771. See *Judge for Yourselves!*, pp. 123-25; note 507.
772. August Neander, *Der heilige Johannes Chrysostomus und die Kirche, besonders des Orients, in dessen Zeitalter* (Berlin: 1822).
773. See Christian Scriver, *Seelen-Schatz*, I-V (Leipzig: 1723), V, 7, para. 25. *ASKB* 261-63. The Danish editions of 1741 and 1888 have the same numbering.
774. See note 28.
775. See *Fear and Trembling*, p. 79; *Fragments*, pp. 101-3, 108-9.
776. See *For Self-Examination* (which was published in 1851), pp. 87-98.
777. Ibid., p. 98.
778. There is a play here on hunger and making a living (*Levebrød*: salary, a living, literally "living-bread").
779. See note 649.
780. See note 675.
781. See James 4:4.
782. See *Fear and Trembling*, pp. 28-29.
783. See note 675.
784. See Exodus 33:20.
785. See Matthew 19:21; Mark 10:21; Luke 18:22.
786. See *Practice* [*Training*] *in Christianity*, p. 44; the present En-

glish edition translates *"ikke en suur Sild værd"* as "not worth a straw," which is hardly adequate and obviously would be a loss here.

787. Ecclesiastes 7:29.
788. See, for example, *For Self-Examination,* pp. 12–21.
789. This is something different.
790. See note 788.
791. Hesiod, *Works and Days,* stanza 40; S. Meisling, *Digte fra Oldtiden,* I–VII (Copenhagen, 1827–32), I, p. 7.
792. Agur; see Proverbs 30:1, 8–9.
793. Danish, *Videnskabeligheder.*
794. See Matthew 16:23.

STATE CHURCH

In the constitution of June 5, 1849, which gave Denmark a parliamentary government, there were several sections pointing toward future legislation concerning the position of the Church. This intensified the debate in progress on the relation between the state and the Church, in which among others N. F. S. Grundtvig, Bishop Mynster, and A. G. Rudelbach took part.

In a journal entry in 1849 Kierkegaard writes of the current situation: "Then I was horrified to see what was understood by a Christian state (this I saw especially in 1848); I saw how the ones who were supposed to rule, both in Church and in state, hid themselves like cowards while barbarism boldly and brazenly raged. ..." And further, "But if what one sees all over Europe is Christendom, a Christian state, then I propose to start here in Denmark to list the price for being a Christian in such a way that the whole concept—state-Church, official appointments, livelihood—bursts open" (X^1 A 541).

Kierkegaard had long realized "all the objections there are which can be leveled from a Christian point of view against a state church, a folk church, an established Church, etc.," and that "in the strictly Christian sense the demand is: separation. This is ideality's maximum requirement." But Kierkegaard also believed that a separation of Church and state ought not be the result of a political decision, since it is first and foremost a religious matter. It could be carried through properly only by "an apostle, at least a witness to the truth." But since there was no man of "religious character" in the age, Kierkegaard saw but one way out, that one must remain with "the established," which was "far preferable to a reformation devoid of character." On the other hand, Kierkegaard more than ever saw it as his task to call for "admissions" from himself and others, admissions that in Christendom "imitation" in the more rigorous sense had been left out (X^4 A 296).

Kierkegaard, therefore, did not take part in the current debate on Church affairs, and when Dr. Rudelbach in *Om det borgerlige Ægteskab* (Copenhagen: 1851) wanted to cite him and his authorship in support of "the emancipation of the Church from the state," Kierkegaard in a pointed article in *Fædrelandet,*

January, 1851, called attention to the fact that never in his authorship had he let fall a single word "about a proposal for external change, suggesting a belief that the problem is lodged in externalities," but on the contrary had seen it as his task "to work for the inward deepening of Christianity in myself and others . . ." (*An Open Letter*, p. 49).

Kierkegaard's disappointment over the position of responsible persons and especially of Bishop Mynster during these years was a contributing factor in his later very sharp statements about the "state church" in the first numbers of *The Moment*. His main criticism is that the state church sets itself up as representing true Christianity and thereby gives men the illusion that they are all Christians, and that the pastors help to confirm this illusion in people, and that furthermore the oath pastors make upon the New Testament is a self-contradiction, since the Christianity of the New Testament is just the opposite of state-church Christianity (see, for example, *The Moment*, no. 3, in *Attack*, pp. 127–29, 130–31). Kierkegaard also points out that the state, too, must ponder whether its relation to Christianity is defensible (pp. 132–33).

Kierkegaard's primary aim in directly attacking the Church was to get people to see that what the state church passed off as Christianity was not true Christianity. This was the reason, too, for his conviction that in the long run a state-church arrangement would be untenable, and that "world development" would carry with it a "separation of state and Church" (XI^2 A 414). But whatever else the external situation, for Kierkegaard the interiorizing of Christianity in the individual person was always decisive.

For references in the works to state church, see, for example, *The Concept of Irony*, p. 188; *Either/Or*, I, p. 101; *An Open Letter* and *Armed Neutrality*, pp. 47–49; "This Has to Be Said," in *Attack*, pp. 63–64; *The Moment*, no. 1, no. 2, ibid., pp. 83–86, 110; "Christ's Judgment," ibid., pp. 115–24; *The Moment*, no. 3, no. 4, no. 6, no. 7, no. 10, ibid., pp. 127–36, 139–40, 184, 202, 288.

795. *Pernilles korte Frøikenstand*, II, 7.
796. See Luke 2:1.
797. See, for example, *Works of Love*, pp. 252–53; INDIVIDUAL.
798. Plato, *Republic*, VIII, 552 b-c, 559 c-d, 564 b-d; *Platons Stat*, tr. Carl. J. Heise, I–III (Copenhagen: 1831), III, pp. 21, 38–39, 49–51. *ASKB* 1167.

STEPHEN

There are very few observations in Kierkegaard's journals and authorship on Stephen, the Christian Church's first martyr. On the other hand it is characteristic of Kierkegaard, when he does mention Stephen, to emphasize strongly the contrast between the human and the Christian, for this contrast is most clearly demonstrated in the life of the martyr.

For this reason Kierkegaard finds it appropriate that St. Stephen's Day, when the account of his martyrdom (Acts 6:8–15 and 7:54–70) is read aloud in church, falls on the day after Christmas, the day of Christ's birth, for Christ was born "in order that the natural man should die" (VIII¹ A 470). And just as, humanly understood, it is the child who looks like an angel, it is, Christianly understood, the dying man who looks that way—as did Stephen, whose face, when he sensed the martyr's death, looked like the face of an angel (VIII¹ A 470). Kierkegaard also mentions that, humanly speaking, the stoning of Stephen was a victory for the enemies, but from a Christian point of view it was a defeat, because Stephen peacefully went to sleep after having prayed for his enemies, while they in their impotent fury were unable to sleep (X⁴ A 434). Stephen's death also makes manifest that the more the world shuts itself to a man, the more heaven opens for him, although it is only "the Christian, especially the martyr," who sees heaven open (X⁴ A 436).

Again, the strong contrast between the human and the Christian in its most radical consequences is what Kierkegaard emphasizes in his last reference to Stephen. This occurs in an article in *Fædrelandet*, no. 24, January 29, 1855, on the occasion of H. L. Martensen's once again having spoken "indefatigably" of the clergy as "witnesses," "witnesses to the truth" (in *Attack*, p. 23), at a consecration of a bishop in Frue Kirke the Second Day of Christmas, St. Stephen's Day. According to Kierkegaard, by such a comparison "either Stephen becomes ridiculous by the help of the 'many witnesses to the truth' who are available to Dr. Martensen," or it is perhaps rather the case that all the pastors, deans, and bishops, "under the illumination of Stephen become ridiculous in the role of witnesses to the truth" (p. 24).

For references in the works to Stephen, see *Upbuilding* [*Edifying*] *Discourses*, IV, pp. 58, 67; article in *Fædrelandet*, no. 24, January 29, 1855, in *Attack*, p. 24.

799. See Acts 7:60.
800. See Matthew 8:24.
801. See Acts 7:60.
802. See Acts 7:55–56.

STOICISM, STOICS

In his book *From the Papers of One Still Living* (1838), Kierkegaard tries to prove his claim that Hans Christian Andersen "completely lacks a philosophy of life." Kierkegaard defines a life-view as "an arduously won confidence in oneself, unshakable by any experience," and maintains that there are two main types of life-views—the human and the Christian. Stoicism is cited as an example of the human life-view. In Stoicism a person tries to maintain an "unshakable confidence in himself" with respect to all the vicissitudes of the world. Kierkegaard thereby defines Stoicism positively, even though he refers to its limitation compared to Christianity, inasmuch as Christianity presupposes contact with "a deeper empiricism" (*S.V.*, XIII, p. 68).

In 1848 Kierkegaard makes his first negatively critical comment on Stoicism: "This is what I desire in a man, something a Stoic uses in an evil sense:

ευκαταφορια εις παθος (IV A 44). While the phrase "disposition to passion" as used by the Stoic Chrysippus expresses a negative view of passion, it is characteristic of Kierkegaard that in stressing the existential, he wants to emphasize the significance of passion.

Later, while reading such Stoics as Marcus Aurelius Antoninus and Epictetus, Kierkegaard criticizes some of Stoicism's points of view from a Christian position. For example, he objects to Marcus Aurelius's praise of suicide and his disapproval of Christian martyrdom on the grounds that the Stoic's position is a "selfishness" which is sufficient unto itself and will not serve a cause. "The Stoical self" is therefore called "the most isolated self" (IX A 373; see *The Sickness unto Death*, p. 202). Kierkegaard also reproaches the Stoic for his pride, which leaves no room for compassion for men (X^3 A 13). When the Stoic maintains suicide as an escape, his position is defined as "the union of pride and cowardice" (X^3 A 14).

While reading Epictetus, Kierkegaard was particularly aware of the clues to Epictetus' slave origin in his teaching, in that he is prepared to submit slavishly to situations that cannot be altered (X^3 A 643). But a comparison of Marcus Aurelius and Epictetus is to the latter's advantage, because he dealt with existential situations in a different and more decisive way than did Marcus Aurelius (X^4 A 576).

Kierkegaard believes that Christianity's superiority over Stoicism, existentially speaking, can be seen in the fact that while Stoicism fails man by commending suicide, Christianity helps man to surmount the wretchedness of the world by asking him to "die to the world" (X^5 A 63) and by affirming a transcendent possibility with significance in time, a healing of despair.

For references in the works to the Stoics and Stoicism, see *The Concept of Irony*, pp. 237, 313; *Either/Or*, p. 97; *Fragments*, pp. 15, 95; *Postscript*, p. 148; *The Sickness unto Death*, pp. 202, 207; article in *Fædrelandet*, no. 10, January 12, 1855, in *Attack*, p. 17.

803. The Danish editors of the *Papirer* point out that Poul Martin Møller (*Efterladte Skrifter*, I–III, Copenhagen: 1839–1843, II, p. 338; *ASKB* 1574-76) designates Empedocles as a disciple of Zeno and suggest that therefore Kierkegaard may have confused that Eleatic Zeno with the later Stoic Zeno.

804. See note 839; ibid., 16, 464 b; *Postscript*, p. 128.

805. See note 544.

806. Disposition to passion.

807. See note 544; *Fragments*, pp. 14–15.

808. See *Postscript*, p. 148.

809. *Epiktets Haandbog*, tr. E. Boye (Copenhagen: 1781), p. 3. *ASKB* 1114.

810. The door, after it is opened, signifies an invitation.

811. See note 595.

812. The *Auktionsprotokol over Søren Kierkegaard's Bogsamling* (*ASKB*)

lists: M[arcus Aurelius] Antoninus Commentarii libri XII, ed. J. M. Schulz (Leipzig: 1829), *ASKB* 1218; *Marcus Aurelius Antonins Unterhaltung mit sich selbst,* tr. J. M. Schulz (Schleswig: 1799), *ASKB* 1219; *Epicteti Manuale et Cebetis Tabula graeci et latine,* ed. J. Schweighauser (Leipzig: 1798), *ASKB* 1113; *Epiktets Haandbog,* tr. E. Boye (Copenhagen: 1781), *ASKB* 1114; *Theophrasti Characteres et: Epicteti Manuale* (Leipzig: 1829), *ASKB* 1205; *Epictets Haandbog,* tr. L. Sahl (Copenhagen: 1785), *ASKB* Ap. I, 156.

813. E. Zeller, *Die Philosophie der Griechen,* I–III$^{1-2}$, (Tübingen: 1844–52), III, pp. 184 ff.

STRIVING

As long as a person lives solely in immediacy, he does not know striving; it is reflection which first moves the individual from desiring to striving when he consciously chooses "the way to the thing sought" (*Three Discourses on Imagined Occasions* [*Thoughts on Crucial Situations*], p. 15). According to Kierkegaard, man's striving has "its source" in "the world of freedom," which is also the reason all essential striving is a striving toward the infinite, thus really "directed toward God," even though it begins as a striving "toward the unknown" (p. 16).

In contrast to this, Kierkegaard characterizes man's so-called striving in finitude as "the pedestrian's peace of mind on the highway of mediocrity," where men who have given up striving for the ideal have learned "triviality" and "contentment" or merely covet temporal goods such as money, esteem, etc. (p. 15). He speaks contemptuously of this calculating striving, particularly in his latest journal entries (see, for example, X^3 A 686, XI^1 A 212, 397, and 398).

The artistic striving described by the esthete A in *Either/Or* is on a higher level, although it, too, lies within the temporal, inasmuch as it has its goal in itself, which is why it is designated as "fragmentary" (*Either/Or,* I, p. 150). The highest this striving can bring a man is to catch a glimpse of the idea.

Only when a person is seized by enthusiasm "for a specific striving can he be led to a striving for something higher: to will one thing by willing the good." Kierkegaard says of this in the *Upbuilding Discourses in Various Spirits,* Part One [*Purity of Heart*]: "But perhaps his striving was still not the good in the deepest sense—so enthusiasm became for him a teacher . . ." (p. 67, ed. tr.). The good in the deepest sense, the good in and for itself, is the goal of ethical striving. Climacus describes this striving in *Concluding Unscientific Postscript,* especially in the section on "the existing subjective thinker" (pp. 74–86). Here Climacus shows how "existence itself, to exist, is a striving" (p. 84, ed. tr.), because man is a composite of "the infinite and the finite, the eternal and the temporal" (p. 85). Ethical striving is essentially an "actualization of infinitude" (p. 84), that is, a continually renewed resolve (see *Upbuilding* [*Edifying*] *Discourses,* IV, pp. 91–95) that every action have the intrinsic good as its goal; it is "a striving which is motivated and is repeatedly refreshed by the crucial passion of the infinite" (*Postscript*, p. 182, ed. tr.).

But a person gradually learns through honest ethical striving how little he is able to achieve, and if he continually maintains "his personal knowledge of the ideal, which requires everything" (p. 488), he eventually will come to comprehend the "totality of guilt-consciousness" (p. 489) and be open to Christ's invitation to forgiveness. But even when a person has accepted God's forgiveness, he is nevertheless to strive after the still higher goal, so that his life "expresses the truth," so that his life "in a striving after truth is approximately the being of truth, a life, as it was in Christ . . ." (*Practice* [*Training*] *in Christianity*, p. 201, ed. tr.). This is the way Anti-Climacus describes man's striving in Christianity. Here the difficulty for man is to understand that now this striving, although it is the utmost strenuousness, "is to be regarded as a jest, a childlike act . . . the Atonement is the earnestness." Kierkegaard adds: "It is detestable, however, for a man to want to use grace, 'since all is grace,' to avoid striving" (X^4 A 491; see also *Judge for Yourselves!*, pp. 177-78). That the emphasis is particularly on striving is clearly expressed in a journal entry from 1851, in which Kierkegaard says: "*Christianly*, the emphasis does not fall so much upon to what extent or how far a person succeeds in meeting or fulfilling the requirement if he actually is striving. . . . No, infinite humiliation and grace, and then a striving born of gratitude—this is Christianity" (X^3 A 734).

Kierkegaard blamed his age and "official Christendom" primarily for not making the slightest effort to make known the Christian requirement so that we can all perceive "at what a distance we are living, and that our lives cannot in the remotest way be called a striving toward a fulfilling the requirement" ("What Do I Want?", *Fædrelandet*, no. 77, March 31, 1855, in *Attack*, p. 38, ed. tr.).

For references in the works to striving, see, for example, *The Concept of Irony*, pp. 146-47, 320-21, 332; *Either/Or*, I, pp. 150, 204; II, pp. 18, 96, 136, 263, 279; *Upbuilding* [*Edifying*] *Discourses*, IV, pp. 87-95; *Three Discourses on Imagined Occasions* [*Thoughts on Crucial Situations*], pp. 14-23; *Stages*, p. 71; *Postscript*, pp. 74-86, 98-99, 110, 121-25, 135-36, 181-82, 238, 353, 356, 364-65, 374-75 fn., 385, 469, 476, 487-88; *Upbuilding Discourses in Various Spirits*, Part One [*Purity of Heart*, pp. 66-67]; *The Sickness unto Death*, p. 208; *Practice* [*Training*] *In Christianity*, pp. 109, 201, 228, 234-50; *For Self-Examination*, p. [i]; *Judge for Yourselves!*, pp. 161, 164-66; *On My Work as an Author*, with *The Point of View*, p. 151 fn.; articles in *Fædrelandet*, no. 77 and no. 83, March 31, and April 11, 1855, in *Attack*, pp. 38, 42; *The Moment*, no. 4, no. 6, no. 7, and no. 9, ibid., pp. 144 and 151, 187, 208-11, and 265-66.

814. One, two, three.
815. See I Corinthians 9:26.
816. See I Corinthians 9:24.

817. See note 675.
818. See, for example, *Works of Love,* passim, especially pp. 62-98.
819. A play on *letsindig* (literally "light-minded") and *tungsindig* (literally "heavy-minded").
820. See *Armed Neutrality* and *An Open Letter,* pp. 33-46, especially p. 37. The first move was the authorship in its ideality; the second would have been the expected admission of accommodation.
821. Ibid., pp. 36-39.
822. See Philippians 4:13.
823. J. L. Heiberg, *Syvsoverdag* (Copenhagen: 1840), I, 15.
824. See *Stages,* p. 377; *Postscript,* p. 228; *The Moment,* no. 10, in *Attack,* pp. 287-88.
825. Ibid.
826. See note 32.

SUBJECTIVITY/OBJECTIVITY

As early as 1835 (during his stay at Gilleleje) Kierkegaard wrote in his journal that he did not want to base the development of his thought "on anything called objective" (I A 75) but wanted to concentrate on his own personal actuality. This marked interest in personal existence (subjectivity) in contrast to an external, objective knowledge Kierkegaard retained all his life. He constantly endeavored to deepen his understanding of man's inner being by way of what he called "anthropological contemplation" (III A 3) and "an inland journey within his own consciousness" (*Prefaces, S.V.,* V, p. 48; see also V B 47:13). In his writings Kierkegaard used the profound inner experience of the actuality of the subject which he attained in this way.

In *Concluding Unscientific Postscript* Johannes Climacus gives a detailed and coherent account of what Kierkegaard understood as subjective actuality and its relation to objectivity. Since Climacus is attempting in this book to permit subjectivity to attain its full right, he very carefully demarcates it from objectivity. Climacus points out that objective knowledge does not in the deeper sense concern the existence of the subject at all. This knowledge includes such branches of knowledge as mathematics, the natural sciences, and also historical knowledge. The sphere of these branches of knowledge lies within finitude, within the quantitative (pertains to "the quantitative 'what' "; *Postscript,* p. 442), and the highest level that can be attained here is an abstract objective description of this phenomenal actuality. Climacus says of this objective form of knowledge: "That knowledge which does not, in the reflection of inwardness, inwardly pertain to existence is essentially accidental knowledge" (p.176, ed. tr.). It is the very opposite of knowledge based on the presupposition that man himself is the most important object of our knowledge, because only in the human subject is the possibility of the eternal to be found, and only in relation to this possibility can there be any question of truth (see TRUTH).

This eternal in man makes itself known as an absolute ethical requirement, and the first awareness of this requirement is essential knowledge. In a person's striving to actualize this knowledge, he is led to religious knowledge, which has God as its ultimate aim. Therefore Climacus calls essential knowledge only that knowledge which is reached by "subjective reflection" (p. 171), that is, by way of "the subjective approach" (p. 173, ed. tr.), and which is to be actualized through "the 'how' of inwardness" (p. 443, ed. tr.). He says of this knowledge: "Therefore only ethical and ethical-religious knowledge are essential knowledge. But all ethical and all ethical-religious knowledge are essentially related to the existing of the knower" (p. 177, ed. tr.). Regarded objectively, the actualization of essential knowledge in existence must be regarded as a paradox, because in this attempt a synthesis of two opposite qualities must be found: finitude and infinitude. The paradox also becomes an indication that one ventures beyond ordinary objective categories.

In *Concluding Unscientific Postscript,* Climacus has scrupulously described the subject's efforts to relate absolutely to the absolute and relatively to relativities (pp. 358–70) and has pointed out the guilt that is the final result of these efforts (pp. 468–93). He shows that the transformation of subjectivity and the encounter with "the object of truth" (p. 515, ed. tr.), Christ, takes place according to very specific laws, which can be stated objectively (pp. 541–42). Kierkegaard writes in a journal entry: "In all the usual talk that Johannes Climacus is mere subjectivity, etc., it has been completely overlooked that he, in addition to all his other concretions, points out in one of the last sections that the remarkable thing is that there is a How with the characteristic that when the How is scrupulously rendered the What is also given, that this is the How of 'faith.' Right here, at its very maximum, inwardness is shown to be objectivity. And this, then, is a turning of the subjectivity-principle, which, as far as I know, has never before been carried through or accomplished in this way" (X^2 A 299). This objectivity could be called the objectivity to the second power, or the objectivity of inwardness, and it is different from the objectivity with which the empirical sciences operate. Thus it cannot be demonstrated directly by visible means; everyone must himself test it by experiencing the How of inwardness. This was also one of the reasons that Climacus retracted his book; he could not directly communicate his experiences to others. On the other hand the objectivity to the second power can be revealed in such a way "that merely by describing the How of his inwardness a man" can indirectly show "that he is a Christian without naming the name of Christ" (p. 542, ed. tr.).

Kierkegaard touches on an essential aspect of the relation of objectivity to subjectivity in an entry entitled "to relate objectively to one's own subjectivity" (XI^2 A 97). Here subjectivity is asked to look soberly and truthfully at itself in its spiritual development, with a sense of responsibility and without the intermingling of accidental and arbitrary points of view, and at the same time to apprehend others as subjects and not as objects.

Bedell, George C. "The Modalities of Existence," in *Kierkegaard and Faulkner; Modalities of Existence*, ch. 7. Baton Rouge: Louisiana State University Press, 1971.

Brown, James. *Kierkegaard, Heidegger, Buber and Barth: Subject and Object in Modern Theology.* New York: Collier, 1962. Originally published as *Subject and Object in Modern Theology.* New York: Macmillan, 1956.

Chervin, Ronda. "The Process of Conversion in the Philosophy of Søren Kierkegaard." Ph.D. dissertation, Fordham, 1967.

Edwards, Paul. "Kierkegaard and the 'Truth' of Christianity." *Philosophy*, 46, April 1971, pp. 89–108.

Eller, Vernard. "Fact, Faith, and Foolishness: Kierkegaard and the New Quest." *Journal of Religion*, 48, January 1968, pp. 54–65.

Fabro, Cornelio. "The 'Subjectivity of Truth' and the Interpretation of Kierkegaard." *Kierkegaard-Studiet* (Copenhagen), 1, 1964, pp. 35–43.

Galati, Michael. "A Rhetoric for the Subjectivist in a World of Untruth: the Tasks and Strategy of Søren Kierkegaard." *Quarterly Journal of Speech*, 55, 1969, pp. 372–80.

Heinecken, Martin J. "Truth is Subjectivity," "Objectivity and the Offense," in *The Moment Before God*, ch. 8, 9. Philadelphia: Muhlenberg, 1956.

Hendel, Charles W. "The Subjective as a Problem." *Philosophical Review*, 62, 3, 1953, pp. 327–54.

Horgby, Ingvar. "Immediacy–Subjectivity–Revelation: An Interpretation of Kierkegaard's Conception of Reality." *Inquiry* (Oslo), 8, 1, 1965, pp. 84–117.

Jennings, Theodore W. "Man as the Subject of Existence: A Study of Post-Hegelian Anthropologies in Continental Theology." Ph.D. dissertation, Emory, 1971.

Keane, Ellen M. "The Equation of Subjectivity and Truth in Kierkegaard's *Postscript.*" Ph.D. dissertation, Notre Dame, 1965.

Lindstrom, Valter. "The Problem of Objectivity and Subjectivity in Kierkegaard," in *A Kierkegaard Critique*, ed. Howard A. Johnson and Niels Thulstrup, ch. 13. New York: Harper, 1962.

Lowry, Charles W. "Existentialism or Subjectivity in Rebound," in *Communism and Christ*, ch. 2(6). New York: Morehouse-Gorham, 1953.

Mackey, Louis. "Kierkegaard and the Problem of Existential Philosophy." *Review of Metaphysics*, 9, 3–4, 1956, pp. 404–19, 569–88.

———. "Poetry of Inwardness," in *The Existential Philosophers*, ed. George Schrader, pp. 45–107. New York: McGraw-Hill, 1967.

McMinn, J. B. "Values and Subjectivity in Kierkegaard." *Review and Expositor*, 53, October 1956, pp. 477–88.

Martin, H. V. "Truth Is Subjectivity," in *Kierkegaard*, ch. 5. London: Epworth, 1950.

Murphy, Arthur E. "On Kierkegaard's Claim that 'Truth is Subjectivity.'" *Reason and the Common Good*, ed. William H. Hay. Englewood Cliffs, N.J.: Prentice-Hall, 1963, pp. 173–79.

Roberts, James Deotis. "Kierkegaard on Truth and Subjectivity." *Journal of Religious Thought*, 17, 1961, pp. 41–56.

Robinson, William. "Objectivity of the Subjective in Kierkegaard." *Shane Quarterly*, 16, July 1955, pp. 144–50.

Schacht, Richard. "Kierkegaard on 'Truth is Subjectivity' and 'The Leap of Faith.'" *Canadian Journal of Philosophy*, 2, March 1973, pp. 297–313.

Schrag, Calvin O. *Existence and Freedom: towards an Ontology of Human Finitude*. Evanston: Northwestern University Press, 1961.

Sefler, George P. "Kierkegaard's Religious Truth: Three Dimensions of Subjectivity." *International Journal for Philosophy of Religion*, 2, Spring 1971, pp. 43–52.

Stein, Waltraut J. "Truth as Subjectivity: the Thought of Søren Kierkegaard." *Religious Humanism*, 4, Spring 1970, pp. 78–82.

Thomas, John Heywood. *Subjectivity and Paradox*. London: Blackwell, 1957.

Van de Pitte, Frederick. "Kierkegaard's 'Approximation.'" *Personalist*, 52, Summer 1971, pp. 483–98.

Wiseman, William James Johnston. "Subjectivity in the Existential Method of Søren Kierkegaard." Ph.D. dissertation, Temple, 1948.

For references in the works to subjectivity and objectivity, see, for example, SELF: *From the Papers of One Still Living, S.V.*, XIII, pp. 73–74; *The Concept of Irony*, pp. 52–53, 72–77, 83, 111, 139, 154, 161, 166–67, 173–74, 191–92, 218, 221, 224, 232–38, 245, 249, 260, 270, 274–75, 279, 281, 288, 290–92, 336, 349; *Either/Or*, I, pp. 85, 128, 141–43, 148, 152, 157–58, 169–71, 338, 384, 418; II, 164, 170–73, 215–36; *Fear and Trembling*, p. 120; *The Concept of Anxiety* [*Dread*], pp. 10, 16, 21, 46, 50–72, 88, 124–37; *Stages*, pp. 218, 223, 388; *Postscript*, passim; *The Sickness unto Death*, p. 253; *Practice* [*Training*] *in Christianity*, pp. 51–52, 87, 227–50; *For Self-Examination*, pp. 23–54; *Judge for Yourselves!*, pp. 216–17; *The Moment*, no. 5, no. 8, in *Attack*, pp. 172, 242.

827. See Luke 17:11.

828. See *Christian Discourses*, pp. 210 ff.

829. See "advance beyond," *Fragments*, pp. 14, 18, 22, 25, 47, 139; "go further," etc., *Fear and Trembling*, pp. 22–23, 37, 43, 57, 79, 98, 109–11, 129–32.

830. See *Fear and Trembling*, p. 108.

831. The ironic reference is to Hegel's world-historical sweep which overlooks the existing individual. See Hegel, *Philosophie der Geschichte, Werke*, I–XVIII (Berlin: 1832–40), IX, pp. 131 ff.; *Fragments*, p. 97; *Postscript*, pp. 119, 138, 232, 272 fn., 383, 415, 419, 445, 485.

832. From sketch of *Postscript;* see pp. 115–18.
833. See *Postscript,* p. 178.
834. Ibid., p. 171.
835. See note 542; ibid., "Themistocles," III, 3. See *Fear and Trembling,* p. 39; *Postscript,* pp. 321–22; *Practice [Training] in Christianity,* p. 185.
836. See, for example, "'The Single Individual,'" together with *The Point of View,* pp. 107–40; *Works of Love,* pp. 17, 53, 80–81, 160; INDIVIDUAL.
837. To be subjective toward all others means to regard and treat others as subjects, not as objects. See IX A 363, XI² A 97.
838. See *Two Discourses at the Communion on Fridays,* with *Judge for Yourselves!,* p. 5.
839. Plutarch, *De cohibenda ira,* 461 d–e; *Plutarchs moralische Abhandlungen,* tr. J. F. S. Kaltwasser (Frankfurt am Main: 1783), IV, p. 280. *ASKB* 1192–96. See III B 30; 4246.
840. See Matthew 10:29–30.
841. See *Christian Discourses,* pp. 199–200.
842. Anti-Climacus, Kierkegaard's new pseudonym, not "against" Johannes Climacus, but "above" him. Anti-Climacus is the author of *The Sickness unto Death,* published July 30, 1849, and of *Practice in Christianity,* to be published the following year (September 25, 1850).
843. See INDIVIDUAL.
844. Dilettantism.
845. See note 280; ibid., I.
846. See note 829.
847. Johannes Climacus, pseudonymous author of *Philosophical Fragments* and *Concluding Unscientific Postscript,* and also of the earlier *Johannes Climacus or De omnibus dubitandum est* (although written in the third person).
848. See *Postscript,* p. 540; X² A 299.
849. In a particular instance.
850. *Practice [Training] in Christianity,* pp. 247–50.
851. For an instance of this constructivist epistemology, see *Works of Love,* pp. 213–30.
852. See Julius Müller, *Die christliche Lehre von der Sünde,* I–II (Breslau: 3 ed., 1849), I, pp. 48–53, 536–38. *ASKB* 689–690.
853. Change into another sphere or kind.
854. See X² A 299.
855. See first stanza of *"Die worte des Glaubens,"* in *Schillers sämmtliche Werke,* I–XII (Stuttgart, Tübingen: 1838), I, p. 403. *ASKB* 1804–15. Kierkegaard has inaccurately recalled the opening lines, although as quoted their substance fits the context.

> *Drei Worte nenn' euch, inhaltschwer,*
> *Sie gehen von Munde zu Munde,*

> *Doch stamnen sie nicht von Auszen her;*
> *Das Herz nur gibt davon Kunde.*
>
> Three words of mighty moment I'll name,
> From mouth to mouth they fly ever,
> Yet the heart alone their great value proclaims,
> For their source from without rises never.

"The Words of Faith," *The Poems of Schiller,* tr. Edgar A. Bowring (London: Bell, 1882), p. 257.

Kierkegaard's version:

> A word
> From mouth to mouth it flies
> The heart does not proclaim it.

856. See *For Self-Examination* (dated August, 1851), pp. 23–61; X^4 A 412.
857. See note 4; ibid., p. 341.
858. See *Works of Love,* pp. 51–52.
859. See *For Self-Examination,* pp. 41–44.
860. See II Samuel 12:7; *For Self-Examination,* pp. 42–43.
861. Ibid.
862. A crucial metaphor in Kierkegaard's thought. See, for example, *Works of Love,* p. 332; *The Sickness unto Death,* pp. 147, 262.
863. See note 478.
864. See Matthew 7:14; *For Self-Examination,* pp. 63–83.
865. See I Corinthians 2:28; James 2:5.
866. See Matthew 7:1.
867. See *The Moment,* no. 7, in *Attack,* p. 208.
868. See VIII^1 A 165, IX A 363.
869. See Matthew 12:1–14; Mark 2:23–28; Luke 6:1–11.

SUFFERING

It appears from Kierkegaard's journals and books that even as a child he had intimate knowledge of human suffering. Many have conjectured as to the nature of his own particular suffering; in any case it is certain that it was linked to the despondency from which his father also suffered and which Kierkegaard believed he had inherited. Kierkegaard's own close relationship to suffering resulted in a lifelong concern with the forms and mystery of suffering.

As Kierkegaard sees it, in order to understand the meaning of suffering in human life and in order to be able to help men bear it, we must distinguish among the various forms of suffering. In a journal entry about "Joyful Notes in the Strife of Suffering" (*Christian Discourses,* II), he says: "The ordinary sermon confusingly lumps distress and adversity—and sin together" (VIII^1 A 504).

Kierkegaard calls the suffering to which all men are exposed through misfortune, sickness, and the loss of near and dear ones "unavoidable suffering" (VIII^1 A 259; see *Practice* [*Training*] *in Christianity*, p. 173: "universally human sufferings"). This form of suffering the Christian as well as the pagan can learn to bear with patience, and it can teach the believer to submit to God's will and in humility and meekness to find comfort and help in God. In several of the eighteen upbuilding discourses (addressed to men still living on the esthetic plane within Christendom), Kierkegaard tries to help men to bear these sufferings with the proper attitude (see, for example, *Upbuilding* [*Edifying*] *Discourses*, I, pp. 34–55; II, pp. 7–26, 67–87; III, pp. 7–35).

But there are also individuals who from the time they are born are innocent victims of a particular fateful suffering of a physical or psychic nature. Kierkegaard is thinking of such a person when he discusses "the essential sufferer" (*Upbuilding Discourses in Various Spirits*, Part One [*Purity of Heart*, pp. 148–69]), whose "innocent suffering" (VIII^1 A 504) is movingly described by Kierkegaard in these words: "Let us speak of a whole life of sufferings, or of one whom nature has wronged, as we are tempted to say, from the very beginning, who was assigned in the beginning the pointless sufferings of being a burden to others and almost a burden to himself, yes, what is worse, being almost a born argument against the goodness of Governance" (*Purity of Heart*, p. 160, ed. tr.). Kierkegaard believes that a form of this suffering by which man "is painfully placed outside the universal" is "the hidden secret in the lives of many of the most eminent world-historical figures" (VIII^1 A 161); it can also be the suffering of the genius and the artist. Kierkegaard's own suffering was of this kind (see, for example, X^2 A 619). In the pseudonymous authorship we meet it in figures such as "The Unhappiest Man" in *Either/Or* and particularly in Quidam in " 'Guilty?'/'Not Guilty?' " (*Stages*, pp. 179–444). It is this suffering which, if it is not borne in humility, can lead to rebellion against God and to the demonic (*Fear and Trembling*, p. 115). The only help a man has in bearing such suffering is the insight that "in relation to God a man always suffers as being guilty" (*Upbuilding Discourses in Various Spirits*, Part Three [*The Gospel of Suffering*, p. 67]). But even when a man tries to bear such a suffering in humility, he is subject to worse spiritual trials than others because he must continually struggle with the thought "whether this is suffering or sin" and whether God would not free him from the suffering if he had sufficient faith (IX A 333; see also V A 49 and IX A 131). When suffering is regarded from the religious position in this way (*Upbuilding* [*Edifying*] *Discourses*, III, pp. 107–10), it is comparable to the suffering Paul calls "a thorn in the flesh" and which he thought was to keep him from becoming haughty because of the "exceedingly lofty revelations that had been given him" (II Corinthians 12:7).

This particular suffering also makes more stringent "the suffering of the God-relationship," as Kierkegaard calls it (VI A 46), that is, the suffering from having to actualize the eternal within temporality. Climacus calls this suffering "religious suffering," the suffering from which no person who involves himself with the religious can ever be free (*Postscript*, p. 405). It culminates in "the suffering of the consciousness of guilt" (p. 476) and within Christianity in "sin-consciousness" (p. 516; *Practice [Training] in Christianity*, p. 72). In "The Gospel of Suffering," Part Three of *Upbuilding Discourses in Various Spirits*, Kierkegaard begins a description of the religious suffering which a person encounters when he tries to "imitate Christ," but he stresses simultaneously "the joy" in the fact that these sufferings help man on his way toward the eternal and to victory over the world. In "Joyful Notes in the Strife of Suffering" in *Christian Discourses*, it is finally pointed out that because they have an end, earthly sufferings, no matter how intense, are not the most dangerous for a man; what he ought to fear is sin as "man's corruption" (p. 108), for it reaches beyond temporality (see VIII^1 A 85). It is really here that "the consolation of Christianity" first begins (VIII^1 A 32).

Religious suffering actually has two sides: in a person's attempt to actualize the good he must learn self-denial and also experience that the good is bound to suffer in this world. This situation is further intensified in Christianity because the one who ventures out into suffering and danger without regard for himself must in addition bear the insults of other men. In *Works of Love*, Kierkegaard calls this the "double danger" contained in "Christian self-denial" (p. 188; see also *Practice [Training] in Christianity*, pp. 217–18).

But even in freely choosing (see *Works of Love*, p. 188) the suffering that accompanies Christian self-denial, a person still has not exposed himself to Christian suffering proper. The only "specifically Christian suffering" (VIII^1 A 259), according to Kierkegaard, is the avoidable suffering to which a person freely exposes himself in proclaiming the Gospel. This was the suffering that the apostles chose when they were whipped (*Postscript*, p. 405) and that in its ultimate form is the suffering of martyrdom (pp. 405–6). In its voluntariness Christian suffering resembles the human side of Christ's suffering, inasmuch as Christ himself "chose to suffer" (VIII^1 A 259). But Kierkegaard also strongly emphasizes that the divine side of Christ's sufferings is totally incomprehensible to men (VIII^1 A 579 and 580).

Colette, Jacques. *Kierkegaard*, tr. Ralph M. McInerny and Leo Turncotte. Notre Dame: University of Notre Dame Press, 1968.

Croxall, T. H. "Seduction and Suffering," in *Kierkegaard Commentary*, ch. 7. London: James Nesbet, 1956.

Dewey, Bradley R. "Kierkegaard on Suffering: Promise and Lack of Fulfillment in Life's Stages." *Humanities*, 9, February 1972, pp. 21–45.

Heinecken, Martin J. "Christianity Is Suffering," "Suffering and Guilt," in *The Moment Before God*, ch. 10, 11. Philadelphia: Muhlenberg Press, 1956.

Koutsowilis, A. "Is Suffering Necessary for the Good Man?" *The Heythrop Journal*, 13, January 1972, pp. 44–53.

Larson, Curtis Walter. "A Comparison of the Views of Paul and Kierkegaard on Christian Suffering." Ph.D. dissertation, Yale, 1953.

Sponheim, Paul. "Kierkegaard and the Suffering of the Christian Man." *Dialog*, 3, 1964, pp. 199–206.

For references in the works to suffering see, for example, *Either/Or*, I, pp. 145–49; *Fear and Trembling*, pp. 21–29; *Upbuilding [Edifying] Discourses*, III, pp. 107–10; IV, pp. 50–73; *Fragments*, pp. 39–42, 91; *Prefaces, S.V.*, V, p. 45; *Stages*, pp. 172–75, 179, 231, 248–49, 251–56, 354–55, 411–28; *Postscript*, pp. 255–58, 384, 386–415, 422, 434–40, 445–46, 452, 459, 468, 476, 522–23, 529; *Upbuilding Discourses in Various Spirits*, Part One [*Purity of Heart*, pp. 121–39, 148–77, 207–11]; Part Three [*The Gospel of Suffering*, passim]; *Works of Love*, pp. 292–305; *Christian Discourses*, passim; *The Lily of the Field and the Bird of the Air*, with *Christian Discourses*, pp. 326–30; "Has a Man the Right to Let Himself Be Put to Death for the Truth?" with *The Present Age*, pp. 105–6; *The Sickness unto Death*, pp. 183–207; *Three Discourses for the Communion on Fridays*, with *Christian Discourses*, pp. 363–69; *Practice [Training] in Christianity*, pp. 21–22, 61–65, 105–7, 110–12, 136–38, 167–79, 185–96; *For Self-Examination*, pp. 63–83, 91–95; *Judge for Yourselves!*, pp. 144, 179–80, 198, 209–17; *The Point of View*, pp. 91, 101–2; articles in *Fædrelandet*, no. 295, December 18, 1854, no. 83, April 11, 1855, in *Attack*, pp. 5–8, 42; "Christ's Judgment," ibid., pp. 121–24; *The Moment*, no. 8, no. 9, ibid., pp. 242–45 and 248, 268–72.

870. See Matthew 11:28; *Practice [Training] in Christianity*, pp. 5–72.
871. See John 3:2.
872. See John 20:19.
873. See *Prefaces, S.V.*, V, p. 58.
874. See Matthew 27:32.
875. See *Upbuilding [Edifying] Discourses*, III, p. 110.
876. "The Thorn in the Flesh," *Fire opbyggelige Taler*, II (August 31, 1844), in *Upbuilding [Edifying] Discourses*, IV, pp. 49–73.
877. See *Postscript*, pp. 391–99.
878. See *Either/Or*, I, pp. 246–47.
879. See *Postscript*, pp. 396–99.
880. See I Corinthians 15:19.
881. See I Timothy 4:8.
882. Plato, *Gorgias*, 511 d ff.; see *Postscript*, p. 77.
883. Wherein the deception lies, in the deceptiveness of finite existence.
884. See *Postscript*, pp. 397–98.
885. See *Upbuilding Discourses in Various Spirits*, Part One [*Purity of Heart*, pp. 64–65].
886. See Hebrews 7:27; 9:12, 26, 28; 10:10.
887. See *Christian Discourses*, pp. 101–10; *Works of Love*, p. 97.
888. See *The Moment*, no. 8, in *Attack*, pp. 244–45, also pp. 246–47.
889. See Note 887.

890. See *Christian Discourses*, pp. 108–9. For another observation on "religious art" see *Practice [Training] in Christianity*, pp. 247–50.
891. See *Christian Discourses*, p. 102.
892. See *The Sickness unto Death*, p. 145.
893. See *Works of Love*, p. 43.
894. See Moriz Carriere, *Die philosophische Weltanschanung der Reformationszeit* (Stuttgart, Tübingen: 1847), *ASKB* 458.

> Let him to whom suffering is like joy
> And joy like suffering,
> Thank God for such equivalence.

895. Presumably the Duke of Gloucester in Shakespeare's *Richard III* (see I, 1); see *Fear and Trembling*, pp. 114–15.
896. See *Fear and Trembling*, p. 116.
897. *For Self-Examination*, pp. 63–78.
898. This entry is the first expression of Kierkegaard's later more developed view that voluntary suffering and the Christian life are bound together. This is also related to his emphasis upon "imitation." See IMITATION; WITNESS.
899. See *Works of Love*, pp. 68–69.
900. See *Practice [Training] in Christianity*, pp. 136–37.
901. See Luke 11:14; *Practice [Training] in Christianity*, p. 26.
902. See Mark 9:49.
903. For Kierkegaard the relation of the paradox and thought is not that the understanding is to be abandoned but that it should understand its limits. See *Fragments*, pp. 46–67; REASON, UNDERSTANDING.
904. See Matthew 26:31; *Practice [Training] in Christianity*, pp. 105–6; OFFENSE.
905. See Matthew 27:46.
906. This presumably is to be understood to mean writing something on the Passion Story. In 1847 he had published "The Gospel of Suffering," Part Three of *Upbuilding Discourses in Various Spirits,* and later in 1849–50 he wrote about the passion story in *Practice [Training] in Christianity*.
907. See Matthew 26:40 ff.
908. See note 1222.
909. See Acts 21:27–26:29; Colossians 1:24–29.
910. See Matthew 10:16–25.
911. Parenthetically.
912. See Matthew 10:24.
913. See Luke 23:34.
914. See Matthew 26:36–45.
915. Danish, *Actuositet*; English, actuosity (*N.E.D.*, abounding activity).
916. See note 78; ibid., XII, 22, 25; Schultz ed., pp. 183, 185.

917. See Matthew 26:21.
918. See *Upbuilding Discourses in Various Spirits,* Part Three [*The Gospel of Suffering,* pp. 33–41].
919. See note 648.
920. See Matthew 26:61.
921. *Evangelisk-christelig Psalmebog* (Copenhagen: 1845), no. 306, p. 221. *ASKB* 197.
922. See note 851.
923. Horace, *Odes,* III, 1, 40; *Q. Horatii Flacci Opera* (Leipzig: 1828). *ASKB* 1248.
924. *Fenelons Werke religiösen Inhalts,* tr. Matthias Claudius, I–III (Hamburg: 1823), I, p. 219. *ASKB* 1914.
925. See Luke 7:11, in 1849 the text on September 23.
926. C. H. Visby preached September 23, 1849, in Vor Frelsers Kirke.
927. In the preeminent sense.
928. Extraordinary endowments and an incumbent extraordinary task.
929. See Acts 14:22.
930. See note 504.
931. See note 515.
932. See II Corinthians 12:9.
933. See Matthew 21:8–10; Mark 11:8–10; Luke 19:37–38; John 12:12–19.
934. See Mark 14:8.
935. Danish *uendelig,* presumably an allusion to what Hegel called "bad infinity," that is, quantitative infinity or quantitative endlessness.
936. See Matthew 5:44.
937. See Plato, *Phaedo,* 117.
938. *Three Discourses at the Communion on Fridays,* together with *Christian Discourses,* pp. 361–69.
939. *Integrum:* integrity, wholeness, prior state; *restitutio:* reestablishment. See note 497; *Repetition* (*Redintegratio in statum pristinum*), p. 26; *The Concept of Anxiety* [*Dread*] (*Redintegration:* tr. "reintegration"), p. 106; *Prefaces* (*redintegratio amoris*), *S.V.,* V, p. 13.
940. See Galatians 6:14.
941. Gottfried A. Bürger, "Lenore," *Bürgers Gedichte* (Gotha, New York: 1828), stanza 7, ll. 5–6.

> O, mother, mother, what is searing me
> No sacrament can soothe.

942. See Luke 10:20.
943. *Evangelisk-christelig Psalmebog* (Copenhagen: 1823), p. 648. *ASKB* 196.
944. See note 772.

945. See Homily VIII on Colossians 3:15. The English translation is from Kierkegaard's Danish version based on the German. The English translation of the original Greek reads: "If then one bears his griefs and gives thanks, he hath gained a crown of martyrdom. For instance, is her little child sick and doth she give thanks? This is a crown to her. What torture is so bad that despondency is not worse? Still it doth not force her to vent a bitter word. It dies: again she hath given thanks. She hath become a daughter of Abraham. For if she sacrificed not with her own hand, yet she was pleased with the sacrifice, which is the same. . . ." *Nicene and Post-Nicene Fathers* (New York: Christian Literature Co., 1889), XIII, p. 298.

946. See Matthew 20:22.
947. See note 28.
948. Ibid.
949. Ibid.
950. Hebrews 12:5.
951. See note 507.
952. See Acts 9:4.
953. See Acts 8:9 ff.
954. See Acts 9:16.
955. See Matthew 10:24; Luke 6:40; John 13:16, 15:20.
956. See Matthew 10:22, 24:9; John 15:18–20.
957. See note 1018.
958. Ibid.
959. See note 82.
960. See Matthew 11:5.
961. See Matthew 10:22; John 16:2.
962. See Matthew 10:35–36.
963. See Matthew 11:28; *Practice [Training] in Christianity*, pp. 2–72.
964. See note 675.
965. Montaigne. *Michael Montaigne's Gedanken und Meinungen über allerley Gegenstände*, I–VII (Berlin: 1793–99), III, p. 84. *ASKB* 681—87.
966. See note 675.
967. See note 601.
968. In the 1853 *Veiviser* (directory), Søren A. Kierkegaard is listed as living at Klædeboderne 5–6 (now Skindergade 5–6) in 1852. This was his last lodging. Earlier annual editions list him at Østerbro 108A (later torn down) in 1851, Nørregade 43 (now 35) in 1850, Rosenborggade 156A (now 7) in 1849. On this subject see F. Brandt and F. Rammel, *Kierkegaard og Pengene* (Copenhagen: 1935), p. 130.
969. See Matthew 4:1–11; Mark 1:12–13; Luke 4:1–13.
970. See Mark 15:34.
971. *For Self-Examination*, p. [i].
972. Narrow passes.

973. See *For Self-Examination*, p. [i].

974. Kierkegaard says in many places in the works that the writer is "without authority," is only a poet. See, for example, *Upbuilding [Edifying] Discourses*, I, p. 5; *Fear and Trembling*, pp. 42–45; *Fragments*, pp. 43–45; *Postscript*, pp. 551–54; *Armed Neutrality*, passim; *For Self-Examination*, pp. 12, 18, 19; *Judge for Yourselves!*, p. 147; *The Point of View*, pp. 75, 130, 147, 155, 159.

975. Jacob Peter Mynster, M. P. Kierkegaard's family friend, Bishop of Sjælland, from whom Søren Kierkegaard had hoped an "admission" would come concerning the cultural-political accommodation of Christianity in Danish Christendom.

976. See Ephesians 2:16; James 4:4.

977. See Matthew 5:20.

978. See note 976.

979. Ibid.

980. [As] a judgment from the heart.

981. See Matthew 27:46.

982. See John 18:37.

983. From no. 328 ("*Jesu, din søde Forening at smage*"), *Psalmebog, samlet og udgivet af Roskilde-Konvents Psalmkomite* (Copenhagen: 1850).

984. See *Practice [Training] in Christianity*, pp. 21–22.

985. T. Lucretius Carus, *De rerum natura*, II, 1 ff. See I. Kant, *Anthropoligie*, para. 66; A. Schopenhauer, *Die Welt als Wille und Vorstellung* (see note 38), I, para. 58.

SUICIDE

In a journal entry from 1839 Kierkegaard writes that he "would like to write a dissertation on suicide" (II A 482), but instead he wrote his dissertation on irony, an outlook on life which at first takes a negative stance toward temporal existence and brings a person into a crisis situation. Later in his authorship Kierkegaard points out that the risk of suicide is greatest during any crisis that arises at the transition from one stage to another. When the prior basis for a man's existence has proved to be untenable, he must either despair or make a decisive leap into a higher view of life. Despair, more less conscious, is always the deeper motive for suicide.

In the esthetic stage, where despair still expresses itself only as anxiety because the eternal in man has not yet made its claim, misfortune can lead to suicide; but it is graver still that one who is aware of anxiety as possibility in freedom is also exposed to the risk of suicide. The pseudonymous writer Vigilius Haufniensis says of this: "But I do not deny that the person who is instructed by possibility is exposed ... to a fall, and it is suicide. If at the beginning of his instruction he misunderstands anxiety so that it does not lead him to faith but away from faith, then he is lost" (*The Concept of Anxiety [Dread]*, p. 142, ed. tr.; see also *Either/Or*, II, pp. 250–51).

Suicide in this stage must be judged more leniently, for as yet one does not have a clear consciousness of the self, and in the pagan world, which does not believe in something eternal in man, suicide might even be regarded as commendable. In any case, Kierkegaard considers it a mistake to explain suicide on esthetic grounds as cowardice, inasmuch as it takes greater existential passion and courage to deprive oneself of life than to hang on in finitude's despair without making the decisive choice, as in the case with "a great many men" (XI^1 A 269; see also I A 330). The pseudonymous writer Johannes Climacus notes a similar lack of passion in the philosophers of the day, for if they had used "modern speculation" in existence with passion, they "would have perceived that suicide was the only satisfactory practical interpretation of its attempt" (*Postscript,* p. 176; see also p. 310). The Hegelian philosophy referred to here was supposed to be able to abrogate the qualitative contradictions of existence, a process whereby everything in life actually loses its meaning.

Seen from an ethical point of view, according to which man is regarded as under obligation to the eternal, to God, suicide must be judged severely, and in several passages Kierkegaard characterizes it as a "jailbreak" from the prison of existence, where man is placed "as guilty of the most crucial sin, rebellion against God" (see, for example, *Upbuilding* [*Edifying*] *Discourses,* IV, p. 79; *The Sickness unto Death,* pp. 179–80). In *The Sickness unto Death* Anti-Climacus points out that "the clearer the consciousness" a person has of himself, the graver is suicide, just as the despair of such a man is far more intense than that of one "whose soul, compared to the other's, is in a confused and darkish state" (p. 182). Suicide will be the most iminent danger for the person who in desperate defiance of God shuts himself up within himself ("the self-encapsulated," p. 199, ed. tr.).

Kierkegaard emphasizes even more strongly that from a Christian point of view suicide is "against Governance." He maintains that it "displeases" God if someone "arbitrarily breaks out of this existence," where it is a matter of bearing the suffering in expectation of an eternal salvation (XI^1 A 292).

Kierkegaard also refers to the possibility of a spiritual suicide, the hazard for a person who has fought for the good "against the world" and now is led into "a new strife" in which he battles with himself and with God over giving God the honor. "If he falls in this struggle, he falls by his own hand," for no one else can spiritually "murder an immortal spirit; spiritually suicide is the only possible death" (*Works of Love,* p. 308). In *Christian Discourses* Kierkegaard refers to the spiritual suicide committed by one who does not want to know anything about God but consciously tries to forget him. "To slay God is the most horrible suicide, utterly to forget God is a man's deepest fall—so deep the animal cannot fall" (p. 70, ed. tr.).

For references in the works to suicide see *The Concept of Irony*, pp. 103 fn., 309, 314, 339; *Either/Or*, I, p. 179; II, pp. 192, 219, 236, 250–51; *Repetition*, p. 136; *Upbuilding [Edifying] Discourses*, IV, p. 79; *The Concept of Anxiety [Dread]*, p. 142; *Stages*, pp. 241, 277, 296, 302, 355, 428, 430–31, 433 fn., 439; *Postscript*, pp. 147–48, 176, 225, 258, 263, 274, 310, 373; *Two Ages [The Present Age]*, p. 3; *Upbuilding Discourses in Various Spirits*, Part One [*Purity of Heart*, p. 149]; *Works of Love*, pp. 39, 308; *Christian Discourses*, p. 70; *The Sickness unto Death*, pp. 153, 179, 182, 199–200.

986. Johannes Ewald, *Samtlige Skrifter*, I–IV (Copenhagen: 1780–91). *ASKB* 1533–36. Kierkegaard also had Ewald's *Samtlige Skrifter*, I–VIII (Copenhagen: 1850–55). *ASKB* 1537–44.

SUPERIORITY

In only a few places does Kierkegaard write about the superiority resulting from what he would call accidental or unessential differences among men: for example, man's superiority in relation to woman (*Either/Or*, I, pp. 208–9; II, p. 58; *The Concept of Anxiety [Dread]*, p. 59; *Stages*, p. 253).

But there is a true superiority which can be attained only through an *existential* relationship to truth, to the eternal, to God. This is why the person who exists "on the strength of the ethical" is actually superior to the esthete, even though the latter may be superior as a dialectician because "he has received all the seductive gifts of understanding and intellect," as Climacus says of the esthete A in *Either/Or* (*Postscript*, p. 227). Socrates, too, on the strength of his existential relation to truth, that is, as an ethicist, was superior to the philosophers of his age, and it was precisely because they were irked by his superiority that he was put to death. Thus in finitude "the power of superiority" can have the appearance of impotence (IX A 453).

The ultimate is the superiority that accompanies Christian love toward other men, the love Kierkegaard has described in *Works of Love*. A good example of the superiority of this love is the parental love which has "the true, serious, concerned view of superiority, grounded in an eternal responsibility to will in truth the best for the child" (p. 222). To the world the superiority of the true love frequently looks like weakness and simplemindedness which can be duped, but in actuality it is an infinite superiority "which is eternally and infinitely secured against being deceived" and the deceiver actually is only deceiving himself (pp. 227–28).

But true superiority also goes hand in hand with increased responsibility. A little essay by the pseudonymous writer H. H., "Has a Man the Right to Let Himself Be Put to Death for the Truth?," says of this: "If a man in relation to others actually has decisive truth on his side, ... then he is in fact decisively the superior. And what is superiority? It is responsibility increasing more and more in direct relation to greater and greater superiority" (p. 104, ed. tr.). An important question for Kierkegaard was whether a "human being" could have an "absolute superiority over others" to the extent that he could take upon himself the responsibility for allowing them to become guilty of his death for the truth (p. 127).

Many of the sketches Kierkegaard gives us of "the infinitely superior" (*Works of Love*, p. 228) and of the superiority of true love are actually analogies intended to help the reader to a deeper understanding of Christ's life, which in its infinite superiority had the appearance of weakness and impotence, inasmuch as it had to suffer in this world (see, for example, *Fragments*, pp. 31–42; "Has a Man the Right . . . ?" with *The Present Age*, p. 134; *Practice* [*Training*] *in Christianity*, pp. 81, 128–31).

For references in the works to superiority, see *Either/Or*, I, pp. 208–9, 300; II, p. 58; *Repetition*, pp. 83, 92–93; *Fragments*, pp. 31–42; *The Concept of Anxiety* [*Dread*], p. 59; *Stages*, pp. 150, 152, 214, 253; *Postscript*, pp. 196–97, 227; *Works of Love*, pp. 222, 227–23; *Christian Discourses*, pp. 136–38; "Has a Man the Right . . . ?" with *The Present Age*, pp. 89–92, 104, 120–24, 127, 131–34; *Practice* [*Training*] *in Christianity*, pp. 81, 128–31; *The Point of View*, p. 91.

987. See Mark 12:41–44; Luke 21:1–4.
988. See note 353.

SUPERSTITION

Through his reading of mythology and folk tales (see Gregor Malantschuk, *Kierkegaard's Thought*, pp. 21–25), Kierkegaard was familiar with the many varieties of superstition, and now and then in his authorship he uses figures or ideas from the world of superstition to illustrate a specific thought (see, for example, *Works of Love*, p. 102; *The Sickness unto Death*, p. 206; *For Self-Examination*, p. 50). But his primary interest was in the nature of superstition, for he perceived that superstition resulted from a specific mentality in man and therefore was to be found not only in paganism and in the primitive religions but on all religious levels, even within Christianity.

According to the pseudonymous writer Vigilius Haufniensis, superstition is essentially identical with unbelief. In *The Concept of Anxiety* [*Dread*] he gives a brief account of the relation between superstition and unbelief, both of which are a manifestation of the demonic (p. 125) and a sign that one lacks inwardness. Instead of steadily fighting to reach the inner certitude of faith, the superstitious person clings to an external, objective security, while the unbeliever in his uncertainty chooses to ridicule faith (pp. 125–26).

In *Concluding Unscientific Postscript* Johannes Climacus discusses particularly the superstition found in Christianity, a sign that the age lacks "inwardness." Thus Climacus criticizes a superstitious belief in science and scholarship, especially in historical-critical theology (pp. 25–55), in reflection, especially as it manifested itself in Hegel's philosophy (p. 311; see also *Fragments*, pp. 96–97 fn., and *The Concept of Anxiety* [*Dread*], p. 27); and he is of the opinion that Grundtvig's "matchless discovery" (*Postscript*, p. 36) conforms to a "craving for a superstitious foothold" and tempts men to use a "shortcut" to faith in the sense of getting "something magical to hold on to" (p. 43, ed. tr.; see also *Either/Or*, II, p. 36). But the external footholds thereby provided for men frustrate the struggle through to the certitude of the true faith. Climacus says: "As soon as I take away the dialectic I become superstitious and attempt to cheat God of each moment's strenuous reacquisition of that which once has been acquired" (p. 35 fn.). Later he says even more pointedly: "If we overleap the dialectical, Christianity as a whole becomes a comfortable delusion, a superstition, and a superstition of the most dangerous kind because it is overbelief in the truth . . ." (p. 385).

While God and Christianity are kept out of life by superstitious belief, there is in paganism, Judaism, and Christianity yet another form of superstition which wants to involve itself with God in order to secure his help for one's own enterprises. Kierkegaard labels "the superstitious man's desire to have God serve him" (*Christian Discourses*, p. 71) as presumption, and in the discourse on "The Cares of Presumption" he says: "Ultimately there is a form of presumption, wanting in a forbidden, a rebellious, an ungodly way to have God's help. This is *superstition*" (p. 70, ed. tr.).

In one of the last sections of *Christian Discourses* Kierkegaard says that even a man's aspiration to bear "his wounds upon his body" is a superstition, because the importance is placed on an external sign that arouses the admiration of men instead of imitation, which brings a man into progressively greater conflict with himself and the world (p. 286; see also VIII^1 A 349).

For references in the works to superstition, see, for example, *Either/Or*, II, p. 36; *Fragments*, pp. 96–97 fn.; *The Concept of Anxiety* [*Dread*], pp. 27, 125–26; *Postscript*, pp. 33, 35, 43, 311, 385; *Works of Love*, p. 102; *Christian Discourses*, pp. 70–71, 286; *The Sickness unto Death*, p. 206; *For Self-Examination*, p. 50.

989. See Plato, *Theaetetus*, 151; *Fragments*, p. 25; *Works of Love*, p. 258.

990. *Paris' sande Mysterier* (Copenhagen: 1851), II, p. 88.

991. Imprinted tracks or footprints.

992. Paul Henry, *Das Leben Johann Calvins*, I–III$^{1-2}$ (Hamburg: 1835–44), I.

TELEOLOGICAL SUSPENSION

In *Fear and Trembling* the pseudonymous writer Johannes de Silentio poses and answers the question: "Is there a teleological suspension of the ethical?" (pp. 64–77). The emphasis is on the word "teleological," which here means for the sake of a higher goal, or even more accurately, for the sake of God. That there is a suspension of the ethical for the sake of inferior goals is easy to demonstrate inasmuch as the pervasiveness of crime and sin in the world always implies a suspension of the ethical (*Postscript*, p. 239).

But for Johannes de Silentio the problem is whether and how a suspension can be in the service of a higher goal. Even in purely human situations he finds relevant examples, such as the sacrifice of a daughter by Agamemnon and Jephtha or of a son by Brutus (pp. 68–69), thereby breaking ethical obligations because of a higher motive—namely, a consideration for the nation or the state. All these violations are comprehensible and justifiable to the public (p. 86).

Johannes de Silentio's question goes beyond these examples in the human sphere and asks whether God can insist on violating the ethical laws he himself has placed in men. Abraham's sacrifice of Isaac answers the question positively. But a suspension of the ethical like that places the individual outside of the universal and isolates him completely. Johannes de Silentio shows how Abraham's undertaking cannot be understood by anyone, because it serves no universally human goal; it is a matter exclusively between Abraham and God, whose will is Abraham's higher duty (p. 70). If Abraham had not had faith that it was God who required the sacrifice of Isaac and had given a "higher hint," Abraham would have been a murderer (pp. 34–35, 41; see also X^6 B 80).

Johannes de Silentio shows that men encounter these same difficulties in Christianity when faced with the demand for a teleological suspension of the ethical in Christ's words: "If anyone comes to me and does not hate his own father and his mother and his wife and his children and his brothers and his sisters, yes, even his own soul, he cannot be my disciple (p. 82; see also *Postscript*, p. 525). Finally, in *Stages on Life's Way*, Judge William poignantly describes the dread the person ("the exception") must experience who undertakes such a teleological suspension of the ethical (pp. 172–75).

There is an essential difference between the violation of the ethical that is a crime and a sin and the violation that serves the good. In the first instance the revocation of the ethical takes place without loving it—indeed, hating it; despite appearances to the contrary, the other suspension presupposes love for that which is suspended and is based on self-denial and trust in God. Johannes de Silentio illustrates these two opposite mentalities in the following words on Abraham's sacrifice of Isaac: "The moment he is willing to sacrifice Isaac, the ethical expression for his act is that he hates Isaac. But if he really hates Isaac, then he can rest assured that God does not require this of him, for Cain and Abraham are not alike. He must love Isaac with his whole soul . . ." (p. 84, ed. tr.). If the suspension is made in hatred, it is in the service of the demonic; if done in faith and love, it is in the service of the good.

The pseudonymous writer Johannes Climacus names yet another form of the teleological suspension of the ethical, in which the individual's attitude either can result in serving the good or can lead to the demonic. Such a suspension takes place when because of congenital conditions an individual is prevented from realizing the universal, as was the case with Kierkegaard himself. The difference between this position and Abraham's is clear. Abraham was "the righteous man," he was still living in the first immediacy, and he knew of no obstacle to a realization of the universal which he was obliged to suspend by his sacrifice. It is quite different with the person suffering the consequences of original sin and prevented by anxiety from realizing the universal. The individual will then face two opposite possibilities: either fighting his way through to faith out of anxiety over the evil (*The Concept of Anxiety* [*Dread*], pp. 101-5), or sinking down into the demonic out of anxiety over the good (pp. 105-21; see especially X^4 A 335). Climacus compares Abraham's situation with that confronting the individual who faces making the decision between these two possibilities: "Just as 'fear and trembling' was the state of teleological suspension because of being tempted by God, so anxiety is the state of mind in the teleological suspension involved in that desperate release from realization of the ethical" (*Postscript*, p. 240, ed. tr.).

Kierkegaard also discusses the suspension of "morals and customs" which the ironist undertakes (*The Concept of Irony*, p. 300). Here again there are two possibilities: that the suspension is made because of something higher, as in the case of Socrates, or that it is made for the benefit of "sensual actuality" (p. 307), as in Fr. Schlegel's *Lucinde*.

A special form of "teleological suspension" discussed by Kierkegaard in *The Point of View for My Work as an Author* is the suspension "with respect to communication of the truth (suppressing something temporarily simply in order that the truth can become more true) . . ." (p. 91).

The problem of teleological suspension in *Fear and Trembling* is very difficult but extremely important. That is one reason for Kierkegaard's writing in a journal entry: ". . . *Fear and Trembling* alone will be enough for an imperishable name as an author. Then it will be read, translated into foreign languages as well. The reader will almost shrink from the frightful pathos of the book" (X^2 A 15). Thus it was especially important for Kierkegaard to provide the essential marks that distinguish the suspension as a crime and a sin and as an expression of the highest religious life.

Bogen, James. "Kierkegaard and the 'Teleological Suspension of the Ethical.'" *Inquiry* (Oslo), 5, 1962, pp. 305-17.

Buber, Martin. "Suspension of Ethics," in Ruth Nanda Anshen, *Moral Principles of Action*, ch. 13. New York: Harper, 1952.

Clive, Geoffrey. "Teleological Suspension of the Ethical in Nineteenth-century Literature." *Journal of Religion*, 34, April, 1954, pp. 75-87.

Donnelly, John J. "Søren Kierkegaard's 'Teleological Suspension of the Ethical': A Reinterpretation." Ph. D. dissertation, Brown, 1970.

Duncan, Elmer H. "Kierkegaard's Teleological Suspension of the Ethical: A Study of Exception-Cases." *The Southern Journal of Philosophy,* 1, 4, 1963, pp. 9–18.

Halevi, Jacob L. "Kierkegaard's Teleological Suspension of the Ethical: Is It Jewish?" *Judaism,* 8, Fall 1959, pp. 291–302.

Kuntz, Paul G. "The God We Find: the God of Abraham, the God of Anselm, and the God of Weiss." *The Modern Schoolman,* 47, May 1970, pp. 433–53.

Mackey, Louis H. "Kierkegaard's Lyric of Faith: A Look at *Fear and Trembling.*" Rice Institute Pamphlets, 47, 1960, pp. 30–34.

———. "The View from Pisgah: A Reading of *Fear and Trembling,*" in *Kierkegaard,* ed. Josiah Thompson, pp. 407–42. New York: Doubleday (Anchor), 1972.

McInerny, Ralph. "The Teleological Suspension of the Ethical." *Thomist,* 20, 1957, pp. 295–310.

Schmitt, Richard. "Kierkegaard's Ethics and Its Teleological Suspension." *The Journal of Philosophy,* 58, 1961, pp. 701–2.

Schrag, Calvin O. "Note on Kierkegaard's Teleological Suspension of the Ethical." *Ethics,* 70, 1, October 1959, pp. 66–68.

For references in the works to teleological suspension see, for example, *The Concept of Irony,* p. 300, 305–8; *Fear and Trembling,* passim, especially pp. 151–58; *Repetition,* passim; *The Concept of Anxiety* [*Dread*], pp. 101–21; *Stages,* pp. 172–75, 218; *Postscript,* pp. 235, 237–40, 525; *The Point of View,* p. 91.

TEMPTATION

Kierkegaard develops his concept of temptation (*Fristelse*) principally on the basis of the Epistle of James 1:13–14. At an early age Kierkegaard found sustenance and admonition in this passage (see II A 310 and 311) and in the second of his first two upbuilding discourses of 1843 he uses it in connection with verse 17 on God's unchangeableness (see *Upbuilding* [*Edifying*] *Discourses,* I, pp. 34–55). He points out that first and foremost God cannot be tempted, either by a man's most urgent prayers or by his righteous (in his own opinion) complaints about his unhappy fate (pp. 42–43).

But it is the second idea in particular, that "God tempts no one but that everyone is tempted when enticed and drawn by his own desires" (p. 43, ed. tr.), which we find most frequently in Kierkegaard's authorship. It corresponds completely with his view that man is responsible for his actions and that the concept of temptation is located within the ethical. In *Concluding Unscientific Postscript* the pseudonymous writer Johannes Climacus says, "When the individual's maximum is the ethical relationship to actuality, then temptation is his greatest danger" (p. 410). Therefore temptation must not be confused either with spiritual trial (*Anfægtelse*) (see rubric), which a person first meets in the sphere of the religious proper, or with testing (*Prøvelse*), by which Kierkegaard understands that God as the transcendent power presents an absolute demand to a man in a specific situation.

According to the pseudonymous writer Johannes de Silentio, the story of Abraham, whom God asks to sacrifice his son, is primarily about a "test," although the Old Testament says that "God tempted Abraham" (pp. 26, 35; see also *Postscript,* p. 235). But the testing contains a special kind of temptation for Abraham—namely, the temptation to take his stand on the ethical instead of "doing God's will" (*Fear and Trembling,* p. 70).

The pseudonymous author Vigilius Haufniensis also uses these words from the Epistle of James to rectify the account in the Old Testament about the Fall, which says that it is the tempter in the form of a serpent that brings man to fall. He thinks that it directly conflicts with the teaching of the Bible and the well-known classic passage in James to have "the temptation come from without" (*The Concept of Anxiety* [*Dread*], p. 43). Later in the book he maintains that "guilt never has any external cause, and anyone who falls into temptation is himself guilty of the temptation" (p. 98, ed. tr.).

According to Kierkegaard's view, the New Testament lays the whole responsibility for falling into temptation on man; and "the way of escape" (I Corinthians 10:13) from the temptation also depends on whether a person relies on himself or, in the temptation, seeks help from God. In the former case the victory as well as the defeat leads to a new fall (*Upbuilding* [*Edifying*] *Discourses,* III, p. 33), whereas in the latter case the temptation as one of the tribulations belonging to the Christian life brings a man closer to God (*Upbuilding Discourses in Various Spirits,* Part Three [*The Gospel of Suffering,* p. 115]), inasmuch as he learns by conquering the temptations of this world to give up this world, which is the way to Christianity (see, for example, *Works of Love,* p. 81) or by succumbing to the temptation he learns humility so that God can "establish him more in the good" (*The Sickness unto Death,* p. 24, ed. tr.).

The best defense against temptation is to be "hidden in God" by means of "unconditioned obedience," because at "the least little hint of ambiguity Satan is powerful and the temptation ensnaring," says Kierkegaard in the first of the "Three Godly Discourses" in *The Lily of the Field and the Bird of the Air,* with *Christian Discourses,* (p. 344, ed. tr.). In the same passage Kierkegaard explains the petition "Lead us not into temptation" this way: "let me never by my disobedience venture out of my hiding place ... outside of which I instantly am led into temptation."

In his discourse on "The High Priest," the first of *Three Discourses for the Communion on Fridays,* Kierkegaard recalls that Christ "can aid those who are tempted" because he himself was "tempted in all things in like manner," yes, he "truly learned to know every temptation by withstanding every temptation" (p. 366). And in *For Self-Examination* he briefly points out that from the very beginning Christ's life was concurrently "a story of temptation" as well as "a story of suffering" (p. 66), even to a special degree inasmuch as Christ at all times "has the possibility in His power to take His calling, His task, in vain" (p. 66; see also X⁴ A 181).

Wood, Forrest E. "Kierkegaardian Light on Ibsen's *Brand*." *Personalist*, 51, Summer 1970, pp. 393-400.

For references in the works to temptation, see, for example, *The Concept of Irony*, p. 289; *Either/Or*, II, pp. 28, 119, 123, 245; *Upbuilding [Edifying] Discourses*, I, pp. 35-36, 42-45, 84, 113; II, p. 9; III, pp. 32-33; IV, pp. 39-40, 108; *Fear and Trembling* [present translation inadequately distinguishes among temptation, test, and spiritual trial], pp. 26-27, 33, 36, 58, 70, 81, 85, 124; *Repetition*, p. 113; *The Concept of Anxiety [Dread]*, pp. 36 fn., 39, 43, 71, 98; *Prefaces, S.V.*, V, p. 56; *Three Upbuilding Discourses on Imagined Occasions* [*Thoughts on Crucial Situations*], p. 99; *Stages*, pp. 86, 192, 355, 400; *Postscript* [see comment on translation of *Fear and Trembling* above], pp. 16, 121, 234-35, 238-39, 366, 410-11, 422; *Upbuilding Discourses in Various Spirits*, Part One [*Purity of Heart*, pp. 51, 70, 72, 78]; Part Three [*The Gospel of Suffering*, p. 115]; *Works of Love*, pp. 81, 130, 179, 224, 270, 276; *Christian Discourses*, pp. 24-25, 38, 78, 187; *The Lily of the Field and the Bird of the Air*, with ibid., p. 344; "Has a Man the Right ... ?" with *The Present Age*, p. 98; *The Sickness unto Death*, pp. 240, 243, 366-68; *Practice [Training] in Christianity*, p. 153; *For Self-Examination*, pp. 15, 66; *Judge for Yourselves!*, p. 118.

993. For we have not a high priest who is unable to sympathize with our weaknesses, but one who in every respect has been tempted as we are, yet without sinning.

994. See II Timothy 4:7.

995. See Matthew 4:1-11, in 1851 the text for March 9.

TERSTEEGEN

Kierkegaard has the following appreciative words to say of Gerhard Tersteegen (1697-1769): "On the whole Tersteegen is incomparable. In him I find genuine and noble piety and simple wisdom" (X³ A 202). This remarkable acknowledgment of Tersteegen's piety is due to Kierkegaard's belief that Tersteegen earnestly tried to apply his being grasped by Christ in practical daily life and in the service of his fellow men. In Tersteegen Kierkegaard found an actualization of the Christian piety that he himself endorsed. Thus it is very significant that he chose the following verse by Tersteegen as the motto for *On My Work as an Author* (1851):

> Whoever believes is great and rich,
> He has God and the kingdom of heaven.
> Whoever believes is small and poor,
> He cries only: Lord, have mercy.

Kierkegaard found this verse in *Auswahl aus Tersteegens Schriften, Nebst dem Leben desselben*, ed. Georg Rapp (Essen: 1841), p. 509 (see X³ A 259). Although

Kierkegaard had Tersteegen's collected works, he referred in his journals to this edition. The quoted verse expresses both Kierkegaard's and Tersteegen's view of the Christian's struggle between faith and despair. Because of their spiritual kinship, Kierkegaard could find in Tersteegen essential points of contact in an understanding of Christian existence in this world, and he underlines Tersteegen's comment on the many who have *"die Worte der Wahrheit, nicht aber die Wahrheit der Worte"* (X^1 A 486), an observation in total agreement with Kierkegaard's comment that there are many who presumably know the truth but do not attempt to actualize it in their lives (X^3 A 210). Just as Kierkegaard did later, Tersteegen perceived that the appropriation of Christianity is a long process, a road with many stations (X^1 A 492).

Kierkegaard also responds to Tersteegen's idea of the absolute incognito of Christ, or of Christ as the absolute paradox unable to communicate directly, when Tersteegen cites the example of the robber on the cross to whom a second person being crucified says: " ... believe on me, I am God ..." (X^3 A 181). Here man faces his supreme test, and it is unconditionally clear that the way to faith in Christ is not direct but that man comes to Christ by the leap of faith.

Kierkegaard could also agree with Tersteegen that salvation and suffering go together. The pseudonymous writer Johannes Climacus has described this at length in *Concluding Unscientific Postscript*, stressing that adherence to the idea of eternal salvation always involves one in suffering (see, for example, pp. 396–400). Kierkegaard also calls it "superb" on Tersteegen's part when he points out that much less attention is paid to books which recommend self-denial and dying to the world than to those which contain only reasoning and speculation (X^1 A 572).

The only direct reference to Tersteegen in the works is in *On My Work as an Author*, with *The Point of View*, p. 142.

996. *Auswahl aus Gerhardt Tersteegens Schriften*, ed. G. Rapp (Essen: 1841), pp. 146, 169, 171–72. *ASKB* 729.

997. See Luke 23:34.

998. See Luke 23:43; Matthew 27:46.

999. "Scholars for the most part (in disputes about terms and distinctions) are guilty of it. But they should consider that not even one in a thousand true believers has a complete grasp of many of their expressions and distinctions, just as a thousand others on the other hand have *the words of truth but not the truth of the words.*" In "Our Faith and Justification." For edition see note 996.

1000. See note 996.

1001. See *Works of Love*, pp. 178–81.

1002. See note 996.

1003. See note 996. "On the Difference and Progress in Godliness." "But why is it that such precious writings are generally so little esteemed and used?

Is it not because curious reason does not find such sustenance in them, and that the old tendency of the flesh and the deep ground of one's own life is assailed in them and because they do not demand *reason and speculation* like others which are a bit more accomodating to the taste of the old Adam and of reason, *but rather mortification and denial?"*

1004.

> To conceal faithlessness and indolence
> Causes one to be counted among the weak;
> One shrinks from [having] a pious appearance
> For appearance's sake,
> When one has no desire to be pious.

1005. See Psalms 77:2. My soul refuses to be comforted.
1006. See Hebrews 12:5.
1007. See note 996.
1008. See note 996; ibid., pp. 123-24.
1009. See note 996; ibid., p. 607.
1010. See note 996. "Yes, souls, cleanse your hearts of your wavering, of the world and of all vanities; for Christ wants to come and be born in us. O, that it may not be said that he found no room in the inn!"
1011. See note 996: ibid., pp. 123 ff.
1012. See note 996: ibid., p. 509.

> He who believes is great and rich,
> He has God and heaven's kingdom.
> He who believes is small and poor,
> He cries only: Lord, have mercy.

1013. See note 996; ibid., p. 81.

> Teach me to live solely in the Spirit,
> As before thine eyes:
> Removed from the world, from time, from senses,
> Secluded with thee within.

TERTULLIAN

There are essential points of similarity between Quintus Septimus Florens Tertullian's (*ca.* 160–220 A.D.) interpretation of Christianity and Kierkegaard's. Kierkegaard calls Tertullian "the unconditionally most consistent and most Christianly two-edged of all the Church Fathers" (X^5 A 98). Precisely because of his rigorous consistency Tertullian could make a sharp distinction between philosophy and faith (see X^4 A 140), and he was one of the first to advance the idea of the paradoxical in Christ's life. In his book *De carne Christi,* para. 5, Tertullian declares: *"Natus est dei filius; non pudet, quia pudendum est: et mortuus est dei filius; prorsus credibile est, quia ineptum est: et septultus resurrexit; certum est, quia impossible."** (God's son is born—it is not shameful, because it is a fact of which one ought to be ashamed; God's son is dead—it is altogether credible, because it is absurd [or foolish]; and after having been buried he rose again —it is certain, because it is impossible.) This statement by Tertullian is the source of the familiar thesis (not Tertullian's formulation) in Christendom: *Credo, quia absurdum* (See *Fragments,* pp. 65, 67; II A 467).

Kierkegaard, too, was rigorously consistent in trying to draw a clear distinction between the sphere of knowledge, which belongs to immanence, and the sphere of faith, which is rooted in transcendence (*The Concept of Anxiety* [*Dread*], pp. 17, 19). This is especially true in *Concluding Unscientific Postscript,* where he criticizes Hegel's commixture of philosophy and theology.

Moreover, it was Kierkegaard's stringently logical thinking that led him to accentuate the person of Christ as "the absolute paradox" (IV C 84), a thought which came to have a decided impact on his entire authorship.

Kierkegaard often mentions in his journals thoughts from Tertullian which touch upon his own problems in presenting Christianity. For example, while reading Tertullian's essay on patience, Kierkegaard discovered that Tertullian struggled with the very same problem he had—namely, to what extent does one have the right to set up ideals for others which one does not himself succeed in honoring (X^1 A 502)? In the publication of *The Sickness unto Death* Kierkegaard deemed it necessary to use a pseudonym in order to indicate that he personally did not meet the ideality presented there. The same is true of *Practice* [*Training*] *in Christianity,* where "the requirement for being a Christian" "is forced up to the highest peak of ideality" (p. 7, ed. tr.).

Kierkegaard commends Tertullian for presenting Christianity not "in man's interest" but "in God's interest." There is hardly a Church Father "who has presented Christianity in God's interest as powerfully as Tertullian has" (X^4 A 137). Kierkegaard also perceived that he himself was being steadily forced by Governance into having to proclaim Christianity in God's interest (XI^2 A 46; see also X^4 A 499 and X^5 A 146).

But Kierkegaard does criticize Tertullian on one point—the idea of "Christianity's perfectibility" (X^5 A 98), which he believes Tertullian accepts, whereas Kierkegaard rejects it (see PERFECTIBILITY).

For references in the works to Tertullian, see *Fragments,* pp. 65, 67; *The Concept of Anxiety* [*Dread*] p. 24.

1014. See note 28; ibid., pp. 287–90.

1015. See *Armed Neutrality* and *An Open Letter,* passim; *The Point of View,* passim.

---

* *Opera,* ed. E. F. Leopold I–IV (Leipzig: 1839–41), IV, p. 66.

1016. See note 28.
1017. See note 31.
1018. See, for example, *Fragments*, pp. 39–42, 69–81; *Postscript*, pp. 187–92, 369, 386 (incognito), 447–55, 473, 531; *Practice [Training] in Christianity*, pp. 96–144.
1019. See note 28.
1020. Ibid.
1021. Ibid.
1022. Ibid.
1023. Ibid., I, 1, p. 288.
1024. Ibid., p. 298.
1025. *De praescriptione haereticorum.* Things that are probable or likely deceive the truth, whether intentionally or not.
1026. Ignaz H. von Wessenberg, *Die grossen Kirchenversammlungen des 15ten und 16ten Jahrhunderts*, I–IV (Constance: 1840).

THEOLOGIANS, THEOLOGY

Kierkegaard began his theological studies in 1830 and took his final university examination in July, 1840. Significantly the major portion of Kierkegaard's early journal entries deals with theological questions, especially issues in dogmatics.

As early as 1834 there is an entry criticizing the dogmatics which regards Christianity merely as doctrine. Instead, according to Kierkegaard, dogmatics should "grow out of Christ's activity," in order to help men to live as "reborn men" according to the example Christ has given us in his life, besides emphasizing redemption by Christ (I A 27 and 28).

Little by little Kierkegaard stiffened his critical position toward the confusion of theological and philosophical concepts in Hegelian philosophy and especially toward its enervation of the particularly Christian concepts such as "faith, incarnation, tradition, inspiration," and even "the concept of redemption," which he found had been "profaned." Therefore he considered it an important task to restore to the words their "lost power and meaning" (I A 328). "The old Christian dogmatic terminology is like an enchanted castle where the most beautiful princes and princesses rest in a deep sleep—it needs only to be awakened, brought to life, in order to stand in its full glory" (II A 110).

But first the boundaries of philosophy must be marked out carefully and dogmatics must be shown to be based on a completely different premise than philosophy is—namely, the revelation in Christ (see, for example, II A 77, II A 440, III A 39, and III A 211). Kierkegaard also gradually perceived that with dogmatics as a presupposition, a truly Christian view of life, anthropology, and psychology could be worked out, and on this foundation Kierkegaard structured his whole authorship.

The more important it became for Kierkegaard to accentuate the existential significance of Christianity, the more distrustful he became of "scholarly critical theology." In the beginning of *Concluding Unscientific Postscript*, Johannes Climacus, who has nothing but respect for honest scholarship, takes this branch of knowledge to task for always making it seem "as if this criticism would suddenly eventuate in something for faith" (p. 27, ed. tr.). By dealing with Christianity scientifically in this way, one can go on holding its intrusive demand at a distance.

In 1847 Kierkegaard wrote in his journal under the heading of a large NB: "What is needed is a new theological science of arms," and he maintained that "theology in our day" must learn that it possesses "the weapons of attack" and not "the weapons of defense" (VIII^1 A 480). This journal entry became the program for a new direction in Kierkegaard's authorship, commencing with *Works of Love* and continuing with *Christian Discourses* and *Practice in Christianity*. These books stress the distinctively Christian in contrast to the human, and the aim is precisely to challenge and to attack. For example, in the preface to part III of *Christian Discourses* Kierkegaard says: "Christianity needs no *defense*, is not served by any defense—it is aggressive . . ." (p. 168, ed. tr.).

It is understandable that in his struggle to accurately describe how a person becomes a Christian, Kierkegaard could speak both sharply and contemptuously about the theology which theologians had blown up to be "the highest wisdom" but which actually was altogether subordinate and unimportant compared to Christianity's demand to be actualized in existence (see, for example, X^1 A 397, XI^1 A 465, and XI^2 A 94).

Aubry, Edwin. "Kierkegaard, Father of Dialectical Theology," in *Present Theological Tendencies*, ch. 2. New York: Harper, 1936.

Cruickshank, A. "Theology and Kierkegaard's *Postscript.*" *Church Quarterly Review*, 170, January 1969, pp. 206–11.

Dupré, Louis. *Kierkegaard as Theologian*. New York: Sheed and Ward, 1963.

Holmer, Paul L. "Kierkegaard and Theology." *Union Seminary Quarterly Review*, 12, March 1957, pp. 23–31.

Humphries, Hugh W. "Søren Kierkegaard's Concept of Sanctification." Ph.D. dissertation, New York University, 1962.

Michalson, Carl. "Kierkegaard's Theology of Faith." *Religion in Life*, 32, Spring 1963, pp. 225–37.

Morrison, C. C. "Liberalism of Neo-Orthodoxy." *Christian Century*, 67, June 21, 1950, pp. 760–63.

O'Neill, Kevin D. "Kierkegaard's Attempt at a Balanced Philosophy of Religion." Ph.D. dissertation, Yale, 1967.

Otani, Hidehito. "The Concept of a Christian in Kierkegaard." *Inquiry* (Oslo), 8, 1965, pp. 74–83.

Owen, H. P. "Existentialism and Ascetical Theology." *Church Quarterly Review*, 160, April-June 1959, pp. 226–31.

Peck, D. W. "The Christianity of Søren Kierkegaard." *Canadian Journal of Theology*, 12, 1966, pp. 85–97.

Sponheim, Paul R. "The Christological Formulations of Schleiermacher and Kierkegaard in Relation to Fundamental Options Discernible in Divergent Strands in their Discussions of God and Man." Ph.D. dissertation, Chicago, 1961.

———. *Kierkegaard on Christ and Christian Coherence*. New York: Harper, 1968.

Thomas, John Heywood. "The Relevance of Kierkegaard to the Demythologizing Controversy." *Scottish Journal of Theology*, 10, 1957, pp. 239–52.

Wand, J. W. C. *The Minds Behind the New Theology: Kierkegaard, Barth, Bultmann, Tillich, Bonhoeffer*. London: Mowbray, 1963.

Wardlaw, H. R. "The Problem of the Theological Method: A Study of Kierkegaard and Tillich." Ph.D. dissertation, Glasgow, 1962.

Wolf, Herbert C. *Kierkegaard and Bultmann*. Minneapolis: Augsburg, 1964.

For references in the works to theology and theologians, see, for example, *Either/Or*, I, p. 416; II, p. 251; "A Little Explanation," *Fædrelandet*, no. 1236, May 16, 1843, *S.V.*, XIII, p. 416; *Fear and Trembling*, pp. 43, 58, 82–83; *Fragments*, p. 66; *The Concept of Anxiety* [*Dread*], pp. 10–21, 35–36, 105, 145; *Prefaces*, *S.V.*, V, pp. 29–30, 54; *Stages*, p. 374; *Postscript*, pp. 14, 18, 27, 29, 31, 35, 161, 249, 271, 312, 331, 337, 472, 489, 513; *Christian Discourses*, p. 168; *Two Ages* [*The Present Age*], p. 7; pp. 73, 154–56; *The Sickness unto Death*, p. 210; *Practice* [*Training*] *in Christianity*, pp. 98, 104, 178; *Judge for Yourselves!*, pp. 126–28, 138; article in *Fædrelandet*, no. 111, May 15, 1855, in *Attack*, pp. 51–52, 53; *The Moment*, no. 3, no. 4, no. 7, ibid., 128–29, 144–46, 208–9.

1027. *King Lear*, IV, 6; *Shakespeares dramatische Werke*, tr. A. W. Schlegel and Ludwig Tieck, I–XII (Berlin: 1839). *ASKB* 1883–88. See *Fragments*, pp. 66, 67.

1028. See I A 285; 4066.

1029. Presumably a reference to Gregorius Cortese (1483–1548).

1030. See Matthew 5:45.

1031. See Genesis 27:1–40.

1032. See *Christian Discourses*, p. 168.

1033. Hans Christian Ørsted (1777–1851), the great Danish physicist and brother of Anders Sandøe Ørsted, jurist and statesman.

1034. "Imaginary" in the sense that the concrete, historical aspects were forgotten; whereas in an historical-philological approach it was forgotten that the Bible is Holy Scripture.

THOMAS à KEMPIS

In his library Kierkegaard had two editions of *De imitatione Christi* by Thomas à Kempis (1380–1471), one in Latin (Paris: 1702) and a Danish translation by J. A. L. Holm (3 ed., 1848). Although there is no mention of Thomas à Kempis in Kierkegaard's published works, he is mentioned in several journal entries. Beginning in 1849, all such entries refer to the Danish translation of *De imitatione Christi.* The comments Kierkegaard makes while reading Thomas à Kempis are not critical and pertain only to peripheral matters, while the essential question of the legitimacy of imitation in the Christian's life is not touched upon at all. This undoubtedly is due to Kierkegaard's agreement with Thomas à Kempis that imitation is an essential part of Christianity. After critically observing Protestant piety, Kierkegaard became convinced that if there is an omission of imitation, which demands of the Christian a constant passionate struggle with himself and the world, the result is superficial secularism. In spite of all the criticism of "the monastic movement of the Middle Ages" (see Climacus in *Postscript,* pp. 362–67, 370–75) for its externality, Kierkegaard attributed a higher worth to it than to the Protestantism of his day. Reflecting on a line by Thomas à Kempis: "Be desirous, my son, to do the will of another rather than thine own," Kierkegaard maintains that this could be done "in those times," because then there were clergymen who could be obeyed without betraying the Christian ideal, but he was sure that if he were to obey any one of the clergymen of his own time, his whole effort would become secularized (X^1 A 400).

Kierkegaard also makes note of several ideas from Thomas à Kempis's book which parallel his own. For example, the statement by Thomas à Kempis: "Adversities do not make a man weak, but they do reveal what strength he has" (X^1 A 550), points to the very same thing Kierkegaard calls attention to in his upbuilding discourses, that a person first discovers the meagerness of his abilities when he encounters difficulties.

Kierkegaard also commends Thomas à Kempis's declaration that the clearer a person's knowledge, the greater his responsibility (X^2 A 93).

There are in the works no direct or obvious indirect references to Thomas à Kempis.

1035. Thomas à Kempis, *Om Christi Efterfølgelse,* tr. J. A. L. Holm (Copenhagen: 3 ed., 1848), bk. I, ch. XVI, pp. 20–21. *ASKB* 273.

1036. Ibid., p. 48. Kierkegaard has *Troskab* (faithfulness) rather than *Reenhed* (purity) as in Holm's translation.

1037. Ibid., p. 3. Kierkegaard quotes the Danish translation accurately, although he has altered the order of the two sentences and added *thi* (for) in the second sentence.

1038. See *Postscript*, p. 243.

1039. See note 1035; ibid., p. 29; the parenthetical portions are Kierkegaard's.

1040. See note 1035; ibid., p. 193. In some English editions this portion is numbered IV, 7.

TIME

In *The Concept of Anxiety* [*Dread*] Kierkegaard, through the pseudonymous writer Vigilius Haufniensis, gives a coherent presentation of the issues involved in the concept of time and its relation to eternity. Time is defined as "infinite succession." V. Haufniensis points out that time in itself cannot be divided into a "present, past, and future" time, because this requires a firm, immovable criterion. In other words, time itself is nothing but a "process (a going-by)" (pp. 76–77). Kierkegaard generally ignores the spatial (astronomical) quality of time, since it pertains to a wholly external, relative definition of time.

Not until it is related to the eternal as the always present does time acquire meaning, not until then can it be divided into the present, which is always passing, and into past and future. That is, eternity always is, while it is the nature of time to pass by, and however long time lasts, it never becomes eternal (see, for example, *Christian Discourses*, p. 103).

On the first level of man's spiritual-mental development, man had as yet no idea of the eternal as the always present; eternity was pictured as infinitely long time, as infinite succession; this is the "parody" of the eternal (*The Concept of Anxiety* [*Dread*], p. 77). As in ancient India, man was swallowed up in the long space of time.

The idea of the eternal as the always present appears at two points in the history of man's spiritual-mental development. In Greece Socrates arrived at the thought of the eternal as the always present through the assumption of the ideas which have a fixed, unalterable being in contrast to the constant change in the sense-world and the stream of time. But the eternity to which Socrates pointed here was still merely an abstraction, whereby "neither time nor eternity received its proper due" (p. 79, ed. tr.).

A new view of the eternal emerged in the Jewish nation through its being addressed by an eternal, transcendent power, whereby time acquired a new meaning. This also awoke a sense for the historical in this nation (see JUDAISM).

The true concept of eternity, and thereby time as well, comes first with Christianity. Here there is the meeting of time and eternity in the moment, its absolute expression, since the moment, which is brought about by the impingement of the eternal on the temporal (see, for example, *The Book on Adler*, VII^2 B 235, p. 163 [*On Authority and Revelation*, p. 130]), first appears in its perfect form in the incarnation of Christ as the "fullness of time."

Man's relation to time now has the characteristic that the more concrete the eternal becomes for a person, the greater significance decision in time has for him. Kierkegaard's authorship, especially the upbuilding writings, attempts to point up the significance a person's decision regarding the eternal has to his temporal life. A person confronts his most important decision when he encounters Christ as the eternal, revealed truth. It is a matter of man's salvation or damnation. Kierkegaard characterizes this decision, seen from man's side, as follows: "an eternal decision in time is the most intensive intensity, the most intensive leap" (XI^1 A 329). Only in this way does a person get the possibility to realize the task assigned him in temporality: "To satisfy eternity —with this task man was sent out into the world, and later the order was unconditionally enjoined by Christianity" (XI^1 A 435; see also MOMENT and ETERNITY, THE ETERNAL).

Bedell, George C. "Kierkegaard's Conception of Time." *Journal of American Academy of Religion*, 37, 1969, pp. 266-69.

Callan, Edward. "W. H. Auden and Kierkegaard: The Artistic Framework of 'For the Time Being.' " *Christian Scholar*, 48, 1965, pp. 211-23.

Colette, Jacques. *Kierkegaard*, tr. Ralph M. McInerny and Leo Turncotte. Notre Dame: University of Notre Dame Press, 1968.

Croxall, T. H. "Hope," "Time–Eternity," in *Kierkegaard Studies*, ch. 7, 8. London: Lutterworth Press, 1948.

Hamilton, Wayne B. "Søren Kierkegaard's Conception of Temporality." Ph.D. dissertation, McGill, 1972.

Heinecken, Martin J. "The Christian Hope," in *The Moment Before God*, ch. 12. Philadelphia: Muhlenberg Press, 1956.

Jones, Ozio T., Jr. "The Meaning of the 'Moment' in Existential Encounter According to Kierkegaard." S.T.D. dissertation, Temple, 1962.

Kroner, Richard. "Existentialism and Christianity." *Encounter*, 17, 3, Summer 1956, pp. 219-44.

Minear, Paul S. "Thanksgiving as a Synthesis of the Temporal and the Eternal." *Anglican Theological Review*, 38, January 1956, pp. 4-14.

Schrag, Calvin. "Kierkegaard's Existential Reflections on Time." *The Personalist*, 42, 1961, pp. 149-64.

Shmuëli, Adi. "The Historicity and Temporality of Consciousness," in *Kierkegaard and Consciousness*, tr. Naomi Handelman, ch. 10. Princeton: Princeton University Press, 1971.

Sulzbach, Marian F. "Time, Eschatology, and the Human Problem." *Theology Today*, 7, October 1950, pp. 321-30.

Taylor, Mark C. "Time and Self in Kierkegaard's Pseudonymous Writings." Ph.D. dissertation, Harvard, 1972.

Thomas, J. Heywood. "Kierkegaard's View of Time." *The British Journal for Phenomenology*, 4, 1, January 1973, pp. 33-40.

Whittemore, Robert C. "On History, Time, and Kierkegaard's Problem." *Journal of Religious Thought*, 9, 2, 1954, pp. 134-55.

Widenman, Robert. "Some Aspects of Time in Aristotle and Kierkegaard." *Kierkegaardiana*, 8, 1971, pp. 7-25.

For references in the works to time, see, for example, *The Concept of Irony*, pp. 49-50, 132, 137; *Either/Or*, I, pp. 25, 67, 279-97; II, pp. 11, 22, 42, 62, 95-98, 106, 119-20, 128-30, 135-44, 174-78, 220, 254, 311-14; *Fear and Trembling*, pp. 45-46, 52-64; *Repetition*, passim, especially pp. 33-35; *Upbuilding [Edifying] Discourses*, II, p. 72; III, pp. 71-93, 103-20; IV, p. 34; *Fragments*, title-page, pp. 22, 73-76, 89-110, 111-30; *The Concept of Anxiety [Dread]*, pp. 74-83, 135-37; *Three Discourses on Imagined Occasions [Thoughts on Crucial Situations]*, pp. 106-7; *Stages*, pp. 149, 224, 280, 350, 356; *Postscript*, pp. 84-87, 176, 182, 184, 186, 226-27, 242, 244, 262-65, 276-78, 360-61, 433, 439, 469, 474, 492, 506, 507-8, 513, 517; *Two Ages*, S.V., VIII, pp. 8-11, 20; *Upbuilding Discourses in Various Spirits*, Part One [*Purity of Heart*, pp. 43, 100-102, 115-16, 135-37, 166-69, 184-97, 210]; Part Three [*The Gospel of Suffering*, pp. 118-37]; *Works of Love*, pp. 46, 81-83, 134-36, 178, 230, 233-43, 283-91, 302, 325-26; *Christian Discourses*, pp. 72-82, 101-18, 139-48, 156-57; *The Crisis [and a Crisis] in the Life of an Actress*, pp. 85-91; "The Difference between a Genius and an Apostle," with *The Present Age*, pp. 150-51; *The Sickness unto Death*, pp. 159-61, 168; *Practice [Training] in Christianity*, pp. 206-8, 215-19; *The Moment*, no. 2, in *Attack*, pp. 95-96.

1041. See Galatians 4:4.

1042. See Plutarch, *Crassus*, 24. A tactic of the Parthians was to simulate retreat and then to attack from the rear.

1043. See *Christian Discourses*, pp. 167-68.

1044. See *Works of Love*, pp. 135-36; *Upbuilding Discourses in Various Spirits*, Part Two [*What We Learn from the Lilies of the Field and the Birds of the Air*, with *The Gospel of Suffering*, pp. 201; 215]].

1045. See *Works of Love*, pp. 135-36.

1046. See *Practice [Training] in Christianity*, pp. 185-87.

1047. See *Fragments*, p. 12 fn.

1048. Johan L. Ussing, *Reisebilleder fra Syden* (Copenhagen: 1846-47), p. 173. *ASKB* U107.

1049. Unforgetting Furies.

1050. [K. W. F.] *Solgers nachgelassene Schriften und Briefwechsel*, ed. L. Tieck and F. von Raumer, I-II (Leipzig: 1826). *ASKB* 1832-33.

1051. "This accompanying consciousness is also time, thought of in a higher, divine sense, and thus *Chronos* is also a god of fate, who regards everything as one and the same . . . . This unknown, obscure, all-seeing being knows very well all the transgressions of men and punishes them, however tardily; for the same [being], in uninterrupted unity, accompanies the present just as [it does] the most distant future."

1052. Plutarch, *Moralia*, "On the Delays of the Divine Vengeance," pp. 548–68; *Plutarchs moralische Abhandlungen*, tr. J. F. S. Kaltwasser, I–IX in V (Frankfurt am Main: 1783–93), V, pp. 1 ff. *ASKB* 1192–96.
1053. See *Practice [Training] in Christianity*, pp. 23–24 (tr. "the obstacle," "halt").
1054. The reference is to Peter in particular, who explicitly denied Christ.
1055. See Philippians 4:4.
1056. Cheap.
1057. See Matthew 6:24; Luke 16:13; *Judge for Yourselves!*, pp. 161–217.
1058. See *Upbuilding Discourses in Various Spirits*, Part One [*Purity of Heart*], passim.
1059. Thomas Moore, *Epicuræeren*, tr. I. C. Magnus (Copenhagen: 1844), pp. 10 ff.
1060. See Luke 16:1 ff.
1061. See Luke 12:14.
1062. See *Fragments*, title-page.
1063. See Luke 16:29, 31.
1064. There had been in Denmark a special tax on holders of titles.
1065. See note 32.

TOLERATION

The word "toleration" or "tolerance" appears only a few times in Kierkegaard's works and, just as in the journals, is used exclusively in connection with Christianity. The word appears first in *Concluding Unscientific Postscript*, where Climacus criticizes his age for its excessive tolerance, which he considers to be essentially "indifference" to the point that it would even be possible for a "real Christian," if he "does not engage in judging others," to "be permitted to go on living in peace" instead of arousing opposition among his associates (p. 503).

But it is far more serious, according to Kierkegaard, when a tolerance or indifference of this nature gains ground among Christians. Numerous entries after 1851 apparently result from the discussion about Church government, which a section in the new Constitution of 1849 (granting religious freedom) had promised. But in addition, demands had been made since the 1830's for greater freedom in religious practices both by the Grundtvigians and certain revival movements.

In his journals Kierkegaard maintains that the tolerance for other beliefs so zealously advocated by these Christian trends actually was "indifference" (X^4 A 10) and thereby "the most extreme falling away from Christianity" (X^4 A 66). According to his conviction that Christianity was the only and the supreme truth, Christianity must be intolerant; it cannot watch with indifference when men go astray in unbelief or in false forms of religion. But Christianity's intolerance is a "suffering" intolerance (X^4 A 10). Kierkegaard expresses this very clearly in an article in *The Moment,* no. 6 (in *Attack,* pp. 183–87), where he points out that both "the Mynsterian view of life" and Grundtvig's so-called tolerance are "indifferentism." He writes: "Let us not forget that while in one sense Christianity certainly is the most tolerant of all religions because it abhors the use of physical force, in another sense it is the most intolerant of all religions because its true followers, knowing no bounds in suffering the constraint of others, constrain them by suffering their mistreatment and persecution" (pp. 184–85, ed. tr.).

For references in the works to tolerance and toleration, see *Postscript,* p. 503; *The Moment,* no. 6, in *Attack,* pp. 183–87.

1066. Nicolai F. S. Grundtvig (1783–1872), Danish pastor, poet, literary historian, politician. Among his many writings are a treatise *"Om Religionsfrihed"* ("On Freedom of Religion"), 1827, and *"Præstefrihed i Folkekirken"* ("Pastoral Freedom in the Folk-Church").

1067. Grundtvig, who belonged to no political party in Parliament (*Rigsdag*), formed a majority coalition including "indifferent" members (particularly the party called *Bondevennerne;* see X^4 A 58) in order to put through changes in the Church law. The same political operation was carried out later in the 1850's with regard to other Church affairs (parish membership, baptism).

1068. Holberg, *Gert Westphaler,* sc. 8; see *Postscript,* p. 175.

1069. Benjamin Franklin, *Leben und Schriften,* tr. A. Binzer, I–IV (Kiel: 1829). *ASKB* 1871–72.

TRAGEDY/COMEDY

As early as 1834 and certainly in part because of his own existential situation, Kierkegaard began to reflect on the nature of the tragic. An important form of the tragic—namely, misunderstanding—is pointed up in an entry in which he mentions the various tragic figures: "Doubtless the most sublime tragedy consists in being *misunderstood*" (I A 33).

Some years later, in the period (1841–42) when his reading of Hegel's *Esthetics* and Aristotle's *Poetics* drew him into literary and esthetic issues, he became especially interested in the fundamental presupposition for the tragic, the misrelation between "idea and actuality," and also in the relation between the tragic and the comic, which are "the two ways" the poet seeks to get people to "reconcile" themselves with the contradictions in existence (see IV C 113 and 114).

Especially significant for Kierkegaard's concept of the tragic was Aristotle's requirement that "the tragic hero must have ἁμαρτία," a flaw or guilt (*Either/Or,* p. 142), but certainly his own personal experiences (e.g., the broken engagement) were also of importance. He now perceived that within the esthetic the most extreme expression of the misrelation between idea and actuality is the tragic guilt that is at one and the same time both guilt and innocence. Then the tragic collision consists in the individual's becoming guilty not merely through his own personal fault but through fate as an external power. Thus the tragic guilt lies within the two extremes: innocence and total guilt. The esthete A discusses this in the section on "Ancient Tragedy as Reflected in the Modern" in *Either/Or:* "If the individual has no guilt whatsoever, then the tragic interest is annulled, for in that case the tragic collision is enervated; if, however, he has total guilt, he no longer has tragic interest for us" (p. 142, ed. tr.). This blending—of innocence and guilt, of suffering and action, of grief and pain—is also the prerequisite if ancient tragedy is to meet its objective, which, according to Aristotle, is "to arouse fear and sympathy in the spectator" (p. 145, ed. tr.).

On the basis of this concept of the tragic, Kierkegaard now has the esthete A undertake a comparison between Greek tragedy and certain modern tragedies. He mainly tries to show that it is "a misunderstanding of the tragic" if because of an interest in "individuality and subjectivity" the tragic hero is held "responsible for everything," for he thereby becomes not tragic but merely bad, and for that reason he lies outside the interest of the esthetic and falls instead under the judgment of the ethical (p. 142). Moreover he believes it is "an illusion" to let the hero be "his own creator" in this way, which only makes him comic, because every man, the hero as well, is dependent on what we today call heredity and milieu. Therefore it is a misunderstanding if there is no reflection of ancient tragedy in modern tragedy; the reflection need not be in the form of fate coming from without but may be in the form of a "dark side" (I, p. 149, ed. tr.), which is now present in the person himself, an expression of his solidarity with his family and the race and their or his own guilt incurred through past actions. Thus in modern tragedy the tragic collision takes place in a person's inner being, and in the sketch of a modern tragedy about Antigone the esthete A indicates how such a collision could take form (I, pp. 152–62).

Johannes de Silentio also speaks critically of the reflective tragic hero who by his "illusory high-mindedness" (*Fear and Trembling,* p. 103, ed. tr.) wants to play providence to others. By assuming the responsibility himself for a whole sequence of events, the hero himself approaches the ethical and total guilt. In such a case the poet must rather begin where he "for so many years has ended," with the action executed, and thereafter let the hero perceive the guilt. In this way the poet could "work hand in hand with the religious" (p. 103, ed. tr; see also III A 199). If this is done, the guilt itself could be made the object of a poetic treatment. A person does not, however, go as swiftly from guilt to repentance and reconciliation, as "the system" seems to maintain (see *Stages,* p. 404), but on the contrary he will long continue to ponder the extent of his guilt. In "Guilty?/Not Guilty?" (pp. 179–444) the pseudonymous

Quidam and Frater Taciturnus give just such a poetic description of the nature of the difficult transition from the dialectical reflections on guilt to the acceptance of the total guilt whereby a person reaches the religious.

Bedell, George C. "The Nature of Tragedy," in *Kierkegaard and Faulkner; Modalities of Existence*, ch. 5. Baton Rouge: Louisiana State University Press, 1971.

Brantl, George E. "The Tragic Commitment: an Essay in Existentialist Metaphysics." Ph.D. dissertation, Columbia, 1957.

Croxall, T. H. "Tragedy, Imagination, Boredom," in *Kierkegaard Commentary*, ch. 6. London: James Nesbet, 1956.

Glenn, John D. "Kierkegaard on the Unity of Comedy and Tragedy." *Tulane Studies in Philosophy*, 19, 1970, pp. 41–53.

Holmer, Paul L. "Søren Kierkegaard: Faith in a Tragic World," in *The Tragic Vision and the Christian Faith*, ed. Nathan A. Scott, Jr., ch. 6. New York: Association Press, 1957.

Krieger, Murray. "Tragedy and the Tragic Vision," in *The Tragic Vision: Variations on a Theme in Literary Interpretation*, pp. 1–21. New York: Holt, 1960.

Mesnard, Pierre. "Is the Category of the Tragic Absent from the Life and Thought of Kierkegaard?" in *A Kierkegaard Critique*, ch. 7. New York: Harper, 1962.

Norton, R. W. "The Concepts of the Tragic of Søren Kierkegaard and Miguel de Unamuno." M.A. thesis, Illinois, 1952.

Ruotolo, Lucio P. "Keats and Kierkegaard: The Tragedy of Two Worlds." *Renascence*, 16, 1964, pp. 175–90.

Schutz, Alfred. "Mozart and the Philosopher." *Social Research*, 23, Summer 1956, pp. 219–42.

Unamuno, Miguel de. *The Tragic Sense of Life in Men and Peoples*. London: Macmillan, 1921.

Wood, Forrest E. "Kierkegaardian Light on Ibsen's *Brand*." *Personalist*, 51, Summer 1970. pp. 393–400.

For references in the works to tragedy/comedy, see, for example, *The Concept of Irony*, pp. 89, 99, 159, 218, 277–78, 334–35; *Either/Or*, I, pp. 135–62, 261; II, 240–44; *Fear and Trembling*, pp. 69–70, 76, 86–89, 93–94, 102–3, 106–7, 122–26; *The Concept of Anxiety* [*Dread*], pp. 13–14, 87, 93; *Stages*, pp. 52, 335–36, 370–71, 374, 378–87, 395, 399, 403, 411–20, 425–26, 438; *Postscript*, pp. 42, 394–95, 459, 462–64.

1070. Holberg, *Jacob von Thyboe*.
1071. See note 941; ibid., pt. I, pp. 48 ff.
1072. Ibid.
1073. See note 1070.
1074. *Poetics* 1449 b. "Through pity and fear it effects relief to these and similar emotions." Loeb ed., tr. W. Hamilton Fyfe. See *Either/Or*, I, p. 145; *Stages*, p. 416.

1075. Gotthold E. Lessing, *Sämmtliche Werke*, I–XXXII (Berlin: 1825–28), XXV, pp. 154 ff. *ASKB* 1747–62.

1076. See Lessing's letter to Friedrich Nicolai, November 13, 1756, ibid., XXVI, pp. 54–63 (vols. XXVI–XXIX contain correspondence with Moses Mendelssohn, F. Nicolai, and others), also letters to Mendelssohn, November 13 and 28, 1756, XXIX, pp. 63–79, to Nicolai, November 29, 1756, XXIX, pp. 90–94, to Mendelssohn, December 18, 1756, XXVI, pp. 91–106, and to Nicolai, April 2, 1757, XXIX, pp. 110–16.

1077. Pity and fear.

1078. See *Stages*, p. 400.

1079. This entry is a reading note in connection with Aristotle's *Poetics* and is a good example of Kierkegaard's customary use of *Virkelighed*.

1080. I. Kant, *Kritik der Urtheilskraft* (2 ed., Berlin: 1793), para. 2. *ASKB* 594. See *The Concept of Anxiety* [*Dread*], p. 16 fn.

1081. See *Stages*, pp. 399–400.

1082. Aristotle, *Poetics*, 1448 b–1449 a; *Aristoteles Dichtkunst*, tr. M. C. Curtius (Hannover: 1753), pp. 6–7. *ASKB* 1094.

1083. Danish: *Skræk og Medlidenhed*. The original Greek of this phrase from the *Poetics* is usually rendered in English as "pity and fear."

1084. Boethius, *De consolatione philosophiæ libri quinque* (Agriæ: 1758). *ASKB* 431. "Who, saith she, hath permitted these tragical harlots to have access to this sick man, which will not only not comfort his grief with wholesome remedies, but also nourish them with sugared poison? For these be they which with the fruitless thorns of affections do kill the fruitful crop of reason, and do accustom men's minds to sickness, instead of curing them." *The Consolations of Philosophy* (Loeb ed., tr. H. F. Stewart), I, ll. 28–34. See *Stages*, p. 400.

1085. The Boethius text reads: *uberem fructibus*.

1086. "So too he was the first to outline for us the general forms of Comedy by producing not a dramatic invective, but a dramatic picture of the Ridiculous. . . ." *Poetics*, 1448 b, ll. 36–38. Beginning should read οὕτω καί τὰ τῆς.

1087. See note 1082.

1088. See *Stages*, p. 400.

1089. See note 1082 for Curtius edition.

1090. See *Stages*, p. 396.

1091. See M. C. Curtius, note 127 in edition cited above in note 1082.

1092. See Lessing's letter to F. Nicolai, January 21, 1758, pp. 144–45, in Lessing edition cited in note 1075; *Stages*, p. 396.

1093. *Poetics*, 1453 b–1454 a; p. 30 in German edition cited in note 1082.

1094. *Nicomachean Ethics*, 1110 b, 14.

1095. See *Stages,* pp. 96, 122–23. "Tragedy is a deception, by which the deceiver seems more righteous than the non-deceiver; and the deceived wiser than the non-deceived."

1096. Heinrich T. Rötscher, *Die Kunst der dramatischen Darstellung* (Berlin: 1841). *ASKB* 1391.

TRUTH

In his elucidation of the concept of truth in *Concluding Unscientific Postscript,* Johannes Climacus first discusses the classical methods of defining the truth: (1) great importance is attached to the empirical and truth is defined "as the conformity of thought with being," that is, with experience; (2) the idea comes first and truth is defined "more idealistically as the conformity of being with thought" (p. 169). In the first case it is empirical being which is primary and ranks higher than thought; in the second case it is the idea (thought) which is the higher authority. In philosophy there are actually only these two logical methods to attain knowledge of the truth. All other methods are but a variation or combination of the two.

Climacus points out that neither of these two attempts to solve the question of truth is satisfactory, because both are too abstract, stress only the objective, and do not touch personal human existence more deeply (see SUBJECTIVITY/OBJECTIVITY). Therefore he gives a definition of truth which lies outside the domain of traditional philosophy and which can be utilized in human existence because it is based on an ethical-religious understanding of existence. The point of departure for this conception of truth is the thesis: "Truth is subjectivity" (p. 169). The statement contains the following elements, which Climacus amplifies in great detail. (1) Truth must always stand in relation to the person, to subjectivity. (2) This truth can only be something eternal, thus not anything that is changeable. In a journal entry Kierkegaard says more specifically: "If there is nothing eternal, there then is neither truth nor freedom" (V B 60, p. 136, draft of *The Concept of Anxiety*). This means that subjectivity must never be confused with subjectivism, in which one arbitrarily decides what is truth, as Nietzsche did, for example. (3) This eternal truth, which has an ethical-religious character, must be actualized by the person, as expressed in the well-known statement that "subjectivity is truth" (consequently not *only* "truth is subjectivity"). When an attempt is made to actualize this truth in subjectivity, objectively considered it is a paradox (p. 183). (4) The only example of the actualization of this truth is provided by him who said: "I am the way, the truth, and the life" (John 14:6). "The eternal truth has come into existence in time," an actualization which must be designated as "the absolute paradox" (pp. 187, 195, ed. tr.). (5) But it is up to each and every person to try to actualize the ethical-religious truth in his life, as expressed in the sentence "subjectivity is truth." (6) Climacus shows that the final result of this effort is that one fails to reach his goal and thereby becomes guilty. This guilt is qualified as sin in the encounter with him who alone could actualize the eternal truth in his earthly life, thereby the sentence "subjectivity is truth" is changed to its opposite—"subjectivity is untruth" (p. 185). By forgiveness a person can once again come into a positive relation to the truth.

Manifestly Climacus's and Kierkegaard's concept of truth is completely oriented to existence and is presented in connection with Christianity's concept of truth in a new and original manner. In contrast to the two classical conceptions of truth, the empirical and the idealistic, Kierkegaard's concept of truth gives man an exceptional place in creation, inasmuch as only man has the possibility of the eternal in him. Climacus strongly emphasizes that only this view of truth embraces a "becoming" (pp. 273, 368), in which the eternal as "the absolute good ... transforms the entire life of the existing individual" (p. 347, ed. tr.). On the other hand, in the two definitions of truth mentioned previously, becoming plays no role, and the individual man is regarded by both views as a vanishing nonentity in a great world process.

Kierkegaard points out that from the beginning of his authorship he operates with an ethical-religious concept of truth which has upbuilding as its goal. He writes: "When I had *Either/Or* end with the clause: 'Only the truth that builds up is truth for you,' only a few, I regret, perceived the outlook involved. There was considerable argument among Greek philosophers about the criterion of truth (see, for example, Tennemann, *Geschichte der Philosophie*, V, p. 311); it would be very interesting to pursue this matter further. Meanwhile I doubt that a more concrete expression will be found" (IV A 42).

Kierkegaard's original concept of truth is not only the basis for his pseudonymous authorship but to an exceptional degree is the basis for all his upbuilding literature.

Crites, Stephen. *In the Twilight of Christendom: Hegel vs. Kierkegaard on Faith and History.* Chambersburg, Pa.: American Academy of Religion, 1971.

Diem, Hermann. "Being in Truth," "Being in Untruth," in *Kierkegaard's Dialectic of Existence,* tr. Harold Knight, ch. 8, 12. Edinburgh and London: Oliver and Boyd, 1959.

Edwards, Paul. "Kierkegaard and the 'Truth' of Christianity." *Philosophy,* 46, April 1971, pp. 89–108.

Fabro, Cornelio. "The 'Subjectivity of Truth' and the Interpretation of Kierkegaard." *Kierkegaard-Studiet,* 1964, pp. 35–43.

Fay, Thomas A. "Communication of Truth and Existential Dialectic in the Thought of Kierkegaard." *Personalist,* 53, Spring 1972, pp. 161–69.

Gill, Jerry H. "Kant, Kierkegaard, and Religious Knowledge." *Philosophy and Phenomenological Research,* 28, December 1967, pp. 188–204. Reprinted in *Essays on Kierkegaard,* ed. Jerry Gill. Minneapolis: Burgess, 1969.

Hare, Peter H. "Is There an Existential Theory of Truth?" *Journal of Existentialism*, 7, Summer 1967, pp. 417-24.

Holmer, Paul L. "Kierkegaard and the Truth: An Analysis of the Presuppositions Integral to His Definition of the Truth." Ph.D. dissertation, Yale, 1946.

Keane, Ellen M. "The Equation of Subjectivity and Truth in Kierkegaard's *Postscript.*" Ph.D. dissertation, Notre Dame, 1965.

LeFevre, Perry. "The Snare of Truth." *Pastoral Psychology*, 19, 187, 1968, pp. 33-44.

Mackey, Louis. "Kierkegaard and the Problem of Existential Philosophy." *Review of Metaphysics*, 9, 3-4, 1956, pp. 404-19, 569-88.

Malantschuk, Gregor. *Kierkegaard's Way to the Truth*, tr. Mary Michelsen. Minneapolis: Augsburg, 1963.

Martin, H. V. "Truth Is Subjectivity," in *Kierkegaard*, ch. 5. London: Epworth, 1950.

Moore, Robert B. "Kierkegaard's Conception of Truth." M.A. thesis, Minnesota, 1958.

Murphy, Arthur E. "On Kierkegaard's Claim that 'Truth is Subjectivity,' " in *Reason and the Common Good*, pp. 173-79. Englewood Cliffs, N.J.: Prentice-Hall, 1963.

Pelikan, Jaroslav. *Human Culture and the Holy. Essays on the True, the Good, and the Beautiful. Kierkegaard, Paul, Dostoievsky, Luther, Nietzsche, Bach.* London: Student Christian Movement Press, 1959.

Popkin, Richard H. "Hume and Kierkegaard." *Journal of Religion*, 31, 4, 1951, pp. 274-81.

——. "Theological and Religious Scepticism." *Christian Scholar*, 39, June 1956, pp. 150-58.

——. "Kierkegaard and Scepticism." *Algemeen Nederlands Tijdschrift voor Wijsbegeerte en Psychologie*, 51, 3, 1958-59, pp. 123-41.

Roberts, James D. "Kierkegaard on Truth and Subjectivity." *Journal of Religious Thought*, 173, 1961, pp. 41-56.

Shmuëli, Adi. "The Christian Consciousness and the Problem of Truth," in *Kierkegaard and Consciousness*, tr. Naomi Handelman, ch. 9. Princeton: Princeton University Press, 1971.

Sikes, Walter W. *On Becoming the Truth: An Introduction to the Life and Thought of Søren Kierkegaard*, St. Louis: Bethany Press, 1968.

Stein, Waltraut J. "Truth as Subjectivity: the Thought of Søren Kierkegaard." *Religious Humanism*, 4, Spring 1970, pp. 78-82.

Van De Pitte, Frederick P. "Kierkegaard's 'Approximation.' " *The Personalist*, 52, 1971, pp. 483-98.

Walker, Jeremy. "Kierkegaard's Concept of Truthfulness." *Inquiry* (Oslo), 12, 1969, pp. 209-24.

Wilshire, Bruce W. "Kierkegaard's Theory of Knowledge and New Directions in Psychology and Psychoanalysis." *Review of Existential Psychology and Psychiatry,* 3, 1963, pp. 249–61.

For references in the works to truth, see, for example, *The Concept of Irony,* pp. 264, 338–41; *Either/Or,* I, pp. 111, 176; II, pp. 334, 356; *Upbuilding* [*Edifying*] *Discourses,* III, pp. 71–72, 119; *Fragments,* passim, especially pp. 11–27, 37–38, 47–48, 63–66, 77, 92, 97–110; *The Concept of Anxiety* [*Dread*], pp. 99, 123–26; *Stages,* pp. 25, 41, 218, 435 fn.; *Postscript,* pp. 23–25, 34 fn., 36, 45–46, 71–113, 169–224, 227, 248–52, 273–82, 287, 306, 312–22, 331; *Three Upbuilding Discourses in Various Spirits,* Part One [*Purity of Heart,* pp. 66–67, 121–22]; Part Three [*The Gospel of Suffering,* pp. 51–52, 65–66, 147–48]; *Works of Love,* pp. 96, 213–30, 312–13, 331–32, 336–39; *Christian Discourses,* pp. 178–79, 287; "Has a Man the Right to Let Himself Be Put to Death for the Truth?" passim, with *The Present Age; Practice* [*Training*] *in Christianity,* pp. 37, 67–68, 87–90, 198–204, 228, 227–50; *The Point of View,* pp. 39–40; " 'The Single Individual,' " with *The Point of View,* pp. 112–21; articles in *Fædrelandet,* no. 24 and no. 83, January 29 and April 11, 1855, in *Attack,* pp. 22–24, 42; *The Moment,* no. 8, no. 9, no. 10, ibid., pp. 248–49, 271–72, 290.

1097. See note 544; ibid., V.

1098. *Adversus Mathematicos* (*Against the Professors*), I, 9. To learn and to teach a discipline.

1099. The wording in this entry corresponds to the German of Tennemann, V, p. 293. See note 544.

1100. See *The Concept of Anxiety* [*Dread*], p. 15.

1101. Publication of *Either/Or* was announced in *Adresseavisen,* no. 43, February 20, 1843.

1102. *Either/Or,* II, p. 356; see IV C 60.

1103. See *Philosophical Fragments,* p. 47.

1104. See note 544; ibid., IV, p. 205.

1105. See John 3:1–15, text for Trinity Sunday, which in 1844 was on June 2.

1106. To hide, [he who] hides well. *"Bene qui latuit, bene vixit."* "Let me tell thee, he who hides well his life lives well; each man ought to remain within his proper position." Ovid. *Tristia,* III, 4, 25.

1107. See " 'The Single Individual,' " with *The Point of View,* pp. 112–21.

1108. See note 407.

1109. See note 1107.

1110. A reference to Kierkegaard's practice of walking about in central Copenhagen and casually conversing with all sorts of people. See Villads Christensen, *Peripatetikeren Søren Kierkegaard* (Copenhagen: Graabrødre Torvs Forlag, 1965), which includes Andrew Hamilton's (*Sixteen Months in the Danish Isles,* I–II, 1852, I, pp. 83–84, 268–70) comments on Kierkegaard's daily walks. See *The Point of View,* p. 47.

1111. See John 18:38.

1112. See John 19:5, which in current English translation reads somewhat differently from the Danish translation.

1113. Ernst Wilhelm Kolthoff (1809–1890), in 1849 a pastor of Helliggeists Kirke in Copenhagen.

1114. See Mark 7:36.

1115. See Luke 17:17–18.

1116. See *For Self-Examination,* p. [i].

1117. See *Fenelons Werke religiösen Inhalts,* tr. Matthias Claudius, I–III (Hamburg: 1823), III, pp. 322–23. *ASKB* 1914.

1118. If I am not mistaken.

1119. See Franz Baader, *Gesammelte Schriften,* I–XVI (Leipzig: 1851–60; photo reprint, Aalen: 1963), p. 127. Kierkegaard had 28 single volumes of Baader's works published from 1815 to 1841. *ASKB* 391–418.

1120. See *Fear and Trembling,* title-page, for another reference to Tarquinius.

1121. Seneca, *Ad Lucilium Epistulae Morales,* VII, 11.

1122. See "The Activity of a Travelling Esthetician," *S.V.,* XIII, p. 429.

1123. See note 81.

1124. See note 1110.

1125. In Schiller's *"Das verschleierte Bild zu Sais"* a young man who wanted to know the truth entered at night the temple in Sais, Egypt, and tore the veil from the statue of the goddess Isis. Afterward he replied to those who pressed him because of his subsequent changed way of life: Woe to those who want to come to the truth as guilty; the truth will never make them happy.

1126. See note 675.

1127. See note 1107.

1128. See note 28; ibid., I, 1, pp. 234–35.

1129. See note 504.

1130. A reference to an expression by Andreas G. Rudelbach in *Fædrelandet,* no. 38, February 14, 1851. See X^4 A 100.

1131. Nicholai P. Nielsen (1795–1860), known especially for his roles as the Nordic hero in Oehlenschläger's dramas.

1132. Johanne Luise Heiberg (1812–90), actress and writer, wife of poet-dramatist-philosopher J. L. Heiberg, and the subject of Kierkegaard's last esthetic work, *The Crisis [and a Crisis] in the Life of an Actress.*

1133. See note 445.

1134. Carl Ritter, *Die Erdkunde in Verhältniss zur Natur und zur Geschichte des Menschen,* I–X (II–X in 19 parts) 2 ed. (Berlin: 1822–59).

1135. A book society formed in 1824 with a very extensive collection of books. Kierkegaard was a member.

1136. Truth emerges more readily from error than from confusion. *Novum Organum,* II, 20. Kierkegaard had *Franz Bacon's neues Organ,* tr. A. T.

Bruck (Leipzig: 1830), and *Oeuvres philosophiques et morales* (Paris: 1797). *ASKB* 420 and 419.

1137. See Mark 7:33.

1138. See note 662.

1139. All the same.

1140. According to legend, Aristeas, in the reign of Ptolemy Philadelphus (284–246 B.C.) had seventy-two interpreters work solitarily for seventy-two days translating the Old Testament into Greek. When they had finished, their translations all agreed. The number was later rounded off to seventy (*Septuagint*, the name for the Alexandrian translation of the Eastern Church). See *Fragments*, p. 115.

UNCHANGEABLENESS

In August, 1855, in the midst of his violent attack on the Danish Church, Kierkegaard published a sermon, *The Unchangeableness of God*, which he had delivered in Citadelskirken on May 18, 1851. In his preface he says, "The text is the first I used; since then it has frequently been unearthed; now I come back to it again." By "the text" Kierkegaard means the Epistle of James 1:17–21, which declares: "Every good and every perfect gift is from above and comes down from the Father of lights, with whom there is no variableness or shadow of turning."

The reason this particular text became so meaningful for Kierkegaard was that during his struggle to find a personal faith he searched primarily for "the Archimedean point ... that point ... outside the restrictions of time and space," which could provide him a fixed place in the middle of this world of relativities, where everything is insecure and perishable (see I A 68).

In Kierkegaard's upbuilding writings, God as the eternal fixed point in the changeable world also becomes the point of departure from which he steers men to greater ethical and religious discernment. The thought of the unchangeableness of God becomes the fixed undercurrent running through all his upbuilding literature.

In the 1855 discourse Kierkegaard amplifies the meaning of the words "God's unchangeableness" and touches on the contrast between the philosophical concept of God as the unmoved mover and the Christian concept of God who "in infinite love" is moved by everything (*The Unchangeableness of God* with *Judge for Yourselves!*, p. 227). Therefore Kierkegaard does not use the adjective "unmoved" for God, but "unchangeable." In 1854 Kierkegaard recorded in his journal several reflections on the concept of God's unchangeableness, which he substantiates by saying that God totally imbues himself with his consciousness and is therefore totally himself, that he is a "self" who is not dependent upon anyone and is therefore always the same (see especially XI^2 A 54, 56, 97, 133).

NOTES   755

In the discourse *The Unchangeableness of God* Kierkegaard formulates this as follows: "In unaltered clarity—yes, this is precisely why he is unchanged, because he is sheer clarity, a clarity with no obscurity and which no obscurity can approach" (p. 231, ed. tr.).

Kierkegaard also emphasizes in this discourse that for man the thought of God's unchangeableness is both terrifying and reassuring—terrifying if a person's will is not unconditionally also God's will, which is unchangeable (see also XI^2 A 56), but reassuring when one learns to renounce his own "changeability" and "arbitrariness" so that he "can rest blessedly" in God's unchangeableness (p. 238, ed. tr.).

The reason that Kierkegaard published this discourse in the middle of the Church battle (after the seventh number of *The Moment*) was that he believed he had now touched bottom in his annihilation of the old; therefore he wanted to point again to the thought which is the source and basis of all positivity—namely, the thought of God's unchangeableness. Only the idea of God as the power who stands firm when everything totters can become the point of departure for the person who has to begin all over again, and thereby for a new ethical and religious composure.

For references in the works to unchangeableness or immutability, see, for example, *Upbuilding [Edifying] Discourses*, II, p. 43; IV, pp. 126, 133–34, 136–37; *Fragments*, p. 95; *Three Discourses on Imagined Occasions* [*Thoughts on Crucial Situations*], pp. 85–86; *Upbuilding Discourses in Various Spirits*, Part One [*Purity of Heart*, pp. 35–36, 51, 60, 209–10]; Part Two [*What We Learn from the Lilies of the Field and the Birds of the Air*, with *The Gospel of Suffering*, p. 202]; Part Three [ibid., p. 132]; *Works of Love*, pp. 49–54, 164, 289–90, 327–28; *Christian Discourses*, pp. 54, 203–4, 230, 275, 292; *Two Discourses at the Communion on Fridays*, with *Judge for Yourselves!*, pp. 14–15; *The Unchangeableness of God*, with *Judge for Yourselves!*, pp. 223–40.

1141. See note 234.

1142. See *The Unchangeableness of God*, with *Judge for Yourselves!*, pp. 223–40.

1143. See notes 1141 and 1142.

UNCONDITIONED, THE

In one of the discourses in the section "What We Learn from the Lilies of the Field and the Birds of the Air," which deals with *how glorious it is to be a human being*, Kierkegaard declares that man is distinguished from the animals by being "this separate entity which is implied in the unconditioned character of those first thoughts" (*Upbuilding Discourses in Various Spirits*, Part Two [with *The Gospel of Suffering*, p. 208, ed. tr.]). This means that man has the qualification to comprehend the eternal ideas, has the possibility of the eternal within him. Thus man alone of all the God, has the possibility to relate to the absolute, to God, who presents his ethical requirements to man. By God's revelation in

Christ these requirements are presented unconditionally to every man in all their unconditionedness. For this reason Kierkegaard generally uses the expression "the unconditioned" when speaking of Christianity, particularly in his Christianly upbuilding writings.

Especially in *Practice in Christianity* Kierkegaard shows that precisely because Christ stepped forth as "the unconditioned" who provided "the criterion of the unconditioned," he had to become "a sacrifice." All too easily men forget "those first thoughts" and desire to see sympathy, love, and mercy practiced only "*to a certain degree*" (p. 64), whereas divine sympathy discloses the falsity of human sympathy. Men's fear of the unconditioned, of being torn out of the "busy worldly life of comparisons" (*Upbuilding Discourses* ..., II [with *The Gospel of Suffering*, p. 207]), has made them substitute "leniency" for "rigorousness" in Christianity and to give "reasons" for the unconditioned, because they themselves do not wish to be convinced unconditionally of its truth (X^4 A 468 and X^5 A 40). But, as a matter of fact, men have thereby abolished Christianity, for "if it is not the unconditioned, it is abolished" (*Practice* ..., p. 221, ed. tr.). Christianity specifically demands "unconditioned surrender," demands that a person seek the kingdom of God *first* (see X^3 A 393 and XI^1 A 427; *Judge for Yourselves!*, pp. 126–27).

Generally speaking, Kierkegaard's authorship after 1847 demonstrates quite clearly that it became ever more urgent for him to present Christianity in all its rigor and unconditionedness as a corrective particularly to the clergy's misrepresentation of Christianity and misuse of grace. For several years he did this vigorously, particularly in *Works of Love*, *Practice in Christianity*, and *Christian Discourses*. But when the leadership went along "vapidly agreeing to everything, everything to a certain degree," he finally had to alter his tactics and utilize the unconditioned "as the beast of prey's lunging leap and the bird of prey's plunging attack" (XI^1 A 526).

This tactic, which Kierkegaard used during the Church battle, was possibly one of the reasons for his not publishing the little book *Judge for Yourselves!* while he lived. Here, as in *Practice in Christianity*, he presents Christ as the prototype who unconditionally has fulfilled the unconditioned requirement (see p. 170, ed. tr.), but he also includes the other side when he declares that "the meaning of the gospel," with its unconditioned requirement, is not that a person must lift it, for then he will be crushed, but that a person, "in humility, is to be lifted by it, believing and worshiping" (p. 165, ed. tr.). But he goes on to emphasize that a person must never beseech God to revoke the unconditioned requirement, for "if the requirement is not the unconditioned, I have nothing to do with God" (p. 177, ed. tr.). This idea is accented in *On My Work as an Author* (with *The Point of View*), p. 164: "To live in the unconditioned, to breathe only the unconditioned, a person cannot do," but at the same time Kierkegaard steadfastly maintains that "without relating himself to the unconditioned a person cannot in the deeper sense 'live.' "

For references in the works to the unconditioned (sometimes translated "the absolute," etc.) see, for example, *Upbuilding Discourses in Various Spirits*, Part Two [*What We Learn from the Lilies of the Field and the Birds of the Air*], with *The Gospel of Suffering*, pp. 207-8; *Christian Discourses*, p. 194; *The Lily of the Field and the Bird of the Air*, with *Christian Discourses*, pp. 336-38, 348-49, 352-55; *Practice* [*Training*] *in Christianity*, pp. 64, 221, 232; *Judge for Yourselves!*, pp. 120, 123-30, 165-70, 177-79, 215-16; *On My Work as an Author*, with *The Point of View*, pp. 163-64; ibid., pp. 69, 88; *The Moment*, no. 1, no. 5, no. 8, no. 10, in *Attack*, pp. 81-82, 160, 208, 243, 287.

1144. See Matthew 8:18-22.

1145. See note 1116.

1146. One catches mice with bacon.

1147. See Matthew 11:28; *Practice* [*Training*] *in Christianity*, pp. 10-72.

1148. See Exodus 3:14.

1149. Goal or end.

1150. An allusion to horse-tails symbolic of the Pasha's status. See *Either/Or*, I, p. 22 ("a three-tailed Pasha"); *Postscript*, p. 483 ("a Pasha with three horse-tails").

1151. Settled.

1152. A transition or change into another sphere or kind.

1153. See Acts 9:3 ff.

1154. See Philipp K. Marheineke, *Geschichte der teutschen Reformation*, I-IV (Berlin: 1816-31), I, p. 37. This important work is not listed in *ASKB*, but in the *Papirer* from 1731-32 there are fourteen pages of notes with page references from Kierkegaard's careful reading of volume I. See I C 1 in supplementary vol. XII of second edition of *Søren Kierkegaards Papirer*.

1155. See Blaise Pascal, *Gedanken über die Religion und einige andere Gegenstände. Voran das Leben Pascals, von seiner Schwester geschrieben*, tr. K. A. Blech, I-II (Berlin: 1840), p. 33 fn. *ASKB* 712-13.

1156. See note 32.

1157. An allusion to a game (something like "Hide the Thimble") in which the others call out to the one who is "it" when he is getting closer, very close, "The whip is burning."

1158. Michael Nielsen (1776-1846), principal of Borgerdydskolen (which Kierkegaard attended 1821 30) 1811-44. Kierkegaard called Nielsen "the unforgettable teacher of my youth, the admired paradigm of my later years" (dedication in volume of *Tre opbyggelige taler*, 1842, which Kierkegaard gave to M. Nielsen). See also appreciative letter to Nielsen, no. 107, *Breve*, I, p. 133.

1159. See note 662.

1160. See Luke 9:61.

1161. See John 11:35.

1162. See John 19:26.

1163. See Matthew 16:22-23; Mark 8:32-33.
1164. See John 8:48.
1165. The reference is to Proudhon; see A. Sundré, *Communismens Historie*, tr. C. Ebeling and J. Beyer (Copenhagen: 1851), pp. 349, 373.
1166. See, for example, *For Self-Examination*, pp. 12-21.
1167. See notes 504 and 975.
1168. See Note 32.
1169. See I John 5:19.
1170. See note 38; ibid., I, para, 36, p. 43.

UNIVERSALISM

According to Kierkegaard Christianity as God's revealed truth must, in contrast to Judaism and the pagan religions, be for all men (see X^4 A 103), who are all saved by God's grace. But the statement "that all who are saved are saved by grace" (X^5 A 108; 1495) does not mean that eternal salvation is guaranteed to all men as a matter of course, as is apparently the general assumption of those who are "brought up in Christianity" (X^5 A 146; see also XI^1 A 143 and 261).

Kierkegaard maintains that on the contrary the New Testament teaches something else; it speaks of "the opposite: a little flock which will be eternally saved, and the remainder" (X^5 A 142) and "clearly rests on the assumption that there is an eternal damnation and —perhaps not one in a million is saved" (X^5 A 146). Therefore the problem for man is not so much "whether God wants to save all or merely some "but whether I, the single individual, will accept salvation" (X^1 A 516). Kierkegaard holds that one of the conditions for becoming a Christian is that a person learns renunciation and becomes "the single individual" who, "unconditionally alone, asks only about his salvation" (X^5 A 86); and yet Kierkegaard must ask himself the question (with Regine particularly in mind) whether a person is not deceiving the people he loves most on earth if he himself lives in a faith "according to which one believes himself to be saved, and then does not get the others to enter into it, and consequently according to the same faith must believe that they are eternally lost—is it not the same as hating them not to abandon his faith and choose to follow the loved ones!" (X^5 A 142).

In his last years Kierkegaard struggled with this thought; on the one hand it was so clear to him "that the New Testament is a terrifying book, for it reckons with precisely this kind of collision with true Christianity," and on the other hand there could be moments when everything was "so infinitely lenient" and when he believed that renunciation perhaps was not an absolute demand, "that it is not demanded of everyone to be a disciple" (X^5 A 146).

But even if Kierkegaard felt compelled to present New Testament Christianity in all its rigor, he nevertheless considered himself to be "without authority, only a poet" and therefore would not make himself out to be "better than others." Thus Bishop Mynster was wrong when he once, as Kierkegaard himself tells, scolded Kierkegaard for speaking "as if the others are going to hell"; and then Kierkegaard goes on to say: "No, ... if the others are going to hell, I am going along with them. But I do not believe that; on the contrary, I believe that we will all be saved, I, too, and this is something that arouses my deepest wonder" (XI³ B 57).

In the works the specific term "universalism" does not appear in the sense of religious universalism. On the universally human, the ethical universal, see THE ETHICAL and the cumulative index. Entry XI¹ A 296 on this theme refers to *Two Ages* (see note 1171).

1171. See *Two Ages, S.V.*, VIII, pp. 99–102 [omitted in *The Present Age*].

UPBUILDING, THE

For Kierkegaard "the upbuilding" (*det opbyggelige*) means everything that contributes to interiorization or inward deepening, that is, the individual's appropriation of ethical and religious truths. In his upbuilding discourses, which Kierkegaard considers the most important part of his authorship, he describes in detail the steps through which the individual moves on the way of interiorization. The descriptions are significant because they are founded on his own inner experiences and struggles in appropriating the ethical and the religious. And just as these experiences led him step by step closer to Christianity, the ultimate aim of the upbuilding literature is to help other individuals along the way to Christianity.

In composing his upbuilding discourses, Kierkegaard used his dialectic of communication, according to which the communicator must carefully consider the receiver's ethical-religious level in order to determine how the ethical-religious truths are to be communicated. When Kierkegaard began his authorship (with *Either/Or*), he paid careful attention to the interplay between the four elements mentioned—that is, the content of the communication, the mode of the communication, the receiver, and the communicator. In this way he was in a position to give a reliable and pedagogically useful exposition of the steps in the individual's interiorization.

The most important prerequisite for the art of communicating is the ability to place oneself where the receiver is, in order, if possible, to lead him further. In *Either/Or*, for example, Kierkegaard had his pseudonyms place themselves on the level where most men live their lives—namely, paganism. Kierkegaard declares that "one must begin with paganism. So I begin with *Either/Or*" (VIII¹ A 548).

The same is true of the upbuilding discourses. The first two discourses are directed to Regine, who still lived in the category of immediacy—that is, looked at existentially, in paganism. She had to be helped in the direction of the religious. But in a wider sense these discourses say something to all who live as pagans under the name of Christian and have not advanced in the direction of the Christian as existence.

Later Kierkegaard saw it as his task as communicator in the succeeding upbuilding discourses to describe the difficult road that leads from giving up the first immediacy and moving in the direction of the religious. In the first step along this road a person perceives the insecurity of the temporal life and his own bondage to this temporality; later he will experience his own nothingness before God, and finally he will be led to what is "man's highest perfection," namely "to need God" (from the title of the first of *Four Upbuilding Discourses,* 1844; *Edifying Discourses,* IV, pp. 7-47). The awareness of this perfection and need became the aim of the first eighteen upbuilding discourses. What Climacus says of the first five discourses applies to all eighteen—that "they employ only ethical categories of immanence" (*Postscript,* p. 229) and thereby remain within "immanence"; but the last four discourses have "a tinge of the humorous," which lies on the border of the religious (pp. 241-42, ed. tr.).

There is, however considerable distance between the substance of the discourses and the specifically Christian upbuilding, which uses "the doubly reflected religious categories in the paradox," as Johannes Climacus says (p. 229). They first appear at the end of *Christian Discourses* and again in *The Sickness unto Death* and *Practice in Christianity.* Between the eighteen upbuilding discourses and the books mentioned lies the sphere of the upbuilding which can be called ethical-religious. This sphere embraces *Upbuilding Discourses in Various Spirits, Works of Love,* and the first sections of *Christian Discourses.* From these books a person can learn to seek a foothold in the transcendent; the transcendent, however, is still in time—that is, Christ as Savior is not yet the central point. Within this sphere the individual strives to be obedient to God and learns to know his disobedience, and thereby he is prepared to encounter Christianity, which leads him to an awareness of his total disobedience to God.

Thus there is a clear "graduated, forward-moving line" (*Two Discourses at the Communion on Fridays,* with *Judge for Yourselves!,* p. 5, ed. tr.) not only through the pseudonymous authorship but especially through the upbuilding literature. The purpose, then, is for the receiver to move steadily closer to Christianity along the same path as the communicator. The communication of the upbuilding conforms entirely to this objective. It is very important to note that Kierkegaard as communicator very conscientiously and scrupulously tried always to qualify his own position and wanted to appear as author of only that part of his upbuilding authorship which existentially corresponded to his own ethical-religious development (*Two Upbuilding Discourses,* 1843, through *Two Discourses at the Communion on Fridays,* 1851).

When Kierkegaard began his writing, he had advanced beyond the esthetic stage, and in the pseudonymous books, particularly up to and including *Concluding Unscientific Postscript,* he described the battle between the esthetic on the one side and the ethical-religious on the other. But in his own mind the most important part of the authorship was the upbuilding writings, which depict his own movement from the esthetic through the ethical to the religious, and which culminate in *Two Discourses at the Communion on Fridays*. Later works in this sequence do not bear Kierkegaard's name as author, because his own existence did not correspond to the claims of higher ideality they express. He presents this higher ideality in *Sickness unto Death* and in *Practice in Christianity* under the pseudonym Anti-Climacus (above Climacus). He summarizes his own relation as communicator to the art of communication in this brief comment: "... there is a stretch which is mine: the upbuilding; behind and ahead lie the lower and the higher pseudonymities; the upbuilding is mine, but not the esthetic, not [the pseudonymous works] for upbuilding, either, and even less those for awakening" (X^1 A 593). Consequently Kierkegaard considered as "the upbuilding" only that writing which corresponded to his own life. The phrases "for the upbuilding and awakening" and "for awakening and inward deepening," which he uses in *The Sickness unto Death* and *Practice in Christianity* respectively, could be used only by someone who existentially stood higher than he did himself. Kierkegaard felt that the two religious books *For Self-Examination* and *Judge for Yourselves!* could be published under his own name inasmuch as they actually were not upbuilding but were regarded as aids to critical self-searching.

For direct references in the works to the upbuilding (usually translated "edifying" in current translations), see, for example, *The Concept of Irony*, pp. 282, 288, 291; *Either/Or*, II, pp. 72, 342, 348–56, 365; *Upbuilding [Edifying] Discourses*, I–IV, passim, especially I, pp. 5, 59, 115; III, pp. 5, 50, 65, 69, 79, 92, 96, 123; IV, p. 5; *Prefaces*, *S.V.*, V, pp. 35–38; *Postscript*, pp. 226, 229, 230 fn., 231, 240, 241–44, 390 fn., 497–98 fn.; *Two Ages*, *S.V.*, VIII, pp. 11, 105 [omitted in *The Present Age*]; *Upbuilding Discourses in Various Spirits*, Part One [*Purity of Heart*, pp. 36, 151, 162, 208, 210]; Part Three [*The Gospel of Suffering*, p. 78]; *Works of Love*, pp. 56, 85, 199–212, 233, 280, 284; *Christian Discourses*, pp. 16, 101–3, 167, 229; *The Lily of the Field and the Bird of the Air*, with *Christian Discourses*, p. 313; *The Sickness unto Death*, p. 141; *Practice [Training] in Christianity*, pp. 5, 260; *Two Discourses for the Communion on Fridays*, with *Judge for Yourselves!*, p. 5; *For Self-Examination*, p. 5; "'The Single Individual,'" with *The Point of View*, p. 126.

The two main factors leading to the translation of *opbygge, opbyggende* as "build up" and "upbuilding" have been (1) Kierkegaard's elemental understanding of the words (see *Works of Love*, pp. 200–201), which cannot be rendered in English by "edify," and (2) the almost complete replacement of "edify" (used in the King James Bible) by some form of "build up" in the Revised Standard Version and others (see, for example, Romans 14:19; I Corinthians 8:1, 10:23, 14:3, 14:12; II Corinthians 10:8, 13:10, 12:19; Ephesians 4:12, 4:16; I Thessalonians 5:11).

1172. The reference is to *En Hverdags-Historie* (literally *An Everyday Story*) by Thomasine C. Gyllembourg-Ehrensvärd, which appeared first in *Kjøbenhavns flyvende Post*, ed. J. H. Heiberg, no. 69–76, 1828; also in Vol. I, *Gamle og nye Noveller af Forfatteren til En Hverdags-Historie*, ed. J. L. Heiberg, I–III (Copenhagen: 1833–34). See *Postscript*, p. 14; *S.V.* XIII, pp. 56–59, 65. Kierkegaard's *Two Ages: A Literary Review*, (part of which is in English under the title *The Present Age*) includes in the subtitle *Novelle af Forfatteren til "En Hverdagshistorie"* (*Novel by the Author of "A Story of Everyday Life"*).

1173. The familiar form of the second personal pronoun, used in address of family, close friends, and God in Christianity.

1174. See Johann Arndt, *Joh. Arndt, Sämtliche geistreiche Bücher vom wahren Christentum* (Tübingen: 1777), V, 5, 4. The figure here is of the hungry child and mother and of the hungering soul and God.

1175. Morning prayer on Tuesday, *Evangeliske christelig Psalmebog* (Copenhagen: 1823), p. 648. *ASKB* 196.

VENTURE, RISK

Kierkegaard believed that men have the freedom to choose among possibilities, which also involves responsibility and risk—thus to act means also to venture.

Most people weigh their possible actions against the prospects of succeeding; they act on the basis of probability. And even though some men, as Kierkegaard puts it, "have stronger will power, greater passion" than others and therefore venture farther out, "one thing stands fast: they never relinquish probability" (*Judge for Yourselves!*, p. 116, ed. tr.). But as long as men act only on the basis of probability, there is no venturing at all. Venturing can be done only in relation to the eternal, only by relinquishing temporal assurance. This happens when men in various life situations act in reliance upon God. Thus, for example, Judge William calls marriage a "venturesome deed" if it is entered into on the basis of love and as the result of an ethical resolution in reliance upon God (*Either/Or*, II, p. 67, ed. tr.; see *Stages*, pp. 157–58).

But not until a person ventures his whole temporal existence for the sake of the eternal is there any venture in the proper sense of the word. Climacus calls Socrates the highest example of venture, since despite "the objective uncertainty" he ventured to believe in "an immortality" and oriented his life accordingly, indeed, ventured to die in this belief (*Postscript*, p. 180). According to Climacus, very few men in Christendom matched Socrates' perception that faith is a "venturesome deed" of this kind (p. 182, ed. tr.), and in *Concluding Unscientific Postscript* Climacus ironizes over a so-called "serious man" who wants to have objective certainty before commencing to aspire to eternal salvation, to say nothing of "venturing" everything for it (p. 378). But when it comes to something in the future, there can never be any certainty, and when it comes to eternal salvation, which is "the highest good," the venturing must be made with infinite passion (pp. 381–82).

It is generally held that Christianity has made it easier to believe in eternal salvation. The evidence here is "resurrection's proof," "a mediator," Christ, and a "gospel." But all this just makes the whole matter more difficult. To believe requires that a person "venture his thought, venture to believe against the understanding" (p. 384, ed. tr.). It is far easier "to cling to a weak hope *in one's own strength* than to gain certainty by virtue of the absurd" (p. 384, ed. tr.). For this reason Climacus calls Christianity "the ultimate venture" (p. 384, ed. tr.). The only certainty offered is suffering. The "serious man mentioned before," who regarded venturing everything without certainty to be madness, will here regard the venturing to be "complete madness" (p. 410, ed. tr.).

Climacus declares that to venture everything in this manner requires "a conscious clarity with regard to oneself which is gained only very slowly" (p. 382, ed tr.). For Kierkegaard personally the question of how far he himself dared to venture with respect to the essentially Christian became a steadily more burning issue. On the one hand a person must always relinquish, yes, even defy, probability when involving himself with God (*Judge for Yourselves!*, pp. 116–20); yet a person must not tempt God either. But again and again Kierkegaard arrives at the conclusion that it is always most dangerous to avoid venturing because of the danger "of avoiding Governance somehow by not coming out so that it can grab hold of a person" (X^5 A 41). The crucial issue is whether a man's venturing is made in reliance upon God. In *Judge for Yourselves!* Kierkegaard stipulates what this means—namely, not that a man is sure of success but, on the contrary, perceives that it is "precisely just as possible that he will be victorious as that he will succumb" (p. 117, ed. tr.). Kierkegaard also believes that the person who ventured too much and lost is more to be forgiven than he who ventured not at all (see X^4 A 501 and IX A 352).

Croxall, T. H. "Choice," in *Kierkegaard Studies*, ch. 1. London: Lutterworth, 1948.

———. "Existence," in *Kierkegaard Commentary*, ch. 2. New York: Harper, 1956.

Ofstad, Harold. "Morality, Choice, and Inwardness." *Inquiry* (Oslo), 8, Spring 1965, pp. 33–72.

Pait, James A. "Kierkegaard and the Problem of Choice." *Emory University Quarterly*, 2, December 1946, pp. 237–45.

Starkloff, C. "The Election: Choice of Faith." *Review for Religious*, 24, 1965, pp. 444–54.

For references in the works to venture or to risk, see, for example, *The Concept of Irony*, p. 140; *Either/Or*, II, p. 67; *Fragments*, pp. 103 fn., 108; *Upbuilding [Edifying] Discourses*, IV, pp. 95, 102, 118; *Three Discourses on Imagined Occasions [Thoughts on Crucial Situations]*, p. 15; *Stages*, pp. 108, 110, 119, 157–58, 163, 166, 170, 180, 182, 188, 269–70, 274, 355, 362, 378–84, 410, 459–60 fn., 487,

538; *Two Ages* [*The Present Age*], pp. 8–9; *Upbuilding Discourses in Various Spirits*, Part One [*Purity of Heart*, pp. 122–30]; *The Sickness unto Death*, pp. 166–67; *Judge for Yourselves!*, pp. 115–20; article in *Fædrelandet*, no. 77, March 31, 1855, in *Attack*, p. 40; *The Moment*, no. 6, no. 10, ibid., pp. 191–92, 281.

1176. The premiere performance of Adam Oehlenschläger's *Aladdin* in its entirety took place April 17, 1839; ten additional performances were given during the following five weeks. See *Either/Or*, I, pp. 21–22.

1177. See Matthew 25:14–30; Luke 19:12–28.

1178. See Matthew 25:30.

1179. See Ephesians 4:30.

1180. See John 7:17.

1181. Kierkegaard's favorite metaphor for existence as venture, as a life of faith. See, for example, *Stages*, pp. 402, 425, 430; *Postscript*, pp. 126, 182; *Works of Love*, p. 334.

1182. See note 1177.

1183. Exact source not located. See Epistle 28: 6–7, although the wording and substance are not quite the same.

1184. See note 675.

1185. See John 5:2–9.

1186. See note 1171.

1187. Presumably a reference to Socrates' discussion of life, death, and immortality at the end of the *Apology*, 40 c–41 a.

VOCATION

The ethical view of life described particularly by Judge William in *Either/Or* requires that every man try to realize the universal in his life. One of the phrases used to designate this universal is "every man has a vocation" (II, p. 296, ed. tr.), which means that every man has a special purpose in such a way that he may regard his present task as a vocation if he relates to it in faithfulness and responsibility to God. While the esthetic view of life holds that the man with a specific talent should egotistically do everything to develop it, the ethical man believes that just as "the most insignificant individual" has a vocation, so even the "most eminent talent" ought to be regarded as a vocation as well; indeed, it does not become beautiful "until it is interpreted as a vocation" (p. 298, ed. tr.). Thus "there is a rational order of things in which every person, if he so chooses, fills his place in such a way that he simultaneously expresses the universally human and the individual" (II, p. 297, ed. tr.). Judge William declares that it is just as great a sin to be unfaithful in the most modest vocation as in the greatest (p. 297).

For Kierkegaard the question was still whether, from a religious point of view, it is ethically satisfactory "to transmute one's talent into one's calling," in other words, whether man's natural qualifications and external conditions alone should determine the choice of a vocation, or whether "the religious" also should be taken into consideration. As far as he was concerned, Kierkegaard felt that he had been obliged "to go through the religious" to his "proper task"; had he not done so but had made his choice solely on human-ethical grounds, he would have been a "police official" (IV A 160; see IX A 430). Here we encounter the problem, touched on by Vigilius Haufniensis in *The Concept of Anxiety* [*Dread*], of "how a religious existence penetrates and operates throughout something external." He mentions how difficult it would be to combine the religious with "an external task such as, for example, being a comic actor" (pp. 94–95). The ethical-religious life is the essential and common calling and catches up into itself one's various specific vocations or roles as worker, citizen, parent, etc.

In one of his upbuilding discourses Kierkegaard later points out that the essential element is the frame of mind in which a person carries out his work, that he is clear in his own mind that his task is his vocation. If he begins with God and is faithful, he will not let himself be confused by thoughts of "the outcome" (*Upbuilding Discourses in Various Spirits*, Part One [*Purity of Heart*, p. 199]). But if he succeeds in his work, a person always faces the temptation of taking his occupation in vain and using it for his own honor or advantage. Even Christ, declares Anti-Climacus, faced the temptation of taking his vocation in vain in such a way that instead of becoming the Savior of the world he "became something great in the world, a king or a ruler" (*For Self-Examination*, pp. 66–67).

Thus for Kierkegaard the concept of vocation had essential meaning in a man's life from both an ethical and a religious point of view. He therefore considered it to be one of the many signs of decay within the Danish Church that in ecclesiastical language a vocation or call had become synonymous with a job (*The Moment*, no. 3, in *Attack*, p. 136; see also *The Sickness unto Death*, p. 233), an official appointment, something to be evaluated solely according to the salary, consequently from an esthetic, to say nothing of materialistic, point of view.

For references in the works to vocation, call, calling, see, for example, *The Concept of Irony*, pp. 75, 198, 200; *Either/Or*, II, pp. 8, 153, 296–302, 328; *Upbuilding* [*Edifying*] *Discourses*, IV, pp. 107–8; *Three Discourses on Imagined Occasions* [*Thoughts on Crucial Situations*], p. 65; *Postscript*, pp. 210, 216, 222, 389; *Upbuilding Discourses in Various Spirits*, Part One [*Purity of Heart*, pp. 198–204]; *Works of Love*, p. 118; "The Difference between a Genius and an Apostle," with *The Present Age*, pp. 139–40, 148, 149, 159; *The Sickness unto Death*, pp. 209, 233. *Practice* [*Training*] *in Christianity*, pp. 180, 183; *For Self-Examination*, pp. 15–16, 66–67; *Judge for Yourselves!*, p. 127; *The Moment*, no. 3, no. 7, in *Attack*, pp. 136, 208.

1188. See *Upbuilding Discourses in Various Spirits*, Part One [*Purity of Heart*], pp. 183, 197–211.

1189. From draft of "Purity of Heart"; see ibid., pp. 40, 215.

VOLUNTARY, THE

During the *Corsair* battle, it became clear to Kierkegaard that the Christian cannot stay in that form of religion which Climacus designates as "hidden inwardness" (see, for example, *Postscript*, pp. 424, 445–46). Christianity must also be expressed visibly in man's action and in his entire relationship to the temporal, and thereby the Christian is brought into conflict with the world. This more exacting Christian action, by which a person exposes himself to difficulties that could be avoided, Kierkegaard calls the "voluntary," and it gradually became apparent to him that the "voluntary" is really "what characterizes the essentially Christian and is also that which creates difficulties . . ." (X^3 A 33). In an earlier journal entry Kierkegaard notes that the "voluntary" does not mean "the dangers to which a person exposes himself for the sake of the truth by witnessing for the truth and against the evil," but "the voluntary giving up of the temporal," and for this reason he is unwilling to call his own deliberate vulnerability to the *Corsair's* attack the voluntary (X^2 A 159).

As early as 1848, in a comparison of Job and "the Apostle" (*Christian Discourses*, pp. 185–86), Kierkegaard expressed the view that the special quality of "the Christian" is the voluntary, and by that he means "voluntarily to give up everything in order to follow Christ" and voluntarily to expose oneself to "insults and persecutions," which in the eyes of the world is madness (pp. 186–88). But a series of journal entries the next year reveals that Kierkegaard was personally far from finished with reflecting on the voluntary (see, for example, X^1 A 416, X^2 A 32, X^3 A 43). This was the year he was seeking to understand what external action was required of him and whether he should be a preacher. It is confirmed for him again and again that Christianity's insistence on self-denial specifically shows that "the *essentially Christian* is the 'voluntary' " (X^3 A 457) and that when Christ speaks of taking up his cross he is speaking of voluntary suffering, the suffering of self-denial, which a man can avoid if he so wishes (see SUFFERING).

Kierkegaard also emphasizes that it is the voluntary that leads man into spiritual trial (IX A 392, X^2 A 32). A person must always ask himself whether his voluntary involvements are not "tempting God" (*Christian Discourses*, p. 186), are not "presumptuous" (X^3 A 617), or whether this very question is not an excuse to avoid exposing himself to "dangers and troubles" for the sake of Christianity. Climacus calls this spiritual trial a "specifically Christian suffering" (*Practice* [*Training*] *in Christianity*, p. 110).

Still another important mark of the voluntary is that it creates a "double-collision, which is the mark of everything essentially Christian, to become hated, cursed, detested, to have to suffer for—one's willingness to suffer" (XI^1 A 327). In his later years Kierkegaard's own experience of the sufferings and insults caused by self-denial made it clear to him that it was voluntary suffering, after all, that he had exposed himself to in the *Corsair* battle, and that by renouncing honor and esteem as an admired author (for which his talents and "sagacity" had provided the possibility), he had demonstrated self-denial for the sake of Christianity (XI^1 A 277 and 484; *The Point of View*, pp. 57–58). Nevertheless, many battles and spiritual trials lay ahead before, as one "stamped by the voluntary," he came to understand what a severe "order" had been issued to him—namely, to pronounce judgment upon Christendom. He had hoped death would free him from saying this quite specifically (see X^6 B 232), but instead the "order" led him out into the crucial battle against official Christianity, which was the conclusion of his work as an author.

For references in the works to the voluntary, see, for example, *Upbuilding Discourses in Various Spirits*, Part One [*Purity of Heart*, pp. 171–74]; *Christian Discourses*, pp. 185–88, 194–95; *Practice* [*Training*] *in Christianity*, pp. 111–12, 177; *For Self-Examination*, pp. 8–9, 78; *Judge for Yourselves!*, p. 202; *The Point of View*, pp. 8, 57–60, 102, 122; article in *Fædrelandet*, no. 295, December 18, 1854, in *Attack*, p. 5.

1190. See note 280; ibid., I, p. 202.

1191. A person's struggle of faith for clarity regarding God's will for him.

1192. See Matthew 19:16–22; Mark 10:17–22; Luke 18:18–23.

1193. See Matthew 8:21; Luke 9:59.

1194. See Matthew 19:29; Mark 10:29–30; Luke 18:29–30.

1195. Only the voluntary (responsibility in freedom) can keep a person closely engaged in Christianity.

WIT

Wit is the ability to draw upon and present the comic sides of life and the human situation. Along with Aristotle, Kierkegaard sees the comic as "painless contradiction" (see, for example, *Postscript*, p. 459). In human existence there are many tragic and painful contradictions, but when they are seen from a higher point of view the tension caused by the contradiction is released in a smile. A good example is the ironist. After having seen through the nothingness of the finite goals in which the majority of men are earnestly engrossed, the ironist from his higher position can find many situations that may trigger a witty comment. When Kierkegaard lived existentially as an ironist (his romantic period), he experienced a great urge to utter witticisms. A phrase he jotted down during this period, "the ubiquity of wit" (I A 164), implies that he had a witticism for every time and every situation. But it must be remembered that as long as an ironist has nothing higher than his irony over the world, his own position is tragic, not comic, for his wit is a mask for his own emptiness and despair. In another journal entry Kierkegaard relates that "witticisms flowed" from his mouth when he was at a party, but as soon as he left he wanted to shoot himself (I A 161).

From the standpoint of the irony that Kierkegaard calls "mastered irony" (*The Concept of Irony*, p. 337), irony governed by a higher point of view, the pseudonymous writer of the "Diapsalmata" (*Either/Or*, I, pp. 19–42) gives samples of the irony which sees through the hollowness and emptiness of finitude. On the whole wit appears in all of Kierkegaard's writing—but according to clear and stringent laws, inasmuch as he treats certain phenomena in human existence comically to prepare the way for something truer and higher. Johannes Climacus in particular has carefully described the principles of this approach in *Concluding Unscientific Postscript* (see pp. 82–84 and especially pp. 458–68), where he shows how not only irony but also humor can be used to illuminate the relation between the various spheres of existence.

Even in a strictly upbuilding book such as *Practice* [*Training*] *in Christianity*, the pseudonymous writer Anti-Climacus uses various forms of wit. In order to stimulate his contemporaries to think, Anti-Climacus describes with wit and humor the effect Christ's appearance in contemporary Copenhagen would have on various representatives of society (pp. 43–55).

Kierkegaard utilized wit most damningly in the Church battle, where it takes its sharpest form. His aim was to hold up to ridicule the practices in the Danish Church, which he believed had nothing to do with true Christianity. Here it is not humor but primarily irony that prevails. Irony is used to annihilate the old in order to make room for the new, whereas humor would presuppose that earnest striving was still going on in ecclesiastical circles—which Kierkegaard no longer believed to be true. For this reason he took on the grave responsibility of holding the established Church up to ridicule (XI^3 B 53 and B 55; see G. Malantschuk, *Kierkegaard's Thought*, pp. 370–71).

For references in the works to wit, see, for example, *The Concept of Irony*, passim; *Either/Or*, I, pp. 19–42; II, pp. 210, 265; *Fragments*, p. 62; *The Concept of Anxiety* [*Dread*], pp. 33, 60, 95, 130; *Stages*, pp. 100, 137, 265, 270–71, 433 fn., 437; *Postscript*, pp. 82–84, 188, 315, 352, 361, 362, 424, 458–68, 552; *Practice* [*Training*] *in Christianity*, pp. 43–55; *On My Work as an Author*, with *The Point of View*, p. 148; *The Point of View*, pp. 19, 29, 54. See HUMOR, IRONY, THE COMIC.

1196. See *Samling af danske Sange*, ed. Henrik Hertz, (Copenhagen: 1836), pp. 36–38.

WITNESS

As early as a journal entry written in his student days about "the profound meaning the word 'witness' has in Christianity," Kierkegaard maintained that to be a witness has two sides: an objective side "inasmuch as Christianity is an objective act," and a subjective side, which corresponds to interiorization, inasmuch as the witnesses "assimilate it" (II A 452).

But it was not until after the *Corsair* battle that Kierkegaard began to ponder what it meant personally to be a witness, especially to be a witness in Christendom, where all are under the illusion of being Christians, where witnessing does not bring direct opposition as it did during the first period of Christianity. The task is not merely to witness for the truth but against untruth (X^4 A 406), as Kierkegaard believed he had done when he challenged the *Corsair*, thereby exposing himself to scorn and ridicule.

During the following years Kierkegaard was very absorbed in the question of what was required to be a witness, since in his opinion only "the witness" could be the proper "proclaimer of Christianity" (X^2 A 557). On this point he says: "A witness is a person who directly demonstrates the truth of the doctrine he proclaims," which he continues throughout his life, demonstrating that it is truth for him, and which he risks death for. "This is the continuing practical proof of the truth of the doctrine." "The basic confusion" in Christendom is "that Christianity is not proclaimed by witnesses but by teachers." A teacher has "proofs and arguments—but he stands outside . . ." (X^3 A 5). In the "Christian Order of Precedence" which Kierkegaard gives in an entry of the same year, he places "the apostles" as no. 1, the witnesses "whose lives express what they teach and are marked by sufferings 'for the sake of the Word' " as no. 2, while the teachers of religion, that is, the clergy, "whose conception of Christianity essentially is that it is a doctrine" and who consequently place major emphasis upon the objective, become no. 3 (X^3 A 570).

The special mark of the witness is that, like Christianity, he is heterogeneous with the world and thus suffers in this world: "he suffers for the truth" (X^4 A 609). He prays not to be exempted from suffering but prays for strength to bear it (X^4 A 565), and yet he does not delude himself into thinking he is benefiting the world or posterity but acts solely out of enthusiasm for the truth and in "unconditioned obedience to God" (X^5 A 18). After having "endured all the mistreatment of his contemporary age," he finally witnesses "with his death" (X^4 A 381). Then the preachers profit by stepping forth as poets and actors and describing his sufferings instead of committing themselves and their listeners by truly bringing his sufferings to bear in the present moment (see also X^3 A 561 and X^4 A 609).

In his writings Kierkegaard too had described Christian suffering, but he believed that he personally had ventured so far out that he was qualified to do it honestly. Actually he struggled hard in those years to clarify his own position with respect to the concept of witness for the truth. But even if he personally felt as one who has been sacrificed and has suffered for the sake of the truth, he nevertheless realized that he had not ventured to the limit and that he was still too much of a poet for his life to meet the requirements of a witness to the truth.

As Kierkegaard gradually came to perceive contemporary Christianity to be a forgery, he realized that the future witness to the truth had to be a kind of sophisticated "police-agent" who first of all (just as Kierkegaard himself) had to "carry out the very important and exhausting task" of disclosing the falsification before he, like the earlier ones, might enter into "a life-and-death struggle" (XI¹ A 185). Kierkegaard believed that the late Bishop Mynster had had a large share in falsifying Christianity and called him "one of the instruments of illusions" (XI² A 57).

It is not strange, therefore, that Kierkegaard, who had so scrupulously delineated the concept of witness to the truth, reacted negatively when Bishop Martensen in an address shortly after Bishop Mynster's death called Mynster, who obviously had lived a pleasant life and had been honored and esteemed as a witness to the truth, one of "the genuine witnesses to the truth" (article in *Fædrelandet*, no. 295, December 1855, in *Attack*, p. 5). This remark was a signal to Kierkegaard to attack the official Church in Denmark and also the Christianity of all Christendom (article in *Fædrelandet*, no. 76, March 30, 1855, in *Attack*, p. 34; see SUFFERING).

Dewey, Bradley R. *The New Obedience.* Washington: Corpus Instrumentorium, 1968.

Diem, Hermann. "The Conception of a Witness to the Truth," in *Kierkegaard's Dialectic of Existence,* trans. Harold Knight, ch. 17. Edinburgh and London: Oliver and Boyd, 1959.

Eller, Vernard. *Kierkegaard and Radical Discipleship: A New Perspective.* Princeton: Princeton University Press, 1968.

For references in the works to witness, see, for example, *Fear and Trembling,* p. 90; *Stages,* p. 419; *Postscript,* pp. 190, 224, 348–50, 353, 539; *Upbuilding Discourses in Various Spirits,* Part One [*Purity of Heart,* p. 136]; Part Three [*The Gospel of Suffering,* p. 149]; *Works of Love,* p. 339; *Christian Discourses,* p. 232; *The Crisis [and a Crisis] in the Life of an Actress,* p. 82; "Has a Man the Right to Let Himself Be Put to Death for the Truth?" with *The Present Age,* pp. 109–11; *Practice [Training] in Christianity,* p. 88; *For Self-Examination,* pp. 11–23; *Judge for Yourselves!,* pp. 118, 140–41, 202–3; *On My Work as an Author,* with *The Point of View,* p. 160; ibid., pp. 117, 132–34; articles in *Fædrelandet,* no. 295, December 18, 1854, no. 304, December 30, 1854, no. 10, January 12, 1855, no. 24, January 29, 1855, no. 67, March 20, 1855, in *Attack,* pp. 2–24; articles in *Fædrelandet,* no. 74, March 28, 1855, no. 83, April 11, 1855, no. 97, April 27, 1855, no. 107, May 10, 1855, no. 120, May 26, 1855, in *Attack,* pp. 33, 43, 45, 48–50, 67–72; *The Moment,* no. 1, no. 2, no. 4, no. 5, no. 6, no. 7, no. 8, no. 9, in *Attack,* pp. 85–86, 88, 105–6, 109, 118–24, 148, 158, 164, 172–74, 188, 208–9, 227, 242, 259–61, 264, 268, 270.

1197. See Johann Georg Hamann, *Schriften,* ed., F. Roth, I–VIII, 1–2 (Berlin: 1821–43), VI, p. 144; II A 438.

1198. See Philippians 2:6. The Danish translation of this passage is closer to the King James Version in English.

1199. See John 21:15–17.

1200. See Genesis 20:1–13.

1201. See John 11:50.

1202. See Plato, *Apology*, 25 a–b; *The Book on Adler*, VII² B 235, p. 49 fn. [omitted in *On Authority and Revelation*, p. 41].

1203. Pleasantly, cozily, comfortably. A German word with a Danish ending.

1204. See Matthew 11:28; *Practice* [*Training*] *in Christianity*, pp. 5–72.

1205. See *Berlingske Tidende*, no. 202, August 27, 1849.

1206. The Danish is *Klangfigur*, Chladni figure, symmetrical configurations of particles on a glass plate in response to sound or to vibrations made by a bow on the plate. See *The Concept of Irony*, pp. 63, 267 (tr. "Chladni figure"); *Either/Or*, II, p. 32 (tr. "musical accord").

1207. Richard Rothe, *Die Anfänge der Christlichen Kirche und ihrer Verfassung*, I (Wittenberg: 1837; vol II was not published under this title, although "the material is all ready," I, p. ix), pp. 25 ff., esp. p. 45.

1208. See Matthew 23:29 ff.

1209. See note 32.

1210. See Matthew 23:29–30.

1211. See *Works of Love*, pt. II, ch. IX, pp. 317–29.

1212. See note 32.

1213. See Matthew 27:46; Mark 15:34.

1214. *For Self-Examination*, p. 74.

1215. Trade, business, commerce.

1216. This phrase (*Tanke-Forsøg*) is very similar to the title (*Tanke-Projekt*) of chapter I, *Fragments*, p. 11.

1217. See John 3:2.

1218. See John 18:36.

1219. See note 32.

1220. See notes 504, 975.

WOMAN/MAN

Kierkegaard's fundamental conception of man, including woman as well, is that man is a synthesis of finitude and infinitude, time and eternity. The synthesis of these two opposite qualities signifies "a task" and presupposes "a historical movement" (*The Concept of Anxiety* [*Dread*], p. 26) which has as its goal the permeating of the temporal by the eternal, whereby man becomes a self, a spiritual person.

Before man has reached so far in his attempt to fulfill the synthesis of becoming a self, the single individual, he must go through specific phases of development in which the feminine and the masculine emerge ever more clearly as seen from the spiritual point of view. In the first phase, designated as the mental phase (I C 126), neither man nor woman can be called persons since both are as yet bound to finitude and serve the race. Metaphorically, "The male and the female are in one flower" (*Either/Or*, I, p. 76, ed. tr.), or "The male and the female are on one stem" (*From the Papers of One Still Living*,

S.V., XIII, p. 75). This means that man and woman are totally subject to the needs of the race; they are only particulars without any genuine personal independence. This relation is very precisely described by the ironist ("the Young Man" in *"In Vino Veritas"*) when he says that in actual fact it is not individuals, that is, man and woman, who pursue their own goal in their union, but that the race stands behind it all. In the union, therefore, the individuals are "the ones deceived, for at the same instant the genus triumphs over the individuals, the genus is victorious, whereas the individuals are subordinated to being in its service" (*Stages*, p. 56, ed. tr.).

The significance of the individual emerges more strongly with the Greeks, for whom the goal is for everyone to be a "beautiful individuality," but this goal, too, lies within finitude. The pseudonymous writer A says of this level of existence that "femininity" or "the idea of the feminine" is not yet perceptible (*Either/Or*, I, p. 87, ed. tr). But the same may also be said of the idea of masculinity.

By means of his thought and life, Socrates, who in so many respects signifies a revolution in paganism, brought out a new factor in connection with man and woman. His ethical attempt to subordinate the finite under the infinite through personal action and his belief that he could do it are genuinely masculine traits. The woman's desire for harmony and her sense for beauty, together with her practical approach to the finite, place her outside of Socrates' efforts.

According to Kierkegaard, Christianity is the first to offer a solution to the relationship between man and woman and the differences between the sexes. Man and woman are on equal footing with respect to the religious. As individuals with consciences both are responsible to God. But Kierkegaard at the same time adds that Christianity never intended to erase the external differences between the sexes. "People," he declares, "have foolishly busied themselves in the name of Christianity to make it obvious in the world that women have equal rights with men—Christianity has never demanded or desired this. It has done everything for woman if she Christianly will be satisfied with what is Christian. If she will not, for her loss she gains only a mediocre compensation in the little fragmentary externals she can win by worldly threats" (*Works of Love*, pp. 139–40).

As early as *Either/Or*, Kierkegaard has Judge William comment on the principal difference between the sexes: "Woman explains the finite, man seeks [an explanation of] the infinite" (*Either/Or*, II, p. 316, ed. tr.). This primary distinction leads to a whole scale of differences: woman is "substance, man is reflection" (I, p. 426); earthly life has its origin in her, and feeling is her element. For this reason, as Vigilius Haufniensis points out, she is "more anxious than man" (*The Concept of Anxiety* [*Dread*], p. 59, ed. tr.). Man's strength lies in reflection, which is why he is continually thrown into doubt and despair. Woman is humble and, faced with the ethical demand, readily perceives her imperfection and her need of grace. Thus she makes the leap into the religious without, strictly speaking, the intermediate stage of the ethical. Man has to fight a mortal battle in the sphere of the ethical first before he surrenders his selfish pride and perceives his inability to realize the absolute good, as Climacus so clearly points out in *Concluding Unscientific Postscript* (see, for example, *Postscript*, p. 504 and IX A 414). Quidam mentions an important psychological difference when he declares that "a woman may possess passion as strong as or even stronger than that of a man, but contradiction in passion is not a task for her, as for example giving up this wish and retaining it at the same time" and that "to will both at once is impossible to her, or even so much as to understand such a thing" (*Stages*, pp. 280 and 281). In other words, woman cannot bear the split in her nature which Kierkegaard calls redoubling and which is the mark of the most rigorous form of religiousness (see XI² A 192).

In his discourse "The Woman Who Was a Sinner," Kierkegaard summarizes woman's special religious characteristics. "Piety or godliness in its essential nature is femininity." Woman has "the humble faith in relation to the extraordinary which does not, as does unbelief, doubtingly ask: Why? What for? How is this possible?" Furthermore, a woman can concentrate herself in "one desire," "one thought." "Grant that man has greater earnestness in matters of thought, but when it comes to feeling, passion, decision, to not fouling up oneself and the decision with thoughts, intentions, resolutions, to not coming very close to decision, yet without making a decision—in this woman has greater earnestness . . ." (with *Practice* [*Training*] *in Christianity*, pp. 261–62, ed. tr.). In *For Self-Examination* Kierkegaard points out how a woman can create "the soft light" in a home by making quietness the "bass chord"; similarly he emphasizes that "domesticity" is a quality just as crucial in woman as "strong personality" is in man (p. 58).

There has been some astonishment over Kierkegaard's sharply critical comments on women in his later journals. These comments can be explained by the fact that at this time Kierkegaard viewed all existence from the strictly ascetic understanding of Christianity, which demands the renunciation of everything worldly. On the ascetic level woman with her charm and loveliness is man's greatest temptation to turn back to temporality. Woman represents for man the longing for finitude, and the experience from which Kierkegaard is speaking here is not exclusive to Christianity but is shared by all who have resolved to make the final decisive break with the world. An analogy is found in Kierkegaard's comment that when a man has to give up woman his life becomes "a Passion Story" (VII¹ B 83; a contemplated addition to *Postscript*, p. 256).

The strongest statement Kierkegaard made about women no doubt is that "woman's element is also a lie" (XI² A 202). Again, the observation must be understood from the perspective that with her sexual attraction woman can drag man back to finitude's delusion ("the lie"). But even if Kierkegaard at this point in time speaks very critically about women and marriage, he nevertheless asks whether anyone "has described marriage and all these aspects of life more beautifully, more charmingly, than I?" (XI^1 A 210). Since woman stands in closer connection to finitude than man, Kierkegaard concedes that "woman gives up more than the man when she renounces this life and marriage" (XI^1 A 141). It may also be added here that Kierkegaard believes that the highest form of religiousness is a unity of the masculine and the feminine. "An eminently masculine intellectuality joined to a feminine submissiveness—this is the truly religious" (XI^2 A 70).

So, according to Kierkegaard, both man and woman have their special tasks in life, and the woman should be wholly woman and the man wholly man. For this reason he had sharp words for the emancipation of women, for which he believed men were also at fault. As early as *Either/Or* he has Judge William say that there is no "more dangerous doctrine for woman," for through it she is completely in man's power, "at the mercy of his conditions; she can be nothing for man but a prey to his caprice, while as woman she can be everything for him" (p. 317).

With respect to man and woman Kierkegaard has an order of categories, for he consistently derives his view of man from the conception of man as a synthesis. For this reason Anti-Climacus, too, can say of the relation between the sexes that if something is "logically correct" it shall and must also "be pertinent" in actuality (*The Sickness unto Death*, p. 183 fn.). This categorical insight permitted Kierkegaard to describe women from many different points of view. In order not to misunderstand Kierkegaard, therefore, one must pay close attention to who is speaking about women and from which point of view. A "seducer," as in *Either/Or*, and an esthete, as in *"In Vino Veritas,"* speak about women in a completely different manner than Judge William in *Either/Or* and in *Stages on Life's Way*, and again quite differently than Vigilius Haufniensis, who as a psychologist speaks very unsentimentally about women. In the upbuilding literature Kierkegaard speaks of women with greater depth, inasmuch as he is speaking from a religious point of view.

Consequently it is Kierkegaard's opinion that there are great physical and mental and spiritual differences between men and women, which can never be set aside by external secular institutions. But he also strongly emphasizes that "in inwardness before God woman is absolutely equal with man" (*Works of Love*, p. 139).

Croxall, T. H. "Woman and Wine," in *Kierkegaard Commentary*, ch. 8. London: James Nesbet, 1956.

Garside, Christine. "Can a Woman Be Good in the Same Way as a Man?" *Dialogue: Canadian Philosophical Review—Revue Canadienne de Philosophie*, 10, 1971, pp. 534–44.

Kainz, Howard P. "The Relationship of Dread to Spirit in Man and Woman, according to Kierkegaard." *The Modern Schoolman*, 47, November 1969, pp. 1–13.

For references in the works to woman/man, see, for example, an article in *Kjøbenhavns flyvende Post*, no. 34, December 17, 1834, *S.V.*, XIII, pp. 5–8; *The Concept of Irony*, pp. 309–12, 314–15, *Either/Or*, I, pp. 11, 76, 87, 113–14, 127, 151, 155–56, 170, 175–213, 292–94, 335–36, 359–60, 386, 422–27, 431–32; II, pp. 21–22, 54, 115–16, 211, 311–20; *Repetition*, pp. 46, 50–52, 123–24; *The Concept of Anxiety* [*Dread*], pp. 42–43, 57–60, 62–63, 65; *Stages*, pp. 40, 56–57, 61, 68–80, 128–29, 133–36, 137–45, 152, 163, 205, 210, 256, 280, 364–65, 381–95; *Postscript*, p. 265; *Upbuilding Discourses in Various Spirits*, Part Two [*What We Learn from the Lilies of the Field and the Birds of the Air*, with *The Gospel of Suffering*, p. 164]; *Works of Love*, pp. 97, 139–43, 153; *The Crisis* [*and a Crisis*] *in the Life of an Actress*, pp. 67–71; article in *Fædrelandet*, no. 1890–91, May 19–20, 1845, with ibid., pp. 97–100; *The Sickness unto Death*, pp. 158, 183–84; *Practice* [*Training*] *in Christianity*, p. 119; *An Upbuilding* [*Edifying*] *Discourse*, with ibid., pp. 255–71; *For Self-Examination*, pp. 54–61; *An Open Letter*, with *Armed Neutrality*, p. 50; *The Moment*, no. 8, no. 9, in *Attack*, pp. 251, 265.

1221. From draft of *The Concept of Anxiety* [*Dread*], p. 59, ll. 33 ff.

1222. Kierkegaard's library included a German edition, *Tausend und eine Nacht*, tr. G. Weil, I-IV (Stuttgart, Pforzheim, 1838–41). ASKB 1414–17.

1223. The editors have been unable to find this allusion in Lavater. In his library Kierkegaard had *Physiognomische Fragmente* (Leipzig, Winterthur: 1775–78); *Physiognomische Reisen* [a parody on Lavater by J. K. A. Musäus] (Altenburg: 1788). ASKB 613–16; 617–18.

1224. Richard Rothe, *Theologische Ethik*, I-III$^{1-2}$ (Wittenberg: 1848), III^2, p. 613. No person of equal birth.

1225. See Luke 14:16–26.

1226. See note 45; ibid., I, ch. IV, II, ch. XXVII, esp. para. 382.

1227. See *Stages*, p. 85. The Danish word (from French) *Mystification*, meaning exploitation of the credulity of another. The word itself does not appear in *Stages* (*S.V.*, VI, p. 75), but the idea, linked to the deceptive momentary appearance of the infinite, is elaborated there.

1228. *Either/Or*, II, pp. 311–21.

1229. *Stages*, p. 84.

1230. See *An Open Letter*, with *Armed Neutrality*, p. 54, fn.

1231. See note 32.

1232. See L. Holberg, *Erasmus Montanus*, I, 4.

WORK

Man's relationship to work is discussed from various points of view in Kierkegaard's writings in both the pseudonymous and the signed works.

The esthete, who is heard especially in *Either/Or*, considers a burden all work that is not done for pleasure but in order to live, consequently, out of necessity. He ironizes over "the meaning of life" defined as work to maintain life (I, p. 30).

In contrast stands the ethical view of life in which "it is every man's duty to work in order to live." But this duty is not an expression of a necessity but of "the universally human," and also an expression of a person's freedom. "Precisely by working man frees himself; by working he becomes lord over nature; by working he demonstrates that he is higher than nature," asserts Judge William in *Either/Or*. Thus it is "an expression of man's perfection that he can work; it is a still higher expression for it that he must" (II, pp. 285-87). We encounter the same idea in *Upbuilding Discourses in Various Spirits*, Part Two, "What We Learn from the Lilies of the Field and the Birds of the Air," in which Kierkegaard shows that by comparing himself with "the poor bird" that cannot work, man learns to perceive "that to work is a perfection," and that by working "for food" man is "God's co-worker" (with *The Gospel of Suffering*, p. 219, ed. tr.).

On the other hand, however, a person must learn to understand that he does not actually achieve anything with his work if it is not blessed by God, but praying for a blessing means that one "dedicates himself and his enterprise to serving God, no matter whether, humanly speaking, it succeeds and prospers or not" (*Christian Discourses*, p. 306). Therefore the kind of work a man does is not important. Even the person who does the most menial work in the eyes of men can serve God through it. In *Works of Love* Kierkegaard says: "Christianity has made every human relation between man and man a relationship of conscience" (p. 137).

Christian conscientiousness with regard to work, just as in other situations, implies the possibility of coming into conflict with society's conception of a man's duty (see, for example, X^3 A 401). This touches the problem of the relation of work to imitation, to which Kierkegaard was attuned very early (see, for example, IV A 62) and which he takes up later in *Judge for Yourselves!*, where he again uses the metaphor of the lilies and the birds to show man's complete dependence on God. He declares that man's work should be regarded almost as a jest, because it actually is God who works—and yet it is earnest because God desires that man also should work (p. 192). But later Kierkegaard points out that this pious view of work is still not "Christianity in the strictest sense," for "the imitation of Christ" can never be a pleasant jest, because here the crucial factor is "suffering because one adheres to God" (p. 196, ed. tr.).

While it does happen in the world of imperfection that one may enjoy a bountiful life without working, in the world of spirit, declares Frater Taciturnus, "only he who works gets bread" (*Fear and Trembling*, p. 38, ed. tr., from II Thessalonians 3:10). Climacus, too, speaks of "the work of inwardness" that one must do in order "to continue to be Christian" (*Postscript*, p. 536, ed. tr.), and Kierkegaard points out that anyone who works to attain the perfect benefits in the world of spirit—faith, hope, and love—does not work solely for himself but "for all; his striving to attain these goods in and for itself directly enriches others" (*Christian Discourses,* p. 122, ed. tr.).

Kierkegaard himself belonged to the so-called favored few who do not need to work for a living. Nevertheless, during most of his life he worked with enormous diligence and discipline, to which his voluminous writing indeed testifies. But with respect to this work he learned to understand that he was not his own master, that he was as if "under arrest"; and he writes in *The Point of View:* "Therefore during all my work as an author I have continually needed God's help in order to do it simply as a job to be done, for which certain hours were assigned each day, beyond which there should be no work. . . . From the outset I have been like one under arrest and at every moment have been aware that it was not I who played the master but that another was the master, aware of this with fear and trembling when he let me detect his omnipotence and my nothingness, aware of this in indescribable blessedness when I was related to him and the work in unconditional obedience" (p. 69).

Standley, Nancy V. "Existentialism: A Philosophical Framework for Vocational Development. A Study in Kierkegaard, Tiedeman, Super." Ph.D. dissertation, Florida State University, 1969.

For references in the works to work, see, for example, *Either/Or,* I, pp. 24, 30, 285–86, 294; II, pp. 122, 193, 200–201, 211–12, 283–302; *Fear and Trembling,* p. 38; *Stages,* pp. 314–16; *Postscript,* pp. 123, 136, 164–67, 208, 349 fn., 382, 553; *Upbuilding Discourses in Various Spirits,* Part One [*Purity of Heart,* pp. 182–84, 197–205]; Part Two [*What We Learn from the Lilies of the Field and the Birds of the Air,* with *The Gospel of Suffering,* pp. 173–74, 184–98, 213–21]; *Works of Love,* p. 334; *Christian Discourses,* pp. 17–39, 76–77, 120–28, 269–73, 305–7; *The Sickness unto Death,* p. 181; *For Self-Examination,* pp. 19–21; *Judge for Yourselves!,* pp. 191–96.

1233. See Moriz Carriere, *Die philosophische Weltanschauung der Reformationszeit* (Stuttgart, Tübingen: 1847), p. 621. *ASKB* 458.

> The one to whom time is as eternity,
> And eternity as time,
> He is freed
> From all strife.

1234. *Faust, Goethe's Werke,* I-LV (Stuttgart, Tübingen: 1828–33), XII, p. 121. *ASKB* 1641–68.

> This work needs skill and knowledge, it is true,
> But it requires some patience too.
> A quiet mind may work for years on end
> But time alone achieves the potent blend.
>   (Mephistopheles)

Tr. C. E. Passage, *Faust* (Indianapolis: Bobbs-Merrill, 1965), ll. 2370–73.

1235. See John 4:34.

1236. See Judges 14:14; *Stages*, p. 27.

1237. J. P. Mynster, *Prædikener*, I (3 ed., 1826)–II (2 ed., 1832) (Copenhagen: 1826–32), I, pp. 53 ff. *ASKB* 228–29.

1238. See notes 504, 975.

1239. August Neander, *Der hellige Bernhard und sein Zeitalter* (Hamburg, Gotha: 2 ed., 1848).

WORLD

By "the world" is meant the total creation, and as such the world can be seen from many different points of view. For example, the world may be looked at from an esthetic, a philosophical, or an ethical-religious perspective. In Kierkegaard's authorship all these points of view are represented, but his emphasis on the ethical-religious view of the world accounts for the contrast central in his thought between the created—that is, the finite—and God as the infinite.

Man as creature, as a temporal being, belongs to the world, but he also has within him the possibility of the eternal, which is the condition for a relationship to God. Thus man is not only a citizen of this world but also has a citizenship in heaven. In complete accord with Christian teaching, the pseudonymous writer Vigilius Haufniensis points out that by his disobedience man has brought and continues to bring sin into the world, or as he puts it: *"Sin came into the world by a sin"* (*The Concept of Anxiety* [*Dread*], p. 29). Thus the world as an expression of man's sinfulness stands in opposition to God, and Kierkegaard or his pseudonymous writers describe the battle that takes place in the interior of man between God and the world. Consequently man must choose, and Kierkegaard says: "The conflict is terrible, the conflict in a man's heart between God and the world" (*Upbuilding Discourses in Various Spirits*, Part Two [*What We Learn from the Lilies of the Field and the Birds of the Air*, with *The Gospel of Suffering*, p. 231]).

Kierkegaard has carefully delineated the different steps in man's attempt to seek his way back to God. Through irony man sees through the nothingness of the world, through resignation he attempts to break the world's power, through penitence he tries to repent himself out of his bondage to the world. In *Either/Or* Judge William says of the person who makes the movement of repentance: he repents himself "back into himself, back into the family, back into the race, until he finds himself in God" (II, p. 220). An even more profound expression for this movement of repentance is found in Climacus, who declares that in repentance a person not only repents himself out of the world but also out of the idea of his own possibility of accomplishing the good. Kierkegaard characterizes the struggle against oneself as even more difficult than the struggle against the world (see *Christian Discourses*, pp. 86–87).

The world has only a relative criterion for the good, which means that it can never have the proper conception of the good. Only the man who as the single individual stands in relationship to God has the absolute criterion; by his life he can and may contribute to a quantitative change in the world's criterion for the good. If the single individuals themselves are not under the absolute criterion, the world's criterion will be changed in a negative direction. This accounts for what Kierkegaard calls a leveling or a demoralization in the world. The demoralization is most obvious to the person who tries to fulfill Christianity's requirement in his life, for Christianity sharpens the contrast between God and the world. Christ as the revealed truth fully discloses the world's wretchedness and sin.

Kierkegaard's observations about the world became especially sharp in his last years, when he was continually trying to come under the Christian requirement. He perceived very well that "the world is beautiful" from an esthetic perspective, but not from the perspective of Christianity. From this vantage point one sees it in all its wretchedness and moral decay (XI^1 A 566). Kierkegaard goes so far as to call the world "a penitentiary" (XI^1 A 286; see also XI^2 A 223).

Since the world has only a relative criterion for the good, there can be no talk of progress in the world in the true sense of the word. In *Practice [Training] in Christianity,* Kierkegaard comments on this situation and on the meaning of the world to the single individual: "For the world goes neither backward nor forward; it remains essentially the same, like the sea, like the air, that is, like an element. It is and will be the element that can provide the test of what it means to be a Christian, who in this world is always a member of the Church militant" (p. 226, ed. tr.).

Eller, Vernard. "The World Well Lost," "The World Well Loved," in *Kierkegaard and Radical Discipleship: A New Perspective,* ch. 8, 9. Princeton: Princeton University Press, 1968.

For references in the works to the world, see, for example, *The Concept of Irony,* pp. 198, 221, 271, 276–78, 292, 312–14, 318–19; *Either/Or,* I, pp. 59–63; II, pp. 19–20, 206–9, 223–25, 244–49, 153–56; *Upbuilding [Edifying] Discourses,* I, pp. 26–27, 93–95, 98–101; II, pp. 45–47, 73–79; *Fear and Trembling,* pp. 38, 48–60; *Repetition,* pp. 114–16, 110–20, 130–31; *The Concept of Anxiety [Dread],* pp. 28–31; *Stages,* p. 313; *Postscript,* pp. 62, 134–35, 164–66, 260–61, 283–84, 364–75, 408–10, 413–14, 502, 518–19; *Upbuilding Discourses in Various Spirits,* Part One [*Purity of Heart,* pp. 56–60, 97–98, 112–13]; Part Two [*What We Learn from the Lilies of the Field and the Birds of the Air,* with *The Gospel of Suffering,* pp. 226–36]; Part Three [ibid.], pp. 18–20, 55–57, 138–64; *Works of Love,* pp. 40–42, 114–31, 179–80, 187, 193–95, 294–99, 340; *Christian Discourses,* pp. 129–30, 151, 232–33; *The Sickness unto Death,* pp. 166–68; *Practice [Training] in Christianity,* pp. 89–90, 169–70, 204–26; *Judge for Yourselves!,* pp. 109, 114, 153–54, 162–63; *The Point of View,* pp. 21, 45, 52, 59–60, 88–89 fn.; "'The Single Individual,'" with ibid., p. 134; article in *Fædrelandet*, no. 76, March 30, 1885, in *Attack*, p. 34; *The Moment*, no. 2, no. 6, no. 9, no. 10, ibid., pp. 108, 111, 181, 183–84, 198, 266, 279, 281.

1240. The bell-shaped glass or ceramic protective cover for cheese.

1241. The play *Verden vil bedrages. Lystspil i 5 Acter efter Scribes franske Original*, tr. N. C. L. Abrahams, was presented a number of times between March 27 and October 16, 1849. See note 445.

1242. See note 1241.

1243. See note 504.

1244. See John 20:19, text for April 18, 1852, the first Sunday after Easter.

1245. Good form.

1246. Presumably a reference to a police order against masquerading in clothes of the other sex, January 21, 1688, concerning "those who disguise themselves, masquerade or blacken their faces." See XI^1 A 530.

1247. See note 453.

1248. See Holberg, *Mester Gert Westphaler*, sc. 10.

1249. Shakespeare, *Richard III*, IV, 4.

1250. See note 1158.

1251. See note 675.

WORSHIP

According to Kierkegaard, man's searching for God, which is the beginning of all worship, always has two factors: "fear and rapture" (*Three Discourses on Imagined Occasions* [*Thoughts on Crucial Situations*], p. 30), corresponding to the feeling of his own smallness and God's loftiness, to man as sinner and God as the holy. In "What It Means to Seek God" he says: "Even the most purified rational worship of God is happiness in fear and trembling, trust in deadly peril, bold confidence in the consciousness of sin" (p. 13, ed. tr.).

For Kierkegaard, then, the essential factor in worship is primarily inwardness. He places less weight upon the outer forms (see, however, X^4 A 654), believing them to have value only to the extent a person can himself invest them with truth. Consequently one's "true worship," as Johannes Climacus declares, must in effect be "to become nothing before God" (*Postscript*, p. 220). The Christian expresses this attitude in his constantly sacrificing his own will "in obedience to God" (*Christian Discourses*, p. 86), or, as stated in *The Moment*, no. 7, "True worship consists quite simply of doing God's will." "But," Kierkegaard goes on to say, "true worship was never to man's taste." On the contrary, in their deep-seated anxiety before God, men try to organize another kind of "worship involving doing one's own will, but in such a way that the name of God, the invocation of God, is connected with it . . ." (in *Attack*, p. 219, ed. tr.). For example, they try to "join together to worship God" either as a state (Hegel) or as a nation (Grundtvig). Thus men in Christendom try to avoid the New Testament demand "as a single individual to become involved with God," which requires exhausting effort and the courage of despair (XI¹ A 248 and 251).

Gradually Kierkegaard came to see that the most shocking and nauseating form of false worship was that practiced within the official Church, where it was taken for granted that all were Christians and the scandal in Christianity was completely omitted. Since Mynster was the highest ranking representative for this Church, commencing in 1847 Kierkegaard hoped by means of his books, especially *Practice [Training] in Christianity,* and several conversations to influence Mynster to admit that Christianity as it was officially practiced did not correspond at all to the New Testament requirement for "being Christian," but the admission did not come.

After Mynster's death in January 1854, Kierkegaard believed that he had no right to wait any longer to challenge the official Church and its worship (see, for example, XI¹ A 1, XI³ B 53). In *Fædrelandet* for March 21, 1855, he posed a "Question of Conscience" to those who "privately know it but officially pretend that nothing is wrong": "Is This Christian Worship or Is It Treating God as a Fool?" (in *Attack,* p. 26). The same year, in a brochure entitled "This Must Be Said, So Let It Be Said," he warned against taking part in "the public worship as it is at present" and thereby sharing in "treating God as a fool by calling something New Testament Christianity that is not New Testament Christianity" (p. 59, ed. tr.).

In the pamphlets entitled *The Moment,* Kierkegaard branded the official worship an insult to God and blasphemy because in their daily lives neither the congregations nor the pastors "could dream of" renouncing the least little comfort or earthly advantage, and yet their worship is called *"Christian worship"* (p. 87). In a brochure entitled "Christ's Judgment of Official Christianity" Kierkegaard says that Christ will judge "Sunday worship" just as severely as he judges the scribes' and Pharisees' ornamenting of the graves of the murdered prophets, namely, as "hypocrisy" and "blood-guilt" (p. 124).

Kierkegaard personally accepted the consequence of his denunciation of the official worship when shortly before his death, although he could pray peacefully and above all for forgiveness, he declined Communion because it could be administered only by a royal office-holder and not by a layman (see *E.P.,* IX, p. 59, an account of Kierkegaard's last day by his old friend, Pastor Emil Boesen).

For references in the works to worship, see, for example, *Either/Or,* II, p. 72; *Three Discourses on Imagined Occasions* [*Thoughts on Crucial Situations*], pp. 13, 30, 77; *Postscript,* pp. 220, 369, 456; *Christian Discourses,* pp. 83–93; *The Point of View,* pp. 67–68; articles in *Fædrelandet,* no. 24, January 29, 1855, no. 68, March 21, 1855, in *Attack,* pp. 18–21, 26; "This Must Be Said," ibid., pp. 59–60; *Christ's Judgment,* ibid., pp. 119–24; *The Moment,* no. 1, no. 7, no. 9, ibid., pp. 84, 87, 202, 208–11, 219, 231–32, 259–60.

1252. See Adolf Helferrich, *Die christliche Mystik,* I–II (Gotha: 1842), II, pp. 427–28.

1253. See *Upbuilding Discourses in Various Spirits,* Part One [*Purity of Heart*], pp. 179–82.

1254. See Hermann Reuchlin, *Pascals Leben* (Stuttgart, Tübingen: 1840), p. 136.

1255. See *The Moment,* no. 4, in *Attack,* p. 140.

ZACHAEUS

In the works there is no reference to Zachaeus.

1256. Zacharais Werner, *Poetische Werke,* I–XIII (Grimma: n.d.) *ASKB* 1851–54.

1257. See Luke 19:2–10.